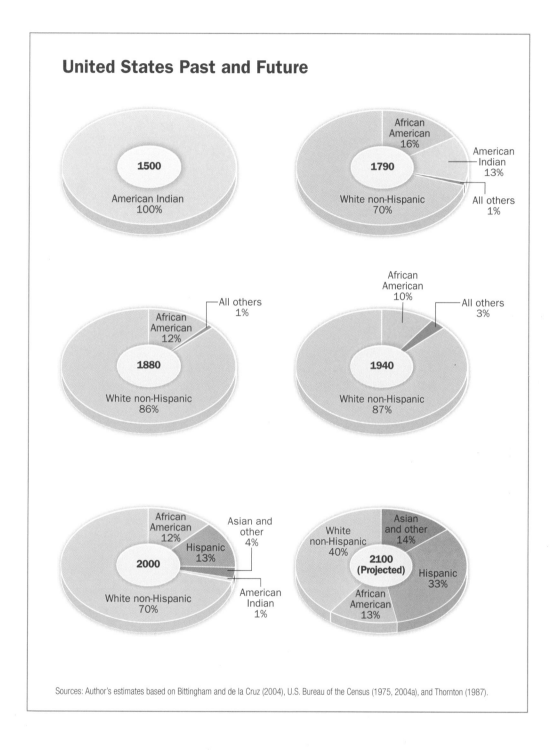

United States Past and Future

1500
American Indian
100%

1790
African American 16%
American Indian 13%
All others 1%
White non-Hispanic 70%

1880
All others 1%
African American 12%
White non-Hispanic 86%

1940
African American 10%
All others 3%
White non-Hispanic 87%

2000
African American 12%
Asian and other 4%
Hispanic 13%
White non-Hispanic 70%
American Indian 1%

2100 (Projected)
White non-Hispanic 40%
Asian and other 14%
Hispanic 33%
African American 13%

Sources: Author's estimates based on Bittingham and de la Cruz (2004), U.S. Bureau of the Census (1975, 2004a), and Thornton (1987).

ELEVENTH EDITION

RACIAL AND ETHNIC GROUPS

RICHARD T. SCHAEFER

DePaul University

PEARSON

Prentice
Hall

Upper Saddle River, New Jersey 07458

Library of Congress Cataloging-in-Publication Data

Schaefer, Richard T.
    Racial and ethnic groups / Richard T. Schaefer.—11th ed.
        p.   cm.
    Includes bibliographical references and index.
    ISBN 0-13-243875-5
        1. Minorities—United States. 2. United States—Ethnic relations. 3. United States—Race relations.
        4. Prejudices—United States. I. Title.
    E184.A1.S3 2007
    305.800973—dc22   2007001933

Editorial Director: Leah Jewell
Executive Editor: Jennifer Gilliland
VP, Director of Production and Manufacturing: Barbara Kittle
Senior Managing Editor: Ann Marie McCarthy
Full-Service Project Management: Linda Martino, Preparé Inc.
Production Liaison: Barbara Reilly
Prepress and Manufacturing Manager: Nick Sklitsis
Prepress and Manufacturing Buyer: Brian Mackey
Director of Marketing: Brandy Dawson
Marketing Manager: Lindsey Prudhomme
Marketing Assistant: Kimberly Caldwell
Editorial Assistant: Lee Peterson

Creative Design Director: Leslie Osher
Art Director/Interior and Cover Design: Kathryn Foot
Line Art Illustrations: Precision Graphics
Director, Image Resource Center: Melinda Patelli
Manager, Rights and Permissions: Zina Arabia
Manager, Visual Research: Beth Brenzel
Image Permissions Coordinator: Joanne Dippel
Photo Researcher: Diane Austin
Cover Photo: Corbis/Bettmann; Shutterstock
Director, Media and Assessment: Shannon Gattens
Senior Media Editor: Deborah O'Connell

This book was set in 10/12 New Baskerville by Preparé/Emilcomp, and was printed and bound by Courier Companies, Inc. The cover was printed by Phoenix Color Corp.

For permission to use copyrighted material, grateful acknowledgment is made to the copyright holders listed on pages 507–8, which is considered an extension of this copyright page.

Pearson Education LTD.
Pearson Education Singapore, Pte. Ltd
Pearson Education, Canada, Ltd.
Pearson Education—Japan
Pearson Education Australia PTY, Limited

Pearson Education North Asia Ltd
Pearson Educación de Mexico, S.A. de C.V.
Pearson Education Malaysia, Pte. Ltd
Pearson Education, Upper Saddle River, New Jersey

10 9 8 7 6 5 4 3 2 1

ISBN-13: 978-0-13-243875-9
ISBN-10: 0-13-243875-5

To the Students in My Classes Who Assist Me
in Understanding a Multicultural Society

Brief Contents

CHAPTER 1
Understanding Race and Ethnicity   2

CHAPTER 2
Prejudice   36

CHAPTER 3
Discrimination   66

CHAPTER 4
Immigration and the United States   94

CHAPTER 5
Ethnicity and Religion   122

CHAPTER 6
The Native Americans   164

CHAPTER 7
The Making of African Americans in a White America   198

CHAPTER 8
African Americans Today   226

CHAPTER 9
Hispanic Americans   252

CHAPTER 10
Mexican Americans and Puerto Ricans   272

CHAPTER 11
Muslim and Arab Americans: Diverse Minorities   298

CHAPTER 12
Asian Americans: Growth and Diversity   322

CHAPTER 13
Chinese Americans and Japanese Americans   350

CHAPTER 14
Jewish Americans: Quest to Maintain Identity   372

CHAPTER 15
Women: The Oppressed Majority   400

CHAPTER 16
Beyond the United States: The Comparative Perspective   424

CHAPTER 17
Overcoming Exclusion   452

Contents

Preface   xv

About the Author   1

PART I
PERSPECTIVES ON RACIAL AND ETHNIC GROUPS

 Understanding Race and Ethnicity   2

What Is a Subordinate Group?   7

Types of Subordinate Groups   8
   Racial Groups   8
   Ethnic Groups   9
   Religious Groups   10
   Gender Groups   11
   Other Subordinate Groups   12

Does Race Matter?   12
   Biological Meaning   12
   Social Construction of Race   14

Sociology and the Study of Race and Ethnicity   15
   Stratification by Class and Gender   15
   Theoretical Perspectives   16

The Creation of Subordinate-Group Status   19
   Migration   20
   Annexation   20
   Colonialism   21

The Consequences of Subordinate-Group Status   22
   Extermination   22
   Expulsion   22
   Secession   23
   Segregation   23
   Fusion   25
   Assimilation   25
   The Pluralist Perspective   26

Who Am I?   29

Resistance and Change   32

■ **LISTEN TO OUR VOICES:** Problem of the Color Line,
W. E. B. Du Bois   10

■ **RESEARCH FOCUS:** Measuring Multiculturalism   30

Prejudice 36

Hate Crimes 39
Prejudice and Discrimination 41
    Merton's Typology 41
    LaPiere's Study 42
Theories of Prejudice 43
    Scapegoating Theory 43
    Authoritarian Personality Theory 45
    Exploitation Theory 45
    Normative Approach 46
The Content of Prejudice: Stereotypes 46
    What Are Stereotypes? 47
    Trends in Stereotypes 47
    Stereotyping in Action: Racial Profiling 49
The Extent of Prejudice 50
    The Social Distance Scale 51
    Trends in Prejudice 52
The Mood of the Oppressed 53
Intergroup Hostility 55
Reducing Prejudice 57
    Education and Mass Media 57
    Equal-Status Contact 59
    Corporate Response: Diversity Training 60
Ways to Fight Hate 63

■ **LISTEN TO OUR VOICES:** Gangsters, Gooks, Geishas, and Geeks, Helen Zia 48

■ **RESEARCH FOCUS:** What's in a Name? 62

3 Discrimination 66

Understanding Discrimination 69
    Relative Versus Absolute Deprivation 69
    Total Discrimination 70
    Institutional Discrimination 72
Low-Wage Labor 75
Discrimination Today 77
    Measuring Discrimination 78
    Eliminating Discrimination 80
Wealth Inequality: Discrimination's Legacy 83
Environmental Justice 84
Affirmative Action 85
    Affirmative Action Explained 86
    The Legal Debate 87
Reverse Discrimination 88
The Glass Ceiling 89

■ **LISTEN TO OUR VOICES:** Of Race and Risk, Patricia J. Williams 70

■ **RESEARCH FOCUS:** Discrimination in Job Seeking 76

PART II
ETHNIC AND RELIGIOUS SOURCES OF CONFLICT

 Immigration and the United States   94

Immigration: A Global Phenomenon   97
Patterns of Immigration to the United States   98
Today's Foreign-Born Population   99
Early Immigration   100
    The Anti-Chinese Movement   101
Restrictionist Sentiment Increases   103
    The National Origin System   104
    The 1965 Immigration and Naturalization Act   104
Contemporary Social Concerns   107
    The Brain Drain   107
    Population Growth   108
Illegal Immigration   109
The Economic Impact of Immigration   114
Women and Immigration   116
The Global Economy and Immigration   117
Refugees   118

■ **LISTEN TO OUR VOICES:** The Wall That Keeps Illegal Workers In,
Douglas S. Massey   110

■ **RESEARCH FOCUS:** How Well Are Immigrants Doing?   115

5 Ethnicity and Religion   122

Ethnic Diversity   124
Why Don't We Study Whiteness?   125
    Whiteness   125
    White Privilege   127
    The Rediscovery of Ethnicity   127
    The Third-Generation Principle   127
    Symbolic Ethnicity   128
The Price Paid by White Ethnics   129
    Prejudice Toward White Ethnic Groups   129
    The Prejudice of Ethnics   130
The Irish Americans   131
    Early Irish Immigration (before 1845)   131
    The Famine Years   132
    Becoming White   133
    Contemporary Irish Americans   134
The Italian Americans   135
Polish Americans   138
    Early Immigration   138
    Polonia   139
    The Contemporary Picture   140
The Language Divide   141
    Bilingual Education   143
    Official Language Movement   145
Religious Pluralism   146

Ethnicity, Religion, and Social Class   151
Religion in the United States   152
 Diversity Among Roman Catholics   153
 Diversity Among Protestants   154
 Women and Religion   156
 Religion and the U.S. Supreme Court   157
Limits of Religious Freedom: The Amish   159
 The Amish Way of Life   159
 The Amish and Larger Society   160

▥ **LISTEN TO OUR VOICES:** I Was Born in Tirana, Harallamb
Terba   142

▥ **RESEARCH FOCUS:** Measuring the Importance of Religion   150

PART III
MAJOR RACIAL AND ETHNIC MINORITY GROUPS
IN THE UNITED STATES

The Native Americans   164

Early European Contacts   167
Treaties and Warfare   168
 The Case of the Sioux   170
Ruling the Native Americans   172
 The Allotment Act   172
 The Reorganization Act   173
Reservation Life and Federal Policies   174
 Native American Legal Claims   175
 The Termination Act   176
 Employment Assistance Program   177
Collective Action   178
 Protest Efforts   178
 Pan-Indianism: An Overview   180
Sovereignty   181
Native Americans Today   182
 Economic Development   183
 Education   187
 Health Care   190
 Religious and Spiritual Expression   192
 Environment   193

▥ **LISTEN TO OUR VOICES:** The Scalpel and the Silver Bear,
Lori Arviso Alvord   191

▥ **RESEARCH FOCUS:** Learning the Navajo Way   189

The Making of African Americans in a White America   198

Slavery   201
 Slave Codes   202
 African Americans and Africa   204
 The Attack on Slavery   204
 Slavery's Aftermath   205
 Reparations for Slavery   206

The Challenge of Black Leadership   208
  The Politics of Accommodation   208
  The Niagara Movement   209
Reemergence of Black Protest   211
The Civil Rights Movement   214
  Struggle to Desegregate the Schools   214
  Civil Disobedience   215
Urban Violence and Oppression   218
Black Power   219
The Religious Force   222

▨ **LISTEN TO OUR VOICES:** Letter from Birmingham Jail,
Martin Luther King, Jr.   217

▪ **RESEARCH FOCUS:** Sundown Towns, USA   212

African Americans Today   226

Education   228
  Quality and Quantity of Education   229
  School Segregation   230
  Acting White, Acting Black, or Neither   231
  Higher Education   232
The Economic Picture   234
  Income and Wealth   234
  Employment   236
Family Life   238
  Challenges to Family Stability   238
  Strengths of African American Families   240
  The African American Middle Class   241
Housing   243
  Residential Segregation   243
Criminal Justice   245
Health Care   245
Politics   248

▨ **LISTEN TO OUR VOICES:** When Work Disappears,
William Julius Wilson   237

▪ **RESEARCH FOCUS:** The Ultimate Penalty: Execution   246

Hispanic Americans   252

Latino Identity   255
The Economic Picture   257
The Growing Political Presence   261
The Borderlands   262
Cuban Americans   264
  Immigration   264
  The Present Picture   266

Central and South Americans 268
    Immigration 268
    The Present Picture 269
◼ **LISTEN TO OUR VOICES:** Leaving Cuba, Alfredo Jimenez 265
◼ **RESEARCH FOCUS:** Latinas: American Style 258

Mexican Americans and Puerto Ricans 272

Mexican Americans 275
    The Immigrant Experience 275
    The Economic Picture 278
    Political Organizations 280
Puerto Ricans 282
    The Bridge Between the Island and the Mainland 283
    The Island of Puerto Rico 284
    The Island Economy 289
The Contemporary Picture of Mexican Americans
and Puerto Ricans 290
    Education 290
    Family Life 292
    Health Care 292
    Religion 294
◼ **LISTEN TO OUR VOICES:** "¡Viva Vieques!", Martín St. Espada 288
◼ **RESEARCH FOCUS:** Assimilation May Be Hazardous
to Your Health 293

Muslim and Arab Americans: Diverse Minorities 298

Muslim and Arab People 300
Arab Americans 301
Muslim Americans 304
    Black Muslims 307
Immigration to the United States 310
Contemporary Life in the United States 311
    Family Life and Gender 312
    Education 314
    Politics 314
Being Arab or Muslim in the United States 316
Issues of Prejudice and Discrimination 319
◼ **LISTEN TO OUR VOICES:** Pendulum Swings on Civil Rights,
James Zogby 317
◼ **RESEARCH FOCUS:** Christian and Muslim Arab American Women's
Gender Roles 313

Asian Americans: Growth and Diversity 322

The "Model Minority" Image Explored 325
    Education and the Economy 326
    The Door Half Open 329

Political Activity   331
Diversity Among Asian Americans   333
Asian Indians   334
    Immigration   334
    The Present Picture   335
Filipino Americans   335
    Immigration Patterns   335
    The Present Picture   337
Southeast Asian Americans   339
    The Refugees   339
    The Present Picture   339
    Case Study: A Hmong Community   341
Korean Americans   342
    Historical Background   342
    The Present Picture   343
Hawaii and Its People   345
    Historical Background   345
    The Present Picture   346

▨ **LISTEN TO OUR VOICES:** Being Pakistani, Muslim, and Female in America, Fatima Arain   326

▧ **RESEARCH FOCUS:** Arranged Marriages in America   336

Chinese Americans and Japanese Americans   350

Chinese Americans   352
    Occupational Profile of Chinese Americans   353
    Chinatowns Today   354
    Family and Religious Life   357
Japanese Americans   359
    The Wartime Evacuation   360
    The Economic Picture   364
    Family and Religious Life   365
Remnants of Prejudice and Discrimination   366

▨ **LISTEN TO OUR VOICES:** From Kawasaki to Chicago, Miku Ishii   366

▧ **RESEARCH FOCUS:** Chinese Christians or Christian Chinese?   358

Jewish Americans: Quest to Maintain Identity   372

The Jewish People: Race, Religion, or Ethnic Group?   376
Immigration of Jews to the United States   377
Anti-Semitism: Past and Present   379
    Origins   379
    The Holocaust   381
    U.S. Anti-Semitism: Past   382
    Contemporary Anti-Semitism   384
Position of Jewish Americans   386
    Employment and Income   387
    Education   388

Organizational Activity   388
Political Activity   389
Religious Life   389
The Orthodox Tradition   390
The Reform Tradition   392
Jewish Identity   393
Role of the Family   394
Role of Religion   395
Role of Cultural Heritage   397

■ **LISTEN TO OUR VOICES:** Night, Elie Wiesel   382

■ **RESEARCH FOCUS:** Intermarriage: The Final Step
to Assimilation?   395

PART IV
OTHER PATTERNS OF DOMINANCE

15   Women: The Oppressed Majority   400

Gender Roles   403
Sociological Perspectives   404
The Feminist Movement   405
The Suffrage Movement   406
The Women's Liberation Movement   406
The Economic Picture   407
Sources of Discrimination   410
Sexual Harassment   413
Feminization of Poverty   414
Education   415
Family Life   416
Child Care and Housework   416
Abortion   420
Political Activity   420
Matrix of Domination: Minority Women   421

■ **LISTEN TO OUR VOICES:** Time for Change, Arlie Russell
Hochschild   408

■ **RESEARCH FOCUS:** Housework and the Gender Divide   418

16   Beyond the United States:
The Comparative Perspective   424

Mexico   426
The Mexican Indian People and the Color Gradient   429
The Status of Women   430
Canada   431
The First Nation   432
The Québécois   433
Immigration and Race   435

Brazil: Not a Racial Paradise   436
   Legacy of Slavery   436
   The "Racial Democracy" Illusion   437
   Brazilian Dilemma   438
Israel and the Palestinians   440
   Arab-Israeli Conflicts   441
   The Intifada   442
   The Search for Solutions Amid Violence   443
Republic of South Africa   445
   The Legacy of Colonialism   445
   Apartheid   446
   The Era of Reconciliation and Moving On   448

▨ **LISTEN TO OUR VOICES:** Africa, It Is Ours!, Nelson Mandela   447

■ **RESEARCH FOCUS:** Listening to the People   449

17   Overcoming Exclusion   452

The Aged: A Social Minority   455
   Who Are the Elderly?   455
   Ageism   456
   The Economic Picture   458
   Advocacy Efforts by the Elderly   459
People with Disabilities: Moving On   460
   Disability in Contemporary Society   461
   Labeling the Disabled   462
   Advocacy for Disability Rights   464
Gays and Lesbians: Coming Out for Equality   466
   Being Gay and Lesbian in the USA   467
   Prejudice and Discrimination   468
   Advocacy for Gay and Lesbian Rights   469
The Glass Half Empty   471

▨ **LISTEN TO OUR VOICES:** The Magic Wand, Lynn Manning   463

■ **RESEARCH FOCUS:** The Face of Ageism   457

Internet Resource Directory   476

Glossary   479

References   484

Photo Credits   507

Index   509

Preface

On October 17, 2006, the United States population hit the 300 million mark. While there is no way to know exactly who is the 300,000,000th American, some analysts suggested that, reflecting the mosaic that makes up contemporary United States, it was a Mexican Latino in Los Angeles County, with parents who speak Spanish at home and with siblings who are bilingual. Just two years earlier, front-page newspaper headlines had read "Minority Majority" when the Census Bureau released its annual population estimates. Now, in 280 counties, whites who are not Hispanic are outnumbered by Latinos, African Americans, Asian Americans, Native American tribal members, and others. However, do these groups wield the power in all these counties? In any of these counties? Does the United States' becoming more diverse signify a significant advancement in the quality of life of people of color relative to gains made by white Americans? These are the real questions, and rarely are they asked and almost never answered. Some people who have not followed these trends seemed stunned that in 2003, Orange County, surf 'n sun capital of southern California and home of Disneyland, now has a minority majority. Nor should one have been surprised that in the wake of Hurricane Katrina in 2005, New Orleans' poor were overwhelmingly African American. Although these changes may not signify a major shift in social inequality among groups, they do underscore the importance of being familiar with the nature of race and ethnicity in the United States.

Race and ethnicity are an important part of the national agenda. Twenty-nine years ago, when the first edition of this book was being written, it was noted that race is not a static phenomenon and that, although it is always a part of the social reality, specific aspects change. At that time, the presence of a new immigrant group, the Vietnamese, was duly noted, and the efforts to define affirmative action were described. Today we seek to describe the growing presence of El Salvadorans, Haitians, and Arab Americans and the attempts to dismantle affirmative action.

Specific issues may change over time, but they continue to play out against a backdrop of discrimination that is rooted in the social structure and changing population composition, as influenced by immigration patterns and reproduction patterns. One unanticipated change is that the breakup of the Soviet Union and further disinterest of the major industrial powers in the political and social events in Africa, Latin America, and much of Asia have made ethnic, language, and religious divisions even more significant sources of antagonism between and within nations. The old ideological debates about communism and capitalism have been replaced by emotional divisions over religious dogma and cultural traditions.

We continue to be reminded about the importance of the social construction of many aspects of racial and ethnic relations. What constitutes a race in terms of identity? What meaning do race and ethnicity have amid the growing number of interracial marriages and marriages across cultural boundaries? Beyond the spectrum of race and ethnicity, we see the socially constructed meaning attached to all religions as members debate who is the "true" keeper of the faith. As we consider matters of gender, we see again that differences are largely the result of social constructions. And finally, as we consider all groups that have been subjected to discrimination, such as the disabled, the elderly, and gays and lesbians, we see, in a similar manner, the power of labeling. The very issue of national identity is also a part of the agenda. The public and politicians alike ask, "How many immigrants can we accept?" and "How much should be done to make up for past discrimination?" We are also witnessing the emergence of race, ethnicity, and national identity as global issues.

Changes in the Eleventh Edition

As with all previous editions, every line, every source, and every number has been rechecked for its currency. We pride ourselves on providing the most current information possible to document the patterns in intergroup relations both in the United States and abroad.

Relevant scholarly findings in a variety of disciplines, including economics, anthropology, and communication sciences, have been incorporated. The feature "Listen to Our Voices" appears in every chapter. These selections include excerpts from the writings or speeches of noted members of racial and ethnic groups such as Martin Luther King, Jr., Elie Wiesel, Patricia J. Williams, and Nelson Mandela. Their writings will help students appreciate the emotional and the intellectual energies felt by subordinate groups.

The eleventh edition includes entirely new sections on Irish Americans, Polish Americans, women and immigration, the matrix of domination, and on race in Brazil.

We also introduce a new feature called **Student Voice** questions to encourage students to think critically about the material. These questions are intended to create a dialogue between the student reader and the material in this book. There are two or three questions in every chapter.

In addition to this new feature, the eleventh edition includes the following additions and changes:

- New key terms such as acting white (Chapter 8), apartheid schools (Chapter 8), arranged marriage (Chapter 12), chain immigration (Chapter 4), cultural capital (Chapter 17), dry foot, wet foot (Chapter 9), intelligent design (Chapter 5), matrix of domination (Chapter 16), mulatto escape hatch (Chapter 17), quinceañera (Chapter 16), quilombo (Chapter 16), social capital (Chapter 17), and sundown towns (Chapter 7)
- A new "Research Focus" on discrimination in employment that seems to show that whites who are ex-convicts have a better chance of getting a job interview than a Black man with no prison record (Chapter 3)
- A new section on immigration as worldwide social phenomenon, which includes a map highlighting major migration streams globally (Chapter 4)
- A new "Listen to Our Voices" box entitled "The Wall That Keeps Illegal Workers In" by Douglas S. Massey (Chapter 4)
- A new section highlighting the special impact that immigration has on women and children (Chapter 4)
- Coverage of white ethnic groups has been increased with separate sections profiling Irish Americans and Polish Americans as well as Italian Americans (Chapter 5)
- To highlight the fact that issues of non-English native speakers reach beyond the Hispanic community, the material on bilingual education has been moved from the chapter on Latinos to the earlier chapter on ethnic groups (Chapter 5)
- A new "Listen to Our Voices" box entitled "I Was Born In Tirana, Albania" by Harallamb Terba (Chapter 5)
- The discussion on the teaching of creationism in schools is updated with a presentation on the debate on intelligent design (Chapter 5)

- A new "Research Focus" on the long history of Sundown Towns where non-whites could work and spend their money but could not live (Chapter 7)
- The Intergroup Relations Continuum has been added to two additional chapters (Chapters 7 and 11)
- A new section that confronts the assertion that some African American youth do poorly in school because they do not want to "act white" (Chapter 8)
- Maps showing the countries of the world that are regarded as either Arab or Muslim to assist students in getting a better global view (Chapter 11)
- A new "Listen to Our Voices" box entitled "Being Pakistani, Muslim, and Female in America" by Fatima Arain (Chapter 12)
- A new "Listen to Our Voices" box entitled "From Kawasaki To Chicago" by Miku Ishii (Chapter 13)
- The discussion of the treatment of gays and lesbians is prefaced by a clarification for the reader about terms such as *homosexual, bisexual, transexual, transgender,* and *transvestites.*
- A new section on the "matrix of domination" documents the intersection of oppression based on race, gender, and class as well as disability status, religion, age, and sexual orientation (Chapter 15)
- In our consideration of ethnic diversity, we have added a new section outlining race in Brazil (Chapter 16)
- A new "Listen to Our Voices" box entitled "Magic Wand" by Lynn Manning (Chapter 17)
- A new coverage of Pierre Bourdieu's cultural capital and social capital has been added as part of a new section, "The Persistence of Equality" (Chapter 17)

In addition, tables, figures, maps, political cartoons, Internet Connections, and Internet sources in the Appendix have been updated.

Complete Coverage in Four Parts

Any constructive discussion of racial and ethnic minorities must do more than merely describe events. Part I, "Perspectives on Racial and Ethnic Groups," includes the relevant theories and operational definitions that ground the study of race and ethnic relations in the social sciences. We specifically present the functionalist, conflict, and labeling theories of sociology in relation to the study of race and ethnicity. We show the relationship between subordinate groups and the study of stratification. We also introduce the dual labor market theory and the irregular economy theory from economics and the reference group theory from psychology. The extensive treatment of prejudice and discrimination covers anti-white prejudice as well as the more familiar topic of bigotry aimed at subordinate groups. Discrimination is analyzed from an economic perspective, including the latest efforts to document discrimination in environmental issues such as location of toxic waste facilities and the move to dismantle affirmative action.

In Part II, "Ethnic and Religious Sources of Conflict," we examine some often-ignored sources of intergroup conflict in the United States: White ethnic groups and religious minorities. Diversity in the United States is readily apparent when we look at the ethnic and religious groups that have resulted from waves of immigration. Refugees, now primarily from Haiti and Central America, also continue to raise major issues.

Any student needs to be familiar with the past to understand present forms of discrimination and subordination. Part III, "Major Racial and Ethnic Minority Groups in the United States," brings into sharper focus the history and contemporary status of Native Americans, African Americans, Latinos, Arab and Muslim Americans, Asian Americans, and Jews in the United States. Social institutions such as education, economy, family, housing, criminal justice system, health care and politics receive special attention for the subordinate groups. The author contends that institutional discrimination, rather than individual action, is the source of conflict between the subordinate and dominant elements in the United States.

Part IV, "Other Patterns of Dominance," includes topics related to American racial and ethnic relations. The author recognizes, as have Gunnar Myrdal and Helen Mayer Hacker before, that relations between women and men resemble those between blacks and whites. Therefore, in this book, we consider the position of women as a subordinate group. Since the first edition of Racial and Ethnic Groups, published more than 25 years ago, debates over equal rights and abortion have shown no sign of resolution. For women of color, we document the matrix of domination suffered because of their subordinate status of race and gender.

Perhaps we can best comprehend intergroup conflict in the United States by comparing it with the ethnic hostilities in other nations. The similarities and differences between the United States and other societies treated in this book are striking. We examine the tensions in Canada, Israel, Mexico, Brazil (added in this edition), and South Africa to document further the diversity of intergroup conflict.

The final chapter highlights other groups that have been the subject of exclusion: the aged, people with disabilities, and gay men and lesbians. This chapter also includes a concluding section that ties together thematically the forces of dominance and subordination and the persistence of inequality that have been the subject of this book.

Features to Aid Students

Several features are included in the text to facilitate student learning. A Chapter Outline appears at the beginning of each chapter and is followed by Highlights, a short section alerting students to important issues and topics to be addressed. To help students review, each chapter ends with a summary Conclusion. The Key Terms are highlighted in bold when they are first introduced in the text and are listed with page numbers at the end of each chapter. Periodically throughout the book, the Intergroup Relations Continuum first presented in Chapter 1 is repeated to reinforce major concepts while addressing the unique social circumstances of individual racial and ethnic groups.

In addition, there is an end-of-book Glossary with full definitions referenced to page numbers. This edition includes both Review Questions and Critical Thinking Questions. The Review Questions are intended to remind the reader of major points, whereas the Critical Thinking Questions encourage students to think more deeply about some of the major issues raised in the chapter. Updated Internet Exercises allow students to do some critical thinking and research on the Web. An Internet Resource Directory has been expanded to allow access to the latest electronic sources. An extensive illustration program, which includes maps and political cartoons, expands the text discussion and provokes thought.

Ancillary Materials

The ancillary materials that accompany this textbook have been carefully created to enhance the topics being discussed.

PRINT AND MEDIA SUPPLEMENTS FOR INSTRUCTORS

Instructor's Resource Manual with Tests ISBN 0-13-243878-X Created by Matthew Jendian, California State Univeristy, Fresno, and Leigh Willis, University of Georgia, each chapter in the manual includes the following resources: Chapter Learning

Objectives; Chapter Overview; Lecture Suggestions and Classroom Discussons; Activities, Handouts, and Demonstrations; Student Assignments and Projects; and Multimedia Resources. Designed to make your lectures more effective and to save you preparation time, this extensive resource gathers together the most effective activities and strategies for teaching your course.

The test bank includes approximately 2,000 multiple-choice, short answer, and essay questions. Each chapter's question types are organized into a test planner called the Total Assessment Guide designed to make creating tests easier by listing all of the test items on an easy-to-reference grid. The Total Assessment Guide organizes all of the test items by text section, question type, and level of difficulty. Additionally, each chapter of the test bank includes a ready-made ten-item quiz with an answer key for immediate use in class.

Prentice Hall's *TestGen* **ISBN 0-13-2438798** Available on one dual platform CD-ROM, this test generator program provides instructors "best in class" features in an easy-to-use program. Create tests using the TestGen Wizard and easily select questions with drag-and-drop or point-and-click functionality. Add or modify text questions using the built-in Question Editor. TestGen also offers algorithmic functionality, which allows for the creation of unlimited versions of a single text. The Quiz Master features allows for online test delivery, complete with an instructor gradebook and full technical support.

NEW **Pearson's MyTest** Pearson MyTest is a powerful assessment generation program that helps instructors easily create and print quizzes and exams. Questions and tests can be authored online, allowing instructors ultimate flexibility and the ability to efficiently manage assessments anytime, anywhere. Contact your Prentice Hall Representative for more information.

OneKey™ for *Racial and Ethnic Groups, Eleventh Edition* Prentice Hall's all-inclusive online resource offers instructors and students all of the teaching and learning resources in one place. For students, OneKey offers a diagnostic test that creates a customized study plan and additional quizzing and study resources to ensure they master the course content and do better on exams. For instructors, OneKey offers all of the lecture and presentation resources to accompany this text, as well as a gradebook. OneKey is available in WebCT™, CourseCompass™, and BlackBoard™ formats. Contact your Prentice Hall representative for further information.

PowerPoint™ Slides with *NEW* **Classroom Response System Questions** Available Online and on the Instructor's Resource CD-ROM.

Created by Rose Hunte, Metropolitan Community College, Nebraska, each chapter's presentations highlight the key points covered in the text and include ten to fifteen questions to incorporate into your course using a Classroom Response System. Available on the Instructor's Resource CD-ROM or online at www.prenhall.com.

Instructor's Resource CD-ROM ISBN 0-13-243880-1 Pulling together all of the media assets available to instructors, this CD-ROM allows instructors to insert media—video, PowerPoint®, and line art—into their classroom presentations. This CD-ROM also includes an electronic version of the Instructor's Manual with Tests.

NEW **ABCNews/Prentice Hall Video Library ISBN 0-13-179107-9** This video library consists of brief segments from award-winning news programs such as *Good Morning America, Nightline, 20/20,* and *World News Tonight.* These brief segments provide contemporary "lecture-launcher" videos and demonstrate the applicability of what students are learning in class to everyday situations.

Films for Humanities and Sciences Video Library Qualified adopters can select full-length feature videos on various topics in Sociology from the extensive library of Films for the Humanities and Sciences. Contact your Prentice Hall representative for a list of videos.

Voices Listen to Our Voices Listen to

- Problem of the Color Line, W. E. B. Du Bois (Chapter 1)
- Gangsters, Gooks, Geishas, and Geeks, Helen Zia (Chapter 2)
- Of Race and Risk, Patricia J. Williams (Chapter 3)
- The Wall That Keeps Illegal Workers In, Douglas S. Massey (Chapter 4)
- I was Born in Tirana, Harallamb Terba (Chapter 5)
- The Scalpel and the Silver Bear, Lori Arviso Alvord (Chapter 6)
- Letter from Birmingham Jail, Martin Luther King, Jr. (Chapter 7)
- When Work Disappears, William Julius Wilson (Chapter 8)

- Leaving Cuba, Alfredo Jimenez (Chapter 9)
- ¡Viva Vieques!, Martín St. Espada (Chapter 10)
- Pendulum Swings on Civil Rights, James Zogby (Chapter 11)
- Being Pakistani, Muslim, and Female in America, Fatima Arain (Chapter 12)
- From Kawasaki to Chicago, Miku Ishii (Chapter 13)
- Night, Elie Wiesel (Chapter 14)
- Time for Change, Arlie Russell Hochschild (Chapter 15)
- Africa, It Is Ours! Nelson Mandela (Chapter 16)
- The Magic Wand Lynn Manning (Chapter 17)

PRINT AND MEDIA SUPPLEMENTS FOR STUDENTS

Study Guide ISBN 0-13-243877-1 Created by Jenifer Kunz, West Texas A&M University, this guide includes Chapter Objectives and a Chapter Overview; Practice Tests; Applications, Exercises and Activities; and a Crossword Puzzle to help students master the core concepts presented in each chapter.

The Prentice Hall Guide to Research Naviator ™ The easiest way to do research! This guide focuses on using **Research Navigator**™—Prentice Hall's own gateway to databases including *The New York Times* Search-by-Subject Archive, *ContentSelect*™ Academic Journal Database powered by EBSCO, *The Financial Times,* and the *Best of the Web* Link Library. It also includes extensive appendices on documenting online sources and on avoiding pla-

giarism. This supplement—which includes an access code to the Research Navigator™ Web site—is available for college adoptions when packaged with a new text.

SafariX WebBooks This Pearson Choice offers students an online subscription to ***Racial and Ethnic Groups, Eleventh Edition,*** online at a 50% savings. With the SafariX WebBook, students can search the text, makes notes online, print out reading assignments and bookmark important passages. Ask your Prentice Hall representative for details or visit www.safarix.com.

Focus Research Focus Research

- Measuring Multiculturalism (Chapter 1)
- What's in a Name? (Chapter 2)
- Discrimination in Job Seeking (Chapter 3)
- How Well Are Immigrants Doing? (Chapter 4)
- Measuring the Importance of Religion (Chapter 5)
- Learning the Navajo Way (Chapter 6)
- Sundown Towns USA (Chapter 7)
- The Ultimate Penalty: Execution (Chapter 8)
- Latinas: American Style (Chapter 9)

- Assimilation May Be Hazardous to Your Health (Chapter 10)
- Christian and Muslim Arab American Women's Gender Roles (Chapter 11)
- Arranged Marriages in America (Chapter 12)
- Chinese Christians or Christian Chinese? (Chapter 13)
- Intermarriage: The Final Step to Assimilation? (Chapter 14)
- Housework and the Gender Divide (Chapter 15)
- Listening to the People (Chapter 16)
- The Face of Ageism (Chapter 17)

Acknowledgments

The eleventh edition benefited from the thoughtful reaction of my students in classes. Data analysis of the General Social Survey and Census Bureau data sets was provided by my faculty colleague Kiljoong Kim of DePaul University. Rachel Hanes, a student at DePaul, assisted with special tasks related to the preparation of the manuscript.

The eleventh edition was improved by the suggestions of:

E.M. Beck	University of Georgia
Deborah Brunson	University of North Carolina, Wilmington
Jac D. Bulk	University of Wisconsin, La Crosse
Ada Sh Cheng	DePaul University
Roberta Rosenberg Farber	Yeshiva University
Celestino Fernandez	University of Arizona.
Black Hawk Hancock	DePaul University
S. Homes Hogue	Mississippi State University
Tomas R. Jimenez	University of California, San Diego
Karen Leonard	University of California, Irvine
Susan Lobo	University of Arizona
Ron Loewe	Mississippi State University
Jackquice Smith-Mahdi	Washburn University
Karyn McKinney Marvasti	Pennsylvania State University, Altoona
Efren N. Padilla	California State University, Hayward
Monique Payne	DePaul University
Kristen M. Wallingford	Davidson College
Carol Ward	Brigham Young University
William Wei	University of Colorado, Boulder
Diane L. Wolf	University of California, Davis
Earl Wright II	Texas Southern University

I would also like to thank my editors at Prentice Hall, Jennifer Gilliland, Nancy Roberts, and Lee Peterson for developing this eleventh edition. They make a great team in the production of academic books.

The truly exciting challenge of writing and researching has always been for me an enriching experience, mostly because of the supportive home I share with my wife, Sandy. She knows so well my appreciation and gratitude, now as in the past and in the future.

Richard T. Schaefer
schaeferrt@aol.com
www.schaefersociology.net

About the Author

R ichard T. Schaefer grew up in Chicago at a time when neighborhoods were going through transitions in ethnic and racial composition. He found himself increasingly intrigued by what was happening, how people were reacting, and how these changes were affecting neighborhoods and people's jobs. In high school, he took a course in sociology. His interest in social issues caused him to gravitate to more sociology courses at Northwestern University, where he eventually received a B.A. in sociology.

"Originally as an undergraduate I thought I would go on to law school and become a lawyer. But after taking a few sociology courses, I found myself wanting to learn more about what sociologists studied and was fascinated by the kinds of questions they raised," Dr. Schaefer says. "Perhaps the most fascinating and, to me, relevant to the 1960s was the intersection of race, gender, and social class." This interest led him to obtain his M.A. and Ph.D. in sociology from the University of Chicago. Dr. Schaefer's continuing interest in race relations led him to write his master's thesis on the membership of the Ku Klux Klan and his doctoral thesis on racial prejudice and race relations in Great Britain.

Dr. Schaefer went on to become a professor of sociology. He has taught sociology and courses on multiculturalism for thirty years. He has been invited to give special presentations to students and faculty on racial and ethnic diversity in Illinois, Indiana, Missouri, North Carolina, Ohio, and Texas.

Dr. Schaefer is author of *Race and Ethnicity in the United States, Fourth Edition* (Prentice Hall, 2007). Dr. Schaefer is the General Editor of the forthcoming three-volume *Encyclopedia of Race, Ethnicity, and Society* (2008). He is also the author of the tenth edition of *Sociology* (2007), the seventh edition of *Sociology: A Brief Introduction* (2008), and the third edition of *Sociology Matters* (2008). His articles and book reviews have appeared in many journals, including *American Journal of Sociology, Phylon: A Review of Race and Culture, Contemporary Sociology, Sociology and Social Research, Sociological Quarterly,* and *Teaching Sociology.* He served as president of the Midwest Sociological Society from 1994 to 1995. In recognition of his achievements in undergraduate teaching, he was named Vincent de Paul Professor of Sociology in 2004.

Understanding Race and Ethnicity

1

CHAPTER OUTLINE

What Is a Subordinate Group?

Types of Subordinate Groups

■ **LISTEN TO OUR VOICES**
Problem of the Color Line
by W. E. B. Du Bois

Does Race Matter?

Sociology and the Study of Race
and Ethnicity

The Creation of
Subordinate-Group Status

The Consequences of
Subordinate-Group Status

Who Am I?

RESEARCH FOCUS
Measuring Multiculturalism

Resistance and Change

Conclusion

Key Terms/Review Questions/Critical Thinking/
Internet Connections—Research Navigator™

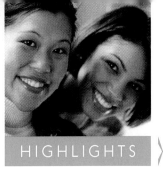

MINORITY GROUPS ARE SUBORDINATED IN TERMS OF POWER and privilege to the majority, or dominant, group. A minority is defined not by being outnumbered but by five characteristics: unequal treatment, distinguishing physical or cultural traits, involuntary membership, awareness of subordination, and in-group marriage. Subordinate groups are classified in terms of race, ethnicity, religion, and gender. The social importance of race is derived from a process of racial formation; its biological significance is uncertain. The theoretical perspectives of functionalism, conflict theory, and labeling offer insights into the sociology of intergroup relations.

Immigration, annexation, and colonialism are processes that may create subordinate groups. Other processes such as expulsion may remove the presence of a subordinate group. Significant for racial and ethnic oppression in the United States today is the distinction between assimilation and pluralism. Assimilation demands subordinate-group conformity to the dominant group, and pluralism implies mutual respect between diverse groups.

Only a few years into the twenty-first century two events shook the country in different ways—the attacks of September 11, 2001, and the devastation left by Hurricane Katrina in 2005.

In the wake of the September 11, 2001 terrorist attacks in the United States, Alexandr Manin, a citizen of Kazakhstan, joined the military in October 2001. He was not joining some far-flung military effort of his country of birth: The 25-year-old from Brooklyn was joining the U.S. Marine Corps. A legal permanent resident, Alexandr can join the U.S. military even though he is not a citizen. His decision is not that unusual. Thousands of immigrants join each year. Some do it for the training or employment possibilities, but others are motivated by allegiance to their new country. As Alexandr said, "It doesn't matter that America is not my country; New York is my city, and what happened shook my life. I feel patriotic, and I have this itch now to go sooner" (Chen and Sengupta 2001, A1).

Hurricane Katrina destroyed more than an enormous part of the Gulf Coast. In its wake people were asking the president if the slow response of the government to provide disaster relief was because large numbers of residents left homeless were poor and Black. Rap star Kanye West weighed in and said that "George Bush doesn't care about Black people." The president denounced such criticism, declaring, "When those Coast Guard choppers . . . were pulling people off roofs, they didn't check the color of a person's skin." Yet the nation was split on this view with 66 percent of African Americans feeling the response would have been faster if the victims had been White compared to only 26 percent of Whites holding that view.

Yet Katrina proved to be more than a Black–White issue. The Asian American community expressed concern over the neglect it saw in assisting Vietnamese Americans who lived in the rural Gulf Coast—themselves only a generation removed from having experienced upheaval during the Vietnam War. Native Americans nationwide reached out to help Gulf Coast reservations whose rebuilding, they felt, was being ignored by the government. And finally, the mayor of New Orleans expressed concern that many of the people arriving to help rebuild the city were Latino and that the first housing likely to be created would be for White residents. The mayor declared that the Almighty wanted the metropolis rebuilt to become a "chocolate" city (Bush 2005; Bustillo 2006; Pew Research Center 2005).

So, in the United States, with its diverse racial and ethnic heritage and new immigrants, is it only major events that bring out social concerns?

- In October 2005, an Elgin high school that is over one-third Hispanic had an assembly in celebration of Mexican Independence Day. A senior refused to stand, fearing that since he was in the process of enlisting in the armed services that honoring another nation's anthem might jeopardize his military status.

- Earlier that same year, residents of Danbury, Connecticut, were seeking to ban volleyball in their parks. Actually, it was "ecuavolley," a form of the game beloved by

Ecuadorian Americans. Played in their backyards, it attracts families and friends and often brings a hundred people together. The Latino community became enraged when the local government, unable to figure out how to ban the sport, tried to convince the federal government to "raid" the backyards looking for illegal immigrants.

- What about trying to stop the sale of methamphetamines? Sounds reasonable, but when in Georgia agents found they now had arrested their forty-ninth convenience store clerk—all of whom were recent Indian immigrants—they realized their "trap" was poorly planned. Undercover agents had gone to the stores asking for cold medicine containing the chemicals, matches, and camping fuel to "finish up a cook." The arrested clerks all stated later that they had merely felt the customer was doing some kind of barbecue and denied that they were assisting in the setting up a meth lab.

- Further north, it was a different immigrant group that attracted unwanted attention. In the old New England town of Lewiston, Maine, hundreds of Somalis have arrived from Africa seeking work and affordable housing thousands of miles from their African hometowns, which had been torn apart by civil strife and famine. Residents expressed alarm over this influx, prompting the mayor to send a letter to all the Somalis already in Lewiston to discourage friends and relatives from relocating there. The pace of Somalis, many of them U.S. citizens, resettling to Lewiston slowed significantly amidst the furor (C. Jones 2003; Malone 2005; Thornburgh 2005; Zernike 2005).

 ASK Yourself

What do you think the Somali immigrants think about this situation?

Relations between racial and ethnic groups are not like relations between family members. The history of the United States is one of racial oppression. It goes well beyond the actions of a mayor in Maine or the plight of people made homeless by a natural disaster in the Gulf Coast. Episodes of a new social identity developing, as in the case of Alexandr Manin, are not unusual, but that does not change the fact that the society is structured to keep some groups of people down and extend privileges automatically to other groups on the basis of race, ethnicity, or gender.

People in the United States and elsewhere are beginning to consider that the same principles that guarantee equality based on race or gender can apply to other groups that are discriminated against. There have been growing efforts to ensure that the same rights and privileges are available to all people, regardless of age, disability, or sexual orientation. These concerns are emerging even as the old divisions over race, ethnicity, and religion continue to fester and occasionally explode into violence that envelops entire nations.

The United States is a very diverse nation, as shown in Table 1.1. According to the 2000 census, about 17 percent of the population are members of racial minorities, and about another 13 percent are Hispanic. These percentages represent almost one out of three people in the United States, without counting White ethnic groups. As shown in Figure 1.1, between 2000 and 2100 the population in the United States is expected to increase from 30 percent Black, Hispanic, Asian, and Native American to 60 percent. Although the composition of the population is changing, the problems of prejudice, discrimination, and mistrust remain.

TABLE 1.1
Racial and Ethnic Groups in the United States, 2000

Classification	Number in Thousands	Percentage of Total Population
RACIAL GROUPS		
Whites (includes 16.9 million White Hispanic)	211,461	75.1
Blacks/African Americans	34,658	12.3
Native Americans, Alaskan Native	2,476	0.9
Asian Americans	10,243	3.6
Chinese	2,433	0.9
Filipinos	1,850	0.7
Asian Indians	1,679	0.6
Vietnamese	1,123	0.4
Koreans	1,077	0.4
Japanese	797	0.2
Other	1,285	0.5
ETHNIC GROUPS		
White ancestry (single or mixed)		
Germans	42,842	15.2
Irish	30,525	10.8
English	24,509	8.7
Italians	15,638	5.6
Poles	8,977	3.2
French	8,310	3.0
Jews	5,200	1.8
Hispanics (or Latinos)	35,306	12.5
Mexican Americans	23,337	8.3
Central and South Americans	5,119	1.8
Puerto Ricans	3,178	1.1
Cubans	1,412	0.5
Other	2,260	0.8
TOTAL (ALL GROUPS)	281,422	

Note: Percentages do not total 100 percent, and subheads do not add up to figures in major heads because of overlap between groups (e.g., Polish American Jews or people of mixed ancestry, such as Irish and Italian).

Source: Brittingham and de la Cruz 2004; Bureau of the Census 2003a; Grieco and Cassidy 2001; Therrien and Ramirez 2001; United Jewish Communities 2003.

FIGURE 1.1 **Population of the United States by Race and Ethnicity, 2005 and 2100 (Projected)**

According to projections by the Census Bureau, the proportion of residents of the United States who are White and non-Hispanic will decrease significantly by the year 2050. By contrast, there will be a striking rise in the proportion of both Hispanic Americans and Asian Americans.

Source: Author's analysis based on American Community Survey 2006 and Bureau of the Census 2004b.

2005

2100 (projected)

What Is a Subordinate Group?

Identifying a subordinate group or a minority in a society seems to be a simple enough task. In the United States, the groups readily identified as minorities—Blacks and Native Americans, for example—are outnumbered by non-Blacks and non–Native Americans. However, minority status is not necessarily the result of being outnumbered. A social minority need not be a mathematical one. A **minority group** is a subordinate group whose members have significantly less control or power over their own lives than do the members of a dominant or majority group. In sociology, *minority* means the same as *subordinate*, and *dominant* is used interchangeably with *majority*.

Confronted with evidence that a particular minority in the United States is subordinate to the majority, some people respond, "Why not? After all, this is a democracy, so the majority rules." However, the subordination of a minority involves more than its inability to rule over society. A member of a subordinate or minority group experiences a narrowing of life's opportunities—for success, education, wealth, the pursuit of happiness—that goes beyond any personal shortcoming he or she may have. A minority group does not share in proportion to its numbers what a given society, such as the United States, defines as valuable.

Being superior in numbers does not guarantee a group control over its destiny and ensure majority status. In 1920, the majority of people in Mississippi and South Carolina were African Americans. Yet African Americans did not have as much control over their lives as Whites, let alone control of the states of Mississippi and South Carolina. Throughout the United States today are counties or neighborhoods in which the majority of people are African American, Native American, or Hispanic, but White Americans are the dominant force. Nationally, 50.8 percent of the population is female, but males still dominate positions of authority and wealth well beyond their numbers.

A minority or subordinate group has five characteristics: unequal treatment, distinguishing physical or cultural traits, involuntary membership, awareness of subordination, and in-group marriage (Wagley and Harris 1958):

1. Members of a minority experience unequal treatment and have less power over their lives than members of a dominant group have over theirs. Prejudice, discrimination, segregation, and even extermination create this social inequality.
2. Members of a minority group share physical or cultural characteristics that distinguish them from the dominant group, such as skin color or language. Each society has its own arbitrary standard for determining which characteristics are most important in defining dominant and minority groups.
3. Membership in a dominant or minority group is not voluntary: People are born into the group. A person does not choose to be African American or White.
4. Minority-group members have a strong sense of group solidarity. William Graham Sumner, writing in 1906, noted that people make distinctions between members of their own group (the in-group) and everyone else (the out-group). When a group is the object of long-term prejudice and discrimination, the feeling of "us versus them" often becomes intense.
5. Members of a minority generally marry others from the same group. A member of a dominant group often is unwilling to join a supposedly inferior minority by marrying one of its members. In addition, the minority group's sense of solidarity encourages marriage within the group and discourages marriage to outsiders.

minority group
A subordinate group whose members have significantly less control or power over their own lives than do the members of a dominant or majority group.

Although "minority" is not about numbers, there is no denying that the majority is diminishing in size relative to the growing diversity of racial and ethnic groups. In Figure 1.2 we see that more and more states have close to a majority of non-Whites or Latinos and that several states have already reached that point today.

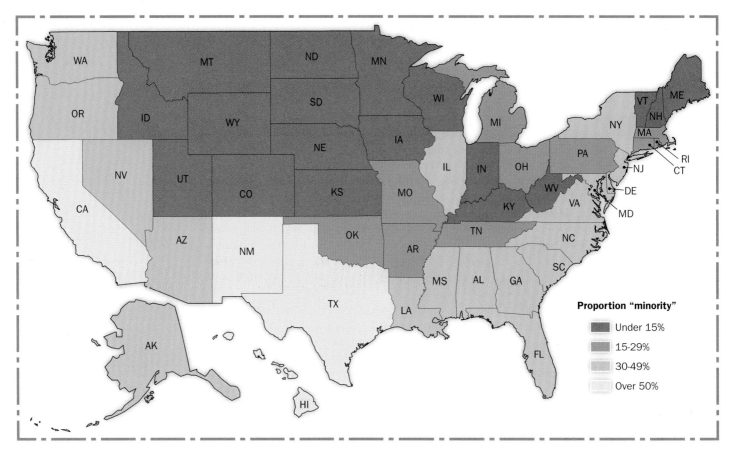

FIGURE 1.2 Race and Ethnic Presence by State (Projected)

According to projections by the Census Bureau, the proportion of residents of the United States who are White and non-Hispanic will decrease significantly by the year 2050. By contrast, there will be a striking rise in the proportion of both Hispanic Americans and Asian Americans.

Source: 2004 data released in 2005 by Bureau of the Census 2005b.

Types of Subordinate Groups

There are four types of minority or subordinate groups. All four, except where noted, have the five properties previously outlined. The four criteria for classifying minority groups are race, ethnicity, religion, and gender.

Racial Groups

The term **racial group** is reserved for minorities and the corresponding majorities that are socially set apart because of obvious physical differences. Notice the two crucial words in the definition: *obvious* and *physical*. What is obvious? Hair color? Shape of an earlobe? Presence of body hair? To whom are these differences obvious, and why? Each society defines what it finds obvious.

In the United States, skin color is one obvious difference. On a cold winter day when one has clothing covering all but one's head, however, skin color may be less obvious than hair color. Yet people in the United States have learned informally that skin color is important and hair color is unimportant. We need to say more than that. In the United States, people have traditionally classified and classify themselves as either Black or White. There is no in-between state except for people readily identified as

racial group
A group that is socially set apart because of obvious physical differences.

Native Americans or Asian Americans. Later in this chapter we will explore this issue more deeply and see how such assumptions have very complex implications.

Other societies use skin color as a standard but may have a more elaborate system of classification. In Brazil, where hostility between races is less than in the United States, numerous categories identify people on the basis of skin color. In the United States, a person is Black or White. In Brazil, a variety of terms, such as *cafuso, mazombo, preto,* and *escuro,* are applied to describe various combinations of skin color, facial features, and hair texture. In Chapter 16, we will be exploring how the people of Brazil consider racial issues there. What makes differences obvious is subject to a society's definition.

The designation of a racial group emphasizes physical differences as opposed to cultural distinctions. In the United States, minority races include Blacks, Native Americans (or American Indians), Japanese Americans, Chinese Americans, Arab Americans, Filipinos, Hawaiians, and other Asian peoples. The issue of race and racial differences has been an important one, not only in the United States but also throughout the entire sphere of European influence. Later in this chapter we will examine race and its significance more closely. We should not forget that Whites are a race, too. As we will consider in Chapter 5, who is White has been subject to change over time as certain European groups were felt historically not to deserve being considered White, but over time, partly to compete against a growing Black population, the "Whiting" of some European Americans has occurred.

Some racial groups may also have unique cultural traditions, as we can readily see in the many Chinatowns throughout the United States. For racial groups, however, the physical distinctiveness and not the cultural differences generally proves to be the barrier to acceptance by the host society. For example, Chinese Americans who are faithful Protestants and know the names of all the members of the Baseball Hall of Fame may be bearers of American culture. Yet these Chinese Americans are still part of a minority because they are seen as physically different.

Ethnic Groups

Ethnic minority groups are differentiated from the dominant group on the basis of cultural differences, such as language, attitudes toward marriage and parenting, and food habits. **Ethnic groups** are groups set apart from others because of their national origin or distinctive cultural patterns.

Ethnic groups in the United States include a grouping that we call Hispanics or Latinos, which includes Mexican Americans, Puerto Ricans, Cubans, and other Latin Americans in the United States. Hispanics can be either Black or White, as in the case of a dark-skinned Puerto Rican who may be taken as Black in central Texas but be viewed as a Puerto Rican in New York City. The ethnic group category also includes White ethnics, such as Irish Americans, Polish Americans, and Norwegian Americans.

The cultural traits that make groups distinctive usually originate from their homelands or, for Jews, from a long history of being segregated and prohibited from becoming a part of the host society. Once in the United States, an immigrant group may maintain distinctive cultural practices through associations, clubs, and worship. Ethnic enclaves such as a Little Haiti or a Greektown in urban areas also perpetuate cultural distinctiveness.

Ethnicity continues to be important, as recent events in Bosnia and other parts of Eastern Europe have demonstrated. Almost a century ago, African American sociologist W. E. B. Du Bois, addressing in 1900 an audience at a world antislavery convention in London, called attention to the overwhelming importance of the color line throughout the world. In "Listen to Our Voices," we read the remarks of Du Bois, the first Black person to receive a doctorate from Harvard, who later helped to organize

ethnic group
A group set apart from others because of its national origin or distinctive cultural patterns.

Voices Listen to Our Voices Listen to

PROBLEM OF THE COLOR LINE

W. E. B. Du Bois

In the metropolis of the modern world, in this the closing year of the nineteenth century, there has been assembled a congress of men and women of African blood, to deliberate solemnly upon the present situation and outlook of the darker races of mankind. The problem of the twentieth century is the problem of the color line, the question as to how far differences of race—which show themselves chiefly in the color of the skin and the texture of the hair—will hereafter be made the basis of denying to over half the world the right of sharing to their utmost ability the opportunities and privileges of modern civilization. . . .

To be sure, the darker races are today the least advanced in culture according to European standards. This has not, however, always been the case in the past, and certainly the world's history, both ancient and modern, has given many instances of no despicable ability and capacity among the blackest races of men.

In any case, the modern world must remember that in this age when the ends of the world are being brought so near together, the millions of black men in Africa, America, and Islands of the Sea, not to speak of the brown and yellow myriads elsewhere, are bound to have a great influence upon the world in the future, by reason of sheer numbers and physical contact. If now the world

of culture bends itself towards giving Negroes and other dark men the largest and broadest opportunity for education and self-development, then this contact and influence is bound to have a beneficial effect upon the world and hasten human progress. But if, by reason of carelessness, prejudice, greed and injustice, the black world is to be exploited and ravished and degraded, the results must be deplorable, if not fatal—not simply to them, but to the high ideals of justice, freedom and culture which a thousand years of Christian civilization have held before Europe. . . .

Let the world take no backward step in that slow but sure progress which has successively refused to let the spirit of class, of caste, of privilege, or of birth, debar from life, liberty, and the pursuit of happiness a striving human soul.

Let not color or race be a feature of distinction between white and black men, regardless of worth or ability. . . .

Thus we appeal with boldness and confidence to the Great Powers of the civilized world, trusting in the wide spirit of humanity, and the deep sense of justice of our age, for a generous recognition of the righteousness of our cause. ■

Source: Du Bois 1900 [1969a]. From pp. 20–21, 23, in **An ABC of Color**, by W. E. B. Du Bois. Copyright 1969 by International Publishers.

the National Association for the Advancement of Colored People (NAACP). Du Bois's observances give us a historic perspective on the struggle for equality. We can look ahead, knowing how far we have come and speculating on how much further we have to go.

Religious Groups

Association with a religion other than the dominant faith is the third basis for minority-group status. In the United States, Protestants, as a group, outnumber members of all other religions. Roman Catholics form the largest minority religion. Chapter 5 focuses on the increasing Judeo-Christian-Islamic diversity of the United States. For people who are not a part of the Christian tradition, such as followers of Islam, allegiance to the faith often is misunderstood and stigmatizes people. This stigmatization became especially widespread and legitimated by government action in the aftermath of the attacks of September 11, 2001.

Religious minorities include such groups as the Church of Jesus Christ of Latter-day Saints (the Mormons), Jehovah's Witnesses, Amish, Muslims, and Buddhists. Cults or sects associated with such practices as animal sacrifice, doomsday prophecy, demon worship, or the use of snakes in a ritualistic fashion would also constitute minorities. Jews are excluded from this category and placed among ethnic groups. Culture is a more important defining trait for Jewish people worldwide than is religious dogma. Jewish Americans share a cultural tradition that goes beyond theology. In this sense, it is appropriate to view them as an ethnic group rather than as members of a religious faith.

Gender Groups

Gender is another attribute that creates dominant and subordinate groups. Males are the social majority; females, although more numerous, are relegated to the position of the social minority, a subordinate status to be explored in detail in Chapter 15. Women are considered a minority even though they do not exhibit all the characteristics outlined earlier (e.g., there is little in-group marriage). Women encounter prejudice and discrimination and are physically distinguishable. Group membership is involuntary, and many women have developed a sense of sisterhood. Women who are members of racial and ethnic minorities face a special challenge to achieving equality. They suffer from greater inequality because they belong to two separate minority groups: a racial or ethnic group plus a subordinate gender group.

Given the diversity in the nation, the workplace is increasingly a place where intergroup tensions may develop.

Source: © Tribune Media Services, Inc. All rights reserved. Reprinted with permission.

Other Subordinate Groups

This book focuses on groups that meet a set of criteria for subordinate status. People encounter prejudice or are excluded from full participation in society for many reasons. Racial, ethnic, religious, and gender barriers are the main ones, but there are others. Age, disabilities, and sexual orientation are among the factors that are used to subordinate groups of people. As a result, in Chapter 16 we will go beyond the title of the book and consider other groups of people who have been excluded from all that society values and witness their fight against prejudice and discrimination.

Does Race Matter?

We see people around us—some of whom may look quite different from us. Do these differences matter? The simple answer is no, but because so many people have for so long acted as if difference in physical characteristics as well as geographic origin and shared culture do matter, distinct groups have been created in people's minds. Race has many meanings for many people. Often these meanings are inaccurate and based on theories discarded by scientists generations ago. As we will see, race is a socially constructed concept (Young 2003).

Biological Meaning

The way the term *race* has been used by some people to apply to human beings lacks any scientific meaning. We cannot identify distinctive physical characteristics for groups of human beings the same way that scientists distinguish one animal species from another. The idea of **biological race** is based on the mistaken notion of a genetically isolated human group.

Even among past proponents who believed that sharp, scientific divisions exist among humans, there were endless debates over what the races of the world were. Given people's frequent migration, exploration, and invasions, pure genetic types have not existed for some time, if they ever did. There are no mutually exclusive races. Skin color among African Americans varies tremendously, as it does among White Americans. There is even an overlapping of dark-skinned Whites and light-skinned African Americans. If we grouped people by genetic resistance to malaria and by fingerprint patterns, Norwegians and many African groups would be of the same race. If we grouped people by some digestive capacities, some Africans, Asians, and southern Europeans would be of one group and West Africans and northern Europeans of another (Leehotz 1995; Shanklin 1994).

Biologically there are no pure, distinct races. For example, blood type cannot distinguish racial groups with any accuracy. Furthermore, applying pure racial types to humans is problematic because of interbreeding. Contemporary studies of DNA on a global basis have determined that 85 percent of human genetic variation is within "local populations" such as within the French or within Afghan people. Another 5 to 89 percent is between local populations thought to be similar in public opinion like the Koreans and Chinese. The remaining 6 to 9 percent of total human variation is what we think of today as constituting races and accounts for skin color, hair form, nose shape, and so forth (Lewontin 2005).

Even the latest research as a part of the Human Genome Project mapping human DNA has only served to confirm genetic diversity with differences within traditionally regarded racial groups (e.g., Black Africans) much greater than that between groups (e.g., between Black Africans and Europeans). Research has also been conducted to determine whether personality characteristics such as temperament and nervous

biological race
The mistaken notion of a genetically isolated human group.

habits are inherited among minority groups. Not surprisingly, the question of whether races have different innate levels of intelligence has led to the most explosive controversy (Bamshad and Olson 2003).

Typically, intelligence is measured as an **intelligence quotient (IQ)**, the ratio of a person's mental age to his or her chronological age, multiplied by 100, where 100 represents average intelligence and higher scores represent greater intelligence. It should be noted that there is little consensus over just what intelligence is, other than as defined by such IQ tests. Intelligence tests are adjusted for a person's age, so that 10-year-olds take a very different test from someone 20 years old. Although research shows that certain learning strategies can improve a person's IQ, generally IQ remains stable as one ages.

A great deal of debate continues over the accuracy of these tests. Are they biased toward people who come to the tests with knowledge similar to that of the test writers? Consider the following two questions used on standard tests.

1. Runner: marathon (A) envoy: embassy, (B) oarsman: regatta, (C) martyr: massacre, (D) referee: tournament.

2. Your mother sends you to a store to get a loaf of bread. The store is closed. What should you do? (A) return home, (B) go to the next store, (C) wait until it opens, (D) ask a stranger for advice.

Both correct answers are B. But is a lower-class youth likely to know, in the first question, what a regatta is? Skeptics argue that such test questions do not truly measure intellectual potential. Inner-city youths often have been shown to respond with A to the second question because that may be the only store with which the family has credit. Youths in rural areas, where the next store may be miles away, are also unlikely to respond with the designated correct answer. The issue of culture bias in tests remains an unresolved concern. The most recent research shows that differences in intelligence scores between Blacks and Whites are almost eliminated when adjustments are made for social and economic characteristics (Brooks-Gunn, Klebanov, and Duncan 1996; Herrnstein and Murray 1994, 30; Kagan 1971; Young 2003).

The second issue, trying to associate these results with certain subpopulations such as races, also has a long history. In the past, a few have contended that Whites have more intelligence on average than Blacks. All researchers agree that within-group differences are greater than any speculated differences between groups. The range of intelligence among, for example, Korean Americans is much greater than any average difference between them as a group and Japanese Americans.

The third issue relates to the subpopulations themselves. If Blacks or Whites are not mutually exclusive biologically, how can there be measurable differences? Many Whites and most Blacks have mixed ancestry that complicates any supposed inheritance of intelligence issue. Both groups reflect a rich heritage of very dissimilar populations, from Swedes to Slovaks and Zulus to Tutus.

In 1994, an 845-page book unleashed a new national debate on the issue of IQ. The latest research effort of psychologist Richard J. Herrnstein and social scientist Charles Murray (1994), published in *The Bell Curve*, concluded that 60 percent of IQ is inheritable and that racial groups offer a convenient means to generalize about any differences in intelligence. Unlike most other proponents of the race–IQ link, the authors offered policy suggestions that include ending welfare to discourage births among low-IQ poor women and changing immigration laws so that the IQ pool in the United States is not diminished. Herrnstein and Murray even made generalizations about IQ levels among Asians and Hispanics in the United States, groups subject to even more intermarriage. It is not possible to generalize about absolute differences between groups, such as Latinos versus Whites, when almost half of Latinos in the United States marry non-Hispanics.

intelligence quotient (IQ)
The ratio of a person's mental age (as computed by an IQ test) to his or her chronological age, multiplied by 100.

Years later, the mere mention of "the bell curve" signals to many the belief in a racial hierarchy with Whites toward the top and Blacks near the bottom. The research present then and repeated today points to the difficulty in definitions: What is intelligence, and what constitutes a racial group, given generations, if not centuries, of intermarriage? How can we speak of definitive inherited racial differences if there has been intermarriage between people of every color? Furthermore, as people on both sides of the debate have noted, regardless of the findings, we would still want to strive to maximize the talents of each individual. All research shows that the differences within a group are much greater than any alleged differences between group averages.

All these issues and controversial research have led to the basic question of what difference it would make if there were significant differences. No researcher believes that race can be used to predict one's intelligence. Also, there is a general agreement that certain intervention strategies can improve scholastic achievement and even intelligence as defined by standard tests. Should we mount efforts to upgrade the abilities of those alleged to be below average? These debates tend to contribute to a sense of hopelessness among some policy makers who think that biology is destiny, rather than causing them to rethink the issue or expand positive intervention efforts.

Why does such IQ research reemerge if the data are subject to different interpretations? The argument that "we" are superior to "them" is very appealing to the dominant group. It justifies receiving opportunities that are denied to others. For example, the authors of *The Bell Curve* argue that intelligence significantly determines the poverty problem in the United States. We can anticipate that the debate over IQ and the allegations of significant group differences will continue. Policy makers need to acknowledge the difficulty in treating race as a biologically significant characteristic.

Social Construction of Race

If race does not distinguish humans from one another biologically, why does it seem to be so important? It is important because of the social meaning people have attached to it. The 1950 (UNESCO) Statement on Race maintains that "for all practical social purposes 'race' is not so much a biological phenomenon as a social myth" (Montagu 1972, 118). Adolf Hitler expressed concern over the "Jewish race" and translated this concern into Nazi death camps. Winston Churchill spoke proudly of the "British race" and used that pride to spur a nation to fight. Evidently, race was a useful political tool for two very different leaders in the 1930s and 1940s.

Race is a social construction, and this process benefits the oppressor, who defines who is privileged and who is not. The acceptance of race in a society as a legitimate category allows racial hierarchies to emerge to the benefit of the dominant "races." For example, inner-city drive-by shootings have come to be seen as a race-specific problem worthy of local officials cleaning up troubled neighborhoods. Yet schoolyard shootouts are viewed as a societal concern and placed on the national agenda.

People could speculate that if human groups have obvious physical differences, then they could have corresponding mental or personality differences. No one disagrees that people differ in temperament, potential to learn, and sense of humor. In its social sense, race implies that groups that differ physically also bear distinctive emotional and mental abilities or disabilities. These beliefs are based on the notion that humankind can be divided into distinct groups. We have already seen the difficulties associated with pigeonholing people into racial categories. Despite these difficulties, belief in the inheritance of behavior patterns and in an association between physical and cultural traits is widespread. It is called **racism** when this belief is coupled with the feeling that certain groups or races are inherently superior to others. Racism is a doctrine of racial supremacy, stating that one race is superior to another (Bash 2001; Bonilla-Silva 1996).

 ASK Yourself

Why are schoolyard massacres national news but school drive-by killings go largely unnoticed?

racism
A doctrine that one race is superior.

We questioned the biological significance of race in the previous section. In modern complex industrial societies, we find little adaptive utility in the presence or absence of prominent chins, epicanthic folds of the eyelids, or the comparative amount of melanin in the skin. What is important is not that people are genetically different but that they approach one another with dissimilar perspectives. It is in the social setting that race is decisive. Race is significant because people have given it significance.

Race definitions are crystallized through what Michael Omi and Howard Winant (1994) called racial formation. **Racial formation** is a sociohistorical process by which racial categories are created, inhibited, transformed, and destroyed. Those in power define groups of people in a certain way that depends on a racist social structure. The Native Americans and the creation of the reservation system for Native Americans in the late 1800s is an example of this racial formation. The federal American Indian policy combined previously distinctive tribes into a single group. No one escapes the extent and frequency to which we are subjected to racial formation.

In the southern United States, the social construction of race was known as the "one-drop rule." This tradition stipulated that if a person had even a single drop of "Black blood," that person was defined and viewed as Black. Today children of biracial or multiracial marriages try to build their own identities in a country that seems intent on placing them in some single, traditional category.

Sociology and the Study of Race and Ethnicity

Before proceeding further with our study of racial and ethnic groups, let us consider several sociological perspectives that provide insight into dominant–subordinate relationships. **Sociology** is the systematic study of social behavior and human groups and, therefore, is aptly suited to enlarge our understanding of intergroup relations. There is a long, valuable history of the study of race relations in sociology. Admittedly, it has not always been progressive; indeed, at times it has reflected the prejudices of society. In some instances, scholars who are members of racial, ethnic, and religious minorities, as well as women, have not been permitted to make the kind of contributions they are capable of making to the field.

Stratification by Class and Gender

All societies are characterized by members having unequal amounts of wealth, prestige, or power. Sociologists observe that entire groups may be assigned less or more of what a society values. The hierarchy that emerges is called stratification. **Stratification** is the structured ranking of entire groups of people that perpetuates unequal rewards and power in a society.

Much discussion of stratification identifies the **class**, or social ranking, of people who share similar wealth, according to sociologist Max Weber's classic definition. Mobility from one class to another is not easy. Movement into classes of greater wealth may be particularly difficult for subordinate-group members faced with lifelong prejudice and discrimination (Gerth and Mills 1958).

Recall that the first property of subordinate-group standing is unequal treatment by the dominant group in the form of prejudice, discrimination, and segregation. Stratification is intertwined with the subordination of racial, ethnic, religious, and gender groups. Race has implications for the way people are treated; so does class. One also has to add the effects of race and class together. For example, being poor and Black is not the same as being either one by itself. A wealthy Mexican American is not the same as an affluent Anglo or as Mexican Americans as a group.

ASK Yourself

Who are we in terms of race or ethnicity? Do you ever ask someone "What are you?" or "Where are you from?" because you are uncomfortable with not knowing? Concepts of race and ethnicity in the United States are socially constructed and, while most of the time we think we correctly identify people around us, sometimes we cannot.

racial formation
A sociohistorical process by which racial categories are created, inhibited, transformed, and destroyed.

sociology
The systematic study of social behavior and human groups.

stratification
A structured ranking of entire groups of people that perpetuates unequal rewards and power in a society.

class
As defined by Max Weber, people who share similar levels of wealth.

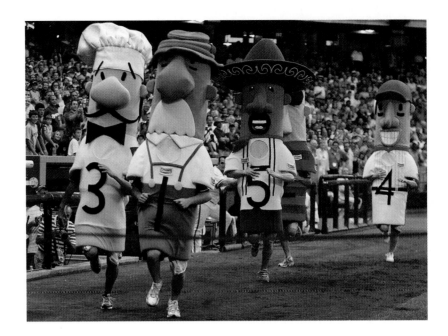

Public discussion of issues such as housing or public assistance often is disguised as discussion of class issues, when in fact the issues are based primarily on race. Similarly, some topics such as the poorest of poor or the working poor are addressed in terms of race when the class component should be explicit. Nonetheless, the link between race and class in society is abundantly clear (Winant 1994).

Another stratification factor that we need to consider is gender. How different is the situation for women as contrasted with men? Returning again to the first property of minority groups—unequal treatment and less control—treatment of women is not equal to that received by men. Whether the issue is jobs or poverty, education or crime, the experience of women typically is more difficult. In addition, the situation faced by women in such areas as health care and welfare raises different concerns than it does for men. Just as we need to consider the role of social class to understand race and ethnicity better, we also need to consider the role of gender.

Theoretical Perspectives

Sociologists view society in different ways. Some see the world basically as a stable and ongoing entity. The endurance of a Chinatown, the general sameness of male–female roles over time, and other aspects of intergroup relations impress them. Some sociologists see society as composed of many groups in conflict, competing for scarce resources. Within this conflict, some people or even entire groups may be labeled or stigmatized in a way that blocks their access to what a society values. We will examine three theoretical perspectives that are widely used by sociologists today: the functionalist, conflict, and labeling perspectives.

Functionalist Perspective In the view of a functionalist, a society is like a living organism in which each part contributes to the survival of the whole. The **functionalist perspective** emphasizes how the parts of society are structured to maintain its stability. According to this approach, if an aspect of social life does not contribute to a society's stability or survival, it will not be passed on from one generation to the next.

It seems reasonable to assume that bigotry between races offers no such positive function, and so we ask, why does it persist? Although agreeing that racial hostility is

functionalist perspective
A sociological approach emphasizing how parts of a society are structured to maintain its stability.

hardly to be admired, the functionalist would point out that it serves some positive functions from the perspective of the racists. We can identify five functions that racial beliefs have for the dominant group.

1. Racist ideologies provide a moral justification for maintaining a society that routinely deprives a group of its rights and privileges.
2. Racist beliefs discourage subordinate people from attempting to question their lowly status; to do so is to question the very foundations of the society.
3. Racial ideologies not only justify existing practices but also serve as a rallying point for social movements, as seen in the rise of the Nazi party.
4. Racist myths encourage support for the existing order. Some argue that if there were any major societal change, the subordinate group would suffer even greater poverty, and the dominant group would suffer lower living standards (Nash 1962).
5. Racist beliefs relieve the dominant group of the responsibility to address the economic and educational problems faced by subordinate groups.

As a result, racial ideology grows when a value system (e.g., that underlying a colonial empire or slavery) is being threatened.

There are also definite dysfunctions caused by prejudice and discrimination. **Dysfunctions** are elements of society that may disrupt a social system or decrease its stability. There are six ways in which racism is dysfunctional to a society, including to its dominant group.

1. A society that practices discrimination fails to use the resources of all individuals. Discrimination limits the search for talent and leadership to the dominant group.
2. Discrimination aggravates social problems such as poverty, delinquency, and crime and places the financial burden of alleviating these problems on the dominant group.
3. Society must invest a good deal of time and money to defend the barriers that prevent the full participation of all members.
4. Racial prejudice and discrimination undercut goodwill and friendly diplomatic relations between nations. They also negatively affect efforts to increase global trade.
5. Social change is inhibited because change may assist a subordinate group.
6. Discrimination promotes disrespect for law enforcement and for the peaceful settlement of disputes.

That racism has costs for the dominant group as well as for the subordinate group reminds us that intergroup conflict is exceedingly complex (Bowser and Hunt 1996; Feagin, Vera, and Batur 2000; Rose 1951).

Conflict Perspective In contrast to the functionalists' emphasis on stability, conflict sociologists see the social world as being in continual struggle. The **conflict perspective** assumes that the social structure is best understood in terms of conflict or tension between competing groups. Specifically, society is a struggle between the privileged (the dominant group) and the exploited (the subordinate groups). Such conflicts need not be physically violent and may take the form of immigration restrictions, real estate practices, or disputes over cuts in the federal budget.

The conflict model often is selected today when one is examining race and ethnicity because it readily accounts for the presence of tension between competing groups. According to the conflict perspective, competition takes place between groups with unequal amounts of economic and political power. The minorities are exploited or, at best, ignored by the dominant group. The conflict perspective is viewed as more

dysfunction
An element of society that may disrupt a social system or decrease its stability.

conflict perspective
A sociological approach that assumes that the social structure is best understood in terms of conflict or tension between competing groups.

radical and activist than functionalism because conflict theorists emphasize social change and the redistribution of resources. Functionalists are not necessarily in favor of inequality; rather, their approach helps us to understand why such systems persist.

Those who follow the conflict approach to race and ethnicity have remarked repeatedly that the subordinate group is criticized for its low status. That the dominant group is responsible for subordination is often ignored. William Ryan (1976) calls this an instance of **blaming the victim**: portraying the problems of racial and ethnic minorities as their fault rather than recognizing society's responsibility.

The recognition that many in society fault the weak rather than embrace the need for restructuring society is not new. Gunnar Myrdal, a Swedish social economist of international reputation, headed a project that produced the classic 1944 work on Blacks in the United States, *The American Dilemma*. Myrdal concluded that the plight of the subordinate group is the responsibility of the dominant majority. It is not a Black problem but a White problem. Similarly, we can use the same approach and note that it is not a Hispanic problem or a Haitian refugee problem but a White problem. Myrdal and others since then have reminded the public and policy makers alike that the ultimate responsibility for society's problems must rest with those who possess the most authority and the most economic resources (Hochschild 1995; Southern 1987).

Labeling Approach Related to the conflict perspective and its concern over blaming the victim is labeling theory. **Labeling theory**, a concept introduced by sociologist Howard Becker, is an attempt to explain why certain people are viewed as deviant and others engaging in the same behavior are not. Students of crime and deviance have relied heavily on labeling theory. According to labeling theory, a youth who misbehaves may be considered and treated as a delinquent if she or he comes from the "wrong kind of family." Another youth, from a middle-class family, who commits the same sort of misbehavior might be given another chance before being punished.

The labeling perspective directs our attention to the role negative stereotypes play in race and ethnicity. The image that prejudiced people maintain of a group toward which they hold ill feelings is called a stereotype. **Stereotypes** are unreliable generalizations about all members of a group that do not take individual differences into account. The warrior image of Native American (America Indian) people is perpetuated by the frequent use of tribal names or even terms such as "Indians" and "Redskins" as sports team mascots. In Chapter 2, we will review some of the research on the stereotyping of minorities. This labeling is not limited to racial and ethnic groups, however. For instance, age can be used to exclude a person from an activity in which he or she is qualified to engage. Groups are subjected to stereotypes and discrimination in such a way that their treatment resembles that of social minorities. Social prejudice exists toward ex-convicts, gamblers, alcoholics, lesbians, gays, prostitutes, people with AIDS, and people with disabilities, to name a few.

The labeling approach points out that stereotypes, when applied by people in power, can have very negative consequences for people or groups identified falsely. A crucial aspect of the relationship between dominant and subordinate groups is the prerogative of the dominant group to define society's values. U.S. sociologist William I. Thomas (1923), an early critic of racial and gender discrimination, saw that the "definition of the situation" could mold the personality of the individual. In other words, Thomas observed that people respond not only to the objective features of a situation (or person) but also to the meaning these features have for them. So, for example, a lone walker seeing a young Black man walking toward him may perceive the situation differently than if the oncoming person is an older woman. In this manner, we can create false images or stereotypes that become real in their social consequences.

blaming the victim
Portraying the problems of racial and ethnic minorities as their fault rather than recognizing society's responsibilities.

labeling theory
A sociological approach introduced by Howard Becker that attempts to explain why certain people are viewed as deviants and others engaging in the same behavior are not.

stereotypes
Unreliable, exaggerated generalizations about all members of a group that do not take individual differences into account.

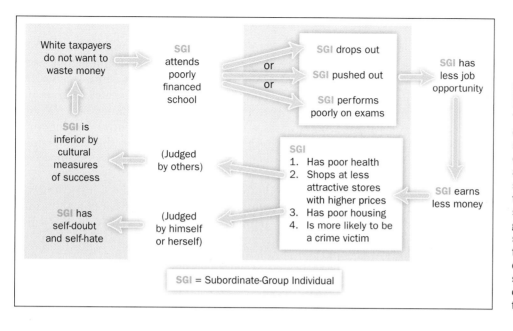

FIGURE 1.3   Self-Fulfilling Prophecy

The self-validating effects of dominant-group definitions are shown in this figure. The subordinate-group individual (SGI) attends a poorly financed school and is left unequipped to perform jobs that offer high status and pay. He or she then gets a low-paying job and must settle for a standard of living far short of society's standards. Because the person shares these societal standards, he or she may begin to feel self-doubt and self-hatred.

In certain situations, we may respond to negative stereotypes and act on them, with the result that false definitions become accurate. This is known as a **self-fulfilling prophecy**. A person or group described as having particular characteristics begins to display the very traits attributed to him or her. Thus, a child who is praised for being a natural comic may focus on learning to become funny to gain approval and attention.

Self-fulfilling prophecies can be devastating for minority groups (Figure 1.3). Such groups often find that they are allowed to hold only low-paying jobs with little prestige or opportunity for advancement. The rationale of the dominant society is that these minority people lack the ability to perform in more important and lucrative positions. Training to become scientists, executives, or physicians is denied to many subordinate-group individuals, who are then locked into society's inferior jobs. As a result, the false definition becomes real. The subordinate group has become inferior because it was defined at the start as inferior and was, therefore, prevented from achieving the levels attained by the majority.

Because of this vicious circle, a talented subordinate-group person may come to see the worlds of entertainment and professional sports as his or her only hope for achieving wealth and fame. Thus, it is no accident that successive waves of Irish, Jewish, Italian, African American, and Hispanic performers and athletes have made their mark on culture in the United States. Unfortunately, these very successes may convince the dominant group that its original stereotypes were valid—that these are the only areas of society in which subordinate-group members can excel. Furthermore, athletics and the arts are highly competitive areas. For every LeBron James and Jennifer Lopez who makes it, many, many more will end up disappointed.

The Creation of Subordinate-Group Status

Three situations are likely to lead to the formation of a subordinate-group–dominant-group relationship. A subordinate group emerges through migration, annexation, and colonialism.

self-fulfilling prophecy
The tendency to respond to and act on the basis of stereotypes, a predisposition that can lead one to validate false definitions.

Migration

People who emigrate to a new country often find themselves a minority in that new country. Cultural or physical traits or religious affiliation may set the immigrant apart from the dominant group. Immigration from Europe, Asia, and Latin America has been a powerful force in shaping the fabric of life in the United States. **Migration** is the general term used to describe any transfer of population. **Emigration** (by emigrants) describes leaving a country to settle in another; **immigration** (by immigrants) denotes coming into the new country. From Vietnam's perspective, the "boat people" were emigrants from Vietnam to the United States, but in the United States they were counted among this nation's immigrants.

Although people may migrate because they want to, leaving the home country is not always voluntary. Conflict or war has displaced people throughout human history. In the twentieth century, we saw huge population movements caused by two world wars; revolutions in Spain, Hungary, and Cuba; the partition of British India; conflicts in Southeast Asia, Korea, and Central America; and the confrontation between Arabs and Israelis.

In all types of movement, even the movement of a U.S. family from Ohio to Florida, two sets of forces operate: push factors and pull factors. Push factors discourage a person from remaining where he or she lives. Religious persecution and economic factors such as dissatisfaction with employment opportunities are possible push factors. Pull factors, such as a better standard of living, friends and relatives who have already emigrated, and a promised job, attract an immigrant to a particular country.

Although generally we think of migration as a voluntary process, much of the population transfer that has occurred in the world has been involuntary. The forced movement of people into another society guarantees a subordinate role. Involuntary migration is no longer common; although enslavement has a long history, all industrialized societies today prohibit such practices. Of course, many contemporary societies, including the United States, bear the legacy of slavery.

Migration has taken on new significance in the twenty-first century partly due to **globalization**. Globalization refers to the worldwide integration of government policies, cultures, social movements, and financial markets through trade and the exchange of ideas. The increased movement of people and money across borders has made the distinction between temporary and permanent migration less meaningful. Although migration has always been fluid, in today's global economy, people are connected across societies culturally and economically like they have never been before. Even after they have relocated, people maintain global linkages to their former country and with a global economy (Richmond 2002).

Annexation

Nations, particularly during wars or as a result of war, incorporate or attach land. This new land is contiguous to the nation, as in the German annexation of Austria and Czechoslovakia in 1938 and 1939 and in the U.S. Louisiana Purchase of 1803. The Treaty of Guadalupe Hidalgo that ended the Mexican-American War in 1848 gave the United States California, Utah, Nevada, most of New Mexico, and parts of Arizona, Wyoming, and Colorado. The indigenous peoples in some of this huge territory were dominant in their society one day, only to become minority-group members the next.

When annexation occurs, the dominant power generally suppresses the language and culture of the minority. Such was the practice of Russia with the Ukrainians and Poles and of Prussia with the Poles. Minorities try to maintain their cultural integrity despite annexation. Poles inhabited an area divided into territories ruled by three countries but maintained their own culture across political boundaries.

migration
A general term that describes any transfer of population.

emigration
Leaving a country to settle in another.

immigration
Coming into a new country as a permanent resident.

globalization
Worldwide integration of government policies, cultures, social movements, and financial markets through trade, movements of people, and the exchange of ideas.

Colonialism in India and elsewhere established for generations a hierarchical relationship between Europeans and much of the rest of the world. Pictured here is a British officer being fanned and pampered by two Indian attendants.

Colonialism

Colonialism has been the most common way for one group of people to dominate another. **Colonialism** is the maintenance of political, social, economic, and cultural dominance over people by a foreign power for an extended period (W. Bell 1991). Colonialism is rule by outsiders but, unlike annexation, does not involve actual incorporation into the dominant people's nation. The long control exercised by the British Empire over much of North America, parts of Africa, and India is an example of colonial domination.

Societies gain power over a foreign land through military strength, sophisticated political organization, and investment capital. The extent of power may also vary according to the dominant group's scope of settlement in the colonial land. Relations between the colonial nation and the colonized people are similar to those between a dominant group and exploited subordinate groups. The colonial subjects generally are limited to menial jobs and the wages from their labor. The natural resources of their land benefit the members of the ruling class.

By the 1980s, colonialism, in the sense of political rule, had become largely a phenomenon of the past, yet industrial countries of North America and Europe still dominated the world economically and politically. Drawing on the conflict perspective, sociologist Immanuel Wallerstein (1974) views the global economic system of today as much like the height of colonial days. Wallerstein has advanced the **world systems theory**, which views the global economic system as divided between nations that control wealth and those that provide natural resources and labor. The limited economic resources available in developing nations exacerbate many of the ethnic, racial, and religious conflicts noted at the beginning of the chapter. In addition the presence of massive inequality between nations only serves to encourage immigration generally and more specifically the movement of many of the most skilled from developing nations to the industrial nations.

A significant exception to the end of foreign political rule is Puerto Rico, whose territorial or commonwealth status with the United States is basically that of a colony. The nearly 4 million people on the island are U.S. citizens but are unable to vote in presidential elections unless they migrate to the mainland. In 1998, 50 percent of Puerto Ricans on the island voted for options favoring continuation of commonwealth status, 47 percent favored statehood, and less than 3 percent voted for independence. Despite their poor showing, proindependence forces are very vocal and enjoy the sympathies of others concerned about the cultural and economic dominance of the U.S. mainland (Navarro 1998; Saad 1998).

colonialism
A foreign power's maintenance of political, social, economic, and cultural dominance over people for an extended period.

world systems theory
A view of the global economic system as divided between nations that control wealth and those that provide natural resources and labor.

internal colonialism
The treatment of subordinate peoples as colonial subjects by those in power.

genocide
The deliberate, systematic killing of an entire people or nation.

ethnic cleansing
Policy of ethnic Serbs to eliminate Muslims from parts of Bosnia.

Colonialism is domination by outsiders. Relations between the colonizer and the colony are similar to those between the dominant and subordinate peoples within the same country. This distinctive pattern of oppression is called **internal colonialism**. Among other cases, it has been applied to the plight of Blacks in the United States and Mexican Indians in Mexico, who are colonial peoples in their own country. Internal colonialism covers more than simple economic oppression. Nationalist movements in African colonies struggled to achieve political and economic independence from Europeans. Similarly, some African Americans also call themselves nationalists in trying to gain more autonomy over their lives (Blauner 1969, 1972).

The Consequences of Subordinate-Group Status

There are several consequences for a group with subordinate status. These differ in their degree of harshness, ranging from physical annihilation to absorption into the dominant group. In this section, we will examine six consequences of subordinate-group status: extermination, expulsion, secession, segregation, fusion, and assimilation. Figure 1.4 illustrates how these consequences can be defined.

Extermination

The most extreme way of dealing with a subordinate group is to eliminate it. Today the term **genocide** is used to describe the deliberate, systematic killing of an entire people or nation. This term is often used in reference to the Holocaust, Nazi Germany's extermination of 12 million European Jews and other ethnic minorities during World War II. The term **ethnic cleansing** was introduced into the world's vocabulary as ethnic Serbs instituted a policy intended to "cleanse"—eliminate—Muslims from parts of Bosnia. More recently, a genocidal war between the Hutu and Tutsi people in Rwanda left 300,000 school-age children orphaned (Chirot and Edwards 2003).

However, genocide also appropriately describes White policies toward Native Americans in the nineteenth century. In 1800, the American Indian population in the United States was about 600,000; by 1850 it had been reduced to 250,000 through warfare with the U.S. Army, disease, and forced relocation to inhospitable environments.

Expulsion

Dominant groups may choose to force a specific subordinate group to leave certain areas or even vacate a country. Expulsion, therefore, is another extreme consequence of minority-group status. European colonial powers in North America and eventually

FIGURE 1.4   Intergroup Relations Continuum
The social consequences of being in a subordinate group can be viewed along a continuum ranging from extermination to forms of mutual acceptance such as pluralism.

the U.S. government itself drove almost all Native Americans out of their tribal lands into unfamiliar territory.

More recently, Vietnam in 1979 expelled nearly 1 million ethnic Chinese from the country, partly as a result of centuries of hostility between the two Asian neighbors. These "boat people" were abruptly eliminated as a minority within Vietnamese society. This expulsion meant that they were uprooted and became a new minority group in many nations, including Australia, France, the United States, and Canada. Thus, expulsion may remove a minority group from one society; however, the expelled people merely go to another nation, where they are again a minority group.

Secession

A group ceases to be a subordinate group when it secedes to form a new nation or moves to an already established nation, where it becomes dominant. After Great Britain withdrew from Palestine, Jewish people achieved a dominant position in 1948, attracting Jews from throughout the world to the new state of Israel. In a similar fashion, Pakistan was created in 1947 when India was partitioned. The predominantly Muslim areas in the north became Pakistan, making India predominantly Hindu. Throughout this century, minorities have repudiated dominant customs. In this spirit, the Estonian, Latvian, Lithuanian, and Armenian peoples, not content to be merely tolerated by the majority, all seceded to form independent states after the demise of the Soviet Union in 1991. In 1999, ethnic Albanians fought bitterly for their cultural and political recognition in the Kosovo region of Yugoslavia.

Some African Americans have called for secession. Suggestions dating back to the early 1700s supported the return of Blacks to Africa as a solution to racial problems. The settlement target of the American Colonization Society was Liberia, but proposals were also advanced to establish settlements in other areas. Territorial separatism and the emigrationist ideology were recurrent and interrelated themes among African Americans from the late nineteenth century well into the 1980s. The Black Muslims, or Nation of Islam, once expressed the desire for complete separation in their own state or territory within the present borders of the United States. Although a secession of Blacks from the United States has not taken place, it has been proposed.

Segregation

Segregation is the physical separation of two groups in residence, workplace, and social functions. Generally, the dominant group imposes segregation on a subordinate group. Segregation is rarely complete, however; intergroup contact inevitably occurs even in the most segregated societies.

Sociologists Douglas Massey and Nancy Denton (1993) wrote *American Apartheid*, which described segregation in U.S. cities based on 1990 data. The title of their book was meant to indicate that neighborhoods in the United States resembled the segregation of the rigid government-imposed racial segregation that prevailed for so long in the Republic of South Africa.

Analyzing the 2000 census results shows little change despite growing racial and ethnic diversity in the nation. Sociologists measure racial segregation using a segregation index or index of dissimilarity. The index ranges from 0 to 100, giving the percentage of a group that would have to move to achieve even residential patterns. For example, Atlanta has an index of 65.6 for Black–White segregation, which means that about 66 percent of either Blacks or Whites would have to move so that each small neighborhood (or census tract) would have the same racial balance as the metropolitan area as a whole. In Figure 1.5, we give the index values for the most and least segregated metropolitan areas among the 50 largest in the nation with respect to the Black–White racial divide.

segregation
The physical separation of two groups, often imposed on a subordinate group by the dominant group.

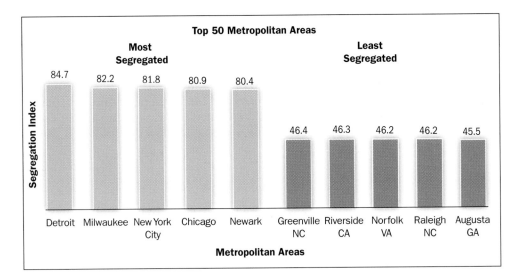

FIGURE 1.5 White–Black Segregation, 2000

Source: From "Ethnic Diversity Grows, Neighborhood Integration Lags Behind." Reprinted by permission of John Logan, Brown University, *http://www.s4.brown.edu* (Also see Lewis Mumford Center 2001).

Overall, the least segregated metropolitan areas tend to be those with the smallest African American populations. For Latinos, the separation patterns are similar, with the highest patterns of isolation occurring in the cities with the larger number of Hispanics (Figure 1.6). There has been little change in overall levels of racial and ethnic segregation from 1990 to 2000. Similarly, Asian–White segregation remains high and showed little change during the 1990s (Lewis Mumford Center 2001).

This focus on metropolitan areas should not cause us to ignore the continuing legally sanctioned segregation of Native Americans on reservations. Although the majority of our nation's first inhabitants live outside these tribal areas, the reservations play a prominent role in the identity of Native Americans. Although it is easier to maintain tribal identity on the reservation, economic and educational opportunities are more limited in these areas segregated from the rest of society.

The social consequences of residential segregation are significant. Given the elevated rates of poverty experienced by racial and ethnic minorities, their patterns of segregation mean that the consequences of poverty (dismal job opportunities, poor health care facilities, delinquency, and crime) are much more likely to be experienced by even the middle-class Blacks, Latinos, and tribal people than it is by middle-class Whites (Massey 2004).

FIGURE 1.6 White–Latino Segregation, 2000

Source: From "Ethnic Diversity Grows, Neighborhood Integration Lags Behind." Reprinted by permission of John Logan, Brown University, *http://www.s4.brown.edu* (Also see Lewis Mumford Center 2001).

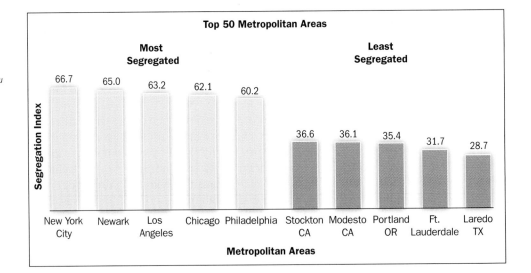

Given segregation patterns, many Whites in the United States have limited contact with people of other racial and ethnic backgrounds. In one study of 100 affluent powerful White men looking at their experiences past and present, it was clear they had lived in a "white bubble"—neighborhoods, schools, elite colleges, and workplaces overwhelmingly White. The continuing pattern of segregation in the United States means our diverse population grows up in very different nations. (Feagin and O'Brien 2003).

Fusion

Fusion occurs when a minority and a majority group combine to form a new group. This combining can be expressed as $A + B + C \rightarrow D$ where A, B, and C represent the groups present in a society, and D signifies the result, an ethnocultural-racial group sharing some of the characteristics of each initial group. Mexican people are an example of fusion, originating as they do out of the mixing of the Spanish and indigenous Indian cultures. Theoretically, fusion does not entail intermarriage, but it is very similar to **amalgamation**, or the process by which a dominant group and a subordinate group combine through intermarriage into a new people. In everyday speech, the words *fusion* and *amalgamation* are rarely used, but the concept is expressed in the notion of a human **melting pot**, in which diverse racial or ethnic groups form a new creation, a new cultural entity (Newman 1973).

The analogy of the cauldron, the "melting pot," was first used to describe the United States by the French observer Crèvecoeur in 1782. The phrase dates back to the Middle Ages, when alchemists attempted to change less valuable metals into gold and silver. Similarly, the idea of the human melting pot implied that the new group would represent only the best qualities and attributes of the different cultures contributing to it. The belief in the United States as a melting pot became widespread in the early twentieth century. This belief suggested that the United States had an almost divine mission to destroy artificial divisions and create a single kind of human. However, the dominant group had indicated its unwillingness to welcome such groups as Native Americans, Blacks, Hispanics, Jews, Asians, and Irish Roman Catholics into the melting pot. It is a mistake to think of the United States as an ethnic mixing bowl. Although there are superficial signs of fusion, as in a cuisine that includes sauerkraut and spaghetti, most contributions of subordinate groups are ignored (Gleason 1980).

Marriage patterns indicate the resistance to fusion. People are unwilling, in varying degrees, to marry outside their own ethnic, religious, and racial groups and indeed through the 1960s there many states where it was illegal to cross racial boundaries. Surveys today show that 20 to 50 percent of various White ethnic groups report single ancestry. When White ethnics do cross boundaries, they tend to marry within their religion and social class. For example, Italians are more likely to marry Irish, who are also Catholic, than they are to marry Protestant Swedes.

Although it may seem that interracial matches are everywhere, there is only modest evidence of a fusion of races in the United States. Racial intermarriage has been increasing, and the number of interracial couples immigrating to the United States has also grown. In 1980, there were 167,000 Black–White couples, but by 2004 there were 413,000. That is still less than one out of every 100 marriages involving a White and Black person.

Among couples in which at least one member is Hispanic, marriages with a non-Hispanic partner account for 27 percent. Taken together all interracial and Hispanic–non-Hispanic couples account for 7.2 percent of married couples today (Bureau of the Census 2005a, 51; A. Coleman 2006; Lee and Edmonston 2005).

Assimilation

Assimilation is the process by which a subordinate individual or group takes on the characteristics of the dominant group and is eventually accepted as part of that group.

? ASK Yourself

Lot's of people seem to date and marry across racial lines. Just how common is it?

fusion
A minority and a majority group combining to form a new group.

amalgamation
The process by which a dominant group and a subordinate group combine through intermarriage to form a new group.

melting pot
Diverse racial or ethnic groups or both, forming a new creation, a new cultural entity.

assimilation
The process by which a subordinate individual or group takes on the characteristics of the dominant group.

Faced with new laws restricting rights of noncitizens, people representing countries from around the world participate in naturalization ceremonies in New York City in 2006 aboard the USS Intrepid. About 18,000 new citizens took the oath during the July 4th week.

Assimilation is a majority ideology in which $A + B + C \rightarrow A$. The majority (A) dominates in such a way that the minorities (B and C) become indistinguishable from the dominant group. Assimilation dictates conformity to the dominant group, regardless of how many racial, ethnic, or religious groups are involved (Newman 1973, 53).

To be complete, assimilation must entail an active effort by the minority-group individual to shed all distinguishing actions and beliefs and the unqualified acceptance of that individual by the dominant society. In the United States, dominant White society encourages assimilation. The assimilation perspective tends to devalue alien culture and to treasure the dominant. For example, assimilation assumes that whatever is admirable among Blacks was adapted from Whites and that whatever is bad is inherently Black. The assimilation solution to Black–White conflict is the development of a consensus around White American values.

Assimilation is very difficult. The person must forsake his or her cultural tradition to become part of a different, often antagonistic culture. Members of the subordinate group who choose not to assimilate look on those who do as deserters.

Assimilation does not occur at the same pace for all groups or for all individuals in the same group. Assimilation tends to take longer under the following conditions:

- The differences between the minority and the majority are large.
- The majority is not receptive or the minority retains its own culture.
- The minority group arrives over a short period of time.
- The minority-group residents are concentrated rather than dispersed.
- The arrival is recent, and the homeland is accessible.

Assimilation is not a smooth process (Warner and Srole 1945).

Assimilation is viewed by many as unfair or even dictatorial. However, members of the dominant group see it as reasonable that people shed their distinctive cultural traditions. In public discussions today, assimilation is the ideology of the dominant group in forcing people how to act. Consequently, the social institutions in the United States, such as the educational system, economy, government, religion, and medicine, all push toward assimilation, with occasional references to the pluralist approach.

The Pluralist Perspective

Thus far, we have concentrated on how subordinate groups cease to exist (removal) or take on the characteristics of the dominant group (assimilation). The alternative to these relationships between the majority and the minority is pluralism. **Pluralism** im-

pluralism
Mutual respect between the various groups in a society for one another's cultures, allowing minorities to express their own culture without experiencing prejudice or hostility.

plies that various groups in a society have mutual respect for one another's culture, a respect that allows minorities to express their own culture without suffering prejudice or hostility. Whereas the assimilationist or integrationist seeks the elimination of ethnic boundaries, the pluralist believes in maintaining many of them.

There are limits to cultural freedom. A Romanian immigrant to the United States could not expect to avoid learning English and still move up the occupational ladder. To survive, a society must have a consensus among its members on basic ideals, values, and beliefs. Nevertheless, there is still plenty of room for variety. Earlier, fusion was described as $A + B + C \rightarrow D$ and assimilation as $A + B + C \rightarrow A$. Using this same scheme, we can think of pluralism as $A + B + C \rightarrow A + B + C$, where groups coexist in one society (Manning 1995; Newman 1973; Simpson 1995).

In the United States, cultural pluralism is more an ideal than a reality. Although there are vestiges of cultural pluralism—in the various ethnic neighborhoods in major cities, for instance—the rule has been for subordinate groups to assimilate. Yet as the minority becomes the numerical majority, the ability to live out one's identity becomes a bit easier. African Americans, Hispanics, and Asian Americans already outnumber Whites in nine of the ten largest cities (Figure 1.7). The trend is toward even greater diversity. Nonetheless, the cost of cultural integrity throughout the nation's history has been high. The various Native American tribes have succeeded to a large extent in maintaining their heritage, but the price has been bare subsistence on federal reservations.

In the United States, there is a reemergence of ethnic identification by groups that had previously expressed little interest in their heritage. Groups that make up the dominant majority are also reasserting their ethnic heritages. Various nationality groups are rekindling interest in almost forgotten languages, customs, festivals, and traditions. In some instances, this expression of the past has taken the form of a protest against exclusion from the dominant society. For example, Chinese youths

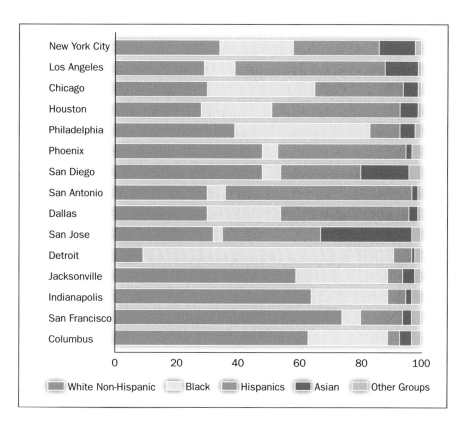

FIGURE 1.7   Race and Ethnicity, 15 Largest Cities, 2005

Source: Author analysis based on American Community Survey 2006 and U.S. Bureau of the Census 2001c.

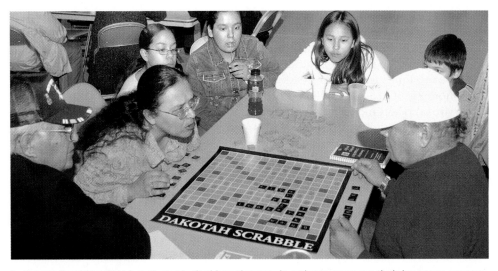

Let's play Scrabble! This is not your typical board game. In order to preserve their language among young people, residents of the Lake Traverse Reservation of the Sisseton Wahpeton Oyate hold Scrabble tournaments where only Dakotah language words are permitted.

chastise their elders for forgetting the old ways and accepting White American influence and control.

The most visible controversy about pluralism is the debate surrounding bilingualism. **Bilingualism** is the use of two or more languages in places of work or education, with each language being treated as equally legitimate. As of 2000, about one of every six people (17 percent) speaks a native language other than English at home. Reflecting this diversity, the demand for interpreters is now unprecedented. One private company, NetworkOmni (2006), provides services to both government and private clients seeking translation services. To meet the need, the business offers interpreters to 911 services, hospitals, and private corporations in 150 languages and dialects ranging from widely spoken languages like Arabic, Spanish, Chinese, and Russian to dozens of lesser-known ones such as Akan, Oromo, and Telagu.

The passionate debate under way in the United States over bilingualism often acknowledges the large number of people who do not speak English at home. In education, bilingualism has seemed to be one way of helping millions of people who want to learn English to function more efficiently within the United States.

Bilingualism for almost two decades has been a political issue. A proposed Constitutional amendment has been introduced that designates English as the "official language of the nation." A major force behind the proposed amendment and other efforts to restrict bilingualism is U.S. English, a nationwide organization that views the English language as the "social glue" that keeps the nation together. This organization supports assimilation. By contrast, Hispanic leaders see the U.S. English campaign as a veiled expression of racism.

The reality of learning English offers little reason for concern about language acquisition. Historically, English is the language of choice by the third generation. By 1970, over 90 percent of the grandchildren of immigrants from Germany, Italy, and Poland spoke only English. In 1990, the grandchildren of Asian immigrants were in the same situation. Today, most of the third generation (64 percent of Mexican and 78 percent of Cuban) speak only English. Given the large Latino enclaves in cities like Miami and the back-and-forth movement along the Mexico–U.S. border, it is surprising that English-only is so high today (Massey et al. 2002).

bilingualism
The use of two or more languages in places of work or education and the treatment of each language as legitimate.

Who Am I?

When Tiger Woods first appeared on *The Oprah Winfrey Show,* he was asked whether it bothered him, the only child of a Black American father and a Thai mother, to be called an African American. He replied, "It does. Growing up, I came up with this name: I'm a Cabalinasian" (White 1997, 34). This is a self-crafted acronym to reflect that Tiger Woods is one-eighth Caucasian, one-fourth Black, one-eighth American Indian, one-fourth Thai, and one-fourth Chinese. Soon after he achieved professional stardom, another golfer was strongly criticized for making racist remarks based on seeing Woods only as African American. If Tiger Woods was not so famous, would most people, upon meeting him, see him as anything but an African American? Probably not. Tiger Woods's problem is really the challenge to a diverse society that continues to try to place people in a few socially constructed racial and ethnic boxes.

The diversity of the United States today has made it more difficult for many people to place themselves on the racial and ethnic landscape. It reminds us that racial formation continues to take place. Obviously, the racial and ethnic landscape, as we have seen, is constructed not naturally but socially and, therefore, is subject to change and different interpretations. Although our focus is on the United States, almost every nation faces the same problems.

The United States tracks people by race and ethnicity for myriad reasons, ranging from attempting to improve the status of oppressed groups to diversifying classrooms. But how can we measure the growing number of people whose ancestry is mixed by anyone's definition? In "Research Focus" we consider how the U.S. Census Bureau dealt with this issue.

Within little more than a generation, we have witnessed changes in labeling subordinate groups from Negroes to Blacks to African Americans, from American Indians to Native Americans or Native Peoples. However, more Native Americans prefer the use of their tribal name, such as *Seminole,* instead of a collective label. The old 1950s statistical term of "people with a Spanish surname" has long been discarded, yet there is disagreement over a new term: *Latino* or *Hispanic.* Like Native Americans, Hispanic Americans avoid such global terms and prefer their native names, such as *Puerto Ricans* or *Cubans.* People of Mexican ancestry indicate preferences for a variety of names, such as *Mexican American, Chicano,* or simply *Mexican.*

Celebrities such as Mariah Carey are unable to protect their privacy. Much has been made about her racial and ethnic identity. She told *Ebony* magazine that she is very aware of her African American heritage, "and I think sometimes it bothers people that I don't say, 'I'm black' and that's it . . . So when people ask, I say I'm, black, Venezuelan, and Irish, because that's who I am" (Carberry 2005, 5).

Focus Research Focus Research Fo

MEASURING MULTICULTURALISM

Approaching Census 2000, a movement was spawned by people who were frustrated by government questionnaires that forced them to indicate only one race. Take the case of Stacey Davis in New Orleans. The young woman's mother is Thai and her father is Creole, a blend of Black, French, and German. People seeing Stacey confuse her for a Latina, Filipina, or Hawaiian. Officially, she has been "White" all her life because she looked White. Congress was lobbied by groups such as Project RACE (Reclassify All Children Equally) for a category "biracial" or "multiracial" that one could select on census forms instead of a specific race. Race is only one of six questions asked of every person in the United States on census day every ten years. After various trial runs with different wordings on the race question, Census 2000 for the first time gave people the option to check off one or more racial groups. "Biracial" or "multiracial" was not an option because pretests showed very few people would use it. This meant that the government recognized in Census 2000 different social constructions of racial identity—that is, a person could be Asian American and White.

Most people did select one racial category in Census 2000. Overall, about 7 million people, or 2.4 percent of the total population, selected two or more racial groups. This was a smaller proportion than many had anticipated. In fact, not even the majority of mixed-race couples identified their children with more than one racial classification. As shown in Figure 1.8, White and American Indian was the most common multiple identity, with about a million people selecting that response. As a group, American Indians were most likely to select a second category and Whites least likely. Race is socially defined.

Complicating the situation is that people are asked separately whether they are Hispanic or non-Hispanic. So a Hispanic person can be any race. In the 2000 Census 94 percent indicated they were one race but 6 percent indicated two or more races; this proportion was three times higher than among non-Hispanics. Therefore, Latinos are more likely than non-Hispanics to indicate a multiracial ancestry.

The Census Bureau's decision does not necessarily resolve the frustration of hun-

---

In the United States and other multiracial, multiethnic societies, panethnicity has emerged. **Panethnicity** is the development of solidarity between ethnic subgroups. The coalition of tribal groups as Native Americans or American Indians to confront outside forces, notably the federal government, is one example of panethnicity. Hispanics or Latinos and Asian Americans are other examples of panethnicity. Although it is rarely recognized by dominant society, the very term *Black* or *African American* represents the descendants of many different ethnic or tribal groups, such as Akamba, Fulani, Hausa, Malinke, and Yoruba (Lopez and Espiritu 1990).

Is panethnicity a convenient label for "outsiders" or a term that reflects a mutual identity? Certainly, many people outside the group are unable or unwilling to recognize ethnic differences and prefer umbrella terms such as *Asian Americans*. For some small groups, combining with others is emerging as a useful way to make themselves heard, but there is always a fear that their own distinctive culture will become submerged. Although many Hispanics share the Spanish language and many are united by Roman Catholicism, only one in four native-born people of Mexican, Puerto Rican,

panethnicity
The development of solidarity between ethnic subgroups, as reflected in the terms Hispanic or Asian American.

esearch Focus Research Focus Research

FIGURE 1.8 **Multiple Race Choices in Census 2000**
This figure shows the percentage distribution of the 6.8 million people who chose two or more races out of 281.4 million total population.
Source: Grieco and Cassidy 2001.

dreds of thousands of people such as Stacey Davis who face on a daily basis people trying to place them in some racial or ethnic category convenient for them. However, it does underscore the complexity of social construction and trying to apply arbitrary definitions to the diversity of the human population. ■

Source: El Nasser 1997; Grieco and Cassidy 2001; Jones and Smith 2001; Tafoya, Johnson, and Hill 2004; K. Williams 2005.

or Cuban descent prefers a panethnic label to nationality or ethnic identity. Yet the growth of a variety of panethnic associations among many groups, including Hispanics, continued through the 1990s (de la Garza et al. 1992; Espiritu 1992).

Add to this cultural mix the many peoples with clear social identities who are not yet generally recognized in the United States. Arabs are a rapidly growing segment whose identity is heavily subject to stereotypes or, at best, is still ambiguous. Haitians and Jamaicans affirm that they are Black but rarely accept the identity of African American. Brazilians, who speak Portuguese, often object to being called Hispanic because of that term's association with Spain. Similarly, there are White Hispanics and non–White Hispanics, some of the latter being Black and others Asian (Bennett 1993; Omi and Winant 1994, 162).

Another challenge to identity is **marginality**, the status of being between two cultures, as in the case of a person whose mother is a Jew and whose father is a Christian. Du Bois (1903) spoke eloquently of the "double consciousness" that Black Americans feel—caught between the concept of being a citizen of the United States but viewed as

marginality
The status of being between two cultures at the same time, such as the status of Jewish immigrants in the United States.

something quite apart from the dominant social forces of society. Incomplete assimilation by immigrants also results in marginality. Although a Filipino woman migrating to the United States may take on the characteristics of her new host society, she may not be fully accepted and may, therefore, feel neither Filipino nor American. The marginalized person finds himself or herself being perceived differently in different environments, with varying expectations (Billson 1988; Park 1928; Stonequist 1937).

As we seek to understand diversity in the United States, we must be mindful that ethnic and racial labels are just that: labels that have been socially constructed. Yet these social constructs can have a powerful impact, whether self-applied or applied by others.

Resistance and Change

By virtue of wielding power and influence, the dominant group may define the terms by which all members of society operate. This is particularly evident in a slave society, but even in contemporary industrialized nations, the dominant group has a disproportionate role in shaping immigration policy, the curriculum of the schools, and the content of the media.

Subordinate groups do not merely accept the definitions and ideology proposed by the dominant group. A continuing theme in dominant–subordinate relations is the minority group's challenge to its subordination. We will see throughout this book the resistance of subordinate groups as they seek to promote change that will bring them more rights and privileges, if not true equality (Moulder 1996).

Resistance can be seen in efforts by racial and ethnic groups to maintain their identity through newspapers, organizations, and in today's technological age, cable television stations and Internet sites. Resistance manifests itself in social movements such as the civil rights movement, the feminist movement, and gay rights efforts. The passage of such legislation as the Age Discrimination Act or the Americans with Disabilities Act marks the success of oppressed groups in lobbying on their own behalf.

Resistance efforts may begin through small actions. For example, residents of a reservation question a second toxic waste dump being located on their land. Although it may bring in money, they question the wisdom of such a move. Their concerns lead to further investigations of the extent to which American Indian lands are used disproportionately to house dangerous materials. This action in turn leads to a broader investigation of the way in which minority-group people often find themselves "hosting" dumps and incinerators. As we will discuss later, these local efforts eventually led the Environmental Protection Agency to monitor the disproportionate placement of toxic facilities in or near racial and ethnic minority communities. There is little reason to expect that such reforms would have occurred if we had relied on traditional decision-making processes alone.

Change has occurred. At the beginning of the twentieth century lynching was practiced in many parts of the country. At the beginning of the twenty-first century, laws punishing hate crimes were increasingly common and embraced a variety of stigmatized groups. Although this social progress should not be ignored, the nation needs to focus concern ahead on the significant social inequalities that remain (Best 2001).

An even more basic form of resistance is to question societal values. In this book, we avoid using the term *American* to describe people of the United States because geographically Brazilians, Canadians, and El Salvadorans are Americans as well. It is very easy to overlook how our understanding of today has been shaped by the way institutions and even the very telling of history have been presented by members of the dominant group. African American studies scholar Molefi Kete Asante (2000) has called for an **Afrocentric perspective** that emphasizes the customs of African cultures and how they have pervaded the history, culture, and behavior of Blacks in the United States and around the world. Afrocentrism counters Eurocentrism and works toward a multiculturalist or pluralist orientation in which no viewpoint is suppressed. The Afrocentric approach could become part of our school curriculum, which has not adequately acknowledged the importance of this heritage.

The Afrocentric perspective has attracted much attention in colleges. Opponents view it as a separatist view of history and culture that distorts both past and present. Its supporters counter that African peoples everywhere can come to full self-determination only when they are able to overthrow White or Eurocentric intellectual interpretations (Early 1994).

In considering the inequalities present today, as we will in the chapters that follow, it is easy to forget how much change has taken place. Much of the resistance to prejudice and discrimination in the past, whether to slavery or to women's prohibition from voting, took the active support of members of the dominant group. The indignities still experienced by subordinate groups continue to be resisted as subordinate groups and their allies among the dominant group seek further change.

afrocentric perspective
An emphasis on the customs of African cultures and how they have pervaded the history, culture, and behavior of Blacks in the United States and around the world.

Conclusion

One hundred years ago, sociologist and activist W. E. B. Du Bois took another famed Black activist, Booker T. Washington, to task for saying that the races could best work together apart, like fingers on a hand. Du Bois felt that Black people had to be a part of all social institutions and not create their own. Today among African Americans, Whites, and other groups, the debate persists as to what form society should take. Should we seek to bring everyone together into an integrated whole? Or do we strive to maintain as much of our group identities as possible while working cooperatively as necessary?

In this first chapter, we have attempted to organize our approach to subordinate–dominant relations in the United States. We observed that subordinate groups do not necessarily contain fewer members than the dominant group. Subordinate groups are classified into racial, ethnic, religious, and gender groups. Racial classification has been of interest, but scientific findings do not explain contemporary race relations. Biological differences of race are not supported by scientific data. Yet as the continuing debate over standardized tests demonstrates, attempts to establish a biological meaning of race have not been swept entirely into the dustbin of history. However, the social meaning given to physical differences is very significant. People have defined racial differences in such a way as to encourage or discourage the progress of certain groups.

The oppression of selected racial and ethnic groups may serve some people's vested interests. However, denying opportunities or privileges to an entire group only leads to conflict between dominant and subordinate groups. Societies such as the United States develop ideologies to justify privileges given to some and opportunities denied to others. These ideologies may be subtle, such as assimilation (i.e., "You should be like us"), or overt, such as racist thought and behavior.

Subordinate groups generally emerge in one of three ways: migration, annexation, or colonialism. Once a group is given subordinate status, it does not necessarily keep it indefinitely. Extermination, expulsion, secession, segregation, fusion, and assimilation remove the status of subordination, although inequality still persists.

Subordinate-group members' reactions include the seeking of an alternative avenue to acceptance and success: "Why should we forsake what we are to be accepted by them?" In response to this question, there has been a resurgence of ethnic identification. Pluralism describes a society in which several different groups coexist, with no dominant or subordinate groups. The hope for such a society remains unfulfilled, except perhaps for isolated exceptions.

Race and ethnicity remains the single most consistent social indicator of where we live, whom we date, what media we watch, where we worship, and even how we vote (Younge 2004).

Subordinate groups have not and do not always accept their second-class status passively. They may protest, organize, revolt, and resist society as defined by the dominant group. Patterns of race and ethnic relations are changing, not stagnant. Furthermore, in many nations, including the United States, the nature of race and ethnicity changes through migration. Indicative of the changing landscape, biracial and multiracial children present us with new definitions of identity emerging through a process of racial formation, reminding us that race is socially constructed.

The two significant forces that are absent in a truly pluralistic society are prejudice and discrimination. In an assimilation society, prejudice disparages out-group differences, and discrimination financially rewards those who shed their past. In the next two chapters, we will explore the nature of prejudice and discrimination in the United States.

Key Terms

Afrocentric perspective 33	ethnic group 9	minority group 7
amalgamation 25	functionalist perspective 16	panethnicity 30
assimilation 25	fusion 25	pluralism 26
bilingualism 28	genocide 22	racial formation 15
biological race 12	globalization 20	racial group 8
blaming the victim 18	immigration 20	racism 14
class 15	intelligence quotient (IQ) 13	segregation 23
colonialism 21	internal colonialism 22	self-fulfilling prophecy 19
conflict perspective 17	labeling theory 18	sociology 15
dysfunction 17	marginality 31	stereotypes 18
emigration 20	melting pot 25	stratification 15
ethnic cleansing 22	migration 20	world systems theory 21

Review Questions

1. In what ways have you seen issues of race and ethnicity emerge? Identify groups that have been subordinated for reasons other than race, ethnicity, or gender.

2. How can a significant political or social issue (such as bilingual education) be viewed in assimilationist and pluralistic terms?

3. How does the concept of "double consciousness" popularized by W. E. B. Du Bois relate to the question "Who am I?"

Critical Thinking

1. How diverse is your city? Can you see evidence that some group is being subordinated? What social construction of categories do you see that may be different in your community as compared to elsewhere?

2. In 2006 "Nuestro Himno" ("Our Anthem") hit the airwaves as a Spanish-language version of Francis Scott Key's original words. Do you think this represents a positive development or a step backward? How does it relate to the Intergroup Relations Continuum pictured on page 22?

3. Identify some protest and resistance efforts by subordinated groups in your area. Have they been successful? Why are some people who say they favor equality uncomfortable with such efforts? How can people unconnected with such efforts either help or hinder such protests?

Internet Connections—Research Navigator™

1. To access the full resources of Research Navigator™, please find the access code printed on the inside cover of OneSearch with Research Navigator™: Sociology. You may have received this booklet if your instructor recommended this guide be packaged with new textbooks. (If your book did not come with this printed guide, you can purchase one through your college bookstore.) Visit our Research Navigator™ site at *www.ResearchNavigator.com*. Once at this site, click on Register under New Users and enter your access code to create a personal Login Name and Password. (When revisiting the site, use the same Login Name and Password.) Browse the features of the Research Navigator™ Web site and search the databases of academic journals, newspapers, magazines, and Web links.

2. For further information relevant to Chapter 1, you may wish to use such keywords as "ethnicity," "IQ," and "biracial," and the search engine will supply relevant and recent scholarly and popular press publications. Use the *New York Times* Search-by-Subject Archive to find recent news articles related to sociology and the Link Library feature to locate relevant Web links organized by the key terms associated with this chapter.

2 Prejudice

CHAPTER OUTLINE

Hate Crimes

Prejudice and Discrimination

Theories of Prejudice

The Content of Prejudice: Stereotypes

■ **LISTEN TO OUR VOICES**
Gangsters, Gooks, Geishas, and Geeks
by Helen Zia

The Extent of Prejudice

The Mood of the Oppressed

Intergroup Hostility

Reducing Prejudice

■ **RESEARCH FOCUS**
What's In a Name?

Ways to Fight Hate

Conclusion

Key Terms/Review Questions/
Critical Thinking/Internet Connections—
Research Navigator™

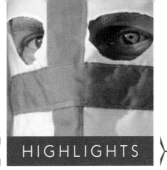
PREJUDICE IS A NEGATIVE ATTITUDE THAT REJECTS AN ENTIRE group; discrimination is behavior that deprives a group of certain rights or opportunities. Prejudice does not necessarily coincide with discrimination, as is made apparent by a typology developed by sociologist Robert Merton. Several theories have been advanced to explain prejudice: scapegoating, authoritarian personality, exploitation, and the normative approach. These explanations examine prejudice in terms of content (negative stereotypes) and extent. Prejudice is not limited to the dominant group; subordinate groups often dislike one another. The mass media seem to be of limited value in reducing prejudice and may even intensify ill feeling. Equal-status contact and the shared-coping approach may reduce hostility between groups. In response to increasing diversity in the workplace, corporations and organizations have mounted diversity training programs to increase organizational effectiveness and combat prejudice. There are also ten identifiable steps that we as individuals can take to stop prejudice and hatred.

African American artist Jacob Lawrence portrays the separate facilities typical of the treatment received by Blacks in the first half of the twentieth century.

Source: The Phillips Collection, Washington, DC, ARS (Artists Rights Society).

On a Web site available since 1995 to anyone with Internet access, one can find the latest reports of Black on White crimes and why "Western civilization" won as well as tips on self-defense. Elsewhere on the Internet you can locate organizations assuring that contributions to them will go only to White victims of Hurricane Katrina. In Pennsylvania a racial slur and the letters "KKK" were spray-painted on the cars, garage doors, and mailbox at the home of a Jamaican immigrant family, Also in 2006, a support center for lesbian, gay, bisexual, and transgender students at Oregon State University was vandalized. Elsewhere in Florida, a dead raccoon hanging from a noose and a racist note were found on the porch of a Methodist church with a predominantly Black congregation. So is it a fringe element that engages in negative views of people based only on their racial, ethnic, or religious affiliation?

In a social science laboratory at the University of Colorado, Boulder, subjects in an experiment played video games as researchers recorded their moves. Presented with a rapid-fire series of pictures showing Black and White men holding various objects—cell phones, cameras, wallets, guns—subjects pressed one button if they considered a character harmless and another button to "shoot" characters they believed to be armed. Researchers were studying people's split-second reactions to tests of decision making involving race and the potential for violence. When they analyzed the results, they found that the subjects, most of whom were White, had reacted more quickly to pictures of Black men with guns than to pictures of White men with guns. Subjects were also more likely to mistakenly shoot an unarmed Black character than an unarmed White character. The results were the same for Black subjects as for White subjects.

These results were not unusual. In a similar study at the University of Washington, psychologists asked college students to distinguish virtual citizens and police officers from armed criminals. They found that subjects were more likely to misperceive and shoot images of Black men than of White men in the video game they created. For the last three decades, in fact, research has suggested that people in the United States are more likely to see Black men as being violent than White men, which translated in this study for the Black men to be more likely to be "shot" at.

Are there limits for this hostility? Apparently not. In the commercially successful "Grand Theft Auto: Vice City" video game, players are encouraged to take very violent actions against a variety of images. At one point players are informed that they have come across a "Stinking nest of Haitians. We gonna kill them all. Kill all the Haitians." Why? "Kill all the Haitians, they are all drug dealers." This game, released by Rockstar Video in 2003, bore a parental code declaring that use was inappropriate for children under 17, but aside from the fact that so many youth access such games, we might be left to ponder why such a "game" with this dialogue would be marketed even to young adults (CBS New York 2003; Correll et al. 2002; Greenwald, Oakes, and Hoffman 2003; Kim 2005; Southern Poverty Law Center 2006b).

Prejudice is so prevalent that it is tempting to consider it inevitable or, even more broadly, just part of human nature. Such a view ignores its variability from individual to individual and from society to society. People must learn prejudice as children before they exhibit it as adults. Therefore, prejudice is a social phenomenon, an acquired characteristic. A truly pluralistic society would lack unfavorable distinctions made through prejudicial attitudes among racial and ethnic groups.

Ill feeling between groups may result from ethnocentrism. **Ethnocentrism** is the tendency to assume that one's culture and way of life are superior to all others. The ethnocentric person judges other groups and other cultures by the standards of his or her own group. This attitude leads people quite easily to view other cultures as inferior. We see a woman with a veil and may regard it as strange and backward, yet find it baffling when other societies see U.S. women in short skirts and view the dress as inappropriate. Ethnocentrism and other expressions of prejudice are voiced very often, but unfortunately they also become the motivation for criminal acts.

ethnocentrism
The tendency to assume that one's culture and way of life are superior to all others.

hate crimes
Criminal offense committed because of the offender's bias against a race, religion, ethnic/national origin group, or sexual orientation group.

Hate Crimes

Although prejudice certainly is not new in the United States, it is receiving increased attention as it manifests itself in neighborhoods, at meetings, and on college campuses. The Hate Crime Statistics Act, which became law in 1990, directs the Department of Justice to gather data on hate or bias crimes. The government defines

an ordinary crime as a **hate crime** *when offenders choose a victim because of some characteristic— for example, race, ethnicity, or religion—and provide evidence that hatred prompted them to commit the crime. Hate or bias crimes which is another name can also be based on hatred because of national origin or sexual orientation. (Harlow 2005:1)*

This law created a national mandate to identify such crimes, whereas previously only twelve states had monitored hate crimes. In 1994, the act was amended to include disabilities, both physical and mental, as factors that could be considered a basis for hate crimes.

In 2005 law enforcement agencies released hate crime data submitted by police agencies covering 86 percent of the United States. Even though many, many hate crimes are not reported, a staggering number of offenses that come to law agencies' attention were motivated by hate. There were official reports of more than 8,800 hate crimes and bias-motivated incidents. As indicated in Figure 2.1, race was the apparent motivation for the bias in about 51 percent of the reports, and religion, sexual orientation, and ethnicity accounted for 13 to 18 percent each. Vandalism and intimidation were the most common, but 43 percent of the incidents against people involved assault, rape, or murder.

These official reports appear to be only the tip of the iceberg. Government-commissioned surveys asking a national cross section indicate that annually people say they have been victims of 192,000 hate crimes of which only half get reported to police.

FIGURE 2.1   Distribution of Reported Hate Crimes in 2005

Source: Department of Justice 2006.

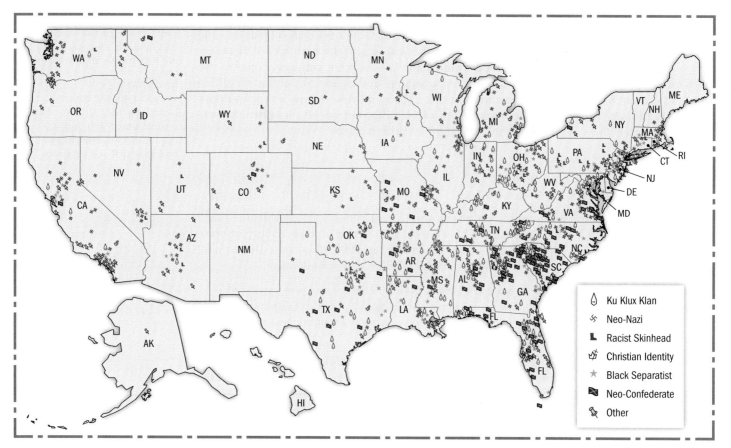

FIGURE 2.2   Active Hate Groups

Source: Map, "Active Hate Groups in the U.S. in the Year 2005," The Intelligence Project of the Southern Poverty Law Center (2006a). Reprinted by permission of Southern Poverty Law Center.

Of these only one out ten according to the victims are confirmed as hate crimes. Although definitions vary, there is obviously a lot of racial hostility in the country that becomes violent (Harlow 2005).

National legislation and publicity have made *hate crime* a meaningful term, and we are beginning to recognize the victimization associated with such incidents. A current proposal would make a violent crime into a federal crime if it were motivated by racial or religious bias. Although passage is uncertain, the serious consideration of the proposal indicates a willingness to consider a major expansion of federal jurisdiction. Currently, federal law prohibits crimes motivated by race, color, religion, or national origin only if they involve violation of a federally guaranteed right, such as voting.

Most hate crimes are the result of people acting alone or with a few others, but there is a troubling pattern of organized hate groups that dates back more than 130 years in the United States to the founding of the Ku Klux Klan. As shown in Figure 2.2, some people organize into groups with the express purpose of showing their hatred toward other groups of people. Law enforcement agencies attempt to monitor such groups but are limited in their actions by constitutional freedoms of speech and assembly.

These hate groups not only serve as a source of hate literature but they also reframe contemporary issues such as abortion, immigration, hurricane victims, crime statistics, school overcrowding, and unemployment to all be the result of the presence of

 ASK Yourself

What kind of role does the Internet play when it comes to bias?

"strangers," such as racial and ethnic minorities and the foreign born (McVeigh and Sikkink 2005).

Victimized groups are not merely observing these events. Watchdog organizations play an important role in documenting bias-motivated violence; among such groups are the Anti-Defamation League (ADL), the National Institute Against Prejudice and Violence, the Southern Poverty Law Center, and the National Gay and Lesbian Task Force.

Established hate groups have even set up propaganda sites on the World Wide Web. This also creates opportunities for previously unknown haters and hate groups to promote themselves. However, hate crime legislation does not affect such outlets because of legal questions involving freedom of speech. An even more recent technique has been to use instant messaging software, which enables Internet users to create a private chat room with another individual. Enterprising bigots use directories to target their attacks through instant messaging, much as harassing telephone calls were placed in the past (Gerstenfeld and Grant 2003; Rivlin 2005).

What causes people to dislike entire groups of other people? Is it possible to change attitudes? This chapter tries to answer these questions about prejudice. Chapter 3 focuses on discrimination.

Prejudice and Discrimination

Prejudice and discrimination are related concepts but are not the same. **Prejudice** is a negative attitude toward an entire category of people. The two important components in this definition are *attitude* and *entire category*. Prejudice involves attitudes, thoughts, and beliefs, not actions. Prejudice often is expressed through the use of **ethnophaulisms**, or ethnic slurs, which include derisive nicknames such as *honky*, *gook*, or *wetback*. Ethnophaulisms also include speaking about or to members of a particular group in a condescending way ("José does well in school for a Mexican American") or referring to a middle-aged woman as "one of the girls."

A prejudiced belief leads to categorical rejection. Prejudice is not disliking someone you meet because you find his or her behavior objectionable. It is disliking an entire racial or ethnic group, even if you have had little or no contact with that group. A college student who requests a room change after three weeks of enduring his roommate's sleeping all day, playing loud music all night, and piling garbage on his desk is not prejudiced. However, he is displaying prejudice if he requests a change on arriving at school and learning that his new roommate is of a different nationality.

Prejudice is a belief or attitude; discrimination is action. **Discrimination** involves behavior that excludes all members of a group from certain rights, opportunities, or privileges. Like prejudice, it must be categorical. If an employer refuses to hire as a typist an Italian American who is illiterate, it is not discrimination. If she refuses to hire any Italian Americans because she thinks they are incompetent and does not make the effort to see whether an applicant is qualified, it is discrimination.

Merton's Typology

Prejudice does not necessarily coincide with discriminatory behavior. In exploring the relationship between negative attitudes and negative behavior, sociologist Robert Merton (1949, 1976) identified four major categories (Figure 2.3). The label added to each of Merton's categories may more readily identify the type of person being described. These are

1. The unprejudiced nondiscriminator: all-weather liberal
2. The unprejudiced discriminator: reluctant liberal

prejudice
A negative attitude toward an entire category of people, such as a racial or ethnic minority.

ethnophaulism
Ethnic or racial slurs, including derisive nicknames.

discrimination
The denial of opportunities and equal rights to individuals and groups because of prejudice or for other arbitrary reasons.

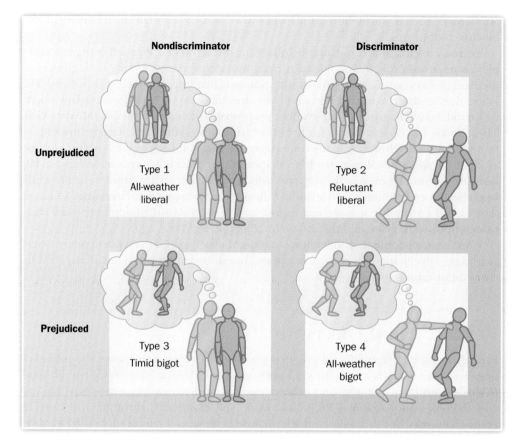

FIGURE 2.3 Prejudice and Discrimination

As sociologist Robert Merton's formulation shows, prejudice and discrimination are related to each other but are not the same.

3. The prejudiced nondiscriminator: timid bigot
4. The prejudiced discriminator: all-weather bigot

As the term is used in types 1 and 2, liberals are committed to equality among people. The all-weather liberal believes in equality and practices it. Merton was quick to observe that all-weather liberals may be far removed from any real competition with subordinate groups such as African Americans or women. Furthermore, such people may be content with their own behavior and may do little to change themselves. The reluctant liberal is not this committed to equality between groups. Social pressure may cause such a person to discriminate. Fear of losing employees may lead a manager to avoid promoting women to supervisory capacities. Equal-opportunity legislation may be the best way to influence the reluctant liberals.

Types 3 and 4 do not believe in equal treatment for racial and ethnic groups, but they vary in their willingness to act. The timid bigot, type 3, will not discriminate if discrimination costs money or reduces profits or if he or she is pressured not to by peers or the government. The all-weather bigot unhesitatingly acts on the prejudiced beliefs he or she holds.

LaPiere's Study

Merton's typology points out that attitudes should not be confused with behavior. People do not always act as they believe. More than a half century ago, Richard LaPiere (1934, 1969) exposed the relationship between racial attitudes and social conduct. From 1930 to 1932 LaPiere traveled throughout the United States with a Chinese couple. Despite an alleged climate of intolerance of Asians, LaPiere observed that the couple were treated courteously at hotels, motels, and restaurants. He was puzzled by the good reception they received; all the conventional attitude surveys showed extreme prejudice by Whites toward the Chinese.

Was it possible that LaPiere had been fortunate during his travels and consistently stopped at places operated by the tolerant members of the dominant group? To test this possibility, he sent questionnaires asking the very establishments at which they had been served whether the owner would "accept members of the Chinese race as guests in your establishment." More than 90 percent responded no, even though LaPiere's Chinese couple had been treated politely at all the establishments. How can this inconsistency be explained? People who returned questionnaires reflecting prejudice were unwilling to act based on those asserted beliefs; they were timid bigots.

The LaPiere study is not without flaws. First, he had no way of knowing whether the respondent to the questionnaire was the same person who had served him and the Chinese couple. Second, he accompanied the couple, but the questionnaire suggested that the arrival would be unescorted (and, in the minds of some, uncontrolled) and perhaps would consist of many Chinese people. Third, personnel may have changed between the time of the visit and the mailing of the questionnaire (Deutscher, Restello, and Restello 1993).

The LaPiere technique has been replicated with similar results. This technique raises the question of whether attitudes are important if they are not completely reflected in behavior. But if attitudes are not important in small matters, they are important in other ways: Lawmakers legislate and courts may reach decisions based on what the public thinks.

This is not just a hypothetical possibility. Legislators in the United States often are persuaded to vote in a certain way by what they perceive as changed attitudes toward immigration, affirmative action, and prayer in public schools. Sociologists have enumerated some of prejudice's functions. For the majority group, it serves to maintain privileged occupations and more power for its members.

The following sections examine the theories of why prejudice exists and discuss the content and extent of prejudice today.

Theories of Prejudice

Prejudice is learned. Friends, relatives, newspapers, books, movies, television, and the Internet all teach it. Awareness begins at an early age that there are differences between people that society judges to be important. Several theories have been advanced to explain the rejection of certain groups in a society. We will examine four theoretical explanations. The first two (scapegoating and authoritarian personality) tend to be psychological, emphasizing why a particular person harbors ill feelings. The second two are more sociological (exploitation and normative), viewing prejudice in the context of our interaction in a larger society.

Scapegoating Theory

Scapegoating theory says that prejudiced people believe they are society's victims. The term *scapegoat* comes from a biblical injunction telling the Hebrews to send a goat into the wilderness to symbolically carry away the people's sins. Similarly, the theory of scapegoating suggests that, rather than accepting guilt for some failure, a person transfers the responsibility for failure to some vulnerable group. In the major tragic twentieth-century example, Adolf Hitler used the Jews as the scapegoat for all German social and economic ills in the 1930s. This premise led to the passage of laws restricting Jewish

scapegoating theory
A person or group blamed irrationally for another person's or group's problems or difficulties.

Many would regard this statue of colonialist Hannah Duston in Massachusetts as perpetuating stereotypes about American Indians. She is honored for killing and scalping ten Abeenaki Indians in 1697 while defending her family. Believed to be the first woman ever honored in the United States with a monument, it portrays her holding a hatchet in her right hand.

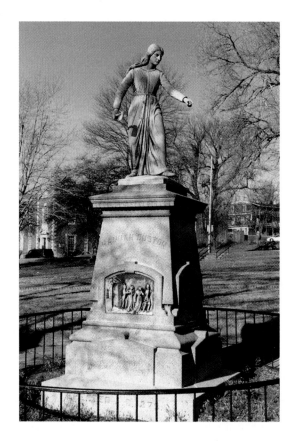

life in pre–World War II Germany and eventually escalated into the mass extermination of Europe's Jews.

Today in the United States, immigrants, whether legal or illegal, often are blamed by "real Americans" for their failure to get jobs or secure desirable housing. The immigrant becomes the scapegoat for one's own lack of skills, planning, or motivation. It is so much easier to blame someone else.

Public figures who should know better express their ill feelings. Longtime civil rights leader Andrew Young in 2006 applauded the expansion of Wal-Mart noting that the big box stores were merely replacing small stores run by Jews, Koreans, and Arabs that ripped off customers. In the same year a drunk Mel Gibson pulled over by a policeman who was Jewish was told by the Hollywood celebrity that "Jews are responsible for all the wars in the world." Both Young and Gibson quickly apologized for their inflammatory remarks, but finding scapegoats among racial and ethnic groups occurs all the time (McGhee 2006; McNamara 2006).

Like exploitation theory, scapegoating theory adds to our understanding of why prejudice exists but does not explain all its facets. For example, scapegoating theory offers little explanation of why a specific group is selected or why frustration is not taken out on the real culprit when possible. Also, both the exploitation and the scapegoating theories suggest that every person sharing the same general experiences in society would be equally prejudiced, but that is not the case. Prejudice varies between individuals who seem to benefit equally from the exploitation of a subordinate group or who have experienced equal frustration. In an effort to explain these personality differences, social scientists developed the concept of the authoritarian personality.

Authoritarian Personality Theory

A number of social scientists do not see prejudice as an isolated trait that anyone can have. Several efforts have been made to detail the prejudiced personality, but the most comprehensive effort culminated in a volume titled *The Authoritarian Personality* (Adorno et al. 1950). Using a variety of tests and relying on more than 2,000 respondents, ranging from middle-class Whites to inmates of San Quentin (California) State Prison, the authors claimed they had isolated the characteristics of the authoritarian personality.

In these authors' view, the basic characteristics of the **authoritarian personality** are adherence to conventional values, uncritical acceptance of authority, and concern with power and toughness. With obvious relevance to the development of intolerance, the authoritarian personality was also characterized by aggressiveness toward people who did not conform to conventional norms or obey authority. According to the researchers, this personality type developed from an early childhood of harsh discipline. A child with an authoritarian upbringing obeyed and then later treated others as he or she had been raised.

This study has been widely criticized, but the very existence of such wide criticism indicates the influence of the study. Critics have attacked the study's equation of authoritarianism with right-wing politics (although liberals can also be rigid); its failure to see that prejudice is more closely related to other individual traits, such as social class, than to authoritarianism as it was defined; and the research methods used. Graham Kinloch (1974), discussing personality research, added a fourth criticism: The authors concentrated on factors behind extreme racial prejudice rather than on more common expressions of hostility.

Exploitation Theory

Racial prejudice often is used to justify keeping a group in a subordinate position, such as a lower social class. Conflict theorists, in particular, stress the role of racial and ethnic hostility as a way for the dominant group to keep its position of status and power intact. Indeed, this approach maintains that even the less affluent White working class uses prejudice to minimize competition from upwardly mobile minorities.

This exploitation theory is clearly part of the Marxist tradition in sociological thought. Karl Marx emphasized exploitation of the lower class as an integral part of capitalism. Similarly, the exploitation or conflict approach explains how racism can stigmatize a group as inferior so that the exploitation of that group can be justified. As developed by Oliver Cox (1942), exploitation theory saw prejudice against Blacks as an extension of the inequality faced by the entire lower class.

The **exploitation theory** of prejudice is persuasive. Japanese Americans were the object of little prejudice until they began to enter occupations that brought them into competition with Whites. The movement to keep Chinese out of the country became strongest during the late nineteenth century, when Chinese immigrants and Whites fought over dwindling numbers of jobs. Both the enslavement of African Americans and the removal westward of Native Americans were to a significant degree economically motivated.

Although many cases support the exploitation theory, it is too limited to explain prejudice in all its forms. First, not all minority groups are exploited economically to the same extent. Second, many groups that have been the victims of prejudice have not been persecuted for economic reasons, such as the Quakers or gays and lesbians. Nevertheless, as Gordon Allport (1979) concludes, the exploitation theory correctly points a finger at one of the factors in prejudice, that is, the rationalized self-interest of the privileged.

ASK Yourself

Suppose you encounter a person whose prejudice is obvious? Will you say or do anything? What if it is a friend who speaks disparagingly of all members of some ethnic or religious group? Will you speak out? When do you speak out?

authoritarian personality
A psychological construct of a personality type likely to be prejudiced and to use others as scapegoats.

exploitation theory
A Marxist theory that views racial subordination in the United States as a manifestation of the class system inherent in capitalism.

TABLE 2.1
Theories of Prejudice

There is no one explanation of why prejudice exists, but several approaches taken together offer insight.

Theory	Proponent	Explanation	Example
Scapegoating	Bruno Bettelheim Morris Janowitz	People blame others for their own failures.	An unsuccessful applicant assumes that a minority member or a woman got "his" job.
Authoritarian	Adorno and associates	Child rearing leads one to develop intolerance as an adult.	The rigid personality type dislikes people who are different.
Exploitation	Oliver C. Cox Marxist theory	People use others unfairly for economic advantage.	A minority member is hired at a lower wage level.
Normative	Thomas Pettigrew	Peer and social influences encourage tolerance or intolerance.	A person from an intolerant household is more likely to be openly prejudiced.

Normative Approach

Although personality factors are important contributors to prejudice, normative or situational factors must also be given serious consideration. The **normative approach** takes the view that prejudice is influenced by societal norms and situations that encourage or discourage the tolerance of minorities.

Analysis reveals how societal influences shape a climate for tolerance or intolerance. Societies develop social norms that dictate not only what foods are desirable (or forbidden) but also what racial and ethnic groups are to be favored (or despised). Social forces operate in a society to encourage or discourage tolerance. The force may be widespread, such as the pressure on White Southerners to oppose racial equality while there was slavery or segregation. The influence of social norms may be limited, as when one man finds himself becoming more sexist as he competes with three women for a position in a prestigious law firm.

We should not view the four approaches to prejudice summarized in Table 2.1 as mutually exclusive. Social circumstances provide cues for a person's attitudes; personality determines the extent to which people follow social cues and the likelihood that they will encourage others to do the same. Societal norms may promote or deter tolerance; personality traits suggest the degree to which a person will conform to norms of intolerance. To understand prejudice, we need to use all four approaches together.

The Content of Prejudice: Stereotypes

On Christmas Day 2001, Arab American Walied Shater boarded an American Airlines flight from Baltimore to Dallas carrying a gun. Immediately, the cockpit crew refused to let him fly, fearing that Shater would take over the plane and use it as a weapon of mass destruction. Yet Walied Shater carried documentation that he was a Secret Service agent, and calls to Washington, DC, confirmed that he was flying to join a presidential protection force at President George W. Bush's ranch in Texas. Nevertheless, the crew could not get past the stereotype of Arab American men posing a lethal threat (Leavitt 2002).

normative approach
The view that prejudice is influenced by societal norms and situations that encourage or discourage the tolerance of minorities.

? ASK Yourself

How do the images we see affect how we view people? On the left is a scene from the familiar motion picture *King and I*. On the right is the real monarch, King Chulalongkorn, and his son. The king in real life bore limited similarity to the portrayal made famous by the Russian-born actor Yul Brynner. Is what we know about many ethnic and religious groups more likely the result of portrayals in the popular media than any actual study of their history and customs?

What Are Stereotypes?

In Chapter 1, we saw that stereotypes play a powerful role in how people come to view dominant and subordinate groups. **Stereotypes** are unreliable generalizations about all members of a group that do not take individual differences into account. Numerous scientific studies have been made of these exaggerated images. This research has shown the willingness of people to assign positive and negative traits to entire groups of people, which are then applied to particular individuals. Stereotyping causes people to view Blacks as superstitious, Whites as uncaring, and Jews as shrewd. Over the last seventy years of such research, social scientists have found that people have become less willing to express such views openly, but as we will see later, prejudice persists (MacRae, Stangor, and Hewstore 1996).

If stereotypes are exaggerated generalizations, why are they so widely held, and why are some traits more often assigned than others? Evidence for traits may arise out of real conditions. For example, more Puerto Ricans live in poverty than Whites, and so the prejudiced mind associates Puerto Ricans with laziness. According to the New Testament, some Jews were responsible for the crucifixion of Jesus, and so, to the prejudiced mind, all Jews are Christ killers. Some activists in the women's movement are lesbians, and so all feminists are seen as lesbians. From a kernel of fact, faulty generalization creates a stereotype.

Labels take on such strong significance that people often ignore facts that contradict their previously held beliefs. People who believe many Italian Americans to be members of the Mafia disregard law-abiding Italian Americans. Muslims are regularly portrayed in a violent, offensive manner that contributes to their being misunderstood and distrusted. We will consider later in the chapter how this stereotype about Muslims has become widespread since the mid-1970s but intensified after the attack on the World Trade Center on September 11, 2001.

In "Listen to Our Voices," journalist Helen Zia comments about how immigrant parents grapple with the prejudice their children feel. Should they teach their children their language and perhaps heighten stereotypes and ill feelings from others or push them to become American as fast as possible?

Trends in Stereotypes

In the last thirty years, we have become more and more aware of the power of the mass media to introduce stereotypes into everyday life. Television is a prime example. Almost

stereotypes
Unreliable, exaggerated generalizations about all members of a group that do not take individual differences into account.

Voices Listen to Our Voices Listen to

GANGSTERS, GOOKS, GEISHAS, AND GEEKS

Ah so. No tickee, no washee. So sorry, so sollee.

Chinkee, Chink. Jap, Nip, zero, kamikaze. Dothead, flat face, flat nose, slant eye, slope. Slit, mamasan, dragon lady. Gook, VC, Flip, Hindoo.

By the time I was ten, I'd heard such words so many times I could feel them coming before they parted lips. I knew they were meant in the unkindest way. Still, we didn't talk about these incidents at home, we just accepted them as part of being in America, something to learn to rise above.

The most common taunting didn't even utilize words but a string of unintelligible gobbledygook that kids—and adults—would spew as they pretended to speak Chinese or some other Asian language. It was a mockery of how they imagined my parents talked to me.

Truth was that Mom and Dad rarely spoke to us in Chinese, except to scold or call us to dinner. Worried that we might develop an accent, my father insisted that we speak English at home. This, he explained, would lessen the hardships we might encounter and make us more acceptable as Americans.

I'll never know if my father's language decision was right. On the one hand, I, like most Asian Americans, have been complimented countless times on my spoken English by people who assumed I was a foreigner. "My, you speak such good English," they'd cluck. "No kidding, I ought to,"

Helen Zia

I would think to myself, then wonder: should I thank them for assuming that English isn't my native language? Or should I correct them on the proper usage of "well" and "good"?

More often than feeling grateful for my American accent, I've wished that I could jump into a heated exchange of rapid-fire Chinese, volume high and spit flying. But with a vocabulary limited to "Ni hao?" (How are you?) and "Ting bu dong" (I hear but don't understand), meaningful exchanges are woefully impossible. I find myself smiling and nodding like a dashboard ornament. I'm envious of the many people I know who grew up speaking an Asian language yet converse in English beautifully.

Armed with standard English and my flat New Jersey "a," I still couldn't escape the name-calling. I became all too familiar with other names and faces that supposedly matched mine—Fu Manchu, Suzie Wong, Hop Sing, Madame Butterfly, Charlie Chan, Ming the Merciless—the "Asians" produced for mass consumption. Their faces filled me with shame whenever I saw them on TV or in the movies. They defined my face to the rest of the world: a sinister Fu, Suzie the whore, subservient Hop Sing, pathetic Butterfly, cunning Chan, and warlike Ming. Inscrutable Orientals all, real Americans none. ■

Source: Excerpt from pp. 109–110 in *Asian-American Dreams* by Helen Zia. Copyright (c) 2000 by Helen Zia. Reprinted by permission of Farrar, Straus and Giroux.

all television roles showing leadership feature Whites. Even urban-based programs such as *Seinfeld* and *Friends* prospered without any major Black, Hispanic, or Asian American characters. A 1998 national survey of boys and girls aged 10 to 17 asked a very simple question and came up with some disturbing findings. The children were asked, "How often do you see your race on television?" The results showed that 71 percent of White children said "very often," compared with only 42 percent of African Americans, 22 percent of Latinos, and 16 percent of Asian Americans. Even more troubling is that generally the children view the White characters as affluent and well educated, whereas they see the minority characters as "breaking the law or rules," "being lazy," and "acting goofy." Later in this chapter we will consider the degree to which the media have changed in presenting stereotyped images (Children Now 1998).

The labeling of individuals has strong implications for the self-fulfilling prophecy. Studies show that people are all too aware of the negative images other people have of them. When asked to estimate the prevalence of hard-core racism among Whites, one in four Blacks agrees that more than half "personally share the attitudes of groups like the Ku Klux Klan toward Blacks"; only one Black in ten says "only a few" share such views. Stereotypes not only influence how people feel about themselves but, perhaps equally important, also affect how people interact with others. If people feel that others hold incorrect, disparaging attitudes toward them, it undoubtedly will make it difficult to have harmonious relations (Sigelman and Tuch 1997).

Do only dominant groups about subordinate groups hold stereotypes? The answer is clearly no. White Americans even believe generalizations about themselves, although admittedly these are usually positive. Subordinate groups also hold exaggerated images of themselves. Studies before World War II showed a tendency for Blacks to assign to themselves many of the same negative traits assigned by Whites. Today, African Americans, Jews, Asians, and other minority groups largely reject stereotypes of themselves.

Stereotyping in Action: Racial Profiling

Five Middle Eastern–looking men were led off the Newark-bound plane by security in 2006. Suspiciously in-flight they had been talking among themselves in a foreign language looking at flight manuals they had aboard. Actually, as the investigation would reveal, they were Portuguese-speaking Angolan and Israeli soldiers returning from government-approved helicopter training in Texas. Reasonable precaution in these days of terrorism? Perhaps. But would air marshals have been as suspicious of White travelers or if the men had been speaking English? Suspicions raised by appearances often related to race or ethnicity are not new.

A Black dentist, Elmo Randolph, testified before a state commission that he was stopped dozens of times in the 1980s and 1990s while traveling the New Jersey Turnpike to work. Invariably state troopers asked, "Do you have guns or drugs?" "My parents always told me, be careful when you're driving on the turnpike" said Dr. Randolph, 44. "White people don't have that conversation" (Purdy 2001:37; also see Frenandez and Fahim 2006).

Little wonder that Dr. Randolph was pulled over. Although African Americans accounted for only 17 percent of the motorists on that turnpike, they were 80 percent of the motorists pulled over. Such occurrences gave rise to the charge that we had added a new traffic offense to the books: DWB, or Driving While Black (Bowles 2000).

In recent years government attention has been given to a social phenomenon with a long history: racial profiling. According to the Department of Justice, **racial profiling** is any police-initiated action based on race, ethnicity, or national

racial profiling
Any arbitrary police-initiated action based on race, ethnicity, or natural origin rather than a person's behavior.

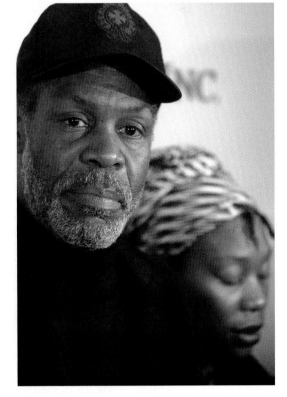

Actor Danny Glover, with his daughter, holds a press briefing after filing a discrimination complaint with a New York taxi company in 1999. A driver refused to let him sit in the front of the car while his daughter and a friend sat in the back.

origin rather than the person's behavior. Generally, profiling occurs when law enforcement officers, including customs officials, airport security, and police, assume that people fitting certain descriptions are likely to be engaged in something illegal. Beginning in the 1980s with the emergence of the crack cocaine market, skin color became a key characteristic. This profiling can be a very explicit use of stereotypes. For example, the federal antidrug initiative, Operation Pipeline, specifically encouraged officers to look for people with dreadlocks or for Latino men traveling together.

The reliance on racial profiling persists despite overwhelming evidence that it is misleading. Whites are more likely to be found with drugs in the areas in which minority group members are disproportionately targeted. A federal study made public in 2005 found little difference nationwide in the likelihood of being stopped by officers, but African Americans were twice as likely to have their vehicles searched and Latinos were five time more likely. A similar pattern emerged in the likelihood of force being used against drivers with it three times more likely among Latinos and Blacks than White drivers (Lichtblau 2005).

In the 1990s increased attention to racial profiling led not only to special reports and commissions but also to talk of legislating against it. This proved difficult. The U.S. Supreme Court in *Whren v. United States* (1996) upheld the constitutionality of using a minor traffic infraction as an excuse to stop and search a vehicle and its passengers. Nonetheless, states and other government units are discussing policies and training that would discourage racial profiling. At the same time, most law enforcement agencies reject the idea of compiling racial data on traffic stops, arguing that it would be a waste of money and staff time.

The effort to stop racial profiling came to an abrupt end after the September 11, 2001 terrorist attacks on the United States. Suspicions about Muslims and Arabs in the United States became widespread. Foreign students from Arab countries were summoned for special questioning. Legal immigrants identified as Arab or Muslim were scrutinized for any illegal activity and were prosecuted for routine immigration violations that were ignored for people of other ethnic backgrounds and religious faiths. In 2003, President George W. Bush issued guidelines that barred federal agents from using race and ethnicity in investigations but specifically exempted cases involving terrorism and national security matters (Withrow 2006).

National surveys showed that those groups most likely to be stigmatized were not as supportive of using profiling. In a national 2004 survey, people were asked if racial profiling was ever justified when passengers are stopped at airport security checkpoints. Less than a third of all African Americans and 40 percent of Latinos supported such profiling compared to 46 percent of non-Hispanic Whites. Nonetheless, racial profiling moved from a questionable local police action to a reaffirmed matter of national policy (Carlson 2004; Coates 2004; Lichtblau 2003).

The Extent of Prejudice

Interest in developing theories of prejudice or studying the concept has been exceeded only by interest in measuring it. From the outset, efforts to measure prejudice have suffered from disagreement over exactly what constitutes intolerance and whether there is such a phenomenon as no prejudice at all. Add to these uncertainties the methodological problems of attitude measurement and the empirical study of prejudice becomes fraught with difficulty.

The extent of prejudice can be measured only in relative differences. For example, we cannot accurately say that prejudice toward Puerto Ricans is four times greater than that toward Portuguese Americans. We can conclude that prejudice is greater toward one group than toward the other; we just cannot quantify how much greater. The social distance scale is especially appropriate to assess differences in prejudice.

The Social Distance Scale

Robert Park and Ernest Burgess first defined **social distance** as the tendency to approach or withdraw from a racial group (1921, 440). Emory Bogardus (1968) conceptualized a scale that could measure social distance empirically. His social distance scale is so widely used that it is often called the **Bogardus scale**.

The scale asks people how willing they would be to interact with various racial and ethnic groups in specified social situations. The situations describe different degrees of social contact or social distance. The items used, with their corresponding distance scores, follow. People are asked whether they would be willing to work alongside, be a neighbor, and, showing the least amount of social distance, be related through marriage. Over the seventy-year period the tests were administered, certain patterns emerge. In the top third of the hierarchy are White Americans and northern Europeans. Held at greater social distance are eastern and southern Europeans, and generally near the bottom are racial minorities (Bogardus 1968; Song 1991).

More recently the concept of social distance has been applied to how people actually function. Sociologists Grace Kao and Kara Joyner released a study in 2004 that considered the responses of more than 90,000 adolescents nationwide in an in-school survey. Among many questions, students were asked to identify their best friend and later to identify that person's race and ethnicity. As we can see in Figure 2.4, most people for their primary friendships chose someone of the same race or ethnicity. While Whites are the numerical majority nationwide, we can see that over 81 percent

social distance
Tendency to approach or withdraw from a racial group.

Bogardus scale
Technique to measure social distance toward different racial and ethnic groups.

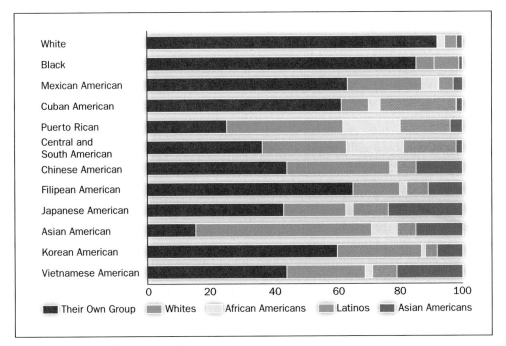

FIGURE 2.4   Who's Your Best Friend?

Source: Adapted from Table I in Grace Kao and Kara Joyner 2002 "Do Race and Ethnicity Matter Among Friends?" p. 564 in *The Sociological Quarterly* Vol. 45 Issue 3.

of White youths had as their best friend someone who was also White. Other racial and ethnic groups are more likely to venture outside their group's boundaries.

Generally, the researchers also found that among the respondents who had friends of different racial and ethnic origin, they were more likely to show greater social distance—that is, they were less likely to have been in each other's homes, share in fewer activities, and were less likely to talk about their problems with each other.

Trends in Prejudice

We hold certain images or stereotypes of each other, and we also may be more prejudiced toward some groups of people than others. However, is prejudice less than it used to be? The evidence we will see is mixed, with some indications of willingness to give up some old prejudices while new negative attitudes emerge.

Over the years, nationwide surveys have consistently shown growing support by Whites for integration, even during the Southern resistance and Northern turmoil of the 1960s. National opinion surveys conducted from the 1950s into the 21st century, with few exceptions, show an increase in the number of Whites responding positively to hypothetical situations of increased contact with African Americans. For example, 30 percent of the Whites sampled in 1942 felt that Blacks should not attend separate schools, but by 1970, 74 percent supported integrated schools, and fully 93 percent responded in that manner in 1991 (Davis et al. 2005).

Attitudes are still important, however. A change of attitude may create a context in which legislative or behavioral change can occur. Such attitude changes leading to behavior changes did occur in some areas in the 1960s. Changes in intergroup behavior mandated by law in housing, schools, public places of accommodation, and the workplace appear to be responsible for making some new kinds of interracial contact a social reality. Attitudes translate into votes, peer pressure, and political clout, each of which can facilitate efforts to undo racial inequality.

Today few Whites are likely to express support for school segregation or endorse beliefs of Black racial inferiority. However, many scholars see the substantial opposition by Whites to immigration reform or affirmative action as merely a more acceptable, veiled way to express deep-felt prejudiced feelings toward ethnic and racial groups. This "new" expression of prejudice has been described as modern racism, color-blind racism, or laissez-faire racism.

When we survey White attitudes toward African Americans, two conclusions are inescapable. First, attitudes are subject to change, and in periods of dramatic social upheaval, dramatic shifts can occur within one generation. Second, less progress was made in the late twentieth century than was made in the 1950s and 1960s. Researchers have variously called these subtle forms of prejudice color-blind racism, modern racism, or laissez-faire racism. People today may not be as openly racist or prejudiced as in the past in expressing the notion that they are inherently superior to others. Yet much of the opposition to policies related to eradicating poverty or immigration is a smokescreen for those who dislike entire groups of racial and ethnic minorities (Bonilla–Silva 2006; Quillian 2006).

In the 1990s, White attitudes hardened still further as issues such as affirmative action, immigration, and crime provoked strong emotions among members of this dominant group as well as members of subordinate groups. Economically less-successful groups such as African Americans and Latinos have been associated with negative traits to the point at which issues such as welfare and crime are now viewed as race issues. Besides making the resolution of very difficult social issues even harder, this is another instance of blaming the victim. These perceptions come at a time when the willingness of government to address domestic ills is limited by increasing opposition to new taxes. Although there is some evidence that fewer Whites are consistently prejudiced on all issues from interracial marriage to school integration, it is also apparent that many Whites continue to endorse some anti-Black statements and that negative images are widespread as they relate to the major domestic issues of the twenty-first century.

The Mood of the Oppressed

Sociologist W. E. B. Du Bois relates an experience from his youth in a largely White community in Massachusetts. He tells how, on one occasion, the boys and girls were exchanging cards, and everyone was having a lot of fun. One girl, a newcomer, refused his card as soon as she saw that Du Bois was Black. He wrote,

> Then it dawned upon me with a certain suddenness that I was different from others . . . shut out from their world by a vast veil. I had therefore no desire to tear down that veil, to creep through; I held all beyond it in common contempt and lived above it in a region of blue sky and great wandering shadows. (Du Bois 1903:2)

In using the image of a veil, Du Bois describes how members of subordinate groups learn that they are being treated differently. In his case and that of many others, this leads to feelings of contempt toward all Whites that continue for a lifetime.

Opinion pollsters have been interested in White attitudes on racial issues longer than they have measured the views of subordinate groups. This neglect of minority attitudes reflects, in part, the bias of the White researchers. It also stems from the contention that the dominant group is more important to study because it is in a better position to act on its beliefs. The results of nationwide surveys conducted in the United States in 2003 offer insight into sharply different views on the state of race relations today (Figure 2.5). African Americans are much less satisfied with the current situation than are White Americans and Hispanics.

We have focused so far on what usually comes to mind when we think about prejudice: one group hating another group. But there is another form of prejudice: A group may come to hate itself. Members of groups held in low esteem by society may, as a result, have low self-esteem themselves. Many social scientists once believed that members of subordinate groups hated themselves or at least had low self-esteem. Similarly, they argued that Whites had high self-esteem. High self-esteem means that an individual has fundamental respect for himself or herself, appreciates his or her own merits, and is aware of personal faults and will strive to overcome them.

The research literature of the 1940s through the 1960s emphasized the low self-esteem of minorities. Usually, the subject was African Americans, but the argument has also been generalized to include any subordinate racial, ethnic, or nationality group. This view is no longer accepted. We should not assume that minority status influences personality traits in either a good or a bad way. First, such assumptions may create a stereotype. We cannot describe a Black personality any more accurately than we can a White personality. Second, characteristics of minority-group members are not entirely the result of subordinate racial status; they are also influenced by low incomes, poor neighborhoods, and so forth. Third, many studies of personality imply that certain values are normal or preferable, but the values chosen are those of dominant groups.

If assessments of a subordinate group's personality are so prone to misjudgments, why has the belief in low self-esteem been so widely held? Much of the research rests on studies with preschool-age Black children asked to express preferences among dolls with different facial colors. Indeed, one such study, by psychologists Kenneth and Mamie Clark (1947), was cited in the arguments before the U.S. Supreme Court in the landmark 1954 case *Brown v. Board of Education*. The Clarks' study showed that Black children preferred White dolls, a finding suggesting that the children had developed

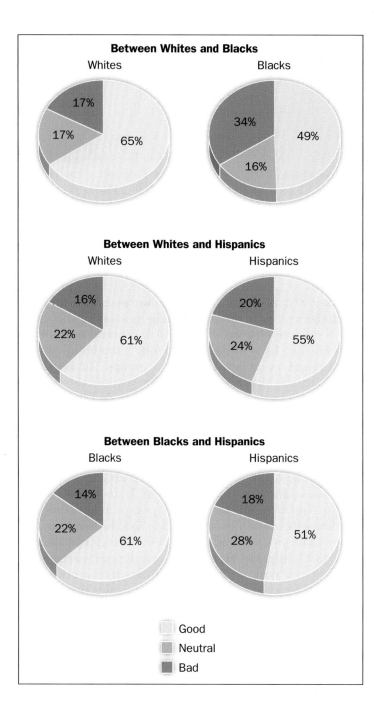

FIGURE 2.5   What Is the State of Race Relations?

Source: AARP 2004, 36, 41, 44.

a negative self-image. Although subsequent doll studies have sometimes shown Black children's preference for white-faced dolls, other social scientists contend that this shows a realization of what most commercially sold dolls look like rather than documenting low self-esteem (Bloom 1971; Powell-Hopson and Hopson 1988).

Because African American children, as well as other subordinate groups' children, can realistically see that Whites have more power and resources and, therefore, rate them higher does not mean that they personally feel inferior. Indeed, studies, even with children, show that when the self-images of middle-class or affluent African Americans are measured, their feelings of self-esteem are more positive than those of comparable Whites (Gray-Little and Hafdahl 2000).

Intergroup Hostility

Prejudice is as diverse as the nation's population. It exists not only between dominant and subordinate peoples but also between specific subordinate groups. Unfortunately, until recently little research existed on this subject except for a few social distance scales administered to racial and ethnic minorities.

A national survey revealed that, like Whites, many African Americans, Hispanic Americans, and Asian Americans held prejudiced and stereotypical views of other racial and ethnic minority groups:

- Majorities of Black, Hispanic, and Asian American respondents agreed that Whites are "bigoted, bossy, and unwilling to share power." Majorities of these non-White groups also believed that they had less opportunity than Whites to obtain a good education, a skilled job, or decent housing.
- Forty-six percent of Hispanic Americans and 42 percent of African Americans agreed that Asian Americans are "unscrupulous, crafty, and devious in business."
- Sixty-eight percent of Asian Americans and 49 percent of African Americans believed that Hispanic Americans "tend to have bigger families than they are able to support."
- Thirty-one percent of Asian Americans and 26 percent of Hispanic Americans agreed that African Americans "want to live on welfare."

Members of oppressed groups obviously have adopted the widely held beliefs of the dominant culture concerning oppressed groups. At the same time, the survey also revealed positive views of major racial and ethnic minorities:

- More than 80 percent of respondents admired Asian Americans for "placing a high value on intellectual and professional achievement" and "having strong family ties."
- A majority of all groups surveyed agreed that Hispanic Americans "take deep pride in their culture and work hard to achieve a better life."
- Large majorities from all groups stated that African Americans "have made a valuable contribution to American society and will work hard when given a chance." (National Conference of Christians and Jews 1994)

Do we get along? Although this question often is framed in terms of the relationships between White Americans and other racial and ethnic groups, we should recognize the prejudice between groups. In a national survey conducted in 2000, people were asked whether they felt they could generally get along with members of other groups. In Figure 2.6, we can see that Whites felt they had the most difficulty getting along with Blacks. We also see the different views that Blacks, Latinos, Asian Americans, and American Indians hold toward other groups.

Curiously, we find that some groups feel they get along better with Whites than with other minority groups. Why would that be? Often, low-income people are competing on a daily basis with other low-income people and do not readily see the larger societal forces that contribute to their low status. As we can see from the survey results, many Hispanics are more likely to see Asian Americans as getting in their way than the White Americans who are actually the real decision makers in their community.

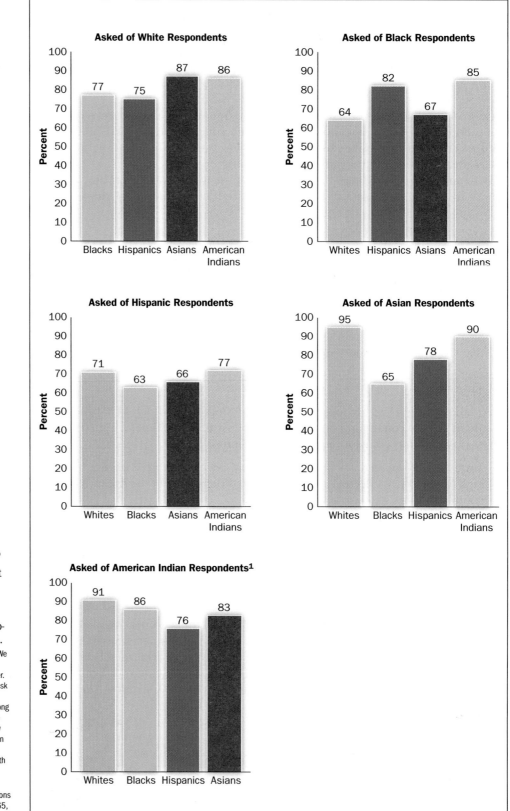

FIGURE 2.6   Do We Get Along?

Percentage saying groups get along with each other (Don't Knows excluded).

[1]Sample size for American Indians is very small and subject to large sample variance.

Note: The wording of the question was: "We hear a lot these days about how various groups in society get along with each other. I'm going to mention several groups and ask whether you think they generally get along with each other or generally do not get along with each other." So, in the Asked of White Respondents graph, Whites are asked how Whites get along with each ethnic group; in the Asked of Black Respondents graph, Blacks are asked how Blacks get along with each ethnic group, and so on.

Source: From Taking America's Pulse III: NCCJ's 2005 Survey of Intergroup Relations in the United States, by T. Smith, 2006:65, National Conference for Community and Justice.

Reducing Prejudice

Focusing on how to eliminate prejudice involves an explicit value judgment: Prejudice is wrong and causes problems for those who are prejudiced and for their victims. The obvious way to eliminate prejudice is to eliminate its causes: the desire to exploit, the fear of being threatened, and the need to blame others for one's own failure. These might be eliminated by personal therapy, but therapy, even if it works for every individual, is no solution for an entire society in which prejudice is a part of everyday life.

The answer appears to rest with programs directed at society as a whole. Prejudice is attacked indirectly when discrimination is attacked. Despite prevailing beliefs to the contrary, we can legislate against prejudice: Statutes and decisions do affect attitudes. In the past, people firmly believed that laws could not overcome norms, especially racist ones. Recent history, especially after the civil rights movement began in 1954, has challenged that common wisdom. Laws and court rulings that have equalized the treatment of Blacks and Whites have led people to reevaluate their beliefs about what is right and wrong. The increasing tolerance by Whites during the civil rights era, from 1954 to 1965, seems to support this conclusion.

Much research has been done to determine how to change negative attitudes toward groups of people. The most encouraging findings point to education, mass media, intergroup contact, and workplace training programs.

Education and Mass Media

Research on the mass media and education consists of two types: research performed in artificially (experimentally) created situations and studies examining the influence on attitudes of motion pictures, television, and advertisements.

Leaflets, radio commercials, comic books, billboards, Web pages, and classroom posters bombard people with the message of racial harmony. Television audiences watch a public service message that for 30 seconds shows smiling White and African American infants reaching out toward each other. Law enforcement and military personnel attend in-service training sessions that preach the value of a pluralistic society. Does this publicity do any good? Do these programs make any difference?

Most research studies show that well-constructed programs do have some positive effect in reducing prejudice, at least temporarily. The reduction is rarely as much as

JEFF STAHLER reprinted by permission of Newspaper Enterprise Association, Inc.

one might wish, however. The difficulty is that a single program is insufficient to change lifelong habits, especially if little is done to reinforce the program's message once it ends. Persuasion to respect other groups does not operate in a clear field because, in their ordinary environments, people are still subjected to situations that promote prejudicial feelings. Children and adults are encouraged to laugh at Polish jokes and cheer for a team named "Redskins." Black adolescents may be discouraged by peers from befriending a White youth. All this undermines the effectiveness of prejudice reduction programs (Allport 1979).

Studies consistently document that increased formal education, regardless of content, is associated with racial tolerance. Research data show that more highly educated people are more likely to indicate respect and liking for groups different from themselves. Why should more years of schooling have this effect? It could be that more education gives a broader outlook and makes a person less likely to endorse myths that sustain racial prejudice. Formal education teaches the importance of qualifying statements and the need to question rigid categorizations, if not reject them altogether. Colleges are increasingly including as a graduation requirement a course that explores diversity or multiculturalism. Another explanation is that education does not actually reduce intolerance but simply makes people more careful about revealing it. Formal education may simply instruct people in the appropriate responses, which in some settings could even be prejudiced views. Despite the lack of a clear-cut explanation, either theory suggests that the continued trend toward a better-educated population will contribute to a reduction in overt prejudice.

However, college education may not reduce prejudice uniformly. For example, some White students will come to believe that minority students did not earn their admission into college. Students may feel threatened to see large groups of people of different racial and cultural backgrounds congregating together and forming their own groups. Racist confrontations do occur outside the classroom and, even if they do involve only a few, the events themselves will be followed by hundreds. Therefore, some aspects of the college experience may only foster "we" and "they" attitudes (Schaefer 1986, 1996).

The mass media, like schools, may reduce prejudice without the need for specially designed programs. Television, radio, motion pictures, newspapers, magazines, and the Internet present only a portion of real life, but what effect do they have on prejudice if the content is racist or antiracist, sexist or antisexist? As with measuring the influence of programs designed to reduce prejudice, coming to strong conclusions on the mass media's effect is hazardous, but the evidence points to a measurable effect.

In late spring 1999, as the television networks prepared their schedules for the 1999–2000 season, an article in the *Los Angeles Times* hit the broadcasting industry like a bombshell. In every new prime-time series—twenty-six of them—set to debut in the coming season, the *Times* reported, all the leading characters and most of the supporting casts would be White. The public response was immediate. The NAACP, alarmed by the "virtual whitewash in programming," threatened a lawsuit, and a national coalition of Latino groups urged viewers to boycott network TV.

By 2004, reports showed improvement in the representation of Blacks on television but little improvement in Hispanic representation (especially if the *George Lopez Show* is excluded). Asian Americans, Arab Americans, and Native Americans continue to be virtually nonexistent. *West Wing* was praised in 2006 when it depicted a Latino, played by Puerto Rican American Jimmy Smits, elected President. Ironically, the long-running show's President Jed Bartlett is played by Martin Sheen. Yet Sheen was born Ramon Estevez and rarely makes mention of his Hispanic roots.

Why the underrepresentation? Incredibly, network executives seemed surprised by the research demonstrating an all-White season. Producers, writers, executives, and advertisers blamed each other for the alleged oversight. In recent years, the rise of both cable TV and the Internet has fragmented the broadcast entertainment market, siphoning viewers away from the general-audience sitcoms and dramas of the past. With the proliferation of cable channels such as Black Entertainment Television (BET) and the Spanish-language Univision and Web sites that cater to every imaginable taste, there no longer seems to be a need for broadly popular series such as *The Cosby Show,* whose tone and content appealed to Whites as well as Blacks in a way that the newer series do not. The UPN and WB networks produce situation comedies and even full nights geared toward African American audiences. The result of these sweeping technological changes has been a sharp divergence in viewer preferences.

While BET and Univision were grabbing minority audiences and offering new outlets for minority talent, network executives and writers remained overwhelmingly White. It is not surprising that these mainstream writers and producers, most of whom live far from ethnically and racially diverse inner-city neighborhoods, tend to write and prefer stories about people like themselves. Even urban-based programs such as the successful *Seinfeld* and *Frazier* lasted years on television with almost no people of color crossing the screen. Television series are only part of the picture. Newscasting is overwhelmingly done by Whites: 89 percent in 2000. Among the top thirty correspondents on the major network evening news shows, one was a Latino, one was an African American, and twenty-eight were White. Ironically, this means that if television were to report the research on television and race, the news correspondent probably would be White (Braxton 1999; Bunche Center 2003; Carter 2001; Children Now 2004; Johnson 2001).

Because we acquire prejudice from our social environment, it follows that the mass media and educational programs, as major elements of that environment, influence the level of prejudice. The movement to eliminate the stereotyping of minorities and the sexes in textbooks and on television recognizes this influence. Most of the effort has been to avoid contributing to racial hostility; less effort has been made to attack prejudice actively, primarily because no one knows how to do that effectively. In looking for a way to attack prejudice directly, many people advocate intergroup contact.

Equal-Status Contact

An impressive number of research studies have confirmed the **contact hypothesis**, which states that intergroup contact between people of equal status in harmonious circumstances will cause them to become less prejudiced and to abandon previously held stereotypes. Most studies indicate that such contact also improves the attitude of subordinate-group members. The importance of equal status in the interaction cannot be stressed enough. If a Puerto Rican is abused by his employer, little interracial harmony is promoted. Similarly, the situation in which contact occurs must be pleasant, making a positive evaluation likely for both individuals. Contact between two nurses, one Black and the other White, who are competing for one vacancy as a supervisor may lead to greater racial hostility (Schaefer 1976).

The key factor in reducing hostility, in addition to equal-status contact, is the presence of a common goal. If people are in competition, as already noted, contact may heighten tension. However, bringing people together to share a common task has been shown to reduce ill feeling when these people belong to different racial, ethnic, or religious groups. A study released in 2004 traced the transformations that occurred over the generations in the composition of the Social Service Employees Union in New York City. Always a mixed membership, the union was founded by Jews and Italian Americans, only to experience an influx of Black Americans. More recently, it is comprised of Latin Americans, Africans, West Indians, and South Asians. At each point, the common goals of representing the workers effectively overcame the very real cultural differences among the rank-and-file of Mexican and El Salvadoran immigrants in Houston. The researchers found when the new arrivals had contact with African Americans, intergroup relations generally improved relations, and the absence of

contact hypothesis
An interactionist perspective stating that intergroup contact between people of equal status in noncompetitive circumstances will reduce prejudice.

Efforts are beginning in the workplace to reduce hostility among workers based on prejudice.

contact tended to foster ambivalent, even negative attitudes (Fine 2004; Foerster 2004; Sherif and Sherif 1969).

National surveys show prejudice directed toward Muslim Americans, but social contact bridges that hatred. In a 2006 survey, 50 percent of people who are not acquainted with a Muslim favor special identification for Muslim Americans, but only 24 percent of those who know a Muslim embrace that same view. Similarly people personally familiar with Muslims are a more than a third less likely to endorse special security checks just for Muslims and are nervous to see a Muslim man on the same flight with themselves. While negative views are common toward Muslim Americans today, they are much less likely to be endorsed by people who have had intergroup contact (Saad 2006a).

As African Americans and other subordinate groups slowly gain access to better-paying and more responsible jobs, the contact hypothesis takes on greater significance. Usually, the availability of equal-status interaction is taken for granted, yet in everyday life intergroup contact does not conform to the equal-status idea of the contact hypothesis as often as we are assured by researchers, who hope to see a lessening of tension. Furthermore, in a highly segregated society such as the United States, contact, especially between Whites and minorities, tends to be brief and superficial (Miller 2002).

Corporate Response: Diversity Training

Prejudice carries a cost. This cost is not only to the victim but also to any organization that allows prejudice to interfere with its functioning. Workplace hostility can lead to lost productivity and even attrition. Furthermore, if left unchecked, an organization, whether a corporation, government agency, or nonprofit enterprise, can develop a reputation for having a "chilly climate." This reputation as a business unfriendly to people of color or to women discourages both qualified people from applying for jobs and potential clients from seeking products or services.

In an effort to improve workplace relations, most organizations have initiated some form of diversity training. These programs are aimed at eliminating circumstances and relationships that cause groups to receive fewer rewards, resources, or opportunities. Typically, programs aim to reduce ill treatment based on race, gender, and ethnicity. In addition, diversity training may deal with (in descending order of frequency) age, disability, religion, and language, as well as other aspects, including citizenship status, marital status, and parental status (Society for Human Resource Management 2002).

It is difficult to make any broad generalization about the effectiveness of diversity training programs because they vary so much in structure between organizations. At one extreme are short presentations that seem to have little support from management. People file into the room feeling that this is something they need to get through quickly. Such training is unlikely to be effective and may actually be counter-productive by heightening social tensions. At the other end of the continuum is a diversity training program that is integrated into initial job training, reinforced periodically, and presented as part of the overall mission of the organization, with full support from all levels of management. In these businesses, diversity is a core value, and management demands a high degree of commitment from all employees (Ely et al. 2006; Lindsley 1998).

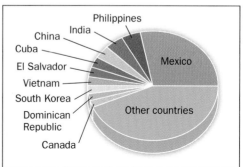

As shown in Figure 2.7, the workforce is becoming more diverse, and management is taking notice. An increasing proportion of the workforce is foreign-born and the numbers of U.S.-born African Americans, Latinos, and Asian Americans is also growing.

It is not in an organization's best interests if employees start to create barriers based on, for example, racial lines. We saw in the previous section that equal-status contact can reduce hostility. However, in the workplace, people compete for promotions, desirable work assignments, and better office space, to name a few sources of friction. When done well, an organization undertakes diversity training to remove ill feelings among workers, often reflected in the prejudices present in larger society.

FIGURE 2.7   Foreign-Born Workers in the United States by Country

About 15 percent of the civilian labor force is foreign-born with Mexico the largest source.
Source: Data for 2004 from the Bureau of Labor Statistics in Moslsa 2006, 48.

The content of diversity training also varies. Generally, it includes sharing information about the diverse composition of the service region, the company, and potential clientele, today and in the future. Videotapes are sometimes used that usually compare proper and awkward ways to handle a situation. Training sessions may break up into smaller group interactions where problem solving and team building are also encouraged.

If it is to have lasting impact on an organization, diversity training should not be separated from other aspects of the organization. For example, even the most inspired program will have little effect on prejudice if the organization promotes a sexist or ethnically offensive image in its advertising. The University of North Dakota launched an initiative in 2001 to become one of the top institutions for Native Americans in the nation. Yet at almost the same time, the administration reaffirmed its commitment, despite tribal objections, to having as its mascot for athletic teams the "Fighting Sioux." It does little to do diversity training if overt actions by an organization propel it in the opposite direction. In 2005, the National Collegiate Athletic Association began a review of logos and mascots that could be considered insulting to Native Americans. Some colleges have resisted suggestions to change or alter their publicity images while others have abandoned the practice (Brownstein 2001; NCAA 2005).

A central function that businesses can perform is to monitor prejudice that may deny opportunities to people largely because of their race, ethnicity, or nationality. In "Research Focus," we consider a recent and innovative experiment to measure prejudice in the workplace.

Although diversity training is increasingly common in the workplace, it may be undertaken primarily in response to major evidence of wrongdoing. In recent years, companies as diverse as Avis Rent-a-Car, Circuit City, Coca-Cola, Mitsubishi, Denny's Restaurants, Morgan Stanley, and Texaco have become synonymous with racism or sexual harassment. Generally, as a part of multimillion-dollar settlements, organizations agree to conduct comprehensive diversity training programs. So common is this pattern that a human resources textbook even cautions that a company should "avoid beginning such training too soon" after a complaint of workplace prejudice or discrimination (Carrell, Elbert, and Hatfield 2000, 266).

Despite the problems inherent in confronting prejudice, an organization with a comprehensive, management-supported program of diversity training can go a long way toward reducing prejudice in the workplace. The one major qualifier is that the rest of the organization must also support mutual respect.

Focus Research Focus Research

WHAT'S IN A NAME?

As a job applicant, you revise and rework that résumé. Do you include that summer job three years ago? Who should you list as a reference? Do you state specific career objectives? But one thing you never ponder—your name.

Yet recent research shows your name may be a big factor if the potential interviewer is able to use it as a means to determine your race or nationality. Would a Mohammad be as likely to get a chance to work as a Michael in the United States? Most likely not, in what could be seen as yet another form of profiling, only this one occurs in the job market. Two economists, Marianne Bertrand and Sendhil Mullainathan, sent out 5,000 job applications for 1,300 job openings advertised in the *Boston Globe* and *Chicago Tribune*. The vacancies covered the gamut of the classified advertisements from cashier jobs to sales management positions. Among this massive undertaking, the researchers decided to see if the name of the job applicant made a difference. Carefully, they tracked responses to two different sets of applicants—one with first names most likely to be African Ameri-

can and the other set being more typical of Whites. Names were selected by examining a random sample of Boston birth certificates that identified a person's race as well as his or her name.

The results of this job-seeking experiment were even startling to the researchers. Applicants with White-sounding names were 50 percent more likely to be called for an interview than those with Black-sounding names. Put another way, typical White applicants were contacted for an interview for every ten résumés they sent out, whereas the "African American" applicant had to send out fifteen applications. Where employers responded positively to more than one résumé, rarely did they contact a "Black" applicant and not also contact a "White" applicant. Because these were hypothetical applicants, we have no way of knowing to what degree these disturbing job results would have continued during the interview, job offer, and salary offered. Yet, clearly, the biggest constraining factor in any person's attempt to get a job is to get that interview.

The researchers took their study one step further. They made conscious efforts to make a portion of the applicants better qualified or to list addresses in more affluent neighborhoods. In both instances, résumés with White-sounding names were given even further advantages, but this had much less positive impact on callbacks to the résumés bearing Black-sounding names. They did find that the apparent pro-White bias was less when employers were located in minority neighborhoods.

This study showed—using a clever, if simple, methodology—that people's prejudices seem to surface even when they scan that top line of a résumé. Many businesspeople apparently read no further if they detect that the applicant is from the wrong group. ■

Source: Bertand and Mullainathan 2003; Krueger 2002.

TABLE 2.2
Names and Interview Success

Name on Résumé	Callback (%)
Brad	15.0
Kristen	13.6
Meredith	10.6
Matthew	9.0
Emily	8.3
Tanisha	6.3
Darnell	4.8
Keisha	3.8
Rasheed	3.0
Aisha	2.2

Ways to Fight Hate

What can schools do? Television and movie producers? Corporate big shots? It is easy to shift the responsibility for confronting prejudice to the movers and shakers, and certainly they do play a critical role. Yet there are definitely actions one can take in the course of everyday day life to challenge intergroup hostility.

The Southern Poverty Law Center (SPLC), founded in 1971 and based in Montgomery, Alabama, organized committed activists all over the country to mount legal cases and challenges against hate groups such as the Ku Klux Klan. The center's courtroom challenges led to the end of many discriminatory practices. Its cases have now gone beyond conventional race-based cases since the center has won equal benefits for women in the armed forces, ended involuntary sterilization of women on welfare, and reformed prison and mental health conditions.

Recognizing that social change can also begin at the individual level, the SPLC has identified ten ways to fight hate based on its experience working at the community level (Carrier 2000).

1. *Act.* Do something. In the face of hatred, apathy will be taken as acceptance even by the victims of prejudice themselves. The SPLC tells of a time when a cross was burned in the yard of a single mother of Portuguese descent in Missouri; one person acted and set in motion a community uprising against hatred.

2. *Unite.* Call a friend or co-worker. Organize a group of like-thinking friends from school or your place of worship or club. Create a coalition that is a diverse coalition and includes the young, the old, law enforcement representatives, and the media. Frustrated when a neo-Nazi group got permission to march in Springfield, Illinois, in 1994, a Jewish couple formed Project Lemonade. Money raised helps to create education projects or monuments in communities that witness such decisive events.

3. *Support the Victims.* Victims of hate crimes are especially vulnerable. Let them know you care by words, by email. If you or your friend is a victim, report it. In the wake of an outbreak of anti–Native American and anti-Jewish activity in Billings, Montana, a manager of a local sports shop replaced all his usual outdoor advertising and print ads with "Not in Our Town," which soon became a community rallying point for a support network of hate victims.

4. *Do Your Homework.* If you suspect a hate crime has been committed, do your research to document it. An Indiana father spotted his son receiving a "pastor's license," did some research, and found that the source was a White supremacist group disguised as a church. It helped explain the boy's recent fascination with Nazi symbols. The father wrote the "church," demanded that the contacts be stopped, and threatened suit.

5. *Create an Alternative.* Never attend a rally where hate is a part of the agenda. Find another outlet for your frustration, whatever the cause. When the Ku Klux Klan held a rally in Madison, Wisconsin, a coalition of ministers organized citizens to spend the day in minority neighborhoods.

6. *Speak Up.* You too have First Amendment rights. Denounce the hatred, the cruel jokes. If you see a news organization misrepresenting a group, speak up. When a newspaper exposed the 20-year-old national leader of the Aryan Nation in Canada, he resigned and closed his Web site.

7. *Lobby Leaders.* Persuade policy makers, business heads, community leaders, and executives of media outlets to take a stand against hate. Levi Strauss contributed $5 million to an antiprejudice project and a program that helps people of color get loans in communities where it has plants: Knoxville, Albuquerque, El Paso, and Valdosta, Georgia.

8. *Look Long Range.* Participate or organize events such as annual parades or cultural fairs to celebrate diversity and harmony. Supplement it with a Web site that can be a 24/7 resource. In Selma, Alabama, a major weekend street fair is held on the anniversary of Bloody Sunday, when voting-rights activists attempting to walk across a bridge to Montgomery were beaten back by police.

9. *Teach Tolerance.* Prejudice is learned and parents and teachers can influence the content of curriculum. In Brooklyn, New York, an interracial basketball program called Flames was founded in the mid-1970s. Since then, it has brought together more than 10,000 youths of diverse backgrounds.

10. *Dig Deeper.* Look into the issues that divide us—social inequality, immigration, and sexual orientation. Work against prejudice. Dig deep inside yourself for prejudices and stereotypes you may embrace. Find out what is happening and act! As former White supremacist Floyd Cochran declared, "It is not enough to hold hands and sing Kumbaya" (Carrier 2000, 22).

Expressing prejudice and expressing tolerance are fundamentally personal decisions. These steps recognize that we have the ability to change our attitudes, resist ethnocentrism and prejudice, and avoid the use of ethnophaulisms and stereotypes.

Conclusion

This chapter has examined theories of prejudice and measurements of its extent. Prejudice should not be confused with discrimination. The two concepts are not the same: Prejudice consists of negative attitudes, and discrimination consists of negative behavior toward a group.

Several theories try to explain why prejudice exists. Some emphasize economic concerns (the exploitation and scapegoating theories), whereas other approaches stress personality or normative factors. No one explanation is sufficient. Surveys conducted in the United States over the past sixty years point to a reduction of prejudice as measured by the willingness to express stereotypes or maintain social distance. Survey data also show that African Americans, Latinos, Asian Americans, and American Indians do not necessarily feel comfortable with each other. They have adopted attitudes toward other oppressed groups similar to those held by many White Americans. Prejudice aimed at Hispanics, Asian Americans, and large recent immigrant groups such as Arab Americans and Muslim Americans is well documented. Issues such as immigration and affirmative action re-emerge and cause bitter resentment. Furthermore, ill feelings exist between subordinate groups in schools, in the streets, and in the workplace.

Equal-status contact may reduce hostility between groups. However, in a highly segregated society defined by inequality, such opportunities are not typical. The mass media can be of value in reducing discrimination but have not done enough and may even intensify ill feeling by promoting stereotypical images. Although strides are being made in increasing the appearance of minorities in positive roles in television and films, one would not realize how diverse our society is by sampling advertisements, TV programs, or movies.

Even though we can be encouraged by the techniques available to reduce intergroup hostility, there are still sizable segments of the population that do not want to live in integrated neighborhoods, that do not want to work for or be led by someone of a different race, and that certainly object to the idea of their relatives marrying outside their own group. People still harbor stereotypes toward one another, and this tendency includes racial and ethnic minorities having stereotypes about one another.

Reducing prejudice is important because it can lead to support for policy change. There are steps we can take as individuals to confront prejudice and overcome hatred. Another real challenge and the ultimate objective is to improve the social condition of oppressed groups in the United States. To consider this challenge, we turn to discrimination in Chapter 3. Discrimination's costs are high to both dominant and subordinate groups. With that fact in mind, we will examine some techniques for reducing discrimination.

Key Terms

authoritarian personality 45

Bogardus scale 51

contact hypothesis 59

discrimination 41

ethnocentrism 39

ethnophaulism 41

exploitation theory 45

hate crimes 39

normative approach 46

prejudice 41

racial profiling 49

scapegoating theory 43

social distance 51

stereotypes 47

Review Questions

1. How are prejudice and discrimination both related and unrelated to each other?
2. How do theories of prejudice relate to different expressions of prejudice?
3. Why does prejudice develop even toward groups with whom people have little contact?
4. Are there steps that you can identify that have been taken against prejudice in your community?

Critical Thinking

1. Identify stereotypes associated with a group of people, such as older adults or people with physical disabilities.
2. What social issues do you think are most likely to engender hostility along racial and ethnic lines?
3. Consider the television programs you have watched the most. In terms of race and ethnicity, how well do the programs you watch tend to reflect the diversity of the population in the United States?

Internet Connections—Research Navigator™

Follow the instructions found on page 35 of this text to access the features of Research Navigator™. Once at the Web site, enter your Login Name and Password. Then, to use the ContentSelect database, enter keywords such as "racism," "racial profiling," and "diversity training," and the research engine will supply relevant and recent scholarly and popular press publications. Use the *New York Times* Search-by-Subject Archive to find recent news articles related to sociology and the Link Library feature to locate relevant Web links organized by the key terms associated with this chapter.

3

Discrimination

CHAPTER OUTLINE

Understanding Discrimination

■**LISTEN TO OUR VOICES**
Of Race and Risk
by Patricia J. Williams

Low-Wage Labor

■**RESEARCH FOCUS**
Discrimination in Job Seeking

Discrimination Today

Wealth Inequality: Discrimination's Legacy

Environmental Justice

Affirmative Action

Reverse Discrimination

The Glass Ceiling

Conclusion

Key Terms/Review Questions/Critical Thinking/
Internet Connections—Research Navigator™

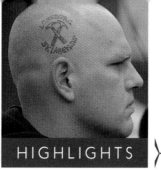

JUST AS SOCIAL SCIENTISTS HAVE ADVANCED THEORIES TO explain why prejudice exists, they have also presented explanations of why discrimination occurs. Social scientists look more and more at the manner in which institutions, not individuals, discriminate. Institutional discrimination is a pattern in social institutions that produces or perpetuates inequalities, even if individuals in the society do not intend to be racist or sexist. Income data document that gaps exist between racial and ethnic groups. Historically, attempts have been made to reduce discrimination, usually as a result of strong lobbying efforts by minorities themselves. Patterns of total discrimination make solutions particularly difficult for people in the informal economy or the underclass. Affirmative action was designed to equalize opportunity but has encountered significant resentment by those who charge that it constitutes reverse discrimination. Despite many efforts to end discrimination, glass ceilings and glass walls remain in the workplace.

Discrimination can take many forms. As the next two incidents indicate, discrimination can be either outright or the result of a complex combination of factors. It can lead to indignities or even death.

Lawrence Otis Graham (1995) had "arrived" by the standards of most people in the United States. He was a graduate of Harvard Law School, married, and had become a well-regarded member of a Manhattan law firm. But he was also Black. Despite his success in securing clients for himself and his firm, Graham had noticed that White attorneys seemed to get a jump on him because of their associations with corporate leaders at private clubs. By tradition, the clubs were exclusively White. Graham decided to take time out from his law firm and learn more about the workings of these private clubs, which allowed some Whites to mingle in an informal atmosphere and so contributed to their establishing networks. These networks, in turn, allowed people to establish contacts that advanced their success in the business world. Rather than present himself as a successful Ivy League college graduate to become a member, he presented himself as a working-class African American seeking a job as a waiter. From the vantage point of a server, Graham figured he could observe the network of these predominantly White country club members. This was not to be the case. He was not given a job at club after club. Despite all sorts of encouragement when he talked to employers over the phone, he was denied a job when he presented himself, and they saw that this articulate, well-mannered young man was Black. Eventually, he obtained a job as a busboy, clearing tables in a club where the White servers commented that he could do their job better than they could.

Cynthia Wiggins was also African American, but she lived in a different world from Lawrence Otis Graham. She was a 17-year-old single mother struggling to make a living. She had sought jobs near her home but had found no employment opportunities. Eventually, she found employment as a cashier, but it was far from her home, and she could not afford a car. Still, she was optimistic and looked forward to marrying the man to whom she was engaged. In 1995, she made the 50-minute bus ride from her predominantly Black neighborhood in Buffalo, New York, to her job at the Galleria, a fancy suburban shopping mall. Every day, charter buses unloaded shoppers from as far away as Canada, but city buses were not allowed on mall property. The bus Wiggins rode was forced to stop across the lot and across a seven-lane highway without sidewalks. On a December day, with the roadway lined with mounds of snow, she tried to cross the highway, only to be struck by a dump truck. She died three weeks later. Later investigation showed that the bus company had been trying to arrange for the bus to stop in the mall parking lot, but the shopping center authorities had blocked the move. Before the incident, the mall said it would consider allowing in suburban buses but not public buses from the city. As one mall storeowner put it, "You'll never see an inner-city bus on the mall premises" (Barnes 1996, 33, Gladwell 1996).

Discrimination has a long history, right up to the present, of taking its toll on people. For some, such as Lawrence Otis Graham, discrimination is being reminded that even when you do try to seek employment, you may be treated like a second-class citizen. For others, such as Cynthia Wiggins, discrimination meant suffering for the unjust decisions made in a society that quietly discriminated. Williams lost her life not because anyone actually intended to kill her but because decisions made it more likely that an inner-city resident would be an accident victim. Despite legislative and court efforts to eliminate discrimination, members of dominant and subordinate groups pay a price for continued intolerance.

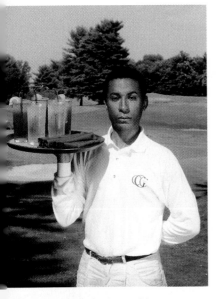

Harvard-educated lawyer Lawrence Otis Graham sought a position as a waiter in exclusive clubs to learn more about contemporary discrimination.

Understanding Discrimination

Discrimination is the denial of opportunities and equal rights to individuals and groups because of prejudice or for other arbitrary reasons. Some people in the United States find it difficult to see discrimination as a widespread phenomenon. "After all," it is often said, "these minorities drive cars, hold jobs, own their homes, and even go to college." Yet this also fails to recognize the lingering legacy of past discrimination. Recently scholarly research documented the history of "sundown towns," communities that for decades had explicit rules ordering Black people out at sundown. They could work and spend their money in these towns, but they could not socialize or live there. Asians and American Indians were also the victim of such policies. Although this explicit practice ended in the post–World War II era, most of these communities still remained all White well into the twenty-first century, we will consider sundown towns in greater detail in Chapter 7. (Loewen 2005).

Even today discrimination is not rare. An understanding of discrimination in modern industrialized societies such as the United States must begin by distinguishing between relative and absolute deprivation.

Relative Versus Absolute Deprivation

Conflict theorists have said correctly that it is not absolute, unchanging standards that determine deprivation and oppression. Although minority groups may be viewed as having adequate or even good incomes, housing, health care, and educational opportunities, it is their position relative to some other group that offers evidence of discrimination.

Relative deprivation is defined as the conscious experience of a negative discrepancy between legitimate expectations and present actualities. After settling in the United States, immigrants often enjoy better material comforts and more political freedom than were possible in their old country. If they compare themselves with most other people in the United States, however, they will feel deprived because, although their standard has improved, the immigrants still perceive relative deprivation.

Absolute deprivation, on the other hand, implies a fixed standard based on a minimum level of subsistence below which families should not be expected to exist. Discrimination does not necessarily mean absolute deprivation. A Japanese American who is promoted to a management position may still be a victim of discrimination if he or she had been passed over for years because of corporate reluctance to place an Asian American in a highly visible position.

Dissatisfaction is also likely to arise from feelings of relative deprivation. The members of a society who feel most frustrated and disgruntled by the social and economic conditions of their lives are not necessarily worse off in an objective sense. Social scientists have long recognized that what is most significant is how people perceive their situations. Karl Marx pointed out that, although the misery of the workers was important in reflecting their oppressed state, so was their position relative to the ruling class. In 1847, Marx wrote,

> *Although the enjoyment of the workers has risen, the social satisfaction that they have has fallen in comparison with the increased enjoyment of the capitalist. (Marx and Engels 1955, 94)*

This statement explains why the groups or individuals who are most vocal and best organized against discrimination are not necessarily in the worst economic and social situation. However, they are likely to be those who most strongly perceive that, relative to others, they are not receiving their fair share. Resistance to perceived discrimination, rather than the actual amount of absolute discrimination, is the key.

discrimination
The denial of opportunities and equal rights to individuals and groups because of prejudice or for other arbitrary reasons.

relative deprivation
The conscious experience of a negative discrepancy between legitimate expectations and present actualities.

absolute deprivation
The minimum level of subsistence below which families or individuals should not be expected to exist.

Voices Listen to Our Voices Listen to Ou

OF RACE AND RISK

Patricia J. Williams

Several years ago, at a moment when I was particularly tired of the unstable lifestyle that academic careers sometimes require, I surprised myself and bought a real house. Because the house was in a state other than the one where I was living at the time, I obtained my mortgage by telephone. I am a prudent little squirrel when it comes to things financial, always tucking away stores of nuts for the winter, and so I meet the criteria of a quite good credit risk. My loan was approved almost immediately.

A little while later, the contract came in the mail. Among the papers the bank forwarded were forms documenting compliance with the Fair Housing Act, which outlaws racial discrimination in the housing market. The act monitors lending practices to prevent banks from redlining—redlining being the phenomenon whereby banks circle certain neighborhoods on the map and refuse to lend in those areas. It is a practice for which the bank with which I was dealing, unbeknownst to me, had been cited previously—as well as since. In any event, the act tracks the race of all banking customers to prevent such discrimination. Unfortunately, and with the creative variability of all illegality, some banks also use the racial informa-

tion disclosed on the fair housing forms to engage in precisely the discrimination the law seeks to prevent.

I should repeat that to this point my entire mortgage transaction had been conducted by telephone. I should also note that I speak a Received Standard English, regionally marked as Northeastern perhaps, but not easily identifiable as black. With my credit history, my job as a law professor, and, no doubt, with my accent, I am not only middle class but apparently match the cultural stereotype of a good white person. It is thus, perhaps, that the loan officer of the bank, whom I had never met, had checked off the box on the fair housing form indicating that I was white.

Race shouldn't matter, I suppose, but it seemed to in this case, so I took a deep breath, crossed out "white" and sent the contract back. That will teach them to presume too much, I thought. A done deal, I assumed. But suddenly the transaction came to a screeching halt. The bank wanted more money, more points, and a higher rate of interest. Suddenly I found myself facing great resistance and much more debt. To make a long story short, I threatened to sue under the act in question, the bank quickly backed down, and I procured the loan on the origi-

Total Discrimination

Social scientists—and increasingly policy makers—have begun to use the concept of total discrimination. **Total discrimination**, as shown in Figure 3.1, refers to current discrimination operating in the labor market and past discrimination. Past discrimination experienced by an individual includes the poorer education and job experiences of racial and ethnic minorities compared with those of many White Americans. When considering discrimination, therefore, it is not enough to focus only on what is being done to people now. Sometimes a person may be dealt with fairly but may still be at a disadvantage because he or she suffered from poorer health care, inferior counseling

total discrimination
The combination of current discrimination with past discrimination created by poor schools and menial jobs.

Listen to Our Voices Listen to Our Voices

nal terms. What was interesting about all this was that the reason the bank gave for its newfound recalcitrance was not race, heaven forbid. No, it was all about economics and increased risk: The reason they gave was that property values in that neighborhood were suddenly falling. They wanted more money to buffer themselves against the snappy winds of projected misfortune.

Initially, I was surprised, confused. The house was in a neighborhood that was extremely stable. I am an extremely careful shopper; I had uncovered absolutely nothing to indicate that prices were falling. It took my realtor to make me see the light. "Don't you get it," he sighed. "This is what always happens." And even though I suppose it was a little thick of me, I really hadn't gotten it: For, of course, I was the reason the prices were in peril. . . .

In retrospect, what has remained so fascinating to me about this experience was the way it so exemplified the problems of the new rhetoric of racism. For starters, the new rhetoric of race never mentions race. It wasn't race but risk with which the bank was so concerned. . . .

By this measure of mortgage-worthiness, the ingredient of blackness is cast not just as a social toll but also as an actual tax. A fee, an extra contribution at the door, an admission charge for the high costs of handling my dangerous propensities, my inherently unsa-

vory properties. I was not judged based on my independent attributes or financial worth; not even was I judged by statistical profiles of what my group actually does. (For, in fact, anxiety-stricken, middle-class black people make good cake-baking neighbors when not made to feel defensive by the unfortunate historical strategies of bombs, burnings, or abandonment.) Rather, I was being evaluated based on what an abstraction of White Society writ large thinks we—or I—do, and that imagined "doing" was treated and thus established as a self-fulfilling prophecy. It is a dispiriting message: that some in society apparently not only devalue black people but devalue themselves and their homes just for having us as part of their landscape.

"I bet you'll keep your mouth shut the next time they plug you into the computer as white," laughed a friend when he heard my story. It took me aback, this postmodern pressure to "pass," even as it highlighted the intolerable logic of it all. For by these "rational" economic measures, an investment in my property suggests the selling of myself. ■

Source: P. Williams (1997). "Of Race and Risk" by Patricia J. Williams. Reprinted with permission from the December 29 issue of *The Nation*. Portions of each week's *The Nation* magazine can be accessed at http://www.thenation.com.

in the school system, less access to books and other educational materials, or a poor job record resulting from absences to take care of brothers and sisters.

Discrimination casts a wide net. Although the poor and less educated are most vulnerable and unable to access resources that might help them, discrimination also is faced by the affluent with professional degrees. In "Listen to Our Voices," respected law professor Patricia J. Williams, an African American, describes her inability to secure a mortgage despite initial approval after an analysis of her financial status but before the bank realized she was Black. Her recent experience is not unusual and helps to explain the persistence of discrimination.

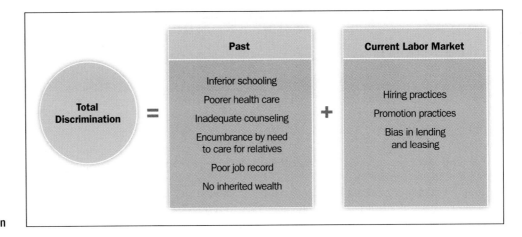

FIGURE 3.1 Total Discrimination

William's experience is not unusual. A study released by the National Fair Housing Alliance and the federal Department of Housing and Urban Development found that discriminatory housing practices were routine. Consider the sobering results of a two-year study conducted in 12 metropolitan areas with 73 real estate firms: White real estate shoppers are steered away from houses in mixed neighborhoods even when they express interest in integrated areas. Latinos and African Americans looking for housing are steered toward minority neighborhoods even when their incomes justify seeing more affluent neighborhoods. The challenge to being a minority home buyer does not stop there. Studies document that Black and Hispanic home buyers tend to pay higher interest rates than Whites with similar credit ratings. All things are hardly equal in home buying (Bocian et al. 2006).

We find another variation of this past-in-present discrimination when apparently nondiscriminatory present practices have negative effects because of prior intentionally biased practices. Although unions that purposely discriminated against minority members in the past may no longer do so, some people are still prevented from achieving higher levels of seniority because of those past practices. Personnel records include a cumulative record that is vital in promotion and selection for desirable assignments. Blatantly discriminatory judgments and recommendations in the past remain part of a person's record.

Institutional Discrimination

Individuals practice discrimination in one-to-one encounters, and institutions practice discrimination through their daily operations. Indeed, a consensus is growing today that this institutional discrimination is more significant than acts committed by prejudiced individuals.

Social scientists are particularly concerned with the ways in which patterns of employment, education, criminal justice, housing, health care, and government operations maintain the social significance of race and ethnicity. **Institutional discrimination** is the denial of opportunities and equal rights to individuals and groups that results from the normal operations of a society.

Civil rights activist Stokely Carmichael and political scientist Charles Hamilton are credited with introducing the concept of institutional racism. Individual discrimination refers to overt acts of individual Whites against individual Blacks; Carmichael and Hamilton reserved the term *institutional racism* for covert acts committed collectively against an entire group. From this perspective, discrimination can take place without an individual intending to deprive others of privileges and even without the individual being aware that others are being deprived (Ture and Hamilton 1992).

institutional discrimination
A denial of opportunities and equal rights to individuals or groups resulting from the normal operations of a society.

Despite numerous laws and steep penalties, discrimination continues in the housing market.

How can discrimination be widespread and unconscious at the same time? The following are a few documented examples of institutional discrimination.

1. Standards for assessing credit risks work against African Americans and Hispanics seeking to establish businesses because many lack conventional credit references. Businesses in low-income areas where these groups often reside also have much higher insurance costs.

2. IQ testing favors middle-class children, especially the White middle class, because of the types of questions included.

3. The entire criminal justice system, from the patrol officer to the judge and jury, is dominated by Whites who find it difficult to understand life in poverty areas.

4. Hiring practices often require several years' experience at jobs only recently opened to members of subordinate groups.

5. Many jobs automatically eliminate a person with felony records or past drug offenses, which disproportionately reduces employment opportunities for people of color.

In some cases, even apparently neutral institutional standards can turn out to have discriminatory effects. African American students at a midwestern state university protested a policy under which fraternities and sororities that wanted to use campus facilities for a dance were required to post a $150 security deposit to cover possible damage. The Black students complained that this policy had a discriminatory impact on minority student organizations. Campus police countered that the university's policy applied to all student groups interested in using these facilities. However, because, overwhelmingly, White fraternities and sororities at the school had their own houses, which they used for dances, the policy affected only African American and other subordinate groups' organizations.

Ten years later, the entire nation scrambled to make aviation safer in the wake of the September, 11 2001 terrorist attacks. The government saw airport security as a weak link and federalized airport screeners under the newly formed Transport

How does institutional discrimination figure in national elections?

Security Administration. Wages improved and training strengthened. The new screeners also had to be U.S. citizens. This latter provision eliminated the many legal immigrants from Asia, Africa, and Latin America who had previously worked as screeners. Airport screening went from overwhelmingly minority to 61 percent White. Clearly, this measure had the unintended consequences of discriminating against people of color (Alonso-Zaldivar and Oldhan 2002).

Even efforts to right injustices can be discriminatory in their outcome. Numerous instances are documented of low-income potential homeowners entering into very undesirable financial agreements eventually leading to foreclosure when they go to buy that first home. In an effort to protect people from being taken advantage of, beginning in 2006, the State of Illinois required buyers with poor credit records in certain areas of Chicago to go through mandatory financial counseling. As a result, over twenty lenders have curtailed granting home loans in these areas, not wanting to deal with the further restrictions. Over eighty percent of the people in the affected area are Black of Latino. A well-intentioned attempt to help people is making it very difficult for people wanting to live in an area overwhelmingly populated by racial and ethnic minorities (Umberger 2006).

The U.S. population is becoming more diversified, and examples of institutional discrimination are confronting more and different groups. Many Asian peoples have distinctive customs honoring their deceased family members. Among these traditions is the burning of incense at the gravesite, placing food on the grave markers, and leaving fake money. These practices stem from ancestor worship but often are followed by Christian Chinese Americans who try to hold onto some of the "old ways." Cemetery proprietors maintain standards of what they regard as proper grave decoration to maintain a tidy appearance. Consequently, people of Asian descent find they are unable to bury their loved ones in the cemeteries most convenient to them and must travel to cemeteries that are more open to different ways of memorializing the dead. Cemeteries do not consciously seek to keep people out because they are Asian, but they develop policies, often with little thought, that fail to recognize the pluralistic nature of society (Eng 1998).

The 2000 presidential election created headlines because it took weeks to resolve who won—Bush or Gore. Yet for 1.4 million African Americans who were denied the right to vote, this seemed like a national issue that had left them on the sidelines. The prohibition was not because they were Black, which would have been clearly racist and legally discriminatory, but because they were convicted felons. In eleven states a felony conviction can result in a band from voting for life even after their prison sentence is served. Because many of these states are in the South and have large Black

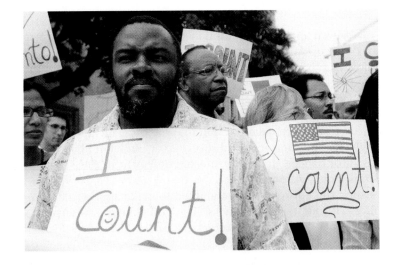

Institutional discrimination takes many forms. The 2000 presidential election highlighted the restriction in many states that ex-convicts can never vote. In these same states the excluded are most likely to be African American. Here Leroy Jones demonstrates for restoration of voting rights for himself and his fellow ex-felons outside a federal court in Miami in April 2003.

populations, disproportionately, the voting prohibition covers African American men. Currently 13 percent of the nation's Black male population is precluded from voting by such laws. Florida was the deciding state in the close 2000 elections, and more than 200,000 potential Black voters were excluded. This case of institutional discrimination may have changed the outcome of a presidential election (Cooper 2004; Sentencing Project 2006).

Institutional discrimination continuously imposes more hindrances on and awards fewer benefits to certain racial and ethnic groups than it does to others. This is the underlying and painful context of American intergroup relations.

Low-Wage Labor

Disproportionate shares of racial and ethnic minority members are either unemployed or employed in low-wage labor. Much of this low-wage labor is in a part of the labor market that provides little opportunities for improvement during one's working years and virtually no protection in terms of health insurance or retirement benefits.

The secondary labor market affecting many members of racial and ethnic minorities has come to be called the **informal economy**. The informal economy (also called the **irregular** or **underground economy**) consists of transfers of money, goods, or services that are not reported to the government. This label describes much of the work in inner-city neighborhoods and poverty-stricken rural areas, which is in sharp contrast to the rest of the marketplace. Workers are employed in the informal economy seasonally or infrequently. The work they do may resemble the work of traditional occupations, such as mechanic, cook, or electrician, but these workers lack the formal credentials to enter such employment. Indeed, workers in the informal economy may work sporadically or may moonlight in the regular economy. The informal economy also includes unregulated child-care services, garage sales, and the unreported income of craftspeople and street vendors.

According to the **dual labor market** model, minorities have been relegated to the informal economy. Although the informal economy may offer employment to the jobless, it provides few safeguards against fraud or malpractice that victimizes the workers. There are also few of the fringe benefits of health insurance and pensions that are much more likely to be present in the conventional marketplace. Therefore, informal economies are criticized for promoting highly unfair and dangerous working conditions. To be consigned to the informal economy is yet another example of social inequality.

informal economy
Transfers of money, goods, or services that are not reported to the government. Common in inner-city neighborhoods and poverty-stricken rural areas.

irregular or underground economy
See informal economy.

dual labor market
Division of the economy into two areas of employment, the secondary one of which is populated primarily by minorities working at menial jobs.

Many people work in the informal economy with little prospect of moving into the primary, better-paying economy. Pictured is a street vendor in New York City.

Focus Research Focus Research

DISCRIMINATION IN JOB SEEKING

A dramatic confirmation of discrimination came with research begun by sociologist Devah Pager in 2003. She sent four men out as trained "testers" to look for entry-level jobs in Milwaukee, Wisconsin, requiring no experience or special training. Each was a 23-year-old college student but each one presented himself as having a high school diploma with similar job histories.

The job-seeking experiences with 350 different employers were vastly different among the four men. Why was that? Two of the testers where Black and two were White. Furthermore, one tester of each pair indicated in the job application that he had served 18 months of jail time for a felony conviction (possession of cocaine with intent to distribute). As you can see in Figure 3.2, applicants with a prison record received significantly fewer callbacks. But as dramatic a difference as a criminal record made, race was clearly more important.

The differences were to the point that a White job applicant with a jail record actual-

ly received more callbacks for further consideration than a Black man with no criminal record. Whiteness has a privilege even when it comes to jail time; race, it seems, was more of a concern to potential employers than a criminal background.

"I expected there to be an effect of race, but I did not expect it to swamp the results as it did," Pager told an interviewer. Her finding was especially significant because the majority of convicts who are released from prison each year (52 percent) are, in fact, Black men. Pager's research, which was widely publicized, eventually contributed to a change in public policy. In his 2004 State of the Union address, and specifically referring to Pager's work, President George W. Bush announced a $300 million monitoring program for ex-convicts who are attempting to reintegrate into society. ▓

Sources: Bordt 2005; Bureau of Justice Statistics 2004; Krueger 2005, Pager 2003; Pager and Quillian 2005.

FIGURE 3.2   Discrimination in Job Seeking

Source: The Mark of A Criminal Record, Devah Pager, *American Journal of Sociology*, 108(5). The University of Chicago Press © 2003. Reprinted by permission of the University of Chicago.

Sociologist Edna Bonacich (1972, 1976) outlined the dual or split labor market that divides the economy into two realms of employment, the secondary one being populated primarily by minorities working at menial jobs. Even when not manual, labor is still rewarded less when performed by minorities. In keeping with the conflict model, this dual market model emphasizes that minorities fare unfavorably in the competition between dominant and subordinate groups.

The workers in the informal economy are ill prepared to enter the regular economy permanently or to take its better-paying jobs. Frequent changes in employment or lack of a specific supervisor leaves them without the kind of résumé that employers in the regular economy expect before they hire. Some of the sources of employment in the informal economy are illegal, such as fencing stolen goods, narcotics peddling, pimping, and prostitution. More likely, the work is legal but not transferable to a more traditional job. An example is an "information broker," who receives cash in exchange for such information as where to find good buys or how to receive maximum benefits from public assistance programs (Pedder 1991).

Workers in the informal economy have not necessarily experienced direct discrimination. Because of past discrimination, they are unable to secure traditional employment. Working in the informal economy provides income but does not lead them into the primary labor market. A self-fulfilling cycle continues that allows past discrimination to create a separate work environment.

Efforts to end discrimination continue to run up against discrimination of all sorts. As described in "Research Focus," although we can document discrimination in research studies, it is often very difficult to prove even if we had the time and money to bring the incident to the attention of the legal system.

Not all low-wage laborers are a part of the informal economy, but many workers are driven into such jobs as better-paying jobs either move far away from where African Americans and Latinos live or even move abroad as globalization creates more and more of an international labor market.

The absence of jobs casts a wider shadow in poor neighborhoods beyond the lousy employment opportunities. People in poor urban neighborhoods often live in what have been called "commercial deserts" where they have little access to major grocers, pharmacies, or other retailers, but have plenty of liquor stores and fast-food restaurants nearby. Not only does this affect the quality of life but also it exacerbates the exodus of good job opportunities (Gallagher 2005; Kelly 2005).

It is commonly believed that there are jobs available for the inner-city poor but that they just do not seek them. A study looked at jobs that were advertised in a help-wanted section of the *Washington Post*. The analysis showed that most of the jobs were beyond the reach of the underclass; perhaps 5 percent of all openings could even remotely be considered reasonable job prospects for people without skills or experience. During interviews with the employers, researchers found that an average of twenty-one people applied for each position, which typically was filled within three days of the time the advertisement appeared. The mean hourly wage was $6.12, 42 percent offered no fringe benefits, and the remaining positions offered meager fringe benefits after six months or one year of employment. This study, like others before it, counters the folk wisdom that there are plenty of jobs around for the underclass (Pease and Martin 1997).

Discrimination Today

In 2003, the Legal Assistance Foundation of Metropolitan Chicago sent matched pairs of a White woman and a Black woman to seek jobs in suburban Chicago. They applied for a variety of jobs that were advertised or that posted "Help Wanted" signs in the window. Many of the jobs were retail positions in shopping centers or malls. Employers were 16 percent more likely to offer jobs to Whites than to Blacks, even though the Black applicant always applied first and presented stronger job-related qualifications. Black applicants were four times as likely to be asked about their absenteeism record and nearly twice as likely to be specifically asked why they left their previous job. This was in 2003, not 1953. It was also where jobs in urban America tend to be available—the suburbs (Lodder, McFarland, and White 2003).

Discrimination is widespread in the United States. It sometimes results from prejudices held by individuals. More significantly, it is found in institutional discrimination and the presence of the informal economy. The presence of an underclass is symptomatic of many social forces, and total discrimination—past and present discrimination taken together—is one of them.

Measuring Discrimination

How much discrimination is there? As in measuring prejudice, problems arise in quantifying discrimination. Measuring prejudice is hampered by the difficulties in assessing attitudes and by the need to take many factors into account. It is further limited by the initial challenge of identifying different treatment. A second difficulty of measuring discrimination is assigning a cost to the discrimination.

Some tentative conclusions about discrimination can be made, however. Figure 3.3 uses income data to show vividly the disparity in income between African Americans and Whites and also between men and women. This encompasses all full-time workers. White men, with a median income of $48,909, earn one-third more than Black men and nearly twice what Hispanic women earn in wages.

Why do Asian American men earn so much if race serve as a barrier? The economic picture is not entirely good, as we consider in Chapters 12 and 13. Some Asian American groups such as Laotians and Vietnamese have high levels of poverty. However, a significant number of Asian Americans with advanced educations have high-earning jobs bringing up the median income. However, as we will see, given their high levels of schooling, their incomes should be even higher.

 ASK Yourself

Just how significant is the annual income gap between racial groups today?

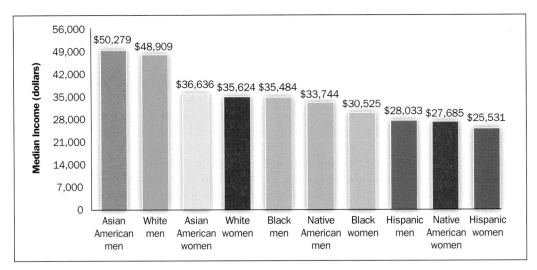

FIGURE 3.3 **Median Income by Race, Ethnicity, and Gender**
Even at the very highest levels of schooling, the income gap remains between Whites and Blacks. Education also has little apparent effect on the income gap between male and female workers. Even a brief analysis reveals striking differences in earning power between White men and other groups in the United States. Furthermore, the greater inequality is apparent for African American and Hispanic women.

Note: Median income is from all sources and is limited to year-round, full-time workers over 25 years old. Data for White men and women are for non-Hispanics.

Note: Data released in 2006 for income earned in 2006.

Source: DeNavas-Walt, Proctor, and Lee 2006; for Native Americans, author's estimate based on Bureau of the Census data in Ogunwale 2006.

Clearly, regardless of race or ethnicity, men outpace women in annual income. This disparity between the incomes of Black women and White men has remained unchanged over the more than fifty years during which such data have been tabulated. It illustrates yet another instance of the greater inequality experienced by minority women. Also, Figure 3.3 includes only data for full-time, year-round workers; it excludes homemakers and the unemployed. Even in this comparison, the deprivation of Blacks, Hispanics, and women is confirmed again.

Are these differences entirely the result of discrimination in employment? No, individuals within the four groups are not equally prepared to compete for high-paying jobs. Past discrimination is a significant factor in a person's present social position. As discussed previously and illustrated in Figure 3.1, past discrimination continues to take its toll on modern victims. Taxpayers, predominantly White, were unwilling to subsidize the public education of African Americans and Hispanics at the same levels as White pupils. Even as these actions have changed, today's schools show the continuing results of this uneven spending pattern from the past. Education clearly is an appropriate variable to control.

In Table 3.1, median income is compared, holding education constant, which means that we can compare Blacks and Whites and men and women with approximately the same amount of formal schooling. More education means more money, but the disparity remains. The gap between races does narrow somewhat as education increases. However, both African Americans and women lag behind their more affluent counterparts. The contrast remains dramatic: Women with a master's degree typically receive $51,412, which means they earn almost $8,608 less than men who complete only a bachelor's degree.

Thinking over the long term, a college-educated woman will work three years to earn over $120,000. The typical male can work two years, take the third year off without pay, and match the woman's earnings. Remember these comparisons are limited to full-time workers.

? ASK Yourself

Have women caught up with men in wages? How big is the male–female income gap?

TABLE 3.1
Median Income by Race and Sex, Holding Education Constant

Even at the very highest levels of schooling, the income gap remains between Whites and Blacks. Education also has little apparent effect on the income gap between male and female workers.

	Race				Sex	
	White Families	Black Families	Asian Families	Hispanic Families	Male	Female
Total	$ 64,663	$ 37,005	$ 71,156	$ 39,053	$ 43,317	$ 33,075
HIGH SCHOOL						
Nongraduate	27,432	20,468	30,086	27,757	27,189	20,125
Graduate	33,090	31,264	40,330	30,610	36,302	26,289
COLLEGE						
Some college	51,148	40,280	50,167	39,653	42,418	31,399
Bachelor's degree	86,553	67,487	87,444	66,717	60,020	42,172
Master's degree	100,000	82,296	98,353	85,121	75,025	51,412
Doctorate degree	141,000	115,000	119,074	118,000	85,864	66,852

Notes: Data released in 2006 for income earned in 2005. Figures are median income from all sources except capital gains. Included are public assistance payments, dividends, pensions, unemployment compensation, and so on. Incomes are for all workers over 25 years of age. High school graduates include those with GEDs. Data for Whites are for White non-Hispanics. "Some college" excludes associate degree holders. Data for doctorate-holder's families are author's estimate.

Source: DeNavas-Walt et al. 2006.

Note what happens to Asian American households. Although the highly educated Asian Americans earn a lot of money, they trail well behind their White counterparts. With a doctorate holder in the family, the typical Asian American household earns an estimated $119,074 compared to $141,000 in a White household. To put this another way, these highly educated Asian Americans will work six years to earn what Whites do in five years.

What do these individual differences look like if we consider them on a national level? Economist Andrew Brimmer (1995), citing numerous government studies, estimates that about 3 or 4 percent of the gross domestic product (GDP, or the value of goods and services) is lost annually by the failure to use African Americans' existing education. There had been little change in this economic cost from the mid-1960s to the mid-1990s. This estimate would be even higher if we took into account economic losses caused by the underuse of the academic talents of women and other minorities.

Now that education has been held constant, is the remaining gap caused by discrimination? No, not necessarily. Table 3.1 uses only the amount of schooling, not its quality. Racial minorities are more likely to attend inadequately financed schools. Some efforts have been made to eliminate disparities between school districts in the amount of wealth available to tax for school support but have met with little success. The inequality of educational opportunity may seem less important in explaining sex discrimination. Although women usually are not segregated from men, educational institutions encourage talented women to enter fields that pay less (nursing or elementary education) than other occupations requiring similar amounts of training.

Eliminating Discrimination

Two main agents of social change work to reduce discrimination: voluntary associations organized to solve racial and ethnic problems and the federal government, including the courts. The two are closely related: Most efforts initiated by the government were urged by associations or organizations representing minority groups, following vigorous protests against racism by African Americans. Resistance to social inequality by subordinate groups has been the key to change. Rarely has any government of its own initiative sought to end discrimination based on such criteria as race, ethnicity, and gender.

All racial and ethnic groups of any size are represented by private organizations that are to some degree trying to end discrimination. Some groups originated in the first half of the twentieth century, but most have been founded since World War II or have become significant forces in bringing about change only since then. These include church organizations, fraternal social groups, minor political parties, and legal de-

What do you think? Do people in a workplace sometimes question the credentials of a minority hire? Do you think minority workers are sometimes viewed by their colleagues at work as taking the place of someone "more qualified?"

fense funds, as well as more militant organizations operating under the scrutiny of law enforcement agencies. The purposes, membership, successes, and failures of these resistance organizations dedicated to eliminating discrimination are discussed throughout this book.

Government action toward eliminating discrimination is also recent. Each branch of the government has taken antidiscrimination actions: the executive, the judicial, and the legislative.

The first antidiscrimination action at the executive level was President Franklin D. Roosevelt's 1943 creation of the Fair Employment Practices Commission (FEPC), which handled thousands of complaints of discrimination, mostly from African Americans, despite strong opposition by powerful economic and political leaders and many southern Whites. The FEPC had little actual power. It had no authority to compel employers to stop discriminating but could only ask for voluntary compliance. Its jurisdiction was limited to federal government employees, federal contractors, and labor unions. State and local governments and any business without a federal contract were not covered. Furthermore, the FEPC never enjoyed vigorous support from the White House, was denied adequate funds, and was part of larger agencies that were hostile to the commission's existence. This weak antidiscrimination agency was finally dropped in 1946, only to be succeeded by an even weaker one in 1948.

The judiciary, charged with interpreting laws and the U.S. Constitution, has a much longer history of involvement in the rights of racial, ethnic, and religious minorities. However, its early decisions protected the rights of the dominant group, as in the 1857 U.S. Supreme Court's *Dred Scott* decision, which ruled that slaves remained slaves even when living or traveling in states where slavery was illegal. Not until the 1940s did the Supreme Court revise earlier decisions and begin to grant African Americans the same rights as those held by Whites. The 1954 *Brown v. Board of Education* decision, which stated that "separate but equal" facilities, including education, were unconstitutional, heralded a new series of rulings, arguing that distinguishing between races in order to segregate was inherently unconstitutional.

It was assumed incorrectly by many that *Brown* and other judicial actions would lead quickly to sweeping change. In fact, little change occurred initially, and resistance to racism continued. The immediate effect of many court rulings was minimal because the executive branch and the Congress did not want to violate the principle of **states' rights**, which holds that each state is sovereign in most of its affairs and has the right to order them without interference from the federal government. In other words, supporters of states' rights felt that the federal government had to allow state governments to determine how soon the rights of African Americans would be protected. Gradually, U.S. society became more committed to the rights of individuals. Legislation in the 1960s committed the federal government to protecting civil rights actively rather than merely leaving action up to state and local officials.

The most important legislative effort to eradicate discrimination was the Civil Rights Act of 1964. This act led to the establishment of the Equal Employment Opportunity Commission (EEOC), which had the power to investigate complaints against employers and to recommend action to the Department of Justice. If the Justice Department sued and discrimination was found, the court could order appropriate compensation. The act covered employment practices of all businesses with more than 25 employees and nearly all employment agencies and labor unions. A 1972 amendment broadened the coverage to employers with as few as 15 employees.

The Civil Rights Act of 1964 prohibited different voting registration standards for White and Black voting applicants. It also prohibited discrimination in public accommodations—that is, hotels, motels, restaurants, gasoline stations, and amusement parks. Publicly owned facilities, such as parks, stadiums, and swimming pools, were

? ASK Yourself

How does government attempt to eliminate discrimination?

states' rights
The principle, reinvoked in the late 1940s, that holds that each state is sovereign and has the right to order its own affairs without interference by the federal government.

also prohibited from discriminating. Another important provision forbade discrimination in all federally supported programs and institutions, such as hospitals, colleges, and road construction projects.

The Civil Rights Act of 1964 covered discrimination based on race, color, creed, national origin, and sex. Although the inclusion of gender in employment criteria had been prohibited in the federal civil service since 1949, most laws and most groups pushing for change showed little concern about sex discrimination. There was little precedent for attention to sex discrimination even at the state level. Only Hawaii and Wisconsin had enacted laws against sex discrimination before 1964. As first proposed, the Civil Rights Act did not include mention of gender. One day before the final vote, opponents of the measure offered an amendment on gender bias in an effort to defeat the entire act. The act did pass with prohibition against sex bias included, an event that can only be regarded as a milestone for women seeking equal employment rights with men.

The Civil Rights Act of 1964 was not perfect. Since 1964, several acts and amendments to the original act have been added to cover the many areas of discrimination it left untouched, such as criminal justice and housing. Even in areas singled out for enforcement in the Civil Rights Act of 1964, discrimination still occurs. Federal agencies charged with its enforcement complain that they are underfunded or are denied wholehearted support by the White House. Also, regardless of how much the EEOC may want to act in a particular case, the person who alleges discrimination has to pursue the complaint over a long time, marked by long periods of inaction. Despite these efforts, devastating forms of discrimination persist. African Americans, Latinos, and others fall victim to redlining. **Redlining** is the pattern of discrimination against people trying to buy homes in minority and racially changing neighborhoods. Research finds that in twenty-five metropolitan areas, housing agents showed fewer housing units to Blacks and Latinos, steered them to minority neighborhoods, and gave them far less assistance in finding housing that met their needs. The concept of redlining is now being applied to areas other than home buying.

People living in predominantly minority neighborhoods have found that service deliverers refuse to go to their area. In one case that attracted national attention in 1997, Kansas City's Pizza Hut refused to deliver forty pizzas to an honor program at a high school in an all-Black neighborhood. A Pizza Hut spokesperson called the neighborhood unsafe and said that almost every city has "restricted areas" to which the company will not deliver. This admission was particularly embarrassing because the high school already had a $170,000-a-year contract with Pizza Hut to deliver pizzas as a part of its school lunch program. Service redlining covers everything from parcel deliveries to repair people as well as food deliveries. The red pencil appears not be have been set aside in cities throughout the United States (Fuller 1998; Rusk 2001; Schwartz 2001; Turner et al. 2002; Yinger 1995).

Although civil rights laws often have established rights for other minorities, the Supreme Court made them explicit in two 1987 decisions involving groups other than African Americans. In the first of the two cases, an Iraqi American professor asserted that he had been denied tenure because of his Arab origins; in the second, a Jewish congregation brought suit for damages in response to the defacement of its synagogue with derogatory symbols. The Supreme Court ruled unanimously that, in effect, any member of an ethnic minority may sue under federal prohibitions against discrimination. These decisions paved the way for almost all racial and ethnic groups to invoke the Civil Rights Act of 1964 (Taylor 1987).

A particularly insulting form of discrimination seemed finally to be on its way out in the late 1980s. Many social clubs had limitations forbidding membership to minorities, Jews, and women. For years, exclusive clubs argued that they were merely selecting friends, but, in fact, a principal function of these clubs is as a forum to transact business. Denial of membership meant more than the inability to attend a luncheon; it also seemed to exclude certain groups from part of the marketplace, as Lawrence Otis

redlining
The pattern of discrimination against people trying to buy homes in minority and racially changing neighborhoods.

Graham observed at the beginning of this chapter. The Supreme Court ruled unanimously, in *New York State Clubs Association v. City of New York* in 1988 that states and cities may ban sex discrimination by large private clubs where business lunches and similar activities take place. Although the ruling does not apply to all clubs and leaves the issue of racial and ethnic barriers unresolved, it did chip away at the arbitrary exclusiveness of private groups (Steinhaver 2006; Taylor 1988).

Memberships and restrictive organizations remain perfectly legal. The rise to national attention of professional golfer Tiger Woods, of mixed Native American, African, and Asian ancestry, made the public aware that there were at least twenty-three golf courses where he would be prohibited from playing by virtue of race. In 2002, women's groups tried unsuccessfully to have the golf champion speak out as the Master's and British Open played on courses closed to women as members (Scott 2003).

The inability of the Civil Rights Act, similar legislation, and court decisions to end discrimination does not result entirely from poor financial and political support, although it does play a role. The number of federal employees assigned to investigate and prosecute bias cases is insufficient. Many discriminatory practices, such as those described as institutional discrimination, are seldom subject to legal action.

Wealth Inequality: Discrimination's Legacy

Discrimination that has occurred in the past carries into the present and future. As noted in Figure 3.1, a lack of inherited wealth is one element of the past. African American and other minority groups have had less opportunity to accumulate assets such as homes, land, and savings that can insulate them and later their children from economic setbacks.

Income refers to salaries and wages, and **wealth** is a more inclusive term encompassing all a person's material assets, including land, stocks, and other types of property. Wealth not only allows one to live better but also even modest assets provide insurance against the effects of job layoffs, natural disasters, and long-term illness, and afford individuals much better interest rates when they need to borrow money. It allows children to graduate from college relatively debt free or perhaps with no college loans to pay back at all. This reminds us that for many it is not a question of wealth in the sense of assets but wealth as measured by indebtedness.

Studies document that the kind of disparities in income we have seen are even greater when wealth is considered. In 2004, only 4 percent of home buyers were

income
Salaries, wages, and other money received.

wealth
An inclusive term encompassing all of a person's material assets, including land and other types of property.

A remaining area of discrimination is the legal provision allowing private clubs to set exclusionary standards. Professional atheletes such as Tiger Woods and Venus and Serena Williams have brought attention to a practice that still continues today.

Although more and more African Americans and Latinos are buying their own homes, the assets of accumulation run well behind that of White households—a legacy, in part, of past and present discrimination.

African Americans—at least one-third of what we would expect. This makes sense, however, because if individuals experience lower incomes throughout their lives, they are less likely to be able to put anything aside. They are more likely to have to pay interest rather than save for their future or their children's future.

A close analysis of wealth shows that typically African American families have $86,000 less wealth than their White counterparts even when comparing members of comparably educated, employed households. Evidence indicates that this inequality in wealth has been growing over the last ten years rather than staying the same or declining (Bureau of the Census 2005a, 623; Oliver and Shapiro 2006).

Environmental Justice

Discrimination takes many forms and is not necessarily apparent, even when its impact can be far reaching. Take the example of Kennedy Heights, a well-kept working-class neighborhood nestled in southeastern Houston. This community faces a real threat, and it is not from crime or drugs. The threat that community residents fear is right under their feet in the form of three oil pits abandoned by Gulf Oil in 1927. The residents, most of whom are African American, argue that they have suffered high rates of cancer, lupus, and other illnesses because the chemicals from the oil fields poison their water supply. The residents first sued Chevron USA in 1985, and the case is still making its way through the courtrooms of no less than six states and the federal judiciary.

Lawyers and other representatives for the residents say that the oil company is guilty of environmental racism because it knowingly allowed a predominantly Black housing development to be built on the contaminated land. They are able to support this charge with documents, including a 1954 memorandum from an appraiser who suggested that the oil pits be drained of any toxic substances and the land filled for "low-cost houses for White occupancy." When the land did not sell right away, an oil company official in a 1967 memorandum suggested a tax-free land exchange with a developer who intended to use the land for "Negro residents and commercial development." For this latter intended use by African Americans, there was no mention of any required environmental cleanup of the land. The oil company counters that it just assumed the developer would do the necessary cleanup of the pits (Maning 1997; Verhovek 1997).

The conflict perspective sees the case of the Houston suburb as one in which pollution harms minority groups disproportionately. **Environmental justice** refers to the efforts to ensure that hazardous substances are controlled so that all communities receive protection regardless of race or socioeconomic circumstance. After the Environmental Protection Agency (EPA) and other organizations documented discrimination in the locating of hazardous waste sites, an Executive Order was issued in 1994 that requires all federal agencies to ensure that low-income and minority communities have access to better information about their environment and have an opportunity to participate in shaping government policies that affect their community's health. Initial efforts to implement the policy have met widespread opposition, including criticism from some proponents of economic development who argue that the guidelines unnecessarily delay or block altogether locating new industrial sites.

Sociologist Robert Bullard (1990) has shown that low-income communities and areas with significant minority populations are more likely to be adjacent to waste sites than are affluent White communities. Undergraduate student researchers at Occidental College in California found in 1995 that the poor, African Americans, Latinos, Asian Americans, and Native Americans were especially likely to be living near Los Angeles County's 82 potential environmental hazards. Another study in 2001 also showed the higher probability that people of color live closer to sources of air pollution. Yet a third study, released in 2003, found that grade schools in Florida nearer environmental hazards are disproportionately Black or Latino. People of color jeopardized by environmental problems also lack the resources and political muscle to do something about it (Institutes of Medicine 1999; Moffat 1995; Polakovic 2001; Streteksy and Lynch 2002).

Issues of environmental justice are not limited to metropolitan areas. Another continuing problem is abuse of Native American reservation land. Many American Indian leaders are concerned that tribal lands are too often regarded as dumping grounds for toxic waste that go to the highest bidder. On the other hand, the economic devastation faced by some tribes in isolated areas has led one tribe in Utah to actually seek out becoming a depot for discarded nuclear waste (*New York Times* 2005a; Skull Valley Goshutes 2006).

As with other aspects of discrimination, experts disagree. There is controversy within the scientific community over the potential hazards of some of the problems, and there is even some opposition within the subordinate communities being affected. This complexity of the issues in terms of social class and race is apparent, as some observers question the wisdom of an executive order that slows economic development coming to areas in dire need of employment opportunities. On the other hand, some counter that such businesses typically employ few less-skilled workers and only make the environment less livable for those left behind. Despite such varying viewpoints, **environmental justice** is an excellent example of resistance and change in the 1990s that could not have been foreseen by the civil rights workers of the 1950s.

Affirmative Action

Affirmative action is the positive effort to recruit subordinate-group members, including women, for jobs, promotions, and educational opportunities. The phrase *affirmative action* first appeared in an executive order issued by President Kennedy in 1961. The order called for contractors to "take affirmative action to ensure that applicants are employed, and that employees are treated during employment, without regard to their race, creed, color, or national origin." However, at this early time, no enforcement procedures were specified. Six years later, the order was amended to prohibit discrimination on the basis of sex, but affirmative action was still defined vaguely.

environmental justice
Efforts to ensure that hazardous substances are controlled so that all communities receive protection regardless of race or socioeconomic circumstances.

affirmative action
Positive efforts to recruit subordinate group members, including women, for jobs, promotions, and educational opportunities.

So desperate are the economic conditions of isolated Indian tribes that they often seek out questionable forms of economic development. The Skull Valley Goshute Indian Reservation in Utah is trying to attract a nuclear waste dump, and local and state officials are trying to block this possibility.

Today, *affirmative action* has become a catchall term for racial preference programs and goals. It has also become a lightning rod for opposition to any programs that suggest special consideration of women or racial minorities.

Affirmative Action Explained

Affirmative action has been viewed as an important tool for reducing institutional discrimination. Whereas previous efforts were aimed at eliminating individual acts of discrimination, federal measures under the heading of affirmative action have been aimed at procedures that deny equal opportunities, even if they are not intended to be overtly discriminatory. This policy has been implemented to deal with both current discrimination and past discrimination outlined earlier in this chapter.

Affirmative action has been aimed at institutional discrimination in such areas as:

- Height and weight requirements that are unnecessarily geared to the physical proportions of White men without regard to the actual characteristics needed to perform the job and, therefore, exclude women and some minorities.
- Seniority rules, when applied to jobs historically held only by White men, that make more recently hired minorities and females more subject to layoff—the "last hired, first fired" employee—and less eligible for advancement.
- Nepotism-based membership policies of some unions that exclude those who are not relatives of members who, because of past employment practices, are usually White.
- Restrictive employment leave policies, coupled with prohibitions on part-time work or denials of fringe benefits to part-time workers, that make it difficult for the heads of single-parent families, most of whom are women, to get and keep jobs and also meet the needs of their families.
- Rules requiring that only English be spoken at the workplace, even when not a business necessity, which result in discriminatory employment practices toward people whose primary language is not English.
- Standardized academic tests or criteria geared to the cultural and educational norms of middle-class or White men when these are not relevant predictors of successful job performance.
- Preferences shown by law and medical schools in admitting children of wealthy and influential alumni, nearly all of whom are White.

- Credit policies of banks and lending institutions that prevent the granting of mortgages and loans in minority neighborhoods or prevent the granting of credit to married women and others who have previously been denied the opportunity to build good credit histories in their own names.

Employers have also been cautioned against asking leading questions in interviews, such as "Did you know you would be the first Black to supervise all Whites in that factory?" or "Does your husband mind your working on weekends?" Furthermore, the lack of minority-group or female employees may in itself represent evidence for a case of unlawful exclusion (Commission on Civil Rights 1981).

The Legal Debate

How far can an employer go in encouraging women and minorities to apply for a job before it becomes unlawful discrimination against White men? Since the late 1970s, a number of bitterly debated cases on this difficult aspect of affirmative action have reached the U.S. Supreme Court. The most significant cases are summarized in Table 3.2. Furthermore, as we will see, the debate has moved into party politics.

In the 1978 *Bakke* case (*Regents of the University of California v. Bakke*), by a narrow 5–4 vote, the Court ordered the medical school of the University of California at Davis to admit Allan Bakke, a qualified White engineer who had originally been denied admission solely on the basis of his race. The justices ruled that the school had violated Bakke's constitutional rights by establishing a fixed quota system for minority students. However, the Court added that it was constitutional for universities to adopt flexible admission programs that use race as one factor in making decisions.

Colleges and universities responded with new policies designed to meet the *Bakke* ruling while broadening opportunities for traditionally underrepresented minority students. However, in 1996 the Supreme Court allowed a lower court decision to stand that affirmative action programs for African American and Mexican American students at the University of Texas law school were unconstitutional. The ruling effectively prohibited schools in the lower court's jurisdiction of Louisiana, Mississippi, and Texas from taking race into account in admissions. In 2003, the Supreme Court made two rulings concerning the admissions policies at the University of Michigan. In one case involving the law school, the Court upheld the right of the school to use applicants' race as criteria for admission decisions but ruled against a strict admissions formula awarding points to minority applicants who applied to the university's undergraduate school. Given the various legal actions, further challenges to affirmative action can be expected (Greenhouse 2003a).

Has affirmative action actually helped alleviate employment inequality on the basis of race and gender? This is a difficult question to answer, given the complexity of the labor market and the fact that there are other antidiscrimination measures, but it does appear that affirmative action has had significant impact in the sectors where it has been applied. Sociologist Barbara Reskin (1998) reviewed available studies looking at workforce composition in terms of race and gender in light of affirmative action policies. She found that gains in minority employment can be attributed to affirmative action policies. This includes both firms mandated to follow affirmative action guidelines and those that took them on voluntarily. There is also evidence that some earnings gains can be attributed to affirmative action. Economists M. V. Lee Badgett and Heidi Hartmann (1995), reviewing twenty-six other research studies, came to similar conclusions: Affirmative action and other federal compliance programs have had a modest impact, but it is difficult to assess, given larger economic changes such as recessions or the rapid increase in women in the paid labor force.

TABLE 3.2
Key Decisions on Affirmative Action

In a series of split and often very close decisions, the Supreme Court has expressed a variety of reservations in specific situations.

Year	Favorable/Unfavorable to Policy	Case	Vote	Ruling
1971	+	*Griggs v. Duke Power Co.*	9-0	Private employers must provide a remedy where minorities were denied opportunities, even if unintentional.
1978	−	*Regents of the University of California v. Bakke*	5-4	Prohibited holding specific number of places for minorities in college admissions.
1979	+	*United Steelworkers of America v. Weber*	5-2	Okay for union to favor minorities in special training programs.
1984	−	*Firefighters Local Union No 1784 (Memphis, TN) v. Stotts*	6-1	Seniority means recently hired minorities may be laid off first in staff reductions.
1986	+	*International Association of Firefighters v. City of Cleveland*	6-3	May promote minorities over more senior Whites.
1986	+	*New York City v. Sheet Metal*	5-4	Approved specific quota of minority workers for union.
1987	+	*United States v. Paradise*	5-4	Endorsed quotas for promotions of state troopers.
1987	+	*Johnson v. Transportation Agency, Santa Clara, CA*	6-3	Approved preference in hiring for minorities and women over better-qualified men and Whites.
1989	−	*Richmond v. Croson Company*	6-3	Ruled a 30 percent set-aside program for minority contractors unconstitutional.
1989	−	*Martin v. Wilks*	5-4	Ruled Whites may bring reverse discrimination claims against Court-approved affirmative action plans.
1990	+	*Metro Broadcasting v. FCC*	5-4	Supported federal programs aimed at increasing minority ownership of broadcast licenses.
1995	−	*Adarand Constructors Inc. v. Peña*	5-4	Benefits based on race are constitutional only if narrowly defined to accomplish a compelling interest.
1996	−	*Texas v. Hopwood*	*	Let stand a lower court decision covering Louisiana, Mississippi, and Texas that race could not be used in college admissions.
2003	+	*Grutter v. Bollinger*	5-4	Race can be a factor in admissions at the University of Michigan Law School.
2003	−	*Gratz v. Bollinger*	6-3	Cannot use a strict formula awarding advantage based on race for admissions to the University of Michigan.

* 5th U.S. Circuit Court of Appeals decision.

Reverse Discrimination

reverse discrimination
Actions that cause better-qualified White men to be passed over for women and minority men.

While researchers debated the merit of affirmative action, the general public—particularly Whites but also some affluent African Americans and Hispanics—questioned the wisdom of the program. Particularly strident were the charges of reverse discrimination: that government actions cause better-qualified White men to be bypassed in favor of women and minority men. **Reverse discrimination** is an emotional term because it conjures up the notion that somehow women and minorities will subject White men in the United States to the same treatment received by minorities during the last three centuries.

Increasingly, critics of affirmative action call for color-blind policies that would end affirmative action and, they argue, allow all people to be judged fairly. However, will that mean an end to the institutional practices that favored Whites? For example, according to the latest data, 40 percent of Harvard's alumni, who are almost all White, are admitted to the university compared to 11 percent of nonalumni. Of major significance, often overlooked in public debates, is that a color-blind policy implies a very limited role for the state in addressing social inequality between racial and ethnic groups (*Economist* 2004b; Pincus 2003).

Is it possible to have color-blind policies prevail in the United States in the twenty-first century? Supporters of affirmative action contend that as long as businesses rely on informal social networks, personal recommendations, and family ties, White men will have a distinct advantage built on generations of being in positions of power. Furthermore, an end to affirmative action should also mean an end to the many programs that give advantages to certain businesses, homeowners, veterans, farmers, and others. Most of these preference holders are White (Kilson 1995; Mack 1996).

Consequently, by the 1990s and into the twenty-first century, affirmative action had emerged as an increasingly important issue in state and national political campaigns. In 2003, the Supreme Court reviewed the admission policies at the University of Michigan which may favor racial minorities (see Table 3.2). In 2006, Michigan citizens by a 58 percent margin voted to restrict all their state universities from using affirmative action in their admissions policies. Generally, discussions have focused on the use of quotas in hiring practices. Supporters of affirmative action argue that hiring goals establish "floors" for minority inclusion but do not exclude truly qualified candidates from any group. Opponents insist that these "targets" are, in fact, quotas that lead to reverse discrimination. (Lewin 2006).

The state of California, in particular, was a battleground for this controversial issue. The California Civil Rights Initiative was placed on the ballot in 1996 as a referendum to amend the state constitution and prohibit any programs that give preference to women and minorities for college admission, employment, promotion, or government contracts. Overall, 54 percent of the voters backed the state proposition, with 61 percent of men in favor compared with only 48 percent of women. Whites, who represented 74 percent of the voters, voted in favor of the measure overwhelmingly, with 63 percent backing Proposition 209. This compares with 26 percent of African Americans, 24 percent of Hispanics, and 39 percent of Asian Americans favoring the end of affirmative action in state-operated institutions. Obviously, the voters—Whites and men—who perceived themselves as least likely to benefit from affirmative action overwhelmingly favored Proposition 209.

Legal challenges continue concerning Proposition 209, which is being implemented unevenly throughout the state. Much of the attention has focused on the impact that reducing racial preference programs will have in law and medical schools, in which competition for admission is very high. The courts have upheld the measures, and in 1998 voters in Washington state passed a similar anti–affirmative action measure (Dolan 2000).

The Glass Ceiling

We have been talking primarily about racial and ethnic groups as if they have uniformly failed to keep pace with Whites. Although that is accurate, there are tens of thousands of people of color who have matched and even exceeded Whites in terms of income. For example, in 2000, more than 815,000 Black households and more than 556,000 Hispanic households earned more than $100,000. What can we say about affluent members of subordinate groups in the United States (Bureau of the Census 2001d)?

SIGNE
PHILADELPHIA DAILY NEWS
Philadelphia
USA

Prejudice does not necessarily end with wealth. Black newspaper columnist De Wayne Wickham (1993) wrote of the subtle racism he had experienced. He heard a White clerk in a supermarket ask a White customer whether she knew the price of an item the computer would not scan; when the problem occurred while the clerk was ringing up Wickham's groceries, she called for a price check. Affluent subordinate-group members routinely report being blocked as they move toward the first-class section aboard airplanes or seek service in upscale stores. Another journalist, Ellis Cose (1993), has called these insults the soul-destroying slights to affluent minorities that lead to the "rage of a privileged class."

Discrimination persists for even the educated and qualified from the best family backgrounds. As subordinate-group members are able to compete successfully, they sometimes encounter attitudinal or organizational bias that prevents them from reaching their full potential. They have confronted what has come to be called the **glass ceiling**. This refers to the barrier that blocks the promotion of a qualified worker because of gender or minority membership (Figure 3.4). Often, people entering non-traditional areas of employment become marginalized and are made to feel uncomfortable, much like the situation of immigrants who feel a part of two cultures, as we discussed in Chapter 1.

The reasons for glass ceilings are as many as the occurrences. It may be that one Black or one woman vice president is regarded as enough, so the second potential candidate faces a block to movement up through management. Decision makers may be concerned that their clientele will not trust them if they have too many people of color or may worry that a talented woman could become overwhelmed with her duties as a mother and wife and thus perform poorly in the workplace.

Concern about women and minorities climbing a broken ladder led to the formation in 1991 of the Glass Ceiling Commission, with the U.S. secretary of labor chairing the twenty-one-member group. Initially, it regarded some of the glass ceiling barriers as:

- Lack of management commitment to establishing systems, policies, and practices for achieving workplace diversity and upward mobility.
- Pay inequities for work of equal or comparable value.
- Sex-, race-, and ethnicity-based stereotyping and harassment.

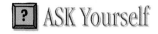 **ASK Yourself**

How does a "glass ceiling" operate?

glass ceiling
The barrier that blocks the promotion of a qualified worker because of gender or minority membership.

FIGURE 3.4 Glass Ceilings and Glass Walls

Women and minority men are moving up in corporations but encounter glass ceilings that block entry to top positions. In addition, they face glass walls that block lateral moves to areas from which executives are promoted. These barriers contribute to women and minority men not moving into the ultimate decision-making positions in the nation's corporate giants.

- Unfair recruitment practices.
- Lack of family-friendly workplace policies.
- "Parent-track" policies that discourage parental leave policies.
- Limited opportunities for advancement to decision-making positions.

This significant underrepresentation of women and minority males in managerial positions results in large part from the presence of glass ceilings. Sociologist Max Weber wrote over a hundred years ago that the privileged class monopolizes the purchase of high-priced consumer goods and wields the power to grant or withhold opportunity from others. To grasp just how White and male the membership of this elite group is, consider the following: Eighty-two percent of the 11,500 people who serve on the boards of directors of *Fortune* 1,000 corporations are non-Hispanic White males. For every 82 White men on these boards, there are 2 Latinos, 2 Asian Americans, 3 African Americans, and 11 White women (Strauss 2002; Weber [1913–1922] 1947).

Glass ceilings are not the only barrier. There are also glass walls. Catalyst, a nonprofit research organization, conducted interviews in 1992 and again in 2001 with senior and middle managers from larger corporations. The study found that even before glass ceilings are encountered, women and racial and ethnic minorities face **glass walls** that

glass wall
A barrier to moving laterally in a business to positions that are more likely to lead to upward mobility.

glass escalator
The male advantage experienced in occupations dominated by women.

keep them from moving laterally. Specifically, the study found that women tend to be placed in staff or support positions in areas such as public relations and human resources and are often directed away from jobs in core areas such as marketing, production, and sales. Women are assigned to and, therefore, trapped in jobs that reflect their stereotypical helping nature and encounter glass walls that cut off access to jobs that might lead to broader experience and advancement (Catalyst 2001; Lopez 1992).

Researchers have documented a differential impact that the glass ceiling has on White males. It appears that men who enter traditionally female occupations are more likely to rise to the top. Male elementary teachers become principals and male nurses become supervisors. The **glass escalator** refers to the male advantage experienced in occupations dominated by women. Whereas females may become tokens when they enter traditionally male occupations, men are more likely to be advantaged when they move out of sex-typical jobs. In summary, women and minority men confront a glass ceiling that limits upward mobility and glass walls that reduce their ability to move into fast-track jobs leading to the highest reaches of the corporate executive suite. Meanwhile, men who do choose to enter female-dominated occupations are often rewarded with promotions and positions of responsibility coveted by their fellow female workers (Budig 2002 ; Cognard-Black 2004).

Conclusion

Discrimination takes its toll, whether or not a person who is discriminated against is part of the informal economy. Even members of minority groups who are not today being overtly discriminated against continue to fall victim to past discrimination. We have also identified the costs of discrimination to members of the privileged group. The attitudes of Whites and even members of minority groups themselves are influenced by the images they have of racial and ethnic groups. These images come from what has been called statistical discrimination, which causes people to act based on stereotypes they hold and the actions of a few subordinate-group members.

From the conflict perspective, it is not surprising to find the widespread presence of the informal economy proposed by the dual labor market model and even an underclass. Derrick Bell (1994), an African American law professor, has made the sobering assertion that "racism is permanent." He contends that the attitudes of dominant Whites prevail, and society is willing to advance programs on behalf of subordinate groups only when they coincide with needs as perceived by those Whites.

The surveys presented in Chapter 2 show gradual acceptance of the earliest efforts to eliminate discrimination, but that support is failing, especially as it relates to affirmative action. Indeed, concerns about doing something about alleged reverse discrimination are as likely to be voiced as concerns about racial or gender discrimination or glass ceilings and glass walls.

Institutional discrimination remains a formidable challenge in the United States. Attempts to reduce discrimination by attacking institutional discrimination have met with staunch resistance. Partly as a result of this outcry from some of the public, especially White Americans, the federal government gradually deemphasized its affirmative action efforts in the 1980s and 1990s. As we turn to examine the various groups that make up the American people, through generations of immigration and religious diversity, look for the types of programs designed to reduce prejudice and discrimination that were discussed here. Most of the material in this chapter has been about racial groups, especially Black and White Americans. It would be easy to see intergroup hostility as a racial phenomenon, but that would be incorrect. Throughout the history of the United States, relations between some White groups have been characterized by resentment and violence. The next two chapters examine the ongoing legacy of immigration and the nature and relations of White ethnic groups.

Key Terms

absolute deprivation 69
affirmative action 85
discrimination 69
dual labor market 75
environmental justice 84
glass ceiling 90
glass escalator 92

glass wall 91
income 83
informal economy 75
institutional
   discrimination 72
irregular or underground
   economy 75

redlining 82
relative deprivation 69
reverse discrimination 88
states' rights 81
total discrimination 70
wealth 83

Review Questions

1. Why might people still feel disadvantaged, even though their incomes are rising and their housing circumstances have improved?
2. Why does institutional discrimination sometimes seem less objectionable than individual discrimination?
3. In what way does an industrial society operate on several economic levels?
4. Why are questions raised about affirmative action while inequality persists?
5. Distinguish between glass ceilings and glass walls. How do they differ from more obvious forms of discrimination in employment?

Critical Thinking

1. Discrimination can take many forms. Select a case of discrimination that you think just about everyone would agree is wrong. Then describe another incident in which the alleged discrimination was of a more subtle form. Who is likely to condemn and who is likely to overlook such situations?
2. Resistance is a continuing theme of intergroup race relations. Discrimination implies the oppression of a group, but how can discrimination also unify the oppressed group to resist such unequal treatment? How can acceptance, or integration, for example, weaken the sense of solidarity within a group?
3. Voluntary associations such as the National Association for the Advancement of Colored People (NAACP) and government units such as the courts have been important vehicles for bringing about a measure of social justice. In what ways can the private sector—corporations and businesses—also work to bring about an end to discrimination?

Internet Connections—Research Navigator™

Follow the instructions found on page 35 of this text to access the features of Research Navigator™. Once at the Web site, enter your Login Name and Password. Then, to use the ContentSelect database, enter keywords such as "informal economy," "affirmative action," and "glass ceiling," and the research engine will supply relevant and recent scholarly and popular press publications. Use the *New York Times* Search-by-Subject Archive to find recent news articles related to sociology and the Link Library feature to locate relevant Web links organized by the key terms associated with this chapter.

4

Immigration and the United States

CHAPTER OUTLINE

Immigration: A Global Phenomenon

Patterns of Immigration to the United States

Today's Foreign-Born Population

Early Immigration

Restrictionist Sentiment Increases

Contemporary Social Concerns

Illegal Immigration

LISTEN TO OUR VOICES
The Wall That Keeps Illegal Workers In
by Douglas S. Massey

The Economic Impact of Immigration

RESEARCH FOCUS
How Well Are Immigrants Doing?

Women and Immigration

The Global Economy and Immigration

Refugees

Conclusion

Key Terms/Review Questions/
Critical Thinking/Internet Connections—
Research Navigator™

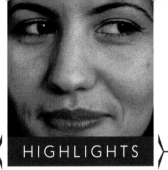

T HE DIVERSITY OF THE AMERICAN PEOPLE IS UNMISTAKABLE evidence of the variety of places from which immigrants have come. Yet each succeeding generation of immigrants found itself being reluctantly accepted, at best, by the descendants of earlier arrivals. The Chinese were the first immigrant group to be singled out for restriction with the passage of the 1882 Exclusion Act. The initial Chinese immigrants became scapegoats for America's sagging economy in the last half of the nineteenth century. Growing fears that too many non-American types were immigrating motivated the creation of the national origin system and the quota acts of the 1920s. These acts gave preference to certain nationalities until the passage of the Immigration and Naturalization Act in 1965 ended that practice. Many immigrants are transnationals who still maintain close ties to their country of origin, sending money back, keeping current with political events, and making frequent return trips. Concern about both illegal and legal immigration has continued through today with increased attention in the aftermath of the September 11, 2001 terrorist attacks. Restrictionist sentiment has grown, and debates rage over whether immigrants, even legal ones, should receive services such as education, government-subsidized health care, and welfare. Controversy also continues to surround the policy of the United States toward refugees.

Two very different experiences of coming of age in the United States point to the different lives of immigrants in the United States.

Growing up in Pennington, New Jersey, Pareha Ahmed watched Hollywood videos and enthusiastically attended with her parents the annual Pakistan Independence Day Parade in New York City. By middle school, however, such outward expressions of her Pakistani heritage had become uncool. She tried to fit in by dying her hair blonde, wearing hazel contact lenses, and even avoiding home-cooked foods that might give her a distinctive odor. In college she began to embrace her heritage and the diversity of cultures of her fellow students. Now at age 23 she gets excited about not only celebrating her Pakistani heritage's special days but also those of her non-Asian friends, such as the Islamic holiday Id-al-Fitr and Christmas—occasions never celebrated in her family's home.

The armed immigration agents arrived at the Petit Jean Poultry Plant in Arkadelphia, Arkansas, just before the 7:30 A.M. early morning shift break for breakfast. Half the shift, 119 workers, was taken away in plastic handcuffs to a detention center where all but six were sent back to Mexico. In the weeks following, the 10,000 residents of Arkadelphia were upset that their community had been disrupted. People they had known as classmates at the local community college, neighbors, customers, fellow churchgoers, and clients had disappeared. Although the people of this Arkansas town usually embrace law enforcement, they did not like what had happened. Some even went so far as to reach the deported workers in Mexico and try to arrange to bring them back to town by crossing the border illegally again (Chu and Mustafa 2006; Hennessy-Fiske 2006).

These dramas being played out in New Jersey and Arkansas illustrate the themes in immigration today. Immigrant labor is needed but concerns over illegal immigration persist and, even for those who arrive legally, the transition can be difficult. For the next generation it gets a little easier and, for some, perhaps too easy as they begin to forget their family's heritage. Many come legally, applying for immigrant visas, but others enter illegally. In the United States we may not like lawbreakers, but often we seek services and low-priced products made by people who come here illegally. How do we control this immigration without violating the principle of free movement within the nation? How do we decide who enters? And how do we treat those who come here either legally or illegally?

The diversity of ethnic and racial backgrounds of Americans today is the living legacy of immigration. Except for descendants of Native Americans or of Africans brought here enslaved, today's population is entirely the product of people who chose to leave familiar places to come to a new country.

The social forces that cause people to emigrate are complex. The most important have been economic: financial failure in the old country and expectations of higher incomes and standards of living in the new land. Other factors include dislike of new regimes in their native lands, racial or religious bigotry, and a desire to reunite families. All these factors push people from their homelands and pull them to other nations such as the United States. Immigration into the United States, in particular, has been facilitated by cheap ocean transportation and by other countries' removal of restrictions on emigration.

Immigration: A Global Phenomenon

Immigration, as we noted in Chapter 1, is a worldwide phenomenon and contributes to globalization as more and more people see the world as their "home" rather than one specific country. As shown in Figure 4.1, people move across national borders throughout the world. Generally immigration is from countries with lower standards of living to those that offer better wages. However, wars and famine may precipitate hundreds of thousands of people moving into neighboring countries and sometimes resettling permanently.

Scholars of immigration often point to *push* and *pull* factors. For example, economic difficulties, religious or ethnic persecution, and political unrest may push individuals from their homelands. Immigration to a particular nation, the pull factors, may be a result of perceptions of a better life ahead or to join a community of their fellow nationals already established abroad.

A potent factor contributing to immigration anywhere in the world is **chain immigration**. Chain immigration refers to an immigrant who sponsors several other immigrants who, upon their arrival, may sponsor still more. Laws that favor people desiring to enter a

chain immigration
Immigrants sponsor several other immigrants who upon their arrival may sponsor still more.

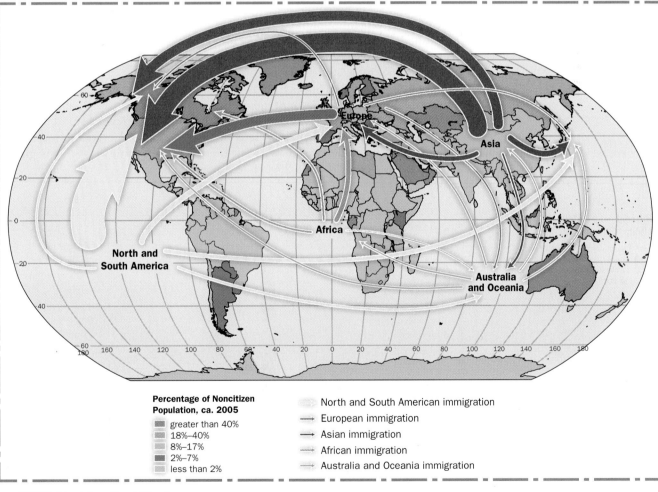

Percentage of Noncitizen Population, ca. 2005

- greater than 40%
- 18%–40%
- 8%–17%
- 2%–7%
- less than 2%

- North and South American immigration
- European immigration
- Asian immigration
- African immigration
- Australia and Oceania immigration

FIGURE 4.1   **International Migration**

Source: Fernandez-Armesto 2007, 1006. Maps designed and produced by DK Education, a division of Dorling Kindersley Limited, 80 Strand London WC2R ORL. DK and the DK logo are registered trademarks of Dorling Kindersley Limited.

given country who already have relatives there or someone who can vouch for them financially may facilitate this sponsorship. But probably the most important aspect of chain immigration is that immigrants anticipate knowing someone who can help them adjust to their new surroundings and find a new job, place to live, and even where to find the kind of foods that are familiar to them. Later in this chapter we will revisit the social impact that immigration has worldwide.

Patterns of Immigration to the United States

There have been three unmistakable patterns of immigration to the United States: The number of immigrants has fluctuated dramatically over time largely due to government policy changes, settlement has not been uniform across the country but centered in certain regions and cities, and the source of immigrants has changed over time. We will first look at the historical picture of immigrant numbers.

Vast numbers of immigrants have come to the United States. Figure 4.2 indicates the high but fluctuating number of immigrants who arrived during every decade from the 1820s through the 1990s. The United States received the largest number of legal immigrants during the 1990s, but because the country was much smaller in the period from 1900 through 1910, the numerical impact was even greater then.

The reception given to immigrants in this country has not always been friendly. Open bloodshed, restrictive laws, and the eventual return of almost one-third of immigrants and their children to their home countries attest to the uneasy feeling toward strangers who want to settle here.

Opinion polls in the United States from 2000 through 2006 have never shown more than 17 percent of the public in favor of more immigration, and usually about 40 to 50 percent want less. Even a survey of Latinos found that only 24 percent wanted immigration increased, 35 percent wanted it left as is, and a sizable 36 percent advocated having immigration levels decreased. We want the door open until we get through, and then we want to close it (Gallup 2006; J. M. Jones 2003a).

FIGURE 4.2 **Legal Migration in the United States, 1820–2010**

Source: Bureau of the Census 2005a:11; Immigration and Naturalization Services 2002; and estimates by the author for the period 2000–2010.

Today's Foreign-Born Population

Before considering the sweep of past immigration policies, let's consider today's immigrant population. About 12 percent of the nation's people are foreign born; this proportion is between the high figure of about 15 percent in 1890 and a low of 4.7 percent in 1970. By global comparisons, the foreign-born population in the United States is large but not unusual. Whereas most industrial countries have a foreign population of around 5 percent, Canada's foreign population is 19 percent and Australia's is 25 percent.

As noted earlier, immigrants have not settled evenly across the nation. As shown in the map in Figure 4.3, the six states of California, New York, Florida, Texas, New Jersey, and Illinois account for 70 percent of the nation's total foreign-born population but less than 40 percent of the nation's total population.

Cities in these states are the focus of the foreign-born population. Almost half (43.3%) live in the central city of a metropolitan area, compared with about one-quarter (27.0%) of the nation's population. More than one-third of residents in the cities of Miami, Los Angeles, San Francisco, San Jose, and New York City are now foreign born (Bureau of Census 2005d; Gibson and Jung 2006;).

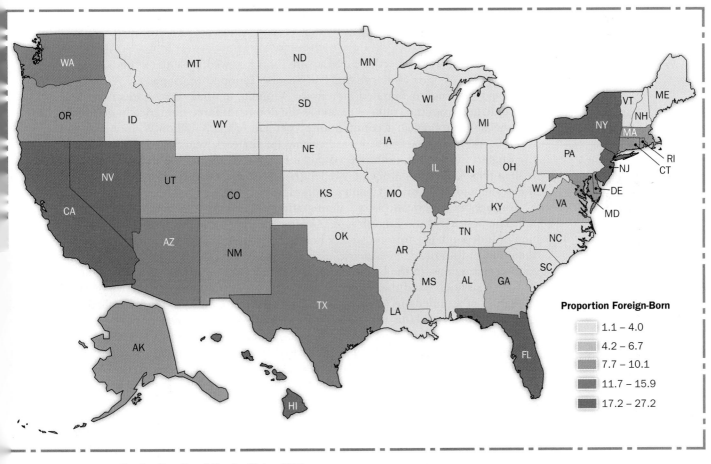

Proportion Foreign-Born

- 1.1 – 4.0
- 4.2 – 6.7
- 7.7 – 10.1
- 11.7 – 15.9
- 17.2 – 27.2

FIGURE 4.3 Foreign-Born Population for States, 2005

Source: Author's estimate based on Census Bureau data in the American Commmunity Survey 2005.

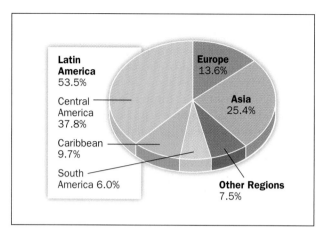

FIGURE 4.4 Foreign Born by World Regions of Birth

Source: Data for 2004 reported in 2005 in Bureau of the Census 2005d.

The third pattern of immigration is that the source of immigrants has changed. As shown in Figure 4.4, the majority of today's 34.2 million foreign-born people are from Latin America. Primarily they are from Central America and, more specifically, Mexico. By contrast, Europeans, who dominated the early settlement of the United States, now account for less than one in seven of the foreign born today.

Early Immigration

European explorers of North America were soon followed by settlers, the first immigrants to the Western Hemisphere. The Spanish founded St. Augustine, Florida, in 1565, and the English founded Jamestown, Virginia, in 1607. Protestants from England emerged from the colonial period as the dominant force numerically, politically, and socially. The English accounted for 60 percent of the 3 million White Americans in 1790. Although exact statistics are lacking for the early years of the United States, the English were soon outnumbered by other nationalities, as the numbers of Scots-Irish and Germans, in particular, swelled. However, the English colonists maintained their dominant position, as Chapter 5 will examine.

Throughout American history, immigration policy has been politically controversial. The policies of the English king, George III, were criticized in the U.S. Declaration of Independence for obstructing immigration to the colonies. Toward the end of the nineteenth century, the American republic itself was criticized for enacting immigration restrictions. In the beginning, however, the country encouraged immigration. At first, legislation fixed the residence requirement for naturalization at five years, although briefly, under the Alien Act of 1798, it was fourteen years, and so-called dangerous people could be expelled. Despite this brief harshness, immigration was unregulated through most of the 1800s, and naturalization was easily available.

Besides holding the mistaken belief that concerns about immigration are something new, we also assume that immigrants to the United States rarely reconsider their decision to come to a new country. Analysis of available records beginning in the early 1900s suggests that about 35 percent of all immigrants to the United States eventually emigrated back to their home country. The proportion varies, with the figures for some countries being much higher, but the overall pattern is clear: About one in three immigrants to this nation eventually chooses to return home (Wyman 1993).

The relative absence of federal legislation from 1790 to 1881 does not mean that all new arrivals were welcomed. **Xenophobia** (the fear or hatred of strangers or foreigners) led naturally to **nativism** (beliefs and policies favoring native-born citizens over

xenophobia
The fear or hatred of strangers or foreigners.

nativism
Beliefs and policies favoring native-born citizens over immigrants.

immigrants). Roman Catholics in general and the Irish in particular were among the first Europeans to be ill-treated. We will look at how organized hostility toward Irish immigrants eventually gave way to their acceptance into the larger society in our next chapter.

However, the most dramatic outbreak of nativism in the nineteenth century was aimed at the Chinese. If there had been any doubt by the mid-1800s that the United States could harmoniously accommodate all and was indeed some sort of melting pot, debate on the Chinese Exclusion Act would negatively settle the question once and for all.

The Anti-Chinese Movement

Before 1851, official records show that only forty-six Chinese had immigrated to the United States. Over the next thirty years, more than 200,000 came to this country, lured by the discovery of gold and the opening of job opportunities in the West. Over-crowding, drought, and warfare in China also encouraged them to take a chance in the United States. Another important factor was improved oceanic transportation; it was actually cheaper to travel from Hong Kong to San Francisco than from Chicago to San Francisco. The frontier communities of the West, particularly in California, looked on the Chinese as a valuable resource to fill manual jobs. As early as 1854, so many Chinese wanted to emigrate that ships had difficulty handling the volume.

In the 1860s, railroad work provided the greatest demand for Chinese labor, until the Union Pacific and Central Pacific railroads were joined at Promontory, Utah, in 1869. The Union Pacific relied primarily on Irish laborers, but 90 percent of the Central Pacific labor force was Chinese because Whites generally refused to do the back-breaking work over the western terrain. Despite the contribution of the Chinese, White workers physically prevented them from attending the driving of the golden spike to mark the joining of the two railroads.

With the dangerous railroad work largely completed, people began to rethink the wisdom of encouraging Chinese to immigrate to do the work no one else would do. Reflecting their xenophobia, White settlers found the Chinese immigrants and their customs and religion difficult to understand. Indeed, few people actually tried to understand these immigrants from Asia. Although they had had no firsthand contact with Chinese Americans, Easterners and legislators were soon on the anti-Chinese bandwagon as they read sensationalized accounts of the lifestyle of the new arrivals.

Even before the Chinese immigrated, stereotypes of them and their customs were prevalent. American traders returning from China, European diplomats, and Protestant missionaries consistently emphasized the exotic and sinister aspects of life in China. The **sinophobes**, people with a fear of anything associated with China, appealed to the racist theory developed during the slavery controversy that non-Europeans were subhuman. Similarly, Americans were beginning to be more conscious of biological inheritance and disease, so it was not hard to conjure up fears of alien genes and germs. The only real challenge the anti-Chinese movement had was to convince people that the negative consequences of unrestricted Chinese immigration outweighed any possible economic gain. Perhaps briefly, racial prejudice had earlier been subordinated to industrial dependence on Chinese labor for the work that Whites shunned, but acceptance of the Chinese was short-lived. The fear of the "yellow peril" overwhelmed any desire to know more about Asian people and their customs (Takaki 1989).

Another nativist fear of Chinese immigrants was based on the threat they posed as laborers. Californians, whose labor force felt the effects of the Chinese immigration first, found support throughout the nation as organized labor feared that the Chinese would be used as strikebreakers. By 1870, Chinese workers had been used for that

 ASK Yourself

How did economic issues influence the move against Chinese immigration to the U.S.?

sinophobes
People with a fear of anything associated with China.

Chinese workers, such as these pictured in 1844, played a major role in building railroads in the West.

purpose as far east as Massachusetts. When Chinese workers did unionize, they were not recognized by major labor organizations. Samuel Gompers, founder of the American Federation of Labor (AFL), consistently opposed any effort to assist Chinese workers and refused to consider having a union of Chinese restaurant employees admitted into the AFL. Gompers worked effectively to see future Chinese immigration ended and produced a pamphlet titled "Chinese Exclusion: Meat vs. Rice: American Manhood Against Asiatic Coolieism—Which Shall Survive?" (Gompers and Gustadt 1908; Hill 1967).

Employers were glad to pay the Chinese low wages, but laborers came to direct their resentment against the Chinese rather than against their compatriots' willingness to exploit the Chinese. Only a generation earlier, the same concerns had been felt about the Irish, but with the Chinese, the hostility reached new heights because of another factor.

Although many arguments were voiced, racial fears motivated the anti-Chinese movement. Race was the critical issue. The labor market fears were largely unfounded, and most advocates of restrictions at the time knew that. There was no possibility that the Chinese would immigrate in numbers that would match those of Europeans at the time, so it is difficult to find any explanation other than racism for their fears (Winant 1994).

From the sociological perspective of conflict theory, we can explain how the Chinese immigrants were welcomed only when their labor was necessary to fuel growth in the United States. When that labor was no longer necessary, the welcome mat for the immigrants was withdrawn. Furthermore, as conflict theorists would point out, restrictions were not applied evenly: Americans focused on a specific nationality (the Chinese) to reduce the overall number of foreign workers in the nation. Because decision making at that time rested in the hands of the descendants of European immigrants, the steps to be taken were most likely to be directed against the least powerful: immigrants from China who, unlike Europeans seeking entry, had few allies among legislators and other policy makers.

In 1882 Congress enacted the Chinese Exclusion Act, which outlawed Chinese immigration for ten years. It also explicitly denied naturalization rights to the Chinese in the United States; that is, they were not allowed to become citizens. There was little debate in Congress, and discussion concentrated on how suspension of Chinese immigration could best be handled. No allowance was made for spouses and children to be reunited with their husbands and fathers in the United States. Only brief visits of Chinese government officials, teachers, tourists, and merchants were exempted.

The rest of the nineteenth century saw the remaining loopholes allowing Chinese immigration closed. Beginning in 1884, Chinese laborers were not allowed to enter

Here women immigrants are undergoing a physical examination before being permitted to enter in 1910.

the United States from any foreign place, a ban that lasted ten years. Two years later, the Statue of Liberty was dedicated, with a poem by Emma Lazarus inscribed on its base. To the Chinese, the poem welcoming the tired, the poor, and the huddled masses must have seemed a hollow mockery.

In 1892 Congress extended the Exclusion Act for another ten years and added that Chinese laborers had to obtain certificates of residence within a year or face deportation. After the turn of the century, the Exclusion Act was extended again. Two decades later, the Chinese were not alone; the list of people restricted by immigration policy had expanded many times.

Restrictionist Sentiment Increases

As Congress closed the door to Chinese immigration, the debate on restricting immigration turned in new directions. Prodded by growing anti-Japanese feelings, the United States entered into the so-called Gentlemen's Agreement, completed in 1908. Japan agreed to halt further immigration to the United States, and the United States agreed to end discrimination against the Japanese who had already arrived. The immigration ended, but anti-Japanese feelings continued. Americans were growing uneasy that the "new immigrants" would overwhelm the culture established by the "old immigrants." The earlier immigrants, if not Anglo-Saxon, were from similar groups such as the Scandinavians, the Swiss, and the French Huguenots. These people were more experienced in democratic political practices and had a greater affinity with the dominant Anglo-Saxon culture. By the end of the nineteenth century, however, more and more immigrants were neither English speaking nor Protestant and came from dramatically different cultures.

In 1917 Congress finally overrode President Wilson's veto and enacted an immigration bill that included the controversial literacy test. Critics of the bill, including

Wilson, argued that illiteracy does not signify inherent incompetence but reflects lack of opportunity for instruction. Such arguments were not heeded, however. The act seemed innocent at first glance—it merely required immigrants to read thirty words in any language—but it was the first attempt to restrict immigration from Western Europe. The act also prohibited immigration from the South Sea islands and other parts of Asia not already excluded. Curiously, this law that closed the door on non–Anglo-Saxons permitted a waiver of the test if the immigrants came because of their home government's discrimination against their race (*New York Times* 1917a, 1917b).

The National Origin System

 ASK Yourself

Who received preference in immigration from the 1920s through 1965?

Beginning in 1921, a series of measures were enacted that marked a new era in American immigration policy. Whatever the legal language, the measures were drawn up to block the growing immigration from southern Europe, such as from Italy and Greece.

Anti-immigration sentiment, combined with the isolationism that followed World War I, caused Congress to severely restrict entry privileges not only of the Chinese and Japanese but of Europeans as well. The national origin system was begun in 1921 and remained the basis of immigration policy until 1965. This system used the country of birth to determine whether a person could enter as a legal alien, and the number of previous immigrants and their descendants was used to set the group's annual immigration cap.

To understand the effect of the national origin system on immigration, it is necessary to clarify the quota system. The quotas were deliberately weighted in favor of immigration from northern Europe. Because of the ethnic composition of the country in 1920, the quotas placed severe restrictions on immigration from the rest of Europe and from other parts of the world. Immigration from the Western Hemisphere (i.e., Canada, Mexico, Central and South America, and the Caribbean) continued unrestricted. The quota for each nation was set at 3 percent of the number of people descended from each nationality recorded in the 1920 census. Once the statistical manipulations were completed, almost 70 percent of the quota for the Eastern Hemisphere went to just three countries: Great Britain, Ireland, and Germany.

The absurdities of the system soon became obvious, but it was nevertheless continued. British immigration had fallen sharply, so most of its quota of 65,000 went unfilled. However, the openings could not be transferred, even though countries such as Italy, with a quota of only 6,000, had 200,000 people who wanted to enter. However one rationalizes the purpose behind the act, the result was obvious: Any English person, regardless of skill and whether related to anyone already here, could enter the country more easily than, say, a Greek doctor whose children were American citizens. The quota for Greece was 305, with the backlog of people wanting to come reaching 100,000.

By the end of the 1920s, annual immigration had dropped to one-fourth of its pre—World War I level. The worldwide economic depression of the 1930s decreased immigration still further. A brief upsurge in immigration just before World War II reflected the flight of Europeans from the oppression of expanding Nazi Germany. The war virtually ended transatlantic immigration. The era of the great European migration to the United States had been legislated out of existence.

The 1965 Immigration and Naturalization Act

The national origin system was abandoned with the passage of the 1965 Immigration and Naturalization Act, signed into law by President Lyndon B. Johnson at the foot of the Statue of Liberty. The primary goals of the act were to reunite families and protect the American labor market. The act also initiated restrictions on immigration from Latin America. After the act, immigration increased by one-third, but the act's influence was primarily on the composition rather than the size of immigration.

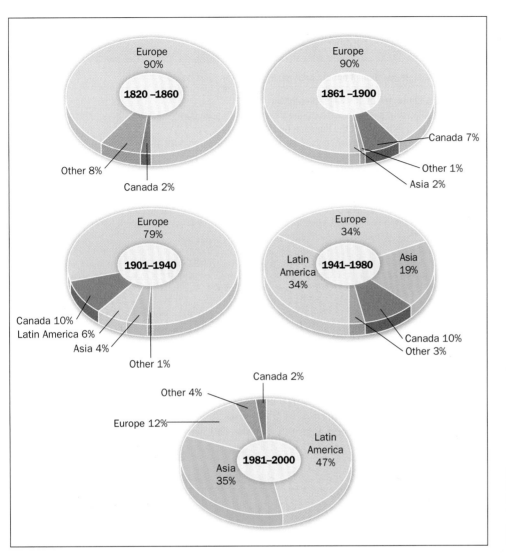

FIGURE 4.5 Legal Immigrants Admitted to the United States by Region of Last Residence, 1820–2000.

Source: Office of Immigration Statistics 2006, 10-13.

The sources of immigrants now included Italy, Greece, Portugal, Mexico, the Philippines, the West Indies, and South America. The effect is apparent when we compare the changing sources of immigration over the last 180 years, as shown in Figure 4.5. The most recent period shows that Asian and Latin American immigrants combined to account for 81 percent of the people who were permitted entry. This contrasts sharply with early immigration, which was dominated by arrivals from Europe.

As reflected in the title of this act, the law set down the rules for becoming a citizen. **Naturalization** is the conferring of citizenship on a person after birth. The general conditions for becoming naturalized in the United States are:

- 18 years of age
- Continuous residence for at least five years (three years for the spouses of U.S. citizens)
- Good moral character as determined by the absence of conviction of selected criminal offenses
- Ability to read, write, speak, and understand words of ordinary usage in the English language
- Ability to pass a test in U.S. government and history

naturalization
Conferring of citizenship on a person after birth.

TABLE 4.1
So You Want to Be a Citizen?

Try these sample questions from the naturalization test (answers below).

1. What do the stripes on the flag represent?
2. How many changes, or amendments, are there to the Constitution?
3. Who is the chief justice of the Supreme Court?
4. What are some of the requirements to be eligible to become president?
5. What are inalienable rights?
6. What is the introduction to the Constitution called and what year was it written?
7. Name one right or freedom guaranteed by the First Amendment.
8. What group of essays supported passage of the U.S. Constitution?

Source: Bureau of Citizenship and Immigrant Services (CIS) 2006 (September 15, 2006). Sample reflects changes proposed by CIS December 1, 2006.

Answers:
1. The first 13 states;   2. 27;   3. John Roberts;   4. Candidates for president must be natural-born citizens, be at least 35 years old, and have lived in the United States for at least 14 years;   5. Individual rights that people are born with;   6. The Preamble and 1787;   7. The rights are freedom of speech, of religion, of assembly, of press, and to petition the government;   8. The Federalist Papers.

In Table 4.1 we offer a sample of the type of questions immigrants face on the citizenship test.

The nature of immigration laws is exceedingly complex and is subjected to frequent, often minor, adjustments. In 2000 and 2004, between 850,000 and 1,100,000 people were legally admitted annually, for the following reasons:

Citizen family unification	
Spouses of citizens	27%
Children and adoptees	11
Parents	8
Other residents	10
Spouses of legal residents	10
Employment based	16
Refugees/people seeking political asylum	7
Diversity (lottery among applications from nations historically sending few immigrants)	5
Other	6

Overall, two-thirds of the immigrants come to join their families, one-seventh because of skills needed in the United States, and one-twelfth because of special refugee status (Office of Immigration Statistics 2006).

We should note that not everything is as simple as suggested by these legal admission categories. A growing problem is families that are "mixed status." One or more members of an immediate family may be legal residents or even citizens but there also may be a member who is in the country illegally. There are almost 7 million families in which the head of the household or spouse is an illegal immigrant. Yet in about one-third of these families one or more of the children are U.S. citizens. This means that some of the issues facing illegal immigrants, whom we will discuss later, will also affect the citizens in the families because they are reluctant to bring attention to themselves for fear of revealing the legal status of their mother or father (Koch 2006a).

Contemporary Social Concerns

brain drain
Immigration to the United States of skilled workers, professionals, and technicians who are desperately needed by their home countries.

Although our current immigration policies are less restrictive than other nations' restrictions, they are the subject of great debate. In Table 4.2, we summarize the benefits and concerns regarding immigration to the United States. We will consider three continuing criticisms of our immigration policy: the brain drain, population growth, and illegal immigration. All three, but particularly illegal immigration, have provoked heated debates and continuing efforts to resolve them with new policies. We will then consider the economic impact of immigration, followed by the nation's policy toward refugees, a group distinct from immigrants.

The Brain Drain

How often have you identified your science or mathematics teacher or your physician as someone who was not born in the United States? This nation has clearly benefited from attracting human resources from throughout the world, but this phenomenon has had its price for the nations of origin.

The **brain drain** is the immigration to the United States of skilled workers, professionals, and technicians who are desperately needed by their home countries. In the mid-twentieth century, many scientists and other professionals from industrial nations, principally Germany and Great Britain, came to the United States. More recently, however, the brain drain has pulled emigrants from developing nations, including India, Pakistan, the Philippines, and several African nations. They are eligible for what are referred to as H-1B visas qualifying for permanent work permits.

One out of four physicians in the United States is foreign born and plays a critical role in serving areas with too few doctors. Thousands of skilled, educated Indians now seek to enter the United States, pulled by the economic opportunity. The pay differential is so great that beginning in 2004, when foreign physicians were no longer favored with entry to the United States, physicians in the Philippines were retraining as nurses so that they could immigrate to the United States where, employed as nurses, they would make four times what they would as doctors in the Philippines (Mullan 2005; *New York Times* 2005b).

The brain drain controversy was evident long before the passage of the 1965 Immigration Act. However, the 1965 act seemed to encourage such immigration by placing the professions in one of the categories of preference. Various corporations, including Motorola and Intel, now find that one-third of their high-tech jobs are held by people born abroad, although many received their advanced education in the United States. Furthermore, these immigrants have links to their old countries and are boosting U.S. exports to the fast-growing economic regions of Asia and Latin America (Bloch 1996).

TABLE 4.2
Immigration Benefits and Concerns

Potential Benefits	Areas of Concern
Provide needed skills	Drain needed resources from home country
Contribute to taxes	Send remittances (or migradollars) home
May come with substantial capital to start business	Less-skilled immigrants compete with those already disadvantaged
Diversify the population (intangible gain)	Population growth
Maintain ties with countries throughout the world	May complicate foreign policy by lobbying the government
	Illegal immigration

Even during times of strongest sentiment against immigration, provisions exist to allow legal entry to overseas technical workers who are in short supply in the United States.

Many foreign students say they plan to return home. Fortunately for the United States, many do not and make their talents available in the United States. One study showed that the majority of foreign students receiving their doctorates in the sciences and engineering are still here four years later. Yet critics note that this supply allows the country to overlook its minority scholars. Presently, for every two minority doctorates, there are five foreign citizens receiving this degree. In the physical sciences, for every doctorate issued to a minority citizen, eleven are received by foreign citizens. More attention needs to be given to encourage African Americans and Latinos to enter high-tech career paths (Hoffer et al. 2001; Wessel 2001).

Conflict theorists see the current brain drain as yet another symptom of the unequal distribution of world resources. In their view, it is ironic that the United States gives foreign aid to improve the technical resources of African and Asian countries while maintaining an immigration policy that encourages professionals in such nations to migrate to our shores. These are the very countries that have unacceptable public health conditions and need native scientists, educators, technicians, and other professionals. In addition, by relying on foreign talent, the United States does not need to take the steps necessary to encourage native members of subordinate groups to enter these desirable fields of employment.

Population Growth

The United States, like a few other industrial nations, continues to accept large numbers of permanent immigrants and refugees. Although such immigration has increased since the passage of the 1965 Immigration and Naturalization Act, the nation's birthrate has decreased. Consequently, the contribution of immigration to population growth has become more significant.

Legal immigration accounted for about 45 to 60 percent of the nation's growth in the early years of the twenty-first century. To some observers, the United States is already overpopulated. The respected environmentalist group Sierra Club debated for several years on taking an official position favoring restricting immigration, recognizing that more people puts greater strain on the nation's natural resources. Thus far the majority of the members have indicated a desire to keep a neutral position rather than enter the politically charged immigration debate (Barringer 2004; Bean et al. 2004).

The patterns of uneven settlement in the United States are expected to continue so that future immigrants' impact on population growth will be felt much more in certain areas: say, California and New York, rather than Iowa or Massachusetts. Although immigration and population growth may be viewed as national concerns, their impact is localized in certain areas such as southern California and large urban centers nationwide (Bean et al. 2004).

Illegal Immigration

The most bitterly debated aspect of U.S. immigration policy has been the control of illegal or undocumented immigrants. These immigrants and their families come to the United States in search of higher-paying jobs than their home countries can provide.

In "Listen to Our Voices," sociologist Douglas Massey ponders the border militarization that has occurred amidst concerns over illegal immigration.

Since, by definition, illegal immigrants are in the country illegally, the exact number of these undocumented or unauthorized workers is subject to estimates and disputes. Based on the best available information, there are more than 11 million illegal immigrants in the United States and probably closer to 12 million. This compares to about 4 million in 1992. Today about 7.2 million are employed accounting for about 5 percent of the entire civilian labor force (Broder 2006; Passel 2006).

Illegal immigrants, and even legal immigrants, have become tied by the public to almost every social problem in the nation. They become the scapegoats for unemployment; they are labeled as "drug runners" and, especially since September 11, 2001, "terrorists." Their vital economic and cultural contribution to the United States is generally overlooked, as it has been for more than a hundred years.

The cost of the federal government's attempt to police the nation's borders and locate illegal immigrants is sizable. There are significant costs for aliens, that is, foreign-born noncitizens, and for other citizens as well. Civil rights advocates have expressed concern that the procedures used to apprehend and deport people are discriminatory and deprive many aliens of their legal rights. American citizens of Hispanic or Asian origin, some of whom were born in the United States, may be greeted with prejudice and distrust, as if their names automatically imply that they are illegal immigrants. Furthermore, these citizens and legal residents of the United States may be unable to find work because employers wrongly believe that their documents are forged.

In the context of this illegal immigration, Congress approved the Immigration Reform and Control Act of 1986 (IRCA) after debating it for nearly a decade. The act marked a historic change in immigration policy compared with earlier laws, as summarized in Table 4.3. Amnesty was granted to 1.7 million illegal immigrants who could

TABLE 4.3
Major Immigration Policies

Policy	Target Group	Impact
Chinese Exclusion Act, 1882	Chinese	Effectively ended all Chinese immigration for more than 60 years
National origin system, 1921	Southern Europeans	Reduced overall immigration and significantly reduced likely immigration from Greece and Italy
Immigration and Naturalization Act, 1965	Western Hemisphere and the less skilled	Facilitated entry of skilled workers and relatives of U.S. residents
Immigration Reform and Control Act of 1986	Illegal immigration	Modest reduction of illegal immigration
Illegal Immigration Reform and Responsibility Act of 1996	Illegal immigration	Greater border surveillance and increased scrutiny of legal immigrants seeking benefits

THE WALL THAT KEEPS ILLEGAL WORKERS IN

The Mexican-American border is not now and never has been out of control. The rate of undocumented migration, adjusted for population growth, to the United States has not increased in 20 years. That is, from 1980 to 2004 the annual likelihood that a Mexican will make his first illegal trip to the United States has remained at about 1 in 100.

Douglas Massey

What has changed are the locations and visibility of border crossings. And that shift, more than anything, has given the public undue fears about waves of Mexican workers trying to flood into America.

Until the 1990s, the vast majority of undocumented Mexicans entered through either El Paso or San Diego. El Paso has around 700,000 residents and is 78 percent Hispanic, whereas San Diego County has three million residents and is 27 percent Hispanic. Thus the daily passage of even thousands of Mexicans through these metropolitan areas was not very visible or disruptive.

This all changed in 1992 when the Border Patrol built a steel fence south of San Diego from the Pacific Ocean to the port of entry at San Ysidro, Calif., where Interstate 5 crosses into Mexico. This fence, and the stationing of officers and equipment behind it, blocked one of the busiest illicit crossing routes and channeled migrants toward the San Ysidro entry station, where their numbers rapidly built up to impossible levels.

Every day the same episode unfolded: the crowd swelled to a critical threshold, whereupon many migrants made what the local press called "banzai runs" into the United States, darting through traffic on the Interstate and clambering over cars.

Waiting nearby were Border Patrol officers, there not to arrest the migrants but to capture the mayhem on video, which was later edited into an agency documentary. Although nothing had changed except the site of border crossings, the video gave the impression that the border was overwhelmed by a rising tide of undocumented migrants.

In response to the ensuing public uproar, the policy of tougher order enforcement was expanded to all of the San Diego and El Paso area in 1993 and 1994. So migrants began going to more remote locations along the border in Arizona. In 1989, two-thirds of undocumented migrants came in through El Paso or San Diego; but by 2004 two-thirds crossed somewhere else. (My statistics on Mexican immigration come from a study I have been undertaking with financing from the National Institutes of Health since 1982.)

document that they had established long-term residency in the United States. Under the IRCA, hiring illegal aliens became illegal, so that employers are subject to fines and even prison sentences. It appears that the act has had mixed results in terms of illegal immigration. According to data compiled by the U.S. Border Patrol, arrests along the border declined substantially in the first three years after the law took effect. However, illegal immigration eventually returned to the levels of the early 1980s.

Many illegal immigrants continue to live in fear and hiding, subject to even more severe harassment and discrimination than before. From a conflict perspective, these immigrants, primarily poor and Hispanic or Asian, are being firmly lodged at the bot-

Listen to Our Voices   Listen to Our Voices

Unlike the old crossing sites, these new locations were sparsely settled, so the sudden appearance of thousands of Mexicans attracted considerable attention and understandably generated much agitation locally. Perceptions of a breakdown at the border were heightened by news reports of rising deaths among migrants; by redistricting flows into harsh, remote terrain the United States tripled the death rate during border crossing.

Less well known is that American policies also reduced the rate of apprehension, because those remote sectors of the border had fewer Border Patrol officers. My research found that during the 1980s, the probability that an undocumented migrant would be apprehended while crossing stood at around 33 percent; by 2000 it was at 10 percent, despite increases in federal spending on border enforcement.

Naturally, public perceptions of chaos on the border prompted more calls for enforcement and the hardening strategy was extended to other sectors. The number of Border Patrol officers increased from around 2,500 in the early 1980s to around 12,000 today, and the agency's annual budget rose to $1.6 billion from $200 million. The boundary between Mexico and the United States has become perhaps the most militarized frontier between two nations at peace anywhere in the world.

Although border militarization had little effect on the probability of Mexicans migrating illegally, it did reduce the likelihood that they would return to their homeland. America's tougher line roughly tripled the average cost of getting across the border illegally; thus Mexicans who had run the gauntlet at the border were more likely to hunker down and stay in the United States. My study has shown that in the early 1980's, about half of all undocumented Mexicans returned home within 12 months of entry, but by 2000 the rate of return migration stood at just 25 percent.

The United States is now locked into a perverse cycle whereby additional border enforcement further decreases the rate of return migration, which accelerates undocumented population growth, which brings calls for harsher enforcement.

The only thing we have to show for two decades of border militarization is a larger undocumented population than we would otherwise have, a rising number of Mexicans dying while trying to cross, and a growing burden on taxpayers for enforcement that is counterproductive.

We need an immigration policy that seeks to manage the cross-border flows of people that are inevitable in a global economy, not to repress them through unilateral police actions. ∎

From: Massey 2006a.

tom of the nation's social and economic hierarchies. However, from a functionalist perspective, employers, by paying low wages, are able to produce goods and services that are profitable for industry and more affordable to consumers. Despite the poor working conditions often experienced by illegal immigrants here, they continue to come because it is still in their best economic interest to work here in disadvantaged positions rather than to seek wage labor unsuccessfully in their home countries.

Little workplace enforcement occurs for the hiring of undocumented workers. Although never a priority, it has fallen to the point where only about five employers are fined annually involving 400 workers nationwide (Echaveste 2005).

In 2006, despite public pressure to crack down on illegal immigrants and counterdemonstrations to make it easier for long-term undocumented workers to become legal, the only major proposal to make it through Congress was to create a wall of several hundred miles between the United States and Mexico.

Amidst heated debate Congress reached a compromise passed, called the Illegal Immigration Reform and Immigrant Responsibility Act of 1996, which emphasized making more effort to keep immigrants from entering the country illegally. Illegal immigrants will not have access to such benefit programs as Social Security and welfare. For now, legal immigrants will be entitled to such benefits, although social service agencies are required to verify their legal status. Another significant element was to increase border control and surveillance.

The illegal aliens or undocumented workers are not necessarily transient. A 2006 estimate indicated 60 percent had been here for at least five years. Many have established homes, families, and networks with relatives and friends in the United States whose legal status might differ. These are the "mixed-status" households noted earlier. For the most part their lives are not much different from legal residents except when they seek services that require citizenship status to be documented (Passel 2006).

Policy makers continue to avoid the only real way to stop illegal immigration, which is to discourage employment opportunities. The public often thinks in terms of greater surveillance at the border. After the terrorist attacks of September 11, 2001, greater control of border traffic took on a new sense of urgency, even though almost all the men who took over the planes had entered the United States legally. It is very difficult to secure the vast boundaries that mark the United States on land and sea.

Reflecting the emphasis on heightened security, a potentially major shake-up recently took place. Since 1940, the Immigration and Naturalization Service (INS) had been in the Department of Justice, but in 2003 it was transferred to the newly formed Department of Homeland Security (see Table 4.4). The various functions of the INS were split into three agencies with a new Bureau of Citizenship and Immigration Services and two other units separately concerned with customs and border protection. For years, immigrant advocates had argued to separate border enforcement from immigration, but the placement of immigrant services in the office responsible for protecting the United States from terrorists sends a chilling message to immigrants.

Numerous civil rights groups and migrant advocacy organizations have expressed alarm over the large number of people now crossing into the United States illegally who perish in their attempt. Death occurs to some in deserts, in isolated canyons, and

TABLE 4.4
Transformation of Immigration Management

Following 9/11, management of immigration in the United States was reorganized, as of March 1, 2003, from INS in the Department of Justice to three new agencies in the new Department of Homeland Security.

Before	After
Located in Department of Justice	Located in Department of Homeland Security
Immigration and Naturalization Services (INS)	INS dissolved
Immigration services Naturalization (citizenship) Applications Visas	U.S. Citizen and Immigration Services (USCIS)
U.S. Border Patrol Inspections at border Deportations at border	U.S. Customs and Borders Protection (CBP)
Immigration enforcement—interior (includes removals and detentions)	U.S. Immigration and Customs Enforcement (ICE)

while concealed in containers or locked in trucks during smuggling attempts. Several hundred die annually in the Southwest, seeking more and more dangerous crossing points as border control has increased. However, this death toll has received little attention, causing one journalist to liken it to a jumbo jet crashing between Los Angeles and Phoenix every year without anyone giving it much notice (del Olmo 2003; K. Sullivan 2005).

What certainly was noticed was the public debate in 2006 over how to stop further illegal immigration and what to do about illegal immigrants already inside the United

States. Debate over hardening the border by erecting a 700-hundred-mile-long double concrete wall brought concerns that desperate immigrants would take even more chances with their lives in order to work in the United States. A Congressional proposal to make assisting an illegal immigrant already here a felony led to strong counter-demonstrations drawing tens of thousands of marchers in cities across the Untied States. Meanwhile the federal government, as it has for a century, struggled between the need to attract workers to do jobs many people here legally would not want to do against the desire to enforce the laws governing legal immigration (Tumulty 2006).

The Economic Impact of Immigration

There is much public and scholarly debate about the economic effects of immigration, both legal and illegal. Varied, conflicting conclusions have resulted from research ranging from case studies of Korean immigrants' dominance among New York City greengrocers to mobility studies charting the progress of all immigrants and their children. The confusion results in part from the different methods of analysis. For example, the studies do not always include political refugees, who generally are less prepared than other refugees to become assimilated. Sometimes the research focuses only on economic effects, such as whether people are employed or on welfare; in other cases it also considers cultural factors such as knowledge of English.

Perhaps the most significant factor is whether a study examines the national impact of immigration or only its effects on a local area. Overall, we can conclude from the research that immigrants adapt well and are an asset to the local economy. In some areas, heavy immigration may drain a community's resources. However, it can also revitalize a local economy. Marginally employed workers, most of whom are either themselves immigrants or African Americans, often experience a negative impact by new arrivals. With or without immigration, competition for low-paying jobs in the United States is high, and those who gain the most from this competition are the employers and the consumers who want to keep prices down (Steinberg 2005).

According to survey data, many people in the United States hold the stereotypical belief that immigrants often end up on welfare and thereby cause increases in taxes. Economist David Card studied the 1980 "Mariel" boatlift that brought 125,000 Cubans into Miami and found that even this substantial addition of mainly low-skilled workers had no measurable impact on the wages or unemployment rates of low-skilled White and African American workers in the Miami area (Card et al. 1998; Lowenstein 2006).

About 70 percent of illegal immigrant workers pay taxes of one type or another. Many of them do not file to receive entitled refunds or benefits. For example, in 2005, the Social Security Administration identified thousands of unauthorized workers contributing to the fund about $7 billion that could not be credited properly (E. Porter 2005).

Social science studies generally contradict many of the negative stereotypes about the economic impact of immigration. A variety of recent studies found that immigrants are a net economic gain for the population. But despite national gains, in some areas and for some groups, immigration may be an economic burden or create unwanted competition for jobs (Fix et al. 2001; Moore 1998; Smith and Edmonston 1997).

In "Research Focus," we consider the most recent research on how immigrants are doing in the United States.

One economic aspect of immigration that has received increasing attention is the effort to measure remittances. **Remittances** (or **migradollars**) are the monies that immigrants return to their country of origin. The amounts are significant and measure in the hundreds of millions of dollars flowing from the United States to a number of countries where they are a very substantial source of support for families and even venture capital for new businesses. Although some observers express concern over this

remittances (or migradollars) The monies that immigrants return to their country of origin.

Focus Research Focus Research

HOW WELL ARE IMMIGRANTS DOING?

In 2001, the respected Urban Institute released its comprehensive study of the progress immigrants are making in the United States, acknowledging that there is great diversity in the immigrant experience between nationality groups. Furthermore, even within the most successful immigrating groups, people have to confront the challenge of adapting to a society that rewards assimilation and typically punishes those who want to maintain cultural practices different from those that dominate society.

Considering contemporary immigrants as a group, we can make some conclusions, which show a mix of some success and evidence that adaptation typically is very difficult.

LESS ENCOURAGING

- Although immigrants have lower divorce rates and are less likely to form single-parent households than natives, their rates equal or exceed these rates by the second generation.
- Children in immigrant families tend to be healthier than U.S.-born children, but the advantage declines.
- Immigrants are less likely to have health insurance.
- Immigrant children attend schools that are disproportionately attended by other poor children and students with limited English proficiency, so they are ethnically, economically, and linguistically isolated.

POSITIVE SIGNS

- Immigrant families and, more broadly, noncitizen households are more likely to be on public assistance, but their time on public assistance is less and they receive fewer benefits. This is even true when considering special restrictions that may apply to noncitizens.
- Second-generation immigrants (i.e., children of immigrants) are overall doing as well as or better than White non-Hispanic natives in educational attainment, labor force participation, wages, and household income.
- Immigrants overwhelmingly (65 %) continue to see learning English as an ethical obligation of all immigrants.

These positive trends diverge between specific immigrant groups, with Asian immigrants doing better than European immigrants, who do better than Latino immigrants. ■

Source: Capps et al. 2002; Farkas 2003; Fix et al. 2001; Myers et al. 2004.

outflow of money, others counter that it probably represents a small price to pay for the human capital that the United States is able to use in the form of the immigrants themselves. Immigrants in the United States send $40 billion to their home countries and worldwide remittances bring $232 billion to developing countries, easily surpassing all other forms of foreign aid.

Remittances are widely recognized as critical to the survival of millions of households worldwide. One estimate concluded that one out of every five people in Mexico regularly receives a payment from abroad. The monies also play a significant role in the financial health of many economies (Hagenbaugh 2006).

States have sought legal redress because the federal government has not seriously considered granting impact aid to heavily burdened states. In 1994, Florida joined California

Remittances from immigrants and overseas relatives are a powerful economic force. As shown here in Mexico these migradollars helps to finance people's businesses and even assist them in buying homes.

in suing the U.S. government to secure strict enforcement of immigration laws and reimbursement for services rendered to illegal immigrants. As frustration mounted, California voters approved a 1994 referendum (Proposition 187) banning illegal immigrants from public schools, public assistance programs, and all but emergency medical care. Although the proposal was later found not to be constitutional, voters heavily favored the referendum. Subsequently, California and other states have tried to enact measures that would partially reflect this view, such as prohibiting illegal immigrants from getting driver's licenses. Only fourteen states knowingly issue driver's licenses to illegal immigrants, reasoning that it is better to regulate driving and document that drivers are insured (Katel 2005).

The concern about immigration today is both understandable and perplexing. The nation has always been uneasy about new arrivals, especially those who are different from the more affluent and the policy makers. Yet most of the last two decades have been marked by low unemployment, low inflation, and much-diminished anxiety about our economic future. This paradoxical situation—a strong economy and concerns about immigration framed in economic arguments—suggests that other concerns, such as ethnic and racial tensions, are more important in explaining current attitudes toward immigration in the United States.

Women and Immigration

? ASK Yourself

What special challenges do women immigrants face?

Immigration is presented as if all immigrants are similar with the only distinctions being made concerning point of origin, education, and employment prospects. Another significant distinction is whether immigrants travel with or without their families. We often think that historical immigrants to the United States were males in search of work. Men dominate much of the labor migration worldwide, but because of the diversified labor force in the United States and some policies that facilitate relatives coming, immigration to the United States generally has been fairly balanced. Actually most immigration historically appears to be families. For example, from 1870 through 1940 men entering the United States only exceeded women by about 10 to 20 percent. Since 1950 to the present women immigrants have actually exceeded men by a modest amount (Gibson and Jung 2006).

Immigration is a challenge
to all family members but
immigrant women must not
only navigate a new culture and
a new country for themselves
but also for their children;
such as in this household
in Colorado.

The second-class status women experience normally in society is reflected in immigration. Most dramatically women citizens who married immigrants who were not citizens actually lost their U.S. citizenship from 1907 through 1922 with few exceptions. However, policy did not apply to men (K. Johnson 2004).

Immigrant women, face all the challenges faced by immigrant men plus some additional ones. Typically they have the responsibility of navigating the new society when it comes to services for their family and, in particular, children. Many new immigrants view the United States as a dangerous place to raise a family and, therefore, remain particularly vigilant of what happens in their children's lives.

Male immigrants are more likely to be consumed with work leaving the women to navigate the bureaucratic morass of city services, schools, medical facilities, and even everyday concerns such as stores and markets. Immigrant women in need of special services for medical purposes or because they are victims of domestic violence are often reluctant to seek outside help. Yet immigrant women are more likely to be the liaison for the household including adult men to community associations and religious organizations (Honhagneu-Sotelo 2003).

Women play a critical role in overseeing the household and for immigrant women the added pressures of being in a new country and trying to move ahead in a different culture heighten this social role.

The Global Economy and Immigration

Immigration exists because of political boundaries that bring the movement of peoples to the attention of national authorities. Within the United States, people may move their residence, but they are not immigrating. For residents in the member nations of the European Union, free movement of people within the union is also protected.

Yet increasingly people recognize the need to think beyond national borders and national identity. As was noted in Chapter 1, **globalization** is the worldwide integration of government policies, cultures, social movements, and financial markets through trade, movement of people, and the exchange of ideas. In this global framework, even immigrants are less likely to think of themselves as residents of only one country. For generations, immigrants have used foreign-language newspapers to keep in touch with

globalization
Worldwide integration of government policies, cultures, social movements, and financial markets through trade, movements of people, and the exchange of ideas.

events in their home country. Today, cable channels carry news and variety programs from their home country, and the Internet offers immediate access to the homeland and kinfolk thousands of miles away.

While bringing the world together, globalization has also sharpened the focus on the dramatic economic inequalities between nations. Today, people in North America, Europe, and Japan consume thirty-two times more resources than the billions of people in developing nations. Thanks to tourism, the media, and other aspects of globalization, the people of less-affluent countries know of this affluent lifestyle and, of course, often aspire to it (Diamond 2003).

Transnationals are immigrants who sustain multiple social relationships linking their societies of origin and settlement. Immigrants from the Dominican Republic identify with Americans but also maintain very close ties to their Caribbean homeland. They return for visits, send remittances (migradollars), and host extended stays of relatives and friends. Back in the Dominican Republic, villages reflect these close ties, as shown in billboards promoting special long-distance services to the United States and by the presence of household appliances sent by relatives. The volume of remittances—perhaps $80 billion worldwide—is easily the most reliable source of foreign money going to poor countries, far outstripping foreign aid programs (Kapur and McHale 2003).

The growing number of transnationals, as well as immigration in general, directly reflects the world systems analysis we considered in Chapter 1. A global economic system that has such sharp contrasts between the industrial haves and the developing have-not nations only serves to encourage movement across borders. The industrial haves gain benefits from it even when they seem to discourage it. The movement back and forth only serves to increase globalization and the creation of informal social networks between people seeking a better life and those already enjoying increased prosperity.

Refugees

Refugees are people living outside their country of citizenship for fear of political or religious persecution. Enough refugees exist to populate an entire "nation". There are approximately 12 to 14 million refugees worldwide. That makes the nation of refugees larger than Belgium, Sweden, or Cuba. The United States has touted itself as a haven for political refugees. However, as we shall see, the welcome to political refugees has not always been unqualified.

The United States makes the largest financial contribution of any nation to worldwide assistance programs. The United States resettles about 70,000 refugees annually and served as the host to a cumulative 1 million refugees between 1990 and 2003. The post-9/11 years have seen the procedures become much more cumbersome for foreigners to acquire refugee status and gain entry to the United States. Many other nations much smaller and much poorer than the United States have many more refugees than the United States., with Jordan, Iran, and Pakistan hosting over a million refugees each (Immigration and Refugee Services of America 2004; U.S. Committee for Refugees 2003).

The United States, insulated by distance from wars and famines in Europe and Asia, has been able to be selective about which and how many refugees are welcomed. Since the arrival of refugees uprooted by World War II, the United States through the 1980s had allowed three groups of refugees to enter in numbers greater than regulations would ordinarily permit: Hungarians, Cubans, and Southeast Asians. Compared with the other two groups, the nearly 40,000 Hungarians who arrived after the unsuccessful

transnationals
Immigrants who sustain multiple social relationships linking their societies of origin and settlement.

refugees
People living outside their country of citizenship for fear of political or religious persecution.

Seen in this 1989 x-ray photo taken by Mexican authorities at the border are a wide shot, on top, and a close-up image of human forms. New technology is used to scan passing trucks to detect human cargo as well as drugs and weapons.

revolt against the Soviet Union of November 1956 were few indeed. At the time, however, theirs was the fastest mass immigration to this country since before 1922. With little delay, the United States amended the laws so that the Hungarian refugees could enter. Because of their small numbers and their dispersion throughout this country, the Hungarians are in little evidence nearly 50 years later. The much larger and longer period of movement of Cuban and Southeast Asian refugees into the United States continues to have a profound social and economic impact.

Despite periodic public opposition, the U.S. government is officially committed to accepting refugees from other nations. According to the United Nations treaty on refugees, which our government ratified in 1968, countries are obliged to refrain from forcibly returning people to territories where their lives or liberty might be endangered. However, it is not always clear whether a person is fleeing for his or her personal safety or to escape poverty. Although people in the latter category may be of humanitarian interest, they do not meet the official definition of refugees and are subject to deportation.

Refugees are people who are granted the right to enter a country while still residing abroad. **Asylees** are foreigners who have already entered the United States and now seek protection because of persecution or a well-founded fear of persecution. This persecution may be based on the individual's race, religion, nationality, membership in a particular social group, or political opinion. Asylees are eligible to adjust to lawful permanent resident status after one year of continuous presence in the United States. The number of asylees is currently limited to 10,000 per year, but there is sharp debate over how asylum is granted.

Because asylees, by definition, are already here, the outcome is either to grant them legal entry or to return them to their home country. It is the practice of deporting people fleeing poverty that has been the subject of criticism. There is a long tradition in the United States of facilitating the arrival of people leaving Communist nations, such as the Cubans. Mexicans who are refugees from poverty, Liberians fleeing civil war, and Haitians running from despotic rule are not similarly welcomed. The plight of Haitians has become one of particular concern.

Haitians began fleeing their country, often on small boats, in the 1980s. The U.S. Coast Guard intercepted many Haitians at sea, saving some of these boat people from death in their rickety and overcrowded wooden vessels. The Haitians said they feared

asylees
Foreigners who have already entered the United States and now seek protection because of persecution or a well-founded fear of persecution.

detentions, torture, and execution if they remained in Haiti. Yet both Republican and Democratic administrations viewed most of the Haitian exiles as economic migrants rather than political refugees and opposed granting them asylum and permission to enter the United States. Once apprehended, the Haitians are returned. In 1993, the U.S. Supreme Court, by an 8–1 vote, upheld the government's right to intercept Haitian refugees at sea and return them to their homeland without asylum hearings.

African Americans and others denounce the Haitian refugee policy as racist. They contrast it to the "wet foot, dry foot" policy toward Cuban refugees. If the government intercepts Cubans at sea, they are returned; but if they escape detection and make it to the mainland, they may apply for asylum. About 75 percent of Cubans seeking asylum are granted refugee status, compared with only 22 percent of Haitians.

Even with only about a thousand Haitians successfully making it into the United States each year, there is an emerging Haitian American presence, especially in southern Florida. An estimated 60,000 immigrants and their descendants live in the Little Haiti portion of Miami, where per capita income is a meager $5,700. Despite continuing obstacles, the community exhibits pride in those who have succeeded, from a Haitian American Florida state legislator to hip-hop musician Wyclef Jean (Dahlburg 2001; U.S. Committee for Refugees 2003).

Conclusion

For its first hundred years, the United States allowed all immigrants to enter and become permanent residents. However, the federal policy of welcome did not mean that immigrants would not encounter discrimination and prejudice. With the passage of the Chinese Exclusion Act, discrimination against one group of potential immigrants became law. The Chinese were soon joined by the Japanese as peoples forbidden by law to enter and prohibited from becoming naturalized citizens. The development of the national origin system in the 1920s created a hierarchy of nationalities with people from northern Europe encouraged to enter, whereas other Europeans and Asians encountered long delays. The possibility of a melting pot, which had always been a fiction, was legislated out of existence.

In the 1960s and again in 1990, the policy was liberalized so that the importance of nationality was minimized, and a person's work skills and relationship to an American were emphasized. This liberalization came at a time when most Europeans no longer wanted to immigrate to the United States.

One out of ten people in the United States is foreign born; many are technical, professional, and craft workers. Also, 34 percent are household workers, and 33 percent of our farm laborers are foreign born. The U.S. economy and society are built on immigrant labor from farm fields to science laboratories (Parker 2001).

Throughout the history of the United States, as we have seen, there has been intense debate over the nation's immigration and refugee policies. In a sense, this debate reflects the deep value conflicts in the U.S. culture and parallels the "American dilemma" identified by Swedish social economist Gunnar Myrdal (1944). One strand of our culture, epitomized by the words "Give us your tired, your poor, your huddled masses," has emphasized egalitarian principles and a desire to help people in their time of need. At the same time, however, hostility to potential immigrants and refugees, whether the Chinese in the 1880s, European Jews in the 1930s and 1940s, or Mexicans, Haitians, and Arabs today, reflects not only racial, ethnic, and religious prejudice but also a desire to maintain the dominant culture of the in-group by keeping out those viewed as outsiders. The conflict between these cultural values is central to the American dilemma of the twenty-first century.

At present the debate about immigration is highly charged and emotional. Some people see it in economic terms, whereas others see the new arrivals as a challenge to the very culture of our society. Clearly, the general perception is that immigration presents a problem rather than a promise for the future.

Today's concern about immigrants follows generations of people coming to settle in the United States. This immigration in the past produced a very diverse country in terms of both nationality and religion, even before the immigration of the last fifty years. Therefore, the majority of Americans today are not descended from the English, and Protestants are just over half of all worshipers. This diversity of religious and ethnic groups is examined in Chapter 5.

Key Terms

asylees 119

brain drain 107

chain immigration 97

globalization 117

nativism 100

naturalization 105

refugees 118

remittances
  (or migradollars) 114

sinophobes 101

transnationals 118

xenophobia 100

Review Questions

1. What are the functions and dysfunctions of immigration?

2. What were the social and economic issues when public opinion mounted against Chinese immigration to the United States?

3. Ultimately, what do you think is the major concern people have about contemporary immigration to the United States: the numbers of immigrants, their legal status, or their nationality?

4. What principles appear to guide U.S. refugee policy?

Critical Thinking

1. What is the immigrant root story of your family? Consider how your ancestors arrived in the United States and also how your family's past has been shaped by other immigrant groups.

2. Can you find evidence of the brain drain in terms of the professionals with whom you come in contact? Do you regard this as a benefit? What groups in the United States may not have been encouraged to fill such positions by the availability of such professionals?

Internet Connections—Research Navigator™

Follow the instructions found on page 35 of this text to access the features of Research Navigator™. Once at the Web site, enter your Login Name and Password. Then, to use the ContentSelect database, enter keywords such as "remittances," "asylum," and "refugees," and the research engine will supply relevant and recent scholarly and popular press publications. Use the *New York Times* Search-by-Subject Archive to find recent news articles related to sociology and the Link Library feature to locate relevant Web links organized by the key terms associated with this chapter.

5 Ethnicity and Religion

CHAPTER OUTLINE

Ethnic Diversity

Why Don't We Study Whiteness?

The Price Paid by White Ethnics

The Irish Americans

The Italian Americans

Polish Americans

The Language Divide

■LISTEN TO OUR VOICES

I Was Born in Tirana,
by Harallamb Terba

Religious Pluralism

■RESEARCH FOCUS

Measuring the Importance of Religion

Ethnicity, Religion, and Social Class

Religion in the United States

Limits of Religious Freedom: The Amish

Conclusion

Key Terms/Review Questions/Critical Thinking/
Internet Connections—Research Navigator™

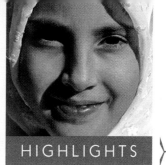

THE UNITED STATES INCLUDES A MULTITUDE OF ETHNIC and religious groups. Do they coexist in harmony or in conflict? How significant are they as sources of identity for their members? Because White is a race, how this identity is socially constructed has received significant attention. Many White ethnic groups have transformed their ethnic status into Whiteness. In the 1960s and 1970s, there was a resurgence of interest in White ethnicity, partly in response to the renewed pride in the ethnicity of Blacks, Latinos, and Native Americans. We have an ethnicity paradox in which White ethnics seem to enjoy their heritage but at the same time seek to assimilate into the larger society. White ethnics are the victims of humor (or respectable bigotry) that some still consider socially acceptable, and they find themselves with little power in big business. Major White ethnic groups such as Irish, Italian, and Polish Americans have experienced similar yet distinctive social circumstances in the United States. Religious diversity continues and expands with immigration and growth in the followings of non-Christian faiths. Religious minorities experience intolerance in the present as they have in the past. Constitutional issues such as school prayer, secessionist minorities, creationism, and public religious displays are regularly taken to the Supreme Court. The Amish are presented as a case study of the experience of a specific religious group in the United States.

Betty O'Keefe is a 60-year-old Californian who is a fifth-generation Irish American, meaning that her grandmother's grandmother came to the United States from Ireland. Sociologist Mary Waters (1990, 97) asked her what it was like growing up in the United States.

When I was in high school my maiden name was Tynan. This was 1940. I was dating some boys from school, and two different times when the parents found out I was an Irish Catholic, they told him he couldn't go out with me. The Protestants were like that. . . . One of his brothers later married someone named O'Flannery and I was so thrilled. I said I hope your mother is turning in her grave. So I am happy that my children have the name O'Keefe. So that people know right away what their background is. I think it is better. They would never be put in the position I was in.
Do you think something like that could happen now?
I don't think so openly. But I think it is definitely still there. You are not as bad (being an Irish Catholic) as a Black, but you are not Protestant. You are not Jewish either, which would be worse, but still you are not of their church.

Their names may be Badovich, Hoggarty, Jablonski, Reggio, or Williams. They may follow any one of thousands of faiths and gather at any of the 360,000 churches, mosques, synagogues, and temples. Our nation's motto is *E Pluribus Unum,* and although there may be doubt that we are truly united into one common culture following a single ideology, there is little doubt about our continuing diversity as a nation of peoples.

Indeed, the very complexity of relations between dominant and subordinate groups in the United States today is partly the result of its heterogeneous population. No one ethnic origin or religious faith encompasses all the inhabitants of the United States. Even though our largest period of sustained immigration is three generations past, an American today is surrounded by remnants of cultures and practitioners of religions whose origins are foreign to this country. Religion and ethnicity continue to be significant in defining a person's identity.

Ethnic Diversity

ASK Yourself

What is the largest ethnic or ancestral group?

The ethnic diversity of the United States at the beginning of the twenty-first century is apparent to almost everyone. Passersby in New York City were undoubtedly surprised once when two street festivals met head-to-head. The procession of San Gennaro, the patron saint of Naples, marched through Little Italy, only to run directly into a Chinese festival originating in Chinatown. Teachers in many public schools often encounter students who speak only one language, and it is not English. Students in Chicago are taught in Spanish, Greek, Italian, Polish, German, Creole, Japanese, Cantonese, or the language of a Native American tribe. In the Detroit metropolitan area, classroom instruction is conveyed in twenty-one languages, including Arabic, Portuguese, Ukrainian, Latvian, Lithuanian, and Serbian. In many areas of the United States, you can refer to a special Yellow Pages and find a driving instructor who speaks Portuguese or a psychotherapist who will talk to you in Hebrew.

Germans are the largest ancestral group in the Untied States; the 2000 census showed almost one-sixth of Americans saying they had at least some German ancestry. Although most German Americans are assimilated, it is possible to see the ethnic tradition in some areas, particularly in Milwaukee, whose population has 48 percent German ancestry. There three Saturday schools teach German, and one can affiliate with thirty-four German American clubs and visit a German library that operates within the public library system. Just a bit to the south in River Forest, a Chicago suburb, *kinderwerksatt* meets weekly to help parents and children alike to maintain German culture (Carvajal 1996; Freedman 2004; Johnson 1992; Usdansky 1992).

Germany is one of twenty-one European nations from which at least 1 million people claim to have ancestry. The numbers are striking when one considers the size of some of the sending countries. For example, there are over 33 million Irish Americans, and the Republic of Ireland had a population of 3.7 million in 1998. Similarly, nearly 5 million people claim Swedish ancestry, and there are 8.9 million people living in Sweden today. Of course, many Irish Americans and Swedish Americans are of mixed ancestry, but not everyone in Ireland is Irish, nor is everyone in Sweden Swedish.

Why Don't We Study Whiteness?

Race is socially constructed, as we learned in Chapter 1. Sometimes we come to define race in a clear-cut manner. A descendant of a Pilgrim is White, for example. But sometimes race is more ambiguous: People who are the children of an African American and Vietnamese American union are biracial or "mixed," or whatever they come to be seen as by others. Our recognition that race is socially constructed has sparked a renewed interest in what it means to be White in the United States. Two aspects of White as a race are useful to consider: the historical creation of whiteness and how contemporary White people reflect on their racial identity.

When the English immigrants established themselves as the political founders of the United States, they also came to define what it meant to be White. Other groups that today are regarded as White, such as Irish, Germans, Norwegians, or Swedes, were not always considered White in the eyes of the English. Differences in language and religious worship, as well as past allegiance to a king in Europe different from the English monarch, all caused these groups to be seen not so much as Whites in the Western Hemisphere but more as nationals of their home country who happened to be residing in North America.

The old distrust in Europe, where, for example, the Irish were viewed by the English as socially and culturally inferior, continued on this side of the Atlantic Ocean. Karl Marx, writing from England, reported that the average English worker looked down on the Irish the way poor Whites in the U.S. South looked down on Black people (Ignatiev 1994, 1995; Roediger 1994).

Whiteness

As European immigrants and their descendants assimilated to the English and distanced themselves from other oppressed groups such as American Indians and African Americans, they came to be viewed as White rather than as part of a particular culture. Writer Noel Ignatiev (1994, 84), contrasting being White with being Polish, argues that "Whiteness is nothing but an expression of race privilege." This strong statement argues that being White, as opposed to being Black or Asian, is characterized by being a member of the dominant group.

Whites as people don't think of themselves as a race or have a conscious racial identity. The only occasion when a White racial identity emerges is momentarily when Whites fill out a form asking for self-designation of race or one of those occasions when they are culturally or socially surrounded by people who are not White.

Many immigrants who were not "White on arrival" had to "become White" in a process long forgotten by today's White Americans. The long documented transparent racial divide that engulfed the South during slavery allowed us to ignore how Whiteness was constructed.

Therefore, contemporary White Americans generally give little thought to "being White." Consequently, there is little interest in studying "Whiteness" or considering "being White" except that it is "not being Black." Unlike non-Whites, who are much more likely to interact with Whites, take orders from Whites, and see Whites as the leading figures in the mass media, Whites enjoy the privilege of not being reminded of their Whiteness.

Unlike racial minorities, Whites downplay the importance of their racial identity while being willing to receive the advantages that come from being White. This means that advocacy of a "color-blind" or "race-neutral" outlook permits the privilege of Whiteness to prevail (Bonilla-Silva 2002; Yancey 2003).

The new interest seeks to look at Whiteness but not from the vantage point of a White supremacist. Rather, focusing on White people as a race or on what it means today to be White goes beyond any definition that implies superiority over non-Whites. It is also recognized that "being White" is not the same experience for all Whites any more than "being Asian American" or "being Black" is the same for all Asian Americans or all Blacks. Historian Noel Ignatiev observes that studying Whiteness is a necessary stage to the "abolition of whiteness"—just as, in Marxist analysis, class consciousness is a necessary stage to the abolition of class. By confronting Whiteness, society grasps the all-encompassing power that accompanies socially constructed race (Lewis 2004; McKinney 2003; Roediger 2006).

White privilege, as described by Peggy McIntosh, includes holding a position in a company without coworkers suspecting it came about because of your race.

White Privilege

Whiteness carries with it a sense of identity of being White as opposed to being, for example, Asian or African. For many people it may not be easy to establish a social identity of Whiteness, as in the case of biracial children. However, one can argue that the social identity of Whiteness exists if one enjoys the privilege of being White.

Scholar Peggy McIntosh of the Wellesley College Center for Research on Women looked at the privilege that comes from being White and the added privilege of being male. The other side of racial oppression is the privilege enjoyed by dominant groups. Being White or being successful in establishing a White identity carries with it distinct advantages. Among those that McIntosh (1988) identified were:

- Being considered financially reliable when using checks, credit cards, or cash.
- Taking a job without having coworkers suspect it came about because of your race.
- Never having to speak for all the people of your race.
- Watching television or reading a newspaper and seeing people of your own race widely represented.
- Speaking effectively in a large group without being called a credit to your race.
- Assuming that if legal or medical help is needed your race will not work against you.

Whiteness does carry privileges, but most White people do not consciously think of them except on the rare occasions when they are questioned. We will return to the concepts of Whiteness and White privilege, but let us also consider the rich diversity of religion in the United States, which parallels the ethnic diversity of this nation.

The Rediscovery of Ethnicity

Robert Park (1950, 205), a prominent early sociologist, wrote in 1913 that "a Pole, Lithuanian, or Norwegian cannot be distinguished, in the second generation, from an American, born of native parents." At one time, sociologists saw the end of ethnicity as nearly a foregone conclusion. W. Lloyd Warner and Leo Srole (1945) wrote in their often-cited *Yankee City* series that the future of ethnic groups seemed to be limited in the United States and that they would be quickly absorbed. Oscar Handlin's *Uprooted* (1951) told of the destruction of immigrant values and their replacement by American culture. Although Handlin was among the pioneers in investigating ethnicity, assimilation was the dominant theme in his work.

Many writers have shown almost a fervent hope that ethnicity would vanish. The persistence of ethnicity was for some time treated by sociologists as dysfunctional because it meant a continuation of old values that interfered with the allegedly superior new values. For example, to hold on to one's language delayed entry into the larger labor market and the upward social mobility it afforded. Ethnicity was expected to disappear not only because of assimilation but also because aspirations to higher social class and status demanded that it vanish. Somehow, it was assumed that one could not be ethnic and middle class, much less affluent.

The Third-Generation Principle

Historian Marcus Hansen's (1952) **principle of third-generation interest** was an early exception to the assimilationist approach to White ethnic groups. Simply stated, Hansen maintained that in the third generation—the grandchildren of the original immigrants—ethnic interest and awareness would actually increase. According to Hansen, "What the son wishes to forget, the grandson wishes to remember."

Hansen's principle has been tested several times since it was first put forth. John Goering (1971), in interviewing Irish and Italian Catholics, found that ethnicity was

How do white people sometimes take for granted what it means to be White?

principle of third-generation interest
Marcus Hansen's contention that ethnic interest and awareness increase in the third generation, among the grandchildren of immigrants.

symbolic ethnicity
Herbert Gans's term that describes emphasis on ethnic food and ethnically associated political issues rather than deeper ties to one's heritage.

more important to members of the third generation than it was to the immigrants themselves. Similarly, Mary Waters (1990), in her interviews of White ethnics living in suburban San Jose, California, and suburban Philadelphia, Pennsylvania, observed many grandchildren wanting to study their ancestors' language, even though it would be a foreign language to them. They also expressed interest in learning more of their ethnic group's history and a desire to visit the homeland.

Social scientists in the past were quick to minimize the ethnic awareness of blue-collar workers. In fact, ethnicity was viewed as merely another aspect of White ethnics' alleged racist nature, an allegation that will be examined later in this chapter. Curiously, the very same intellectuals and journalists who bent over backward to understand the growing solidarity of Blacks, Hispanics, and Native Americans refused to give White ethnics the academic attention they deserved (Wrong 1972).

The new assertiveness of Blacks and other non-Whites of their rights in the 1960s unquestionably presented White ethnics with the opportunity to reexamine their own position. "If solidarity and unapologetic self-consciousness might hasten Blacks' upward mobility, why not ours?" asked the White ethnics, who were often only a half step above Blacks in social status. The African American movement pushed other groups to reflect on their past. The increased consciousness of Blacks and their positive attitude toward African culture and the contributions worldwide of African Americans are embraced in what we called the Afrocentric perspective (Chapter 1). Therefore, the mood was set in the 1960s for the country to be receptive to ethnicity. By legitimizing Black cultural differences from White culture, along with those of Native Americans and Hispanics, the country's opinion leaders legitimized other types of cultural diversity.

Symbolic Ethnicity

Observers comment both on the evidence of assimilation and on the signs of ethnic identity that seem to support a pluralistic view of society. How can both be possible?

First, there is the very visible evidence of **symbolic ethnicity**, which may lead us to exaggerate the persistence of ethnic ties among White Americans. According to sociologist Herbert Gans (1979), ethnicity today increasingly involves the symbols of ethnicity, such as eating ethnic food, acknowledging ceremonial holidays such as St. Patrick's Day, and supporting specific political issues or the issues confronting the old country. One example was the push in 1998 by Irish Americans to convince state legislatures to make it compulsory in public schools to teach about the Irish potato

For many Irish American participants in a St. Patrick's Day Parade, this is their most visible expression of symbolic ethnicity during an entire year.

famine, which was a significant factor in immigration to the United States. This symbolic ethnicity may be more visible, but this type of ethnic heritage does not interfere with what people do, read, or say, or even whom they befriend or marry.

The ethnicity of the twenty-first century embraced by English-speaking Whites is largely symbolic. It does not include active involvement in ethnic activities or participation in ethnic-related organizations. In fact, sizable proportions of White ethnics have gained large-scale entry into almost all clubs, cliques, and fraternal groups. Such acceptance is a key indicator of assimilation. Ethnicity has become increasingly peripheral to the lives of the members of the ethnic group. Although they may not relinquish their ethnic identity, other identities become more important.

Second, the ethnicity that does exist may be more a result of living in the United States than actual importing of practices from the past or the old country. Many so-called ethnic foods or celebrations, for example, began in the United States. The persistence of ethnic consciousness, then, may not depend on foreign birth, a distinctive language, and a unique way of life. Instead, it may reflect the experiences in the United States of a unique group that developed a cultural tradition distinct from that of the mainstream. For example, in Poland the *szlachta,* or landed gentry, rarely mixed socially with the peasant class. In the United States, however, even with those associations still fresh, they interacted together in social organizations as they settled in concentrated communities segregated physically and socially from others (Glazer 1971; Glazer and Moynihan 1970; Lopata 1994).

Third, maintaining ethnicity can be a critical step toward successful assimilation. This **ethnicity paradox** facilitates full entry into the dominant culture. The ethnic community may give its members not only a useful financial boost but also the psychological strength and positive self-esteem that will allow them to compete effectively in larger society. Thus, we may witness people participating actively in their ethnic enclave while trying to cross the bridge into the wider community (Lal 1995).

Therefore, ethnicity gives continuity with the past in the form of an affective or emotional tie. The significance of this sense of belonging cannot be emphasized enough. Whether reinforced by distinctive behavior or by what Milton Gordon (1964) called a sense of "peoplehood," ethnicity is an effective, functional source of cohesion. Proximity to fellow ethnics is not necessary for a person to maintain social cohesion and in-group identity. Fraternal organizations or sports-related groups can preserve associations between ethnics who are separated geographically. Members of ethnic groups may even maintain their feelings of in-group solidarity after leaving ethnic communities in the central cities for the suburban fringe.

The Price Paid by White Ethnics

Many White ethnics have shed their past and want only to be Americans with no ancestral ties to another country. Some ethnics do not want to abandon their heritage, but to retain their past as a part of their present, they must pay a price because of prejudice and discrimination. Although the levels of present and past intolerance toward White ethnics are much less than those we saw in Chapters 2 and 3 toward African Americans, Latinos, Asian Americans, and Native Americans, this intolerance is a part of multicultural America.

Prejudice Toward White Ethnic Groups

Our examination of immigration to the United States in Chapter 4 pointed out the mixed feelings that have greeted European immigrants. They are apparently still not well received. In 1944, well after most immigration from Poland had ended, the Polish-American Congress, an umbrella organization of forty Polish fraternities, was

ethnicity paradox
The maintenance of one's ethnic ties in a way that can assist with assimilation in larger society.

founded to defend the image of Polish Americans. Young Polish Americans are made to feel ashamed of their ethnic origin when teachers find their names unpronounceable and when they hear Polish jokes bandied about in a way that anti-Black or anti-Semitic humor is not. One survey found that half of second-generation Polish Americans encounter prejudice.

Curiously, it was socially proper to condemn the White working class as racist but improper to question the negative attitude of middle-class people toward White ethnics. Michael Lerner (1969) called this hostility toward White ethnics **respectable bigotry**. Polish jokes are acceptable, whereas anti-Black humor is considered to be in poor taste.

White ethnics in the early 1970s felt that the mass media unfairly ridiculed them and their culture while celebrating Black Power and African culture. For instance, Italian Americans remain concerned that their image is overwhelmed by stereotypes of organized crime, spaghetti, overweight mothers, and sexy women. Even television's Italian police seem to conform to the old stereotypes. In response to such stereotyping, the Columbian Coalition, founded in 1971, employs lawyers to handle cases of Italian Americans who claim they are victims of bigotry.

Even the broad group of White ethnics who still dominate Roman Catholicism have expressed feelings of being victimized. In 2000, a Roman Catholic was appointed chaplain of the U.S. House of Representatives for the first time. This led to angry sentiments against a Catholic being granted this symbolic position rather than keeping it in the hands of the Protestant clergy. About the same time, candidate George W. Bush appeared at the avowedly anti-Catholic Bob Jones University during the South Carolina primary campaign. The response to this appearance raised questions in some quarters about lingering hostility toward Roman Catholics and the Roman Catholic Church. A national survey taken of Roman Catholics at that time found that the majority (56 percent) did not believe such a bias existed, but one-third did perceive the presence of anti-Catholic bias in the country (Bendyna and Pearl 2000).

The Prejudice of Ethnics

In the 1960s, as the civil rights movement moved north, White ethnics replaced the southern White as the typical bigot portrayed in the mass media. The chanting of protestors resulted in ugly incidents that made White ethnics and bigots synonymous. This stereotype of the prejudiced White ethnic has rarely been questioned. The danger of this and any stereotype is that it becomes indistinguishable from fact. David Matza (1964, 1) referred to these mental pictures that "tend to remain beyond the reach of such intellectual correctives as argument, criticism and scrutiny. . . . . Left unattended, they return to haunt us by shaping or bending theories that purport to explain major social phenomena." This 1964 picture of ethnics and the degree of truth behind it must be examined.

The first issue to resolve is whether White ethnic groups are more prejudiced than other Whites. Sociologist Andrew Greeley (1974a, 1977; Nie, Curry, and Greeley 1974) examined attitudes toward race, social welfare, and U.S. involvement in Vietnam. The evidence pointed to minimal differences between ethnics and others. Some of the differences actually showed greater tolerance and liberalism among White ethnics. For example, White ethnics were more in favor of welfare programs and more opposed to this country's participation in the Vietnam War.

Even when more sophisticated statistical analysis is introduced, the overall finding remains unchanged. No evidence supports the image of White ethnics as bigots. Greeley (1974a, 202) concludes, "Our argument is not that ethnics are the last bastion of liberalism in America today, but rather that it is a misrepresentation of the facts to picture them as a vanguard of conservatism." However, working-class ethnic neighborhoods have undeniably been the scene of ugly racial confrontations. If ethnics are no

respectable bigotry
Michael Lerner's term for the social acceptance of prejudice against White ethnics, when intolerance against non-White minorities is regarded as unacceptable.

more bigoted than others, how have such incidents come to occur, and how has this reputation developed? For that answer, the unique relationship between White ethnic groups and African Americans must be understood.

In retrospect, it should be no surprise that one group that has been antagonistic to African Americans is the White ethnics. For many citizens, including White ethnics, the United States they remembered from the 1950s seemed to change. When politicians told people in the 1960s, "We must fight poverty and discrimination," this translated to White ethnics as, "Share your job, share your neighborhood, but pay more taxes." Whites recalled how, in several generations, they had moved from membership in a poor immigrant group to becoming a prosperous part of the working class. Government assistance to the poor was almost nonexistent then, public education was more limited, and subsidized training programs were absent. Why was it different now? Many White ethnics found it difficult to understand why African Americans seemed to be singled out as a cause for concern in the 1960s when they perceived that they, too, had real needs (Glazer and Moynihan 1970; Novak 1996; Sanders and Morawska 1975; Tyler 1972).

White ethnics went so far as to turn their backs on federal aid offered them because they did not want to have their neighborhoods marked as "poverty pockets," nor did they want to be associated with Black-oriented programs. In Newark, New Jersey, Italians successfully prevented an antipoverty office from being established and thereby cut off the jobs its programs would have created (Barbaro 1974). This ethnic opposition to publicly sponsored programs was not new. James Wilson and Edward Banfield (1964) studied elections in seven major cities between 1956 and 1963 for referenda to build new hospitals, parks, and schools. The results indicated that the least support came from White ethnics, who would have paid the least and benefited the most.

White ethnics first learned that they are not considered part of the dominant group, but in time, through assimilation, they came to be redefined to enjoy most of the White privileges we identified earlier. We now look at three different White ethnic groups to explore how the sense of privilege can change over time.

The Irish Americans

The Irish presence in the United States stretches back to the 1600s and reflects a diversity based on time of entry, settlement area, and religion. Irish Americans have been visible both in a positive way in terms of playing a central role in American life and also in a negative way at certain historical periods being victimized like so many other immigrant groups.

Early Irish Immigration (before 1845)

The Protestants dominated the early Irish immigration to the colonies even though these Presbyterians from Ireland of Scotch descent accounted for only one out of ten, at most one out of seven, of the island of Ireland's residents in the eighteenth century. Motivating the early immigrants was the lure of free land in North America, which was in sharp contrast to Ireland where more and more tenants had to compete for land. The powerful landlords there took full advantage by squeezing more and more profits out of the tenants, making migration to colonial America attractive.

The Roman Catholics among the early immigrants were a diverse group. Some were extensions of the privileged classes seeking even greater prosperity. Protestant settlers of all national backgrounds were united in their hatred of Catholicism. In most of the colonies, Catholics could not practice their faith openly and either struggled inwardly or converted to Anglicanism. Other Roman Catholics and some Protestants came as an alternative to prison or after signing articles of indenture arriving bound to labor for periods of customarily three to five years but sometimes as long as seven years (Meagher 2005).

The American Revolution temporarily stopped the flow of immigration, but soon deteriorating economic conditions in Ireland spurred even greater movement to North America. British officials, by making passage to the newly formed republic of the United States expensive, diverted many immigrants to British North America (Canada). Yet the numbers to the United States remained significant and, although still primarily Protestant, drew from a broader spectrum of Ireland both economically and geographically.

Many mistakenly overlook this early immigration and begin with Irish immigration during the Great Famine. Yet the Irish were the largest group after the English among immigrants during the colonial period. The historical emphasis on the famine immigrants is understandable given the role it played in Ireland and its impetus for the massive transfer of population from Ireland to the United States.

The Famine Years

In 1845, a fungus wiped out the potato crop of Ireland, as well as much of western Europe and even coastal America. Potatoes were particularly central to the lives of the Irish and the devastating starvation did not begin to recede until 1851. Mortality was high especially among the poor and in the more agricultural areas of the island. Predictably to escape catastrophe, some 2 million fled mostly to England but then many continued on to the United States. From 1841 through 1890, over 3.2 million Irish arrived in the United States. (See Figure 5.1)

This new migration fleeing the old country was much more likely to consist of families rather than single men. This arrival of entire households and extended kinship networks increased significantly the rapid formation of Irish social organizations in the United States. This large influx of immigrants led to the creation of ethnic neighborhoods complete with parochial schools and parish churches serving as focal points. Fraternal organizations such as the Ancient Order of Hibernians, corner saloons, local political organizations, and Irish nationalist groups seeking the ouster of Britain from Ireland rounded out neighborhood social life.

Even in the best of times, the lives of the famine Irish would have been challenging in the United States but they arrived at a very difficult time. Nativist—that is, anti-Catholic and anti-immigrant—movements were already emerging and being embraced by politicians.

FIGURE 5.1 Immigration from Ireland, Italy, and Poland

Note: Immigration after 1925 from Northern Ireland not included. No separate data for Poland from (1900 to 1920.

Source: Office of Immigration Statistics. *Yearbook of Immigration Statistics 2005.* Washington, DC: Office of Immigration Statistics, 2006. Table 2.

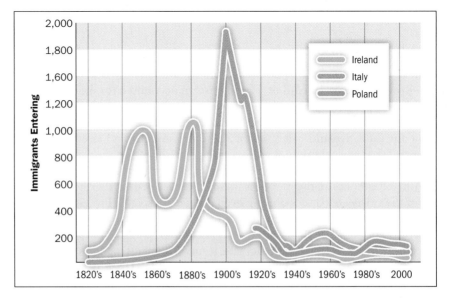

From independence until around 1820, little evidence appeared of the anti-Catholic sentiment of colonial days, but the cry against Roman Catholicism grew as Irish immigration increased. Prominent citizens encouraged hatred of these new arrivals. Samuel F. B. Morse, inventor of the telegraph and an accomplished painter, wrote a strongly worded anti-Catholic work in 1834 titled *A Foreign Conspiracy Against the Liberties of the United States*. Morse felt that the Irish were shamefully illiterate and deserved no respect. In the minds of prejudiced people, the Irish were particularly unwelcome because they were Catholic. Many readily believed Morse's warning that the Pope planned to move the Vatican to the Mississippi River Valley.

This antagonism was not limited to harsh words. From 1834 to 1854, mob violence against Catholics across the country led to death, the burning of a Boston convent, the destruction of a Catholic church and the homes of Catholics, and the use of Marines and state militia to bring peace to American cities as far west as St. Louis.

In retrospect, the reception given to the Irish is not difficult to understand. Many immigrated after the potato crop failure and famine in Ireland. They fled not so much to a better life as from almost certain death. The Irish Catholics brought with them a celibate clergy, who struck the New England aristocracy as strange and reawakened old religious hatreds. The Irish were worse than Blacks according to the dominant Whites, because unlike the slaves and even the freed Blacks, who "knew their place," the Irish did not suffer their maltreatment in silence. Employers balanced minorities by judiciously mixing immigrant groups to prevent unified action by the laborers. For the most part, nativist efforts only led the foreign born to emphasize their ties to Europe.

By the 1850s, nativism became an open political movement pledged to vote only for "native" Americans, to fight Catholicism, and to demand a twenty-one-year naturalization period. Party members were instructed to divulge nothing about their program and to say that they knew nothing about it. As a result, they came to be called the Know-Nothings. Although the Know-Nothings soon vanished, the anti-alien mentality survived and occasionally became formally organized into such societies as the Ku Klux Klan in the 1860s and the anti-Catholic American Protective Association in the 1890s. Revivals of anti-Catholicism continued well into the twentieth century.

Mostly of peasant backgrounds, the Irish arriving were ill-prepared to compete successfully for jobs in the city. Their children found it much easier to improve their occupational status over that of their fathers as well as experiencing upward mobility in their own lifetimes.

Becoming White

Ireland had a long antislavery tradition including practices that prohibited Irish trade in English slaves. Some 60,000 Irish signed an address in 1841 petitioning Irish Americans to join the abolitionist movement in the United States. Many Irish Americans already opposed to slavery applauded the appeal, but they were soon drowned out by fellow immigrants with denouncing or questioning the authenticity of the petition.

The Irish immigrants, subjected to derision and menial jobs, sought to separate themselves from the even lower classes and particularly Black Americans and especially the slaves. It was not altogether clear that the Irish were "white" during the antebellum period. Irish character was rigidly cast in negative racial typology. Although the shared experiences of oppression could have led Irish Americans to allay with Black Americans, they grasped for Whiteness at the margins of their life in the United States. Direct competition was not common between the two groups. For example, in 1855, Irish immigrants made up 87 percent of New York City's unskilled laborers whereas free Blacks accounted for only 3 percent (Greeley 1981; Ignatiev 1995; Roediger 1994).

In 1863, the Union government implemented a national conscription law to fight in the Civil War. Men could avoid service by presenting an acceptable substitute or paying $300. Irish Americans already experiencing heavy losses had grown tired of the war. Opposition to conscription was widespread but especially visible in Boston and New York City. The opposition grew violent in New York City with participants, mostly poor Irish American, striking out first against symbols of the government and then targeting African American organizations and even individual Blacks. The vandalism and violence were aimed at those even weaker than the working-class Irish who resented "a rich man's war and a poor man's fight." The "Draft Riots of 1863," as they came to be called, violently showed the dilemma many Irish Americans felt of fighting for the freedom of their Negro competitors in the labor market. Eventually the rioters were quelled with the dispatch of troops fresh from Gettysburg including Irish American soldiers.

As Irish immigration continued in the latter part of the nineteenth century until Irish independence in 1921, they began to see themselves favorably in comparison to the initial waves of Italian, Polish, and Slovak Roman Catholic immigrants. The Irish Americans began to assume more leadership positions in politics and labor unions. Loyalty to the church still played a major role. By 1910, the priesthood was the professional occupation of choice for second-generation men. Irish women were more likely than their German and English immigrant counterparts to become schoolteachers. In time Irish Americans' occupational profiles diversified and they began to experience slow advancement and gradually were welcomed into the White working class as their identity as "White" overcame any status as "immigrant."

With mobility came social class distinctions within Irish America. The immigrants and their children who began to move into the more affluent urban areas were derogatorily referred to as the "lace-curtain Irish." The lower-class Irish immigrants they left behind, meanwhile, were referred to as the "shanty Irish." But as immigration from Ireland slowed and upward mobility quickened, fewer and fewer Irish qualified as the poor cousins of their predecessors.

In the 1950s, as in the nineteenth century, economic hard times in Ireland spurred immigration to the United States. However, a cap of 2,000 immigrants from any one European country led to the sporadic influx of illegal immigrants from the Republic of Ireland. Congressional action in 1987 included a provision that resulted in another 16,000 visas for Irish immigrants. This recent experience with immigration controls led several national and local Irish American organizations to stand with those in 2006 who protested for procedures to allow illegal immigrants to apply for citizenship.

In the twentieth century, the most visible components of Irish American life had roots that are still visible in the twenty-first century. Extended formal schooling was stressed and entering professions, especially the law, was encouraged. The Irish with their long struggle for political independence comprehended the essentials of representative government. Politics and civic employment opportunities, such as law enforcement, became a critical path both to influence and upward mobility. This pattern continues today. Indeed, of the 345 firefighters who perished in New York City's Twin Trade Towers collapse of September 11, 2001, 145 were members of the Emerald Society, the fire department's Irish American fraternal group (Meagher 2005, 610).

For the Irish American man, the priesthood was viewed as a desirable and respected occupation. Irish Americans furthermore played a leadership role in the Roman Catholic Church in the United States. The Irish dominance persisted long after other ethnic groups swelled the ranks of the faithful (Fallows 1979; Lee and Casey 2006).

Contemporary Irish Americans

In the 2000 census, people identifying as Irish accounted for 30.5 million people—second only to German ancestry. Yet this represented a decline of over 8.2 million people self-identifying as Irish from 1990, a product of assimilation rather than to any out-migration.

Contemporary Irish immigration is relatively slight accounting for perhaps 1 out of 1,000 legal arrivals today compared to over a third of all immigrants in the 1840s and 1850s. About 202,000 people in the United States were born in Ireland—comparable to the numbers of Portuguese born in the United States. Today's Irish American typically enjoys the symbolic ethnicity of food, dance, and music. Gaelic language instruction is limited to less than thirty colleges. Visibility as a collective ethnic group is greatest with the annual St. Patrick's Day celebrations when everyone seems to be Irish or with the occasional fervent nationalism aimed at curtailing Great Britain's role in Northern Ireland. Yet some stereotypes remain concerning excessive drinking despite available data indicating that alcoholism rates are no higher and sometimes lower among people of Irish ancestry compared to descendants of other European immigrant groups.

St. Patrick's Day celebrations, as noted previously, offer an example of how ethnic identity evolves over time. The Feast of St. Patrick has a long history but the public celebrations with parties, concerts, and parades originated in the United States, which were then exported to Ireland in the latter part of the twentieth century.

Well-known Irish Americans span society including the celebrity chef Bobby Flay, actor Philip Seymour Hoffman, comedian Conan O'Brien, and author Frank McCourt as well as the political dynasties of Kennedy in Massachusetts and Daley in Chicago. Reflecting growing rates of intermarriage, Irish America also includes singer Mariah Carey (her mother Irish and her father African American and Venezuelan).

The Irish were the first immigrant group to encounter prolonged organized resistance. Strengthened by continued immigration, facility with the English language, building on strong community and family networks, and familiarity with representative politics, Irish Americans became an integral part of the Untied States.

The Italian Americans

Although each European country's immigration to the United States has created its own social history, the case of Italians, though not typical of every nationality, offers insight into the White ethnic experience. Italians immigrated even during the colonial period, and they played prominent roles during the American Revolution and the early days of the republic. Mass immigration began in the 1880s, peaking in the first twenty years of the twentieth century, when Italians accounted for one-fourth of European immigration.

Italian Americans celebrate a religious festival in Cambridge, Massachusetts.

Italian immigration was concentrated not only in time but also by geography. The majority of the immigrants were landless peasants from rural southern Italy, the Mezzogiorno. Although many people in the United States assume that Italians are a nationality with a single culture, this is not true either culturally or economically. The Italian people recognize multiple geographic divisions reflecting sharp cultural distinctions. These divisions were brought with the immigrants to the New World.

Many Italians, especially in the early years of mass immigration in the nineteenth century, received their jobs through an ethnic labor contractor, the *padrone*. Similar arrangements have been used by Asian, Hispanic, and Greek immigrants, where the labor contractors, most often immigrants, have mastered sufficient English to mediate for their compatriots. Exploitation was common within the padrone system through kickbacks, provision of inadequate housing, and withholding of wages. By World War I, 90 percent of Italian girls and 99 percent of Italian boys in New York City were leaving school at age 14 to work, but by that time Italian Americans were sufficiently fluent in English to seek out work on their own, and the padrone system had disappeared.

Along with manual labor, the Catholic Church was a very important part of Italian Americans' lives at this time. Yet they found little comfort in a Catholic church dominated by an earlier immigrant group: the Irish. The traditions were different; weekly attendance for Italian Americans was overshadowed by the religious aspects of the *feste* (or festivals) held throughout the year in honor of saints (the Irish viewed the feste as practically a form of paganism). These initial adjustment problems were overcome with the establishment of ethnic parishes, a pattern repeated by other non-Irish immigrant groups. Thus, parishes would be staffed by Italian priests, sometimes imported for that purpose. Although the hierarchy of the church adjusted more slowly, Italian Americans were increasingly able to feel at home in their local parish church. Today, more than 70 percent of Italian Americans identify themselves as Roman Catholics (Luconi 2001).

As assimilation proceeded, Italian Americans began to construct a social identity as a nationality group rather than viewing themselves in terms of their village or province. As shown in Figure 5.2, over time, Italian Americans shed old identities for a new one. As immigration from Italy declined, the descendants' ties became more nationalistic. This move from local or regional to national identity was followed by Irish and Greek Americans. The changing identity of Italian Americans reflected the treatment they received in the United States, where non-Italians did not make those regional distinctions. However, they were not treated well. For example, in turn-of-the-century New Orleans, Italian Americans established special ties to the Black community because both groups were marginalized in southern society. Gradually, Italian Americans became White and enjoyed all the privileges that come with it. Today it would be inconceivable to imagine that Italian Americans of New Orleans would reach out to the African American community as their natural allies on social and political issues (Guglielmo and Salemo 2003; Luconi 2001).

FIGURE 5.2 Constructing Social Identity Among Italian Immigrants

Over time Italian Americans moved from seeing themselves in terms of their provincial or village identity to their national identity, and then they successfully became indistinguishable from other Whites.

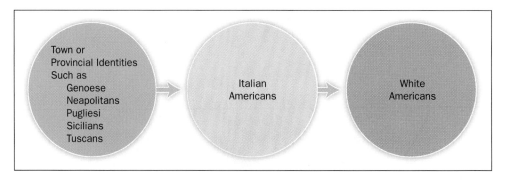

A controversial aspect of the Italian American experience involves organized crime, as typified by Al Capone (1899–1947). Arriving in U.S. society in the bottom layers, Italians lived in decaying, crime-ridden neighborhoods that became known as Little Italies. For a small segment of these immigrants, crime was a significant means of upward social mobility. In effect, entering and leading criminal activity was one aspect of assimilation, though not a positive one. Complaints linking ethnicity and crime actually began in colonial times with talk about the criminally inclined Irish and Germans, and they continue with contemporary stereotyping about such groups as Colombian drug dealers and Vietnamese street gangs. Yet the image of Italians as criminals has persisted from Prohibition-era gangsters to the view of mob families today. As noted earlier, it is not at all surprising that groups such as the Columbian Coalition have been organized to counter such negative images.

The fact that Italians often are characterized as criminal, even in the mass media, is another example of what we have called respectable bigotry toward White ethnics. The persistence of linking Italians, or any other minority group, with crime probably is attributable to attempts to explain a problem by citing a single cause: the presence of perceived undesirables. Many Italian Americans still see their image tied to old stereotypes. A 2001 survey of Italian American teenagers found that 39 percent felt the media presented their ethnic group as criminal or gang members and 34 percent as restaurant workers (Girardelli 2004; National Italian American Foundation 2001).

The immigration of Italians was slowed by the national origin system, described in Chapter 4. As Italian Americans settled permanently, the mutual aid societies that had grown up in the 1920s to provide basic social services began to dissolve. More slowly, education came to be valued by Italian Americans as a means of upward mobility. Even becoming more educated did not ward off prejudice, however. In 1930, for example, President Herbert Hoover rebuked Fiorello La Guardia, then an Italian American member of Congress from New York City, stating that "the Italians are predominantly our murderers and bootleggers" and recommending that La Guardia "go back to where you belong" because, "like a lot of other foreign spawn, you do not appreciate this country which supports you and tolerates you" (Baltzell 1964:30).

While U.S. troops, including 500,000 Italian Americans, battled Italy during World War II, some hatred and sporadic violence emerged against Italian Americans and their property. However, they were not limited to actions against individuals. Italian Americans were even confined by the federal government in specific areas of California by virtue of their ethnicity alone, and 10,000 were relocated from coastal areas. In addition, 1,800 Italian Americans who were citizens of Italy were placed in an internment camp in Montana. The internees were eventually freed on Columbus Day 1942 as President Roosevelt lobbied the Italian American community to gain full support for the impending land invasion of Italy (Department of Justice 2001a; Fox 1990).

In politics, Italian Americans have been more successful, at least at the local level, where family and community ties can be translated into votes. However, political success did not come easily because many Italian immigrants anticipated returning to their homeland and did not always take neighborhood politics seriously. It was even more difficult for Italian Americans to break into national politics.

Not until 1962 was an Italian American named to a cabinet-level position. Geraldine Ferraro's nomination as the Democratic vice presidential candidate in 1984 was every bit as much an achievement for Italian Americans as it was for women. The opposition to the nomination of Judge Samuel Alito to the Supreme Court in 2006 struck many as bordering on anti–Italian American sentiments in the manner it was advanced. Numerous critics used the phrase "Judge Scalito" in obvious reference to the sitting Italian American on the Court, Justice Antonio Scalia (Cornacchia and Nelson 1992; National Italian American Foundation 2006).

A recent study of the members of the American Academy of Arts and Sciences, a group of nearly 4,000 members drawn from throughout the academic and scientific worlds, showed that Italian Americans are represented well below their representation on the nation's faculties. Ethnic disadvantage has not disappeared entirely (Alba and Abdel-Hady 2005).

There is no paucity of famous Italian Americans. They include athletes like Joe DiMaggio and Joe Paterno, politician Rudolph Giullani, director Francis Ford Coppola, singer Madonna, comedian Jay Leno, writer Mario Puzo, actor Nicholas Cage, chef Rachel Ray, and auto racing legend Mario Andretti.

In 2000, the 15.9 million people of Italian ancestry accounted for about 6 percent of the population, although only a small fraction of them had actually been born in Italy. Italian Americans still remain the seventh-largest immigrant group. Just how ethnically conscious is the Italian American community? Although the number is declining, 1 million Americans speak Italian at home; only six languages are spoken more frequently at home (Spanish, French, Chinese, Vietnamese, Tagalog [Philippines], and German). For another 14-plus million Italian Americans, however, the language tie to their culture is absent, and depending on their degree of assimilation, only traces of symbolic ethnicity may remain. In a later section we will look at the role that language plays for many immigrants and their children (Shin and Bruno 2003).

Polish Americans

Immigrants from Poland have had experiences similar to that of the Irish and Italians. They had to overcome economic problems and personal hardships just to make the journey. Once in the United States they found themselves often assigned to the jobs many citizens had not wanted to do. They had to adjust to a new language, a familiar yet different culture. And always they were looking back to the family members left behind who either wanted to join them in the United States or, in contrast, never wanted them to leave in the first place.

Like other arrivals, many Poles sought improvement in their lives, the *Za Chlebem* (For Bread) migration. The Poles who came were, at different times, more likely than many other European immigrants to see themselves as forced immigrants and were often described by and themselves adopted the terminology directly reflecting this social roles *exiles, refugees, displaced persons* or *émigrés*. The primary force for this exodus was the changing political status of Poland itself through most the 19th and 20th centuries, which was as turbulent as were the lives of the new arrivals.

Early Immigration

Polish immigrants were among the settlers at Jamestown, Virginia in 1608 to help develop the colony's timber industry but it was the Poles that came later in that century that made a lasting mark. The successful exploits of Polish immigrants such as cavalry officer Casimir Pulaski and military engineer Thaddeus Kosciuszko are still commemorated today in communities with large Polish American populations. As we can see in Figure 5-1, it was not until the 1890s that Polish immigration was significant in comparison to some other European arrivals. Admittedly it is difficult to document exactly the size of this immigration because Poland or parts of the country became part, at various historical periods, of Austria-Hungary, Germany (Prussia), and the Soviet Union so that the migrants were not officially coming from a nation called "Poland."

Many of the Polish immigrants were adjusting not only to a new culture but also to a more urban way of life. Sociologists William I. Thomas and Florian Znaniecki in their classic study *The Polish Peasant in Europe and America* traced the path from rural Poland to urban America. Many of the peasants did not necessarily come directly to the United States but first traveled through other European countries. This pattern is not unique and reminds us that, even today, many immigrants have crossed several countries sometimes establishing themselves for a period of time before finally settling in the United States (Thomas and Znaniecki 19187–1920).

Like the Italians and Irish, they arrived at the large port cities of the East Coast but, unlike them, the Polish immigrants were more likely to settle in cities further inland or work in mines in Pennsylvania. In such areas they would join kinfolk or acquaintances through the process of chain migration described in the previous chapter.

The reference to coal mining as an occupation reflects the continuing tendency of immigrants at work in jobs avoided by U.S. citizens because they paid little or were dangerous or both. For example, in September 1897, a group of miners in Lattimer, Pennsylvania, marched to demand safer working conditions and an end to special taxes placed only on foreign-born workers. In the ensuing confrontation with local officials, police officers shot at the protesters killing nineteen people, most of whom were Polish, the others Lithuanians and Slovaks (Duszak 1997).

Polonia

With growing numbers, the emergence of *Polonia* (meaning Polish American communities) became more common in cities throughout the Midwest. Male immigrants who came alone often took shelter through a system of inexpensive boarding houses called *tryzmanie bortnków* (brother-keeping), which allowed the new arrival to save and send money back to Poland to support his family. These funds eventually provided the financial means necessary to bring family members over, adding to the size of Polonia in such cities as Buffalo, Cleveland, Detroit, Milwaukee, Pittsburgh, and above all in Chicago where the population of Poles was second only to Warsaw, Poland.

Religion has played an important role among the Polish immigrants and their descendants. Most of the Polish immigrants who came to the United States prior to World War I were Roman Catholic. They quickly established their own parishes where new arrivals could feel welcomed. Although religious services at that time were in the Latin language, as they had been in Poland, the many service organizations around the parish, not to mention the Catholic schools, kept the immigrants steeped in the Polish language and the latest happenings back home. Jewish Poles began immigrating during the first part of the twentieth century to escape the growing hostility they felt in Europe that culminated in the Holocaust. Their numbers swelled greatly until movement from Poland stopped with the invasion of Poland by Germany in 1939 and then resumed again after the war.

Although the Jewish–Catholic distinction may be the most obvious distinguishing factor among Polish Americans, there are other divisions as well. Regional subgroups such as the Kashubes, the Górali, and the Mazurians have often carried great significance. Some Poles emigrated from areas where German actually was the language of origin.

Feelings about Poland and its future have both served to unify Polonia and at time reflect the political, economic, and culture divisions of the poles' ancestral homeland, which they have been able to follow through the dozens of Polish-language local and national newspapers, magazines, radio stations, and cable television news shows.

As with other immigrant groups, Polish Americans could make use of a rich structure of self-help voluntary associations that was already well established by the 1890s. Besides providing economic assistance and social networks, these organizations also directed attention to the political and ideological controversies that swirled around back in Poland. Groups like the Polish National Alliance and the Polish Roman Catholic Union, both headquartered in Chicago, had well over a hundred thousand members for most of the twentieth century.

Richie Sambora, guitarist with the rock group Bon Jovi, is one of many well-known Polish Americans.

Like many other newcomers, Poles have been stigmatized as outsiders but also stereotyped as simple and uncultured—the typical biased view of working-class White ethnics. Their struggles in manual occupations placed them in direct competition with other White ethnics and African Americans, which occasionally led to labor disputes and longer-term tense and emotional rivalries. "Polish jokes" continue now to have a remarkable shelf life in casual conversation well into the twenty-first century. Jewish Poles suffer the added indignities of anti-Semitism.

The Contemporary Picture

Today Polonia numbers 9 million. Although this may not seem significant in a country of over 300 million, we need to recall that today Poland itself has a population of only about 39 million. Whether it was to support the efforts of Lech Walesa, Solidarity movement leader confronting the Soviet Union in the 1980s, or to celebrate the elevation of Karol Józef Wojtyla as Pope John Paul II in 1978, Polish Americans are a central part of the global Polish community.

Aging Polish American communities have received an influx of new arrivals since 1989 as elections in Poland marked the end of Soviet dominance, allowing Poles to join their relatives and facilitating immigration of entire households. Poland's entry into NATO in 1999 and the European Union in 2004 smoothed the way even further for Poles to migrate to Western Europe and on to the United States.

Many Polish Americans have retained little of their rich cultural traditions and may barely acknowledge even symbolic ethnicity. Others are still immersed in Polonia and their lives still revolve around many of the same religious and social institutions that were the center of Polonia a century ago. For example, as of 2006, fifty-four Roman Catholic churches in the metropolitan Chicago area still offer Polish-language masses. Although in many of these parishes there may only be one service in Polish serving a declining number of celebrants, a few traditional "Polish" churches actually still have Polish-speaking priests in residence.

Polish core neighborhoods and strips of stores proudly proclaiming their Polish connections still abound but increasingly Polish Americans have moved into suburban communities—first to inner-ring suburbs and then out to the further reaches of metropolitan centers. This migration outward from the traditional ethnic enclaves is evidence of upward mobility and growing diversity in occupations and leisure-time pursuits.

In the latter part of the twentieth century some of the voluntary associations relocated or built satellite centers to serve the outlying Polish American populations. These social organizations also reached out of the central cities in order to tap into the financial resources of suburban Poles to sustain their activities financially. Yet also increasingly people of Polish descent have now made their way into the same social networks populated by Irish, Italian, and other ethnic Americans (Bukowcyk 1996; Erdmans 1998, 2006; Jaroszynska-Kirchman 1996; Lopata 1994; Mocha 1998; Polzin 1973).

Among the many Polish Americans well known or remembered today are actor Adrien Brody, home designer Martha (Kostyra) Stewart, comedian Jack Benny (Benjamin Kubelsky), guitarist Richie Sambora of the rock group Bon Jovi, actress Jane Kaczmarek of *Malcolm and the Middle*, entertainer Liberace, *Wheel of Fortune* host Pat Sajak, baseball star Stan Musial, football star Mike Ditka, Senator Barbara Mikulski, singer Bobby Vinton (Stanley Ventula, Jr.), polio vaccine pioneer Albert Sabin, and director Stanley Kubrick.

The Language Divide

One evening in Chicago, Audrey Cho faced her ten adult students holding a handout listing federal holidays and asked, "Who is Washington?" Confused looks came over the faces of the Korean, Mexican, Peruvian, and Mongolian immigrants. Finally, someone raised his hand and said, "February 16th?" Cho, herself having immigrated from South Korea, remained patient and stated "No, it's who, not when." Learning English may not be easy but many immigrants of all ages are trying (Kaneya 2004 6).

In "Listen to Our Voices," Albanian immigrant Harallamb Terba speaks to his efforts to attend Truman College, the Chicago city college, and become a part of American society. Language is both a barrier and a means to accomplishing that.

Language is key to people's functioning in a society, and it is critical in relation to how they see themselves. But when that language is different from the dominant tongue, it can be the source of hardship and stigmatization. About 18 percent of the population speaks a language other than English, as shown in Figure 5.3 (Shin and Bruno 2003).

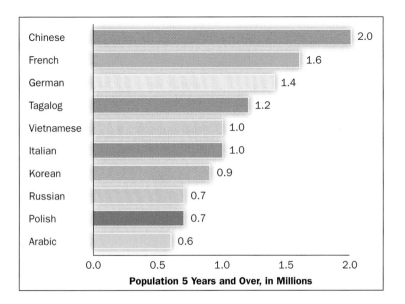

FIGURE 5.3   Ten Languages Most Frequently Spoken at Home Other Than English and Spanish

Source: Data for 2000 released in 2003 in Shin and Bruno 2003.

Voices Listen to Our Voices Listen to

I WAS BORN IN TIRANA

My name is Harallamb Terba. I was born in Tirana, Albania in November 21st, 1965. I came here exactly in March 25, 1996. It was afternoon, 5:00 Chicago time, but my watch say 12:00 in the night because it is seven hours different from my country to here. [Laughs.]

I'm in college now. My major is computer information system. I think after I will be graduating from school, I'm gonna start working, maybe for a company. I love working in computer, computer programming, designing and building programs, applications. I think my life is gonna be good. I always think about that. My wife is in school, too. She's taking sign language. She loves working with deaf people. So I think she is gonna get a good job. . . .

Home is the place where you live. I think about my home in my country. It's the place where you born. But this is the life. The life change. You have to move. You have to try and when you try for the best, it's better for you. I like my country. I like the people there, but I feel this is my home now. I don't feel that about Albania now. I feel that when I was in Albania, I have this thought in my mind that, "I will go. One day I will go in the United States. Everything that I did here it's nothing. I have to get my education. I have to work. I have to do, but everything it's gonna start when I go in the United States." That's why I wish to came here younger.

I think to have my own home, years after. I think about that. It's not important,

Harallamb Terba

but I always loved having my own home, my yard. I always loved that because I have been grow up with big home with a yard in front, so that's why I love that. But now I'm living in apartment and everything is OK. I like that.

In the future I want plan for to have children. I'm going to tell my children in the future that they will be American because they will be born here, but I always am gonna tell them from where they are, their parents are. So they have to know about their country because this was the country that grow us, their father and their mother. So they have to know about their culture. Maybe I'm gonna advise them that when they go in Albanian, to be more Albanian than Albanians are, because Albanians are gonna see them just, "Hey, you are from America. You're American." You know what happens.

America to me means freedom, and the land where everyone can do what he dreams. Dreams come true. It's a hard work to do what you want, but finally you can do that. I came from one country that you want to do something, but no one lets you to do that. You can only do what they say to you. So here, if you want to do that, if you like to do that, you can do that. It's hard. I know it's hard. Nothing is easy in our life today, but you can do that. And this is more important for our life, to do what we want. ∎

Source: Harallamb Terba. 2004, In Jeff Libman, 2004 *An Immigrant Class: Oral Histories from Chicago's Newest Immigrants.* Chicago: Flying Kite, pp. 185, 194–195 in pp. 184–195. Reprinted with permission of Flying Kite, Inc.

As of 2002, about 23 percent of Mexican Americans are English dominant, 26 percent are bilingual, and 51 percent are Spanish dominant. Puerto Ricans in the United States tend to be more English language oriented, with 39 percent English-dominant, 40 percent bilingual, and 21 percent Spanish dominant. At the other extreme, Salvadorans, Dominicans, Colombians, and other Central and South Americans tend to be more Spanish dominant, and they are also more likely to be more recent immigrants. Nationally, about 70 percent of Latino schoolchildren report speaking Spanish at home (Brodie et al. 2002; Bureau of the Census 2003a, 158).

The myth of Anglo superiority has rested in part on language differences. (The term *Anglo* in the following text is used to mean all non-Hispanics but primarily Whites.) First, the criteria for economic and social achievement usually include proficiency in English. By such standards, Spanish-speaking pupils are judged less able to compete until they learn English. Second, many Anglos believe that Spanish is not an asset occupationally. Only recently, as government agencies have belatedly begun to serve Latino people and as businesses recognize the growing Latino consumer market, have Anglos recognized that knowing Spanish is not only useful but also necessary to carry out certain tasks. However, as we see in education, voting, and language practices, many people in the United States are concerned and suspicious about the public use of any language other than English.

Bilingual Education

Until the last twenty or thirty years, there was a conscious effort to devalue Spanish and other languages and to discourage the use of foreign languages in schools. In the case of Spanish, this practice was built on a pattern of segregating Hispanic schoolchildren from Anglos. In the recent past in the Southwest, Mexican Americans were assigned to Mexican schools to keep Anglo schools all White. These Mexican schools, created through de jure school segregation, were substantially underfunded compared with the regular public schools. Legal action against such schools dates back to 1945, but it was not until 1970 that the U.S. Supreme Court ruled, in *Cisneros v. Corpus Christi Independent School District*, that the de jure segregation of Mexican Americans was unconstitutional. Appeals delayed implementation of that decision, and not until September 1975 was the de jure plan forcibly overturned in Corpus Christi, Texas (Commission on Civil Rights 1976).

Even in integrated schools, Latino children were given separate, unequal treatment. "No Spanish" was a rule enforced throughout the Southwest, Florida, and New York City by school boards in the 1960s. Children speaking Spanish on school grounds, even on the playground, might be punished with detention after school, fines, physical reprimands, and even expulsion for repeated violations. From 1855 to as recently as 1968, teaching in any language other than English was illegal in California. Such laws existed despite a provision in the 1848 Treaty of Guadalupe Hidalgo between the United States and Mexico that guaranteed the right of Mexicans to maintain their culture. All official publications were to be bilingual, but "English only" became the social norm.

Is it essential that English be the sole language of instruction in schools in the United States? **Bilingualism** is the use of two or more languages in places of work or educational facilities, according each language equal legitimacy. Thus, a program of **bilingual education** may instruct children in their native language (such as Spanish) while gradually introducing them to the language of the dominant society (English). If such a program is also bicultural, it will teach children about the culture of both linguistic groups. Bilingual education allows students to learn academic material in their own language while they are learning a second language. Proponents believe that,

bilingualism
The use of two or more languages in places of work or education and the treatment of each language as legitimate.

bilingual education
Program designed to allow students to learn academic concepts in their native language while they learn a second language.

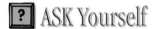 ASK Yourself

What different forms can bilingual education take?

ideally, bilingual education programs should also allow English-speaking pupils to be bilingual, but generally they are directed only at making non-English speakers proficient in more than one language.

Programs to teach English as a second language (ESL) have been the cornerstones of bilingual education, but they are limited in approach. For example, ESL programs tend to emphasize bilingual but not bicultural education. As a result, the method can unintentionally contribute to ethnocentric attitudes, especially if it seems to imply that a minority group is not really worthy of attention. As conflict theorists are quick to note, the interests of the less powerful—in this case, millions of non-English-speaking children—are those least likely to be recognized and respected. One alternative to the ESL approach, viewed with much less favor by advocates of bilingualism, is **English immersion**, in which students are taught primarily in English, using their native languages only when they do not understand their lessons. In practice, such instruction usually becomes an English-only "crash program" (Hechinger 1987).

Since its introduction into U.S. schools, bilingual education has been beset by problems. Its early supporters were disillusioned by the small number of English-speaking children participating and by the absence of a bicultural component in most programs. However, the frustration has been most clearly visible in the lack of consensus among educators on how best to implement bilingual programs. Even when a school district decides what methods it prefers, superintendents find it difficult to hire qualified instructors, although this varies depending on the language and the part of the country. The problem is further complicated by the presence of children speaking languages other than the predominant second language, so superintendents may want to mount bilingual programs in many languages.

Do bilingual programs help children to learn English? It is difficult to reach firm conclusions on the effectiveness of the bilingual programs in general because they vary so widely in their approach to non-English-speaking children. The programs differ in the length of the transition to English and how long they allow students to remain in bilingual classrooms. A major study released in 2004 analyzed more than three decades of research, combining seventeen different studies, and found that bilingual education programs produce higher levels of student achievement in reading. The most successful are paired bilingual programs—those offering ongoing instruction in a native language and English at different times of the day (Slavin and Cheung 2003).

Drawing on the perspective of conflict theory, we can understand some of the attacks on bilingual programs. The criticisms do not necessarily result from careful educational research. Rather, they stem from the effort to assimilate children and to deprive them of language pluralism. This view, that any deviation from the majority is bad, is expressed by those who want to stamp out foreigners, especially in our schools. Research findings have little influence on those who, holding such ethnocentric views, try to persuade policy makers to follow their thinking. This perspective does not take into account that success in bilingual education may begin to address the problem of high school dropouts and the paucity of Hispanics in colleges and universities.

As one might expect, Latinos tend to be very supportive of bilingual programs. A 2003 national survey found that 72 percent of Hispanics (and a similar proportion of African Americans) favor school districts offering such programs compared to 53 percent of non-Hispanic Whites. Nonetheless, opposition to bilingualism can be quite strong among some Hispanics. A few are very active in organized efforts to stop such programs, and some Latino parents pressure schools to keep their children out of

English immersion
Teaching in English by teachers who know the students' native language but use it only when students do not understand the lessons.

classrooms where Spanish may be spoken out of the misguided notion that English-only education, even for the youngest children, is the key to success (Freedman 2004; Mason 2003; Soltero 2004).

Official Language Movement

Attacks on bilingualism both in voting and in education have taken several forms and have even broadened to question the appropriateness of U.S. residents using any language other than English. Federal policy has become more restrictive. Local schools have been given more authority to determine appropriate methods of instruction; they have also been forced to provide more of their own funding for bilingual education.

In the United States, repeated efforts have been made to introduce a constitutional amendment declaring English as the nation's official language. In 2006, a congressional proposal for a national language arose during debates over immigration. Legislative leaders who were struggling to reach a compromise introduced a proposal to make English the national language. The legislation would not completely outlaw bilingual or multilingual government services. It would, however, require that such services be called for specifically as in the Voting Rights Act of 1965, which requires voting information to be available in multiple languages.

As shown in Figure 5.4, non-English speakers cluster in certain states, but bilingualism attracts nationwide passions. The release in 2006 of "Nuestro Himmo", the Spanish-language version of "The Star-Spangled Banner", led to a strong reaction with 69 percent of people saying it was only appropriate to be sung in English. Yet at least one congressman decrying the Spanish version sang the anthem himself in English with incorrect lyrics. Similarly, a locally famous restaurant owner in Philadelphia posted signs at his Philly steak sandwich diner announcing he would only accept orders in English. Passions remain strong as policy makers debate how much support should be given to prople who speak other languages (Carroll 2006; Koch 2006b).

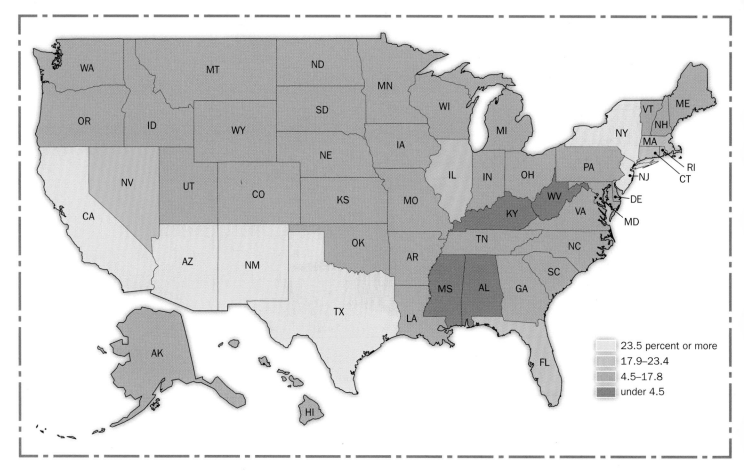

FIGURE 5.4   People Who Speak a Language Other Than English at Home
Source: U.S. data for 2000 released in Shin and Bruno 2003, 8.

Legend:
- 23.5 percent or more
- 17.9–23.4
- 4.5–17.8
- under 4.5

Religious Pluralism

In popular speech, the term *pluralism* has often been used in the United States to refer explicitly to religion. Although certain faiths figure more prominently in the worship scene, there has been a history of greater religious tolerance in the United States than in most other nations. Today there are more than 1,500 religious bodies in the United States, ranging from the more than 66 million members of the Roman Catholic Church to sects with fewer than 1,000 adherents.

How do we view the United States in terms of religion? It is now more accurate to speak of the country as Judeo-Christian-Islamic or Abrahamic (referring to the historical religious leader common to the three faiths). There is an increasingly non-Christian presence in the United States. In 1900, an estimated 96 percent of the nation was Christian, just over 1 percent nonreligious, and about 3 percent all other faiths. In 2005, it is estimated that the nation is 82 percent Christian, nearly 11 percent nonreligious, and another 7 percent all other faiths. The United States has a long Jewish tradition, and Muslims number close to 5 million. A smaller but also growing number of people adhere to such Eastern faiths as Hinduism, Buddhism, Confucianism, and Taoism (Barrett and Johnson 2001; Baylor Institute for Studies of Religion 2006).

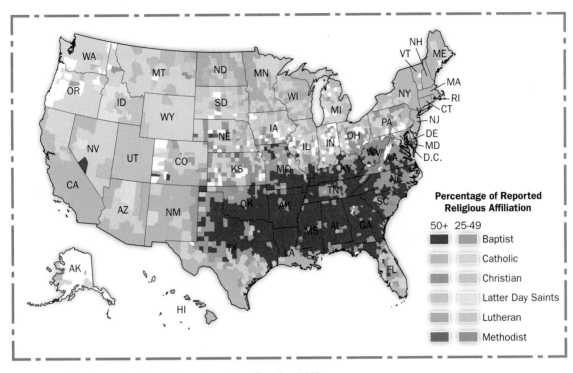

FIGURE 5.5 Predominant Christian Denominations by Counties, 2000

The diversity of Christian religious life in the United States is apparent in the map. Many Christian denominations account for 25 percent or more of the church members in a county. Among non-Christian faiths, only Judaism figures so significantly—in New York County (Manhattan) of New York City and in Dade County, Florida (which includes Miami Beach).

Source: Major Religious Families By Counties of the United States 2000 from "Religious Congregations and Memberships in the United States 2000," Dale E. Jones, et al. Nashville, TN: Glenmary Research Center © 2002 Association of Statisticians of American Religious Bodies. (All rights reserved.) This material may not be printed or reproduced in any electronic format except for individual use and may not be distributed for profit.

The diversity of religious life in the United States is apparent in Figure 5.5, which numerically shows the Christian faiths that dominate various areas of the country. For many nations of the world, a map of religions would hardly be useful because one faith accounts for almost all religious followers in the country. The diversity of beliefs, rituals, and experiences that characterizes religious life in the United States reflects both the nation's immigrant heritage and the First Amendment prohibition against establishing a state religion.

Sociologists use the word **denomination** for a large, organized religion that is not linked officially with the state or government. By far the largest denomination in the United States is Catholicism, yet at least twenty-four other Christian religious denominations have 1 million or more members (Table 5.1).

There are also at least four non-Christian religious groups in the United States whose numbers are comparable to any of these large denominations. Jews, Muslims, Buddhists, and Hindus in the United States all number more than 1 million. Within each of these groups, there are branches or sects that distinguish themselves from each other. For example, in the United States and the rest of the world, some followers of Islam are Sunni Muslims and others are Shiites. There are further divisions within these groups, just as there are among Protestants and in turn among Baptists (Kosmin, Mayer, and Keysar 2001).

One notable characteristic of religious practice in the United States is its segregated nature at the local level. In 2006, arsonists victimized ten churches in Alabama, and

denomination
A large, organized religion not officially linked with the state or government.

TABLE 5.1
Churches with More Than a Million Members

Denomination Name	Inclusive Membership
The Roman Catholic Church	67,820,835
Southern Baptist Convention	16,267,494
The United Methodist Church	8,186,254
The Church of Jesus Christ of Latter-day Saints	5,599,177
The Church of God in Christ	5,499,875
National Baptist Convention, U.S.A., Inc.	5,000,000
Evangelical Lutheran Church in America	4,930,429
National Baptist Convention of America, Inc.	3,500,000
Presbyterian Church (U.S.A.)	3,189,573
Assemblies of God	2,779,095
Progressive National Baptist Convention, Inc.	2,500,000
African Methodist Episcopal Church	2,500,000
National Missionary Baptist Convention of America	2,500,000
The Lutheran Church–Missouri Synod (LCMS)	2,463,747
Episcopal Church	2,284,233
Greek Orthodox Archdiocese of America	1,500,000
Pentecostal Assemblies of the World, Inc.	1,500,000
Churches of Christ	1,500,000
African Methodist Episcopal Zion Church	1,432,795
American Baptist Churches in the U.S.A.	1,424,840
United Church of Christ	1,265,786
Baptist Bible Fellowship International	1,200,000
Christian Churches and Churches of Christ	1,071,616
Orthodox Church in America	1,064,000
Jehovah's Witness	1,029,092

Note: Most recent data as of 2006. Membership reporting year ranges from 1992 to 2004.

Source: "Membership Statistics in the United States" in *Yearbook of American and Canadian Churches 2006* edited by Reverend Eileen W. Lindner, Ph.D. Copyright (c) 2006 by National Council of the Churches of Christ in the USA. Reprinted by permission [www.ncccusa.org].

some feared that these fires could be racially motivated. But state and national authorities reassured the public that since five churches were "White" and five churches were "Black," racism was unlikely to be a motivating factor. The irony is that the legacy of racism in religious expression leads to the very segregation in worship that allows churches to be easily identified as "Black" or "White" (Associated Press 2006a).

Even if religious faiths have broad representation, they tend to be fairly homogeneous at the local church level. This is especially ironic, given that many faiths have played critical roles in resisting racism and trying to bring together the nation in the name of racial and ethnic harmony (Orfield and Liebowitz 1999).

Broadly defined faiths show representation of a variety of ethnic and racial groups. In Figure 5.6, we consider the interaction of White, Black, and Hispanic race with religions. Muslims, Pentecostals, and Jehovah's Witnesses are much more diverse than Presbyterians or Lutherans. Religion plays an even more central role for Blacks and Latinos than Whites. A 2004 national survey indicated that 65 percent of African Americans and 51 percent of Latinos attend a religious service every week, compared to 44 percent of non-Hispanic Whites (Winseman 2004b).

About two in three Americans (66 percent) are counted as church members, but it is difficult to assess the strength of their religious commitment. A persuasive case can be

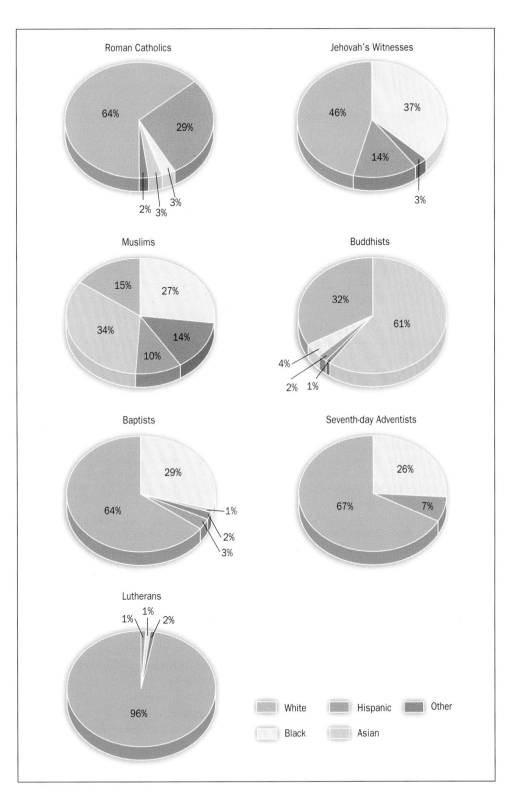

FIGURE 5.6   Racial and Ethnic Makeup of Selected Religions in the United States

Note: More recent study (Latino Coalition 2006) shows 44 percent of Roman Catholics to be Hispanic. Totals do not always sum to 100 percent due to rounding.

Source: "Racial and Ethnic Make-Up of Selected Religions," in *American Religious Identification Survey, 2001* by Egon Mayer et al., The Graduate Center of the City University of New York. Reprinted with permission.

MEASURING THE IMPORTANCE OF RELIGION

Social scientists and scholars of religious behavior have tried to measure the importance that religion has for people. Studies center on the holding of religious beliefs ("Do you believe in God?"), declarations of membership, contributions of money or time, and attendance at or participation in religious services.

We will focus on how people perceive the importance of religion to themselves and to others. This is a reasonable step because it does not make any assumptions about a specific religion, as if one were to ask people whether they read the Bible or attended church. In addition, we have reliable national data covering a long period of time with the same questions being asked using largely the same survey techniques.

In Figure 5.7 we see the responses over the last twenty-five years to two questions: how important people feel religion is to them and whether they feel religion is increasing its influence on the United States as a whole.

Two patterns emerge. First, somewhere between 53 and 61 percent of adults see religion as "very important" in their daily lives. Second, a much smaller proportion of people, usually around 35 percent, see religion's influence increasing, but this has fluctuated more widely. Of particular note across this time period is the dramatic increase in 2001. The events of September 11, 2001, had a pronounced impact on how people saw religion as influencing the nation. In 2000, about 36 percent of the people felt religion was increasing its influence and 55 percent felt it was losing its hold on the nation—pretty typical responses for the twenty-year period. Yet by December 7, 2001, 35 percent felt religion was increasing its influence and only 24 percent saw it losing. By the next year it dropped back to 48 percent.

Will this dramatic shift in the perception of how the nation was influenced translate into people's own lives? Probably not. There was little lasting change in how people saw religion playing in their own lives: 58 percent saw it as "very important" in May 2001, 60 percent by December. Media accounts spoke of a possible reawakening because religious houses of worship were packed in the weeks after the

made that religious institutions continue to grow stronger through an influx of new members despite mounting secularism in society. Some observers think that, after reaching a low in the 1960s, religion is becoming more important to people again. The past upheavals in U.S. religious life are reflected on the covers of *Time* magazine, which have cried out variously, "Is God Dead?" (April 8, 1966), "Is God Coming Back to Life?" (December 26, 1969), and "The Jesus Revolution" (June 21, 1971). Much more recently, *Newsweek* proclaimed that "Science Finds God" (July 20, 1998). At present, there is little statistical support for the view that the influence of religion on society is diminishing (Moore 2002).

In "Research Focus," we consider how social scientists examine religious fervor in the United States and what recent studies have indicated.

It would also be incorrect to focus only on older religious organizations. Local churches that developed into national faiths in the 1990s, such as the Calvary Chapel, Vineyard, and Hope Chapel, have created a following among Pentecostal believers, who embrace a more charismatic form of worship devoid of many traditional ornaments, with pastors and congregations alike favoring informal attire. New faiths develop with increasing rapidity in what can only be called a very competitive market for individual religious faith. In addition, many people, with or without religious affiliaesearch Focus Research Focus Research

September 11 terrorist attacks, but it appeared to be a short-term gathering out of a sense of grieving rather than a transformation.

These research data show the importance of not using a single measure to analyze something as complex as attitudes about reli-gion. They also show the importance of con-sidering a broader historical perspective rather than attempting to reach a conclu-sion from a single snapshot. ■

Sources: Gallup 2004a, 2006b,; Goodstein 2001; Sherkat and Ellison 1999.

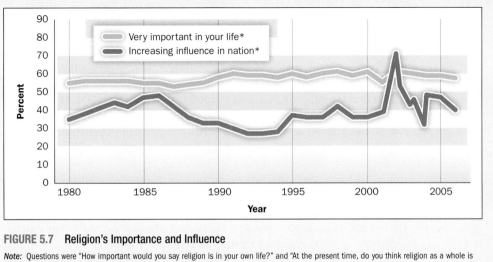

FIGURE 5.7   **Religion's Importance and Influence**

Note: Questions were "How important would you say religion is in your own life?" and "At the present time, do you think religion as a whole is increasing its influence on American life or losing its influence?"

Source: Gallup 2004a, 2006b. Copyright The Gallup Organization. Princeton, NJ. Reprinted with permission.

tion, become fascinated with spiritual concepts such as angels or become a part of loose-knit fellowships such as the Promise Keepers, an all-male movement of evangeli-cal Christians founded in 1990. Religion in the United States is an ever-changing social phenomenon (Dudley and Roozen 2001; Miller and Schaefer 1998).

Ethnicity, Religion, and Social Class

Generally, several social factors influence a person's identity and life chances. Pioneer sociologist Max Weber described **life chances** as people's opportunities to provide themselves with material goods, positive living conditions, and favorable life experi-ences. Religion, ethnicity, or both may affect life chances.

Religion and ethnicity do not necessarily operate together. Sometimes, they have been studied as if they were synonymous. Groups have been described as Irish Catholics, Swedish Lutherans, Muslim Arabs, or Russian Jew, as if religion and ethnici-ty had been merged into some type of national church. In the 1990s, the religion—ethnicity tie took on new meaning as Latin American immigration invigorated the

life chances
People's opportunities to pro-vide themselves with material goods, positive living condi-tions, and favorable life experiences.

Roman Catholic Church nationwide, and West Indian immigration, particularly to New York City, brought new life to the Episcopal Church.

In the 1960s, sociologists felt that religion was more important than ethnicity in explaining behavior. They based this conclusion not on data but on the apparently higher visibility of religion in society. Using national survey data, Andrew Greeley came to different conclusions. He attempted to clarify the relative importance of religion and ethnicity by measuring personality characteristics, political participation, support for civil rights, and family structure. The sample consisted of German and Irish Americans, both Protestant and Catholic. If religion was more significant than ethnicity, Protestants, whether of German or Irish ancestry, and Catholics, regardless of ethnicity, would have been similar in outlook. Conversely, if ethnicity was the key, then the similarities would be among the Germans of either faith or among the Irish as a distinct group. On seventeen of the twenty-four items that made up the four areas measured, the differences were greater between German Catholics and Irish Catholics than between German Catholics and Protestants or between Irish Catholics and Protestants. Ethnicity was a stronger predictor of attitudes and beliefs than religion. In one area—political party allegiance—religion was more important, but this was the exception rather than the rule. In sum, Greeley found ethnicity to be generally more important than religion in predicting behavior. In reality, it is very difficult to separate the influences of religion and ethnicity on any one individual, but Greeley's research cautions against discounting the influence of ethnicity in favor of religion (Glazer and Moynihan 1970; Greeley 1974a, 1974b; Herberg 1983).

In addition, as already noted several times, social class is yet another significant factor. Sociologist Milton Gordon (1978) developed the term **ethclass** (ethnicity and class) to denote the importance of both factors. All three factors—religion, ethnicity, and class—combine to form one's identity, determine one's social behavior, and limit one's life chances. For example, in certain ethnic communities, friendships are limited, to a degree, to people who share the same ethnic background and social class. In other words, neither race and ethnicity nor religion nor class alone places one socially. One must consider several elements together, as reflected in ethclass.

Religion in the United States

Divisive conflicts along religious lines are muted in the United States compared with those in, say, Northern Ireland or the Middle East. Although not entirely absent, conflicts about religion in the United States seem to be overshadowed by civil religion. **Civil religion** is the religious dimension in U.S. life that merges the state with sacred beliefs.

Sociologist Robert Bellah (1967) borrowed the phrase *civil religion* from eighteenth-century French philosopher Jean-Jacques Rousseau to describe a significant phenomenon in the contemporary United States. Civil religion exists alongside established religious faiths, and it embodies a belief system incorporating all religions but not associated specifically with any one. It is the type of faith to which presidents refer in inaugural speeches and to which American Legion posts and Girl Scout troops swear allegiance. In 1954, Congress added the phrase "under God" to the pledge of allegiance as a legislative recognition of religion's significance. Presidents of the United States, beginning with Ronald Reagan and continuing through George W. Bush, typically concluded even their most straightforward speeches with "God Bless the United States of America," which in effect evokes the civil religion of the nation.

Functionalists see civil religion as reinforcing central American values that may be more expressly patriotic than sacred in nature. Often, the mass media, following major societal upheavals, from the 1995 Oklahoma City bombing to the 2001 terrorist attacks, show church services with clergy praying and asking for national healing. Bellah (1967)

ethclass
The merged ethnicity and class in a person's status.

civil religion
The religious dimension in American life that merges the state with sacred beliefs.

sees no sign that the importance of civil religion has diminished in promoting collective identity, but he does acknowledge that it is more conservative than during the 1970s.

In the following section, we will explore the diversity among the major Christian groups in the United States, such as Roman Catholics and Protestants. However, as already noted, significant numbers of people in the United States now practice religions long established in other parts of the world, such as Islam, Hinduism, Judaism, and Buddhism. The greater visibility of religious diversity in the United States is primarily the result of immigrants bringing their religious faith with them and not assimilating to the dominant Christian rituals.

Diversity Among Roman Catholics

Social scientists have persistently tended to ignore the diversity within the Roman Catholic Church in the United States. Recent research has not sustained the conclusions that Roman Catholics are melding into a single group, following the traditions of the American Irish Catholic model, or even that parishioners are attending English-language churches. Religious behavior has been different for each ethnic group within the Roman Catholic Church. The Irish and the French Canadians left societies that were highly competitive both culturally and socially. Their religious involvement in the United States is more relaxed than it was in Ireland and Quebec. However, the influence of life in the United States has increased German and Polish involvement in the Roman Catholic Church, whereas Italians have remained largely inactive. Variations by ethnic background continue to emerge in studies of contemporary religious involvement in the Roman Catholic Church (Eckstrom 2001).

Since the mid-1970s, the Roman Catholic Church in America has received a significant number of new members from the Philippines, Southeast Asia, and particularly Latin America. Although these new members have been a stabilizing force offsetting the loss of White ethnics, they have also challenged a church that for generations was dominated by Irish, Italian, and Polish parishes. Perhaps the most prominent subgroup in the Roman Catholic Church is the Latinos, who now account for one-third of all Roman Catholic parishioners. In the 2006 new class of priests ordained, nearly one-third were foreign born. Some Los Angeles churches in or near Latino neighborhoods must schedule fourteen masses each Sunday to accommodate the crowds of worshipers. By 2006, Latinos constituted 44 percent of Roman Catholics nationwide (Chicago Tribune 2006; Murphy and Banerjee 2005).

The Roman Catholic Church, despite its ethnic diversity, has clearly been a powerful force in reducing the ethnic ties of its members, making it also a significant assimilating

The Roman Catholic Church has experienced growth through immigration from Latin America but has had difficulty recruiting men into the priesthood. Here we see an ordination ceremony at the Holy Name Cathedral in Chicago, Illinois, in 2003.

force. The irony in this role of Catholicism is that so many nineteenth-century Americans heaped abuse on Catholics in this country for allegedly being un-American and having a dual allegiance. The history of the Catholic Church in the United States may be portrayed as a struggle within the membership between the Americanizers and the anti-Americanizers, with the former ultimately winning. Unlike the various Protestant churches that accommodated immigrants of a single nationality, the Roman Catholic Church had to Americanize a variety of linguistic and ethnic groups. The Catholic Church may have been the most potent assimilating force after the public school system. Comparing the assimilationist goal of the Catholic Church and the present diversity in it leads us to the conclusion that ethnic diversity has continued in the Roman Catholic Church despite, not because of, this religious institution.

Diversity Among Protestants

Protestantism, like Catholicism, often is portrayed as a monolithic entity. Little attention is given to the doctrinal and attitudinal differences that sharply divide the various denominations in both laity and clergy. However, several studies document the diversity. Unfortunately, many opinion polls and surveys are content to learn whether a respondent is a Catholic, a Protestant, or a Jew. Stark and Glock (1968) found sharp differences in religious attitudes within Protestant churches. For example, 99 percent of Southern Baptists had no doubt that Jesus was the divine Son of God as contrasted to only 40 percent of Congregationalists. We can identify four "generic theological camps":

1. **Liberals:** United Church of Christ (Congregationalists) and Episcopalians
2. **Moderates:** Disciples of Christ, Methodists, and Presbyterians
3. **Conservatives:** American Lutherans and American Baptists
4. **Fundamentalists:** Missouri Synod Lutherans, Southern Baptists, and Assembly of God

Roman Catholics generally hold religious beliefs similar to those of conservative Protestants, except on essentially Catholic issues such as papal infallibility (the authority of the spiritual role in all decisions regarding faith and morals). Whether or not there are four distinct camps is not important: The point is that the familiar practice of contrasting Roman Catholics and Protestants is clearly not productive. Some differences between Roman Catholics and Protestants are inconsequential compared with the differences between Protestant sects.

Secular criteria as well as doctrinal issues may distinguish religious faiths. Research has consistently shown that denominations can be arranged in a hierarchy based on social class. As Figure 5.8 reveals, members of certain faiths, such as Episcopalians, Jews, and Presbyterians, have a higher proportion of affluent members. Members of other faiths, including Baptists, tend to be poorer. Of course, all Protestant groups draw members from each social stratum. Nonetheless, the social significance of these class differences is that religion becomes a mechanism for signaling social mobility. A person who is moving up in wealth and power may seek out a faith associated with a higher social ranking. Similar contrasts are shown in formal schooling in Figure 5.9.

Protestant faiths have been diversifying, and many of their members have been leaving them for churches that follow strict codes of behavior or fundamental interpretations of Biblical teachings. This trend is reflected in the decline of the five mainline churches: Baptist, Episcopalian, Lutheran, Methodist, and Presbyterian. In 2004, these faiths accounted for about 34 percent of total membership, compared with 75 percent in the 1970s. With a broader acceptance of new faiths and continuing immigration, it is unlikely that these mainline churches will regain their dominance in the near future (Davis, Smith, and Marsden 2005, 170).

Although Protestants may seem to define the civil religion and the accepted dominant orientation, some Christian faiths feel they, too, experience the discrimination

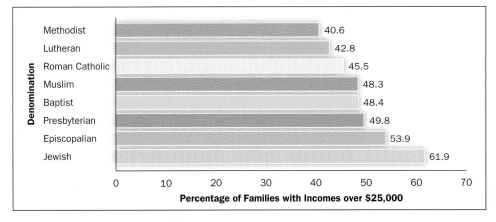

FIGURE 5.8 Income and Denominations

Denominations attract different income groups. All groups have both affluent and poor members, yet some have a higher proportion of members with high incomes and others are comparatively poor.

Source: General social survey, 1994 through 2004. See Davis, Smith, and Marsden 2005.

usually associated with non-Christians such as Jews and Muslims. For example, representatives of the liberal and moderate faiths dominate the leadership of the military's chaplain corps. For example, there are 16 Presbyterian soldiers for every Presbyterian chaplain, 121 Full Gospel worshippers for every Full Gospel chaplain, and 339 Muslim soldiers for every Muslim chaplain (Cooperman 2005).

As another example of denominational discrimination, in 1998 the Southern Baptist Convention amended its basic theological statements of beliefs to include a strong statement on family life. However, the statement included a declaration that a woman should "submit herself graciously" to her husband's leadership. There were widespread attacks on this position, which many Baptists felt was inappropriate because they were offering guidance for their denomination's members. In some respects, Baptists felt this was a form of respectable bigotry. It was acceptable to attack them for their views on social issues even though such criticism would be much more muted for many more liberal faiths that seem free to tolerate abortion (Bowman 1998; Niebuhr 1998).

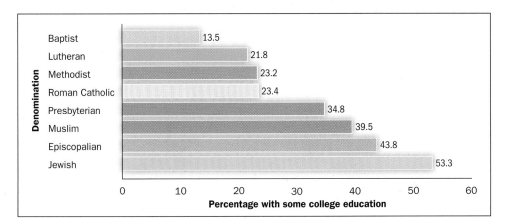

FIGURE 5.9 Education and Denominations

There are sharp differences in the proportion of those with some college education by denomination.

Source: General social survey, 1994 through 2004. See Davis et al. 2005.

Women and Religion

Religious beliefs have often placed women in an exalted but protected position. As religions are practiced, this position has often meant being "protected" from becoming leaders. Perhaps the only major exception in the United States is the Christian Science church, in which the majority of practitioners and readers are women. Women may be evangelists, prophets, and even saints, but they find it difficult to enter the clergy within their own congregations.

Even today, the largest denomination in the United States, Roman Catholicism, does not permit women to be priests. A 2005 national survey found that 62 percent of Roman Catholics in this country favor the ordination of women, compared with only 29 percent in 1974 but the church hierarchy has continued to maintain its long-standing requirement that priests be male (Briggs 1996; Snyder 2006).

The largest Protestant denomination, the Southern Baptist Convention, has voted against ordaining women (although some of its autonomous churches have women ministers). Other religious faiths that do not allow women clergy include the Lutheran Church—Missouri Synod, the Greek Orthodox Archdiocese of North and South America, the Orthodox Church in America, the Church of God in Christ, the Church of Jesus Christ of Latter-Day Saints, and Orthodox Judaism.

Despite these restrictions, there has been a notable rise in female clergy in the last twenty years. The Bureau of the Census (2005a) shows that 6 percent of clergy were women in 1983, but that figure had increased to 14 percent in 2005. Increasingly, some branches of Protestantism and Judaism have been convinced that women have the right to become spiritual leaders. Yet a lingering question remains: Once women are ordained as spiritual leaders, do congregations necessarily accept these female ministers and rabbis? Will they advance in their calling as easily as

Women play a significant role as unpaid volunteers, but relatively few become members of the clergy with leadership responsibilities. Pictured is Barbara Harris as she was ordained the first female bishop in the Episcopalian Church in 1989.

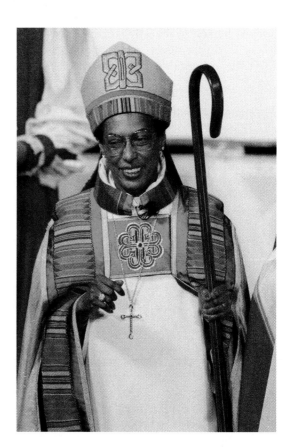

their male counterparts, or will they face blatant or subtle discrimination in their efforts to secure desirable posts within their faiths?

It is too early to offer any definitive answers to these questions, but thus far, women clearly continue to face lingering sexism after ordination. Evidence to date indicates that women find it more difficult than men to secure jobs in larger, more prestigious congregations. Although they may be accepted as junior clergy or as copastors, women may fail to receive senior clergy appointments. A national study found that 70 percent of men had moved on to midsize or larger congregations by their second decade compared to only 37 percent of the women. In both Reform and Conservative Judaism, the largest and best-known congregations rarely hire women rabbis. Consequently, women clergy in many denominations are gathered at the low end of the pay scale and the hierarchy (Banerjee 2006; Chang 1997; Religion Watch 1995a).

Religion and the U.S. Supreme Court

Religious pluralism owes its existence in the United States to the First Amendment declaration that "Congress shall make no law respecting an establishment of religion, or prohibiting the free exercise thereof." The U.S. Supreme Court has consistently interpreted this wording to mean not that government should ignore religion but that it should follow a policy of neutrality to maximize religious freedom. For example, the government may not help religion by financing a new church building, but it also may not obstruct religion by denying a church adequate police and fire protection. We will examine four issues that continue to require clarification: school prayer, secessionist minorities, creationism (including intelligent design), and the public display of religious symbols.

Among the most controversial and continuing disputes has been whether prayer has a role in the schools. Many people were disturbed by the 1962 Supreme Court decision in *Engel v. Vitale* that disallowed a purportedly nondenominational prayer drafted for use in the New York public schools. The prayer was "Almighty God, we acknowledge our dependence upon Thee, and we beg Thy blessings upon us, our

secessionist minority
Groups, such as the Amish, that reject both assimilation and coexistence.

creationists
People who support a literal interpretation of the biblical book of Genesis on the origins of the universe and argue that evolution should not be presented as established scientific thought.

parents, our teachers, and our country." Subsequent decisions overturned state laws requiring Bible reading in public schools, laws requiring recitation of the Lord's Prayer, and laws permitting a daily one-minute period of silent meditation or prayer. Despite such judicial pronouncements, children in many public schools in the United States are led in regular prayer recitation or Bible reading.

What about prayers at public gatherings? In 1992, the Supreme Court ruled 5–4 in *Lee v. Weisman* that prayer at a junior high school graduation in Providence, Rhode Island, violated the U.S. Constitution's mandate of separation of church and state. A rabbi had given thanks to God in his invocation. The district court suggested that the invocation would have been acceptable without that reference. The Supreme Court did not agree with the school board that a prayer at a graduation was not coercive. The Court did say in its opinion that it was acceptable for a student speaker voluntarily to say a prayer at such a program (Marshall 2001).

Several religious groups have been in legal and social conflict with the rest of society. Some can be called **secessionist minorities** in that they reject both assimilation and coexistence in some form of cultural pluralism. The Amish are one such group that comes into conflict with outside society because of its beliefs and way of life. The Old Order Amish shun most modern conveniences, and later in this chapter we will consider them as a case study of maintaining a lifestyle dramatically different from that of larger society.

Are there limits to the free exercise of religious rituals by secessionist minorities? Today, tens of thousands of members of Native American religions believe that ingesting the powerful drug peyote is a sacrament and that those who partake of peyote will enter into direct contact with God. In 1990, the Supreme Court ruled that prosecuting people who use illegal drugs as part of a religious ritual is not a violation of the First Amendment guarantee of religious freedom. The case arose because Native Americans were dismissed from their jobs for the religious use of peyote and were then refused unemployment benefits by the State of Oregon's employment division. In 1991, however, Oregon enacted a new law permitting the sacramental use of peyote by Native Americans (*New York Times* 1991).

In another ruling on religious rituals, in 1993, the Supreme Court unanimously overturned a local ordinance in Florida that banned ritual animal sacrifice. The High Court held that this law violated the free-exercise rights of adherents of the Santeria religion, in which the sacrifice of animals (including goats, chickens, and other birds) plays a central role. The same year Congress passed the Religious Freedom Restoration Act, which said the government may not enforce laws that "substantially burden" the exercise of religion. Presumably, this action will give religious groups more flexibility in practicing their faiths. However, many local and state officials are concerned that the law has led to unintended consequences, such as forcing states to accommodate prisoners' requests for questionable religious activities or to permit a church to expand into a historic district in defiance of local laws (Greenhouse 1996).

The third area of contention has been whether the biblical account of creation should be or must be presented in school curricula and whether this account should receive the same emphasis as scientific theories. In the famous "monkey trial" of 1925, Tennessee schoolteacher John Scopes was found guilty of teaching the scientific theory of evolution in public schools. Since then, however, Darwin's evolutionary theories have been presented in public schools with little reference to the biblical account in Genesis. People who support the literal interpretation of the Bible, commonly known as **creationists**, have formed various organizations to crusade for creationist treatment in U.S. public schools and universities.

In a 1987 Louisiana case, *Edwards v. Aguillard*, the Supreme Court ruled that states may not require the teaching of creationism alongside evolution in public schools if the primary purpose of such legislation is to promote a religious viewpoint. Neverthe-

 ASK Yourself

What is meant by creationism? Intelligent Design?

less, the teaching of evolution and creationism has remained a controversial issue in many communities across the United States (Applebome 1996).

Beginning in the 1980s, those who believe in a divine hand in the creation of life have advanced **intelligent design** (ID). Although not explicitly drawn on the biblical account, creationists feel comfortable with ID. Intelligent design is the idea that life is so complex it could only have been created by a higher intelligence. Supporters of ID advocate it is a more accurate account than Darwinism or, at the very least, that it be taught as an alternative alongside the theory of evolution. In 2005 a federal judge in *Kitzmiller v. Dove Area School District* ended a Pennsylvania school district intention to require the presentation of ID. In essence the judge found ID to be "a religious belief" that was only a subtler way of finding God's fingerprints in nature than traditional creationism. Because the issue continues to be hotly debated, future court cases are certain to come (Clemmitt 2005; Goodstein 2005).

The fourth area of contention has been a battle over public displays that depict symbols of or seem associated with a religion. Can manger scenes be erected on public property? Do people have a right to be protected from large displays such as a cross or a star atop a water tower overlooking an entire town? In a series of decisions in the 1980s through to 1995, the Supreme Court ruled that tax-supported religious displays on public government property may be successfully challenged but are not permissible if they are made more secular. Displays that combine a crèche, the Christmas manger scene depicting the birth of Jesus, or the Hanukkah menorah and also include Frosty the Snowman or even Christmas trees have been ruled secular. These decisions have been dubbed "the plastic reindeer rules." In 1995, the Court clarified the issue by stating that privately sponsored religious displays may be allowed on public property if other forms of expression are permitted in the same location. The final judicial word has not been heard, and all these rulings should be viewed as tentative because the Court cases have been decided by close votes. Changes in the Supreme Court composition also may alter the outcome of future cases (Bork 1995; Hirsley 1991; Mauro 1995).

Limits of Religious Freedom: The Amish

The Amish began migrating to North America early in the eighteenth century and settled first in eastern Pennsylvania, where a large settlement is still found. Those who continued the characteristic lifestyle of the Amish are primarily members of the Old Order Amish Mennonite Church. By 2003, there were about 1,400 Old Order Amish settlements in the United States and Canada. Estimates place this faith at about 180,000, with approximately 75 percent living in three states: Ohio, Pennsylvania, and Indiana.

The Amish Way of Life

Amish practice self-segregation, living in settlements divided into church districts that are autonomous congregations composed of about 75 baptized members. If the district becomes much larger, it is again divided because the members meet in each other's homes. There are no church buildings. Amish homes are large, with the main floor often having removable walls so a household can take its periodic turn hosting the Sunday service.

Each Amish district has a bishop, two to four preachers, and an elder but there are no general conferences, mission groups, or cooperative agencies. The Amish differ little from the Mennonites in formal religious doctrine. Holy Communion is celebrated twice each year, and both groups practice washing of feet. Adults are baptized when they are admitted to formal membership in the church at about age 17 to 20. Old Order Amish services are conducted in German with a mixture of English, commonly known as Pennsylvania Dutch (from *Deutsch,* the German word for "German").

intelligent design
View that life is so complex that it must have been created by a higher intelligence.

The Amish are best known for their plain clothing and their nonconformist way of life. Sociologists sometimes use the term *secessionist minorities* to refer to groups such as the Amish, who reject assimilation and practice coexistence or pluralism with the rest of society primarily on their own terms. The practice of *Meidung*, or shunning, persists, and sociologists view it as central to the Amish system of social control. The social norms of this secessionist minority that have evolved over the years are known as the *Ordnung*. These "understandings" specify the color and style of clothing, color and style of buggies, the use of horses for fieldwork, the use of the Pennsylvania Dutch dialect, worship services in the homes, unison singing without instruments, and marriage within the church, to name a few.

The Amish shun telephones and electric lights, and they drive horses and buggies rather than automobiles. The *Ordnung* also prohibits filing a lawsuit, entering military service, divorce, using air transportation, and even using wall-to-wall carpeting. They are generally considered excellent farmers, but they often refuse to use modern farm machinery. Concessions have been made but do vary from one Amish settlement to another. Among common exceptions to the *Ordnung* is the use of chemical fertilizers, insecticides, and pesticides, the use of indoor bathroom facilities, and modern medical and dental practice.

The Amish and Larger Society

The Amish have made some concessions to the dominant society, but larger society has made concessions to the Amish to facilitate their lifestyle. For example, the 1972 U.S. Supreme Court, in *Yoder v. Wisconsin*, allowed Wisconsin Amish to escape prosecution from laws that required parents to send their children to school to age 18. Amish education ends at about age 13 because the community feels their members have received all the schooling necessary to prosper as Amish people. States waive certification requirements for Amish teaching staff (who are other Amish people), minimum wage requirements for the teachers, and school building requirements.

The Amish today do not totally reject social change. For example, until the late 1960s, church members could be excommunicated for being employed in other than agricultural pursuits. Now their work is much more diversified. Although you will not find Amish computer programmers, there are Amish engaged as blacksmiths, harness makers, buggy repairers, and carpenters. Non-Amish often hire these craftspeople as well.

The movement by the Amish into other occupations is sometimes a source of tension with larger society, or the "English," as the Amish refer to non-Amish people. Conflict theorists observe that as long as the Amish remained totally apart from dominant society in the United States, they experienced little hostility. As they entered the larger economic sector, however, intergroup tensions developed in the form of growing prejudice. The Amish today may underbid their competitors. The Amish entry into the commercial marketplace has also strained the church's traditional teaching on litigation and insurance, both of which are to be avoided. Mutual assistance has been the historical path taken, but that does not always mesh well with the modern businessperson. After legal action taken on their behalf, Amish businesses typically have been allowed to be exempt from paying Social Security and workers' compensation, another sore point with English competitors.

The Amish entrepreneur represents an interesting variation of the typical ethnic businessperson one might encounter in a Chinatown, for example. Research on ethnic businesses often cites discrimination against minorities and immigrants as a prime force prodding the development of minority enterprises. The Amish are a very different case because their own restrictions on education, factory work, and certain occupations have propelled them into becoming small business owners.

The Amish, as shown in this group of young women on a farm in Kentucky, have made relatively few accommodations with the larger culture—the culture of outsiders referred collectively to by the Amish as the "English."

However, stratification is largely absent among the Old Order Amish. The notion of ethclass would have no meaning, as the Amish truly regard one another as equal.

Children are not sent to high schools. This practice caused the Amish some difficulty because of compulsory school attendance laws, and some Amish parents have gone to jail rather than allow their children to go to high school. Eventually, as noted earlier, the Supreme Court, in *Yoder v. Wisconsin,* upheld a lower court's decision that a Wisconsin compulsory education law violated the Amish right to religious freedom. However, not all court rulings have been friendly to Amish efforts to avoid the practices and customs of the English. In another case, the effort by the Amish to avoid using the legally mandated orange triangles for marking slow-moving vehicles (such as their buggies) was rejected. If you travel through Amish areas, you can now see their horse-drawn buggies displaying this one symbol of modernity.

Living alongside this modernity, Amish youth often test their subculture's boundaries during a period of discovery called *rumspringe,* a term that means "running around." Amish young people attend barn dances where taboos like drinking, smoking, and driving cars are commonly broken. Parents often react by looking the other way, sometimes literally. For example, when they hear radio sounds from a barn or motorcycle entering their property in the middle of the night, they don't immediately investigate and punish their offspring. Instead, they pretend not to notice, secure in the comfort that their children almost always return to the traditions of the Amish lifestyle. In 2004, UPN aired the "Amish in the City" reality program featuring five Amish youths allegedly on *rumspringe* moving in with six city-wise young adults in Los Angeles. Critics on behalf of the Amish community noted that this exploitation showed how vulnerable the Amish are, since no program was developed to try to show the conversion of Muslim or Orthodox Jewish youth.

A growing area of Amish–English legal clashes is over the custom of young Amish children working as laborers. Amish families in western and central Pennsylvania in 1998 protested the federal government's enforcement of labor laws that are intended to protect children from workplace hazards. The Amish are turning to new businesses, such as sawmills and wood shops, as their available farmland begins to disappear. That means more children on the shop floor. The Amish contend that their religious and cultural traditions hold that children should work, but the U.S. Labor Department had taken a different view. The Amish argued that letting children work alongside their fathers instills core values of hard work, diligence, cooperation, and responsibility, values that they say are central to their faith. English businesses see this underage employment as another form of unfair competition by the Amish. In 2004, Congress passed the law with the Amish in mind that exempted such child labor as long as machinery is not operated and adults are present.

The Old Order Amish have developed a pluralistic position that has become increasingly difficult to maintain as their numbers grow and as they enter the economy in competition with the English, or the non-Amish (Dart 1998; *The Economist* 2004a; Kraybill 2001, 2003; Kraybill and Nolt 1995; Public Broadcasting System 1998).

Conclusion

Considering ethnicity and religion reinforces our understanding of the patterns of intergroup relations first presented in Chapter 1. Figure 5.10 shows the rich variety of relationships as defined by people's ethnic and religious identity. The profiles of Irish, Italian, and Polish Americans reflect the variety of White ethnic experiences.

Any study of life in the United States, but especially one focusing on dominant and subordinate groups, cannot ignore religion and ethnicity. The two are closely related, as certain religious faiths predominate in certain nationalities. Both religious activity and interest by White ethnics in their heritage continue to be prominent features of the contemporary scene. People have been and continue to be ridiculed or deprived of opportunities solely because of their ethnic or religious affiliation. To get a true picture of people's place in society, we need to consider both ethnicity and social class (or what has been called ethclass) in association with their religious identification.

Religion is changing in the United States. As one commercial measure, Hallmark created its first greeting card in 2003 for the Muslim holiday Eid-al-fitr, which marks the end of the monthlong feast of Ramadan. The issue of the persistence of ethnicity is an intriguing one. Some people may only casually exhibit their ethnicity and practice what has been called symbolic ethnicity. However, can people immerse themselves in their ethnic culture without society punishing them for their will to be different? The tendency to put down White ethnics through respectable bigotry continues. Despite this intolerance, ethnicity remains a viable source of identity for many citizens today. There is also the ethnicity paradox, which finds that practicing one's ethnic heritage often strengthens people and allows them to move successfully into the larger society.

The issue of religious expression in all its forms also raises a variety of intriguing questions. How can a country increasingly populated by diverse and often non-Christian faiths maintain religious tolerance? How might this change in decades ahead? How will the courts and society resolve the issues of religious freedom? This is a particularly important issue in such areas as school

FIGURE 5.10 **Intergroup Relations Continuum**

prayer, secessionist minorities, creationism, intelligent design, and public religious displays. Some examination of religious ties is fundamental to completing an accurate picture of a person's social identity.

Ethnicity and religion are a basic part of today's social reality and of each individual's identity. The emotions, disputes, and debate over religion and ethnicity in the United States are powerful indeed.

Key Terms

bilingual education 143
bilingualism 143
civil religion 152
creationists 158
denomination 147

English immersion 144
ethclass 152
ethnicity paradox 129
intelligent design 159
life chances 151

principle of third-generation
  interest 127
respectable bigotry 130
secessionist minority 158
symbolic ethnicity 128

Review Questions

1. In what respects are ethnic and religious diversity in the United States related to each other?
2. Is assimilation automatic within any given ethnic group?
3. Apply "Whiteness" to Irish, Italian, and Polish Americans.
4. To what extent has a non-Christian tradition been developing in the United States?
5. How have court rulings affected religious expression?

Critical Thinking

1. When do you see ethnicity becoming more apparent? When does it appear to occur only in response to other people's advancing their own ethnicity? From these situations, how can ethnic identity be both positive and perhaps counterproductive or even destructive?
2. Why do you think we are so often reluctant to show our religion to others? Why might people of certain faiths be more hesitant than others?
3. How does religion reflect conservative and liberal positions on social issues? Consider services for the homeless, the need for child care, the acceptance or rejection of gay men and lesbians, and a woman's right to terminate a pregnancy versus the fetus's right to survive.

Internet Connections—Research Navigator™

Follow the instructions found on page 35 of this text to access the features of Research Navigator™. Once at the Web site, enter your Login Name and Password. Then, to use the ContentSelect database, enter keywords such as "Mormons," "Amish," and "Whiteness studies," and the research engine will supply relevant and recent scholarly and popular press publications. Use the *New York Times* Search-by-Subject Archive to find recent news articles related to sociology and the Link Library feature to locate relevant Web links organized by the key terms associated with this chapter.

6 The Native Americans

CHAPTER OUTLINE

Early European Contacts

Treaties and Warfare

Ruling the Native Americans

Reservation Life and Federal Policies

Collective Action

Sovereignty

Native Americans Today

■ RESEARCH FOCUS
Learning the Navajo Way

■ LISTEN TO OUR VOICES
"The Scalpel and the Silver Bear"
by Lori Arviso Alvord

Conclusion

Key Terms/Review Questions/
Critical Thinking/Internet Connections—
Research Navigator™

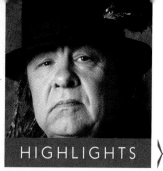
T HE ORIGINAL INHABITANTS OF NORTH AMERICA WERE THE first to be subordinated by the Europeans. The Native Americans who survived contact with the Non-Indian people usually were removed, often far away, from their ancestral homes. The U.S. government weakened tribal institutions through a succession of acts, beginning with the Allotment Act of 1887. Even efforts to strengthen tribal autonomy, such as the 1934 Reorganization Act, did so by encouraging Native Americans to adopt White society's way of life. The modern period of Native American–Non-Indian relations is much the same, as shown by such measures as the Termination Act and the Employment Assistance Program. Today, the pan-Indian movements speak for a diverse Native American people with many needs: settlement of treaty violations, economic development, improved educational programs, effective health care, religious and spiritual freedom, control over natural resources, and greater self-rule.

The computer says "Zik" followed by "Cax sep." This is not the latest space adventure from the local arcade but instead the words for "squirrel" and "eagle" as spoken by a Ho-Chunk elder. Preschoolers gather around the computer at a Head Start program in Wisconsin, where Ho-Chunk children learn the language of their tribe. The Ho-Chunk, formerly known as the Winnebago tribe, are using modern technology to keep their language and, therefore, their culture alive. The challenge is immense, as Two Bears, an anthropologist who works at the tribe's cultural center, observes:

> There was a whole generation by the 1980s that didn't know a word. Turning that around will be a long process—we figure it'll take two years to advance our language curriculum up one grade level in the schools that Ho-chunk kids attend. (Salopek 1996, 2)

It is critical to use schools to restore the Ho-Cak language of the Ho-Chunk people. Only 350 of the 6,200 tribal members speak their language fluently, and none of them have young children of their own (Kozlowicz 2001).

The concern of the Ho-Chunk tribal elders is also faced by most of the tribes in the United States. It is estimated that children are actively learning only 20 of the surviving 154 Native American languages. While much of the country debates the need for a larger percentage of new immigrants to master English, the first Americans' major concern is maintaining the tie to their linguistic past and making it a viable part of the present. In Chicago, adult students gather to learn the languages of their tribes, Kalota and Ojibwee, and in Window Rock, Arizona, the 1996 Super Bowl was broadcast in Navajo for the first time. All these efforts and many more are aimed at maintaining tribal identity within American society (Brooke 1998; Mitchel 1996; Reyhner 2001a).

Education on reservations stresses American Indian and tribal culture more than in the past. Pictured is a classroom on the Crow Reservation in Montana.

Although our focus in this chapter is on the Native American experience in the United States, the pattern of land seizure, subjugation, assimilation, and resistance to domination has been repeated with indigenous people in nations throughout the world. Indeed, in Chapter 16, we will consider the experiences of the tribal people in Mexico and Canada. Hawaiians, another native people who fell under the political, economic, and cultural control of the United States, are considered in Chapter 12. Indigenous peoples on almost every continent are familiar with the patterns of subjugation and the pressure to assimilate. So widespread is this oppression that the United Nations (1997) and even its precursor organization, the League of Nations, have repeatedly considered this issue.

The common term *American Indians* tells us more about the Europeans who explored North America than it does about the native people. The label reflects the initial explorers' confusion in believing that they had arrived in "the Indies" of the Asian continent. However, reference to the diversity of tribal groups either by American Indians or Native Americans comes as a result of the forced subordination to the dominant group.

It is estimated that there were 2,357,544 Native Americans/Alaskan natives in the United States in 2006. This represents an increase of about 40 percent over the 1990s. In addition to this 2.4 million people who gave American Indian or Alaskan Native as their sole racial identification, there were another 1.4 million people who listed multiple responses that included American Indian. As was shown in Figure 1.8, American Indian and White was the most common dual racial response given in Census 2000 (American Community Survey 2006).

Early European Contacts

The Native Americans have been misunderstood and ill-treated by their conquerors for several centuries. Assuming that he had reached the Indies, Christopher Columbus called them "people of India." The European immigrants who followed Columbus did not understand them any more than the Native Americans could have anticipated the destruction of their way of life. But the Europeans had superior weaponry, and the diseases they brought wiped out huge numbers of indigenous people throughout the Western Hemisphere.

The first explorers of the Western Hemisphere came long before Columbus and Leif Eriksson. The ancestors of today's Native Americans were hunters in search of wild game, including mammoths and long-horned bison. For thousands of years, these people spread through the Western Hemisphere, adapting to its many physical environments. Hundreds of cultures evolved, including the complex societies of the Maya, Inca, and Aztec (Deloria 1995, 2004).

It is beyond the scope of this chapter to describe the many tribal cultures of North America, let alone the ways of life of Native Americans in Central and South America and the islands of the Caribbean. We must appreciate that the term *Indian culture* is a convenient way to gloss over the diversity of cultures, languages, religions, kinship systems, and political organizations that existed—and, in many instances, remain—among the peoples referred to collectively as Native Americans or American Indians. For example, in 1500, an estimated 700 distinct languages were spoken in the area north of Mexico. For simplicity's sake, we will refer to these many cultures as Native American, but we must be always mindful of the differences this term conceals. Similarly, we will refer to non–Native Americans as Non-Indians recognizing in this context this term encompasses many groups, including Whites, African Americans, and Hispanics in some instances (J. Schwartz 1994; Swagerty 1983).

Columbus commented in his diary, "It appears to me that the people [of the New World] are ingenious and would be good servants. . . . These people are very unskilled in arms. . . . With fifty men they could all be subjected to do all that one wishes" (Akwesasne Notes 1972, 22). The words of the first European explorer were prophetic. The period between initial European contact and the formation of the United States was characterized by cultural and physical conflict between Native Americans and Whites.

The number of Native Americans north of the Rio Grande, estimated at about 10 million in 1500, gradually decreased as their food sources disappeared and they fell victim to diseases such as measles, smallpox, and influenza. By 1800 the Native American population was about 600,000, and by 1900 it had been reduced to less than 250,000. This loss of human life can only be judged as catastrophic. The United States does not bear total responsibility. The pattern had been well established by the early Spaniards in the Southwest and by the French and English colonists who sought to gain control of the eastern seaboard. As Figure 6.1 reminds us, there were many tribal nations here for many centuries before European contact (Edmonds 1995).

Native Americans did have warfare between tribes, which presumably reduces the guilt for European-initiated warfare. However, their conflicts differed significantly from those of the conquerors. The Europeans launched large campaigns against the tribes, resulting in mass mortality. In contrast, in the Americas, the tribes limited warfare to specific campaigns designed for very specific purposes, such as recapturing a resource or avenging a loss.

Not all the initial contacts led to deliberate loss of life. Some missionaries traveled well in advance of settlement in efforts to Christianize the Native Americans before they came into contact with other less-tolerant Europeans. Fur trappers, vastly outnumbered by Native Americans, were forced to learn their customs, but these trappers established routes of commerce that more and more Whites were to follow (Snipp 1989; Swagerty 1983; Thornton 1991).

Gradually, the policies directed from Europe toward the indigenous peoples of North America resembled the approach described in the world systems theory. As introduced in Chapter 1, the **world systems theory** takes the view that the global economic system is divided between nations that control wealth and those that provide natural resources and labor. The indigenous peoples and, more important to the Europeans, the land they occupied were regarded as targets of exploitation by Spain, England, France, Portugal, and other nations with experience as colonizers in Africa and Asia (Chase-Dunn and Hall 1998).

Treaties and Warfare

The United States formulated a policy during the nineteenth century toward Native Americans that followed the precedents established during the colonial period. The government policy was not to antagonize the Native Americans unnecessarily. Yet if the needs of tribes interfered with the needs, or even the whims, of Whites, Whites were to have precedence. For example, the exploits of the Forty-Niners, the nineteenth-century gold miners in northern California, have been long glorified. However, 150,000 native people inhabited the areas they entered near Sacramento. Authorities offered bounties to the settlers for the heads of American Indians, and the state spent about $1 million to reimburse people for the bullets used to shoot them. Within twenty-five years, the native population had plummeted to about 30,000 (Ybarra 1996).

By this time, the tribes were viewed as separate nations, to be dealt with by treaties arrived at through negotiations with the federal government. Fair-minded as that policy might seem, it was clear from the very beginning that the Non-Indian people's gov-

world systems theory
A view of the global economic system as divided between nations that control wealth and those that provide natural resources and labor.

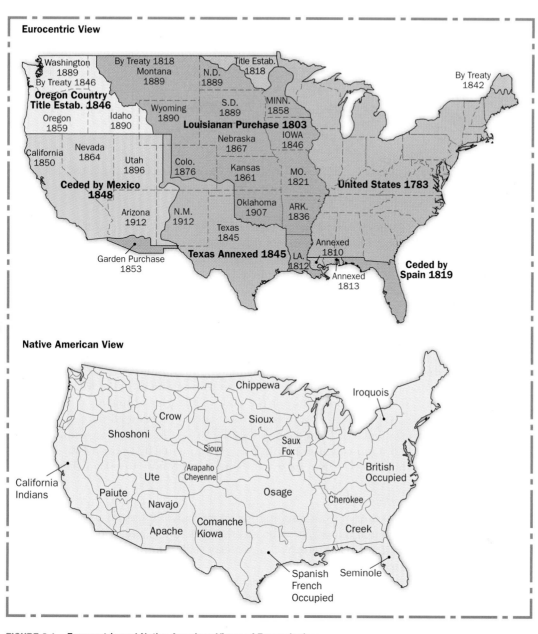

FIGURE 6.1 **Eurocentric and Native American Views of Expansionism**

Students typically are presented with a view that the United States gained its lands through settlement and from Mexico, Spain, France, and Great Britain. This depiction glosses over the land held by tribal groups.

Source: Maps from *Atlas of American History*, © 1993 by Rand McNally, R.L. #04-S-104. Reprinted by permission of Rand McNally.

ernment would deal harshly with the tribal groups that refused to agree to treaties. Federal relations with the Native Americans were the responsibility of the secretary of war. Consequently, when the Bureau of Indian Affairs was created in 1824 to coordinate the government's relations with the tribes, it was placed in the War Department. The government's primary emphasis was on maintaining peace and friendly relations along the frontier. Nevertheless, as settlers moved the frontier westward, they encroached more and more on land that Native Americans had inhabited for centuries.

By Jeff Kerr © 1999 *Indian Country Today.*

The Indian Removal Act, passed in 1830, called for the relocation of all Eastern tribes across the Mississippi River. The Removal Act was very popular with Whites because it opened more land to settlement through annexation of tribal land. Almost all Whites felt that the Native Americans had no right to block progress, defining progress as movement by White society. Among the largest groups relocated were the five tribes of the Creek, Choctaw, Chickasaw, Cherokee, and Seminole, who were resettled in what is now Oklahoma. The movement, lasting more than a decade, has been called the Trail of Tears because the tribes left their ancestral lands under the harshest conditions. Poor planning, corrupt officials, little attention to those ill from a variety of epidemics, and inadequate supplies characterized the forced migration (Remini 2001).

The Removal Act disrupted Native American cultures but didn't move the tribes far enough or fast enough to stay out of the path of the ever-advancing White settlers. After the Civil War, settlers moved westward at an unprecedented pace. The federal government negotiated with the many tribes but primarily enacted legislation that affected them with minimal consultation. The government's first priority was almost always to allow the settlers to live and work regardless of Native American claims.

The Case of the Sioux

The nineteenth century was devastating for every Native American tribe in the areas claimed by the United States. No tribe was the same after federal policy touched it. The treatment of the Great Sioux Nation was especially cruel and remains fresh in the minds of tribal members even today.

In an effort to safeguard White settlers, the United States signed the Fort Laramie Treaty of 1868 with the Sioux, then under the leadership of Red Cloud. The government agreed to keep Whites from hunting or settling on the newly established Great Sioux Reservation, which included all of the land that is now South Dakota west of the Missouri River. In exchange, the Sioux relinquished most of the remaining land they occupied at that time. The first few years saw relative peace, except for some raids by warrior bands under the leadership of medicine man Sitting Bull. Red Cloud even made a much-publicized trip to Washington and New York in 1870.

A flood of Non-Indian people eventually entered the Sioux territory, spurred on by Colonel George Custer's exaggerated 1874 reports of gold in the Black Hills. Hostilities followed, and bands of Native Americans were ordered to move during the winter, when travel was impossible. When the Sioux failed to move, Custer moved in to pacify them and the neighboring Cheyenne. Relying on Crow scouts, Custer underestimated the strength of the Sioux warriors under the leadership of Crazy Horse. The ensuing Battle of the Little Big Horn in 1876 was the last great Sioux victory. After the battle, the large encampment of warriors scattered throughout the plains into small bands, which were defeated one by one by a Congress and an Army more determined than ever to subdue the Sioux.

In this famous Alexander Gardner photograph at the time of the 1868 Fort Laramie Treaty talks the military leaders are identified by name, shown sitting on chairs, and facing the camera. Reflecting the hierarchy of the situation, tribal leaders are not identified, seated on the ground and with their backs to the camera.

In 1876, the Sioux reluctantly sold the Black Hills and agreed to the reduction of the Great Sioux Reservation to five much smaller ones. The Sioux, unable to hunt game as they traditionally had, found life unbearable on the reservation. They sought escape through the supernatural: the Ghost Dance. The Ghost Dance was a religion that included dances and songs proclaiming the return of the buffalo and the resurrection of dead ancestors in a land free of Non-Indian people. The religion soon became what social scientists call a **millenarian movement**, a movement founded on the belief that a cataclysmic upheaval would occur in the immediate future, followed by collective salvation. The movement originated among the Paiutes of Nevada and, ironically, spread northward to the Plains Indians via the cornerstone of the government's assimilationist policy: the schools. The English that Native Americans learned in the mission or government schools gave them the means to overcome the barriers of tribal languages and communicate with one another. By 1890, about 65 percent of the tribes in the West, according to sociologist Russell Thornton (1981), were involved in this movement.

From a functionalist perspective, this millenarian movement can be viewed as a means of coping with the domination of Non-Indian intruders. Although the Ghost Dance was harmless to Whites, they feared that the new tribal solidarity encouraged by the movement would lead to renewed warfare. As a result, more troops were summoned to areas where the Ghost Dance had become popular.

In late December 1890, anticipating that a massive Ghost Dance would be staged, a cavalry division arrived at an encampment of Teton Sioux at Wounded Knee Creek on the Pine Ridge, South Dakota, reservation. When the soldiers began to disarm the warriors, a random shot was fired at the soldiers, touching off a close-range battle. The cavalry then turned its artillery on men, women, and children. Approximately 300 Sioux and 25 government soldiers were killed in the ensuing fighting, which is now called the Battle of Wounded Knee. One Sioux witness later recalled, "We tried to run, but they shot us like we were a buffalo. I know there are some good white people, but the soldiers must be mean to shoot children and women" (D. Brown 1971, 417).

For the federal government, what it considered the Indian problem remained. Despite the effects of disease and warfare, nearly 250,000 Indians still lived, according to the 1890 census. The reservation system constructed in the last decades of the nineteenth century to provide settlements for Native American peoples has formed the basis of the relationship of Native Americans to the government from then until the present.

millenarian movements
Movements, such as the Ghost Dance, that prophesy a cataclysm in the immediate future, to be followed by collective salvation.

internal colonialism
The treatment of subordinate peoples as colonial subjects by those in power.

Ruling the Native Americans

Along with the military defeat of the tribes, the federal government tried to limit the functions of tribal leaders. If tribal institutions were weakened, it was felt, the Native Americans would assimilate more rapidly. The government's intention to merge the various tribes into White society was unmistakably demonstrated in the 1887 Dawes, or General Allotment, Act. This failure to assist Native American people was followed by a somewhat more admirable effort: the Indian Reorganization Act of 1934. The Allotment Act and the Reorganization Act established the government's paternalistic approach.

The more significant federal actions that continue up to the present are summarized in Table 6.1.

These early policies also reflect the oppression of **internal colonialism**. As we presented in Chapter 1, internal colonialism is the treatment of subordinate groups like colonial subjects by those in power. Native Americans found themselves to be the subordinate group on land that they once occupied alone. Now they were being treated like a colonized people by the newly formed government, which itself had successfully broken from the colonial hold of Great Britain. Ironically, the former colony was practicing internal colonialism toward the indigenous people of the new land.

The Allotment Act

The Allotment Act of 1887 bypassed tribal leaders and proposed to make individual landowners of tribal members. Each family was given up to 160 acres under the government's assumption that, with land, they would become more like the White homesteaders who were then flooding the not-yet-settled areas of the West.

The effect of the Allotment Act on the Native Americans was disastrous. To guarantee that they would remain homesteaders, the act prohibited their selling the land for 25 years. Yet no effort was made to acquaint them with the skills necessary to make the land productive. Many tribes were not accustomed to cultivating land and, if anything, considered such labor undignified, and they received no assistance in adapting to homesteading.

TABLE 6.1
Major Federal Policies

Year	Policy	Central Feature
1830	Removal Act	Relocated Eastern tribes westward
1887	Allotment Act	Tribal lands subdivided into individual household plots
1934	Reorganization Act	Required tribes to develop election-based governments and leaders
1934	Johnson-O'Malley Act	Aid to public school districts with Native American enrollments
1946	Indian Claims Commission	Adjudicates litigation by tribes against the federal government
1952	Employment Assistance Program	Relocates reservation people to urban areas for jobs
1953	Termination Act	Closes reservations and their federal services
1971	Alaska Native Settlement Act	Recognizes legally the lands of tribal people
1986	Indian Gaming Regulation Act	States can negotiate gaming rights to reservations
1990	Native American Graves and Repatriation Act	Return of native remains to tribes with authentic claims
1990	Indian Arts and Crafts Act	Monitors authenticity of crafts
1994	American Indian Religious Freedom Act	Seeks to protect tribal spirituality including use of peyote

Much of the land initially deeded under the Allotment Act eventually came into the possession of White landowners. The land could not be sold legally, but it could be leased with the Bureau of Indian Affairs (BIA) serving as the trustee. In this role, the federal government took legal title that included the duty to collect on behalf of the tribal members any revenues generated by non-Indians through mining, oil, timber operations, grazing, or similar activities. The failure of the government to carry this out has been an issue for well over a century.

Large parcels of land eventually fell into the possession of non-Indians. For Native Americans who managed to retain the land, the BIA required that, upon the death of the owner, the land be divided equally among all descendants, regardless of tribal inheritance customs. In documented cases, this division resulted in as many as 30 people trying to live off an 80-acre plot of worthless land. By 1934, Native Americans had lost approximately 90 million of the 138 million acres in their possession before the Allotment Act. The land left was generally considered worthless for farming and marginal even for ranching.

The sad legacy of the Allotment Act lives on in the *Corbell* lawsuit. This investigation into the government mishandling of billions of dollars of trust money will be considered later when we look at contemporary land claims (Blackfeet Reservation Development Fund 2006; Deloria and Lytle 1983).

The Reorganization Act

The assumptions behind the Allotment Act and the missionary activities of the nineteenth century were that it was best for Native Americans to assimilate into the White society, and each individual was best considered apart from his or her tribal identity. Very gradually, in the twentieth century, government officials have accepted the importance of tribal identity. The Indian Reorganization Act of 1934, known as the Wheeler-Howard Act, recognized the need to use, rather than ignore, tribal identity. But assimilation, rather than movement toward a pluralistic society, was still the goal.

Many provisions of the Reorganization Act, including revocation of the Allotment Act, benefited Native Americans. Still, given the legacy of broken treaties, many tribes at first distrusted the new policy. Under the Reorganization Act, tribes could adopt a written constitution and elect a tribal council with a head. This system imposed foreign values and structures. Under it, the elected tribal leader represented an entire reservation, which might include several tribes, some hostile to one another. Furthermore, the leader had to be elected by majority rule, a concept alien to many tribes. Many full-blooded Native Americans resented the provision that mixed-bloods were to have full voting rights. The Indian Reorganization Act did facilitate tribal dealings with government agencies, but the dictating to Native Americans of certain procedures common to White society and alien to the tribes was another sign of forced assimilation.

Tribal people have generally been supportive of a strong military. Fittingly, the first casualty of the War in Iraq was Lori Pestewa, shown on the right, a Hopi woman of Hispanic descent. On the left is her friend Jessica Lynch, whose capture and subsequent rescue made the headlines while Pestewa's death largely went unnoticed outside the Native American community.

As had been true of earlier government reforms, the Reorganization Act sought to assimilate Native Americans into the dominant society on the dominant group's terms. In this case, the tribes were absorbed within the political and economic structure of the larger society. Apart from the provision about tribal chairmen who were to oversee reservations with several tribes, the Reorganization Act solidified tribal identity. Unlike the Allotment Act, it recognized the right of Native Americans to approve or reject some actions taken on their behalf. The act still maintained substantial non–Native American control over the reservations. As institutions, the tribal governments owed their existence not to their people but to the BIA. These tribal governments rested at the bottom of a large administrative hierarchy (Cornell 1984; Deloria 1971; McNickle 1973; Washburn 1984; Wax and Buchanan 1975).

In 2000, on the 175th anniversary of the BIA, its director, Kevin Guer, a Pawnee, declared that it was "no occasion for celebration as we express our profound sorrow for what the agency has done in the past." A formal apology followed (Stout 2000).

Reservation Life and Federal Policies

Today, over one-third of Native Americans live on 557 reservations and trust lands in 33 states, which account for a bit more than 2 percent of the land throughout the United States. Even for those residing far away from the tribal lands, the reservations play a prominent role in the identity of the Native American peoples (Ogunwole 2006) (Figure 6.2).

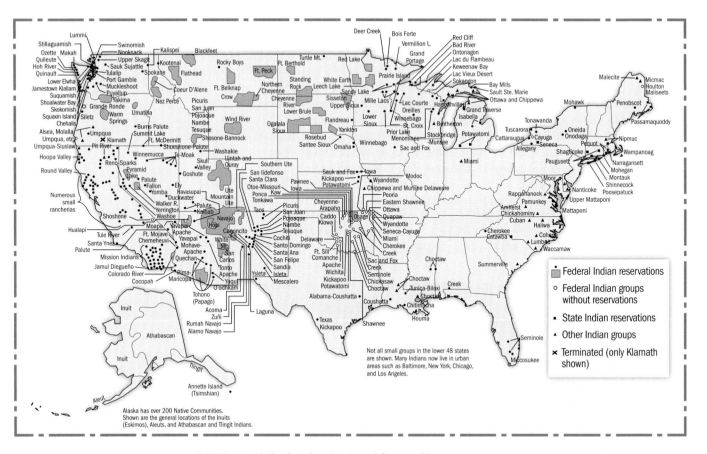

FIGURE 6.2   Native American Lands and Communities

Source: Bureau of Indian Affairs 1986, 12–13.

More than any other segment of the population, with the exception of the military, the reservation Native American finds his or her life determined by the federal government. From the condition of the roads to the level of fire protection to the quality of the schools, the federal government through such agencies as the BIA and the Public Health Service effectively controls reservation life. Tribes and their leaders are now consulted more than in the past, but the ultimate decisions rest in Washington, DC, to a degree that is not true for the rest of the civilian population.

As early as April 1954, an editorial in the *Washington Post* expressed approval of efforts of the federal government to "get out of the Indian business." Many of the policies instituted by the BIA in the 20th century have been designed with this purpose in mind. Most Native Americans and their organizations do not quarrel with this goal. They may only wish that the government and the White people had never gotten into Indian business in the first place. Disagreement between the BIA and the tribes and among Native Americans themselves has focused on how to reduce federal control and subsidies, not on whether they should be reduced. The government has taken three steps in this direction since World War II. Two of these measures have been the formation of the Indian Claims Commission and the passage of the Termination Act. The following section shows how the third step, the Employment Assistance Program, has created a new meeting place for Native Americans in cities, far from their native homelands and the reservations (Tyler 1973).

Native American Legal Claims

Native Americans have had a unique relationship with the federal government. As might be expected, little provision was ever made for them as individuals or tribes to bring grievances against the government. From 1863 to 1946, Native Americans could bring no claim against the government without a special act of Congress, a policy that prevented most charges of treaty violations. Only 142 claims were heard during those 83 years. In 1946, Congress created the Indian Claims Commission, with authority to hear all tribal cases against the government. The three-member commission was given a five-year deadline. During the first five years, however, nearly three times as many claims were filed as had been filed during the 83 years of the old system. Therefore, the commission's term was extended and extended again, and its size was expanded. The commission was disbanded in 1978, with its cases now being heard by the U.S. Court of Claims. As of 1997, the commission and Court, over a period of more than 50 years, paid claims totaling an average of $1,000 for each American Indian for all treaty violations and related claims. In 2006, Congress was still trying to settle cases still left over from the Commission almost thirty years after being disbanded, (Associated Press 2006; Drabelle 1997; Nagel 1996).

In 1986, a member of the Blackfeet tribe in Montana, Eloise Corbell, brought a class-action lawsuit on behalf of a half-million American Indians charging that the government had cheated them of about $137 billion in royalties under the trust arrangements created by the Allotment Act of 1887. Annually the government pays beneficiaries about $500 from the fund, which exceeds an estimated $3 billion. Even by federal standards, this is all a lot of money and the Interior Department quickly defended itself that nothing was wrong. This has not proven to be true. The courts have found that the BIA and other government agencies had extremely poor records even from recent times much less going back in time. The judge presiding over the case has called the handling of the trust fund "The gold standard for mismanagement by the federal government for more than a century" (Files 2004, A17).

How bad has been the federal government defense in the *Corbell* case? The BIA has shut down its Web site for years over fear that any information it gives out about almost anything could be wrong. The Department of Interior by its own accounts is spending

ASK Yourself

What is the importance of the Corbell case?

over $100 million annually in attempts to clean up the record keeping in a manner that will allow it to defend itself in court eventually. Congressional sources estimate that just the cost of accounting, not including any payouts, will probably exceed $3 billion. Efforts to get the *Corbell* case thrown out have failed. Therefore, the secretary of interior declared in 2006 that trust reform was her biggest priority. It is likely to have priority for many years to come before settlements are reached (Department of Interior 2005; IndianTrust 2006).

In specific land issues apart from the *Corbell* class action lawsuit, Native Americans often express a desire to recover their land rather than accept any financial settlements. After numerous legal decisions favoring the Sioux Indians, including a ruling of the U.S. Supreme Court, Congress finally agreed to pay $106 million for the land that was illegally seized in the aftermath of the Battle of the Little Big Horn, described earlier in this chapter. The Sioux rejected the money and lobbied for measures such as the 1987 Black Hills Sioux Nation Act in Congress, to return the land to the tribe. No positive action has yet been taken on these measures. In the meantime, however, the original settlement, the subsequent unaccepted payments, and the interest brought the 1991 total of funds being held for the Sioux to more than $330 million. Despite the desperate need for housing, food, health care, and education, the Sioux still would prefer to regain the land lost in the 1868 Fort Laramie Treaty and, as of 2006, have not accepted payment.

The Termination Act

The Termination Act of 1953 initiated the most controversial government policy toward reservation Native Americans in the twentieth century. Like many such policies, the act originated in ideas that were meant to benefit Native Americans. The BIA commissioner, John Collier, had expressed concern in the 1930s over extensive government control of tribal affairs. In 1947, congressional hearings were held to determine which tribes had the economic resources to be relieved of federal control and assistance. The policy proposed at that time was an admirable attempt to give Native Americans greater autonomy and at the same time to reduce federal expenditures, a goal popular among taxpayers.

The services the tribes received, such as subsidized medical care and college scholarships, should not have been viewed as special and deserving to be discontinued. These services were not the result of favoritism but merely fulfilled treaty obligations. The termination of the Native Americans' relationship to the government then came to be viewed by Native Americans as a threat to reduce services rather than a release from arbitrary authority. Native Americans might be gaining greater self-governance but at a high price.

Unfortunately, the Termination Act as finally passed in 1953 emphasized reducing costs and ignored individual needs. Recommendations for a period of tax immunity were dropped. According to the act, federal services such as medical care, schools, and road equipment were supposed to be withdrawn gradually. Instead, when the Termination Act's provisions began to go into effect, federal services were stopped immediately, with minimal coordination between local government agencies and the tribes to determine whether the services could be continued by other means. The effect of the government orders on the Native Americans was disastrous, with major economic upheaval on the affected tribes, who were unable to establish some of the most basic services—such as road repair and fire protection—which the federal government had previously provided. The federal government resumed these services in 1975 with congressional action that signaled the end of another misguided policy intended to be good for tribal peoples (Deloria 1969; Fixico 1988; Tyler 1973; Wax and Buchanan 1975).

Employment Assistance Program

The depressed economic conditions of reservation life might lead one to expect government initiatives to attract business and industry to locate on or near reservations. The government could provide tax incentives that would eventually pay for themselves. However, such proposals have not been advanced. Rather than take jobs to the Native Americans, the federal government decided to lead the more highly motivated away from the reservation. This policy has further devastated the reservations' economic potential.

In 1952, the BIA began programs to relocate young Native Americans. One of these programs, after 1962, was called the Employment Assistance Program (EAP). Assistance centers were created in Chicago, Cleveland, Dallas, Denver, Los Angeles, Oakland, San Jose, Oklahoma City, Tulsa, and Seattle. In some cities, the Native American population increased as much as fivefold in the 1950s, primarily because of the EAP. By 1968, more than 100,000 people had participated in the program, and 200,000, or one-fourth of the Native American population, had moved to urban areas. They have tended not to spread throughout urban areas but to remain somewhat segregated. Though not as segregated as African Americans or Hispanics, Native Americans often experience moderate segregation, similar to that of European ethnic groups (Bohland 1982).

The EAP's primary provision was for relocation, individually or in families, at government expense, to urban areas where job opportunities were greater than those on the reservations. The BIA stressed that the EAP was voluntary, but as Howard Bahr (1972, 408) correctly states, this voluntary aspect was "a fiction to the extent that the white man has structured the alternatives in such a way that economic pressures force the Indian to relocate." The program was not a success for the many Native Americans who found the urban experience unsuitable or unbearable. By 1965, one-fourth to one-third of the people in the EAP had returned to their home reservation. So great was the rate of return that in 1959 the BIA stopped releasing data on the percentage of returnees, fearing that they would give too much ammunition to critics of the EAP.

The movement of Native Americans into urban areas has had many unintended consequences. It has further reduced the labor force on the reservation. Because those who leave tend to be better educated, it is the Native American version of the brain drain described in Chapter 4. Urbanization unquestionably contributed to the development of an intertribal network or pan-Indian movement, described later in this chapter. The city became the new meeting place of Native Americans, who learned of their common predicament both in the city and on the federally administered reservations. Government agencies also had to develop a policy of continued assistance to nonreservation Native Americans; despite such efforts, the problems of Native Americans in cities persist.

Most reservations today have a measure of self-government through an elected tribal council. Pictured is the Apache tribal council at work.

Programs have emerged to meet the needs of city-dwelling Native Americans. Founded in 1975, the Native American Education Service College in Chicago is an independent, accredited college trying to partially provide for the education of that city's 10,000 Native Americans, who represent 100 tribes. It offers college degrees, with specialized courses in Native American language and history. The college emphasizes small classes and individualized instruction. This institution is unusual not only in higher education but also in offering urban Native Americans a pluralistic solution to being an American Indian in White America (Lauerman 1993).

Collective Action

The growth of pan-Indian activism is an example of both panethnicity and social protest. As we noted in Chapter 1, the panethnic development of solidarity among ethnic subgroups has been reflected in terms such as Hispanic, Latino, and Asian American. **Pan-Indianism** refers to intertribal social movements in which several tribes, joined by political goals but not by kinship, unite in a common identity. Today, these pan-Indian efforts are most vividly seen in cultural efforts and political protests of government policies (Cornell 1996).

Proponents of this movement see the tribes as captive nations or internal colonies. They generally see the enemy as the federal government. Until recently, pan-Indian efforts usually failed to overcome the cultural differences and distrust between tribal groups. However, some efforts to unite have succeeded. The Iroquois made up a six-tribe confederation dating back to the seventeenth century. The Ghost Dance briefly united the Plains tribes in the 1880s, some of which had earlier combined to resist the U.S. Army. But these were the exceptions. It took nearly a century and a half of BIA policies to accomplish a significant level of unification.

The National Congress of American Indians (NCAI), founded in 1944 in Denver, Colorado, was the first national organization representing Native Americans. The NCAI registered itself as a lobby in Washington, DC, hoping to make the Native American perspective heard in the aftermath of the Reorganization Act described earlier. Concern about "White people's meddling" is reflected in the NCAI requirement that White members pay twice as much in dues. The NCAI has had its successes. Early in its history, it played an important role in creating the Indian Claims Commission, and it later pressured the BIA to abandon the practice of termination. It is still the most important civil rights organization for Native Americans and uses tactics similar to those of the NAACP, although the problems facing African Americans and Native Americans are legally and constitutionally different.

A later arrival was the more radical American Indian Movement (AIM), the most visible pan-Indian group. The AIM was founded in 1968 by Clyde Bellecourt (of the White Earth Chippewa) and Dennis Banks (of the Pine Ridge Oglala Sioux), both of whom then lived in Minneapolis. Initially, AIM created a patrol to monitor police actions and document charges of police brutality. Eventually, it promoted programs for alcohol rehabilitation and school reform. By 1972, AIM was nationally known not for its neighborhood-based reforms but for its aggressive confrontations with the BIA and law enforcement agencies.

Protest Efforts

Fish-ins began in 1964 to protest interference by Washington State officials with Native Americans who were fishing, as they argued, in accordance with the 1854 Treaty of Medicine Creek and were not subject to fine or imprisonment, even if they did violate White society's law. The fish-ins had protesters fishing en masse in restricted waterways. This protest was initially hampered by disunity and apathy, but several hundred

pan-Indianism
Intertribal social movements in which several tribes, joined by political goals but not by kinship, unite in a common identity.

fish-ins
Tribes' protests over government interference with their traditional rights to fish as they like.

Native Americans were convinced that civil disobedience was the only way to bring attention to their grievances with the government. Legal battles followed, and the U.S. Supreme Court confirmed the treaty rights in 1968. Other tribes continued to fight in the courts, but the fish-ins brought increased public awareness of the deprivations of Native Americans. One of the longest battles continues to the present: The Chippewas have rights to 50 percent of the fish, timber, and wildlife across the upper third of Wisconsin. In 1991, Wisconsin agreed with this long-standing treaty right, but Whites continue to demonstrate against what they feel is the unfair advantage extended to the Native Americans (Bobo and Tuan 2006; Jolidon 1991; Steiner 1968).

The fish-ins were only the beginning. After the favorable Supreme Court decision in 1968, other events followed in quick succession. In 1969, members of the San Francisco Indian Center seized Alcatraz Island in San Francisco Bay. The 13-acre island was an abandoned maximum-security federal prison, and the federal government was undecided about how to use it. The Native Americans claimed "the excess property" in exchange for $24 in glass beads and cloth, following the precedent set in the sale of Manhattan more than three centuries earlier. With no federal response and the loss of public interest in the demonstration, the protesters left the island more than a year later. The activists' desire to transform it into a Native American cultural center was ignored. Despite the outcome, the event gained international publicity for their cause. Red Power was born, and Native Americans who sympathized with the BIA were labeled "Uncle Tomahawks" or "apples" (red on the outside, white on the inside).

The federal government did not totally ignore calls for a new policy that involved Native Americans in its formulation. Nevertheless, no major breakthroughs came in the 1960s. One significant step was passage of the Alaska Native Settlement Act of 1971. Alaskan Native American people—the 100,000 Inuit Eskimo and other Aleuts— have maintained their claim to the land since Alaska was purchased from Russia in 1867. The federal government had allowed the natives to settle on about one-third of the land they claimed but had not even granted them title to that land. The discovery of huge oil reserves in 1969 made the issue more explosive as the state of Alaska auctioned off mineral rights, ignoring Inuit occupation of the land.

The Alaskan Federation of Natives (AFN), the major native Alaskan group, which had been organized in 1967, moved quickly to stop "the biggest land grab in the history of the U.S.," as the AFN called it. An AFN-sponsored bill was revised, and a compromise, the Native Claims Settlement Act, was passed in late 1971. The final act, which fell short of the requests by the AFN, granted control and ownership of 44 million acres to Alaska's 53,000 Inuits, Aleuts, and other peoples and gave them a cash settlement of nearly $1 billion. Given the enormous pressures from oil companies and conservationists, the Native Claims Settlement Act can be regarded as one of the more reasonable agreements reached between distinctive tribal groups of Native Americans and the government. Further reforms in 1988 helped to safeguard the original act, but as a major trade-off the Alaskan Native Americans surrendered future claims to all aboriginal lands (Cornell and Kalt 2003; Ogunwole 2002).

The most dramatic confrontation between Native Americans and the government came early the next year in the battle of Wounded Knee II. In January 1973, AIM leader Russell Means led an unsuccessful drive to impeach Richard Wilson as tribal chairman of the Oglala Sioux tribe on the Pine Ridge Reservation. In the next month, Means, accompanied by some 300 supporters, started a 70-day occupation of Wounded Knee, South Dakota, site of the infamous cavalry assault in 1890 and now part of the Pine Ridge Reservation. The occupation received tremendous press coverage.

However, the coverage did not affect the outcome. Negotiations between AIM and the federal government on the occupation itself brought no tangible results. Federal prosecutions were initiated against most participants. AIM leaders Russell Means and Dennis Banks eventually faced prosecution on a number of felony charges, and both men were imprisoned. AIM had less visibility as an organization then. Russell Means wryly remarked in 1984, "We're not chic now. We're just Indians, and we have to help ourselves" (Hentoff 1984, 23; also see Nagel 1988, 1996; Smith and Warrior 1996; T. Johnson 1996).

The most visible recent AIM activity has been its efforts to gain clemency for one of its leaders, Leonard Peltier. Imprisoned since 1976, Peltier was given two life sentences for murdering two FBI agents the year before on the embattled Sioux reservation of Pine Ridge, South Dakota. Fellow AIM leaders such as Dennis Banks organized a 1994 Walk for Justice to bring attention in Washington, DC, to the view that Peltier is innocent. This view was supported in two 1992 movie releases: the documentary *Incident at Oglala*, produced by Robert Redford, and the more entertaining, fictionalized *Thunderheart*. To date, clemency appeals to the president to lift the federal sentence have gone unheeded, but this issue remains the rallying point for today's remnants of AIM (Matthiessen 1991).

Pan-Indianism: An Overview

Pan-Indianism, an example of panethnicity, has created a greater solidarity among Native Americans as they seek solutions to common grievances with government agencies. Research shows that tribal people born since the collective action efforts of the 1960s are more likely to reject negative and stereotypic representations of American Indians than those born before the self-determination efforts. Whether through moderate groups such as the NCAI or the more activist AIM, these pan-Indian developments have awakened Whites to the real grievances of Native Americans and have garnered the begrudging acceptance of even the most conservative tribal members, who are more willing to cooperate with government action (Schulz 1998).

However, the results of pan-Indianism have not all been productive, even when viewed from a perspective sympathetic to Native American self-determination. The national organizations are dominated by Plains tribes, not only politically but culturally as well. Pow-wow styles of dancing, singing, and costuming derived from the Plains tradition are spreading nationwide as common cultural traits (see Figure 6.3 for the ten largest tribes).

FIGURE 6.3 Ten Largest American Indian Tribal Groupings, 2000

Source: Ogunwole 2002, 10.

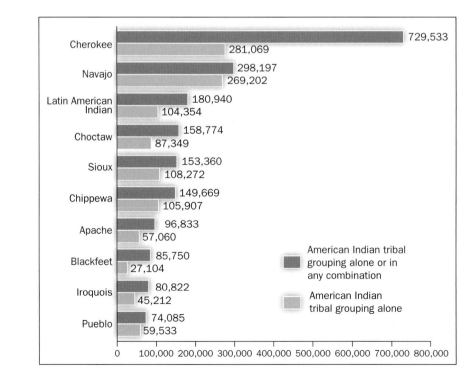

Tribe	alone or in any combination	alone
Cherokee	729,533	281,069
Navajo	298,197	269,202
Latin American Indian	180,940	104,354
Choctaw	158,774	87,349
Sioux	153,360	108,272
Chippewa	149,669	105,907
Apache	96,833	57,060
Blackfeet	85,750	27,104
Iroquois	80,822	45,212
Pueblo	74,085	59,533

American Indian tribal grouping alone or in any combination

American Indian tribal grouping alone

Powwows such as this one in California have become important social, cultural, and economic events that bring together members of many different tribes.

The growing visibility of **powwows** is symbolic of Native Americans in the 1990s. The phrase *pau wau* referred to the medicine man or spiritual leader of the Algonquian tribes, but Europeans who watched medicine men dance thought that the word referred to entire events. Over the last hundred years, powwows have evolved into gatherings in which Native Americans of many tribes come to dance, sing, play music, and visit. More recently, they have become organized events featuring competitions and prizes at several thousand locations. The general public sees them as entertainment, but for Native Americans, they are a celebration of their cultures (Eschbach and Applbaum 2000).

Sovereignty

Although the collective gathering of tribes in pan-Indian efforts cannot be minimized, there continues to be a strong effort to maintain tribal sovereignty. Simply put, **sovereignty** refers in this context to tribal self-rule. Supported by every U.S. president since the 1960s, sovereignty is recognition for tribes to have vibrant economic and cultural lives. At the same time, numerous legal cases, including many at the level of the Supreme Court, continue to clarify to what extent a recognized tribe may rule itself and to what degree it is subject to state and federal laws. In 2004, the U.S. Supreme Court ruled 7–2 in *United States v. Lara* that a tribe has the inherent right to prosecute all American Indians, regardless of affiliation, for crimes that occur on the reservation. However, other cases in lower courts continue to chip away at tribal self-government (Indianz.com 2004).

This legal relationship can be quite complex. For example, tribal members always pay federal income, Social Security, unemployment, and property taxes but do not pay state income if they live and work only on the reservation. Whether tribal members on reservations pay sales, gasoline, cigarette, or motor vehicle taxes has been negotiated on a reservation-by-reservation basis in many sites.

Focused on the tribal group, sovereignty remains linked to both the actions of the federal government and the actions of individual American Indians. The government ultimately determines which tribes are recognized, and although tribal groups may argue publicly for their recognition, self-declaration carries no legal recognition. This has always been an issue, but given the rise of casino gambling to be discussed shortly, the determination of who constitutes a sovereign tribe and who does not may carry significant economic benefits.

Powwows
Native American gatherings of dancing, singing, music playing, and visiting, accompanied by competitions.

sovereignty
Tribal self-rule.

TABLE 6.2 Urban Native Americans, 2000	

According to Census 2000, there are seven cities with more than 10,000 Native Americans. By comparison, there are only four reservations with that many residents.

New York City	41,289
Los Angeles	29,412
Phoenix	26,696
Anchorage	18,941
Tulsa	18,551
Oklahoma City	17,743
Albuquerque	17,444
Tucson	11,038
Chicago	10,290

Source: Ogunwole 2002, 8.

The federal government takes this gatekeeping role of sovereignty very seriously—the irony of the conquering people determining who are "Indians" is not lost upon many tribal activists. In 1978, the Department of the Interior established what it called the acknowledgment process to decide whether any more tribes should have a government-to-government relationship. They must show that they were a distinct group and trace continuity since 1900. Through 2004, 294 groups have sought sovereignty, with just 16 acknowledged and another 9 receiving it though special congressional action.

So sometimes entire tribes are declared not to be tribes. For recognized tribes, they did have to establish a standard of ancestry or descent to determine who is a tribal member. This causes some individuals or entire extended families to be disenrolled. Those disenrolled can appeal to U.S. courts but typically they are reluctant to interfere with the recognized tribes' authority to determine who is a member or not (Beiser 2006).

Individual American Indians play a role as well. For most, their tribal affiliation is fairly clear, but for others it may be more problematic. Certainly if they are members of a group that has yet to receive federal recognition, a long and often costly legal battle is ahead for them to receive the recognition they already feel is their right. For those who have close descendants of more than one tribe, they usually can elect which tribe to belong to legally. Although they may recognize the cultural heritage they have as belonging to more than one tribe, federal laws and most tribal governments require that they declare membership (sometimes also referred to as "enrollment" status) in one tribe (Kalt and Singer 2004; Martinez 2006a; A. Wagner 2004).

Tribal groups and sympathetic others have questioned the appropriateness of creating mascots purporting to celebrate native tradition. Here Chief Illiniwek appears on behalf of the University of Illinois-Champaign Urbana. The NCAA has banned the mascot's appearance at its tournaments.

Native Americans Today

The United States has taken most of the land originally occupied by or deeded to Native Americans; restricted their movement; unilaterally severed agreements; created a special legal status for them; and, after World War II, attempted to move them again. As a result of these efforts and generally poor economic conditions of most reservations, substantial numbers of Native Americans live in the nation's cities (Table 6.2).

How are Native Americans being treated today? A very public insult is the continuing use of American Indian names as mascots for athletic teams of schools, including colleges and many professional sports teams in the United States. Almost all American Indian organizations, including AIM, have brought attention to the use of Native Americans as the mascots of sports teams, such as the Washington Redskins, and to such spectator practices as the "Tomahawk chop" associated with the Atlanta Braves baseball team.

Many sports fans and college alumni find it difficult to understand why Native Americans take offense at a name such as "Braves" or even "Redskins" if it is meant to represent a team about which they have positive feelings. For Native Americans, however, the use of such mascots trivializes their past and their presence today. This at best puzzles if not infuriates most native people, who already face a variety of challenges today. The NCAA, which oversees college athletics, has asked colleges to "explain" their use of mascot names, nicknames, or logos such as savages, braves, warriors, chieftains, redmen, and Indians to name a few. In some cases, the NCAA has already banned the appearance of students dressed as such mascots in tournaments. Typically college alumni and most students wonder what the fuss is about, while most Native people question why should they be so "honored" if they don't want to be (NCAA 2003a, 2003b; Weiberg 2006).

Any discussion of Native American socioeconomic status today must begin with an emphasis on the diversity of the people. Besides the variety of tribal heritages already noted, the contemporary Native American population is split between those on and off reservations and those living in small towns and in central cities. Life in these contrasting social environments is quite different, but enough similarities exist to warrant some broad generalizations on the status of Native Americans in the United States today.

The sections that follow summarize the status of contemporary Native Americans in economic development, education, health care, religious and spiritual expression, and the environment.

Economic Development

Native Americans are an impoverished people. Even to the most casual observer of a reservation, the poverty is a living reality, not merely numbers and percentages. Some visitors seem unconcerned, arguing that because Native Americans are used to hardship and lived a simple life before the Europeans arrived, poverty is a familiar and traditional way of life. In an absolute sense of dollars earned or quality of housing, Native Americans are no worse off now. But in a relative sense that compares their position with that of Whites, they are dismally behind on all standards of income and occupational status. A 1995 national survey showed that overall unemployment is more than 30 percent. Among those who do have jobs, a third earned less than $10,000.

In 1997, the federal government introduced a welfare program that limited how long people can receive public assistance. This clearly will have impact on many tribal reservations, where high proportions of people depend on public assistance because of the lack of training or job opportunities. For example, in South Dakota, American Indians make up 7 percent of the population but account for 53 percent of the welfare recipients. State officials declared they could give five tribes a one-time infusion of start-up money, but after that they would be on their own (Belluck 1997; Egan 1998).

Given the lower incomes and higher poverty rates, it is not surprising that the occupational distribution of Native Americans is similarly bleak. Those who are employed are less likely to be managers, professionals, technicians, salespeople, or administrators. This pattern of low-wage employment is typical of many of the racial and ethnic minorities in the United States, but Native Americans differ in three areas: their roles in tourism, casino gambling, and government employment.

 ASK Yourself

What special role does tourism play for Native Americans?

Tourism Tourism is an important source of employment for many reservation residents, who either serve the needs of visitors directly or sell souvenirs and craft items. Generally, such enterprises do not achieve the kind of success that improves the tribal economy significantly. Even if they did, sociologist Murray Wax (1971, 69) argued, "It requires a special type of person to tolerate exposing himself and his family life to the gaze of tourists, who are often boorish and sometimes offensively condescending in their attitudes."

Tourism, in light of exploitation of tribal people, is a complex interaction of the outside with the Native American. Interviews with tourists visiting museums and reservations found that, regardless of the presentation, many visitors interpreted their brief experiences to be consistent with their previously held stereotypes of and prejudices toward Native Americans. Yet, at the other extreme, some contemporary tourists conscious of the historical context are uncomfortable taking in native foods and purchasing crafts at tribal settlements despite the large economic need many reservations have for such commerce (Laxson 1991; Padget 2004).

Craftwork rarely realizes the profits most Native Americans desire and need. The trading-post business has also taken its toll on Native American cultures. Many craft workers have been manipulated by other Native Americans and Whites to produce what the tourists want. Creativity and authenticity often are replaced by mechanical duplication of "genuine Indian" curios. There continues to be concern and controversy surrounding art such as paintings and pottery that may not be produced by real

Gaming or gambling, whatever you call it, has become big business for a few of the nation's tribes. Shown here are patrons at Mystic Lake Casino operated by the Shakopee Mdewakanton Sioux outside Minneapolis Minnesota.

Native Americans. In 1935, the federal government had created the Indian Arts and Crafts Board to promote tribal arts. The influx of fraudulent crafts was so great that Congress added to its responsibilities the Indian Arts and Crafts Act, which severely punishes anyone who offers to sell an object as produced by a Native American artisan when it was not. The price of both economic and cultural survival is very high (McCoy 2004).

Casino Gambling A more recent source of significant income and some employment has been the introduction of gambling on reservations. Forms of gambling, originally part of tribal ceremonies or celebrations, existed long before Europeans arrived in the Western Hemisphere. Today, however, commercial gambling is the only viable source of employment and revenue available to several tribes.

Under the 1988 Indian Gaming Regulatory Act, states must negotiate gambling agreements with reservations and cannot prohibit any gambling already allowed under state law. By 2006, in 30 states, 228 tribal governments were operating a variety of gambling operations, including off-track betting, casino tables such as blackjack and roulette, lotteries, sports betting, video games of chance, telephone betting, slot machines, and high-stakes bingo. The gamblers, almost all non–Native Americans, sometimes travel long distances for the opportunity to wager money. The actual casinos are a form of tribal government enterprise as opposed to private business operations.

The economic impact on some reservations has been enormous, and nationwide receipts amounted to $22.6 billion in 2005 from reservation casino operations, compared to $20 billion for all Nevada state casino operations. However, the wealth is uneven: About two-thirds of the recognized Indian tribes have no gambling ventures. A few successful casinos have led to staggering windfalls, such as the profits to the 820 members of the Connecticut Mashantucket Pequot Indians, whose Foxwoods Resort Casino, with gambling receipts annually well over $1.5 billion, provides generous benefits to anyone who can establish that he or she is at least one-sixteenth Pequot. Gaming money from the about 25 very successful operations not only supports tribal members but has been used to buy back tribal lands and even to help underwrite the cost of the Smithsonian Museum of the American Indian, which opened in 2004 (Katel 2006; Werner 2006).

The more typical picture is of moderately successful gambling operations associated with tribes whose social and economic needs are overwhelming. Tribes that have opened casinos have experienced drops in unemployment and increases in household income not seen on nongaming reservations. However, three important factors need to be considered.

- First, the tribes do pay taxes. They pay $6 billion in gambling-generated taxes to local, state, and federal governments. That does still leave significant profits, which can be paid out to tribal members or reinvested in collective tribal operations.

- Second, nationwide the economic and social impact of this revenue is limited. The tribes that make substantial revenue from gambling are a small fraction of all Native American people.

- Third, even on the reservations that benefit from gambling enterprises, the levels of unemployment are substantially higher and the family income significantly lower than for the nation as a whole (Bartlett and Steele 2002; Katel 2006, 365; National Indian Gaming Association 2006; Sahagun 2004; Taylor and Kalt 2005).

Criticism is not hard to find, even among Native Americans, some of whom oppose gambling both on moral grounds and because it is marketed in a form that is incompatible with Native American cultures. Opponents are concerned about the appearance of compulsive gambling among some tribal members. The majority of the gamblers are not Native Americans, and almost all of the reservation casinos, though owned by the tribes, are operated by White-owned businesses. Some tribal members feel that the casinos trivialize and cheapen their heritage. The issue of who shares in gambling profits also has led to heated debates in some tribal communities about who is a member of the tribe. In addition, established White gaming interests lobby Congress to restrict the tribes, even though Native Americans generate only 23 percent of the nation's total of legal gambling revenue, including lotteries and racing (National Indian Gaming Association 2006).

Native Americans' voting clout is very weak compared to that of even African Americans and Latinos, but their lobbying power has become significant. Casino money fueled the 2006 scandal involving lobbyist Jack Abramoff, who cheated several tribes by pretending to lobby on their behalf. But although many of the political donations Native Americans make are aimed at protecting reservation casinos, federal grants for education, roads, housing, and other projects also occupy tribes' political agendas.

Although income from gambling has not dramatically changed the lifestyle of most Native Americans, it has been a magnet of criticism from outsiders. Critics question the special status being afforded to Native Americans and contend that there should be an even playing field. This view certainly would have been endorsed by tribal members, because most of what passed for government policies over the last 200 years placed tribes at a major disadvantage. Attention is drawn to some tribes that had made contributions to politicians involved in policies concerning gambling laws. Although some of these contributions may have been illegal, the national media attention was far more intense than was warranted in the messy area of campaign financing. It is another example of how the notion that Native Americans are now playing the White man's game of capitalism "too well" becomes big news (Drinkard 2006; Glionna 2004).

Government Employment Another major source of employment for Native Americans is the government, principally the BIA, but also other federal agencies, the military, and state and local governments. As recently as 1970, one of every four employed Native Americans worked for the federal government. More than half the BIA's employees have tribal ancestry. In fact, since 1854, the BIA has had a policy of giving employment preference to Native Americans over Whites. This policy has been questioned, but the U.S. Supreme Court (*Morton v. Mancari*) upheld it in 1974. Although this is a significant source of employment opportunity, other tribe members have leveled many criticisms at Native American government workers, especially federal employees.

These government employees form a subculture in Native American communities. They tend to be Christians, educated in BIA schools, and sometimes the third generation born into government service. Discrimination against Native Americans in private industry makes government work attractive, and once a person is employed and has seniority, he or she is virtually guaranteed security. Of course, this security may lead some people (whether Native Americans or Whites) to work inefficiently (Bureau of Indian Affairs 1970; Rachlin 1970).

We have examined the sources of economic development, such as tourism, government service, and legalized gambling, but the dominant feature of reservation life is, nevertheless, unemployment. A government report issued by the Full Employment Action Council opened with the statement that such words as *severe, massive,* and *horrendous* are appropriate to describe unemployment among Native Americans. Official unemployment figures for reservations range from 23 percent to 90 percent. It is little wonder that the 1990 census showed that the poorest county in the nation was wholly on tribal lands: Shannon County, South Dakota, of the Pine Ridge Reservation, had a 63 percent poverty rate. Unemployment rates for urban-based Indians are also very high; Los Angeles reports more than 40 percent, and Minneapolis, 49 percent (Cornell and Kalt 1990; Kanamine 1992; Knudson 1987; Sullivan 1986).

The economic outlook for Native Americans need not be bleak. A single program is not the solution; the diversity of both Native Americans and their problems demands a multifaceted approach. The solutions need not be unduly expensive; indeed, because the Native American population is very small compared with the total population, programs with major influence may be financed without significant federal expenditures. Murray Wax (1971) observed that reformers viewing the economically depressed position of Native Americans often seize on education as the key to success. As the next section shows, improving educational programs for Native Americans would be a good place to start.

Paul Moss is giving an Arapaho name to his newborn great-grandson, Raphael, who lies in his arms. The name he chose to give the infant is the one his own deceased son held, Himookoonit, or Golden Eagle. At his feet are cloth goods and cash offerings given to the elder who has given the name.

Education

Government involvement in the education of Native Americans dates as far back as a 1794 treaty with the Oneida Indians. In the 1840s, the federal government and missionary groups combined to start the first school for American Indians. By 1860, the government was operating schools that were free of missionary involvement. Today, laws prohibit federal funds for Native American education from going to sectarian schools. Also, since the passage of the Johnson-O'Malley Act in 1934, the federal government has reimbursed public school districts that include Native American children.

Federal control of the education of Native American children has had mixed results from the beginning. Several tribes started their own school systems at the beginning of the nineteenth century, financing the schools themselves. The Cherokee tribe developed an extensive school system that taught both English and Cherokee, the latter using an alphabet developed by the famed leader Sequoyah. Literacy for the Cherokees was estimated by the mid-1800s at 90 percent, and they even published a bilingual newspaper. The Creek, Chickasaw, and Seminole also maintained school systems. But by the end of the nineteenth century, all these schools had been closed by federal order. Not until the 1930s did the federal government become committed to ensuring an education for Native American children. Despite the push for educational participation, by 1948 only a quarter of the children on the Navajo reservation, the nation's largest, were attending school (Pewewardy 1998).

Educational Attainment   A serious problem in Native American education has been the unusually low level of enrollment. Many children never attend school, or they leave while in elementary school and never return. Enrollment rates are as low as 30 percent for Alaska Eskimos (or Inupiats). This high dropout rate is at least 50 percent higher than that of Blacks or Hispanics and nearly three times that of Whites. The term *dropout* is misleading because many tribal American schoolchildren have found their educational experience so hostile that they had no choice but to leave. In 2005 the South Dakota Supreme Court ruled that a school serving the Lakota Sioux tribe was routinely calling in the police to deal with the slightest misbehavior. The youth soon developed a juvenile record leading to what was termed "school-to-discipline pipeline" (Dell'Angela 2005; James et al. 1995).

Rosalie Wax (1967) conducted a detailed study of the education among the Sioux on the Pine Ridge Reservation of South Dakota. She concluded that terms such as **kickout** or **pushout** are more appropriate. The children are not so much hostile toward school as they are set apart from it; they are socialized by their parents to be independent and not to embarrass their peers, but teachers reward docile acceptance and expect schoolchildren to correct one another in public. Socialization is not all that separates home from school. Teachers often are happy to find parents not "interfering" with their job. Parents do not visit the school, and teachers avoid the homes, a pattern that only furthers the isolation of school from home. This lack of interaction results partly from the predominance of non–Native American teachers, many of who do not recognize the learning styles of American Indian students, although the situation is improving (Hilberg and Tharp 2002).

Quality of Schooling   The quality of Native American education is more difficult to measure than is the quantity. How does one measure excellence? And excellence for what? White society? Tribal life? Both? Chapter 1 discussed the disagreement over measuring intellectual achievement (how much a person has learned) and the greater hazards in measuring intellectual aptitude (how much a person is able to learn). Studies of reservation children, using tests of intelligence that do not require a knowledge of English, consistently show scores at or above the levels of middle-class urban children.

kickouts or pushouts
Native American school dropouts who leave behind an unproductive academic environment.

crossover effect
An effect that appears as previously high-scoring Native American children score as below average in intelligence when tests are given in English rather than their native languages.

Yet in the upper grades, a **crossover effect** appears when tests used assume lifelong familiarity with English. Native American students drop behind their White peers and so would be classified by the dominant society as underachievers (Bureau of Indian Affairs 1988; Coleman et al. 1966; Fuchs and Havighurst 1972).

Preoccupation with such test results perhaps avoids the more important question: educational excellence for what? It would be a mistake to assume that the tribal peoples have reached a consensus. However, they do want to see a curriculum that, at the very least, considers the unique aspects of their heritage. Charles Silberman (1971, 173) reported visiting a sixth-grade English class in a school on a Chippewa reservation where the students were all busily at work writing a composition for Thanksgiving: "Why We Are Happy the Pilgrims Came." A 1991 Department of Education report titled "Indian Nations at Risk" still found the curriculum presented from a European perspective. It is little wonder that in 2004, only 1 percent of Native American high school seniors even attempted the SATs compared to 63 percent of White seniors. In Figure 6.4 we compare educational attainment of the largest tribal groups with all non-Hispanic Whites (Henig 2006).

	Less than high school graduate	High school graduate	Some college or associate's degree	Bachelor's degree or more
Total Non-Hispanic population	11.4	33.1	26.8	28.7
American Indian and Alaska Native	29.1	29.2	30.2	11.5
American Indian	27.4	29.0	31.5	12.1
Apache	31.0	29.0	31.5	8.5
Cherokee	23.4	28.3	32.6	15.7
Chippewa	22.1	31.7	35.9	10.3
Choctaw	20.4	30.6	33.0	16.3
Creek	18.1	30.1	34.6	17.1
Iroquois	20.4	30.3	33.0	16.3
Lumbee	35.3	29.0	23.2	12.5
Navajo	37.3	27.7	28.1	6.9
Pueblo	23.7	33.4	33.3	9.6
Sioux	23.8	30.5	34.9	10.8
Alaska Native	25.4	39.3	27.9	7.4
Alaska Athabascan	24.6	39.6	28.6	7.2
Aleut	22.5	39.6	29.9	7.9
Eskimo	29.7	40.9	23.4	6.0
Tlingit-Haida	17.6	34.6	37.3	10.6

FIGURE 6.4 Educational Attainment 2000

Source: Ogunwole 2006, 8. Data for non-Hispanic Whites from *Current Population Reports 2001.* Washington, DC: U.S. Government Printing Office: Table 10.

Focus Research Focus Research

LEARNING THE NAVAJO WAY

What leads to academic success? Often the answer is a supportive family, but this has not always been said about Native Americans. Educators rooted in the European education traditions often argue that American Indian families whose children are faithful to the traditional culture cannot succeed in schools. This assimilationist view argues that to succeed in larger White-dominated society, it is important to begin to shed the "old ways" as soon as possible. Interestingly, research done in the last ten years questions the assimilationist view and concludes that American Indian students can improve their academic performance through educational programs that are less assimilationist and use curricula that build on what the Native American youth learn in their homes and communities.

Representative of this growing research is the study completed by sociologist Angela A. A. Willeto among her fellow Navajo tribal people. She studied a random sample of 451 Navajo high school students from eleven different Navajo Nation schools. She examined the impact of the students' orientation toward traditional Navajo culture on their per-

formance. Willeto acknowledges that the prevailing view has been that all that is inherently Navajo in a child must be eliminated and replaced with mainstream White society beliefs and lifestyles.

The Navajo tradition was measured by a number of indicators, such as participating in Navajo dances, consulting a medicine man, entering a sweat bath to cleanse oneself spiritually, weaving rugs, living in a traditional hogan, and using the Navajo language. School performance was measured by grades, commitment to school, and aspirations to attend college. She found that the students who lived a more traditional life among the Navajo succeeded in school just as well and were just as committed to success in school and college as high schoolers leading a more assimilated life.

These results are important because many Native Americans themselves accept an assimilationist view. Even within the Navajo Nation, where Navajo language instruction has been mandated in all reservation schools since 1984, many Navajos still equate learning only with the mastery of White society's subject matter. ■

Sources: Reyhner 2001b; Willeto 1999.

Some positive changes are occurring in education. At the beginning of the chapter, we noted the example of the Ho-Chunk preschoolers learning their native language. About 23 percent of the students in BIA-funded schools receive bilingual education. There is growing recognition of the need to move away from past policies that suppressed or ignored the native language and to acknowledge that educational results may be optimized when the native language is included. In "Research Focus: Learning the Navajo Way," we consider the importance of incorporating native teachings and cultures (Bureau of Indian Affairs 1988; James et al. 1995; Reese 1996; Wells 1991).

Higher Education The picture for Native Americans in higher education is decidedly mixed, with some progress and some promise. Enrollment in college increased steadily from the mid-1970s through the mid-1990s, but degree completion, especially the completion of professional degrees, may actually be declining. The economic and educational background of Native American students, especially reservation residents, makes considering entering a predominantly White college a very difficult decision. Native American students may soon feel isolated and discouraged, particularly if the college does not help them understand the alien world of American-style higher education. Even at campuses with large numbers of Native Americans in their student bodies, few Native American faculty or advisors are present to serve as role models. About 53 percent of the students leave at the end of their first year (Carnegie Foundation for the Advancement of Teaching 1990; Wells 1989).

Another encouraging development in higher education in recent years has been the creation of tribally controlled colleges, usually two-year community colleges. The Navajo Community College (now called Diné College), the first such institution, was established in 1968, and by 2006 there were thirty-four nationwide in thirteen states with over 27,000 students enrolled. Besides serving in some rural areas as the only educational institution for many miles, tribal colleges also provide services such as counseling and child care. Tribal colleges enable the students to maintain their cultural identity while training them to succeed outside the reservation (American Indian Higher Education Consortium 2006).

At higher levels, Native Americans largely disappear from the educational scene. In 2003, of the 34,398 doctorates awarded to U.S. citizens, 196 went to Native Americans, compared with more than 11,000 that went to citizens of foreign countries. This production of doctorates among Native Americans has not changed significantly since at least as far back as 1981 (Bureau of the Census 2005a, 186).

Summary "Dine bizaad beeyashti!" Unfortunately, this declaration, of "I speak Navajo!" is not commonly heard from educators. Gradually, schools have begun to encourage the preservation of native cultures. Until the 1960s, BIA and mission schools forbade speaking in the native languages, so it will take time to produce an educated teacher corps knowledgeable in and conversant with native cultures (Linthicum 1993).

As we have seen, there are many failures in our effort to educate, not just assimilate, the first Americans. The problems include:

- Underenrollment at all levels, from the primary grades through college
- The need to adjust to a school with values sometimes dramatically different from those of the home
- The need to make the curriculum more relevant
- The underfinancing of tribal community colleges
- The unique hardships encountered by reservation-born Native Americans who later live in and attend schools in large cities
- The language barrier faced by the many children who have little or no knowledge of English

Other problems include lack of educational innovation (the BIA had no kindergartens until 1967) and a failure to provide special education to children who need it.

Health Care

For Native Americans, "health care" is a misnomer, another broken promise in the array of unmet pledges the government has made. Native Americans compared to other groups are more likely to have poorer health and unmet medical needs and not be able to afford the care. They are more likely to have higher levels of diabetes, trouble hearing, and activity limitations and to have experienced serious psychological distress (Barnes et al. 2005).

In 1955, amidst criticism even then, the responsibility for health care through the Indian Health Service (IHS) transferred from the BIA to the Public Health Service.

Voices Listen to Our Voices Listen to

THE SCALPEL AND THE SILVER BEAR

I knew that Navajo people mistrusted Western medicine, and that Navajo customs and beliefs, even Navajo ways of interacting with others, often stood in direct opposition to the way I was trained at Stanford to deliver medical care. I wanted to make a difference in the lives of my people, not only by providing surgery to heal them but also by making it easier for them to understand, relate to, and accept Western medicine. By speaking some Navajo with them, by showing respect for their ways, and by being one of them, I could help them. I watched my patients. I listened to them. Slowly I began to develop better ways to heal them, ways that respected their culture and beliefs. I desired to incorporate these traditional beliefs and customs into my practice. . . .

Navajo patients simply didn't respond well to the brusque and distanced style of Western doctors. To them it is not acceptable to walk into a room, quickly open someone's shirt and listen to their heart with a stethoscope, or stick something in their mouth or ear. Nor is it acceptable to ask probing and personal questions. As I adapted my practice to my culture, my patients relaxed in situations that could otherwise have been highly stressful to them. As they became more comfortable and at ease, something even more remarkable—astonishing, even—happened. When patients

Lori Arviso Alvord

were trusting and accepting before surgery, their operations seemed to be more successful. If they were anxious, distrustful, and did not understand, or had resisted treatment, they seemed to have more operative or post-operative complications. Could this be happening? The more I watched, the more I saw it was indeed true. Incorporating Navajo philosophies of balance and symmetry, respect and connectedness into my practice, benefited my patients and allowed everything in my two worlds to make sense.

Navajos believe in *hózh̜ó* or *hózh̜óni*—"Walking in Beauty"—a worldview in which everything in life is connected and influences everything else. A stone thrown into a pond can influence the life of a deer in the forest, a human voice and a spoken word can influence events around the world, and all things possess spirit and power. So Navajos make every effort to live in harmony and balance with everyone and everything else. Their belief system sees sickness as a result of things falling out of balance, of losing one's way on the path of beauty. In this belief system, religion and medicine are one and the same. ■

Although their health has improved markedly in absolute terms since the mid-1960s, their overall health is comparatively far behind all other segments of the population. The Commission on Civil Rights (2003) found that the federal per capita expenditure for health care of prison inmates was 50 percent higher than it was for Native Americans.

With the pressure to assimilate Native Americans in all aspects of their lives, there has been little willingness to recognize their traditions of healing and treating illnesses. Native treatments tend to be noninvasive, with the patient encouraged to contribute actively to the healing benefits and prevent future recurrence. In the 1990s, a pluralistic effort was slowly emerging to recognize alternative forms of medicine, including those practiced by Native Americans. In addition, reservation health care workers began to accommodate traditional belief systems as they administered the White culture's medicine (Angier 1993; Fox 1992; *Indian Country* 1999).

Some gifted health practitioners have been able to bridge the gap between the traditional Native American ways of healing and those developed out of the Western medical tradition. In "Listen to Our Voices," Dr. Lois Arviso Alvord, the first Navajo woman to become a surgeon, describes her effort to bridge the cultural gap. Dropping the impersonal clinical manner she had learned in medical school, Alvord reached out to her Navajo patients, acknowledging their faith in holistic healing practices.

Contributing to the problems of health care and mortality on reservations are often high rates of reported crime. Poverty and few job opportunities offer an excellent environment for the growth of youth gangs and drug trafficking. All the issues associated with crime can be found on the nation's reservations. There are 171 tribal enforcement agencies operating nearly 70 jails or detention facilities. As with other minority communities dealing with poverty, Native Americans strongly support law enforcement but at the same time contend their people are being abused by those very individuals selected to protect them. As with efforts for improving health care, the isolation and vastness of some of the reservations make them uniquely vulnerable to crime (Hickman 2003; Major et al. 2004; Minton 2002).

Religious and Spiritual Expression

Like other aspects of Native American cultures, the expression of religion is diverse, reflecting the variety of tribal traditions and the assimilationist pressure of the Europeans. Initially, missionaries and settlers expected Native Americans simply to forsake their traditions for European Christianity, and, as in the case of the repression of the Ghost Dance, sometimes force was used to do so. Today, many Protestant churches and Roman Catholic parishes with large tribal congregations incorporate customs such as the sacred pipe ceremony, native incenses, sweat lodges, ceremonies affirming care for the earth, and services and hymns in native languages.

Whether traditional in nature or reflecting the impact of Europeans, native people typically embrace a broad world of spirituality. Whereas Christians, Jews, and Muslims adhere to a single deity and often confine spiritual expression to designated sites, traditional American Indian people see considerably more relevance in the whole of the world, including animals, water, and the wind.

After generations of formal and informal pressure to adopt Christian faiths and their rituals, in 1978 Congress enacted the American Indian Religious Freedom Act, which declares that it is the government's policy to "protect and preserve the inherent right of American Indians to believe, express, and practice their traditional religions." However, the act contains no penalties or enforcement mechanisms. For this reason, Hopi leader Vernon Masayesva (1994, 93) calls it "the law with no teeth." Therefore, Native Americans are lobbying to strengthen this 1978 legislation. They are seeking protection for religious worship services for military personnel and incarcerated Native Americans, as well as better access to religious relics, such as eagle feathers, and better safeguards against the exploitation of sacred lands (Burgess 1992; Deloria 1992; Friends Committee on National Legislation 1993).

A major spiritual concern is the stockpiling of Native American relics, including burial remains. Contemporary Native Americans are increasingly seeking the return of their ancestors' remains and artifacts, a demand that alarms museums and archeologists. The Native American Graves Protection and Repatriation Act (NAGPRA) of 1990 requires an inventory of such collections and provides for the return of materials

Efforts to keep sacred sites holy are difficult when they become popular tourist attractions, such as Devil's Tower National Monument in Wyoming.

if a claim can be substantiated. This has had significant impact on many anthropological and archaeological collections.

Many scholars believe the ancient bones and burial artifacts to be valuable clues to humanity's past. In part, however, this belief reflects a difference in cultural traditions. Yet the return, or repatriation, of these remains has been very uplifting to tribes and individual Native American families who often greet the arrival with elaborate and emotionally touching ceremonies (G. Johnson 2005).

In recent years, significant publicity has been given to an old expression of religion: the ritual use of peyote, which dates back thousands of years. The sacramental use of peyote was first observed by Europeans in the 1640s. In 1918, the religious use of peyote, a plant that creates mild psychedelic effects, was organized as the Native American Church (NAC). At first a Southwest-based religion, the NAC has spread since World War II among northern tribes. The use of the substance is a small part of a long and moving ritual. The exact nature of NAC rituals varies widely. Clearly, the church maintains the tradition of ritual curing and the seeking of individual visions. However, practitioners also embrace elements of Christianity, representing a type of religious pluralism of Indian and European identities.

Peyote is a hallucinogen, however, and the government has been concerned about NAC use of it. Several states passed laws in the 1920s and 1930s prohibiting the use of peyote. In the 1980s, several court cases involved the prosecution of Native Americans who were using peyote for religious purposes. Finally, in 1994, Congress amended the American Indian Religious Freedom Act to allow Native Americans the right to use, transport, and possess peyote for religious purposes (J. Martin 2001).

Today's Native Americans are asking that their traditions be recognized as an expression of pluralist rather than assimilationist coexistence. These traditions are also closely tied to religion. The sacred sites of Native Americans, as well as their religious practices, have been under attack. In the next section, we will focus on aspects of environmental disputes that are anchored in the spiritualism of Native Americans (Kinzer 2000; Mihesuah 2000).

Environment

Environmental issues bring together many of the concerns we have previously considered surrounding Native Americans: land rights, environmental justice, economic development, and spiritualism.

First, we can find in some of today's environmental literature stereotypes of native peoples as the last defense against the encroachment of "civilization." This image tends to trivialize native cultures, making them into what one author called a "New Age savage" (Waller 1996).

Second, many environmental issues are rooted in continuing land disputes arising from treaties and agreements more than a century old. Reservations contain a wealth of natural resources and scenic beauty. In the past, Native Americans often lacked the technical knowledge to negotiate beneficial agreements with private corporations, and when they did have this ability, the federal government often stepped in and made the final agreements more beneficial to the non–Native Americans than to the residents of the reservations. The native peoples have always been rooted in their land. It was their land that became the first source of tension and conflict with the Europeans. At the beginning of the twenty-first century, it is not surprising that land and the natural resources it holds continue to be major concerns. In 1967, the Council of Energy Resource Tribes (CERT) was formed by the leaders of twenty-five of the West's largest tribes. This new council reasoned that by organizing together it could ensure more revenue from the tribes' vast mineral resources. CERT, which by 2005 represented sixty tribes in the United States and Canada, has provided numerous services to tribes. Working with consultants, CERT helps them develop their resources by marketing natural gas more effectively and dealing with deregulation of utilities (Archuleta 1998; CERT 2006).

Third, environmental issues reinforce the tendency to treat the first inhabitants of the Americas as inferior. This is manifested in **environmental justice**—a term introduced in Chapter 3 describing efforts to ensure that hazardous substances are controlled so that all communities receive protection regardless of race or socioeconomic circumstances. Reservation representatives often express concern about how their lands are used as dumping grounds. For example, the Navajo reservation is home to almost 1,100 abandoned uranium mines. After legal action, the federal government finally provided assistance in 2000 to Navajos who had worked in the mines and were showing ill effects from radiation exposure. Although compensation has been less than was felt necessary, the Navajos continue to monitor closely new proposals to use their land. Few reservations have escaped negative environmental impact, and some observers contend that Native American lands are targeted for nuclear waste storage. Critics see this as a de facto policy of nuclear colonialism, whereby reservations are forced to accept all the hazards of nuclear energy, but the Native American people have seen few of its benefits (Daitz 2003).

Fourth, environmental concerns by American Indians often are balanced against economic development needs, just as they are in the larger society. On some reservations, authorization by timber companies to access hardwood forests led to very conflicted feelings among American Indians. However, such arrangements often are the only realistic source of needed revenue, even if they mean entering into arrangements that more affluent people would never consider. The Skull Valley Goshote tribe of Utah has tried to attract a nuclear waste dump over state government objections. Eventually, the federal government rejected the tribe's plans. Even on the Navajo reservation, a proposed new uranium mine has its supporters, those who consider the promises of royalty payments coupled with alleged safety measures sufficient to offset the past half-century of radiation problems (Bryan 2006; Foy 2006).

Fifth, spiritual needs must be balanced against demands on the environment. For example, numerous sacred sites lie in such public areas as the Grand Canyon, Zion, and Canyonlands National Parks that, though not publicized, are accessible to outsiders. Tribal groups have sought vainly to restrict entry to such sites. The

environmental justice
Efforts to ensure that hazardous substances are controlled so that all communities receive protection regardless of race or socioeconomic circumstances.

San Carlos Apaches unsuccessfully tried to block the University of Arizona from erecting an observatory on their sacred Mt. Graham. Similarly, Plains Indians have sought to ban tourists from climbing Devil's Tower, long the site of religious visions, where prayer bundles of tobacco and sage were left behind by native peoples (Martin 2001).

Conclusion

Native Americans have to choose between assimilating to the dominant White culture and maintaining their identity. In Figure 6.5 we revisit the continuum of intergroup relations as it relates to Native Americans. Recently there is evidence of pluralism, but the desire to improve themselves economically usually drives them toward assimilation.

It is not easy to maintain one's tribal identity outside a reservation. One has to consciously seek out one's cultural heritage amid the pressure to assimilate. Even on a reservation, it is not easy to integrate being Native American with elements of contemporary society. The dominant society needs innovative approaches to facilitate pluralism.

The reservations are economically depressed, but they are also the home of the Native American people spiritually and ideologically, if not always physically. Furthermore, the reservation's isolation means that the frustrations of reservation life and the violent outbursts against them do not alarm large numbers of Whites, as do disturbances in urban centers. Native Americans today, except in motion pictures, are out of sight and out of mind. Since the BIA was created in 1824, the federal government has had much greater control over Native Americans than over any other civilian group in the nation. For Native Americans, the federal government and White people are virtually synonymous. However, the typical White tends to be more sympathetic, if not paternalistic, toward Native Americans than toward African Americans.

Subordinate groups in the United States, including Native Americans, have made tremendous gains and will continue to do so in the years to come. But the rest of the population is not standing still. As Native American income rises, so does White income. As Native American children stay in school longer, so do White children. American Indian health care improves, but so does White health care. Advances have been made,

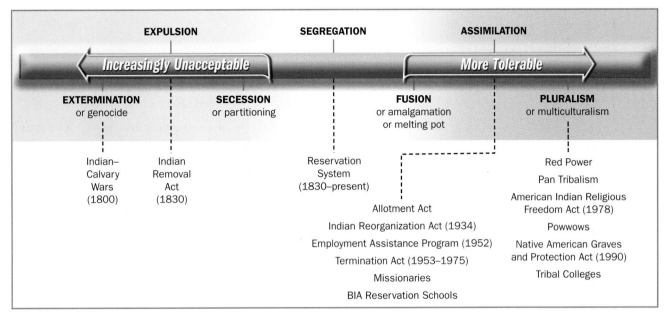

FIGURE 6.5   Intergroup Relations Continuum

but the gap remains between the descendants of the first Americans and those of later arrivals. Low incomes, inadequate education, and poor health care spurred relations between Native Americans and Whites to take a dramatic turn in the 1960s and 1970s, when Native Americans demanded a better life in America.

As Chapter 7 will show, African Americans have achieved a measure of recognition in Washington, DC, that Native Americans have not. Only 5 percent as numerous as the Black population, Native Americans have a weaker collective voice even with casino money fueling lobbying efforts. Only a handful of Native Americans have ever served in Congress, and many of the Whites representing states with large numbers of Native Americans have emerged as their biggest foes rather than their advocates.

The greatest challenge to and asset of the descendants of the first Americans is their land. Over 130 years after the Allotment Act, Native American peoples are still seeking what they feel is theirs through the *Corbell* lawsuit. The land they still possess, although only a small slice of what they once occupied, is an important asset. It is barren and largely unproductive agriculturally, but some of it is unspoiled and often rich in natural resources. No wonder many large businesses, land developers, environmentalists, and casino managers covet their land for their own purposes. For Native Americans, the land they still occupy, as well as much of that occupied by other Americans, represents their roots, their homeland.

One Thanksgiving Day, a scholar noted that, according to tradition, at the first Thanksgiving in 1621 the Pilgrims and the Wampanoag ate together. The descendants of these celebrants increasingly sit at distant tables with equally distant thoughts of equality. Today's Native Americans are the "most undernourished, most short-lived, least educated, least healthy." For them, "that long ago Thanksgiving was not a milestone, not a promise. It was the last full meal" (Dorris 1988, A23).

Key Terms

crossover effect 188	kickouts or pushouts 187	sovereignty 181
environmental justice 194	millenarian movements 171	world systems theory 168
fish-ins 178	pan-Indianism 178	
internal colonialism 172	powwows 181	

Review Questions

1. Identify three policies or actions taken by the federal government that have significant impact today in the daily lives of Native Americans.
2. How have land rights been a continuing theme in White–Native American relations?
3. How much are Native Americans expected to shed their cultural heritage to become a part of contemporary society?
4. Do casinos and other gaming outlets represent a positive force for Native American tribes today?
5. What challenges are there to reservation residents receiving effective health care?

Critical Thinking

1. Consider Independence Day and Thanksgiving Day. How do these national holidays remind Native Americans today of their marginal status?

2. Chronicle how aspects of leisure time from schoolyard games to Halloween costumes to team mascots trivialize Native Americans. What experience have you had with such episodes or seen in the mass media?

3. Why do you think that many people in the United States hold more benevolent attitudes toward Native Americans than they do toward other subordinate groups such as African Americans and Latinos?

Internet Connections—Research Navigator™

Follow the instructions found on page 35 of this text to access the features of Research Navigator™. Once at the Web site, enter your Login Name and Password. Then, to use the ContentSelect database, enter keywords such as "Trail of Tears," "Navajo," and "Apache," and the research engine will supply relevant and recent scholarly and popular press publications. Use the *New York Times* Search-by-Subject Archive to find recent news articles related to sociology and the Link Library feature to locate relevant Web links organized by the key terms associated with this chapter.

The Making of African Americans in a White America

7

CHAPTER OUTLINE

Slavery

The Challenge of Black Leadership

Reemergence of Black Protest

RESEARCH FOCUS
Sundown Towns, USA

The Civil Rights Movement

LISTEN TO OUR VOICES
"Letter from Birmingham Jail"
by Martin Luther King, Jr.

Urban Violence and Oppression

Black Power

The Religious Force

Conclusion

Key Terms/Review Questions/
Critical Thinking/Internet Connections—
Research Navigator™

T HE AFRICAN PRESENCE IN THE UNITED STATES BEGAN almost simultaneously with permanent White settlement. Unlike most Europeans, however, the African people were brought involuntarily and in bondage. The end of slavery heralded new political rights during Reconstruction, but this was a short-lived era of dignity. Despite advocacy of nonviolence by leaders such as the Reverend Martin Luther King, Jr., the civil rights movement met violent resistance throughout the South. In the mid-1960s, the nation's attention was diverted to urban violence in the North and the West. Blacks responded to their relative deprivation and rising expectations by advocating Black Power, which in turn met with White resistance. Although African Americans have made significant gains, the gap between Blacks and Whites remains remarkably unchanged in the last half century. Religion continues to be a major force in the African American community.

The Gee's Bend Ferry resumed service crossing the Alabama River in 2006. This is especially noteworthy because, it represented the end of several decades of keeping Blacks from voting in Camden, Alabama. In 1962, as Blacks began to vote in larger numbers, ending the ferry service meant a key concentration of 700 African American citizens would have to travel an hour rather than 15 minutes to get to the county seat to register to vote. In 2003, the City Council of Zephyrhills, a community of 11,000 people 35 miles northeast of Tampa, Florida, voted to rename a street in honor of Martin Luther King, Jr. In taking this step they joined company with about 650 other cities in 41 states that have renamed streets in honor of the civil rights worker. Although a few responded to the creation of Martin Luther King, Jr. Avenue with pleasure, the city council was unprepared for the strong protest that accompanied its decision. Protesters became more vocal over the action, with critics saying they did not want to have to change their address. Observers noticed that all the townspeople who spoke against the policy were White, and most of the supporters were African American. In May, the council reversed itself and King Avenue again became Sixth Avenue. This is not the story of just one town, because this has occurred again and again. Efforts to recognize significant figures in African American history have often been controversial. The people of San Diego were so incensed about renaming a street after Martin Luther King, Jr., that they successfully got the issue on the ballot in 1987 and had the former name restored. More recently in 2003, the people of Muncie, Indiana, defeated the idea of renaming a street after the slain civil rights leader, and similarly in Portsmouth, New Hampshire, the suggestion to name a city park after King did not succeed (Good enough 2004 Linn 2006).

Relationships between Whites and Blacks in the United States have been marked by many episodes like these, sometimes a step backward and occasionally a step forward.

The United States, with more than 38 million Blacks, has the eighth-largest Black population in the world; only Brazil, Congo, Ethiopia, Nigeria, South Africa, Sudan, and Tanzania have larger Black populations. Despite their large numbers, Blacks in this country have had almost no role in major national and political decisions and have been allowed only a peripheral role in many crucial decisions that influenced their own destiny.

The history of African Americans is, to a significant degree, the history of the United States. Black people accompanied the first explorers, and a Black man was among the first to die in the American Revolution. The enslavement of Africans was responsible for the South's wealth in the nineteenth century and led to the country's most violent domestic strife. After Blacks were freed from slavery, their continued subordination led to sporadic outbreaks of violence in the rural South and throughout urban America. This chapter concentrates on the history of African Americans into the 1990s. Their contemporary situation is the subject of Chapter 8.

As with European immigrants described in Chapter 4, Black Africans brought with them a variety of cultural traditions. As illustrated in Figure 7.1, although most of the people brought forcibly to North America from Africa came from a limited geographic area of the African continent, they represented diverse cultural experiences. Today, we rarely remember these tribal or ethnic variations among the descendants of the Africans in the way we customarily do among Europeans.

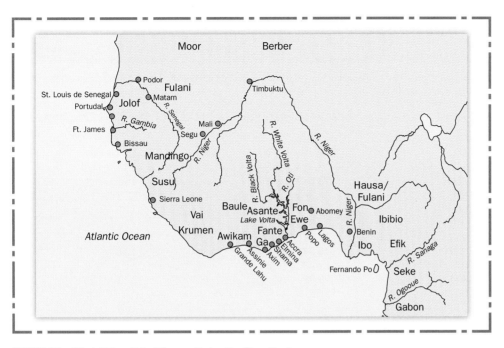

FIGURE 7.1 **West African Tribal Groups During the Slave Trade**

Most Africans who were forcibly brought to the United States came from a limited area of Africa but brought with them a rich variety of cultural traditions, as reflected on this map.

Source: From Historical and Cultural Atlas of African Americans, 1st ed., by M.K. Asante & M.T. Mattson, 1991. Reprinted with permission of Gale, a division of Thomson Learning: www.thomsonrights.com. Fax: 800-730-2215

The Black experience in what came to be the United States began as something less than citizenship, yet slightly better than slavery. In 1619, twenty Africans arrived in Jamestown as indentured servants. Their children were born free people. These Blacks in the British colonies were not the first in the New World, however; some Blacks had accompanied European explorers, perhaps even Columbus. But all this is a historical footnote. By the 1660s, the British colonies had passed laws making Africans slaves for life, forbidding interracial marriages, and making children of slaves bear the status of their mother regardless of their father's race. Slavery had begun in North America; more than three centuries later we still live with its legacy.

Slavery

Slavery seems far removed from the debates over issues that divide Whites and Blacks today. However, contemporary institutional and individual racism, which is central to today's conflicts, has its origins in the institution of slavery. Slavery was not merely a single aspect of American society for three centuries; it has been an essential part of our country's life. For nearly half of this country's history, slavery was not only tolerated but also legally protected by the U.S. Constitution as interpreted by the U.S. Supreme Court.

In sharp contrast to the basic rights and privileges enjoyed by White Americans, Black people in bondage lived under a system of repression and terror. Nearly one out of five people were Black and enslaved in the United States (see Table 7.1). Because the institution of slavery was so fundamental to our culture, it continues to influence Black–White relations in the twenty-first century.

TABLE 7.1
Black Population, 1790–2050

Blacks accounted for a decreasing proportion of the total population until the 1940s, primarily because White immigration to the United States far outdistanced population growth by Blacks.

Census	Black Population (in thousands)	Black Percentage (of Total Population)
1790	757	19.3
1810	1,378	19.0
1830	2,329	18.1
1850	3,639	15.7
1870	4,880	12.7
1890	7,489	11.9
1910	9,828	10.7
1930	11,891	9.7
1950	15,042	10.0
1970	22,580	11.1
1990	29,986	12.1
2000	35,818	12.7
2010 (projection)	40,454	13.1
2050 (projection)	61,361	14.6

Source: Bureau of the Census 2002a, 2004b, Table 1a.

Slave Codes

Slavery in the United States rested on five central conditions: Slavery was for life, the status was inherited, slaves were considered mere property, slaves were denied rights, and coercion was used to maintain the system (Noel 1972). As slavery developed in colonial America and the United States, so did **slave codes,** laws that defined the low position of slaves in the United States. Although the rules varied from state to state and from time to time and were not always enforced, the more common features demonstrate how completely subjugated the Africans were:

1. A slave could not marry or even meet with a free Black.
2. Marriage between slaves was not legally recognized.
3. A slave could not legally buy or sell anything except by special arrangement.
4. A slave could not possess weapons or liquor.
5. A slave could not quarrel with or use abusive language toward Whites.
6. A slave could not possess property (including money), except as allowed by his or her owner.
7. A slave could make no will, nor could he or she inherit anything.
8. A slave could not make a contract or hire him or herself out.
9. A slave could not leave a plantation without a pass noting his or her destination and time of return.
10. No one, including Whites, was to teach a slave (and in some areas even a free Black) to read or write or to give a slave a book, including the Bible.
11. A slave could not gamble.
12. A slave had to obey established curfews.
13. A slave could not testify in court except against another slave.

slave codes
Laws that defined the low position held by slaves in the United States.

For many generations, Africans were treated by their White slave owners as property, with none of the rights extended to people. Pictured is a slave auction in Richmond, Virginia, in 1861.

Violations of these rules were dealt with in a variety of ways. Mutilation and branding were not unknown. Imprisonment was rare; most violators were whipped. An owner was largely immune from prosecution for any physical abuse of slaves. Because slaves could not testify in court, a White's actions toward enslaved African Americans were practically above the law (ACLU 1996; Elkins 1959; Franklin and Moss 2000; Stampp 1956).

Slavery, as enforced through the slave codes, controlled and determined all facets of the lives of the enslaved Africans. The organization of family life and religious worship were no exceptions. Naturally, the Africans had brought to America their own cultural traditions. In Africa, people had been accustomed to a closely regulated family life and a rigidly enforced moral code. Slavery rendered it impossible for them to retain these family ties in the New World.

The slave family had no standing in law. Marriages between slaves were not legally recognized, and masters rarely respected them in selling adults or children. Slave breeding—a deliberate effort to maximize the number of offspring—was practiced with little attention to the emotional needs of the slaves themselves. The slaveholder, not the parents, decided at what age children should begin working in the fields. The slave family could not offer its children shelter or security, rewards or punishments. The man's only recognized family role was that of siring offspring, being the sex partner of a woman. In fact, slave men often were identified as if they were the woman's possession, for example, as "Nancy's Tom." Southern law consistently ruled that "the father of a slave is unknown to our law." This does not imply that the male slave did not occupy an important economic role. Men held almost all the managerial positions open to slaves (Du Bois 1970; Stampp 1956).

Unlike the family structure, to which slavery dealt near-mortal blows, a strong religious tradition survived. In fact, a slaveholder wanting to do "God's work on Earth" would encourage the slave church, finding it functional in dominating the slaves. Of course, African religions were forbidden, and the White people's Christianity flourished, but Blacks still used West African concepts in the new way of life that slavery brought. The preacher maintained an intense relationship with the congregation, similar to the role played by the elder in West Africa. The Christianity to which the slaves were introduced stressed obeying their owner. Complete surrender to Whites meant salvation and eternal happiness in the hereafter. In contrast, to question God's will or to fight slavery caused everlasting damnation. Obviously, this twisted version of Christianity was intended to make slaves acquiesce to their holders' wishes in return for reward after death. To some degree, however, religion did keep the desire for freedom alive in slaves, and to some extent it formed the basis of their struggle for freedom: Nightly prayer meetings and singing gave them a sense of unity and common destiny necessary for that struggle. On a more personal level, religion made the slaves' daily lives more bearable (Frazier 1964; Rawick 1972; Stampp 1956).

African Americans and Africa

The importance of Africa to Black Americans can be seen in the aspects of African culture that became integral parts of Blacks' lives in the United States. This importance was recognized long before the emergence of the Afrocentric perspective in the 1990s. Black scholars W. E. B. Du Bois (1939) and Carter Woodson (1968) and respected White anthropologist Melville Herskovits (1930, 1941) have all argued persuasively for the continued influence of the African heritage.

Scholars debate to what degree African culture was able to persist despite efforts by slaveholders to replace any vestige of African tradition. The survival of African culture can be most easily documented in folklore, religion, language, and music. It is difficult to clarify the degree of survival, however, because Africans came from many different cultures. When we think of ethnic origins, our thoughts turn to European groups such as Poles or Greeks, but within Africa are the Ibos, Gas, and Yorubas, to name a few of the sources of slaves from Africa (see Figure 7.1). Thus, to speak of a single source of African culture ignores the complexity of social life on that continent. Furthermore, as the **Afrocentric perspective** argues, some aspects of African culture, such as certain art forms, have so permeated Western culture that we mistakenly believe their origins are European.

Africa has had and will always have an importance to Blacks that many Blacks and most Whites do not appreciate, and this importance is unlikely to be changed by the continued debate over which aspects of Black life today can be traced back to African culture. The significance of Africa to Black Americans is one of the most easily identifiable themes in the Black experience. During certain periods (the 1920s and the late 1960s), the Black cultural tradition was the rallying point of many Blacks, especially those living in the cities. Studies continue to document the survival of African culture in North America.

Research has identified remnants of grammar and sentence construction in the speech patterns of low-income and rural Blacks. **Ebonics** is the distinctive dialect, with a complex language structure, that is found among Black Americans. Although the term *Ebonics* (*ebony* and *phonics*) was coined in the 1970s, there has long been a recognition of a distinctive language pattern, sometimes called "Black English," that includes some vocabulary and grammar rules that reflect the West African origins of Black Americans. In 1996, Ebonics became a national issue after the Oakland, California, school board's recognition of it as the primary language of schoolchildren who were then learning mainstream American English. This debate aside, there is consensus that, a century after slavery, remnants of African cultural traditions survive (Applebome 1997).

The Attack on Slavery

Although the slave was vulnerable to his or her owner's wishes, slavery as an institution was vulnerable to outside opinion. For a generation after the American Revolution, restrictions on slaves increased as Southerners accepted slavery as permanent. Slave revolts and antislavery propaganda only accelerated the intensity of oppression. This change led to the ironic situation that as slavery was attacked from within and without,

afrocentric perspective
An emphasis on the customs of African cultures and how they have pervaded the history, culture, and behavior of Blacks in the United States and around the world.

Ebonics
Distinctive dialect with a complex language structure found among many Black Americans.

its conditions became harsher and its defenders became more outspoken in asserting what they saw as its benefits.

Antislavery advocates, or **abolitionists**, included both Whites and free Blacks. Many Whites who opposed slavery, such as Abraham Lincoln, did not believe in racial equality. In their minds, even though slavery was a moral evil, racial equality was still unimaginable. This apparent inconsistency did not lessen the emotional fervor of the efforts to end slavery. Antislavery societies had been founded even before the American Revolution, but the Constitution dealt the antislavery movement a blow. To appease the South, the framers of the Constitution recognized and legitimized slavery's existence. The Constitution even allowed slavery to increase Southern political power. A slave was counted as three-fifths of a person in determining population representation in the House of Representatives.

Abolitionists, both Black and White, continued to speak out against slavery and the harm it was doing not only to the slaves but also to the entire nation, which had become economically dependent on bondage. Frederick Douglass and Sojourner Truth, both freed slaves, became very visible in the fight against slavery through their eloquent speeches and publications. Harriet Tubman, along with other Blacks and sympathetic Whites, developed the Underground Railroad to convey escaping slaves to freedom in the North and Canada (Franklin and Moss 2000).

Another aspect of Black enslavement was the slaves' own resistance to servitude. Slaves did revolt, and between 40,000 and 100,000 actually escaped from the South and slavery. Yet fugitive slave acts provided for the return even of slaves who had reached free states. Enslaved Blacks who did not attempt escape, at least in part because failure often led to death, resisted slavery through such means as passive resistance. Slaves feigned clumsiness or illness; pretended not to understand, see, or hear; ridiculed Whites with a mocking, subtle humor that their owners did not comprehend; and destroyed farm implements and committed similar acts of sabotage (Bauer and Bauer 1942; L. Bennett 1966; Oakes 1993).

Slavery's Aftermath

On January 1, 1863, President Lincoln issued the Emancipation Proclamation. The document created hope in slaves in the South, but many Union soldiers resigned rather than participate in a struggle to free slaves. The proclamation freed slaves only in the Confederacy, over which the president had no control. Six months after the surrender of the Confederacy in 1865, abolition became law when the Thirteenth Amendment abolished slavery throughout the nation.

From 1867 to 1877, during the period called Reconstruction, Black–White relations in the South were unlike anything they had ever been. The Reconstruction Act of 1867 put each southern state under a military governor until a new state constitution could be written, with Blacks participating fully in the process. Whites and Blacks married each other, went to public schools and state universities together, and rode side by side on trains and streetcars. The most conspicuous evidence of the new position of Blacks was their presence in elected office. In 1870, the Fifteenth Amendment was ratified, prohibiting the denial of the right to vote on grounds of race, color, or previous condition of servitude. Black men put their vote to good use; Blacks were elected as six lieutenant governors, sixteen major state officials, twenty members of the House of Representatives, and two U.S. senators. Despite accusations that they were corrupt, Black officials and Black-dominated legislatures created new and progressive state constitutions. Black political organizations, such as the Union League and the Loyal League, rivaled the church as the focus of community organization (Du Bois 1969b; Foner 2006).

Reconstruction was ended as part of a political compromise in the election of 1876 and, consequently, segregation became entrenched in the South. Evidence of Jim Crow's reign

abolitionists
Whites and free Blacks who favored the end of slavery.

Jim Crow
Southern laws passed in the late 19th century that kept Blacks in their subordinate position.

white primary
Legal provisions forbidding Black voting in election primaries, which in one-party areas of the South effectively denied Blacks their right to select elected officials.

slavery reparations
Act of making amends for the injustices of slavery.

was apparent by the close of the nineteenth century. The term **Jim Crow** appears to have its origin in a dance tune, but by the 1890s it was synonymous with segregation and referred to the statutes that kept African Americans in an inferior position. Segregation often preceded Jim Crow laws and in practice often went beyond their provisions. The institutionalization of segregation gave White supremacy its ultimate authority. In 1896, the U.S. Supreme Court ruled in *Plessy v. Ferguson* that state laws requiring "separate but equal" accommodations for Blacks were a "reasonable" use of state government power (L. Bennett 1966; Woodward 1974).

It was in the political sphere that Jim Crow exacted its price soonest. In 1898, the Court's decision in *Williams v. Mississippi* declared constitutional the use of poll taxes, literacy tests, and residential requirements to discourage Blacks from voting. In Louisiana that year, 130,000 Blacks were registered to vote. Eight years later only 1,342 were. Even all these measures did not deprive all African Americans of the vote, and so White supremacists erected a final obstacle: the **White primary,** which forbade Black voting in election primaries. By the turn of the century, the South had a one-party system, making the primary the significant contest and the general election a mere rubber stamp. Beginning with South Carolina in 1896 and spreading to twelve other states within twenty years, statewide Democratic party primaries were adopted. The party explicitly excluded Blacks from voting, an exclusion that was constitutional because the party was defined as a private organization that was free to define its own membership qualifications. The White primary brought an end to the political gains of Reconstruction (Lacy 1972; Lewinson 1965; Woodward 1974).

Reparations for Slavery

The legacy of slavery lives on more than 150 years after its end in the United States. We can see it in the nation's Capitol and the White House, which were built with slave labor, but we can also see it in the enduring poverty that grips a large proportion of the descendants of slavery.

For more than thirty years, there has been serious discussion about granting reparations for slavery. **Slavery reparations** refers to the act of making amends for the injustice of slavery. Few would argue that slavery was wrong and continues to be wrong

Larry Wright, The Detroit News

caglecartoons.com

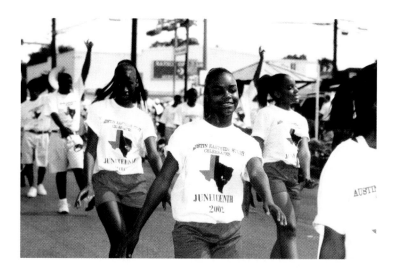

Within all racial and ethnic groups, celebrations emerge to reflect their distinctive experience. Juneteenth celebration is spreading across the United States and marks the anniversary of the emancipation of the slaves in Texas on June 19, 1864.

where it is practiced in parts of the world even today. However, what form should the reparations take? Since 1989, Congressman John Conyers, a Black Democrat from Detroit, has annually introduced in Congress a bill to acknowledge the "fundamental injustice, cruelty, brutality, and inhumanity of slavery" and calls for the creation of a commission to examine the institution and to make recommendations on appropriate remedies. This bill has never made it out of committee, but the discussion continues outside the federal government.

There has not been an official government apology for slavery even though the U.S. government has apologized for injustices to the American Indians and to the Japanese Americans placed in internment camps during World War II. The absence of an official apology angers many African Americans today and those sympathetic to the reparation issue, but the true controversy surrounds what form a remedy should take. Should the government develop and fund some major program to assist the African American community? Should there be direct payments to all African Americans or only to people who can prove that they are descended from enslaved people? Each of these possibilities raises a variety of questions about fairness and equity, but many object in principle to giving any money to people who themselves were not enslaved.

Beginning in the late 1990s, legal researchers raised yet another issue as documentation emerged that private companies that still exist today benefited from slavery. Although it is not too difficult to see how much of the plantation economy of the South was built on enslaved people, the corporate profits from slavery go well beyond the cotton fields. The railroad industry depended heavily on slave labor for construction of railway systems still in use today. Insurance companies even in the North during slavery collected a substantial number of insurance premiums from slaveholders who insured their slaves, much as they would other forms of property. Proponents of slavery reparations argue that these companies owe payments to today's descendants similar to efforts to get payments from German companies that profited from the Jewish Holocaust during World War II.

Government policy makers, for the most part, have not been willing to endorse the concept of slave reparations in any way. A few cities and the state of California have adopted resolutions to explore the issue, but the federal government has not acted. A national survey taken in 2002 showed that only a third of Whites and two-thirds of African Americans feel that corporations that benefited from slavery should even make an apology, although some, such as Aetna Insurance, have already done so. Attitudes

? ASK Yourself

Is there evidence of the nation's slavery past in your area? Perhaps it is present in a segregated cemetery, historic markers, local accounts of the Underground Railroad, or even in the names of streets.

are clearly divided along racial lines on government cash payments: Only 6 percent of Whites and 55 percent of Black Americans endorse some kind of cash payment to the descendants of slaves. Although it may be futile to try to put a price on the cost of slavery, most African Americans and some other citizens are disappointed by the unwillingness to debate the issue in Washington, D.C. (Cox 2002; Dawson and Popoff 2004; Foner 2006; Salzberger and Turck 2004).

The Challenge of Black Leadership

The institutionalization of White supremacy precipitated different responses from African Americans, just as slavery had. In the late 1800s and early 1900s, a number of articulate Blacks attempted to lead the first generation of freeborn Black Americans. Most prominent were Booker T. Washington and W. E. B. Du Bois. The personalities and ideas of these two men contrasted with one another. Washington was born a slave in 1856 on a Virginia plantation. He worked in coal mines after emancipation and attended elementary school. Through hard work and driving ambition, Washington became the head of an educational institute for Blacks in Tuskegee, Alabama. Within fifteen years, his leadership brought the Tuskegee Institute national recognition and made him a national figure. Du Bois, on the other hand, was born in 1868 of a free family in Massachusetts. He attended Fisk University and the University of Berlin and became the first Black to receive a doctorate from Harvard. Washington died in 1915, and Du Bois died in self-imposed exile in Africa in 1963.

The Politics of Accommodation

Booker T. Washington's approach to White supremacy is called the politics of accommodation. He was willing to forgo social equality until White people saw Blacks as deserving of it. Perhaps his most famous speech was made in Atlanta on September 18, 1895, to an audience that was mostly White and mostly wealthy. Introduced by the governor of Georgia as "a representative of Negro enterprise and Negro civilization," Washington (1900) gave a five-minute speech in which he pledged the continued dedication of Blacks to Whites:

> *As we have proved our loyalty to you in the past, in nursing your children, watching by the sick-bed of your mothers and fathers, and often following them with tear-dimmed eyes to their graves, so in the future, in our humble way, we shall stand by you with a devotion that no foreigner can approach, ready to lay down our lives, if need be, in defense of yours. (p. 221)*

The speech catapulted Washington into the public forum, and he became the anointed spokesperson for Blacks for the next twenty years. President Grover Cleveland congratulated Washington for the "new hope" he gave Blacks. Washington's essential theme was compromise. Unlike Frederick Douglass, who had demanded the same rights for Blacks as for Whites, Washington asked that Blacks be educated because it would be a wise investment for Whites. He called racial hatred "the great and intricate problem which God has laid at the doors of the South." The Blacks' goal should be economic respectability. Washington's accommodating attitude ensured his popularity with Whites. His recognition by Whites contributed to his large following of Blacks, who were not used to seeing their leaders achieve fame among Whites.

It is easy in retrospect to be critical of Washington and to write him off as simply a product of his times. Booker T. Washington entered the public arena when the more militant proposals of Douglass had been buried. Black politicians were losing political contests and influence. To become influential as a Black, Washington reasoned, required White acceptance. His image as an accommodator allowed him to fight discrimination covertly. He assisted Presidents Roosevelt and Taft in appointing Blacks to patronage positions. Washington's goal was for African Americans eventually to have the same rights and opportunities as Whites. Just as people disagree with leaders today, some Blacks disagreed over the means that Washington chose to reach that goal. No African American was more outspoken in his criticism of the politics of accommodation than W. E. B. Du Bois (Conyers 1996; Harlan 1972; Hawkins 1962; Meier and Rudwick 1966 Pinkney 2001).

The Niagara Movement

The rivalry between Washington and Du Bois has been exaggerated. Actually, they enjoyed fairly cordial relations for some time. In 1900, Washington recommended Du Bois, at his request, for superintendent of Black schools in Washington, D.C. By 1905, however, relations between the two had cooled. Du Bois spoke critically of Washington's influence, arguing that his power was being used to stifle African Americans who spoke out against the politics of accommodation. He also charged that Washington had caused the transfer of funds from academic programs to vocational education. Du Bois's greatest objection to Washington's statements was that they encouraged Whites to place the burden of the Blacks' problems on the Blacks themselves (Du Bois 1961; Hawkins 1962).

As an alternative to Washington's program, Du Bois (1903) advocated the theory of the *talented tenth*, which reflected his atypical educational background. Unlike Washington, Du Bois was not at home with both intellectuals and sharecroppers. Although the very words talented tenth have an elitist ring to them, Du Bois argued that these privileged Blacks must serve the other nine-tenths. This argument was also Du Bois's way of criticizing Washington's emphasis on vocational education. He thought education for African Americans should emphasize academics, which would be more likely to improve their position. Drawing on the talented tenth, Du Bois invited twenty-nine Blacks to participate in a strategy session near Niagara Falls in 1905. Out of a series of meetings came several demands that unmistakably placed the responsibility for the problems facing African Americans on the shoulders of Whites.

Pictured is a 1935 lynching in Ft. Lauderdale of Rubin Stacy, an African American who had been charged with "threatening and frightening" a White woman. Note the reaction of some of the onlookers. Over 3,000 Blacks were executed by lynching between 1889 and 1938.

The Niagara Movement, as it came to be called, was closely monitored by Booker T. Washington. Du Bois encountered difficulty gaining financial support and recruiting prominent people, and Du Bois (1968) himself wrote, "My leadership was solely of ideas. I never was, nor ever will be, personally popular" (p. 303). The movement's legacy was the education of a new generation of African Americans in the politics of protest. After 1910, the Niagara Movement ceased to hold annual conventions. In 1909, however, the National Association for the Advancement of Colored People (NAACP), with White and Black members, was founded by the Niagara Movement leaders. It was through the work of the NAACP that the Niagara Movement accomplished most of the goals set forth in 1905. The NAACP also marked the merging of White liberalism and Black militancy, a coalition unknown since the end of the abolition movement and Reconstruction (L. Bennett 1966; Conyers 1996; Rudwick 1957).

In 1900, 90 percent of African Americans lived in the South. Blacks moved out of the South and into the West and North, especially the urban areas in those regions, during the post–Civil War period and continued to migrate through the 1950s and 1960s. By the 1980s and 1990s, a migration to the South began as job opportunities grew in that part of the country and most vestiges of Jim Crow vanished in what had been the states of the Confederacy. By 2000, 55 percent of African Americans lived in the South, compared to 33 percent of the rest of the population (Figure 7.2).

The pattern of violence, with Blacks usually the victims, started in the South during Reconstruction and continued into the twentieth century, when it also spread northward. In 1917, a riot in East St. Louis, Illinois, claimed the lives of thirty-nine Blacks

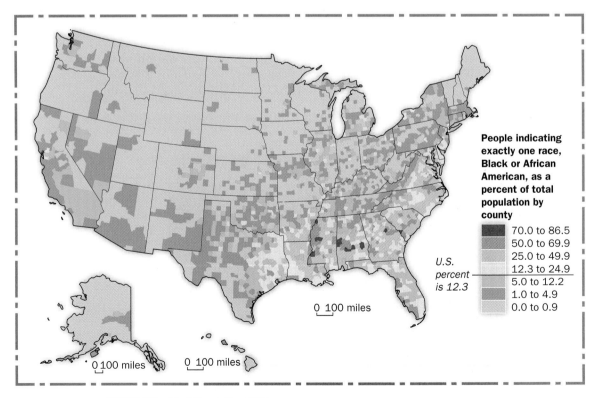

People indicating exactly one race, Black or African American, as a percent of total population by county

70.0 to 86.5
50.0 to 69.9
25.0 to 49.9
12.3 to 24.9
5.0 to 12.2
1.0 to 4.9
0.0 to 0.9

U.S. percent is 12.3

0 100 miles

FIGURE 7.2   Black Population, 2000

Source: Bureau of the Census data map in C. Brewer and Suchan 2001.

and nine Whites. The several days of violence resulted from White fear of social and economic gains made by Blacks. The summer of 1919 saw so much violence that it is commonly called the "red summer." Twenty-six riots broke out throughout the country as White soldiers who returned from World War I feared the new competition that Blacks represented. This period of violence against African Americans also saw a resurgence of the Ku Klux Klan, which at its height had nearly 9 million members (Grimshaw 1969; Schaefer 1971, 1980).

By no stretch of the imagination, and certainly as documented by historians and sociologists, the South had no monopoly on racism. In "Research Focus" we consider the evidence of communities called sundown towns that kept Blacks out at night and were found throughout the North beginning in 1890 and continuing well into the last quarter of the twentieth century.

Reemergence of Black Protest

American involvement in World War II signaled improved economic conditions for both Whites and Blacks. Nearly a million African Americans served in the military in rigidly segregated units. Generally, more Blacks could participate in the armed services in World War II than in previous military engagements, but efforts by Blacks to contribute to the war effort at home were hampered by discriminatory practices in defense plants. A. Philip Randolph, president of the Brotherhood of Sleeping Car Porters, threatened to lead 100,000 Blacks in a march on Washington in 1941 to ensure their employment. Randolph's proposed tactic was nonviolent direct action, which he modeled on Mahatma Gandhi's practices in India. Randolph made it clear that he intended the march to be an all-Black event because he saw it as neither necessary nor desirable for Whites to lead Blacks to their own liberation. President Franklin Roosevelt responded to the pressure and agreed to issue an executive order prohibiting discrimination if Randolph would call off the march. Although the order and the Fair Employment Practices Commission (FEPC) it set up did not fulfill the original promises, a precedent had been established for federal intervention in job discrimination (Garfinkel 1959).

Racial turmoil during World War II was not limited to threatened marches. Racial disturbances occurred in cities throughout the country, the worst riot occurring in Detroit in June 1943. In that case, President Roosevelt sent in 6,000 soldiers to quell the violence, which left twenty-five Blacks and nine Whites dead. The racial disorders were paralleled by a growth in civil disobedience as a means to achieve equality for Blacks. The Congress of Racial Equality (CORE) was founded in 1942 to fight discrimination with nonviolent direct action. This interracial group used sit-ins to open restaurants to Black patrons in Chicago, Baltimore, and Los Angeles. In 1947, CORE sent "freedom riders" to test a court ruling that prohibited segregation in interstate bus travel. In contrast to the red summer of 1919, the end of World War II was not followed by widespread racial violence, in part because the continued expansion of the postwar economy reduced competition between Whites and Blacks for employment (Grimshaw 1969; Meier and Rudwick 1966).

The war years and the postwar period saw several U.S. Supreme Court decisions that suggested the Court was moving away from tolerating racial inequities. The White primary elections endorsed in Jim Crow's formative period were finally challenged in the 1944 *Smith v. Allwright* decision. The effectiveness of the victory was limited; many states simply passed statutes that used new devices to frustrate African American voters.

A particularly repugnant legal device for relegating African Americans to second-class status was restrictive covenants. A **restrictive covenant** was a private contract entered into by neighborhood property owners stipulating that property could not

restrictive covenants
Private contracts or agreements that discourage or prevent minority-group members from purchasing housing in a neighborhood.

SUNDOWN TOWNS, USA

Sundown towns are communities where non-Whites were systematically excluded from living. They emerged in the late nineteenth century and persisted for a hundred years into the late twentieth century. Sundown towns existed throughout the nation, but more often they were located in northern states that were not pre–Civil War Slave states. Although the precise number of sundown towns in the United States is unknown, it is estimated that there were several thousand such towns throughout the nation. As shown in Figure 7.3, sundown towns were common in the southern part of the nonslave state of Illinois.

The dotted line in the map is the "dead line," north of which Blacks were not allowed to live (except in unbolded towns). South of this line, Blacks still lived alongside Whites plantation-style.

The term *sundown town* comes from signs once posted at the city limits reading "Nigger, Don't Let the Sun Set on YOU." In addition to excluding African Americans from many small towns, Chinese Americans, Japanese Americans, Mexican Americans, Jews, and Native Americans—citizens and noncitizens alike—were also subject to such exclusions. In some cases, the exclusion was official town policy. In others cases, the racism policy was enforced through intimidation. This intimidation could occur in a number of ways, including harassment by

law enforcement officers with the blessing of the local citizens.

Although to many today the thought of sundown towns may seem a relic of the past, sociologist James Loewen estimates that by 1970, still *more than half* of all incorporated communities outside the traditional South probably excluded African Americans. Many of these communities had no history of Blacks in residence. Such laws persisted even throughout the era of the civil rights movement. The city council of New Market, Iowa, for example, suspended its sundown ordinance for one night in the mid-1980s to allow an interracial band to play at a town festival, but it went back into effect the very next day.

So what is it like today in these communities? Few sundown towns today have significant populations of excluded people. Some towns where colleges are located have benefited from efforts to desegregate their hometown. Such has been the case with initiatives by Lawrence University in Appleton, Wisconsin. What Loewen calls "recovering" sundown towns face continuing challenges to developing good race relations to attract African American families, including biased school curricula and overwhelmingly White teaching staffs. Practices that discourage desegregation persist across the country. ■

Source: Loewen 2005, 2008.

---

be sold or rented to certain minority groups, thus ensuring that they could not live in the area. In 1948, the Supreme Court finally declared in *Shelley v. Kramer* that restrictive covenants were not constitutional, although it did not actually attack their discriminatory nature. The victory was in many ways less substantial than it was symbolic of the new willingness by the Supreme Court to uphold the rights of Black citizens.

The Democratic administrations of the late 1940s and early 1950s made a number of promises to Black Americans. The party adopted a strong civil rights platform in 1948, but its provisions were not enacted. Once again, union president Randolph

sundown towns
Communities where non-Whites were systematically excluded from living.

search Focus Research Focus Research

FIGURE 7.3   Sundown Towns: A Sampling in Southern Illinois

Source: Loewen 2005, 63.

threatened Washington, D.C., with a march. This time he insisted that as long as Blacks were subjected to a peacetime draft, the military must be desegregated. President Truman responded by issuing an executive order on July 26, 1948, desegregating the armed forces. The U.S. Army abolished its quota system in 1950, and training camps for the Korean War were integrated. Desegregation was not complete, however, especially in the reserves and the National Guard, and even today charges of racial favoritism confront the armed forces. Whatever its shortcomings, the desegregation order offered African Americans an alternative to segregated civilian life (Moskos and Butler 1996).

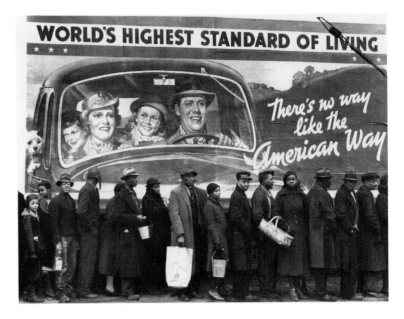

In this classic Margaret Bourke-White photograph, a line of Black Americans awaits food handouts in 1937 in Louisville, Kentucky.

The Civil Rights Movement

It is difficult to say exactly when a social movement begins or ends. Usually, a movement's ideas or tactics precede the actual mobilization of people and continue long after the movement's driving force has been replaced by new ideals and techniques. This description applies to the civil rights movement and its successor, the continuing struggle for African American freedom. Before 1954, there were some confrontations of White supremacy: the CORE sit-ins of 1942 and efforts to desegregate buses in Baton Rouge, Louisiana, in 1953. The civil rights movement gained momentum with a Supreme Court decision in 1954 that eventually desegregated the public schools, and it ended as a major force in Black America with the civil disorders of 1965 through 1968. However, beginning in 1954, toppling the traditional barriers to full rights for Blacks was the rule, not the exception.

Struggle to Desegregate the Schools

For the majority of Black children, public school education meant attending segregated schools. Southern school districts assigned children to school by race rather than by neighborhood, a practice that constituted de jure segregation. **De jure segregation** is segregation that results from children being assigned to schools specifically to maintain racially separate schools. It was this form of legal humiliation that was attacked in the landmark decree of *Linda Brown et al. v. Board of Education of Topeka, Kansas.*

Seven-year-old Linda Brown was not permitted to enroll in the grade school four blocks from her home in Topeka, Kansas. Rather, school board policy dictated that she attend the Black school almost two miles away. This denial led the NAACP Legal Defense and Educational Fund to bring suit on behalf of Linda Brown and twelve other Black children. The NAACP argued that the Fourteenth Amendment was intended to rule out segregation in public schools. Chief Justice Earl Warren of the Supreme Court wrote the unanimous opinion that "in the field of public education the doctrine of 'separate but equal' has no place. Separate educational facilities are inherently unequal."

The freedom that African Americans saw in their grasp at the time of the *Brown* decision essentially amounted to a reaffirmation of American values. What Blacks sought was assimilation into White American society. The motivation for the *Brown* suit did not come

de jure segregation
Children assigned to schools specifically to maintain racially separated schools.

In this often-reproduced photograph, civil rights hero Rosa Parks is shown defying *de jure* segregation by sitting in the White section of the bus that launched the Montgomery, Alabama, bus boycott in 1955. Actually, while the event was very real, there were no journalists present at the time and this iconic photography was a re-creation with an Associated Press reporter seated behind Rosa Parks.

merely because Black schools were inferior, although they were. Blacks were assigned to poorly ventilated and dilapidated buildings, with overcrowded classrooms and unqualified teachers. Less money was spent on Black schools than on White schools throughout the South in both rural and metropolitan areas. The issue was not such tangible factors, however, but the intangible effect of not being allowed to go to school with Whites. All-Black schools could not be equal to all-White schools. Even in this victory, Blacks were reaffirming White society and the importance of an integrated educational experience.

Although *Brown* marked the beginning of the civil rights movement, the reaction to it showed just how deeply prejudice was held in the South. Resistance to court-ordered desegregation took many forms: Some people called for impeachment of all the Supreme Court justices; others petitioned Congress to declare the Fourteenth Amendment unconstitutional; cities closed schools rather than comply; and the governor of Arkansas used the state's National Guard to block Black students from entering a previously all-White high school in Little Rock (Figure 7.4).

The issue of school desegregation was extended to higher education, and Mississippi state troopers and the state's National Guard confronted each other over the 1962 admission of James Meredith, the first African American accepted by the University of Mississippi. Scores were injured, and two were killed in this clash between segregationists and the law. A similar defiant stand was taken a year later by Governor George Wallace, who "stood in the schoolhouse door" to block two Blacks from enrolling in the University of Alabama. President Kennedy federalized the Alabama National Guard to guarantee admission of the students. *Brown* did not resolve the school controversy, and many questions remain unanswered. More recently, the issue of school segregation resulting from neighborhood segregation has been debated. In Chapter 8, another form of segregation, called de facto segregation, is examined more closely (Butler 1996).

Civil Disobedience

The success of a yearlong boycott of city buses in Montgomery, Alabama, dealt Jim Crow another setback. On December 1, 1955, Rosa Parks defied the law and refused to give her seat on a crowded bus to a White man. Her defiance led to the organization of the Montgomery Improvement Association, headed by 26-year-old Martin Luther King, Jr., a Baptist minister with a Ph.D. from Boston University. The bus boycott was

Civil Rights Movement

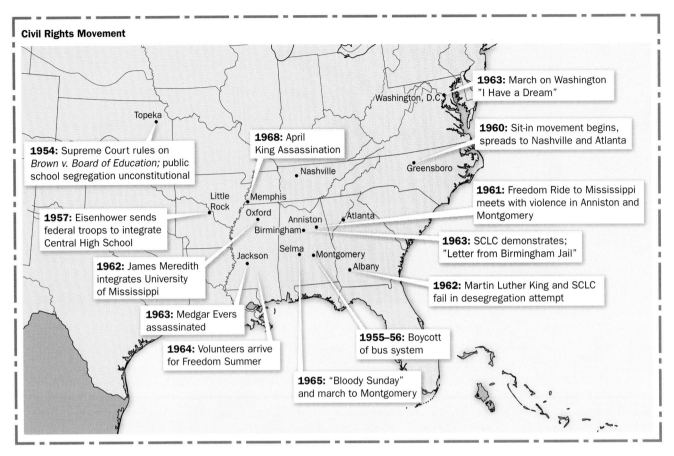

FIGURE 7.4 **Major Events of the Civil Rights Movement**

the first of many instances in which Blacks used nonviolent direct action to obtain the rights that Whites already enjoyed. The boycott eventually demanded the end of segregated seating. The *Brown* decision woke up all of America to racial injustice, but the Montgomery boycott marked a significant shift away from the historical reliance on NAACP court battles (Killian 1975).

Civil disobedience is based on the belief that people have the right to disobey the law under certain circumstances. This tactic was not new; it had been used before in India and also by Blacks in the United States. Under King's leadership, however, civil disobedience became a widely used technique and even gained a measure of acceptability among some prominent Whites. King distinguished clearly between the laws to be obeyed and those to be disobeyed: "A just law is a man-made law of God. An unjust law is a code that is out of harmony with the moral law" (1963, 82). In disobeying unjust laws, King (1958) developed this strategy:

civil disobedience
A tactic promoted by Martin Luther King, Jr., based on the belief that people have the right to disobey unjust laws under certain circumstances.

- Active nonviolent resistance to evil
- Not seeking to defeat or humiliate opponents but to win their friendship and understanding
- Attacking the forces of evil rather than the people who happen to be doing the evil
- Willingness to accept suffering without retaliating
- Refusing to hate the opponent
- Acting with the conviction that the universe is on the side of justice (pp. 101–107)

Voices Listen to Our Voices Listen to

LETTER FROM BIRMINGHAM JAIL

You may well ask: "Why direct action? Why sit-ins, marches and so forth? Isn't negotiation a better path?" You are quite right in calling for negotiation. Indeed, this is the very purpose of direct action. Nonviolent direct action seeks to create such a crisis and foster such a tension that a community which has constantly refused to negotiate is forced to confront the issue. It seeks so to dramatize the issue that it can no longer be ignored. My citing the creation of tension as part of the work of the nonviolent-resister may sound rather shocking. But I must confess that I am not afraid of the word "tension." I have earnestly opposed violent tension, but there is a type of constructive, nonviolent tension which is necessary for growth. Just as Socrates felt that it was necessary to create a tension in the mind so that individuals could rise from the bondage of myths and half-truths to the unfettered realm of creative analysis and objective appraisal, so must we see the need for nonviolent gadflies to create the kind of tension in society that will help men rise from the dark depths of prejudice and racism to the majestic heights of understanding and brotherhood.

Martin Luther King, Jr.

The purpose of our direct-action program is to create a situation so crisis-packed that it will inevitably open the door to negotiation. I therefore concur with you in your call for negotiation. Too long has our beloved Southland been bogged down in a tragic effort to live in monologue rather than dialogue. . . .

You express a great deal of anxiety over our willingness to break laws. This is certainly a legitimate concern. Since we so diligently urge people to obey the Supreme Court's decision of 1954 outlawing segregation in the public schools, at first glance it may seem rather paradoxical for us consciously to break laws. One may well ask: "How can you advocate breaking some laws and obeying others?" The answer lies in the fact that there are two types of laws: just and unjust. I would be the first to advocate obeying just laws. One has not only a legal but a moral responsibility to obey just laws. Conversely, one has a moral responsibility to disobey unjust laws. I would agree with St. Augustine that "an unjust law is no law at all." ▪

Source: "Letter from Birmingham Jail," in *Why We Can't Wait,* by Martin Luther King, Jr. Copyright © 1963 by Martin Luther King, Jr. Renewed 1991 by Coretta Scott King. Reprinted by arrangement with The Estate of Martin Luther King, Jr., c/o Writer's House as agents for the proprietor.

King, like other Blacks before him and since, made it clear that passive acceptance of injustice was intolerable. He hoped that by emphasizing nonviolence, southern Blacks would display their hostility to racism in a way that would undercut violent reaction by Whites.

The pattern had now been established and a method devised to confront racism. But civil disobedience did not work quickly. The struggle to desegregate buses in the South, for example, took seven years. Civil disobedience was also not spontaneous. The success of the civil rights movement rested on a dense network of local efforts. People were spontaneously attracted to the efforts, but organized tactics and targets were crucial to dismantling racist institutions that had existed for generations (Payne 1995).

Beginning in April 1963, the Southern Christian Leadership Conference (SCLC), founded by King, began a series of marches in Birmingham to demand fair employment opportunities, desegregation of public facilities, and the release of 3,000 people arrested for participating in the marches. King, himself arrested, tells in "Listen to Our Voices" why civil disobedience and the confrontations that followed were necessary. In May, the Birmingham police used dogs and water from high-pressure hoses on the marchers, who included many schoolchildren.

Congress had still failed to enact any sweeping federal barrier to discrimination. Following the example of A. Philip Randolph in 1941, Blacks organized the March on Washington for Jobs and Freedom on August 28, 1963. With more than 200,000 people participating, the march was the high point of the civil rights movement. The mass of people, middle-class Whites and Blacks looking to the federal government for support, symbolized the struggle. However, a public opinion poll conducted shortly before the march documented the continuing resentment of the majority of Whites: Sixty-three percent were opposed to the rally (G. Gallup 1972).

King (1971, 351) delivered his famous "I Have a Dream" speech before the large crowd; he looked forward to a time when all Americans "will be able to join hands and sing in the words of the old Negro spiritual, 'Free at last! free at last! Thank God almighty, we are free at last!'" Just eighteen days later, a bomb exploded in a Black church in Birmingham, killing four little girls and injuring twenty others.

Despair only increased as the November 1963 elections saw segregationists successful in their bids for office. Most distressing was the assassination of President Kennedy on November 22. As president, Kennedy had appealed to Blacks despite his previously mediocre legislative record in the U.S. Senate. His death left doubt as to the direction and pace of future actions on civil rights by the executive branch under President Lyndon Baines Johnson. Two months later, the Twenty-Fourth Amendment was ratified, outlawing the poll tax that had long prevented Blacks from voting. The enactment of the Civil Rights Act on July 2, 1964, was hailed as a major victory and provided at least for a while what historian John Hope Franklin called "the illusion of equality" (Franklin and Moss 2000).

In the months that followed the passage of the act, the pace of the movement to end racial injustice slowed. The violence continued, however, from the Bedford-Stuyvesant section of Brooklyn to Selma, Alabama. Southern state courts still found White murderers of Blacks innocent, and they had to be tried and convicted in federal civil, rather than criminal, court on the charge that by killing a person one violates that person's civil rights. Government records, which did not become public until 1973, revealed a systematic campaign by the FBI to infiltrate civil rights groups in an effort to discredit them, in the belief that such activist groups were subversive. It was in such an atmosphere that the Voting Rights Act was passed in August 1965, but this significant, positive event was somewhat overshadowed by violence in the Watts section of Los Angeles in the same week (Blackstock 1976).

Urban Violence and Oppression

Riots involving Whites and Blacks did not begin in the 1960s. As we saw earlier in this chapter, urban violence occurred after World War I and even during World War II, and violence against Blacks in the United States is nearly 350 years old. But the urban riots of the 1960s influenced Blacks and Whites in the United States and throughout the world so extensively that they deserve special attention. However, we must remember that most violence between Whites and Blacks has not been large-scale collective action but has involved only a small number of people.

The summers of 1963 and 1964 were a prelude to riots that gripped the country's attention. Although most people knew of the civil rights efforts in the South and legislative victories in Washington, everyone realized that the racial problem was national after several cities outside the South experienced violent disorders. In April 1968, after the assassination of Martin Luther King, Jr., more cities exploded than had in all of 1967. Even before the summer of 1968 began, there were 369 civil disorders. Communities of all sizes were hit (Oberschall 1968).

As the violence continued and embraced many ghettos, a popular explanation was that riot participants were mostly unemployed youths who had criminal records, often involving narcotics, and who were vastly outnumbered by the African Americans who repudiated the looting and arson. This explanation was called the **riff-raff theory** or the rotten-apple theory because it discredited the rioters and left the barrel of apples, White society, untouched. On the contrary, research shows that the Black community expressed sympathetic understanding toward the rioters and that the rioters were not merely the poor and uneducated but included middle-class, working-class, and educated residents (Sears and McConahay 1969, 1973; Tomlinson 1969; R. Turner 1994).

Several alternatives to the riff-raff theory explain why Black violent protest increased in the United States at a time when the nation was seemingly committed to civil rights for all. Two explanations stand out. One ascribes the problem to Black frustration with rising expectations in the face of continued deprivation relative to Whites.

The standard of living of African Americans improved remarkably after World War II, and it continued to do so during the civil rights movement. However, White income and occupation levels also improved, so the gap between the groups remained. Chapter 3 showed that feelings of relative deprivation often are the basis for perceived discrimination. **Relative deprivation** is the conscious feeling of a negative discrepancy between legitimate expectations and present actualities (W. Wilson 1973).

It is of little comfort to African Americans that their earning power matches that of Whites ten or more years earlier. As shown in Figure 7.5, Black family income has increased significantly, but so has that of White families, leaving the gap between the two largely unchanged. Relative to Whites, most Blacks made no tangible gains in housing, education, jobs, or economic security. African Americans were doing better in absolute numbers, but not relative to Whites.

At the same time that African Americans were feeling relative deprivation, they were also experiencing growing discontent. **Rising expectations** refers to the increasing sense of frustration that legitimate needs are being blocked. Blacks felt that they had legitimate aspirations to equality, and the civil rights movement reaffirmed that discrimination had blocked upward mobility. As the horizons of African Americans broadened, they were more likely to make comparisons with Whites and feel discontented. The civil rights movement gave higher aspirations to Black America, yet for the majority, life remained basically unchanged. Not only were their lives unchanged, but also the feeling was widespread that the existing social structure held no prospect for improvement (Garner 1996; Sears and McConahay 1970; Thomas and Thomas 1984).

Black Power

The riots in the northern ghettos captured the attention of Whites, and Black Power was what they heard. Appropriately enough, Black Power was born not of Black but of White violence. On June 6, 1966, James Meredith was carrying out a one-person march from Memphis to Jackson, Mississippi, to encourage fellow African Americans to overcome their own fears and vote after the passage of the Voting Rights Act. During that

riff-raff theory
Also called the rotten-apple theory; the belief that the riots of the 1960s were caused by discontented youths rather than by social and economic problems facing all African Americans.

relative deprivation
The conscious experience of a negative discrepancy between legitimate expectations and present actualities.

rising expectations
The increasing sense of frustration that legitimate needs are being blocked.

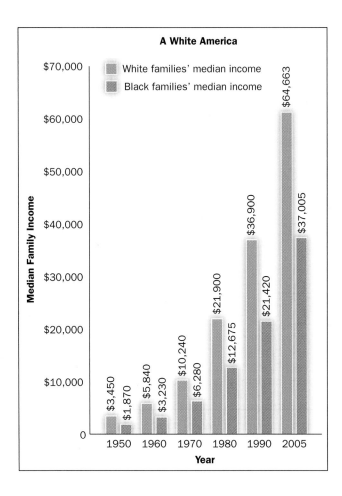

A White America

■ White families' median income

■ Black families' median income

Median Family Income (y-axis): $70,000, $60,000, $50,000, $40,000, $30,000, $20,000, $10,000, 0

Year (x-axis): 1950, 1960, 1970, 1980, 1990, 2005

Year	White	Black
1950	$3,450	$1,870
1960	$5,840	$3,230
1970	$10,240	$6,280
1980	$21,900	$12,675
1990	$36,900	$21,420
2005	$64,663	$37,005

FIGURE 7.5   Black–White Income Gap

For the over 50 years of available data, median Black family income has been only about half that of White family income.

Note: 2005 data are for White, non-Hispanic households.

Sources: Bureau of the Census 1975, 297; 2002c; DeNavas-Walt et al. 2006. HINC.

march, an unidentified assailant shot and wounded Meredith. Blacks from throughout the country immediately continued the march. During the march, Stokely Carmichael of the Student Nonviolent Coordinating Committee (SNCC) proclaimed to a cheering Black crowd, "What we need is Black Power." King and others later urged "Freedom Now" as the slogan for the march. A compromise dictated that no slogan would be used, but the mood of Black America said otherwise (King 1967; Lomax 1971).

In retrospect, it may be puzzling that the phrase *Black Power* frightened Whites and offended so many Blacks. It was not really new. The National Advisory Commission on Civil Disorders (1968, 234–235) correctly identified it as old wine in new bottles: Black consciousness was not new, even if the phrase was.

By advocating Black Power, Carmichael was distancing himself from the assimilationism of King. Carmichael rejected the goal of assimilation into White middle-class society. Instead, he said, Blacks must create new institutions. To succeed in this endeavor, Carmichael argued that Blacks must follow the same path as the Italians, Irish, and other White ethnic groups. "Before a group can enter the open society, it must first close ranks. . . . Group solidarity is necessary before a group can operate effectively from a bargaining position of strength in a pluralistic society" (Ture and Hamilton 1992, 44). Prominent Black leaders opposed the concept; many feared that Whites would retaliate even more violently. King (1967) saw Black Power as a "cry of disappointment" but acknowledged that it had a "positive meaning."

Eventually Black Power gained wide acceptance among Blacks and even many Whites. Although it came to be defined differently by nearly every new proponent,

Since the riots of the 1960s, inner-city neighborhoods such as South Central Los Angeles (renamed South Los Angeles in 2003 to try to symbolically erase the stigma) have undergone only modest redevelopment and much less than originally anticipated by the residents. Santa Ana Pines development, pictured here, is one of the few examples of economic investment in the community.

support of Black Power generally implied endorsing Black control of the political, economic, and social institutions in Black communities. One reason for its popularity among African Americans was that it gave them a viable option for surviving in a segregated society. The civil rights movement strove to end segregation, but the White response showed how committed White society was to maintaining it. Black Power presented restructuring society as the priority item on the Black agenda (Carmichael and Thelwell 2003; Pinkney 2001).

One aspect of Black Power clearly operated outside the conventional system. The Black Panther Party was organized in October 1966 in Oakland, California, by Huey Newton, age 24, and Bobby Seale, age 30, to represent urban Blacks in a political climate that the Panthers felt was unresponsive. The Panthers were controversial from the beginning, charging police brutality and corruption among government officials. They engaged in violent confrontations with law enforcement officers. From 1969 to 1972, internal weaknesses, a long series of trials involving most of the leaders, intraparty strife, and several shoot-outs with police combined to bring the organization to a standstill. Although they were often portrayed as the most separatist of the Black militant movements, the Panthers were willing to form alliances with non-Black organizations, including Students for a Democratic Society (SDS), the Peace and Freedom Party, the Young Lords, the Young Patriots, and the Communist Party of the United States. Despite, or perhaps because of, such coalitions, the Panthers were not a prominent force in shaping contemporary Black America. Newton himself admitted in 1973 that the party had alienated Blacks and had become "too radical" to be accepted by the Black community (Cleaver 1982; Joseph 2006; C. Woodward 1974).

The militant Black Panthers encountered severe difficulties in the 1970s and fell victim to both internal political problems and external surveillance. Finally, their formerly outspoken leaders moved in new directions. Eldridge Cleaver became a born-again Christian and confined himself to lecturing on the virtues of his evangelical faith. Cofounder Bobby Seale ran unsuccessfully for mayor of Oakland, California, in the kind of traditional campaign he had formerly denounced as unproductive. After that unsuccessful bid, Seale became an organizer of moderate community groups. Former Panther defense minister Bobby Rush became deputy chairman of the Illinois State Democratic Party, was elected to the U.S. Congress in 1992, and has been re-elected to eight more terms. The role of spokesperson for a minority group in the United States is exhausting, and people who have assumed that role for a time often turn to more conventional, less personally demanding roles, especially if public support for their programs wanes.

The Religious Force

 ASK Yourself

Does the place where your family has traditionally worshipped show much evidence of diversity among those who attend regularly?

It is not possible to overstate the role religion has played, good and bad, in the social history of African Americans. Historically, Black leaders have emerged from the pulpits to seek out rights on behalf of all Blacks. Churches have served as the basis for community organization in neighborhoods abandoned by businesses and even government. Religion may be a source of antagonism as well.

As we saw earlier in this chapter, because the Africans who were brought involuntarily to the Western Hemisphere were non-Christian, they were seen as heathens and barbarians. To "civilize" the slaves in the period before the Civil War, Southern slaveholders encouraged and often required their slaves to attend church and embrace Christianity. The Christian churches to which Blacks were introduced in the United States encouraged them to accept the inferior status enforced by Whites, and the religious teaching that the slaves received equated whiteness with salvation, presenting whiteness as an acceptable, if not preferred, object of reverence.

Despite being imposed in the past by Whites, the Christian faiths are embraced by most African Americans today. As shown in Figure 7.6, African Americans are overwhelmingly Protestant, with half being Baptist. Methodists and Roman Catholics account for another 9 percent each. Therefore, almost seven out of ten African Americans are members of these three faiths, compared with less than half of Whites.

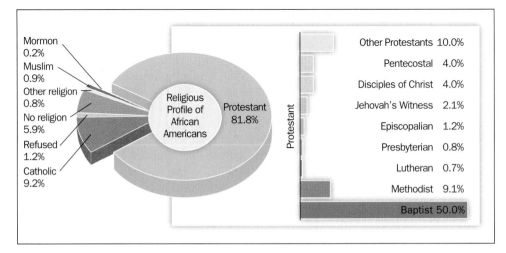

FIGURE 7.6 **Religious Profile of African Americans**

Based on a 1990 national sample, most African Americans are Baptist, Roman Catholic, or Methodist.

Source: From *One Nation Under God* by Seymour P. Lachman and Barry A. Kosmin. Copyright © 1993 by Seymour P. Lachman and Barry A. Kosmin. Reprinted by permission of Harmony Books, a division of Random House Inc.

Especially in urban centers, recent immigrants from Africa have begun to provide a new diversity to the Black community in the United States. Here a Senegalese restaurateur is shown in front of her Philadelphia restaurant.

The Black church continues to be socially involved in the community. Even when upwardly mobile African Americans move out of the central city, many travel long distances to return to their congregations to support them financially and spiritually (Watson 2004).

However, a variety of non-Christian groups have exerted a much greater influence on African Americans than the reported numbers of their followers suggest. The Nation of Islam, for example, which became known as the Black Muslims, has attracted a large number of followers and received the most attention. We will look at this group in grater detail in Chapter 11 when we consider the large Muslim community in the United States.

Conclusion

The dramatic events affecting African Americans today have their roots in the forcible bringing of their ancestors to the United States as slaves. In the South, whether as slaves or later as victims of Jim Crow, Blacks were not a real threat to any but the poorest Whites, although even affluent Whites feared the perceived potential threat that Blacks posed. During their entire history here, Blacks have been criticized when they rebelled and praised when they went along with the system. During the time of slavery, revolts were met with increased suppression; after emancipation, leaders calling for accommodation were applauded.

The Black migration to the urban North helped to define a new social order. Yet many of the communities they may have settled in were sundown towns where the welcome mat had been replaced with covert and overt racism. Whites found it more difficult to ignore Blacks as residents of the ghetto than as sharecroppers in the rural

South. No longer excluded by the White primary as in the South, the Black urban voter had potential power. The federal government and city halls slowly began to acknowledge the presence of Blacks. From the Black community came voices that spoke of pride and self-help: Douglass, Tubman, Washington, Du Bois, King, and Malcolm X.

Most people today look back at the civil rights movement and accept the significance of its legacy but, like so many things in society, Black and White perceptions differ. A national survey found that 46 percent of Whites compared to 75 percent of Blacks felt the movement was extremely important. Half of Whites felt that most of the goals of the civil rights movement have been achieved, while only 30 percent of African Americans were similarly convinced (Ludwig 2004).

Blacks, in their efforts to bring about change, have understandably differed in their willingness to form

FIGURE 7.7   Intergroup Relations Continuum

coalitions with Whites. Resisting African Americans, in the days of either slavery or the civil rights movement (see the intergroup relations continuum in Figure 7.7), would have concurred with Du Bois's (1903) comment that a Black person "simply wishes to make it possible to be both a Negro and an American, without being cursed and spit upon by his fellows, without having the door of opportunity closed roughly in his face"(pp.3–4). The object of Black protest seems simple enough, but for many people, including presidents, the point was lost.

How much progress has been made? When covering several hundred years, beginning with slavery and ending with rights recognized constitutionally, it is easy to be impressed. Yet let us consider Topeka, Kansas, the site of the 1954 *Brown v. Board of Education* case. Linda Brown,

one of the original plaintiffs, was recently touched by another segregation case. In 1992, the courts held that Oliver Brown, her grandchild, was being victimized because the Topeka schools were still segregated, now for reasons of residential segregation. The remedy to separate schools in this Kansas city is still unresolved (Hays 1994).

Chapter 8 assesses the status of African Americans today. Recall the events chronicled in this chapter as you consider the advances that have been made. These events are a reminder that any progress has followed years—indeed, generations—of struggle by African Americans, enlisting the support of Whites seeking to end second-class status for African Americans in the United States.

Key Terms

abolitionists 205

afrocentric perspective 204

civil disobedience 216

de jure segregation 214

Ebonics 204

Jim Crow 206

relative deprivation 219

restrictive covenants 211

riff-raff theory 219

rising expectations 219

slave codes 202

slavery reparations 206

sundown towns 212

white primary 206

Review Questions

1. In what ways were slaves defined as property?

2. How did slavery provide a foundation for both White and Black America today?

3. If civil disobedience is nonviolent, why is so much violence associated with it?

4. How did observers of the urban riots tend to dismiss any social importance to the outbreaks?

5. Why has religion proved to be a force for both unity and disunity among African Americans?

Critical Thinking

1. How much time do you recall spending in school thus far learning about the history of Europe? How about Africa? What do you think this says about the way education is delivered or what we choose to learn?

2. What would you consider the three most important achievements in civil rights for African Americans since 1900? What roles did Whites and Blacks play in making these events happen?

3. Growing numbers of Blacks are immigrating to the United States (especially to the eastern United States) from the Caribbean. What impact may this have on what it means to be Black or African American in the United States? What would the social construction of race say about this development?

Internet Connections—Research Navigator™

To access the full resources of Research Navigator™, please find the access code printed on the inside cover of OneSearch with Research Navigator ™: Sociology. You may have received this booklet if your instructor recommended this guide be packaged with new textbooks. (If your book did not come with this printed guide, you can purchase one through your college bookstore). Visit our Research Navigator™ site atx www.ResearchNavigator.com. Once at this site, click on **REGISTER** under New Users and enter your access code to create a personal Login Name and Password. (When revisiting the site, use the same Login Name and Password.) Browse the features of the Research Navigator ™ Web site and search the databases of academic journals, newspapers, magazines, and Web links.

For further information relevant to Chapter 7, you may wish to use such keywords as "slavery," "Martin Luther King," and "civil rights movement," and the search engine will supply relevant and recent scholarly and popular press publications. Use the *New York Times* Search-by-Subject Archive to find recent news articles related to sociology and the Link Library feature to locate relevant Web links organized by the key terms associated with this chapter.

8 African Americans Today

CHAPTER OUTLINE

Education

The Economic Picture

■**LISTEN TO OUR VOICES**
When Work Disappears
by **William Julius Wilson**

Family Life

Housing

Criminal Justice

Health Care

■**RESEARCH FOCUS**
The Ultimate Penalty: Execution

Politics

Conclusion

Key Terms/Review Questions/Critical
Thinking/Internet Connections—
Research Navigator™

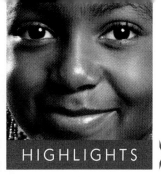

A

FRICAN AMERICANS HAVE MADE SIGNIFICANT PROGRESS IN many areas, but they have not kept pace with White Americans in any sectors. African Americans have advanced in formal schooling to a remarkable degree, although in most areas residential patterns have left many public schools predominantly Black or White. Higher education also reflects the legacy of a nation that has operated two schooling systems: one for Blacks and another for Whites. Gains in earning power have barely kept pace with inflation, and the gap between Whites and Blacks has remained largely unchanged. African American families are susceptible to the problems associated with a low-income group that also faces discrimination and prejudice. Housing in many areas remains segregated, despite growing numbers of Blacks in suburban areas. African Americans are more likely to be victims of crimes and to be arrested for violent crimes. The subordination of Blacks is also apparent in health care delivery. African Americans have made substantial gains in elective office but still are underrepresented compared with their numbers in the general population.

J ohn and Glenn are alike in almost every way: about the same age, Big Ten college graduates, similar jobs, and active sports enthusiasts. But they find that they have very dissimilar experiences in such everyday activities as walking into a shopping mall to buy shoes or look over the latest CDs. John typically receives instant attention when he walks even near the shoe department, but the same salesperson fails to acknowledge Glenn even though he has been waiting five minutes. A little later John casually picks up some CDs in a record store. At the very same time, Glenn is engaged in exactly the same behavior in the same store, but he is closely shadowed by a store employee, who observes Glenn's every move.

John is White and Glenn is Black, which makes all the difference even in this everyday shopping behavior. They were part of an experiment conducted by the television newsmagazine *Primetime Live* in St. Louis to assess the impact of race on the day-to-day lives of average African Americans and Whites. Over a period of three weeks, the program closely monitored the two researchers, who had been trained to present themselves in an identical manner in a variety of situations.

In a televised report on this experiment, *Primetime Live* host Diane Sawyer acknowledged that, at times, the two men were treated equally. However, Sawyer added that not once or twice but "every single day," there were instances of differential treatment. At an employment agency, Glenn was lectured on laziness and told that he would be monitored "real close." John, by contrast, was encouraged to pursue job leads, and staff members made it clear that he could expect to find a suitable position (ABC News 1992).

Race is socially constructed, but that does not mean that being Black does not have consequences and being White carries privileges. Despite the publicity given to obvious discrimination that has persisted well into the present, a superficial sense of complacency about the position of African Americans in the United States exists now in the twenty-first century.

As you read this chapter, try to keep in perspective the profile of African Americans in the United States today. This chapter will assess education, the economy, family life, housing, criminal justice, health care, and politics among the nation's African Americans. Progress has occurred, and some of the advances are nothing short of remarkable. The deprivation of the African American people relative to Whites remains, however, even if absolute deprivation has been softened. A significant gap remains between African Americans and the dominant group, and to this gap a price is assigned: the price of being African Americans in the United States.

Education

The African American population in the United States has placed special importance on acquiring education, beginning with its emphasis in the home of the slave family and continuing through the creation of separate schools for Black children because the public schools were closed to them by custom or law. Today, long after the old civil rights coalition has disbanded, education remains a controversial issue. Because racial and ethnic groups realize that formal schooling is the key to social mobility, they want to maximize this opportunity for upward mobility and, therefore, want better schooling. White Americans also appreciate the value of formal schooling and do not want to do anything that they perceive will jeopardize their own position.

Quality and Quantity of Education

Several measures document the inadequate education received by African Americans, starting with the quantity of formal education. The gap in educational attainment between Blacks as a group and Whites as a group has always been present. Despite programs directed at the poor, such as Head Start, White children are still more likely to have formal prekindergarten education than are African American children. Later, Black children generally drop out of school sooner and, therefore, are less likely to receive high school diplomas, let alone college degrees. Table 8.1 shows the gap in the amount of schooling African Americans receive compared to Whites. It also illustrates progress in reducing this gap in recent years. Despite this progress, however, the gap remains substantial, with nearly twice the proportion of Whites holding a college degree as Blacks in 2004.

A second aspect of inadequate schooling, many educators argue, is that many students would not drop out of school were it not for the combined inadequacies of their education. Among the deficiencies noted have been:

- Insensitive teachers
- Poor counseling
- Unresponsive administrators
- Overcrowded classes
- Irrelevant curricula
- Dilapidated school facilities

Although several of these problems can be addressed with more adequate funding, some are stalemated by disagreements over what changes would lead to the best outcome. For example, there is significant debate among educators and African Americans in general over the content of curriculum that is best for minority students. Some schools have developed academic programs that take an Afrocentric perspective and

TABLE 8.1
Years of School Completed (Percentages of People 25 Years and Older)

	1960	1980	2004
COMPLETING HIGH SCHOOL			
BLACK			
Male	18.2%	50.8%	80.4%
Female	21.8	51.5	80.9
WHITE			
Male	41.6	69.6	89.9
Female	44.7	68.1	90.1
COMPLETING COLLEGE			
BLACK			
Male	2.8	8.4	16.6
Female	3.3	8.3	18.5
WHITE			
Male	10.3	21.3	32.9
Female	6.0	13.3	28.4

Note: Data for Whites are for non-Hispanic Whites.

Source: Bureau of the Census 2005a, 147; 2005c, Table 10.

immerse students in African American history and culture. Yet a few of these programs have been targeted as ignoring fundamentals, as in the debate in Oakland, California, noted in Chapter 7, over recognizing Ebonics as a language in the classroom. On other occasions, the Afrocentric curriculum has even been viewed as racist against Whites. The debates over a few controversial programs attract a lot of attention, clouding the widespread need to reassess the curriculum for racial and ethnic minorities.

Middle- and upper-class children occasionally face these barriers to a high-quality education, but they are more likely than the poor to have a home environment that is favorable to learning. Even African American schoolchildren who stay in school are not guaranteed equal opportunities in life. Many high schools do not prepare students who are interested in college for advanced schooling. The problem is that schools are failing to meet the needs of students, not that students are failing in school. Therefore, the problems with schooling were properly noted as a part of the past discrimination component of total discrimination illustrated in Figure 3.1.

School Segregation

It has been more than fifty years since the U.S. Supreme Court issued its unanimous ruling in *Brown v. Board of Education of Topeka, Kansas,* that separate educational facilities are inherently unequal. What has been the legacy of that decision? Initially, the courts, with the support of the federal government, ordered Southern school districts to end racial separation. But as attention turned to larger school districts, especially in the North, the challenge was to have integrated schools even though the neighborhoods were segregated. In addition, some city school districts were predominantly African American and Hispanic, surrounded by suburban school districts that were predominantly White. This type of school segregation, which results from residential patterns, is called **de facto segregation**.

Initially, courts sought to overcome de facto segregation just as they had de jure school segregation in the *Brown* case. Typically, students were bused within a school district to achieve racial balance, but in a few cases Black students were bused to predominantly White suburban schools and White children were bused into the city. In 1974, however, the Supreme Court ruled in *Millikin v. Bradley* that it was improper to order Detroit and the suburbs to have a joint metropolitan busing solution. These and other Supreme Court decisions have effectively ended initiatives to overcome residential segregation, once again creating racial isolation in the schools. Indeed, even in Topeka, one-third of the schools are segregated today (Orfield et al. 1996).

Racial diversity in individual schools was still largely absent in schools in 2000. White students typically attend public schools that on the average are 80 percent White. Trend data since the 1960s indicate that public schools are increasingly becoming all-White or all-Black or all-Hispanic. New initiatives such as charter schools to provide better education, as well as increases in homeschooling, contribute to greater school segregation.

So enduring has been school segregation, the term *apartheid schools* has been coined to refer to schools that are all Black. An analysis released in 2003 by the Civil Rights Project of Harvard University documented that one in six of the nation's Black students attends an **apartheid school**, and this proportion rose to one out of four in the Northeast and Midwest. If there has been any trend, it is that the typical African American student was less likely to have White classmates in 2000 than in 1970 (Frankenberg et al. 2003; Renzulli and Evans 2005).

Although studies have shown positive effects of integration, a diverse student population does not guarantee an integrated, equal schooling environment. For example, **tracking** in schools, especially middle and high schools, intensifies segregation at the classroom level. Tracking is the practice of placing students in specific curriculum groups on the basis of test scores and other criteria. It also has the effect of decreasing

de facto segregation
Segregation that is the result of residential patterns.

apartheid schools
All-Black schools.

tracking
The practice of placing students in specific curriculum groups on the basis of test scores and other criteria.

White–Black classroom interaction as African American children are disproportionately assigned to general classes, and more White children are placed in college preparatory classes. It is estimated that about 60 percent of elementary schools in the United States and about 80 percent of secondary schools use some form of tracking. Studies indicate that African American students are more likely than White students to be classified as learning disabled or emotionally disturbed. Although there are successes in public education, integration clearly is not one of them (Eitle 2002; Hallinan 2003; Sadker and Sadker 2003).

Acting White, Acting Black, or Neither

A common view advanced by some educators is that the reason African Americans, especially males, do not succeed in school is that they don't want to be caught "**acting White**." That is, they avoid at all costs taking school seriously and do not accept the authority of teachers and administrators. Whatever the accuracy of such a generalization, it clearly shifts the responsibility of low school attainment from the school to the individual and, therefore, can be seen as yet another example of blaming the victim (Fryer 2006; Ogbu with Davis 2003).

"Acting White" sparks strong emotions. In 2004, comedian Bill Cosby sparked the latest round of debates on the subject in a NAACP-sponsored speech he made to mark the fiftieth anniversary of the *Brown* decision. He criticized Black families for tolerating their children not taking school seriously. Social scientists and pundits quickly weighed in not only to deal with the issue but also to question the appropriateness of a Black person criticizing other Blacks in public.

To what extent do Blacks not want to act White in the context of high achievers? Many scholars have noted that individuals' efforts to avoid looking like they want an

acting white
Taking school seriously and accepting the authority of teachers and administrators

 ASK Yourself

How common do you think it is for any student to hide his or her interest in school or even to underperform to be cool?

Is there a difference between Black and White schoolchildren in achievement orientation? Although some feel that African American youth avoid "acting White," research points to no difference in this respect. Members of high school science clubs, whether Black or White, are equally likely to overcome being regarded as "geeks" or "nerds."

Pictured here is Howard University, founded in 1867 in Washington DC, continues to serve as pivotal institutions in the education of African Americans.

education has a long history and is hardly exclusive to any one race. Back in the 1950s, one heard disparaging references to "teacher's pet" and "brown nosing." Does popularity come to high school debaters and National Honor Society students or to cheerleaders and athletes? Academic-oriented classmates are often viewed as social misfits, nerds, and geeks and are seen as socially inept even if their skill building will later make them more economically independent and often more socially desirable. For minority children, including African Americans, to take school seriously means they must overcome their White classmates' same desire to be cool and not a nerd. In addition, Black youth must also come to embrace a curriculum and respect teachers who are much less likely to look or sound like them (Tyson et al. 2005).

The "acting White" thesis overemphasizes personal responsibility rather than structural features such as quality of schools, curriculum, and teachers. Therefore, it locates the source of Black miseducation—and by implication the remedy—in the African American household. As scholar Michael Dyson (2005) observes, "When you think the problems are personal, you think the solutions are the same." If we could only get African American parents to encourage their children to work a little harder and act better (that is, White), everything would be fine. As Dyson notes, "It's hard to argue against any of these things in the abstract; in principle such suggestions sound just fine."

Of course, not all Whites "act White." To equate "acting White" with high academic achievement has little empirical or cultural support. Although more Whites ages 18–19 are in school, the differences are hardly dramatic—64.4 percent of Whites compared to 61.9 percent of Blacks. Studies comparing attitudes and performance show that Black students have the same attitudes—good and bad—about achievement as their White counterparts. Too often we tend to view White slackers who give a hard time to the advanced placement kids as "normal," but when low-performing African Americans do the same thing, it becomes a systemic pathology undermining everything good about schools. The primary stumbling block is not acting White or acting Black but being presented with similar educational opportunities (Bureau of the Census 2005a: 144; Tough 2004; Tyson et al. 2005).

Higher Education

Higher education for Blacks reflects the same pattern: The overall picture of African American higher education is not promising. Although strides were made in the period after the civil rights movement, a plateau was reached in the mid-1970s. African Americans are more likely than Whites to be part-time students and to need financial aid, which began to be severely cut in the 1980s. They are also finding the social climate on predominantly White campuses less than positive. As a result, the historically Black colleges and universities (HBCUs) are once again playing a significant role in educating African Americans. For a century, they were the only real source of college degrees for Blacks. Then, in the 1970s, predominantly White colleges began to recruit African Americans. As of 2006, however, the 105 HBCUs still accounted for about one-quarter of all Black college graduates (White House Initiative 2006).

As shown in Table 8.1, although African Americans are more likely today to be college graduates, the upward trend has declined. Several factors account for this reversal in progress:

1. A reduction in financial aid and more reliance on loans than on grants-in-aid, coupled with rising costs, have tended to discourage students who would be the first members of their families to attend college.
2. Pushing for higher standards in educational achievement without providing remedial courses has locked out many minority students.

3. Employment opportunities, though slight for African Americans without some college, have continued to lure young people who must contribute to their family's income and who otherwise might have gone to college.

4. Negative publicity about affirmative action may have discouraged some African Americans from even considering college.

5. Attention to what appears to be a growing number of racial incidents on predominantly White college campuses has also been a discouraging factor.

Colleges and universities seem uneasy about these problems; publicly, the schools appear committed to addressing them.

There is little question that special challenges face the African American student at a college with an overwhelmingly White student body, faculty, advisors, coaches, and administrators. The campus culture may be neutral at best, and it is often hostile to members of racial minorities. The high attrition rate of African American students on predominantly White college campuses confirms the need for a positive environment.

Because fewer African Americans complete their higher education, fewer are available to fill faculty and administrative positions. This means that despite increases in the numbers of Blacks who enter college, there are no more, and perhaps fewer, role models in college classrooms for students from subordinate groups to see.

The disparity in schooling becomes even more pronounced at the highest levels, and the gap is not closing. Only 3.3 percent of all doctorates awarded in 2001 were to native-born African Americans; that proportion was about the same (i.e., 3.9 percent) in 1981 (Bureau of the Census 2005a, 186; 2005c, Table 10).

In summary, the picture of education for Black Americans is uneven—marked progress in absolute terms (much better educated than a generation ago), but relative to Whites the gap in educational attainment remains at all levels. Fifty years ago, the major issue appeared to be school desegregation, but at the heart it was to improve the quality of education received by Black schoolchildren. Today the concerns of African American parents and most educators are similar—quality education. W. E. B. Du Bois (1935) advanced the same point in 1935—that what a Black student needs "is neither segregated schools nor mixed schools. What he needs is Education" (p. 335).

Few but growing in number, African Americans are entering positions that few people of any color reach. Ayana Howard, with an Electrical Engineering Ph.D., sits beside SmartNav, a prototype for the Mars rover, on a set of the planet at NASA's Jet Propulsion Laboratory in California.

income
Salaries, wages, and other money received.

wealth
An inclusive term encompassing all of a person's material assets, including land and other types of property.

ASK Yourself

What kind of difference do you think it makes for a typical family of four to earn just over $64,000 annually compared to about $37,000?

The Economic Picture

The general economic picture for African Americans has been gradual improvement over the last fifty years, but this improvement is modest compared with that of Whites, whose standard of living has also increased. Therefore, in terms of absolute deprivation, African Americans are much better off today but have experienced much less significant improvement with respect to their relative deprivation to Whites on almost all economic indicators. We will consider income and wealth, employment, and African American–owned businesses.

Income and Wealth

There are two useful measures of the overall economic situation of an individual or household: income and wealth. **Income** refers to salaries, wages, and other money received; **wealth** is a more inclusive term encompassing all of a person's material assets, including land and other types of property.

There is a significant gap between the incomes of Black and White households in the United States. As we saw in Figure 7.5, Black income has been increasing steadily, but so has that of Whites. In 2005, the median income of Black families was $37,005, compared with $64,663 for White non-Hispanic households. Another way to consider the gap is that Black income today resembles that of Whites more than ten years ago. This lag has been present since World War II. In Figure 8.1, we look at the overall distribution of Black and White household income. Even a casual glance at the figure will show very different income profiles for Blacks and Whites today.

FIGURE 8.1 Income Distribution: Black Versus White

Note: Income data for 2005 were reported in 2006, and these data are for White non-Hispanics.

Source: DeNavas-Walt et al. 2006; U.S. Census Bureau, Current Population Reports, *P60–231, Income, Poverty and Health Insurance Coverage in the United States: 2005.* Washington, D.C.: U.S. Government Printing Office.

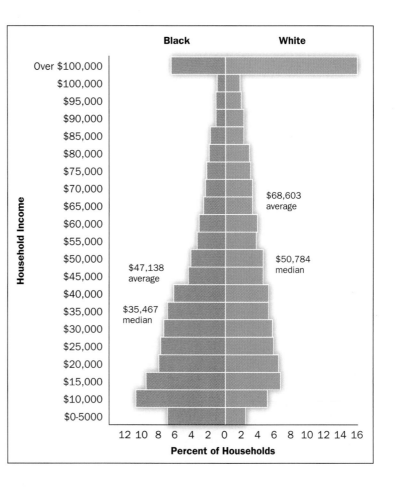

The underside of the income picture is people trapped in poverty. In 2005, 24.7 percent of Black people lived below the poverty level, compared with 8.4 percent of non-Hispanic Whites. Low incomes are counterbalanced to some extent by Medicare, Medicaid, public assistance, and food stamps. However, that an African American family is three times more likely to be poor shows that social inequality is staggering (DeNavas-Walt et al. 2006).

Wealth is more difficult to measure because it takes more effort to determine accurately how much people own and owe, as opposed to how much they earn in a given year. Yet wealth is very important in that it protects individuals against financial hardship and may offer a way to pass money or property to future generations, giving them a good start. On the other hand, the lack of wealth or even the presence of debt can place young people at a severe disadvantage as they seek to become independent.

The wealth picture in the United States shows even greater disparity between Whites and Blacks than does income. Sociologists Melvin Oliver and Thomas Shapiro (1995) drew on data from more than 12,000 households and conducted in-depth interviews with a range of Black and White families. There is clearly a significant difference in wealth patterns because generations of social inequality have left African Americans, as a group, unable to accumulate the kind of wealth that Whites, as a group, have. This is particularly true in the ability to own a home, most people's biggest asset. The inability of many Blacks to own a home and develop this asset results not only from lower incomes but also from discriminatory lending practices, which we consider later in this chapter. Of course, there are poor Whites and very rich Blacks, but the group differences that the researchers documented are unmistakable. The most striking differences are seen when we compare Blacks and Whites in their thirties and when we compare the most educated Blacks with the most educated Whites. Both the young adults and the more educated African Americans would have benefited the most from efforts to reduce inequality, but the gap remains (Shapiro 2004).

As shown in Figure 8.2, most Whites are not in debt in terms of assets, and 30 percent have a net worth over $100,000. In contrast, more than 40 percent of African Americans have a net worth of less than $1,000, with only 8 percent showing assets worth more than $100,000. Assets are valuable as a means to protect people from falling into poverty if all sources of income are interrupted. About 57 percent of all Whites can stay out of poverty for at least six months if all income ends, but only 17 percent of African Americans are in a similar situation.

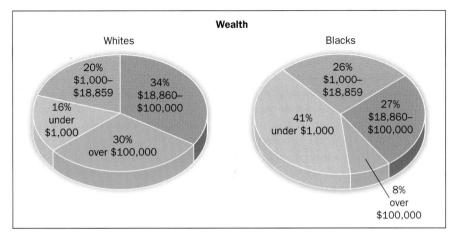

FIGURE 8.2   Wealth Distribution: Black Versus White Comparing Wealth

Note: The wealth data for 1988 were reported in 1996.

Sources: Melvin Oliver and Thomas Shapiro, *Black Wealth/White Wealth: A New Perspective on Racial Equality.* Copyright © 1996. Reproduced by permission of Routledge/Taylor & Francis Books, Inc.

Assets are important both to insulate households against short-term crises and to help other family members, whether for furthering their education, paying insurance premiums, buying the latest computer, or even starting to furnish their first home.

Employment

This precarious situation for African Americans—the lack of dependable assets—is particularly relevant as we consider their employment picture. Higher unemployment rates for Blacks have persisted since the 1940s, when statistics were first documented. Since 1990, the national unemployment rate for Whites has ranged from 3 percent to 6 percent, whereas for Blacks it has ranged from 7 percent to 11 percent. This means that, even in the best economic times, the Black unemployment rate is still significantly higher than it is for Whites during recessions. Obviously, when there is a national economic downturn, the results for the African American community are disastrous. Recessions take a heavy toll on African Americans (Bureau of the Census 2005a).

The employment picture is especially grim for African American workers aged 16 to 24. Many live in the central cities and fall victim to the unrecorded, irregular—perhaps illegal—economy outlined in Chapter 3. Many factors have been cited by social scientists to explain why official unemployment rates for young African Americans exceed 30 percent:

- Many African Americans live in the depressed economy of the central cities.
- Immigrants and illegal aliens present increased competition.
- White middle-class women have entered the labor force.
- Illegal activities at which youths find they can make more money have become more prevalent.

None of these factors is likely to change soon, so depression-like levels of unemployment probably will persist.

The picture grows even more somber when we realize that we are considering only official unemployment. The federal government's Bureau of Labor Statistics counts as unemployed only people who are actively seeking employment. Therefore, to be counted as unemployed, a person must not hold a full-time job, must be registered with a government employment agency, and must be engaged in writing job applications and seeking interviews.

Quite simply, the official unemployment rate leaves out millions of Americans, Black and White, who are effectively unemployed. It does not count people so discouraged that they have temporarily given up looking for employment. The problem of unemployment is further compounded by underemployment. The term **underemployment** refers to working at a job for which one is overqualified, involuntarily working part-time, or being employed only intermittently.

Studies continue to show the deepening plight economically for young Black men. In the nation's inner cities, especially, young Black men often lack the schooling and find appropriate jobs few and far between. In many cities, they face increased competition from immigrants often willing to accept jobs at low pay, no benefits, and no job security. In "Listen to Our Voices," respected sociologist William Julius Wilson describes the employment problem that exists where there are few employers (Eckholm 2006).

The official unemployment rate for African American male high school dropouts is about 72 percent, well above the 25 percent jobless rate for the nation as a whole during the Depression of the 1930s and the 34 percent unemployment rate of White dropouts. Again, such official statistics do not include youths who have dropped out of the system: those who are not at school, not at work, and not looking for a legitimate job. If we add to the official figures the discouraged job seeker, the rate of unemployment and underemployment of

underemployment
Work at a job for which the worker is overqualified, involuntary part-time instead of full-time employment, or intermittent employment.

Voices Listen to Our Voices Listen to

WHEN WORK DISAPPEARS

It is interesting to note how the media perceptions of "underclass" values and attitudes contrast sharply with the views actually expressed by the residents of the inner-city ghetto. For example, a 28-year-old unmarried welfare mother of two children who lives in one of Chicago's large public housing projects described to one of the Urban Poverty and Family Life Study (UPFLS) interviewers how the media create the impression that the people who live in her housing project are all bad or are thugs and killers.

William Julius Wilson

OK, I don't know where you live at, but you read the papers . . . they say, . . . Oh, Cabrini! Oh, they have gang killings . . . they have gang killings on the South Side! But the media and . . . and I guess the public, you know, they build it up so big. I mean, it's bad everywhere. Did anyone offend you when you came up here? My neighbor stopped you and gave you the message. You're white, you're white and they don't know you here, see, see, but you read the paper and your parents will say "don't go over there, girl!" I read where they said, you know, well, I read where there they kill blacks . . . whites, and they do this and they do that, and they, I mean, we're people, too. But it's . . . that's just the system. It makes us look like we're all the same, and we're all bad. . . . But that's not true.

A 28-year-old welfare mother from another South Side housing project raised a similar point:

'Cause a lot of people when they meet me, they say, "You live in a project?" I say "yeah." "Well, you don't look like the type of person." "How is a person supposed to look?" You know, like I tell them, the project don't make nobody, you make yourself. Now, if you want to get out there and carry that project name, be tough and rowdy and sloppy, disrespectful, well, shoot, that's lowlife. "You don't look like the type that lives in a project!" "Well, how am I supposed to look?" Just because I live in a project, that don't mean I have to come outside looking like a tramp, because I'm not. But they all, they like, "You too nice to be living in a project." You know, sometimes I get offended. . . . That just really gets on my nerves. You know, don't no building make you, you make yourself. You live in a home, you know. Look at all these people that's got Hollywood kids, busted for cocaine, o.d. 'in' on it, you know, what's happened to them?

Our research reveals that the beliefs of inner-city residents bear little resemblance to the blanket media reports asserting that values have plummeted in impoverished inner-city neighborhoods or that people in the inner city have an entirely different value system. What is so striking is that despite the overwhelming joblessness and poverty, black residents in inner-city ghetto neighborhoods actually verbally endorse, rather than undermine, the basic American values concerning individual initiative. ■

Source: Excerpt from *When Work Disappears* by William Julius Wilson. Copyright © 1996 by William Julius Wilson. Reprinted by permission of Alfred A. Knopf, a division of Random House, Inc.

African American teenagers in central-city areas climbs to 90 percent. As discouraging as these data are, the picture becomes even grimmer as we consider studies showing that underemployment remains high for young African Americans (Eckholm 2006).

Although few African Americans have crashed through the glass ceiling and made it into the top echelons of business or government, more have entered a wider variety of jobs.

TABLE 8.2
Percentages of African American Employees in Selected Occupations, 1972 and 2004

Occupation	1972	2004
Engineers	2%	5%
Lawyers and judges	2	5
Physicians	3	6
Registered nurses	6	10
College teachers	4	6
Other teachers	8	9
Social workers	16	20
Managers	3	6
Sales workers	3	9
Service workers	17	16
Cleaners and servants	64	18
Firefighters	4	8
Police and detectives	8	16

Source: Bureau of the Census 2005a, 401–404.

The taboo against putting Blacks in jobs in which they would supervise Whites has weakened, and the percentage of African Americans in professional and managerial occupations rose from 4 percent in 1949 to 8.2 percent in 2000, a remarkable improvement. However, most of this advancement came before 1980. Little advancement has occurred since then.

As shown in Table 8.2, African Americans, who constitute 13 percent of the population, are underrepresented in high-status, high-paying occupations. Less than 6 percent of lawyers, judges, physicians, financial managers, public relations specialists, architects, pharmacists, and dentists are African American. On the other hand, they account for more than 15 percent of cooks, health aides, hospital orderlies, maids, janitors, and stock handlers.

Even when they enter highly paid, prestigious positions, Black men typically earn less than their White male colleagues in similar positions. For example, Black lawyers make 79 cents to the "White dollar" and 80 cents compared to White physicians. This is not to say they don't do well. African American physicians enjoy high wages—$134,000 annually in 2001—but this compares to $166,890 among White male physicians. Although they have high prestige, such professionals must build a client base, and a White professional is at an advantage as he seeks to gain the respect of high-paying, largely White potential clients (Grodsky and Pager 2001; Tran 2001).

Family Life

In its role as a social institution providing for the socialization of children, the family is crucial to its members' life satisfaction. The family also reflects the influence, positive or negative, of income, housing, education, and other social factors. For African Americans, the family reflects both amazing stability and the legacy of racism and low income across many generations.

Challenges to Family Stability

Although it is the conventional view that a female heads the typical African American family, most children are still in two-parent households. About one-third of African American children had both a father and a mother present in 2005 (see Figure 8.3).

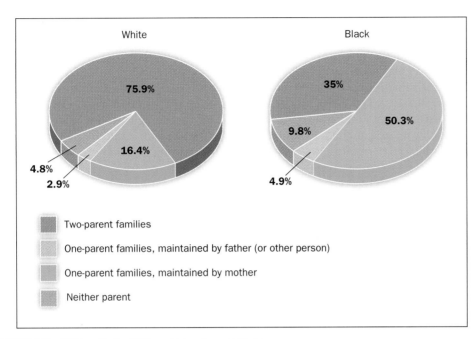

FIGURE 8.3 Children Under 18 Years Living Arrangements

Note: Data for 2005 in 2006.

Source: Bureau of the Census 2006C, Table C3.

Although single-parent African American families are common, they are not universal. In comparison, such single-parent arrangements were also present in about one in five White families.

It is as inaccurate to assume that a single-parent family is necessarily deprived as it is to assume that a two-parent family is always secure and happy. Nevertheless, life in a single-parent family can be extremely stressful for all single parents and their children and not just for those who are members of subordinate groups. Because the absent parent is more often the father, lack of the male presence almost always means the lack of a male income. This monetary impact on a single-parent household cannot be overstated (A. Hacker 1995; Tucker and Mitchell-Kernan 1995).

Looming behind the issue of female-headed families is the plight of the African American man. Simply stated, the economic status of Black men has been deteriorating for several generations. Despite the negative outlook, leaders within the Black community continue to call on men to assume responsibility for the family. In 1995, Nation of Islam Minister Louis Farrakhan organized the Million Man March in Washington, D.C., to assert the role of Black men in their family and in their community. As noted earlier in the chapter, entertainer Bill Cosby and others have raised the issue of "acting White" in criticizing African American youth for not taking on more responsibility.

Historically, female-headed families have not always been a significant economic problem. Despite the absence of legal protection for the slave family, African Americans were nevertheless able to establish significant kinship relationships with the sharing of economic resources, meager as they might be. After emancipation, men preferred that their wives remain at home because a working woman was considered a mark of slavery. But it was hard for many Black men to find work as anything other than strikebreakers, so women were the more important source of wages anyway.

For many single African American women living in poverty, having a child is an added burden. However, the tradition of extended family among African Americans eases this burden somewhat. The absence of a husband does not mean that no one shares in child care: Out-of-wedlock children born to Black teenage mothers live with their grandparents and form three-generation households.

No one explanation accounts for the rise in single-parent households. Sociologists attribute the rapid expansion in the number of such households primarily to shifts in the economy that have kept Black men, especially in urban areas, out of work. The phenomenon certainly is not limited to African Americans. Increasingly, both unmarried White and Black women bear children. More and more parents, both White and Black, divorce; so even children born into a two-parent family end up living with only one parent.

Strengths of African American Families

In the midst of ever-increasing single parenting, another picture of African American family life becomes visible: success despite discrimination and economic hardship. Robert Hill (1999), of the National Urban League and Morgan State University, listed five strengths of African American families that allow them to function effectively in a hostile (racist) society.

1. *Strong kinship bonds.* Blacks are more likely than Whites to care for children and the elderly in an extended family network.

2. *A strong work orientation.* Poor Blacks are more likely to be working, and poor Black families often include more than one wage earner.

3. *Adaptability of family roles.* In two-parent families, the egalitarian pattern of decision making is the most common. The self-reliance of Black women who are the primary wage earners best illustrates this adaptability.

4. *Strong achievement orientation.* Working-class Blacks indicate a greater desire for their children to attend college than do working-class Whites. Even a majority of low-income African Americans want to attend college.

5. *A strong religious orientation.* Since the time of slavery, Black churches have been the impetus behind many significant grass-roots organizations.

Social workers and sociologists have confirmed through social research the strengths that Hill noted first in 1972. In the African American community, these are the sources of family strength (Hudgins 1992).

Family reunions are important annual events for many African Americans.

Increasingly, social scientists are learning to look at both the weaknesses and the strengths of African American family life. Expressions of alarm about instability date back to 1965, when the Department of Labor issued the report *The Negro Family: The Case for National Action*. The document, commonly known as the Moynihan Report, after its principal author, sociologist Daniel Patrick Moynihan, outlined a "tangle of pathology" with the Black family at its core. More recently, two studies, the Stable Black Families Project and the National Survey of Black Americans, sought to learn how Black families encounter problems and resolve them successfully with internal resources such as those that Hill outlined in his highly regarded work (Department of Labor 1965; Gary et al. 1983).

The most consistently documented strength of African American families is the presence of an extended family household. The most common feature is having grandparents residing in the home. Extended living arrangements are much more common among Black households than among White ones. These arrangements are recognized as having the important economic benefit of pooling limited economic resources. Because of the generally lower earnings of African American heads-of-household, income from second, third, and even fourth wage earners is needed to achieve a desired standard of living or, in all too many cases, simply to meet daily needs (Bryson and Casper 1999).

The African American Middle Class

Many characterizations of African American family life have been attacked because they overemphasize the poorest segment of the African American community. An opposite error is the exaggeration of the success African Americans have achieved. Social scientists face the challenge of avoiding a selective, one-sided picture of Black society. The problem is similar to viewing a partially filled glass of water. Does one describe it as half-empty and emphasize the need for assistance? Or does one describe the glass as half-full to give attention to what has been accomplished? The most complete description would acknowledge both perspectives (Gouldner 1970).

A clearly defined African American middle class has emerged. In 2000, nearly one-third of African Americans earned more than the median income for Whites. At least 29 percent of Blacks, then, are middle class or higher. Many have debated the character of this middle class. E. Franklin Frazier (1957), a Black sociologist, wrote an often critical study of the African American middle class in which he identified its overriding goal as achieving petty social values and becoming acceptable to White society (DeNavas-Walt et al. 2006).

African Americans are still aware of their racial subordination even when they have achieved economic equality. The Black middle class may not be militant, but its newest members do not forget their roots. They are more likely than Whites to be first-generation middle class, dependent on two or more sources of income, and precariously close to the lower class both financially and residentially. Yet with their relative success has come a desire to live in better surroundings. The migration of middle-class African Americans out of the ghetto in the 1970s and 1980s has left a vacuum. They may still care about the problems of the Black poor, but they are no longer present as role models.

Members of the African American middle class do not automatically accept all aspects of the White middle class. For years, for example, Whites have relied on books and magazines on infant and child care; such materials treated African American children as if they did not exist. To counter this neglect, James Comer and Alvin Poussaint wrote *Raising Black Children* (1992), in which the authors advise parents on how to deal with questions such as "What is Black?", a child's first encounter with prejudice, and a teenage girl being watched by store security.

Directing attention to the Black middle class also requires that we consider the relative importance of the two components in ethclass, Milton Gordon's concept introduced in Chapter 5. The degree to which affluent Blacks identify themselves in class terms or racial terms is an important ideological question. W. E. B. Du Bois (1952)

class
As defined by Max Weber, people who share similar levels of wealth.

argued that when racism decreases, class issues become more important. As Du Bois saw it, exploitation would remain, and many of the same people would continue to be subordinate. Black elites might become economically successful, either as entrepreneurs (Black capitalists) or professionals (Black white-collar workers), but they would continue to identify with and serve the dominant group's interest.

Social scientists have long recognized the importance of class. **Class** is a term used by sociologist Max Weber to refer to people who share a similar level of wealth and income. The significance of class in people's lives is apparent to all. In the United States today, roughly half the lower-class population suffers from chronic health conditions that limit their activity, compared with only one in eleven among the affluent. The poor are more likely to become victims of crime, and they are only about half as likely as the affluent to send their children to colleges or vocational schools. When considering class difference, remarkable similarities exist in child-rearing practices between Black and White households (Lareau 2002).

The complexity of the relative influence of race and class was apparent in the controversy surrounding the publication of sociologist William J. Wilson's *The Declining Significance of Race* (1980). Pointing to the increasing affluence of African Americans, Wilson concluded that "class has become more important than race in determining black life-chances in the modern world" (p. 150). The policy implications of his conclusion are that programs must be developed to confront class subordination rather than ethnic and racial discrimination. Wilson did not deny the legacy of discrimination reflected in the disproportionate number of African Americans who are poor, less educated, and living in inadequate and overcrowded housing. However, he pointed to "compelling evidence" that young Blacks were competing successfully with young Whites.

Critics of Wilson comment that focusing attention on this small educated elite ignores vast numbers of African Americans relegated to the lower class (Pinkney 1984; Willie 1978, 1979). Wilson himself was not guilty of such an oversimplification and indeed expressed concern over lower-class, inner-city African Americans' seemingly falling even further behind, like those who become a part of the irregular economy discussed in Chapter 3. He pointed out that the poor are socially isolated and have shrinking economic opportunities (1988, 1996). However, it is easy to conclude superficially that because educated Blacks are entering the middle class, race has ceased to be of concern.

Black parents have a special challenge in raising a child to deal with racism.

Zoning laws that may stipulate expensive building materials help keep out the less affluent, who are more likely to be African American home buyers.

Housing

Housing plays a major role in determining the quality of a person's life. For African Americans, as for Whites, housing is the result of personal preferences and income. However, African Americans differ from Whites in that their housing has been restricted through discrimination in a manner that it has not for Whites. We devote significant attention to housing because, for most people, housing is critical to their quality of life and often represents their largest single asset.

Although Black housing has improved, as indicated by statistics on home ownership, new construction, density of living units, and quality as measured by plumbing facilities, African Americans remain behind Whites on all these standards. The quality of Black housing is inferior to that of Whites at all income levels, yet Blacks pay out a larger proportion of their income for shelter.

Housing was the last major area to be covered by civil rights legislation. The delay was not caused by its insignificance; quite the contrary, it was precisely because housing touches so many parts of the American economy and relates to private property rights that legislators were slow to act. After an executive order by President Kennedy, the government required nondiscrimination in federally assisted housing, but this ruling included only 7 percent of the housing market. In 1968, the Federal Fair Housing Law (Title VIII of the 1968 Civil Rights Act) and the U.S. Supreme Court decision in *Jones v. Mayer* combined to outlaw all racial discrimination in housing. Enforcement has remained weak, however, and many aspects of housing, real estate customs, and lending practices remain untouched.

Residential Segregation

Typically in the United States, as noted, White children attend predominantly White schools, Black children attend predominantly Black schools, and Hispanic children attend predominantly Hispanic schools. This school segregation is not only the result of the failure to accept busing but also the effect of residential segregation. In their studies on segregation, Douglas Massey and Nancy Denton (1993) concluded that racial separation "continues to exist because white America has not had the political will or desire to dismantle it." (p. 8) In Chapter 1, we noted the persuasiveness of residential segregation as reflected in Census 2000 (refer back to Figure 1.4). This racial isolation in neighborhoods has not improved since the beginnings of the civil rights movement in the 1950s (Massey 2005).

What factors create residential segregation in the United States? Among the primary factors are the following:

- Because of private prejudice and discrimination, people refuse to sell or rent to people of the "wrong" race, ethnicity, or religion.
- The prejudicial policies of real estate companies steer people to the "correct" neighborhoods.
- Government policies enforce antibias legislation ineffectively.
- Public housing policies today, as well as past construction patterns, reinforce housing for the poor in inner-city neighborhoods.
- Policies of banks and other lenders create barriers based on race to financing home purchasing.

This last issue of racial-basis financing deserves further explanation. In the 1990s, new attention was given to the persistence of **redlining**, the practice of discrimination against people trying to buy homes in minority and racially changing neighborhoods. As we noticed in "Listen to Our Voices" in Chapter 3, Patricia Williams eloquently spoke about her being a victim of discrimination of housing lending practices.

It is important to recall the implications of this discrimination in home financing for the African American community. Earlier in the chapter, we noted the great disparity between Black and White family wealth and the implications this had for both the present and future generations. The key factor in this inequality was the failure of African Americans to accumulate wealth through home buying. Now we see that discrimination plays a documented role in this barrier to what is possible; in 2004, just under half of Blacks were homeowners, compared with 73 percent of non-Hispanic Whites (Bureau of the Census 2005a, 39, 41).

Although the African American concentration in the central cities has increased, a small but growing number of Blacks have moved into suburban areas. By 2000, 39 percent of the nation's metropolitan African Americans lived in suburban areas. Although more than one out of three seems significant, it compares to 71 percent of Whites, 58 percent of Asians, and 49 percent of Latinos. Yet the most significant growth in the percentage of suburban African Americans has come from movement into suburbs that are predominantly Black or are adjacent to predominantly Black areas. In many instances, therefore, it represents further ghettoization and spillover from city slums; it is not necessarily a sign of two cars and a backyard pool. In many instances, the suburbs with large Black populations are isolated from surrounding White communities and residents have less satisfactory housing and municipal services but, ironically, pay higher taxes (Logan 2001b).

A dual housing market is part of today's reality, although attacks continue against the remaining legal barriers to fair housing. In theory, **zoning laws** are enacted to ensure that specific standards of housing construction will be satisfied. These regulations can also separate industrial and commercial enterprises from residential areas. However, some zoning laws in suburbs have seemed to curb the development of low- and moderate-income housing that would attract African Americans who want to move out of the central cities.

For years, the construction of low-income public housing in the ghetto has furthered racial segregation. The courts have not ruled consistently in this matter in recent years so, as with affirmative action, public officials lack clear guidance. Even if court decisions continue to dismantle exclusionary housing practices, the rapid growth of integrated neighborhoods is unlikely. In the future, African American housing probably will continue to improve and remain primarily in all-Black neighborhoods. This gap is greater than can be explained by differences in social class.

redlining
The pattern of discrimination against people trying to buy homes in minority and racially changing neighborhoods.

zoning laws
Legal provisions stipulating land use and the architectural design of housing, often used to keep racial minorities and low-income people out of suburban areas.

Criminal Justice

A complex, sensitive topic affecting African Americans is their role in criminal justice. It was reported in 2005 that Blacks constitute 4.7 percent of the lawyers, 15.7 percent of police, 17.1 percent of the detectives, and 28.4 percent of security guards but 39 percent of jail inmates (Bureau of the Census 2005a, 219, 399–401).

Data collected annually in the FBI's Uniform Crime Report show that Blacks account for 28 percent of arrests, even though they represent only about 13 percent of the nation's population. Conflict theorists point out that the higher arrest rate is not surprising for a group that is disproportionately poor and, therefore, much less able to afford private attorneys, who might be able to prevent formal arrests from taking place. Even more significantly, the Uniform Crime Report focuses on index crimes (mainly property crimes), which are the type of crimes most often committed by low-income people.

These numbers are staggering but, as dramatic as they are, it is not unusual to hear exaggerations presented as facts, such as "more Black men are in prison than in college." The reality is sobering enough. About one in sixteen White males can expect to go to a state or federal prison during his lifetime, yet for Black males this lifetime probability is one out of three (Bureau of the Census 2005a, 39, 41; Gaines 2005).

Most (actually 70 percent) of all the violent crimes against Whites are perpetrated by Whites, according to the FBI. In contrast to popular misconceptions about crime, African Americans and the poor are especially likely to be the victims of serious crimes. This fact is documented in **victimization surveys**, which are systematic interviews of ordinary people carried out annually to reveal how much crime occurs. These Department of Justice statistics show that African Americans are 35 percent more likely to be victims of violent crimes than are Whites (Catalano 2006).

Central to the concern that minorities often express about the criminal justice system is **differential justice;** that is, Whites are dealt with more leniently than are Blacks, whether at the time of investigation, arrest, indictment, conviction, sentencing, incarceration, or parole. Studies demonstrate that police often deal with African American youths more harshly than with White youngsters (Engen et al. 2002; E. Lotke 2004). The "Research Focus" considers the application of differential justice to the harshest judgment that can be made in the legal system—the death penalty.

There is also a reluctant acceptance that the government cannot be counted on to address inner-city problems. When a schoolchild walks into a cafeteria or schoolyard with automatic weapons and kills a dozen children and teachers, it becomes a case of national alarm as with Columbine. When children kill each other in drive-by shootings, it is viewed as a local concern reflecting the need to clean up a dysfunctional neighborhood. Many African Americans note that the main difference between these two situations is not the death toll but who is being killed: middle-class Whites in the schoolyard shootings and Black ghetto youth in the drive-bys.

Health Care

The price of being an African American took on new importance with the release of a shocking study in a prestigious medical journal revealing that two-thirds of boys in Harlem, a predominantly Black neighborhood in New York City, can expect to die young or in mid adulthood—that is, before they reach age 65. In fact, they have less chance of surviving even to age 45 than their White counterparts nationwide have of reaching age 65. The medical researchers noted that it is not the stereotyped images of AIDS and violence that explain the staggering difference. Black men are much more likely to fall victim to unrelenting stress, heart disease, and cancer (Fing et al. 1996).

victimization surveys
Annual attempts to measure crime rates by interviewing ordinary citizens who may or may not have been crime victims.

differential justice
Whites being dealt with more leniently than Blacks, whether at the time of arrest, indictment, conviction, sentencing, or parole.

Focus Research Focus Research

THE ULTIMATE PENALTY: EXECUTION

The death penalty in the United States is enormously controversial partly because many states do not even permit it and because increasingly the United States is marginalized as more of the world's nations have ceased to rely on it as a method of punishment. But given that the death penalty continues to be used in the United States—sixty executions in 2005—what role does being African American play in its use?

Although Blacks and Whites are relatively equal in numbers of homicide perpetrators, a U.S. Department of Justice study indicated that Blacks were the defendants in 72 percent of the cases in which the attorney general approved the death penalty. As disturbing as this finding is alone, it also points to the clearest and most consistent research finding—the race of the victim is the best indicator of whether an execution will occur. If the victim is White, the defendant is more likely to be tried under the death penalty and later executed than if the victim is Black. This reflects the broader concern that the Black-on-Black crime was not being dealt with as seriously as when Whites were victimized. Researchers on crime have come to call this victim discounting, which is society's tendency to view crimes as less socially significant if the victim is viewed as less worthy.

Clearly the use of the death penalty is the most extreme form of **victim discounting**. Numerous studies show that homicide defendants are more likely to be sentenced to death if their victims are White rather than Black. So even in a murder case, a Black death counts less. About 79 percent of the victims in death penalty cases are White, even though only 50 percent of all murder victims are White.

There is also some evidence that Black defendants, who constituted 42 percent of all death row inmates in 2006, are more likely to face execution than Whites in the same legal circumstances. There is even evidence that capital case clients receive poor legal services because of racist attitudes of their own defense counsel. Although racism in the criminal justice system is never acceptable, it is particularly devastating when the process results in an execution. ■

Sources: Cole 1999; Death Penalty Information Center 2006; Swarns 2004.

The morbidity and mortality rates for African Americans as a group, and not just Harlem men, are equally distressing. Compared with Whites, Blacks have higher death rates from diseases of the heart, pneumonia, diabetes, and cancer. The death rate from strokes was twice as high among African Americans as it was among Whites. Such epidemiologic findings reflect in part the higher proportion of Blacks found among the nation's lower classes. White Americans can expect to live 75.0 years if male and 80.2 years if female. By contrast, life expectancy for African Americans is only 68.6 years for males and 75.5 years for females (Arias and Smith 2003).

Drawing on the conflict perspective, sociologist Howard Waitzkin (1986) suggests that racial tensions contribute to the medical problems of African Americans. In his view, the stress resulting from racial prejudice and discrimination helps to explain the higher rates of hypertension found among African Americans (and Hispanics) than among Whites. Death due to hypertension is twice as common in Blacks as in Whites; it is believed to be a critical factor in Blacks' high mortality rates from heart disease,

victim discounting
Tendency to view crime as less socially significant if the victim is viewed as less worthy.

kidney disease, and stroke. Although medical experts disagree, some argue that the stress resulting from racism and suppressed hostility exacerbates hypertension among African Americans (Cooper et al. 1999).

The previous section noted that African Americans are underrepresented among lawyers in the criminal justice system. A similar phenomenon is visible in health care. Blacks represent about 6 percent of practicing physicians. This is especially significant given that communities with a high proportion of African American residents are four times more likely to have a physician shortage than are White neighborhoods. There is little reason to expect this to improve soon. Among the students entering medical school in the fall of 2004, only 6.5 percent were African American. There is also evidence of a declining presence of minorities among medical school faculty members; currently 3.1 percent are Black, reflecting disenchantment with rolling back of affirmative action in many professional schools (Association of American Medical Colleges 2005).

Related to the health care dilemma is the problem of environmental justice, which was introduced in Chapter 3 and again in Chapter 6 with reference to Native Americans. Problems associated with toxic pollution and hazardous garbage dumps are more likely to be faced by low-income Black communities than their affluent counterparts. This disproportionate exposure to environmental hazards can be viewed as part of the complex cycle of discrimination faced by African Americans and other subordinate groups in the United States (Pinderhughes 1996).

Just how significant is the impact of poorer health on the lives of the nation's less educated people, less affluent classes, and subordinate groups? Drawing on a variety of research studies, population specialist Evelyn Kitagawa (1972) estimated the "excess mortality rate" to be 20 percent. In other words, 20 percent more people were dying than otherwise might have because of poor health linked to race and class. Using Kitagawa's model, we can calculate that if every African American in the United States were White and had at least one year of college education, some 58,000 fewer Blacks would have died in 2005 and in each succeeding year (author's estimate based on Bureau of the Census 2005a).

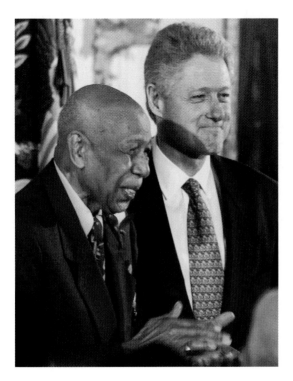

Here in the White House in 1997, after receiving an official apology from President Bill Clinton, is Herman Shaw, age 94, one of the last known survivors of the infamous Tuskegee Syphilis study. This federal government study knowingly infected Black men with syphilis to observe the progression of the disease. Despite discovery of treatments, the men were never given medical assistance until the program was revealed decades later. Such events cause contemporary African Americans to be particularly leery of the medical establishment.

gerrymandering
Redrawing districts bizarrely to create politically advantageous outcomes.

Politics

African Americans have never received an equal share of the political pie. After Reconstruction, it was not until 1928 that a Black was again elected to Congress. Now, more than seventy years and several civil rights acts later, there are still only thirty-eight African American congressional representatives. Recent years have brought some improvement. In fact, between 1970 and 2001, the number of Black elected officials has increased by more than fivefold (Figure 8.4).

Yet there are major problems in the continued success of African American politicians. Locally elected Black officials find it difficult to make the jump to statewide office. Voters, particularly non-Black voters, have difficulty seeing Black politicians as anything other than representatives of the Black community and express concern that the view of Whites and other non-Blacks will not be represented by an African American.

The political gains by African Americans, as well as Hispanics, had been placed in jeopardy by legal actions that questioned race-based districts. Boundaries for elective office, ranging from city council positions to the U.S. House of Representatives, have been drawn in such a way so as to concentrate enough members of a racial or ethnic group to create a "safe majority" to make it likely a member of that group will get elected.

The creation of these minority districts redrawn in this manner raised cries of **gerrymandering**. A practice dating from 1810, gerrymandering is the bizarre outlining of districts to create politically advantageous outcomes. Although creating race-based districts may seem discriminatory, boundaries have routinely been drawn based on a commonality of interests, such as rural versus urban interests, or even to maximize the likelihood of electing a representative from a certain political party. For over a decade, the legality of these actions has been debated, and finally in 2003, the Supreme Court ruled 5–4 that a state might consider overall minority influence in the political process. In Figure 8.5, we look at the admittedly bizarre shape of one congressional district (Bendavid 2004).

As was noted in Chapter 3, in the wake of the very close 2000 presidential election between George W. Bush and Al Gore, another long-standing legal issue and a troubling example of institutional discrimination came to the forefront nationally. Ex-felons are barred from voting for life after leaving prison leaving 13 percent of Black voters disenfranchised. Although little progress has been made to reform this area, other national legislation has been more promising.

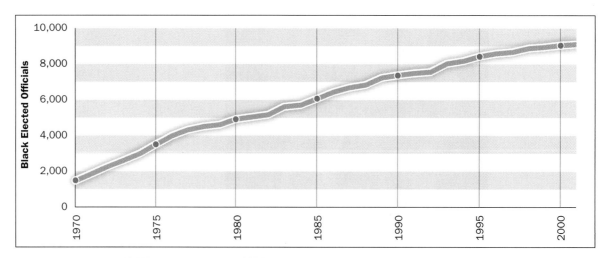

FIGURE 8.4 Black Elected Officials, 1970–2001
Although the rate of increase has leveled off, the number of Black elected officials has steadily increased over three decades.
Source: From *Black Elected Officials: A Statistical Summary 2001* by David Bositis. Reprinted by permission of the Joint Center for Political and Economic Studies.

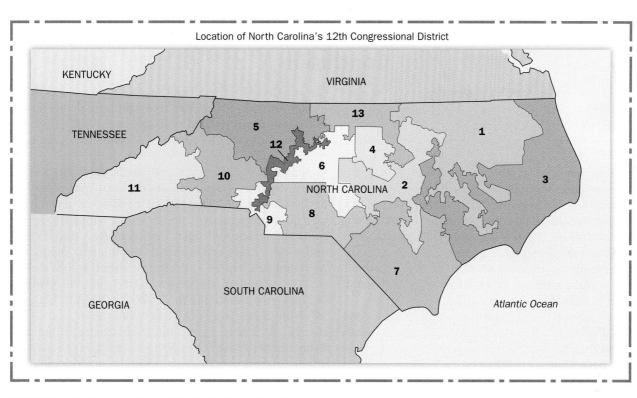

Location of North Carolina's 12th Congressional District

FIGURE 8.5   Developing a Minority District: North Carolina 12th

In areas with a history of keeping African Americans from voting, courts have approved oddly drawn districts to increase the likelihood of a Black being elected to office. The 12th Congressional District in North Carolina zigzags along I-85 from Charlotte to Winston-Salem to create a district that is 45 percent Black and has consistently elected a Black to the House of Representatives.

In 2006, President George W. Bush signed into law the Fannie Lou Hamer, Rosa Parks, and Coretta Scott King Voting Rights Reauthorization and Amendments Act of 2006. Congress and the president rejected attempts to dilute the original intent of the bill and passed a "clean" reauthorization bill, which renews key provisions of the Voting Rights Act dating back to 1965 that would have otherwise expired in 2007. For example, one potent provision requires jurisdictions, whether a school district or an entire state, with significant histories of discrimination in voting to get federal approval of any new voting practices or procedures and to show that these procedures do not have a discriminatory purpose or effect.

The changing racial and ethnic landscape can be expected to have an impact on future strategies to elect African Americans to office, especially in urban areas. However, now that the number of Hispanics exceeds the number of Blacks nationwide, observers wonder how this might play out in the political world. A growing number of major cities, including Los Angeles and Chicago, are witnessing dramatic growth in the Hispanic population. Latinos often settle near Black neighborhoods or even displace Blacks who move out into suburbs, making it more difficult to develop safe African American districts. For example, South Central Los Angeles, the site of rioting in 1992 described in the previous chapter, is now largely a Latino neighborhood. The full impact has not been felt yet because the Latino population tends to be younger, with many not yet reaching voting age. Even more significantly, many Latino adults have not yet obtained their citizenship. As the Hispanic population becomes eligible to vote, the impact is going to be particularly felt by African Americans, who have just begun to enjoy success in local elections (Schodolski 2002).

Conclusion

Black and White Americans have dealt with the continued disparity between the two groups by endorsing several ideologies, as shown in Figure 8.6. Assimilation was the driving force behind the civil rights movement, which sought to integrate Whites and Blacks into one society. People who rejected contact with the other group endorsed separatism. As Chapter 2 showed, both Whites and Blacks generally lent little support to separatism. In the late 1960s, the government and various Black organizations began to recognize cultural pluralism as a goal, at least paying lip service to the desire of many African Americans to exercise cultural and economic autonomy. Perhaps on no other issue is this desire for control more evident than in the schools.

As the future of African American people in the United States unfolds, one element of the population generally unnoticed thus far may move into prominence. An ever-growing proportion of the Black population consists of people of foreign birth. In the 1980 census, 816,000 foreign-born Blacks were counted, or 3.1 percent of the Black population, the highest level ever recorded. By 2000, the number had tripled to 2,100,000, which constituted 8.6 percent of the Black population. In cities such as New York City, Miami, Ft. Lauderdale, and Boston, the foreign-born population of the Black community is at least 25 percent. The immigration numbers are expected to increase, as is the proportion of the African American population that is foreign born. Diversity exists to a significant degree in the Black community today (Logan and Deane 2003).

Twice in this nation's history, African Americans have received significant attention from the federal government and, to some degree, from the larger White society. The first period extended from the Civil War to the end of Reconstruction. The second period was during the civil rights movement of the 1960s. In both periods, the government acknowledged that race was a major issue, and society made commitments to eliminate inequality. As noted in Chapter 7, Reconstruction was followed by decades of neglect, and on several measures the position of Blacks deteriorated in the United States. Although the 1980s and 1990s were not without their successes, race is clearly not a major issue on today's national agenda. Even inner-city violence only diverts much of the nation's attention for a few fleeting moments, while attacks on school integration and affirmative action persist.

The gains that have been made are substantial, but will the momentum continue? Improvement has occurred in a generation inspired and spurred on to bring about change. If the resolve to continue toward that goal lessens in the United States, the picture may become bleaker, and the rate of positive change may decline further.

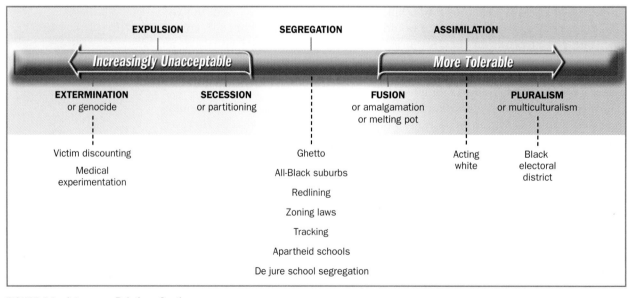

FIGURE 8.6   Intergroup Relations Continuum

Key Terms

acting White 231

apartheid schools 230

class 242

de facto segregation 230

differential justice 245

gerrymandering 248

income 234

redlining 244

tracking 230

underemployment 236

victim discounting 246

victimization surveys 245

wealth 234

zoning laws 244

Review Questions

1. To what degree have the civil rights movement initiatives in education been realized, or do they remain unmet?

2. What challenges face the African American middle class?

3. What are the biggest assets and problems facing African American families?

4. How are differential justice and victim discounting related?

5. How is race-based gerrymandering related to affirmative action?

Critical Thinking

1. Without the comparison to John, Glenn might have taken the shoe salesman to be merely incompetent at his job rather than purposefully avoiding selling to African Americans. Drawing on the case of John and Glenn, what are other types of situations in which people may be victims of discrimination but be unaware of it?

2. What has been the ethnic and racial composition of the neighborhoods you have lived in and the schools you have attended? Consider how the composition of one may have influenced the other. What steps would have been necessary to ensure more diversity?

3. How are the problems in crime, housing, and health interrelated?

˙Internet Connections—Research Navigator™

To access the full resources of Research Navigator™, please find the access code printed on the inside cover of *OneSearch with Research Navigator™: Sociology*. You may have received this booklet if your instructor recommended this guide be packaged with new textbooks. (If your book did not come with this printed guide, you can purchase one through your college bookstore.) Visit our Research Navigator™ site at www.ResearchNavigator.com. Once at this site, click on REGISTER under New Users and enter your access code to create a personal Login Name and Password. (When revisiting the site, use the same Login Name and Password.) Browse the features of the Research Navigator™ Web site and search the databases of academic journals, newspapers, magazines, and Web links.

For further information relevant to Chapter 1, you may wish to use such keywords as "defacto Segregation," "Historically Black Colleges and Universities," and the research engine will supply relevant and recent scholarly and popular press publications. Use the *New York Times* Search-by-Subject Archive to find recent news articles related to sociology and the Link Library feature to locate relevant Web links organized by the key terms associated with this chapter.

9 Hispanic Americans

CHAPTER OUTLINE

Latino Identity

The Economic Picture

■**RESEARCH FOCUS**
Latinas: American Style

The Growing Political Presence

The Borderlands

Cuban Americans

■**LISTEN TO OUR VOICES**
"Leaving Cuba"
by Alfredo Jimenez

Central and South Americans

Conclusion

Key Terms/Review Questions/Critical Thinking/Internet Connections—Research Navigator™

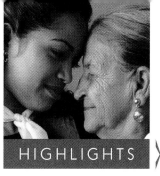

THE GROUP LABEL *HISPANIC* OR *LATINO AMERICAN* LINKS a diverse population that mostly shares a common language heritage but otherwise has many significant differences. The language barrier in an assimilation-oriented society has been of major significance to Hispanics. For generations, schools made it difficult for Spanish-speaking children to succeed. The United States has only recently made any effort to recognize its bilingual, bicultural heritage and to allow those whose native language is not English to use it as an asset rather than a liability. Latinos include several major groups, of which Mexican Americans, Puerto Ricans, and Cubans are the largest in the United States. Cuban Americans constitute a significant presence in southern Florida. Increasingly, immigrants and refugees from Central and South America have also established communities throughout the United States.

The Los Angeles Coliseum is rocking with a crowd of 92,000. Is it the USC Trojan football team playing at home? Britney Spears in a sold-out concert? No, it is Mexico and Argentina playing futbol (soccer) to a crowd with partisan fans cheering on Mexico. Although it took until 2003, AOL now offers customer support in Spanish; Latinos are expected to account for $1 trillion in online purchases by 2007. Consequently, Microsoft MSN launched a Spanish-language personal site and Yahoo en Español publishes news from *La opinión*, the nation's largest Spanish-language newspaper, and Notimex, Mexico's leading wire service.

The governor of the state with the largest Latino presence speaks and declares Puerto Ricans and Cubans are particularly feisty because of their mixed Black and Latino "blood." What was Arnold Schwarzenegger thinking of when he made these statements in 2006? He soon apologized when they became public, but what is interesting is not so much his political misstep, but rather the fact that we have a German-speaking, Austrian-born man who did not immigrate until he was 20 years old became a naturalized citizen in 1983—becoming who has so assimilated that he readily and nonchalantly expresses old-fashioned American stereotypes among friends.

As recently as 1997, American Airlines was roundly criticized for the contents of its manual for pilots flying between the United States and Latin America. A section called "Surviving in Latin America" included guidelines concerning mountainous areas near some local airports but also advised that Latin American fliers like to drink alcohol before a flight and "unruly and/or intoxicated passengers are not infrequent" (Blood 2006; O'Connor 1999; Swartz 2003; UPI 1997).

More than one in eight people in the U.S. population are of Spanish or Latin American origin. Collectively this group is called *Hispanics* or *Latinos,* two terms that we use interchangeably in this book. The Census Bureau estimates that by the year 2100, Hispanics will constitute about one-third of the U.S. population (refer again to Figure 1.1 on p. 6).

Already by 2005, population data showed 41.9 million Latinos, outnumbering the 39 million African Americans. The Latino population is very diverse. Today, nearly 27 million, or two-thirds of Hispanics in the United States, are Mexican Americans, or Chicanos. The diversity of Latinos and their geographical distribution in the United States are shown in Figures 9.1 and 9.2.

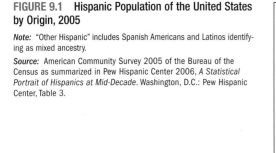

FIGURE 9.1 Hispanic Population of the United States by Origin, 2005

Note: "Other Hispanic" includes Spanish Americans and Latinos identifying as mixed ancestry.

Source: American Community Survey 2005 of the Bureau of the Census as summarized in Pew Hispanic Center 2006, *A Statistical Portrait of Hispanics at Mid-Decade*. Washington, D.C.: Pew Hispanic Center, Table 3.

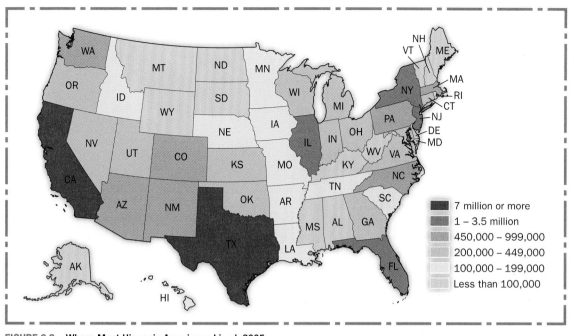

FIGURE 9.2 **Where Most Hispanic Americans Lived, 2005**

Source: American Community Survey 2005 of the Bureau of the Census as summarized in Pew Hispanic Center 2006, *A Statistical Portrait of Hispanics at Mid-Decade.* Washington, D.C.: Pew Hispanic Center, Table 10.

The Latino influence is everywhere. Motion pictures such as *Tortilla Soup, Spanglish, Real Women Have Curves, Quinceañera, Stand and Deliver, Frida,* and *My Family/Mi Familia,* to name a few, did not cater only to Hispanic audiences. MTV offers a channel, MTV Ritmo, featuring all-Latin music. The number-one radio stations in Los Angeles and Miami broadcast in Spanish. Comedian George Lopez, in his television sitcom and motion pictures, enjoys broad appeal. In their speeches, politicians address the needs and desires of Latino Americans.

Some prevailing images of Hispanic settlements in the United States are no longer accurate. Latinos do not live in rural areas. They are generally urban dwellers: 91 percent live in metropolitan areas, in contrast to 78 percent of non-Hispanic Whites. In addition, some Hispanics have moved away from their traditional areas of settlement. Many Mexican Americans have left the Southwest, and many Puerto Ricans have left New York City. In 1940, 88 percent of Puerto Ricans residing in the United States lived in New York City, but by the 2000 census the proportion had dropped to less than a third (J. Logan 2001a; Ramirez and de la Cruz 2003).

Latino Identity

Is there a common identity among Latinos? Is a panethnic identity emerging? **Panethnicity** is the development of solidarity between ethnic subgroups. We noted in Chapter 1 that ethnic identity is not self-evident in the United States and may lead to heated debates even among those who share the same ethnic heritage. Non-Hispanics often give a single label to the diverse group of native-born Latino Americans and immigrants. This labeling by the out-group is similar to the dominant group's way of viewing "American Indians" or "Asian Americans" as one collective group. For example, sociologist Clara Rodríquez has noted that Puerto Ricans, who are American citizens, are often mistakenly viewed as an immigrant group and lumped with all Latinos or Hispanics. She observes that, to most Anglos,

panethnicity
The development of solidarity between ethnic subgroups, as reflected in the terms Hispanic or Asian American.

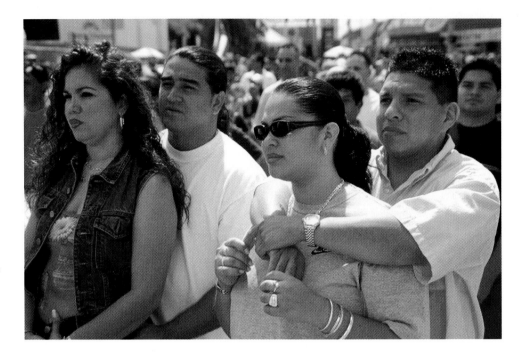

A very fluid issue is how successive generations of Latinos will identify themselves. Will they continue to see themselves in terms of their nationality background, such as Nicaraguan, or will they begin to converge toward a more panethnic identity?

"All Hispanics look alike. It's the tendency to see all Latinos as the same. It's an unfortunate lack of attention to U.S. history" (Rodríquez 1994, 32).

Are Hispanics or Latinos themselves developing a common identity? Indicators vary. The collective term itself is subject to debate with regional variations; for example, *Latino* is more common in the West, and *Hispanic* is used more often in the East and is the term employed by the federal government. Whatever the term, the actions of the dominant group have an impact to some degree in defining cultural identity. Latinos are brought together through language, national cable TV stations such as Univision and Telemundo, and periodicals aimed at them in both English and Spanish.

Sharp divisions remain among Hispanics on the identity issue. Only a minority, about 24 percent, prefers to use panethnic names such as *Hispanic* or *Latino*. In Miami, one can see bumper stickers proclaiming "No soy Hispano, soy Cubano": "I am not Hispanic, I am Cuban." Among U.S.-born Latinos, there is clearly a move away from using the native country as a means of identity. Among this segment of the Latino population, 46 percent say they either first use or only use *American* to describe themselves, and 29 percent use their parents' country of origin. This contrasts sharply with foreign-born Latinos, a group in which only 21 percent use *American* and 54 percent use *Mexican* or *Colombian* or similar national terms of reference (Brodie et al. 2002).

Such name issues—or language battles, as they have been called—are not inconsequential, but they do distract these groups' attention from working together for common concerns. For example, bridging differences is important in politics, where the diverse Latino or Hispanic groups meet to support candidates or legislative initiatives. When specifically asked in a 2003 survey whether Hispanics from different countries are working together to achieve common political goals or not working together politically, their own perception was evenly split between believing in panethnic terms or not. Interestingly, income and education do not seem to influence Hispanics' perceptions, but the younger generation does seem to be thinking more in panethnic terms (Brodie et al. 2002).

Class complicates the identity issue for Latinos in the United States. In Chapter 5, we introduced the term **ethclass**, which describes the merging of ethnicity and class in a person's status. For Latino households that have achieved a measure of economic security—and there is a significant and growing middle class—the issue of identity is complicated as they move economically and perhaps socially further from their roots. In "Research Focus," we examine the special challenges that face many immigrant Latinas in the United States.

ethclass
The merged ethnicity and class in a person's status.

The Economic Picture

Although there are many indicators of how well a group is doing economically in the United States, probably the best one is income. As we can see in Figure 9.3, the median household income of Latinos has gradually increased over the last twenty-five years, with some fluctuations. However, relative to non-Hispanic Whites, the income gap has remained. Generally over the recent years, the Latino household can expect to earn about 70 cents on the dollar received by its White counterpart.

Income is just part of the picture. Low wealth, total assets less debt, is characteristic of Hispanic households. Although they appear to have slightly higher levels of median wealth than African American households, Hispanic households average less than 10 cents for every dollar in wealth owned by White households. Also the trend is not encouraging. During a recent five-year period, Latino wealth increased by 14 percent

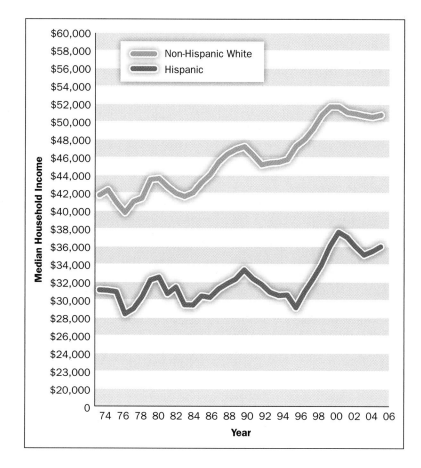

FIGURE 9.3 **Household Income Trends, 1972–2005**

Source: Bureau of the Census data in DeNavas-Walt et al. 2006, pp. 33, 36.

LATINAS: AMERICAN STYLE

Being an adolescent in the United States is difficult—so many demands and changes in one's own desires that are difficult to manage. Add to this mix being an immigrant and the challenges escalate dramatically.

For adolescent Hispanics, it is particularly challenging because of close-knit family ties. For example, a 2002 national survey of Latinos documented the emphasis on maintaining the household with a more traditional view. For example, 78 percent said it was better that children continue to live with their parents until they get married, compared to less than half of Whites and African Americans. The feelings are even stronger among foreign-born Latinos, with 91 percent wanting their unmarried children at home.

Traditions do continue that tie young Latinas to their cultural heritage. The **Quinceañera** or **Quinceañero** (among Puerto Ricans), meaning *fifteen years*, is a celebration of a young woman's fifteenth birthday. The festive occasion may be for the extended family or may resemble more of a debutante ball with the families of several Latinas joining together to mark the occasion for their daughters.

To get a more personal perspective of what is happening in the lives of young Latinas or Hispanic girls, a group of researchers interviewed at length Spanish-speaking Latinas at an urban midwestern school. They found that the Latinas are subject to harsher control both within the family and from the conformist school culture, which marks them as outsiders.

The Latinas are expected to help their family succeed through child care and housekeeping chores. These demands are much greater in the United States than they would have been in their home country because here virtually all the adult family members have to work, and they often do so at odd hours.

This expectation for the young Latinas to be at home when not at school effectively prevents them from working for wages like so many teenage girls, and that makes them seem different to their school peers. Without money from jobs, they are less able to "look American." The Latinas talk about how they wear inexpensive supermarket-brand tennis shoes, which stigmatizes them not only from other high school girls but also even from their brothers, who manage to acquire more respectable footwear through their jobs. Indeed, they commented that even Mexican Americans snubbed them. Added to their household responsibilities is the greater supervision that young Latinas receive from their elders whenever they are not at home and especially at nonschool-related events.

Meanwhile their brothers are encouraged to work outside the home, which gives them greater freedom from the family and also gives them greater opportunities to practice English-language skills with coworkers and customers. This in turn may lead to networking for future employment. Participation in high school sports is also encouraged for Latino boys, and this furthers their acceptance within the high school culture. The gender structure of the family diminishes opportunities available to Latinas outside the family.

Quinceañera (or Quinceañero)
Celebration of Latinas turning 15 years of age.

Quinceañera marks the fifteenth birthday of Latinas but also can be viewed as another step between the worlds of Latino and Anglo America. Here an Ecuadoran immigrant celebrates Quinceañera in New York City.

The Latinas described are typical of many teenage girls who are concerned with how they fit in. They want to belong, but family expectations keep them removed from the very culture into which they want to assimilate. This research and survey data remind us of the special challenges faced by many immigrant girls, and especially those who do not speak English, a situation that, at least initially, serves to isolate them from others. They struggle to overcome being stigmatized as different. One Latina said that her classmates think Latinas "travel on burros" and that "we are called Maria." At the same time that they are trying to acquire skills in school, they are also faced with moving between identifying with the culture of their family and that of the society at large. ■

Sources: Brodie et al 2002; L. Williams et al 2002.

compared to 17 percent of non-Hispanic Whites. So not only are Latinos likely to earn much less annually, but also they have fewer financial resources to fall back on (Kochhar 2004; Pew Hispanic Center 2006a).

The trend in poverty rate reflects that of the pattern in income. At the beginning of 2006, 21.8 percent of Latinos were below the poverty level compared to 8.3 percent of non-Hispanic Whites. This meant that one out of five Latinos at the start of 2006 was in a household of two adults and two children, for example, and earned less than $19,806. Typically over the last quarter century, the proportion of Latinos in poverty has been two or three times that of non-Hispanic Whites (see Figure 9.4).

Looking at income and poverty trends of Latino households shows how much, but also how little, has been accomplished to reduce social inequality between ethnic and racial groups. Although the income of Latinos has gradually increased over the last thirty years, so has White income. The gap between the two groups in both income and poverty level has remained relatively constant. Indeed, the income of the typical Latino household in 2005 was over $10,000 behind the typical 1972 non-Hispanic White household.

Previously in Chapter 8, William Julius Wilson used the term *underclass* to describe the growing proportion of poor African Americans who find obtaining meaningful

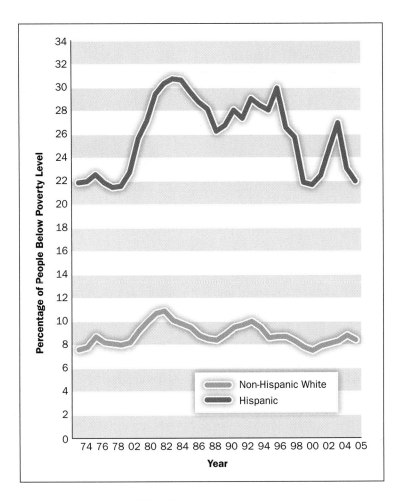

FIGURE 9.4 People in Poverty Trends, 1973–2005

Source: Bureau of the Census data in DeNavas-Walt et al. 2006, pp. 48, 51.

work increasingly difficult. Although this also has been said of today's poor Latinos, their situation is much more difficult to predict. On one hand, as a group poor Latinos are more mobile geographically than poor African Americans, which offers some prospects for a brighter future. On the other hand, nearly half of Latinos send money abroad to help relatives, which obviously puts a greater strain on supporting themselves in the United States (Latino Coalition 2006).

The Growing Political Presence

In the last thirty years, the major political parties have begun to acknowledge that Latinos form a force in the election process. This recognition has come primarily through the growth of the Hispanic population and also through policies that have facilitated non-English voters.

In 1975, Congress moved toward recognizing the multilingual background of the U.S. population. Federal law now requires bilingual or even multilingual ballots in voting districts where at least 5 percent of the voting-age population or 10,000 of the population do not speak English. Even before Congress acted, the federal courts had been ordering cities such as Chicago, Miami, and New York City to provide bilingual ballots where necessary. In the November 2002 elections, some 296 counties and municipalities in 30 states issued multilingual ballots (*Migration News* 2002b).

These voting reforms did not have the impact that many of their advocates had hoped for. The turnout was poor because, although Hispanics were interested in voting, many were ineligible to vote under the U.S. Constitution because they were noncitizens. At the time of the 2004 presidential election, 41 percent of Hispanics of voting age were noncitizens compared with only 2 percent of White non-Hispanics (Holder 2006).

The potential for a greater Latino political presence is strong. Anticipating the greater turnout, political parties are advancing more Hispanic candidates. Generally, the Democrats have been more successful in garnering the Hispanic vote: Democrat challenger John Kerry garnered 53 percent of the Hispanic vote in 2004, compared with 44 percent for the Republican incumbent George W. Bush. Generally surveys show only 21 percent of Latinos saying they typically vote for a Republican candidate with 18 percent undecided and 61 percent leaning to the Democrat candidate. However, observers agree that this is not as much a pro-Democrat vote as a stand against the Republicans, who favor reducing legal immigration, limiting welfare benefits to

Latino political involvement is often frustrated by old-time politics that favor those long in power. Here former Texas State Senator Gonzalo Barrientos holds a proposed redistricting map for defining boundaries to elect state representatives that many felt would not reflect the growing presence of Hispanics in his state.

REXBABIN IN THE SACRAMENTO BEE

The GOP (the Republican Party) has literally tangled itself up in its strong position on curbing illegal immigration, which has hampered its candidates from getting support from the Latino community.

legal immigrants, and eliminating bilingual education. Latinos as a group are not nearly as pro-Democrat as, for example, African Americans (Latino Coalition 2006; Pearson and McCormick 2004).

Unlike the Black vote, the major political parties are more likely to see the Latino vote still in play. The 2004 Bush-Cheney ticket heavily promoted the "agenda del Presidente," while Kerry-Edwards encouraged "contribuya al Partido Democrático." Indeed, evidence shows that younger Hispanics are becoming more conservative and more likely to consider Republican candidates. All these factors among Hispanics—rapidly growing population, higher proportions of voter registration, higher participation in elections, less commitment to a single political party—will increase efforts by politicians to elicit their support (Keen and Benedetto 2001 Pew Hispanic Center 2006c; Suro and Escobar 2006).

Like African Americans, many Latinos resent the fact that every four years political movers and shakers rediscover they exist. In between major elections, little effort is made to court their interest except by Latino elected officials.

The Borderlands

"The border is not where the U.S. stops and Mexico begins," said Mayor Betty Flores of Laredo, Texas. "It's where the U.S. blends into Mexico" (Gibbs 2001, 42). The term **borderlands** here refers to the area of a common culture along the border between Mexico and the United States. Though particularly relevant to Mexicans and Mexican Americans, the growing Mexican influence is relevant to the other Latino groups that we will discuss.

Legal and illegal emigration from Mexico to the United States, day laborers crossing the border regularly to go to jobs in the United States, the implementation of the North American Free Trade Agreement (NAFTA), and the exchange of media across the border all make the notion of separate Mexican and U.S. cultures obsolete in the borderlands.

borderlands
The area of a common culture along the border between Mexico and the United States.

FIGURE 9.5 The Borderlands

In search of higher wages, undocumented Mexicans often attempt to cross the border illegally, risking their lives in the process. Maquiladoras located just south of the U.S.–Mexican border employ Mexican workers at wages far lower than those earned by U.S. workers. The Mexican workers and Mexican Americans send large amounts of money, called remittances, to assist kinfolk and communities in Mexico.

Source: Author based on Cañas 2006; Martinez 2006b; Thompson 2001.

maquiladoras
foreign-owned companies on the Mexican side of the border with the United States.

remittances (or migradollars)
The monies that immigrants return to their country of origin.

hometown clubs
Nonprofit organizations that maintain close ties to immigrants' hometowns in Mexico and other Latin American countries.

The economic position of the borderlands is complex in terms of both businesses and workers. Very visible is the presence of **maquiladoras** on the Mexican side (Figure 9.5). Maquiladoras are foreign-owned companies that establish operations in Mexico yet are exempt from Mexican taxes and are not required to provide insurance or benefits for their workers. Pay at $2.00 to $2.50 an hour is considered very good by prevailing wage standards in Mexico. However, this one example of international trade soon became trumped by another aspect of globalization. As low as these hourly wages seem to people in industrial countries, multinational corporations soon found even lower wages in China. Over 40 percent of the 700,000 new maquiladora jobs created in the 1990s were eliminated by 2003 (*Migration* News 2002c, 2004).

Immigrant workers have a significant economic impact on their home country while employed in the United States. Many Mexicans, as well as other Hispanic groups we will be discussing, send some part of their earnings back across the border to family members remaining in their native country. This substantial flow of money, sometimes called **remittances** (or **migradollars**), was estimated at a minimum of $20 billion in 2005. Most of the money is spent to pay for food, clothing, and housing, but increasingly a growing proportion is being invested to create small businesses (Cañas et al. 2006).

The closeness culturally and economically of the home country found in the borderlands is applicable to other Latino groups. We will see the continuing prominent role that economic and political events have on immigrants and their children, and even grandchildren, in the United States.

Inland from the border, **hometown clubs** have sprung up well into northern cities with large settlements of Mexicans. Hometown clubs typically are nonprofit organizations that maintain close ties to immigrants' hometowns in Mexico and other Latin

Maquiladoras are foreign-owned manufacturers located in Mexico along the United States border. Workers assemble components for export to the United States at a plant in Nueva Laredo, Mexico.

American countries. Hometown clubs collect money for improvements in hospitals and schools that are beyond the means of the local people back home. The impact of hometown clubs has become so noticeable that some states in Mexico have begun programs whereby they will match funds from hometown clubs to encourage such public-spirited efforts. The work of over 1,500 hometown clubs in the United States or Mexican communities alone reflects the blurring of border distinctions within the Latino community (Korecki 2003; *Migration News* 2000).

As we have noted, the Latino or Hispanic community is made up of several nationalities. The Mexican Americans, the people of the borderlands and beyond, and the Puerto Ricans are by far the two largest and are considered separately in Chapter 10. We will continue in this chapter by considering the other Latino groups.

Cuban Americans

Third in numbers only to Mexican Americans and Puerto Ricans, Cuban Americans are a significant ethnic Hispanic minority in the United States. Their presence in this country has a long history, with Cuban settlements in Florida dating back to as early as 1831. These settlements tended to be small, close-knit communities organized around a single enterprise, such as a cigar-manufacturing firm.

Until recently, however, the number of Cuban Americans was very modest. The 1960 census showed that 79,000 people who had been born in Cuba lived in the United States. By 2005, more than 1.4 million people of Cuban birth or descent lived in the United States. This tremendous increase followed Fidel Castro's assumption of power after the 1959 Cuban Revolution.

Immigration

Cuban immigration to the United States since the 1959 revolution has been continuous, but there have been three significant influxes of large numbers of immigrants through the 1980s. First, the initial exodus of about 200,000 Cubans after Castro's assumption of power lasted about three years. Regular commercial air traffic continued despite the United States' severing of diplomatic relations with Cuba. This first wave stopped with the missile crisis of October 1962, when all legal movement between the two nations was halted.

An agreement between the United States and Cuba in 1965 produced the second wave through a program of freedom flights: specially arranged charter flights from Havana to Miami. Through this program, more than 340,000 refugees arrived between 1965 and 1973. Despite efforts to encourage these arrivals to disperse into other parts of the United States, most settled in the Miami area (M. Abrahamson 1996).

The third major migration, the 1980 Mariel boatlift, has been the most controversial. In 1980, more than 124,000 refugees fled Cuba in the "freedom flotilla." In May of that year, a few boats from Cuba began to arrive in Key West, Florida, with people seeking asylum in the United States. President Carter, reflecting the nation's hostility toward Cuba's communist government, told the new arrivals and anyone else who might be listening in Cuba that they were welcome "with open arms and an open heart." As the number of arrivals escalated, it became apparent that Castro had used the invitation as an opportunity to send prison inmates, patients from mental hospitals, and addicts. However, the majority of the refugees were neither marginal to the Cuban economy nor social deviants.

Other Cubans soon began to call the refugees of this migration **Marielitos**. The word, which implies that these refugees were undesirable, refers to Mariel, the fishing port west of Havana from which the boats departed, where Cuban authorities herded people into boats. The term *Marielitos* remains a stigma in the media and in Florida. Because of their negative reception by longer-established Cuban immigrants, as well as

ASK Yourself

What has been the pattern of immigration from Cuba to the US?

Marielitos
People who arrived from Cuba in the third wave of Cuban immigration, most specifically those forcibly deported by way of Mariel Harbor. The term is generally reserved for refugees seen as especially undesirable.

Voices Listen to Our Voices Listen to

LEAVING CUBA

At the age of eight I first realized my family was planning on leaving Cuba when my mother went to my second grade school in Havana to inform the principal that my brother and I would not be returning. I remember my teacher was not surprised that we were leaving but was surprised that we were *gusanos*, literally meaning worms or political dissidents. I returned home as my family waited to receive word that we were allowed to leave.

We waited about a week when a policeman knocked at our door in the middle of the night on May 17, 1980, and handed my father a document granting permission to leave Cuba. Within hours we had to get to the processing center, so my parents woke us up and prepared my grandmother who was in a wheelchair. At the center, the Cuban government confiscated our passports, searched us keeping all valuables including my parents' wedding rings. From there it was to Mariel Port three hours away by a special bus.

The trip on the bus was tough for an eight year old as people along the entire route beat on our bus with bats, sticks, stones, eggs, and

Alfredo Jimenez

tomatoes. Once at the Port, my brother and I managed to get away from the adults to play with other children at the beach where I remember playing with small crabs in the sand. My parents got very upset when our pant legs got wet. They had written on the inside of our pant legs the names, addresses, and phone numbers of friends and family in the United States and Spain.

Days of waiting and we were finally able to board an overcrowded boat headed for Florida. Already filled to the brim, the boat in the middle of the night rescued 12 people from another boat that was sinking. After twelve hours, we arrived in Key West to be greeted by waving American flags. Soon we headed on to Tampa to live with an aunt and her family—she had come to America soon after Fidel Castro assumed power.

The entire trip was an experience that my family values very much to this day. As young as my brother and I were, we didn't appreciate how difficult it was for my parents to leave everything behind. ∎

Source: Jiminez 2005.

---

the group's modest skills and lack of formal education, this group had a great deal of difficulty in adjusting to their new life in the United States.

Now a Chicago real estate broker, Alfredo Jimenez tells in "Listen to Our Voices" of the experience he had as a young child being taken by his family and leaving everything behind in Cuba to go to the United States.

The difficult transition for many members of this freedom flotilla is linked with other factors as well. Unlike the earlier waves, they grew up in a country bombarded with anti-American images. Despite these problems, their eventual acceptance by the Hispanic community has been impressive, and many members of this third significant wave have found employment. Most have applied for permanent resident status. Government assistance to these immigrants was limited, but help from some groups of Cuban Americans in the Miami area was substantial. However, for a small core group, adjustment was impossible. The legal status of a few of these detainees (i.e., arrivals who were held by the

dry foot, wet foot
Policy toward Cuban immigrants allowing entry to those who manage to reach the US (dry foot) to remain, while those picked-up at sea (wet foot) are sent back to Cuba.

government pending clarification of their refugee or immigrant status) was ambiguous because of alleged offenses committed in Cuba or the United States (Peréz 2001).

Since 1994, the United States has a **dry foot wet foot**, policy with respect to arrivals from Cuba. This refers to government policy that generally allows Cuban nationals who manage to actually reach the United States ("dry foot") to remain whereas those who are picked up at sea ("wet foot") are sent back to Cuba. Unfortunately, this policy has people taking great risks at crossing the Florida Straits with an unknown number perishing before reaching the mainland or being intercepted by the Coast Guard.

The Cuban refugee situation continues to be caught up in the strong anti-Castro, anticommunist feelings of most Cuban Americans and many others in the United States. Cuban refugees have a special advantage over other refugees in terms of public opinion. The issue of refugee rights came to an emotional and headline-grabbing climax with the decision to return 6-year-old Elián Gonzalez to Cuba in 2000. His mother had drowned as she sought to bring him to the United States. After months of vehement protests by the Cuban American community to allow the boy to remain in the United States with some cousins, the federal government returned the boy to his father, with the full understanding that the boy would be returned to Cuba. In 2004, the Bush administration launched a series of steps including restricting travel to Cuba and remittances as a means to punish the Castro regime. Although refugee/immigrant issues often are driven by economics, the issue of communist governments still overshadows many people's attitudes about our relationship with Cuba. However, among Cuban Americans, the anti-Cuban movement is waning as a smaller proportion of people have any memories of life in Cuban prior to Castro's rise to power (Dahlburg 2004b; Warren 2000; Williams 2006b).

The Present Picture

Compared with other recent immigrant groups and with Latinos as a whole, Cuban Americans are doing well. As shown in Table 9.1, Cuban Americans have college completion rates twice those of other Latinos. In this and all other social measures, the pattern is similar. Cuban Americans in 2000 compared favorably with other Hispanics, although recent arrivals as a group trail behind White Americans.

The presence of Cubans has been felt in urban centers throughout the United States but most notably in the Miami, Florida area. Throughout their various immigration phases, Cubans have been encouraged to move out of southern Florida, but many have returned to Dade County (metropolitan Miami), with its warm climate and proximity to other Cubans and Cuba itself. As of 2000, 55 percent of all Cuban Americans

---

TABLE 9.1
Selected Social and Economic Characteristics of Cubans and South Americans, 2000

	Total Non-Hispanic White	Total Hispanic	Cuban	Central and South American
Percentage completing college, 25 years and over	28.1	10.6	23.0	17.4
Percentage unemployed	3.4	6.8	5.8	5.1
Percentage of families with a single parent	17.4	32.1	22.9	35.0
Percentage living below poverty level	7.7	22.8	17.3	16.7
Median family income	$54,906	$33,077	$39,432	$34,806

Source: Therrien and Ramirez 2001, Tables 1, 4.1, 7.1, 9.2, 14.1.

lived in the Miami area; another 15 percent lived elsewhere in Florida. Metropolitan Miami itself now has a Hispanic majority of 57 percent of the total population, compared with a Hispanic presence of only 4 percent in 1950 (J. Logan 2001a).

Probably no ethnic group has had more influence on the fortunes of a city in a short period of time than have the Cubans on Miami. Most consider the Cubans' economic influence to be positive. The Cuban and other Latin American immigrants have transformed Miami from a quiet resort to a boomtown. To a large degree, they have recreated the Cuba they left behind. Today, the population of metropolitan Miami is more than 35 percent foreign born—more than any other city. Residents like to joke that one of the reasons they like living in Miami is that it is close to the United States (Clary 1997b).

The relations between Miami's Cuban Americans and other groups have not been perfect. For example, Miami's other Hispanics, including Venezuelans, Ecuadorians, and Colombians, resent being mistaken for Cubans and feel that their own distinctive nationalities are being submerged. Cubans now find in Miami's Little Havana area that storefronts advertise Salvadorans corn pancakes and waitresses hail from El Salvador. Cuban Miamians are also slowly adjusting to sharing their influence with the growing diversity of Hispanics. One obvious symbol is the investment of the park district in building more and more soccer fields—Cubans traditionally play baseball (Dahlburg 2004a).

All Cuban immigrants have had much to adjust to, and they have not been able to immediately establish the kind of life they sought. Although some of those who fled Cuba were forced to give up their life's savings, the early immigrants of the first wave were generally well educated, had professional or managerial backgrounds, and, therefore, met with greater economic success than later immigrants. However, regardless of the occupations the immigrants were able to enter, there was tremendous adjustment for the family. Women who typically did not work outside the home often had to seek employment. Immigrant parents found their children being exposed to a foreign culture. All the challenges typically faced by immigrant households were complicated by uncertainty surrounding those they left behind in Cuba.

The primary adjustment among South Florida's Cuban Americans is more to each other than to Whites, African Americans, or other Latinos. The prolonged immigration now stretching across two generations has led to differences between Cuban Americans in terms of ties to Cuba, social class, and age. There is not a single Cuban American lifestyle.

The long-range prospects for Cubans in the United States depend on several factors. Of obvious importance are events in Cuba, for many Cuban refugees publicly proclaim their desire to return if the communist government is overturned. A powerful force in politics in Miami is the Cuban-American National Foundation, which takes a strong anti-Castro position. They have actively opposed any proposals that the United States develop a more flexible policy toward Cuba. More moderate voices in the Cuban exile community have not been encouraged to speak out. Indeed, sporadic violence has even occurred within the community over U.S.–Cuban relations. In addition, artists or speakers who come from Cuba receive a cold reception in Miami unless they are outspoken critics of Fidel Castro (L. Martin 1996).

Cuban Americans have selectively accepted Anglo culture. But Cuban culture has been tenacious; the Cuban immigrants do not feel that they need to forget Spanish while establishing fluency in English, the way other immigrant children have shunned their linguistic past. Still, a split between the original exiles and their children is evident. Young people are more concerned about the Miami Dolphins football team than they are about what is happening in Havana. They are more open to reestablishing relations with a Castro-led Cuba. However, the more recent wave of immigrants, the *recién llegados* (recently arrived), have again introduced more openly anti-Castro feelings, as evidenced in the battles over Elián Gonzalez in 2000 and travel restrictions in 2004.

of them being identified in the census as "nonwhite." Immigration is often through Mexico, which may serve as a brief stop along the way or represent a point of settlement for six months to three years or even longer (López 2004).

Since the mid-1970s, increasing numbers of Central and South Americans have fled unrest. Although Latinos as a whole are a fast-growing minority, Central and South Americans increased in numbers even faster than Mexicans or any other group in the 1980s. In particular, from about 1978, war and economic chaos in El Salvador, Nicaragua, and Guatemala prompted many to seek refuge in the United States. The impact of the turmoil cannot be exaggerated. It is estimated that anywhere from 13 percent in Guatemala to 32 percent in El Salvador of the total population left the country. Not at all a homogeneous group, they range from Guatemalan Indian peasants to wealthy Nicaraguan exiles. These latest arrivals probably had some economic motivation for migration, but this concern was overshadowed or at least matched by their fear of being killed or hurt if they remained in their home country (Camarillo 1993; López 2004).

The immigrants who fled violence and poverty often have difficulty in adjusting initially because they received little preparation for their movement to a foreign culture. Mario fled to the United States from Nicaragua when he was 16. As he writes, the initial years were trying:

> *At first it was difficult to adjust. People are very materialistic in the U.S. I was starting from zero. I had nothing. They made fun of my clothes. They treated me differently. They pushed me out of their circle. Luckily, I met a friend from school back home who had been in the U.S. eight years. He took care of me. (Cerar 1995, 57)*

Eventually Mario felt comfortable enough to help immigrants and to serve as a tutor at the local community college. His experience has been played out before in the United States and undoubtedly will be again many times.

The Present Picture

Two issues have clouded the recent settlement of Central and South Americans. First, many of the arrivals are illegal immigrants. Among those uncovered as undocumented workers, citizens from El Salvador, Guatemala, and Colombia are outnumbered only by Mexican nationals. Second, significant numbers of highly trained and skilled people have left these countries, which are in great need of professional workers. We noted in Chapter 4 how often immigration produces a **brain drain:** immigration to the United States of skilled workers, professionals, and technicians.

As a group, Central and South Americans experience high unemployment levels compared with Whites, yet they are better educated than most Hispanics, as shown in Table 9.1. This reflects the plight that often faces recent immigrants. Upon relocating to a new country, they initially experience downward mobility in terms of occupational status.

The challenges to immigrants from Latin America are reflected in the experience of Colombians, numbering close to a half million in the United States. The initial arrivals from this South American nation after World War I were educated middle-class people who quickly assimilated to life in the United States. Rural unrest in Colombia in the 1980s triggered large-scale movement to the United States, where the Colombian immigrants had to adapt to a new culture and to urban life. The adaptation of this later group has been much more difficult. Some have found success through catering to other Colombians. For example, enterprising immigrants have opened bodegas (grocery stores) to supply traditional, familiar foodstuffs. Similarly, Colombians have established restaurants, travel agencies, and real estate firms that serve other Colombians. However, many find themselves obliged to take menial jobs and to combine the income of several family members to meet the high cost of urban life. Colombians of mixed African descent face racial as well as ethnic and language barriers (Guzmán 2001).

What is likely to be the future of Central and South Americans in the United States? Although much will depend on future immigration, they could assimilate over the course of

? ASK Yourself

What have been the different reasons behind immigration from Latin America?

brain drain
Immigration to the United States of skilled workers, professionals, and technicians who are desperately needed by their home countries.

Latinos rarely appear on television in central roles, much less on successful television programs. Although animated, *Dora the Explorer* on Nickelodeon is an exception to this rule.

generations. One alternative is that they will become trapped with Mexican Americans as a segment of the dual labor market of the urban areas where they have taken residence. A more encouraging possibility is that they will retain an independent identity, like the Cubans, while also establishing an economic base. For example, nearly 600,000 Dominicans (from the Dominican Republic) settled in the New York City area, where they make up a significant 7 percent of the population. In some neighborhoods, such as Washington Heights, one can easily engage in business, converse, and eat just as if one were in the Dominican Republic. People continue to remain attentive to events in Dominican politics, which often command greater attention than events in the United States. However, within their local neighborhoods, Dominicans here are focused on improving employment opportunities and public safety (J. Logan 2001a; Pessar 1995; Suro 1998).

Conclusion

The signals are mixed. Many movies and television programs and much music have a Hispanic flavor. Candidates for political office seek Latino votes and sometimes even speak Spanish to do so. Yet the poverty rate of Latino families reported in 2006 was more than 22 percent, compared with less than 8 percent for White Americans.

This mixture of positive and negative trends is visible in other areas. Ballots are printed in Spanish and other languages. Many Latinos feel that to be bilingual is not to be less a part of the United States. Espousing pluralism rather than assimilation is not un-American.

The contrast of images and substance will be evident again in Chapter 10. "In World War II, more Latinos won Medals of Honor than any other ethnic group," said Democratic Representative Matthew Martinez, a former U.S. Marine who represented part of Los Angeles. "How much blood do you have to spill before you prove you are a part of something?" Much more recently, we might not be surprised to know that many of the soldiers in Iraq are Hispanic. Perhaps a bit surprising to the general public would be to learn that at least twenty-two Mexican citizens resident in the United States died in the military during the first two years of the Iraq War for their adopted country. Typically Congress passes a resolution making these fallen soldiers citizens after their death. Under a new rule, families of the deceased can now use the deceased as a sponsor for their own residency papers (P. Jonsson 2006; McKinley 2005; Whitman 1987, 49). Still a contrasting image is offered by the refrain "Si usted no habla inglés puede quedarse rezagado" ("If you don't speak English, you might be left behind").

Key Terms

borderlands 262

brain drain 269

color gradient 268

dry foot, wet foot 266

ethclass 257

hometown clubs 263

maquiladoras 263

Marielitos 264

panethnicity 255

Quinceañera
  (or Quinceañero) 258

remittances (or migradollars) 263

Review Questions

1. What different factors seem to unite and to divide the Latino community in the United States?

2. How do Hispanics view themselves as a group? How are they viewed by others?

3. Identify the factors that serve to contribute and to limit to the political power of Latinos as a group in the United States?

4. To what extent has the Cuban migration been positive, and to what degree do significant challenges remain?

5. How have Central and South Americans contributed to the diversity of the Hispanic peoples in the United States?

Critical Thinking

1. Language and culture are almost inseparable. How do you imagine your life would change if you were not permitted to speak your native language? Or how has it been affected if you have been expected to speak some other language?

2. How have you witnessed the presence of a different culture in the United States? At what times have you found it to be interesting and intriguing? Are there times you felt threatened by it or felt its presence to be unfair?

3. Why do you think the borderlands of the U.S.–Mexico border region have been the subject of such close scrutiny, whereas there is little attention to similar areas along the U.S.–Canada border?

Internet Connections—Research Navigator™

To access the full resources of Research Navigator™, please find the access code printed on the inside cover of *OneSearch with Research Navigator™: Sociology*. You may have received this booklet if your instructor recommended this guide be packaged with new textbooks. (If your book did not come with this printed guide, you can purchase one through your college bookstore.) Visit our Research Navigator™ site at www.ResearchNavigator.com. Once at this site, click on REGISTER under New Users and enter your access code to create a personal Login Name and Password. (When revisiting the site, use the same Login Name and Password.) Browse the features of the Research Navigator™ Web site and search the databases of academic journals, newspapers, magazines, and Web links.

For further information relevant to Chapter 9, you may wish to use such keywords as "Maquiladoras," "Salvadoran Americans," and "Marielitos," and the search engine will supply relevant and recent scholarly and popular press publications. Use the *New York Times* Search-by-Subject Archive to find recent news articles related to sociology and the Link Library feature to locate relevant Web links organized by the key terms associated with this chapter.

10

Mexican Americans
and Puerto Ricans

CHAPTER OUTLINE

Mexican Americans

Puerto Ricans

LISTEN TO OUR VOICES
"¡Viva Vieques!"
by Martín St. Espada
The Contemporary Picture of Mexican
Americans and Puerto Ricans

RESEARCH FOCUS

*Assimilation May Be Hazardous
to Your Health*

Conclusion

Key Terms/Review Questions/Critical
Thinking/Internet Connections—
Research Navigator™

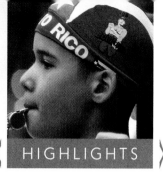

THE HISTORY OF MEXICAN AMERICANS IS CLOSELY TIED TO immigration, which has been encouraged (the *bracero* program) when Mexican labor is in demand or discouraged (repatriation and Operation Wetback) when Mexican workers are unwanted. The Puerto Rican people are divided between those who live in the island commonwealth and those who live on the mainland. Puerto Ricans who migrate to the mainland most often come in search of better jobs and housing. Both Mexican Americans and Puerto Ricans, as groups, have lower incomes, less formal education, and greater health problems than White Americans. Both the family and religion are sources of strength for the typical Puerto Rican or Mexican American.

Citizenship is the basic requirement for receiving one's legal rights and privileges in the United States. However, for both Mexican Americans and Puerto Ricans, citizenship has been an ambiguous concept at best. Mexican Americans (or Chicanos) have a long history in the United States, stretching back before the nation was even formed to the early days of European exploration. Santa Fe, New Mexico, was founded more than a decade before the Pilgrims landed at Plymouth. The Mexican American people trace their ancestry to the merging of Spanish settlers with the Native Americans of Central America and Mexico. This ancestry reaches back to the brilliant Mayan and Aztec civilizations, which attained their height about C.E. 700 and 1500, respectively. However, roots in the land do not guarantee a group dominance over it. Over several centuries, the Spaniards conquered the land and merged with the Native Americans to form the Mexican people. In 1821, Mexico obtained its independence, but this independence was short-lived, for domination from the north began less than a generation later (Meier and Rivera 1972).

Today, Mexican Americans are creating their own destiny in the United States while functioning in a society that is often concerned about immigration both legal and illegal. In the eyes of some, including a few in positions of authority, to be Mexican American is to be suspected of being in the country illegally or, at least, of knowingly harboring illegal aliens.

For no other minority group in the United States is citizenship so ambiguous as it is for Puerto Ricans. Even Native Americans, who are subject to some unique laws and are exempt from others because of past treaties, have a future firmly dominated by the United States. This description does not necessarily fit Puerto Ricans. Their island home is the last major U.S. colonial territory and, for that matter, one of the few colonial areas remaining in the world. Besides assessing the situation of Puerto Ricans on the mainland, we will also need to consider the relationship of the United States to Puerto Rico.

The Roman Catholic Church has a long history among Mexicans and Mexican Americans. The Mission San Xavier del Bac in Arizona was founded in 1700.

Mexican Americans

Wars play a prominent part in any nation's history. The United States was created as a result of the colonies' war with England to win their independence. In the 1800s, the United States acquired significant neighboring territory in two different wars. The legacy of these wars and the annexation that resulted were to create the two largest Hispanic minorities in the United States: Mexican Americans and Puerto Ricans.

A large number of Mexicans became aliens in the United States without ever crossing any border. These people first became Mexican Americans with the conclusion of the Mexican–American War. This two-year war culminated with a U.S. occupation of eleven months. Today Mexicans visit the Museum of Interventions in Mexico City, which outlines the war and how Mexico permanently gave up half its country. The war is still spoken of today as "the Mutilation" (T. Weiner 2004).

In the war-ending Treaty of Guadalupe Hidalgo, signed February 2, 1848, Mexico acknowledged the annexation of Texas by the United States and ceded California and most of Arizona and New Mexico to the United States for $15 million. In exchange, the United States granted citizenship to the 75,000 Mexican nationals who remained on the annexed land after one year. With citizenship, the United States was to guarantee religious freedom, property rights, and cultural integrity—that is, the right to continue Mexican and Spanish cultural traditions and to use the Spanish language.

The beginnings of the Mexican experience in the United States were as varied as the people themselves. Some Mexican Americans were affluent with large land holdings. Others were poor peasants barely able to survive. Along such rivers as the Rio Grande, commercial towns grew up around the increasing river traffic. In New Mexico and Arizona, many Mexican American people welcomed the protection that the U.S. government offered against several Native American tribes. In California, life was quickly dominated by the gold miners, and Anglos controlled the newfound wealth. One generalization can be made about the many segments of the Mexican American population in the nineteenth century: They were regarded as a conquered people. In fact, even before the war, many Whites who traveled into the West were already prejudiced against people of mixed blood (in this instance, against Mexicans). Whenever Mexican American and Anglo interests conflicted, Anglo interests won.

A pattern of second-class treatment for Mexican Americans emerged well before the twentieth century. Gradually, the Anglo system of property ownership replaced the Native American and Hispanic systems. Mexican Americans who inherited land proved no match for Anglo lawyers. Court battles provided no protection for poor Spanish-speaking landowners. Unscrupulous lawyers occasionally defended Mexican Americans successfully, only to demand half the land as their fee. Anglo cattle ranchers gradually pushed out Mexican American ranchers. By 1892, the federal government was granting grazing privileges on public grasslands and forests to anyone except Mexican Americans. Effectively, the people who were now Mexican *Americans* had become outsiders in their own homeland. The ground was laid for the social structure of the Southwest in the twentieth century, an area of growing productivity in which minority groups have increased in size but remain largely subordinate.

The Immigrant Experience

Nowhere else in the world do two countries with such different standards of living and wage scales share such an open border. Immigration from Mexico is unique in several respects. First, it has been a continuous large-scale movement for most of the last hundred years. The United States did not restrict immigration from Mexico through legislation until 1965. Second, the proximity of Mexico encourages past immigrants to maintain strong cultural and language ties with the homeland through friends and relatives.

Return visits to the old country are only one- or two-day bus rides for Mexican Americans, not once-in-a-lifetime voyages, as they were for most European immigrants. The third point of uniqueness is the aura of illegality that has surrounded Mexican migrants. Throughout the twentieth century, the suspicion in which Anglos have held Mexican Americans has contributed to mutual distrust between the two groups.

The years before World War I brought large numbers of Mexicans into the expanding agricultural industry of the Southwest. The Mexican revolution of 1909–1922 thrust refugees into the United States, and World War I curtailed the flow of people from Europe, leaving the labor market open to the Mexican Americans. After the war, continued political turmoil in Mexico and more prosperity in the Southwest brought still more Mexicans across the border.

Simultaneously, corporations in the United States, led by agribusiness, invested in Mexico in such a way as to maximize their profits but minimize the amount of money remaining in Mexico to provide needed employment. Conflict theorists view this investment as part of the continuing process in which American businesses, with the support and cooperation of affluent Mexicans, have used Mexican people when it has been in corporate leaders' best interests. The Mexican workers are used either as cheap laborers in their own country by their fellow Mexicans and by Americans or as undocumented workers here who are dismissed when they are no longer judged to be useful (Guerin-Gonzales 1994).

? ASK Yourself

What role does economics play in permitting immigration from Mexico?

Beginning in the 1930s, the United States embarked on a series of measures aimed specifically at Mexicans. The Depression brought pressure on local governments to care for the growing number of unemployed and impoverished. Government officials developed a quick way to reduce welfare rolls and eliminate people seeking jobs: Ship Mexicans back to Mexico. This program of deporting Mexicans in the 1930s was called repatriation. As officially stated, the program was constitutional because only illegal aliens were to be **repatriated.** Actually, it was much more complex. Border records were incomplete because, before 1930, the United States had shown little interest in whether Mexicans entered with all the proper credentials. Also, many Mexicans who could be classified as illegal aliens had resided in the United States for decades. Because they had children who were citizens by birth, they could not legally be deported. The legal process of fighting a deportation order was overwhelming, however, especially for a poor Spanish-speaking family. The Anglo community largely ignored this outrage against the civil rights of those deported and did not show interest in helping repatriates to ease the transition (Meier and Rivera 1972).

When the Depression ended, Mexican laborers again became attractive to industry. In 1942, when World War II was depleting the labor pool, the United States and Mexico agreed to a program allowing migration across the border by contracted laborers, or **braceros.** Within a year of the initiation of the bracero program, more than 80,000 Mexican nationals had been brought in; they made up one-eleventh of the farm workers on the Pacific Coast. The program continued with some interruptions until 1964. It was devised to recruit labor from poor Mexican areas for U.S. farms. In a program that was supposed to be supervised jointly by Mexico and the United States, minimum standards were to be maintained for the transportation, housing, wages, and health care of the braceros. Ironically, these safeguards placed the braceros in a better economic situation than Mexican Americans, who often worked alongside the protected Mexican nationals. The Mexicans were still regarded as a positive presence by Anglos only when useful, and the Mexican American people were merely tolerated.

Like many policies of the past relating to disadvantaged racial and ethnic groups, the bracero program lives on. After decades of protests, the Mexican government finally issued checks of $3,500 to former braceros and their descendants. The payments were to resolve disputes over what happened to the money the U.S. government gave to the Mexican government to assist in resettlement. To say this has been regarded as

repatriation
The 1930s program of deporting Mexicans.

bracero
Contracted Mexican laborers brought to the United States during World War II.

too little, much too late is an understatement (Associated Press 2005; Galarza 1964; Stoddard 1973).

Another crackdown on illegal aliens was to be the third step in dealing with the perceived Mexican problem. Alternately called Operation Wetback and Special Force Operation, it was fully inaugurated by 1954. The term wetbacks, or **mojados**, the derisive slang for Mexicans who enter illegally, refers to those who secretly swim across the Rio Grande. Like other roundups, this effort failed to stop the illegal flow of workers. For several years, some Mexicans were brought in under the bracero program while other Mexicans were being deported. With the end of the bracero program in 1964 and stricter immigration quotas for Mexicans, illegal border crossings increased because legal crossings became more difficult (W. Gordon 1975; Stoddard 1973, 1976a, 1976b).

More dramatic than the negative influence that continued immigration has had on employment conditions in the Southwest is the effect on the Mexican and Mexican American people themselves. Routinely, the rights of Mexicans, even the rights to which they are entitled as illegal aliens, are ignored. Of the illegal immigrants deported, few have been expelled through formal proceedings. The Mexican American Legal Defense and Education Fund (MALDEF) has repeatedly expressed concern over the government's handling of illegal aliens.

Against this backdrop of legal maneuvers is the tie that the Mexican people have to the land both in today's Mexico and in the parts of the United States that formerly belonged to Mexico. Assimilation may be the key word in the history of many immigrant groups, but for Mexican Americans the key term is La Raza. **La Raza** literally means "the people," but among contemporary Mexican Americans the term connotes pride in a pluralistic Spanish, Native American, and Mexican heritage. Mexican Americans cherish their legacy and, as we shall see, strive to regain some of the economic and social glory that once was theirs.

Despite passage of various measures designed to prevent illegal immigration, neither the immigration nor the apprehension of illegal aliens is likely to end. Mexican Americans will continue to be more closely scrutinized by law enforcement officials because their Mexican descent makes them more suspect as potential illegal aliens. The Mexican American community is another group subject to racial profiling that renders, in the eyes of many, their presence in the United States suspect (Aguirre 2004).

In the United States, Mexican Americans have mixed feelings toward the illegal Mexican immigrants. Many are their kin, and Mexican Americans realize that entry into the United States brings Mexicans better economic opportunities. However,

mojados
"Wetbacks"; derisive slang for Mexicans who enter illegally, supposedly by swimming the Rio Grande.

La Raza
"The People"—a term referring to the rich heritage of Mexican Americans and therefore used to denote a sense of pride among Mexican Americans today.

Mexican migrants harvest strawberries in California.

culture of poverty
A way of life that involves no future planning, no enduring commitment to marriage, and no work ethic; this culture follows the poor even when they move out of the slums or the barrio.

numerous deportations only perpetuate the Anglo stereotype of Mexican and Mexican American alike as surplus labor. Mexican Americans, largely the product of past immigration, find that the continued controversy over illegal immigration places them in the ambivalent role of citizen and relative. Mexican American organizations opposing illegal immigration must confront people to whom they are closely linked by culture and kinship, and they must cooperate with government agencies they deeply distrust.

The Economic Picture

As shown in Table 10.1, both Mexican Americans and Puerto Ricans have higher unemployment rates, higher rates of poverty, and significantly lower incomes than White Americans. Six percent of all managerial and professional positions were held by Latinos. When considering their economic situation, two topics deserve special attention: the debate over what has been called the culture of poverty and the effort to improve the status of migrant workers (Bureau of the Census 2005a).

The Culture of Poverty Like the African American families described in Chapter 8, Mexican American families are labeled as having traits that, in fact, describe poor families rather than specifically Mexican American families. Indeed, as long ago as 1980, a report of the Commission on Civil Rights (1980, 8) stated that the two most prevalent stereotypical themes appearing in works on Hispanics showed them as exclusively poor and prone to commit violence.

Social scientists have also relied excessively on the traits of the poor to describe an entire subordinate group such as Mexican Americans. Anthropologist Oscar Lewis (1959, 1965, 1966), in several publications based on research conducted among Mexicans and Puerto Ricans, identified the **culture of poverty**. According to its theorists, the culture of poverty embraces a deviant way of life that involves no future planning, no enduring commitment to marriage, and absence of the work ethic. This culture supposedly follows the poor, even when they move out of the slums or the barrio.

The culture-of-poverty view is another way of blaming the victim: The affluent are not responsible for social inequality, nor are the policy makers; it is the poor who are to blame for their own problems. This stance allows government and society to attribute the failure of antipoverty and welfare programs to Mexican Americans and other poor people rather than to the programs themselves. These are programs

---

TABLE 10.1
Selected Social and Economic Characteristics of Mexican Americans and Puerto Ricans, 2000

	Total Non-Hispanic White	Total Hispanic	Mexican Americans	Puerto Ricans
Percentage completing college, 25 years and over	28.1	10.6	6.9	13.0
Percentage unemployed	3.4	6.8	7.0	8.1
Percentage of families with a single parent	17.4	32.1	30.0	43.2
Percentage living below poverty level	7.7	22.8	24.1	25.8
Median family income	$54,906	$33,077	$32,345	$31,312

Source: Therrien and Ramirez 2001, Tables 1, 4.1, 7.1, 9.2, 14.1.

designed and too often staffed by middle-class, English-speaking Anglo professionals. Conflict theorists, noting a similar misuse of the more recent term *underclass*, argue that it is unfair to blame the poor for their lack of money, low education, poor health, and low-paying jobs (Ryan 1976).

Lewis's hypothesis about the culture of poverty came to be used indiscriminately to explain continued poverty. Critics argue that Lewis sought out exotic, pathological behavior, ignoring the fact that even among the poor, most people live fairly conventionally and strive to achieve goals similar to those of the middle class. A second criticism challenges the use of the term *culture of poverty* to describe an entire ethnic group. Because Lewis's data were on poor people, social scientists have increasingly stressed that his conclusions may be correct as far as the data permit, but the data cannot be generalized to all Latinos. His sample was not a representative cross section drawn from different economic and educational levels (Gans 1995; Valentine 1968).

More recent social science research, unlike Lewis's, research does sample Mexican American families across a broad range of socioeconomic levels. This research shows that when Anglo and Mexican American families of the same social class are compared, they differ little in family organization and attitudes toward child rearing. In addition, comparisons of work ethics find no significant differences between Mexican Americans and Anglos. Poverty is present among Mexican Americans; there is no doubt about that. However, that does not mean there is a culture of poverty or a permanent underclass. Institutions such as the family and the church seem viable, but the schools are in despair, and the picture on businesses is mixed. However, to question the label *culture of poverty* does not deny the poor life chances facing many Mexican Americans (Aponte 1991; Moore and Pinderhughes 1993; Winkler 1990).

Chávez and the Farm Laborers   The best-known Hispanic labor leader for economic empowerment was César Chávez, the Mexican American who crusaded to organize migrant farm workers. Efforts to organize agricultural laborers date back to the turn of the twentieth century, but Chávez was the first to enjoy any success. These laborers had never won collective bargaining rights, partly because their mobility made it difficult for them to organize into a unified group.

In 1962, Chávez, then 35 years old, formed the National Farm Workers Association, later to become the United Farm Workers (UFW). Organizing migrant farm workers was not easy, for they had no savings to pay for organizing or to live on while striking. Growers could rely on an almost limitless supply of Mexican laborers to replace the Mexican Americans and Filipinos who struck for higher wages and better working conditions.

Chávez's first success was the grape boycott launched in 1965, which carried the struggle into the kitchens of families throughout the country. The UFW launched the boycott with the aim of damaging growers economically until they accepted the union and improved working conditions. It took five years for the grape growers to sign three-year contracts with Chávez's union, which had affiliated with the AFL-CIO. This victory signaled a new era in labor relations and made Chávez a national folk hero (Levy 1975).

Despite their success, Chávez and the UFW were plagued with continual opposition by agribusiness and many lawmakers. This was about the time the UFW was also trying to heighten public consciousness of the pesticides used in the fields. Research into the long-term effects of pesticides had only begun. Although Chávez's 1988 fast to bring attention to this issue was widely publicized, his efforts did not gain the support he had hoped for.

Chávez had difficulty fulfilling his objectives. By 1993, union membership had dwindled from a high of 80,000 in 1970 to 21,000 (it stood at 27,000 in 2004). Nevertheless, what he and the UFW accomplished was significant. First, they succeeded in making federal and state governments more aware of the exploitation of migrant laborers. Second, the migrant workers, or at least those organized in California, developed a sense of their own power and worth that will make it extremely difficult for growers to

César Chávez in 1990.

 ASK Yourself

Is it more likely for you to see members of racial and ethnic minorities doing backbreaking work for lower wages?

FARM WORKERS' SANITATION FACILITIES...

Recently, farm workers have protested their working conditions and the pesticide use that may threaten their lives.

Source: © Gary Huck/UE, Huck/Konopacki Labor Cartoons

abuse them in the future as they had in the past. Third, working conditions improved. California agricultural workers were paid an average of less than $2 an hour in the mid-1960s. By 1987, they were being paid an average of about $5.85 an hour (Mandelbaum 2000; Pawel 2006; Sanchez 1998; Triplett 2004).

Migrant workers still face a very harsh life. An ongoing study of agricultural workers found they are much more likely to suffer from high blood pressure, dental disease, anemia, and poor nutrition, which is ironic because they are harvesting the nation's food. About 70 percent of the workers lack health insurance, and most make less than $10,000 a year, which makes obtaining health care very difficult. Women have far better access to medical treatment because of special maternal and child health services, but a third of the men surveyed said they had never been to a physician or a clinic (Rainey 2000).

César Chávez died in 1993. Although his legacy is clear, many young people, when they hear mention of Chávez, are more likely to think of professional boxer Julio Cesar Chavez. By the beginning of the twenty-first century, the primary challenge came from efforts to permit more foreign workers, primarily from Mexico and Central America, to enter the United States temporarily at even lower wages. About three-quarters of all farm workers are Mexican or Mexican American. The problems of migrant farm workers are inextricably tied to the lives of both Latinos and Latin Americans (S. Greenhouse 2001; Triplett 2004).

Political Organizations

As noted in Chapter 9, Latinos are becoming more involved in party politics in the United States. Though tending to support Democratic candidates (with the exception of Cuban Americans, who typically back Republicans), Latinos are showing a willingness to be more independent voters. As one might expect, given their growing numbers and greater voting power, more Latinos are successfully seeking elective office. This has not always been the case. Politically oriented Mexican Americans such as Rodolfo "Corky" Gonzales in Denver turned to grassroots community organizing. Frustrated by the lack of responsiveness of established politicians, Mexican Americans for a brief period created their own independent party in Texas. La Raza Unida (LRU) was a third party supporting candidates who offered alternatives to the Democratic and Republican parties (Hero 1995; Rosales 1996).

The social protests that characterized much of the political activity in the United States of the mid-1960s touched the Mexican American community as well. In southern California in 1966, young Chicanos in college were attracted to the ideology of **Chicanismo** (or *Chicanozaje*) and joined what is popularly called the Chicano movement. Like Black Power, Chicanismo has taken on a variety of meanings, but all definitions stress a positive self-image and place little reliance on conventional forms of political activity. Followers of Chicanismo, unlike the more assimilation-oriented older generations, have been less likely to accept the standard claim that the United States is equally just to all.

Besides a positive self-image, Chicanismo and the movement of La Raza include renewed awareness of the plight of Chicanos at the hands of Anglos. Mexican Americans are a colonial minority, as Joan Moore (1970) wrote, because their relationship with Anglos was originally involuntary. Mexican culture in the United States has been either transformed or destroyed by Anglos, and the Mexican American people themselves have been victims of racism. The colonial model points out the ways in which societal institutions have failed Mexican Americans and perpetuated their problems. Militant Mexican Americans refer to assimilationists, who they say would sell out to the White people, as *vendidos*, or traitors. The ultimate insult is the term *Malinche*, the name of the Mexican American woman who became the mistress of Spanish conqueror Cortés. Many in the Chicano movement believe that if one does not work actively in the struggle, one is working against it (Rosales 1996; see also Barrera et al. 1972; Moore and Pachon 1985).

Perhaps as well as any recent Mexican American, Reies López Tijerina captures the spirit of Chicanismo. Born in a cotton field worked by migrant farmers, Tijerina became a Pentecostal preacher and in the late 1950s took an interest in old Spanish land grants. From research in Mexico, Spain, and the Southwest, he concluded that the Mexican Americans—and, more specifically, the Hispanos—had lost significant tracts of land through quasi-legal and other questionable practices. In 1963, he formed the Atlanza Federal de Mercedes (Federal Alliance of Land Grants), whose purpose is to recover the lost land. To publicize his purpose when few Anglos would pay attention, he seized part of the Kit Carson National Forest in New Mexico. Tijerina spent the next few years either in jail or awaiting trial. Tijerina's quest for restoration of land rights has been accompanied by violence, even though he advocates civil disobedience. However, the violence led him to be criticized by some Hispanics as well as Anglos (Nabokov 1970; Rosales 1996).

Thirty years later, Tijerina's arguments, which had seemed outrageous to most, were beginning to be endorsed by politicians. In 1997, Republican members of Congress introduced the Guadalupe-Hidalgo Treaty Claims Act to review Latino land claims especially as they relate to government-held forestland. Clearly, the Republicans were trying to garner support from Hispanic voters, but most important, this action showed that the goals of Tijerina and his followers are finally being considered seriously.

Organized in 1967, the Mexican American Legal Defense and Education Fund (MALDEF) has emerged as a potent force to protect Mexican Americans' constitutional rights. Although it does not endorse candidates, it has made itself felt in the political arena, much as the NAACP has for African Americans. On the education side, it has addressed segregation, biased testing, inequities in school financing, and failure to promote bilingualism. MALDEF has been involved in litigation concerning employment practices, immigration reform, and voting rights. It has emerged as the primary civil rights group for Mexican Americans and other Latinos (Vigil 1990).

The late 1990s saw the Mexican community in the United States faced with a new political challenge. Beginning in 1998, Mexicans in the United States could acquire rights as Mexican nationals under Mexico's new dual nationality law. Their children, even if U.S. born, are also eligible for Mexican nationality. The United States does not prohibit dual nationality, and it is estimated that anywhere from 5 to 10 million Mexican Americans are

Chicanismo
An ideology emphasizing pride and positive identity among Mexican Americans.

eligible for such dual nationality. Although many dual-nationality people will not be allowed to vote in Mexico's elections, this measure is likely to further their interest in political life south of the border. As we will now see with Puerto Rico, Latinos in the United States find political issues of importance outside the fifty states (*Migration News* 1998).

Puerto Ricans

Puerto Ricans' current association with the United States, like that of the Mexican people, began as the result of the outcome of a war. The island of Borinquén, subsequently called Puerto Rico, was claimed by Spain in 1493. The native inhabitants, the Taino Indians, were significantly reduced in number by conquest, slavery, and genocide. Although for generations the legacy of the Taíno was largely thought to be archaeological in nature, recent DNA tests revealed that more than 60 percent of Puerto Ricans today have a Taíno ancestor (Cockburn 2003, 41).

After Puerto Rico had been ruled by Spain for four centuries, the island was seized by the United States in 1898 during the Spanish-American War. Spain relinquished control of it in the Treaty of Paris. The value of Puerto Rico for the United States, as it had been for Spain, was mainly its strategic location, which was advantageous for maritime trade (Figure10.1).

The beginnings of rule by the United States quickly destroyed any hope that Puerto Ricans—or Boricua, as Puerto Ricans call themselves—had for self-rule. All power was given to officials appointed by the president, and any act of the island's legislature could

FIGURE 10.1   Puerto Rico

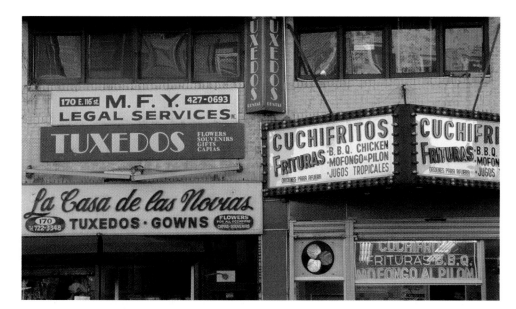

New York City has hosted a large Puerto Rican community for three generations.

be overruled by Congress. Even the spelling was changed briefly to Porto Rico to suit North American pronunciation. English, previously unknown on the island, became the only language permitted in the school systems. The people were colonized—first politically, then culturally, and finally economically (Aran et al. 1973; Christopulos 1974).

Citizenship was extended to Puerto Ricans by the Jones Act of 1917, but Puerto Rico remained a colony. This political dependence altered in 1948, when Puerto Rico elected its own governor and became a commonwealth. This status, officially Estado Libre Asociado, or Associated Free State, extends to Puerto Rico and its people privileges and rights different from those of people on the mainland. Although Puerto Ricans are U.S. citizens and elect their own governor, they may not vote in presidential elections and have no voting representation in Congress. They are subject to military service, Selective Service registration, and all federal laws. Puerto Ricans have a homeland that is and at the same time is not a part of the United States.

The Bridge Between the Island and the Mainland

Despite their citizenship, Puerto Ricans are occasionally challenged by immigration officials. Because other Latin Americans attempt to enter the country posing as Puerto Ricans, Puerto Ricans find their papers scrutinized more closely than do other U.S. citizens.

Puerto Ricans came to the mainland in small numbers in the first half of the century, often encouraged by farm labor contracts similar to those extended to Mexican braceros. During World War II, the government recruited hundreds of Puerto Ricans to work on the railroads, in food manufacturing plants, and in copper mines on the mainland. But migration has been largely a post–World War II phenomenon. The 1940 census showed fewer than 70,000 on the mainland. In 2005, there were more than 3.8 million Puerto Ricans on the mainland and 3.9 million residents on the island.

Among the factors that have contributed to migration are the economic pull away from the underdeveloped and overpopulated island, the absence of legal restrictions against travel, and the growth of cheap air transportation. As the migration continues, the mainland offers the added attraction of a large Puerto Rican community in New York City, which makes adjustment easier for new arrivals.

New York City still has a formidable population of Puerto Ricans, but significant changes have taken place. First, Puerto Ricans no longer dominate the Latino scene in New York City, making up only a little more than a third of the city's Hispanic population.

Neoricans
Puerto Ricans who return to the island to settle after living on the mainland of the United States (also Nuyoricans).

Second, Puerto Ricans are now more dispersed throughout the mainland's cities, with sizable numbers in New Jersey, Illinois, Florida, California, Pennsylvania, and Connecticut. The Puerto Ricans who have moved out of the large ethnic communities in cities such as New York City, Chicago, and Philadelphia are as a group more familiar with U.S. culture and the English language. This movement from the major settlements also has been hastened by the loss of manufacturing jobs in these cities, a loss that hits Puerto Rican men especially hard (Logan 2001a; Navarro 2000).

As the U.S. economy underwent recession in the 1970s and 1980s, unemployment among mainland Puerto Ricans, always high, increased dramatically. This increase shows in migration. In the 1950s, half of the Latino arrivals were Puerto Rican. By the 1970s, they accounted for only 3 percent. Indeed, in some years of the 1980s, more Puerto Ricans went from mainland to the island than the other way around.

Puerto Ricans returning to the island have become a significant force. Indeed, they have come to be given the name **Neoricans** (or *Nuyoricans*), a term the islanders also use for Puerto Ricans in New York. Longtime islanders direct a modest amount of hostility toward these Neoricans. They usually return from the mainland with more formal schooling, more money, and a better command of English than native Puerto Ricans have. Not too surprisingly, Neoricans compete very well with islanders for jobs and land.

The ethnic mix of the nation's largest city has gotten even more complex over the last ten years as Mexican and Mexican American arrivals in New York City have far outpaced any growth among Puerto Ricans. New York City is now following the pattern of other cities such as Miami, where the Latino identity is not defined by a single group (Kugel 2004; Muschkin 1993).

The Island of Puerto Rico

Puerto Rico, located about a thousand miles from Miami, has never been the same since Columbus discovered it in 1493. The original inhabitants of the island were wiped out in a couple of generations by disease, tribal warfare, hard labor, unsuccessful rebellions against the Spanish, and fusion with their conquerors. These social processes are highlighted in the intergroup relations continuum that summarizes the experience of Latinos in the United States (Figure 10.2).

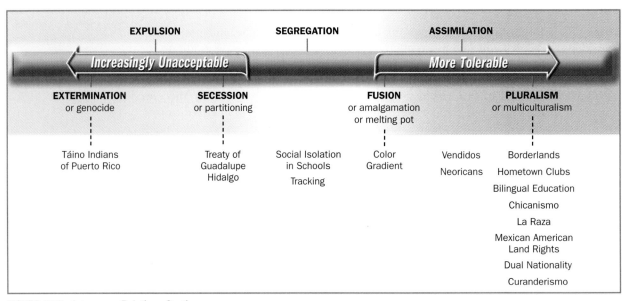

FIGURE 10.2   **Intergroup Relations Continuum**

Among the institutions imported to Puerto Rico by Spain was slavery. Although slavery in Puerto Rico was not as harsh as in the southern United States, the legacy of the transfer of Africans is present in the appearance of Puerto Ricans today, many of whom are seen by people on the mainland as Black.

The commonwealth period that began in 1948 has been a significant one for Puerto Rico. Change has been dramatic, although whether it has all been progress is debatable. On the positive side, Spanish has been reintroduced as the language of classroom instruction, but the study of English is also required. The popularity in the 1980s of music groups such as Menudo shows that Puerto Rican young people want to maintain ties with their ethnicity. Such success is a challenge because Puerto Rican music is almost never aired on non-Hispanic radio stations. The Puerto Rican people have had a vibrant and distinctive cultural tradition, as seen clearly in their folk heroes, holidays, sports, and contemporary literature and drama. Dominance by the culture of the United States makes it difficult to maintain their culture on the mainland and even on the island itself.

Puerto Rico and its people reflect a phenomenon called **neocolonialism**, which refers to continuing dependence of former colonies on foreign countries. Initially, this term was introduced to refer to African nations that, even after gaining their political independence from Great Britain, France, and other European nations, continued to find their destiny in the hands of the former colonial powers. Although most Puerto Ricans today are staunchly proud of their American citizenship, they also want to have their own national identity, independent of the United States. This has not been and continues not to be easy.

From 1902, English was the official language of the island, but Spanish was the language of the people, reaffirming the island's cultural identity independent of the United States. In 1992, however, Puerto Rico also established Spanish as an official language.

In reality, the language issue is related more to ideology than to substance. Although English is once again required in primary and secondary schools, textbooks may be written in English while the classes are conducted in Spanish. Indeed, Spanish remains the language of the island; only 8 percent of the islanders speak only English, and among Spanish-speaking adults about one-third speak it "well" or "very well" (Bureau of the Census 2004c).

neocolonialism
Continuing dependence of former colonies on foreign countries.

Puerto Ricans generally maintain dual identity proudly, celebrating Puerto Rican Day each June by observing independence of the island from Spain.

Issues of Statehood and Self-Rule Puerto Ricans have periodically argued and fought for independence for most of the 500 years since Columbus landed. They continued to do so in the 1990s. The contemporary commonwealth arrangement is popular with many Puerto Ricans, but others prefer statehood, whereas some call for complete independence from the United States. In Table 10.2 we summarize the advantages and disadvantages of the current status as a territory or commonwealth and the alternatives of statehood and independence.

TABLE 10.2	
Puerto Rico's Future	

CONTINUING TERRITORIAL STATUS (STATUS QUO)

Pros	Cons
⚬ Island is under U.S. protection.	⚬ United States has ultimate authority over island matters.
⚬ Islanders enjoy U.S. citizenship with a distinct national identity.	⚬ Residents cannot vote for president.
⚬ Residents don't pay federal income taxes (they do pay into Social Security, Medicare, and 32% to island tax collectors).	⚬ Residents who work for any company/organization that is funded by the United States must pay federal income taxes.
⚬ United States provides federal funds in the sum of $22 billion annually and has other tax advantages.	⚬ Although Puerto Rico has a higher standard of living compared to other Caribbean islands, it has half the per capita income of the poorest U.S. States.
⚬ Island would retain representation in the Miss Universe Pageant and Olympic Games.	⚬ Island cannot enter into free trade agreements.

STATEHOOD

Pros	Cons
⚬ Permanent and guaranteed U.S. citizenship and an end to U.S. colonial rule over the island.	⚬ Possibility of English-only requirements (loss of cultural/national identity).
⚬ The island would receive federal money to build the infrastructure.	⚬ An increased standard of living could result in greater economic deterioration due to the current muddled economic situation.
⚬ The island would be able to enjoy an open market trade with U.S. allies.	⚬ Businesses that take advantage of certain tax benefits could pull out of island and future businesses might not consider working there.
⚬ The island would acquire six seats in the House of Representatives and two seats in the Senate enabling the island to have more political clout and the right to vote in presidential elections.	⚬ Island would lose representation in the Miss Universe Pageant and Olympic Games.

INDEPENDENCE

Pros	Cons
⚬ Island would retain language and culture.	⚬ Lose U.S. citizenship.
⚬ Island would be able to participate in the global economy.	⚬ Lose U.S. protection.
⚬ End U.S. colonial rule over the island.	⚬ Lose federal funds.

Sources: Author based on *Let Puerto Rico Decide* 2005; President's Task Force on Puerto Rico's Status 2005; C. Williams 2006a.

The possible use of Vieques as a military bombing site is strongly opposed by most Puerto Ricans both in Puerto Rico and on the mainland.

Source: Steve Benson. Reprinted by permission of United Feature Syndicate, Inc.

The arguments for continuation of commonwealth status include both the serious and the trivial. Among some island residents, the idea of statehood invokes the fear of higher taxes and an erosion of their cultural heritage. Some even fear the end of separate Puerto Rican participation in the Olympics and the Miss Universe pageant. On the other hand, although independence may be attractive, commonwealth supporters argue that it includes too many unknown costs, so they embrace the status quo. Others view statehood as a key to increased economic development and expansion for tourism.

Proponents of independence have a long, vocal history of insisting on the need for Puerto Rico to regain its cultural and political autonomy. Some of the supporters of independence have even been militant. In 1950, nationalists attempted to assassinate President Truman, killing a White House guard in the process. Four years later, another band of nationalists opened fire in the gallery of the U.S. House of Representatives, wounding five members of Congress. Beginning in 1974, a group calling itself the Armed Forces of National Liberation (FALN, for Fuerzas Armadas de Liberación Nacional) took responsibility for more than 100 explosions that continued through 1987. The FALN is not alone; at least four other militant groups advocating independence were identified as having been at work in the 1980s. The island itself is occasionally beset by violent demonstrations, often reacting to U.S. military installations there—a symbol of U.S. control (Bosque-Pérez and Colon Morera 2006).

The use for more than sixty years of a portion of Puerto Rico as a bombing target by the military had been to many an obvious example of colonial oppression. Protests for years focused on the bombing practice runs over Vieques, an island located six miles off its southeastern coast (see Figure 10.1). Residents were evicted with little compensation. Long after this exodus, residents of remaining areas of Vieques objected to continued bombing. The death of a civilian hit by a misguided bomb in 1999 launched a series of marches, sit-ins, blockades, and other acts of civil disobedience reminiscent of the civil rights era (Ayala and Carro-Figueroa 2006; Colón Morera and Santana 2006).

The federal government ended the bombing in 2003, but islanders continue to be upset that more has not been done sooner to clean up the leftover bombs. In "Listen to Our Voices," poet and professor Martín St. Espada questioned the continued bombing and urged people on the mainland to join Puerto Ricans on the island in calling for an immediate halt to the military exercises (Quintanilla 2006).

Voices Listen to Our Voices Listen to

¡VIVA VIEQUES!

Martín St. Espada

More than eighty years ago, Puerto Rican poet and political leader Jose de Diego wrote, "Puerto Ricans do not know how to say no." And yet, he pointed out, "The no of the oppressed has been the word, the genesis, of the liberation of peoples." De Diego warned: "We must learn to say no."

Today, the people of Puerto Rico say no; the people of Vieques say no; the Puerto Rican community in the U.S. says no. We say no to the Navy, no to the bombing of Vieques. The admirals and apologists of the Navy say they cannot find anywhere else in the world to play their war games. Still we say no. They say they will use dummy bombs. Still we say no. They promise a referendum some day. Still we say no. The word no is the same in English and Spanish. Since translation is not the problem, we must assume they cannot hear us. So we must say it louder: *No.*

Vieques is an offshore island municipality of Puerto Rico. It is controlled, like the rest of Puerto Rico, by the United States. More than 9,300 people live in Viéques. Yet since 1941, the U.S. Navy has occupied two-thirds of this inhabited island for war games and live-ammunition target practice. According to journalist Juan Gonzalez, "Practice at the range goes on for as many as 200 days a year. Combat planes bomb and strafe the island. Destroyers bomb it from the sea. . . . Maneuvers have included, on occasion, practice with depleted uranium shells, napalm, and cluster bombs."

Federal tax dollars go directly to the military budget, and thus to support the Navy presence in Vieques. We share a responsibility to the people of Vieques to protest the injustice our dollars make possible. Keep in mind, too, that Puerto Rico lacks a voting representative in Congress. Given the absence of democratic representation for the people of Puerto Rico, the people of the United States must speak for them.

We Puerto Ricans must keep saying no. And by saying no, we say yes. As Eduardo Galeano has written, "By saying no to the devastating empire of greed whose center lies in North America, we are saying yes to another possible America. . . . In saying no to a peace without dignity, we are saying yes to the sacred right of rebellion against injustice." ◾

Source: "¡Viva Vieques!" by Martín St. Espada, *The Progressive*, July 2000, vol. 64, pp. 27–29. Copyright © 2000 by *The Progressive*. Reprinted by permission of *The Progressive*, 409 E. Main Street, Madison, WI 53703. www.progressive.org.

The issue of Puerto Rico's political destiny is in part ideological. Independence is the easiest way for the island to retain and strengthen its cultural and political identity. Some nationalists express the desire that an autonomous Puerto Rico develop close political ties with communist Cuba. The crucial arguments for and against independence probably are economic. An independent Puerto Rico would no longer be required to use U.S. shipping lines, which are more expensive than those of foreign competitors. However, an independent Puerto Rico might be faced by a tariff wall when trading with its largest current customer, the mainland United States. Also, Puerto Rican migration to the mainland could be restricted.

Puerto Rico's future status most recently faced a vote in 1998. In the latest nonbinding referendum, 50 percent favored continuing commonwealth status, and 47 percent backed statehood. Less than 3 percent favored independence. Interestingly, a

1998 survey of people on the mainland found the population evenly split, with a third favoring each option. Given the lack of overwhelming feelings for statehood on the island, it is unlikely that there will be sufficient support in Congress to move toward statehood. Yet with half the island population expressing a preference for a change, it is clear that discontent with the current arrangement prevails and remains a "colonial dilemma" (Navarro 1998; Saad 1998).

The Social Construction of Race   The most significant difference between the meaning of race in Puerto Rico and on the mainland is that Puerto Rico, like so many other Caribbean societies, has a **color gradient**. The phrase *color gradient* describes distinctions based on skin color made on a continuum rather than by sharp categorical separations. The presence of a color gradient reflects past fusion between different groups (see Figure 10.2). Rather than being either "black" or "white," people are judged in such societies as "lighter" or "darker" than others. Rather than seeing people as either black or white in skin color, Puerto Ricans perceive people as ranging from pale white to very black. Puerto Ricans are more sensitive to degrees of difference and make less effort to pigeonhole a person into one of two categories.

The presence of a color gradient rather than two or three racial categories does not necessarily mean that prejudice is less. Generally, however, societies with a color gradient permit more flexibility, and therefore, are less likely to impose specific sanctions against a group of people based on skin color alone. Puerto Rico has not suffered interracial conflict or violence; its people are conscious of different racial heritages. Studies disagree on the amount of prejudice in Puerto Rico, but all concur that race is not as clear-cut an issue on the island as it is on the mainland.

Racial identification in Puerto Rico depends a great deal on the attitude of the individual making the judgment. If one thinks highly of a person, he or she may be seen as a member of a more acceptable racial group. A variety of terms is used in the color gradient to describe people racially: *Blanco* (white), *trigueño* (bronze- or wheat-colored), *moreno* (dark-skinned), and *negro* (black) are a few of these. Factors such as social class and social position determine race, but on the mainland race is more likely to determine social class. This situation may puzzle people from the mainland, but racial etiquette on the mainland may be just as difficult for Puerto Ricans to comprehend and accept. Puerto Ricans arriving in the United States may find a new identity thrust on them by the dominant society (Landale and Oropesa 2002; Rodríguez 1997, 2000).

The Island Economy

The United States' role in Puerto Rico has produced an overall economy that, though strong by Caribbean standards, remains well below that of the poorest areas of the United States. For many years, the federal government exempted U.S. industries locating in Puerto Rico from taxes on profits for at least ten years. In addition, the federal government's program of enterprise zones, which grants tax incentives to promote private investment in inner cities, has been extended to Puerto Rico. Unquestionably, Puerto Rico has become attractive to mainland-based corporations. Skeptics point out that, as a result, the island's agriculture has been largely ignored. Furthermore, the economic benefits to the island are limited. Businesses have spent the profits gained on Puerto Rico back on the mainland.

Puerto Rico's economy is in severe trouble compared with that of the mainland. Its unemployment rate has been about three times that of the mainland. In addition, the per capita income is less than half that of Mississippi, the poorest state. Efforts to raise the wages of Puerto Rican workers only make the island less attractive to labor- intensive businesses, that is, those employing larger numbers of unskilled people. Capital-intensive companies, such as the petrochemical industries, have found Puerto Rico attractive, but they have not created jobs for the semiskilled. A growing problem is that Puerto Rico is

color gradient
The placement of people on a continuum from light to dark skin color rather than in distinct racial groupings by skin color.

emerging as a major gateway to the United States for illegal drugs from South America, which has led the island to experience waves of violence and the social ills associated with the drug trade (Castañeda 1996; Hemlock 1996; Navarro 1995).

Puerto Rico is an example of the world systems theory initially presented in Chapter 1. **World systems theory** is the view of the global economic system as divided between certain industrialized nations that control wealth and developing countries that are controlled and exploited. Although Puerto Rico may be well off compared with many other Caribbean nations, it clearly is at the mercy of economic forces in the United States and, to a much lesser extent, other industrial nations. Puerto Rico continues to struggle with the advantages of citizenship and the detriment of playing a peripheral role in the economy of the United States.

Another major factor in Puerto Rico's economy is tourism. Government subsidies have encouraged the construction of luxury hotels. After U.S. citizens' travel to Cuba was cut off in 1962, tourists discovered Puerto Rico's beaches and warm climate. Critics complain that the major economic beneficiaries of tourism are not local but are primarily investors from the mainland and that high prices prevent the less affluent from visiting, thus unnecessarily restricting tourism. As has been true of other aspects of the island's economic development, the tourist boom has had little positive effect on most Puerto Ricans.

Puerto Rico continues to face new challenges. First, with congressional approval in 1994 of the North American Free Trade Agreement (NAFTA), Mexico, Canada, and the United States became integrated into a single economic market. The reduction of trade barriers with Mexico, coupled with that nation's lower wages, may combine to undercut Puerto Rico's commonwealth advantage. Second, many more island nations now offer sun-seeking tourists from the mainland alternative destinations to Puerto Rico. In addition, cruise ships present another attractive option for tourists. Given the economic problems of the island, it is not surprising that many Puerto Ricans migrate to the mainland (Rivera-Batiz and Santiago 1996; Rohter 1993).

For years, migration to the mainland has served as a safety valve for Puerto Rico's population, which has grown annually at a rate 50 percent faster than that of the rest of the United States. Typically, migrants from Puerto Rico represent a broad range of occupations. There are seasonal fluctuations as Puerto Rican farm workers leave the island in search of seasonal employment. Puerto Ricans, particularly agricultural workers, earn higher wages on the mainland, yet a significant proportion returns despite the higher wages (Meléndez 1994).

The Contemporary Picture of Mexican Americans and Puerto Ricans

We will now consider the major social institutions of education, the family, health care, and religion, noting the similarities in their organization between Puerto Ricans and Mexican Americans.

Education

Both Mexican Americans and Puerto Ricans, as groups, have experienced gains in formal schooling but still lag behind White Americans in many standards of educational attainment. As is apparent in Table 10.1, Mexican Americans and Puerto Ricans lag well behind other Latinos and even further behind Anglos. Although bilingual education is still endorsed in the United States, the implementation of effective, high-quality programs has been difficult, as Chapter 9 showed. In addition, attacks on the funding of bilingual education has continued into the present.

Latinos, including Mexican Americans and Puerto Ricans, have become increasingly isolated from non-Latinos. In 1968, 55 percent of all Hispanics attended predominantly

ASK Yourself

Have you ever been a tourist in an area where it seemed most local people were relatively poor?

world systems theory
A view of the global economic system as divided between nations that control wealth and those that provide natural resources and labor.

Latino college students look for the same social experiences as do non-Hispanics. Fraternities and sororities oriented to attracting Hispanics have experienced tremendous increases in the last decade. Here are hot-stepping members of Lambda Upsilon Lambda at Rutgers-Newark.

minority schools: that is, schools where at least half of the students were members of minorities. Just a little over three decades later, this had increased to 76 percent. During the 2000–2001 school year, the typical Latino student was in a school that was 54 percent Hispanic. Over a third of Latinos were in schools that were at least 90 percent non-White. Furthermore, as we noted in Chapter 1, the separation continues, with the highest patterns of residential segregation occurring in the cities with the largest number of Hispanics (Frankenburg et al. 2003; Orfield 2002).

Three factors explain this increasing social isolation of Mexican Americans and Puerto Ricans from other students in school. First, Latinos are increasingly concentrated in the largest cities, where minorities dominate. Second, the numbers of Latinos have increased dramatically since the 1970s, when efforts to desegregate schools began to lose momentum. Third, schools once desegregated have become resegregated as the numbers of school-aged Mexican Americans in an area have increased and as the determination to maintain balances in schools has lessened.

Even where Anglos and Latinos live in the same school district, the problem of social isolation in the classroom is often furthered through tracking. **Tracking** is the practice of placing students in specific classes or curriculum groups on the basis of test scores and other criteria. Tracking begins very early in the classroom, often in reading groups during first grade. These tracks may reinforce the disadvantages of Hispanic children from less affluent families and non-English-speaking households that have not been exposed to English reading materials in their homes during early childhood (Rodríguez 1989; Schaefer 2007).

Students see few teachers and administrators like themselves because few Latino university students have been prepared to serve as teachers and administrators. In 2000, only 51 percent of Mexican Americans and 64 percent of Puerto Ricans aged 25 or over had completed high school, compared with 88 percent of non-Hispanic Whites. Mexican Americans and Puerto Ricans who do choose to continue their education beyond high school are more likely to select a technical school or community college to acquire work-related skills (Therrien and Ramirez 2001).

Mexican Americans and Puerto Ricans are underrepresented in higher education in all roles. Recent reports have documented the absence of Hispanics among college teachers and administrators: Less than 6 percent of all college teachers were Latino in 2002. The situation is similar in this respect to that of Blacks; however, there are no Latino counterparts to historic Black colleges, such as Tuskegee Institute, to provide a source of leaders (Bureau of the Census 2005a, 402).

tracking
The practice of placing students in specific curriculum groups on the basis of test scores and other criteria.

Motivation does not appear to be the barrier to school achievement, at least among Mexican immigrants. A Harvard University study of the attitudes of Mexican immigrant adolescents showed that 84 percent felt that school was the most important thing, compared with 40 percent of White teenagers. Again, 68 percent of immigrant children felt that doing their homework was more important than helping a friend, compared with only 20 percent of White adolescents who held the same priorities. However, there is evidence that as these children assimilate, they begin to take on the prevailing White views. The same survey showed second-generation Mexican Americans still giving education a higher priority but not as high as their immigrant counterparts. We will consider shortly how assimilation has a similar effect on health (Crosnoe 2005; Woo 1996).

With respect to higher education, Latinos face challenges similar to those that Black students meet on predominantly White campuses. Given the social isolation of Latino high schools, Mexican Americans are likely to have to adjust for the first time to an educational environment almost totally populated by Anglos. They may experience racism for the first time, just as they are trying to adjust to a heavier academic load.

Family Life

The most important organization or social institution among Latinos, or for that matter any group, is the family. The structure of the Mexican American family differs little from that of all families in the United States, a statement remarkable in itself, given the impoverishment of a significant number of Mexican Americans.

Latino households are described as laudably more familistic than others in the United States. **Familism** means pride and closeness in the family, which results in family obligation and loyalty coming before individual needs. The family is the primary source of both social interaction and caregiving.

Familism has been viewed as both a positive and a negative influence on individual Mexican Americans and Puerto Ricans. It may have the negative effect of discouraging youths with a bright future from taking advantage of opportunities that would separate them from their family. Familism is generally regarded as good, however, because an extended family provides emotional strength in times of crisis. Close family ties maintain the mental and social well-being of the elderly. Most Latinos, therefore, see the intact, extended family as a norm and as a nurturing unit that provides support throughout a person's lifetime. The many significant aspects of familism include the importance of *campadrazgo* (the godparent–godchild relationship), the benefits of the financial dependency of kin, the availability of relatives as a source of advice, and the active involvement of the elderly in the family.

This traditional value of familism, whether judged good or bad, is expected to decline in importance with urbanization, industrialization, and the acquisition of middle-class status. It will also mean taking on some practices more common in the United States, such as divorce. Characteristics that marked differences between Latino and Anglo family life were sharper in the past. Even among past generations, the differences were of degree, not of kind; that is, Hispanic families tended to exhibit some traits more than Anglos, not different traits altogether. A comparison between similar Anglo and Mexican American families in San Diego found no significant differences in family life between the two groups. In short, the Mexican American and Puerto Rican families display all the variety of American families in general, while also suffering higher levels of poverty (Alárcon 1995; Kanellos 1994; Landale and Ogena 1995; Vega et al. 1986; Zambrana 1995).

Health Care

Earlier, in Chapter 5, we introduced the concept of **life chances,** which are people's opportunities to provide themselves with material goods, positive living conditions, and favorable life experiences. We have consistently seen Latino groups as having more limited life chances. Perhaps in no other area does this apply so much as in the health care system.

familism
Pride and closeness in the family that result in placing family obligation and loyalty before individual needs.

life chances
People's opportunities to provide themselves with material goods, positive living conditions, and favorable life experiences.

Focus Research Focus Research

ASSIMILATION MAY BE HAZARDOUS TO YOUR HEALTH

Immigrants come to the United States seeking a better life, but the transition can be very difficult. We are familiar with the problems new arrivals experience in finding good jobs, but we may be less aware of how pervasive the challenges are.

Researchers continuously show that immigrants often encounter health problems as they leave behind old health networks and confront the private pay system of medical care in the United States. The outcome is that the health of immigrants often deteriorates. Interestingly, this occurs with Puerto Ricans, who are citizens upon arrival and obviously do not experience as much culture shock as other new arrivals. Scholars Nancy Landale, R. S. Orapesa, and Bridget Gorman looked at the implications for infant mortality of migration from Puerto Rico to the United States. Their analysis showed that children of migrants have lower rates of infant mortality than do children of mainland-born Puerto Rican women. This means that babies of Puerto Rican mothers who are born in the United States are more likely to die than those of mothers who migrated from Puerto Rico.

Why does this happen? Immigrants generally are still under the protection of their fellow travelers. They are still networked with other immigrants, who assist them in adapting to life in the United States. However, as life in a new country continues, these important social networks break down as people learn to navigate the new social system—in this example, the health care system. The researchers do note that Puerto Ricans in the United States, regardless of recency of arrival, still experience better health than those in Puerto Rico. Of course, this finding only further indicates the colonial relationship of Puerto Rico to the United States. ■

Source: Landale et al. 2000; also see Lara et al. 2005.

Hispanics as a group are locked out of the health care system more often than any other racial or ethnic group. A third had no health insurance (or other coverage such as Medicaid) for all of 2005, compared with 11.2 percent of White non-Hispanics and 19.3 percent of Blacks. Predictably, the uninsured are less likely to have a regular source of medical care. This means that they wait for a crisis before seeking care. Fewer are immunized, and rates of preventable diseases such as lead poisoning are higher. No coverage is increasing, a circumstance that may reflect a further breakdown in health care delivery or may be a result of continuing immigration (DeNavas-Walt et. al. 2006:22).

The health care problem facing Mexican Americans and other Hispanic groups is complicated by the lack of Hispanic health professionals. Hispanics accounted for 5 percent or less of dentists and physicians, yet they are about 15 percent of the population. Obviously, one does not need to be administered health care by someone in one's own ethnic group, but the paucity of Hispanic professionals increases the likelihood that the group will be underserved (Bureau of the Census 2005a).

Given the high proportion of uninsured people and the low number of Latino health care personnel, it is not surprising to learn of the poor status of Latinos' health care as a group. Interestingly, once they settle in the United States, immigrants from Latin America may well experience a decline in their health care. The "Research Focus" considers the impact that immigration may have on a family's health.

Some Mexican Americans and many other Latinos have cultural beliefs that make them less likely to use the medical system. They may interpret their illnesses according

curanderismo
Hispanic folk medicine.

to folk practices or **curanderismo**: Latino folk medicine, a form of holistic health care and healing. This orientation influences how one approaches health care and even how one defines illness. Most Hispanics probably use folk healers, or *curanderos*, infrequently, but perhaps 20 percent rely on home remedies. Although these are not necessarily without value, especially if a dual system of folk and establishment medicine is followed, reliance on natural beliefs may be counterproductive. Another aspect of folk beliefs is the identification of folk-defined illnesses such as *susto* (or fright sickness) and *atague* (or fighting attack). Although these complaints, alien by these names to Anglos, often have biological bases, they must be dealt with carefully by sensitive medical professionals who can diagnose and treat illnesses accurately (Belliard and Ramírez-Johnson 2005; Dansie 2004; Lara et al. 2005).

Religion

The most important formal organization in the Hispanic community is the church. Most Puerto Ricans and Mexican Americans express a religious preference for the Catholic Church. In 2004, about 63 percent of Hispanics were Catholic. In Figure10.3, we examine a more detailed background done ten years earlier that shows specific religious affiliations indicated by Mexican Americans and Puerto Ricans (Winseman 2004b).

The Roman Catholic Church took an assimilationist role in the past, whether with Hispanic Catholics or with other minority Catholics. The church has only sporadically

FIGURE 10.3 Religious Preferences

Using national data, we see that the majority of both Mexican Americans and Puerto Ricans expressed a preference for the Roman Catholic Church.

Source: One Nation Under God by Barry A. Kosmin and Seymour P. Lachman. Copyright © 1993 by Barry A. Kosmin and Seymour P. Lachman. Used by permission of Harmony Books, a division of Random House, Inc.

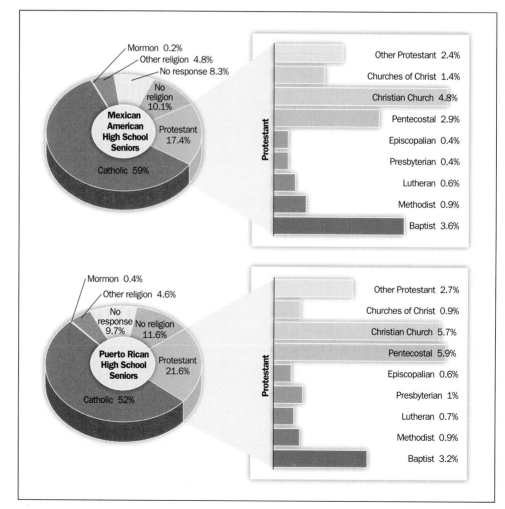

involved itself in the Chicano movement, and rarely in the past did the upper levels of the church hierarchy support Chicanismo. For example, only with some prodding did the Roman Catholic Church support the United Farm Workers, a group whose membership was predominantly Catholic.

Recently the Roman Catholic Church has become more community oriented, seeking to identify Latino, or at least Spanish-speaking, clergy and staff to serve Latino parishes. The lack of Spanish-speaking priests has been complicated by a smaller proportion of a declining number training for the priesthood who speak Spanish (Ramirez 2000; Rosales 1996).

Not only is the Catholic Church important to Hispanics, but Hispanics also play a significant role for the church. The population growth of Mexican Americans and other Hispanics has been responsible for the Catholic Church's continued growth in recent years, whereas mainstream Protestant faiths have declined in size. Hispanics account for more than a third of Catholics in the United States. The church is trying to adjust to Hispanics' more expressive manifestation of religious faith, with frequent reliance on their own patron saints and the presence of special altars in their homes. Catholic churches in some parts of the United States are even starting to accommodate observances of the Mexican Día de los Muertos, or Day of the Dead. Such practices are a tradition from rural Mexico, where religion was followed without trained clergy. Yet even today in the United States, Hispanics continue to be underrepresented among priests, with only 4.4 percent nationwide being Hispanic (O'Connor 1998).

Although Latinos are predominantly Catholic, their membership in Protestant and other Christian faiths is growing. According to a national survey of the University of Notre Dame, first-generation Latinos are 74 percent Catholic, but by the third generation only 62 percent are Catholic (Watanabe and Enriquez 2005).

Pentecostalism, a type of evangelical Christianity, is growing in Latin America and is clearly making a significant impact on Latinos in the United States. Adherents to Pentecostal faiths hold beliefs similar to those of the evangelicals but also believe in the infusion of the Holy Spirit into services and in religious experiences such as faith healing. Pentecostalism and similar faiths are attractive to many because they offer followers the opportunity to express their religious fervor openly. Furthermore, many of the churches are small and, therefore, offer a sense of community, often with Spanish-speaking leadership. Gradually, the more established faiths are recognizing the desirability of offering Latino parishioners a greater sense of belonging (Hunt 1999).

Pentecostalism
A religion similar in many respects to evangelical faiths that believes in the infusion of the Holy Spirit into services and in religious experiences such as faith healing.

Conclusion

David Gomez (1971) described Mexican Americans as "strangers in their own land." Puerto Ricans, on the other hand, are still debating what should be the political destiny of their island nation. All of this makes nationality a very real part of the destiny of Mexican Americans and Puerto Ricans. Can they also preserve their cultures along with a sense of national fervor, or will these be a casualty of assimilation?

As we have seen, even when we concentrate on just Mexican Americans or Puerto Ricans out of the larger collective group of Hispanics or Latinos, diversity remains. As shown in Table 10.3, large concentrations of Latinos live in a number of our largest U.S. cities.

Mexican Americans are divided among the Hispanos and the descendants of earlier Mexican immigrants and the more recent arrivals from Mexico. Puerto Ricans can be divided by virtue of residency and the extent to which they identify with the island culture. For many Puerto Ricans, the identity dilemma is never truly resolved: "No soy de aquí ni de allá," "I am not from here nor from there" (Comas-Díaz et al. 1998).

TABLE 10.3
Cities with the Largest Latino Concentrations, 2005

City	Number of Latinos	Proportion of City's Population
New York City	2,221,906	27.9%
Los Angeles	1,824,373	48.9
Houston	820,510	42.3
Chicago	778,234	28.8
San Antonio	735,456	61.2
Phoenix	575,436	41.8
Dallas	482,024	42.1
El Paso	431,875	76.6
San Diego	312,767	25.9
San Jose	279,420	31.5
Santa Ana	257,097	76.1
Miami	243,874	67.4

Note: Data for Santa Ana and El Paso for 2000. San Juan, Puerto Rico, reported 413,328 Latinos for 98 percent of its population in 2000.

Sources: Author based on American Community Survey 2005 and Bureau of the Census 2001e.

Economic change is also apparent. Poverty and unemployment rates are high, and new arrivals from Mexico and Puerto Rico are particularly likely to enter the lower class, or working class at best, upon arrival. However, there is a growing middle class within the Hispanic community.

Mexican culture is alive and well in the Mexican American community. Some cultural practices that have become more popular here than in Mexico are being imported back to Mexico, with their distinctive Mexican American flavor. All this is occurring in the midst of a reluctance to expand bilingual education and a popular move to make English the official language. In 1998, Puerto Rico observed its 500th anniversary as a colony: four centuries under Spain and another century under the United States. Its dual status as a colony and as a developing nation has been the defining issue for Puerto Ricans, even those who have migrated to the mainland (Perusse 1990).

Key Terms

bracero 276
Chicanismo 281
color gradient 289
culture of poverty 278
curanderismo 294

familism 292
La Raza 277
life chances 292
mojados 277
neocolonialism 285

Neoricans 284
Pentecostalism 295
repatriation 276
tracking 291
world systems theory 290

Review Questions

1. In what respects has Mexico been viewed as both a source of workers and as a place to leave unwanted laborers?

2. In what respects are Hispanic families similar to and different from Anglo households?

3. How does Chicanismo relate to the issue of Hispanic identity?

4. How does the case of Puerto Rico support the notion of race as a social concept?

5. What role does religion play in the Latino community?

Critical Thinking

1. Consider what it means to be patriotic and loyal in terms of being a citizen of the United States. How do the concerns that Puerto Ricans have for the island's future and the Mexican concept of dual nationality affect those notions of patriotism and loyalty?

2. The phrase *territorial minorities* has been used to apply to subordinate groups that have special ties to their land, such as Native American tribes. How would you apply this to Mexican Americans?

3. The family is often regarded by observers as a real strength in the Latino community. How can this strength be harnessed to address some of the challenges that Mexican Americans and Puerto Ricans face in the United States?

4. Are Mexican Americans assimilated and are recent Mexican immigrants likely to assimilate overtime?

Internet Connections—Research Navigator™

To access the full resources of Research Navigator™, please find the access code printed on the inside cover of *OneSearch with Research Navigator™: Sociology.* You may have received this booklet if your instructor recommended this guide be packaged with new textbooks. (If your book did not come with this printed guide, you can purchase one through your college bookstore.) Visit our Research Navigator™ site at www.ResearchNavigator.com. Once at this site, click on REGISTER under New Users and enter your access code to create a personal Login Name and Password. (When revisiting the site, use the same Login Name and Password.) Browse the features of the Research Navigator™ Web site and search the databases of academic journals, newspapers, magazines, and Web links.

For further information relevant to Chapter 10, you may wish to use such keywords as "Chicano," "bracero," and "neocolonialism," and the search engine will supply relevant and recent scholarly and popular press publications. Use the *New York Times* Search-by-Subject Archive to find recent news articles related to sociology and the Link Library feature to locate relevant Web links organized by the key terms associated with this chapter.

Muslim and Arab Americans: Diverse Minorities

11

CHAPTER OUTLINE

Muslim and Arab People

Arab Americans

Muslim Americans

Immigration to the United States

Contemporary Life in the United States

RESEARCH FOCUS
Christian and Muslim Arab American Women's Gender Roles

Being Arab or Muslim in the United States

LISTEN TO OUR VOICES
"Pendulum Swings on Civil Rights"
by James Zogby

Issues of Prejudice and Discrimination

Conclusion

Key Terms/Review Questions/Critical Thinking/Internet Connections—Research Navigator™

MUSLIM AND ARAB AMERICANS ARE DIFFERENT GROUPS IN the United States; although they overlap with some Muslim Americans being of Arab ancestry, they are distinct from each other. Most Arab Americans are not Muslim and most Muslim Americans are not of Arab background. Within each group is a significant diversity that can be seen by differences in forms of religious expression, ancestral background, and recentness of arrival in the United States. Both groups have been seen and stereotyped in the West through the lens of Orientalism. This stigmatizing of people grew more all-encompassing with the outbreak of terrorism and specifically the events of September 11, 2001. Even without these violent events, it is a challenge for Muslim and Arab Americans to sort out their identity, but nonetheless both function in strong and growing communities in the United States.

In downtown Chicago, Jahan Ghaemi stops the taxi he operates and briefly changes roles to become an outreach worker for the Sabeel Food Pantry, the nation's first Muslim-run pantry. The Iranian immigrant takes time from his job to give food to an obviously needy man on the street who is most likely neither Muslim nor Arab. Speaking of his action, he observes, "It doesn't matter what religion you are. It's everyone's responsibility to help others."

Meanwhile in Seattle, Iraqi-born Jawad al-Gheezi has lately come to tell people when they ask that he is from Mesopotamia, especially since one of his "buddies" on his construction crew spray painted his car "Go Home Terrorist."

In contrast, Rebecca Coury of Cleveland directly tells people she is Arab American rather than perhaps the safer answer of Lebanese. She is the fourth-generation descendant of Joseph Coury, who at age 12 left a southern Lebanese port city and stowed away on a boat to the United States, where he became a coal miner. Rebecca cannot speak Arabic, and most of her family members no longer remember the meanings behind the script that adorns the Maronite Church they attend, a Christian faith with roots in the fourth century.

At a political rally in Houston, Texas, during the 2004 presidential campaign, Black Muslims and Muslim immigrants joined together in a get-out-the-vote campaign because many issues, such as U.S. foreign policy and racial profiling, are ones in which they have a common interest (Basu 2004; Brachear 2003; Clemetson 2004; Rosin 2002).

There are two objectives for considering Arab and Muslim Americans together in this chapter. One is to clarify the distinctions between two groups often incorrectly referred to as the same population. Second is to overcome the prism of Orientalism through which many contemporary Americans view the Arab and Muslim world. **Orientalism** is the simplistic view of the people and history of the Orient, with no recognition of change over time or the diversity within its many cultures. Palestinian American literary scholar Edward Said (1978) stressed how so many in North America and Europe came to define, categorize, and study the Orient and, therefore, created a static stereotype of hundreds of millions of people stretched around the globe.

The diversity of Arabs and Muslims is thereby discounted, which allows the outsider to come up with simplistic descriptions and often simplistic policies. Orientalism has led people to see a sweeping unity in both Arab and Muslim societies. It is also an unchanging and clearly a nonmodern image. One must focus on smaller culturally consistent groups or countries rather than surrender to the temptation of a single broad generalization.

Muslim and Arab People

orientalism
The simplistic view of the people and history of the Orient with no recognition of change over time or the diversity within its many cultures.

The Arab American and Muslim American communities are among the most rapidly growing subordinate groups in the United States. Westerners often confuse the two groups. Actually, Arabs are an ethnic group, and Muslims are a religious group. Typically, Islam is the faith (like Christianity), and a Muslim is a believer of that religion (like a Christian). Worldwide, many Arabs (12 million) are not Muslims, and most (85 percent) Muslims are not Arabs (David and Ayouby 2005).

Arab Americans

Coptic Christians

Christian or Secular
Jordanians
Lebanese
Palestinians
Syrians

**Saudis
Muslims from**
Algeria
Egypt
Iraq
Morocco
Sudan
Syria
Tunisia
Yemen

Muslim Americans

**Practicing Muslims
from**
Afghanistan
Albania
Azerbaijan
Bangladesh
India
Indonesia
Iran
Malaysia
Nigeria
Pakistan
Philippines
Somalia
Turkey
Turkmenistan

**African Americans
Nation of Islam
and other Muslim
groups**

Kurds

FIGURE 11.1   Relationship Between Muslim and Arab Americans
Many Arab Americans are not Muslims, and most Muslim Americans are not Arabs.

This relationship between religion and an ethnic group that crosses many nationalities is illustrated in Figure 11.1. As we can see, one cannot accurately identify the Muslim faithful by nationality alone, and clearly being Arab does not define one as being a follower of Islam.

Arab Americans

The name *Arab Americans* refers to the immigrants and their descendants from the countries that now comprise the Arab world (see Figure 11.2). These are the twenty-two nations, as defined by the membership of the League of Arab States, of North Africa and what is popularly called the Middle East, including Morocco, Syria, Iraq, Saudi Arabia, and Somalia.

Not all people living in these countries are necessarily Arab (e.g., the Kurds of Iraq), and some Arab Americans may have immigrated from non-Arab countries such as Great Britain or France, where their families have lived for generations. Further complicating the use of collective terms of identity such as *Arabs* and *Muslim* is evoking the term *Middle Eastern.* The Middle East is an ambiguous geographic designation that includes large numbers of people who are neither Muslim or Arab (such as Israeli Jews) but is also frequently used. (Marvasti 2005; Marvasti and McKinney 2004).

The Arabic language is the single most-unifying force among Arabs, although not all Arabs and certainly not all Arab Americans can read and speak Arabic. As the language has evolved over the centuries, people in different parts of the Arab world speak with a different dialect using their own choices of vocabulary and pronunciation. Although most Arab Americans are not Muslim, the fact that the Qur'an was originally in

? ASK Yourself

What is the difference between Muslim and Arab Americans?

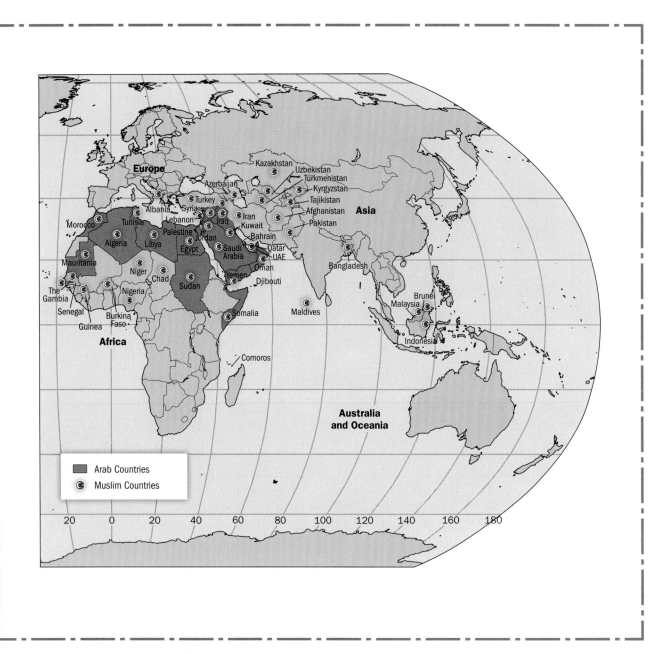

FIGURE 11.2   Arab and Muslim Countries

Sources: Developed by author based on Chambers 2005 and Coogan 2003.

Arabic 1,400 years ago gives the knowledge of Arabic special importance. This is similar to many Jews' reading of the Torah in Hebrew, but unlike Christians, who almost always read the Bible in a translation to their native tongue.

Estimates of the size of the Arab American community differ widely. Despite efforts of the Census Bureau to enlist the assistance of experts, census results are often regarded as severely undercounting the Arab American community. The government only counts those individuals who have identified their ancestry from the countries of the Arab world and, therefore, would not include those descended from other large overseas Arab communities. The Arab American community doubled in size during the 1990s, and even by the official census count, would be equivalent to that of Greek Americans.

By some estimates, there are up to 3 million people with Arab ancestry in the United States. Among those identifying themselves as Arab American, the largest single source of ancestry was Lebanon, followed by Syria, Egypt, and Palestine. These four groups account for two-thirds of Arab Americans in 2000. As with other racial and ethnic groups, Arab Americans, as shown in Figure 11.3, are not uniformly distributed throughout the United States. This rising population has led to the development of Arab retail centers in several cities, including Dearborn and Detroit, Michigan; Los Angeles; Chicago; New York City; and Washington, D.C. (Wertsman 2001).

Diversity underlies virtually everything about Arab Americans. First, there are variations in time of arrival. Many Arab Americans have lived for several generations in the United States, whereas others are foreign born. A second aspect of diversity is point of origin, ranging from urban Cairo, Egypt, to rural Morocco. Third, there is a rich variety of religious tradition that can include Christian or Muslim, practicing or nonpracticing, and so forth. It becomes impossible to characterize Arab Americans having a family type or a gender role or an occupational pattern (David 2004).

As with any ethnic or immigrant community, divisions arise over who can truly be counted as a member of the community. Sociologist Gary David (2003, 2006) developed the concept of the **deficit model of ethnic identity**. This states that one's identity is viewed by others as a factor of subtracting away characteristics corresponding to some ideal ethnic type. Each factor encompassing a perfect ethnic identity missing from a person's background or identity leads the person to be viewed by others as more assimilated and less ethnic. In the case of Arab Americans, if they are unable to speak Arabic,

deficit model of ethnic identity
One's ethnicity is viewed by others as a factor of subtracting away the characteristics corresponding to some ideal ethnic type.

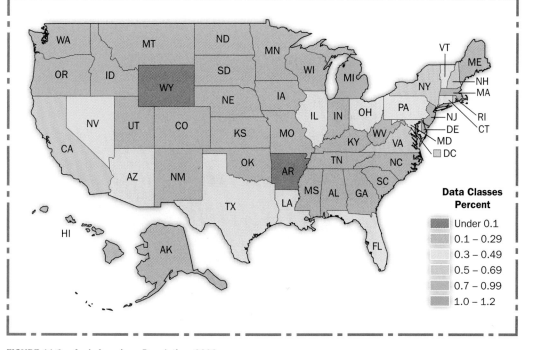

FIGURE 11.3   Arab American Population, 2000

Source: U.S Census Bureau data reported in de la Cruz and Brittingham 2003.

that makes them less Arab to some; if they are married to non-Arabs, less ethnic; if they have never been to the home country, less ethnic. Depending on one's perspective, an Arab American can come to regard another Arab American as either "too American" or "too Arab." Arab American organizations, magazines, and associations may seek to cater to the entire Arab American community, but, more likely, cater to certain segments based on nationality, religion, or degree of assimilation, groups that gravitate to one or the other depending on the perception of what it means to be an Arab American.

Muslim Americans

Islam, with approximately 1.3 billion followers worldwide, is second to Christianity among the world's religions. Although news events and a worldview of Orientalism suggest an inherent conflict between Christians and Muslims, the two faiths are similar in many ways. Both are monotheistic (i.e., based on a single deity) and indeed worship the same God. Allah is the Arabic word for God and refers to the God of Moses, Jesus, and Muhammad. Both Christianity and Islam include a belief in prophets, an afterlife, and a judgment day. In fact, Islam recognizes Jesus as a prophet, though not the son of God. Islam reveres both the Old and New Testaments as integral parts of its tradition. Both faiths impose a moral code on believers, which varies from fairly rigid proscriptions for fundamentalists to relatively relaxed guidelines for liberals.

Although they have some beliefs in common with Christians, Islam is guided by the teachings of the Qur'an (or Koran), which Muslims believe was revealed to the Prophet Muhammad, the collected sayings or hadeeth, and deeds of the seventh-century Prophet Muhammad, called Sunnah or the way of the Prophet. He grew up an orphan and became a respected businessman who rejected the widespread polytheism of his day and turned to the one God (Allah) as worshipped by the region's Christians and Jews. Islam says that he was visited by the angel Gabriel, who began reciting the Word of Allah, the Qur'an. Muslims see Muhammad as the last in a long line of prophets, preceded by Abraham, Moses, and Jesus. Islam is communal, encompassing

Although the Muslim presence in the United States has only been recognized by the general public very recently, it has a long history. Yarrow Marmout, an African Muslim and former slave, was painted in this portrait by famed artist Charles Wilson Peele in 1819.

Source: Charles Wilson Peale, "Yarrow Marmout." Courtesy of The Historical Society of Pennsylvania Collection, Atwater Kent Museum of Philadelphia.

all aspects of one's life. Consequently, in countries that are predominantly Muslim, the separation of religion and the state is not considered necessary or even desirable. In fact, governments in Muslim countries often reinforce Islamic practices through their laws. Muslims do vary in their interpretation of several traditions, some of which—such as the requirement for women to wear face veils—are disputed.

Like other religious systems, certain rituals referred to as the "pillars of wisdom" characterize Islam. Muslims fast during the month of Ramadan, which marks the revelation of the Qur'an to the Prophet Muhammad; pray to Allah facing Mecca five times a day; make charitable donations; and say, where possible, Friday afternoon prayers within their community. They also undertake the **hajj**, the pilgrimage, at least once in their lifetime, to Mecca. This city in contemporary Saudi Arabia is home of the House of Allah, or Ka'aba, built by Abraham and his son Ismael. Muslims perform the hajj in accordance with the Qur'an and in the manner prescribed by the Prophet Muhammed in his Sunnah.

Islamic believers are divided into a variety of faiths and sects, such as Sunnis and Shi'is (or Shiites). These divisions sometimes result in antagonisms between the members, just as there are religious rivalries between Christian denominations. The large majority of Muslims in the United States are Sunni Muslims—literally those who follow the Sunnah, the way of the Prophet. Compared to other Muslims, they tend to be more moderate in their religious orthodoxy. The Shi'ia (primarily from Iraq, Iran, and southern Lebanon) are the second largest group. The two groups differ on who should have been the Caliph, or ruler, after the death of the Prophet Muhammad. This disagreement resulted in different understandings of beliefs and practices, concluding in the Sunni and Shi'ia worshipping separately from each other. They worship separately even if it means crossing national and linguistic lines to do so—provided there are sufficient numbers of Shi'ia to support their own mosque or masjid.

There are many other expressions of Islamic faith and even divisions among Sunnis and Shi'is, so to speak of Muslims as Sunni or Shi'i would be akin to speaking of Christians as Roman Catholic or Baptist, forgetting that there are other denominations as well as sharp divisions within the Roman Catholic and Baptist faiths. Furthermore, there are Muslim groups unique to the United States; later we will focus on the largest one—Islam among African Americans.

Verses in the Qur'an prescribe to Muslims **jihad** or struggle against the enemies of Allah. Typically, jihad is taken by Muslims to refer to their internal struggle for spiritual purity. Today, a very visible minority of Muslims in the world see this as a pretext to carry out an armed struggle against what they view as the enemies of the Palestinians such as Israel and the United States. Such interpretations, even if held by a few, cannot be dismissed because Islam is a faith without an established hierarchy; there is no Muslim pope to deliver the one true interpretation, and there is no provision for excommunication. Individual imams who serve as the clergy for a mosque can offer guidance and scholarship, but Islam's authority rests with the scripture and the teachings of the Prophet (Belt 2002).

It is even more difficult to estimate the number of Muslim Americans in the United States than the number of Arab Americans. There are no census data available, and Islamic institutions such as mosques operate independently. Therefore, even considering the most scientific analyses brings wide variation in estimates. Based on the most recent studies, there are at least 2 million and perhaps as many as 5.7 million Muslims in the United States. About two-thirds are U.S.-born citizens. In terms of ethnic and racial background, the more acceptable estimates still vary widely. Estimates range as follows:

- 20–42 percent African American
- 24–33 percent South Asian (Afghan, Bangladeshi, Indian, and Pakistani)
- 12–32 percent Arab
- 10–22 percent "other" (Bosnian, Iranian, Turk, and White and Hispanic converts)

? ASK Yourself

Who comprises the Muslim population of the United States?

hajj
Pilgrimage to Mecca to be completed at least once in a Muslim's lifetime.

jihad
Struggle against the enemies of Allah, usually taken to mean one's own internal struggle.

306 Chapter 11 *Muslim and Arab Americans: Diverse Minorities*

blended identity
Self-image and worldview that is a combination of religious faith, cultural background based on nationality, and current residency.

There appears to be total agreement that the Muslim population in the United States is growing rapidly through immigration and conversion (Ba-Yunus and Kone 2004; Institute for Social Policy and Understanding 2004; P. King 2004b; Paik 2001; T. Smith 2001).

Reflecting the growth of the Muslim population in the United States, the number of mosques has grown to more than 1,700. Mosques (more properly referred to as masjids) do not maintain identifiable membership rolls as do churches, but scholars have observed that mosques and the imam, the leader or spiritual guide of a mosque, are today taking some of the characteristics of a congregation. In order to maintain their tax-exempt status, mosques are forced to incorporate boards and bylaws. Imams in the United States are more likely to take on a pastoral role relating to nonreligious functions, such as helping immigrants adjust, and representing the Muslim community to other nonprofit groups serving the larger community.

However more common mosques are in the United States, these symbols of faith and houses of worship still attract a different kind of attention than a steeple atop a Lutheran church. For many people in the United States, the mosque does not represent religious freedom and diversity or even a curiosity but a foreign threat in yet another example of Orientalism. Mosques are occasionally the focus of either government-initiated surveillance or police protection from anti-Muslim attacks. Muslim groups have found some communities blocking their efforts to build religious centers. Local authorities may require that the building be stripped of cultural symbols and even forgo the traditional dome.

Existing mosques have also experienced city councils blocking their efforts to publicly broadcast their call to prayer over loudspeakers even when neighboring churches just as loudly ring bells to signal the start of worship. Even after accepting some community-driven changes, mosques or Islamic centers often are victims of vandalism. However, there are also signs of acceptance. College campuses experiencing growing numbers of Muslims are adjusting by hiring part-time imams to minister to their needs, dedicating space for Muslims' prayer to be said five times a day, and providing for the restrictions of the Muslim diet (Ba-Yunus and Kone 2004; Leinwand 2004; Leonard 2003; S. Simon 2004; Wilgoren 2001).

In summary, Muslim Americans reflect a blended identity. **Blended identity** is the self-image and worldview that is a combination of religious faith, cultural background based on nationality, and the status of being a resident of the United States. As shown in Figure 11.4,

FIGURE 11.4 Blended Identity of Muslim Americans

Muslim Americans, as shown in this illustration of a Pakistani Muslim living in the United States, form their identity by bringing together three different identities: their faith, their homeland, and the United States.

Malcolm X, reflecting his conversion to Islam, made a pilgrimage to the Muslim holy city of Mecca. On this trip in 1964, the year before his assassination in New York City, he also met with area leaders such as Prince Faisal al-Saud of Saudi Arabia.

Muslims often find their daily activities defined by their faith, their nationality, and their status as American, however defined in terms of citizenship. Younger Muslims especially can move freely among the different identities. In Chicago, Muslim college students perform hip-hop in Arabic with lyrics like "La ilaha ila Allah" ("There is no God but Allah"). In Fremont, California, high school Muslim girls and some of their non-Muslim girlfriends hold an alternative prom decked out in silken gowns, dancing to both 50 Cent and Arabic music, dining on lasagna, but pausing at sunset to face toward Mecca and pray (Abdo 2004a; P. Brown 2003; Mostofi 2003).

There is one remaining but basic question: What, if anything, is different about being Muslim in the United States as opposed to an Islamic country? In the United States, we have a Muslim population that numbers in the millions but reflects the diversity of the worldwide Islamic faith, and practices their rituals and beliefs in a nation where the expression of Christianity dominates culturally. Some scholars of Islam argue that the experience of democracy and the history of religious diversity and free expression have facilitated a stronger and even more correct Islamic practice—uninhibited by the more totalitarian regimes many find in their homelands. Certainly there is disagreement over what is correct, but there is little pressure outside the Muslim community in the United States about how to precisely follow the teachings of the Prophet Muhammad.

Other scholars contend that what makes the American Muslim experience unique is that followers must place an even stronger focus on Islam in order to survive in a culture that is so permissive and, indeed, encourages so much behavior that is prohibited by either Islamic law or cultural traditions. For many Muslims in the United States, pop culture looks like old-fashioned paganism, a cult that celebrates money and sex. In the United States, many Muslims experience both the freedom to be Muslim and the pressure to be Muslim (Belt 2002).

Black Muslims

African Americans who embrace Islam form a significant segment within the Muslim American community. Islam is also a significant expression of religious beliefs among Black Americans. They number around 1.6 to 1.7 million or about 5 percent of all African Americans, yet they are estimated to account for 90 percent of all converts to Islam in the United States.

The history of Black American Islam begins in the seventeenth century, when members of some Muslim tribes were forcibly brought to the American colonies. It is estimated that 10 percent of African slaves were Muslim. Slave owners discouraged anything that linked them culturally to Africa including then spiritual beliefs. Furthermore, many in the South saw making slaves Christians as part of their mission in civilizing the enslaved people. Enslaved Muslims in the colonies and elsewhere often resisted the pressure to assimilate to the dominant group's faith and maintained their dedication to Islam (Ba-Yunus and Kone 2004; Leonard 2003; McCloud 1995).

It was exceedingly difficult, if not impossible, for a collective Muslim community to survive slavery. Organized Muslim groups within the African American community grew and dispersed in the late nineteenth century and the first half of the twentieth century. Resurgence of Islam among Black Americans often centered around the leadership of charismatic people such as West Indian born Edward Wilmot Blyden and North Carolinian Noble Drew Ali, who founded the Moorish Science Temple. Typically, followers of the movements dispersed at the death of the central leader, but with each movement, the core of converts to Islam grew within the African American community (R. Turner 2003).

Like other Muslims, generally African Americans who follow Islam are not tightly organized into a single religious fellowship. However, most today trace their roots either to the teachings of W. Fard Muhammad or, just as significantly, to those who responded against his version of the faith. Little is known of the early years of the immigrant W. Fard Muhammad, who arrived in Detroit around 1930, introducing the teaching of Islam to poor African Americans. He spoke strongly against adultery and alcohol consumption (which are forbidden by Islamic tradition) and smoking and dancing (which are prohibited among some Muslims). However, he also spoke of the natural superiority of Black people that would cause them to win out in the inevitable struggle between Blacks and Whites, but only if they adopted their "natural religion" and reclaimed their identity as Muslims (Lincoln 1994; R. Turner 2003).

Under the leadership of Elijah Muhammad, Fard's most trusted follower and his successor, the Nation of Islam became a well-known and controversial organization. This Muslim group preached racial hatred and experienced internal dissension, but they also gradually built a financial empire not unlike many of the large Christian denominations in the United States. The group also maintained very strong feelings toward Africa specifically and Arabs in general, even if its more unorthodox beliefs left it alienated from Muslim immigrants to the United States. Despite the controversies, many members of White society respected the Nation of Islam for its impressive use of capitalism to the organization's advantage and for the strict moral code its members followed. Warith Deen Muhammad, successor and son of Elijah Muhammad, aligned his followers in 1975 with the practices of the Sunni Muslim faith and included people of all races, although he acknowledged that the American Society of Muslims (ASM), as it is called today, is basically an African American organization (Abdo 2004b; Ansari 2004).

Malcolm X, originally a member of the Nation of Islam, became the most powerful and brilliant voice of Black self-determination in the 1960s. He was an authentic folk hero to his sympathizers and to many people today, more than a generation after his death. Besides his own followers, he commanded an international audience and is still referred to in a manner befitting a prophet. Indeed, Spike Lee's 1993 movie, based on the *Autobiography of Malcolm X*, reintroduced him to another generation. Malcolm X was highly critical of the civil rights movement in general and of Martin Luther King, Jr., in particular.

Malcolm X is remembered for his sharp attacks on other Black leaders, for his break with the Nation of Islam, and for his apparent shift to support the formation of coalitions with progressive Whites. He is especially remembered for teaching Blacks lessons that came to concern the champions of nonviolent direct action, among them that Blacks must resist violence "by any means necessary." By the last year of his life, Malcolm X (by then known as Malik El-Shabazz) had taken on a very different orientation. He created the secular Organization of Afro-American Unity, which was meant to internationalize the civil rights movement. Malcolm X's life was ended by three assassins in 1964. "His philosophy can be summarized as pride in Blackness, the necessity of knowing Black history, Black autonomy, Black unity, and self-determination for the Black community" (Pinkney 1975, 213; see also Dyson 1995; Kieh 1995).

In recent years, Minister Louis Farrakhan, despite leading a small proportion of Black Muslims, has been the most visible spokesperson among the various Muslim groups in the African American community. Farrakhan broke with W. Deen Muhammad in 1977 and named his group Nation of Islam, adopting, along with the name used by the earlier group, the more unorthodox-to-Islam ideas of Elijah Muhammad, such as Black moral superiority. Farrakhan jumped into the limelight, although his public statements about Jews and Israel gave an anti-Semitic taint to his teachings. W. Deen Muhammad resigned as leader of the ASM in 2003. Although Mohammed remains its spiritual guide, ASM mosques now tend to operate more independently of each other. The split between Farrakhan and Muhammad is not new to the Black followers of Islam, as Malcolm X's life indicates (Abdo 2004b; Henry 1994; Lincoln 1994).

Although Farrakhan's statements against Whites—Jews in particular—and his anti-Israel foreign policy have attracted the media's attention, many of his speeches and writings reflect the basic early tenets of the Nation of Islam. Abortion, drugs, and homosexuality are condemned. Self-help, bootstrap capitalism, and strict punishment are endorsed. Farrakhan is not pessimistic about the future of race relations in the United States. As leader of the 1995 Million Man March, he encouraged those present and African Americans nationwide to register to vote and work for positive change (Bositis 1996; Loury 1996).

Compared to most faiths, an unusual source of converts to Islam has been in the nation's prisons. One estimate released in 2002 states that 32 percent of all incarcerated African Americans in the New York State prison system have embraced Islam. A 2004 report of federal prisons would place the estimate lower but is still at least 20 percent. The Muslim prayer, a different diet, and commitment to a highly moral lifestyle help the inmates create an alternative social space within the prison (Dannin 2002; Office of the Inspector General 2004).

Traditionally, there has been little contact, at best, and actually some friction between the African American Muslim community, particularly those who adhere to the

Colleges and employers are inceasingly setting aside areas in which Muslim students and employees can carry out their daily prayers. Here at Massachusetts Institute of Technology in Cambridge, Massachusetts, worshippers gather for a afternoon prayers.

Nation of Islam, and immigrant Muslims and their descendants. Black Muslims may feel that the larger Islamic community does not speak to what they feel is the unique oppression faced by people who are Black and Muslim in the United States. Meanwhile, other Muslims often assume incorrectly that all African American Muslims embrace the Black superiority view and do not follow orthodox Muslim traditions. It is likely that a single dominating voice of Islam will not emerge among African Americans. That is not surprising because a pluralistic interpretation of faith is common to Muslims worldwide just as it is to Christians and Jews (Abdo 2004; McCloud 2004).

Immigration to the United States

The history of both Muslims and Arabs in the United States is a long one, but their visibility as a true immigrant presence is more of a twentieth-century phenomenon. As has already been noted, a significant proportion of African slaves were followers of Islam. Even earlier, Spanish Muslims accompanied explorers and conquistadores to the Americas. In the nineteenth century, contingents of Arabs made dramatic impressions at a series of world's fairs held in Philadelphia, St. Louis, and Chicago, where millions of fair goers had certainly their first contact and probably their first awareness of Arab culture. Although often viewed through the lens of Orientalism, fair goers came away with an awareness of cultures previously unknown to them. Positive reports of the reception of these delegations began to encourage Arabs, particularly from Syria and Lebanon, to immigrate to the United States. At about the same time, other Arabs immigrated as the result of encouragement from U.S.-funded missionary programs in the Middle East.

Just as immigration of Arabs and, to a lesser extent, practicing Muslims began to annually number in the thousands in the early twentieth century, World War I intervened and then the restrictive National Origins System (see Chapter 4), with its pro-Western and Northern Europe bias, slowed the movement to the United States. As with so many other immigrant groups, the pattern was for immigration to be disproportionately male and the destination to be cities of the East Coast. Pressure to assimilate caused many newcomers to try to reduce the differences between themselves and the host country. So, for example, many women ceased to cover their heads—a practice common to both Christian Arab and Muslim women.

In the wake of professional-preference clauses within the 1965 Immigration and Naturalization Act, immigration increased among both Muslims and Arabs. This movement of skilled workers greatly benefited the United States, as the law intended, but obviously contributed to the brain drain experienced throughout the Arab and Muslim worlds. With the Arab defeat in the 1967 Arab-Israeli War, there was a noticeable rise in immigration, with many Arab and Muslim Americans seeking to bring family members to join them from throughout the Middle East (Naff 1980). Since 1970, an increasing proportion of Arabs immigrating was Muslim. In addition, as some countries restricted their immigration policies, notably Great Britain, more Muslims came from non-Arab countries like Pakistan and Bangladesh as well as from Muslim areas of Africa (Camaruto 2002).

The immediate aftermath of 9/11 led to a decline of about 30 percent of Arabs and Muslims immigrating to the United States due to apprehension over the reception they would receive and increased scrutiny their entry documents received by the federal government. For example, numbers of tourists and students declined nearly by half. However, recently numbers have begun to rebound. In 2005, there were more than 40,000 arrivals from Muslim countries seeking permanent residency resulting in the highest annual numbers since 2000. Some new residents even argue they are better off in post–9/11 America because Islam centers are more organized and free legal help is more accessible (Elliott 2006).

New media outlets, such as *Azizah* magazine, have developed to serve the Muslim American community.

The growth and continuing vibrancy of an Arab presence in the Dearborn, Michigan, area is a unique development in the history of Arab immigration. A few Lebanese immigrants of the late nineteenth century were joined by fellow countrymen and women. Also immigrants from Lebanon came who were largely Christian, as well as from Yemen who were typically Sunni Muslims. With the expansion of the automobile industry during the 1910s, Arabs came to work in the area's many factories. Pleased by their treatment and wages, more immigrants joined them. By 1919, the first mosque was established and a variety of service agencies began to serve the needs of the immigrant community.

As of 2003, there were 33 mosques in the metropolitan Detroit area, serving an estimated 200,000 Muslims. With at least 40 percent of this area's population of Arab ancestry today, it is hard for a visitor not to see the evidence of this century-long immigration. Business establishments often feature greetings for Christmas, Ramadan, New Year's, and the two Islamic holidays called "Eids" in both English and Arabic. Today, it is by far the largest concentration of Arab Americans as well as Muslims. Indeed, this is probably the largest Arab community outside of the Arab world (Abraham and Shryock 2000; Bagby 2004; David and Ayouby 2004; S. Gold 2001).

Contemporary Life in the United States

As has already been noted, Arab Americans tended to immigrate to urban areas. There they have filled a variety of occupational roles, and immigrants, since the 1965 Immigration and Naturalization Act, have been filling skilled and professional roles in the United States. Another area in which Arab Americans often find opportunities for upward mobility is to become self-employed merchants or entrepreneurs. They typically are financially unable to buy into prosperous businesses or high-end retail stores. Rather, they have tended to become involved in precisely those businesses that privileged Whites have long since left behind or avoided altogether. To some degree, Arabs

For many people in the United States, such as this couple in Los Angeles, their primary interaction with the Arab community is by dining at Middle Eastern restaurants.

follow a pattern of Jewish and Korean immigrant entrepreneurs, operating stores in low-income areas of central cities that major retailers ignore. Opportunities for success are great, but it also means that the Arab American merchant faces the challenges of serving a low-income population with few consumer choices and a history of being exploited by outsiders (Cainkar 2006).

Family Life and Gender

The family, as with any people, plays a central role in the lives of both Muslim and Arab Americans. Given the diversity within both groups, it is impossible to generalize about typical patterns. Traditionally, Islam permitted men to have multiple wives—a maximum of four. The Qur'an admonished Muslim men to do justice economically and emotionally to their wives, and if they could not, then they should have only one wife. In some non-Islamic countries, this practice of multiple marriages is legal but is exceedingly rare for Muslim households in countries where the law is not supportive.

In the United States, for those who are recent immigrants or the children of immigrants, family patterns are more likely to be affected by the traditions of their homeland than by the fact that they are Muslim or Arab. Certainly, the role of women receives a great deal of attention because their outer clothing is a conspicuous symbol that to some seems to represent repression of women in society. There is a full range of views of women among Muslims and Arabs, just as there is among Christians and other ethnicities. However, Islam does stress that women need to be protected and should present themselves modestly in public. This code is operationalized very differently among countries where Muslims dominate and varies within Muslim populations in the United States (Haeri 2004).

Sexism and sexist behavior are universal. However, the perception of gender practices in Muslim societies have received special attention in the Western media. Dress codes particularly have been the focus of attention both within and outside the Muslim community. Individually, all Muslims, men and women alike, must cover themselves and avoid revealing clothes designed to accentuate contours of the body and emphasize its physical beauty. According to the Qur'an, more revealing garments can be worn in private with one's family or before members of the same sex, so in some Muslim countries some beaches and public pools are designated for use by men or by women.

Although the Qur'an dictates that women should wear a head covering that also covers their upper chest and neck, the Prophet Muhammad did clarify in his Sunnah that the female body should be covered except the face, hands, and feet. Hence, traditional Muslim women should wear head coverings. The **hijab** refers to a variety of garments that allow women to follow the guidelines of modest dress. It may include head coverings or a face veil and can take the form of a headscarf rather than something that actually covers the face; the latter would be dictated by a cultural tradition, not Islam. U.S. Muslims select from an array of traditional garments from Muslim countries. These garments include long, loose overgarments, which are tailored coats, or a loose black overgarment along with a scarf and perhaps a face veil. U.S. Muslim women are just as apt to wear long skirts or loose pants and overblouses that they may buy at any local retail outlet (Haeri 2004).

When it comes to the hijab, or outer garments, research has identified three perspectives among Muslim women in the United States and other settlements outside Islamic countries. Younger, better-educated women who support wearing the hijab in public draw on Western ideas of individual rights, arguing in favor of veiling as a form of personal expression. In contrast, older, less-educated women who also support the wearing of hijab tend to make their arguments without any reference to Western ideology. They cannot see why veiling should be an issue in the first place. A third group of women, of all ages and educational backgrounds, oppose the hijab. Some countries, notably France, have come under fire for taking official positions banning the hijab or headscarf in public schools. Generally this has not been an issue in the United States;

hijab
Refers to a variety of garments that allow women to follow the guidelines of modest dress.

Focus Research Focus Research

CHRISTIAN AND MUSLIM ARAB AMERICAN WOMEN'S GENDER ROLES

Few issues concerning Islam and Arabs spark more discussion than the role of women. Images of both groups tend to assume women's role is very limited and that any deviation from that role is heavily sanctioned. Sociologist Jen'nan Ghazal Read conducted a national survey of Arab American women in 2000. She was able to compare attitudes on gender roles between Christian and Muslim Arab Americans. The gender role questions highlighted such issues as attitudes on marital roles (who should make the decisions), parenting (mothers with preschool children working full-time), and nontraditional public roles such as women leading religious services.

Read found that Muslim women were more gender traditional than their non-Muslim peers in the Arab American community. However, she also noted that the Muslim respondents were more likely to be immigrants, to have an Arab spouse, and to be more conservative in their faith compared to Christian Arab women. Once she considered these differences, being Muslim seemed to have no impact on how the women viewed gender roles. For example, both the Bible and Qur'an encourage women to be more domestic and less public. Hence, she found that devout Christian and devout Muslim women were conservative in their gender attitudes compared to those of both faiths who were less inclined to accept their holy scripture literally.

Research into the views of Arab and Muslim Americans is just beginning, and Read's research underscores the importance of considering immigrant status and commitment to one's faith. The next step is to collect such data including also a comparable non-Muslim, non-Arab sample. ■

Sources: Marshall and Read 2003; Read 2003, 2004.

however, one 11-year-old had to go to federal court to be able to attend school in Muskogee, Oklahoma, wearing a headscarf. Interestingly, the Department of Justice supported the girl in her lawsuit (C. Killian 2003; *Religious Diversity News* 2004).

In "Research Focus," sociologist Jen'nan Ghazal Read reports on research showing how Christian and Muslim Arab American women view gender roles.

Gender-role differences among Muslims are not limited to the home and the family. There are differences in the role of women within the faith and in the mosque or masjid. In part, this reflects the differences in Islamic practices worldwide. For example, in Pakistan and Bangladesh, women are rarely allowed to enter most mosques. However, in Mecca and Medina, Saudi Arabia, the most holy mosques in Islam, women pray apart from the men but not in separate areas or behind curtains. In the United States, it is not unusual for women to be members of the boards of mosques, and it is also common for women worshippers to be relegated to praying in rooms outside the mosques. In many mosques, the explanation for segregating the sexes is the lack of space necessary to maintain modesty while kneeling for prayer, and it is true that many mosques are little more than small storefronts. However, even newly built mosques do not necessarily accommodate women worshippers in the same way they do men. In mosques that attract more U.S.-born Muslims, these issues remain points of contention and anxiety within the Muslim community (Goodstein 2004).

Education

Muslim and Arab Americans recognize the importance of education, and many of the recent immigrants have high levels of formal education and have benefited by the immigration policy that gave preference to those having job skills needed to enter the United States. Muslims also value formal instruction in their faith, and there are several hundred elementary and secondary schools, the majority attached to mosques, that offer what is been referred to in other religious contexts as a parochial school education.

Schools are specific to particular expressions of Islam and specific nationalities, and some schools serve principally Black Muslims. Qur'anic or Sunday schools also coexist, offering specifically religious instruction either to those attending mosque schools or as a supplement for children enrolled in public schools. A major growth industry has emerged in North America, providing curriculum materials and software to serve these schools, which range from preschool and continue through college, including graduate education (K. Leonard 2003).

Children attending public schools encounter the type of adjustment experienced by those of a religious faith different from the dominant one of society. Although public schools are intended to be secular, it is difficult to escape the orientation of many activities to Christmas and Easter or dietary practices that may not conform to the cultural tradition of the children's families. In some school districts with larger Muslim student populations, strides have been made to recognize the religious diversity. A few have granted Eid-al-Fitr, the day marking the end of Ramadan, as an official school holiday for all students (Avila 2003).

Politics

Muslim and Arab Americans are politically aware and often active. For those who identify with their homeland, politics may take the form of closely monitoring international events as they affect their home country and perhaps their kinfolk who still live there. Admittedly, since U.S. foreign policy often is tilted against some areas such as Palestine, the concerns that Arab Americans may have about events abroad may not be reduced by statements and actions taken by government officials in the United States. On a different level, Muslims and Arab Americans are increasingly involved in politics in the United States. Certainly the most visible Arab American in politics has been consumer advocate Ralph Nader, who has tried to open up presidential politics to consider a true alternative to the two-party system.

Within the traditional two-party system, Arab and Muslim Americans have moved away from the conservative family values policy of the Republicans because of the con-

Although many Muslim children attend public schools in the United States, others attend private or parochial schools. A teacher at the American Islamic Academy in Dearborn, Michigan, reminds her young students to be quiet when walking through school hallways.

Images of either Muslim or Arab Americans rarely focus on the routine daily activities that occupy most of their time that are just like the activities of other citizens. Muslim American girls enjoy the merry-go-round at Coney Island, New York.

tinuing concerns about government actions and policies in countries such as Afghanistan, Iraq, Lebanon, and the occupied territories of Palestine. In 2000, 42 percent of Muslim Americans voted for George Bush whereas four years after he only received 7 percent of their vote. In 2006, marking a new age, Keith Ellison, an African American Democrat from Minneapolis, was elected to the House of Representatives, the First Muslim American to serve. (Boorstein 2006; Mac Farquhar 2006).

Muslims in the United States often express the view that their faith encourages political participation. They note that as Prophet Muhammad lay on his deathbed, he explicitly refused to name a successor to his rule, preferring that the people choose their own leaders. Individual Arabs and Muslims have sought elective office and have been appointed to high-level positions. As voters, they are eagerly sought out by the major parties because they are concentrated in states such as Michigan, Pennsylvania, Ohio, and Florida that often play a critical role in close presidential elections.

There is a clear distancing that one can observe between the major parties and Muslims and Arab Americans. Although there are frequent official welcoming statements of support, close identification as might be shown in routine dinners and convention appearances are rare. This represents a contrast to how politicians cater to African Americans and Latinos to gain votes and more closely resembles the arm's-length relationship to gay and lesbian voters. As charges have escalated in the last decade that some organizations and charities in the Arab and Muslim community were financially assisting overseas groups unfriendly to Israel or even supportive of terrorist objectives, U.S. politicians began to take the safe position of refusing campaign money from virtually any group linked to the Muslim or Arab community. Needless to say, this did not make U.S. citizens who also happen to be of Arab decent or followers of Islam feel very welcomed in the political process (Clemetson 2003; Hassaballa 2004; Marvasti and McKinney 2004).

Despite being ignored presently by politicians, Arab and Muslim Americans are seeking to organize themselves as voters. For example, the Washington-based Muslim American Society has stepped up efforts to register Muslims to vote. Arab and Muslim Americans are following the time-honored tradition of other racial and ethnic minority groups by making themselves heard in electoral politics (Boorstein 2006).

Being Arab or Muslim in the United States

News events have fueled anti-Arab, anti-Muslim feeling. Activities carried out by Arabs or Muslims, including the 1972 terrorist raid at the Munich Olympics and the 1998 bombings of the U.S. embassies in Kenya and Tanzania, contributed to the negative image. The attack of September 11, 2001, engineered by Arab Muslim terrorists, caused many Americans to associate Arab and Muslim Americans with America's enemy in the war against terrorism. As the economy softened and taxpayers paid for increased security, Arab and Muslim Americans became the scapegoat in many people's minds. Vandalism of mosques, attacks on Arab-speaking people, and calls for widespread dragnets based on ethnicity or religion were common. Terrorism, even domestic terrorism, often is the product of homegrown troublemakers, as evidenced by hundreds of attacks on abortion clinics and the 1995 bombing of the federal building in Oklahoma City, Oklahoma.

Following the 1972 Munich Olympics attack, President Richard Nixon initiated Operation Boulder, which allowed for coordinated intelligence activities by the CIA, FBI, and other agencies to spy on and harass any Arab Americans engaging in political activity. With the objective to block support for the Palestinian cause, the three-year effort was to be directed against anyone of Arabic background (David and Ayouby 2004).

The immediate aftermath of the 1995 bombing of the federal building in Oklahoma City showed the willingness of the public to accept stereotypes. Many television news reports indicated that Islamic fundamentalists or Arab terrorists were the prime suspects. A Jordanian American who lives in Oklahoma City was arrested in London but cleared of any involvement in the terrorist attack. Nevertheless, in the first three days after the bombing, there were at least 222 attacks against Muslims in the United States. In the end, two White American men were convicted in the bombing, but this hardly erased the pain felt by many Arab Americans and Muslim Americans about the way in which they were scapegoated (Brooke 1995; Zogby 1998).

The events of September 11, 2001, catapulted the United States to focus on segments of the population with a scrutiny that had not been witnessed since the attack on Pearl Harbor sixty years earlier. President George W. Bush (2001) assured the nation, speaking from the Washington, D.C., Islamic Center within days of the hijacking of four airliners, that "the face of terror is not the true faith of Islam. . . . Islam is peace" and that "Muslims make an incredibly valuable contribution to our country." However, much harm had already been done. Follow-up remarks in the days to come were made by the president and other administrative officials in front of mosques or in the presence of representatives of the Muslim and Arab American community. Even the USA PATRIOT Act passed in October 2001, which has been sharply criticized for contributing to fear within the Arab and Muslim communities, has specific provisions condemning discrimination against Arab and Muslim Americans. Although these were positive symbols of reaching out, the further stigmatization of Muslim and Arab Americans was unstoppable.

In light of these suspicions, some citizens have found themselves under special surveillance because of racial profiling at airports and border checkpoints. As noted earlier in Chapter 2, racial profiling is any arbitrary police-initiated action based on race, ethnicity, or national origin rather than a person's behavior. Profiling of Arabs and Muslims became especially intense after September 11, 2001. The profiling has moved into everyday life. Muslim women who choose to don hair scarves, in keeping with their tradition to dress modestly, encounter harassment from strangers in the street and find many employers insisting that they shed the covering if they want to get a job or expect to be promoted. These citizens find it difficult to understand these attitudes in a nation of immigrants that is grounded in religious freedom (Amnesty International 2004; Institute for Social Policy and Understanding 2004).

Voices Listen to Our Voices Listen to

PENDULUM SWINGS ON CIVIL RIGHTS

There is growing concern that the Department of Justice (DOJ) has in the post–9/11 period, implementing several programs that have caused harm to Arab and Muslim immigrants and visitors to the United States.

Of particular concern have been: the large number of detentions and deportations that took place right after the 2001 terrorist attacks; the so-called "voluntary call-in" of 8,000 young Arab and Muslim immigrants; and the special registration program that has targeted visitors from twenty-five Arab and Muslim countries. . . .

These programs created suspicion as well. Some Americans came to feel that if the DOJ was targeting tens of thousands of Arabs and Muslims, based on their religion and ethnicity, then maybe there was reason to suspect these individuals. So even while President Bush was urging Americans not to discriminate against Arabs and Muslims, a different message was being sent by those DOJ initiatives. . . .

As a frequent traveler to the Arab world, I am aware of yet another negative impact of these DOJ initiatives. They have damaged the U.S. image and harmed our credibility and our relationship with the people of the region.

Because the effects of these DOJ programs have been well publicized in the Arab world there is a growing perception that Arab immigrants and visitors are not welcome in the United States. As a result many fewer Arabs are coming to the United States for medical treatment, tourism, study or business.

The good news is that there is a growing political coalition committed to challenging these practices, and they are having an impact. Broad coalitions of immigrant rights advocates have formed to demand an end to profiling, the registration program and other violations of civil liberties. Similarly, affected institutions like universities, hospitals and

James Zogby

major businesses have mobilized to pressure for changes in the restrictive visa procedures that have made the United States appear to be less open to visitors and immigrants. And major studies have been done both by reputable independent institutions and official government oversight bodies that have called into question the legality of some of these practices and their effectiveness.

Last year, for example, the Justice Department's own Inspector General issued a report that vindicated our concerns. The IG found that the Justice Department classified 762 of the detainees as "September 11 detainees." The IG concluded that none of these detainees were charged with terrorist-related offenses, and that the decision to detain them was "extremely attenuated" from the 9/11 investigation. The IG concluded that the Justice Department's designation of detainees of interest to the 9/11 investigation was "indiscriminate and haphazard" and did not adequately distinguish between terrorism suspects and other immigration detainees. . . .

Last week I testified before a Senate Judiciary Committee hearing on "America after 9/11: Freedom Preserved or Freedom Lost?"

There was strong support for change. Many Senators expressed their concern with the behavior of the DOJ and there are now a number of bills in the House and Senate that seek to correct the post 9/11 abuses. In fact, the American public wants civil liberties to be protected, wants the United States to remain open and welcoming to Arab visitors, students and immigrants. . . .

Two years after the United States was traumatized by terror, the pendulum now appears to be swinging back. ■

Source: "Pendulum Swings on Civil Rights" by James Zogby as posted on www.aaiusa.org/wwatch/112303.htm (November 23, 2003).

Reprinted by permission of the Arab American Institute.

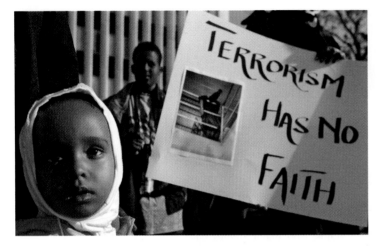

There is no question that 9/11 has brought attention to the many patriotic and law-biding Arab and Muslim Americans.

In those weeks after 9/11, surveys showed that both Muslim and Arab Americans supported the president's policy of going after terrorists. At the same time, they were fearful that continued military action would hurt how the United States is viewed. In the wake of 9/11, expressions and proof of loyalty were forced on Arab and Muslim Americans. Based on interviews with Muslim American college students in New York City, analysis of the responses showed that many felt the same sense of frustration and anger from the terrorist attacks. However, they also expressed an obligation to show their sorrow to others and, if true, indicate that they were born in the United States and actively supported the war on terrorism. In a national survey of Muslim Americans, completed in November 2001, 41 percent reported being more patriotic toward the United States and only 5 percent less patriotic despite the majority having experienced anti-Muslim discrimination in the weeks following 9/11 (P. King 2004a Muslims in the American Public Square 2001; Peek 2002; Zogby 2001).

In an effort to locate domestic terrorists, the U.S. Department of Justice required that all foreign-born Muslim men report to the Bureau of Citizenship and Immigration Services to be photographed, fingerprinted, and interviewed. Some questions were mundane: Where did they work? Were they married? Did they have children? Some were more pointed: Had they been asked by any Arabs or Muslims to teach them to fly airplanes? With very little public notice, 144,513 Muslim men from 25 countries reported during a five-month period ending in 2003. Of those who reported, about 13,000 faced deportation because of visa violations such as overstaying their visas, and 11 remained in custody because they were suspected terrorists.

The registration deepened fear and disillusionment among the many law-abiding Muslims in the United States. Many of the over 144,000 men interviewed were embarrassed to even be questioned, since their code of behavior (no drinking or illegal drugs) meant they were less likely to have faced routine encounters with law enforcement officials. Immigration advocates argued that the government was selectively enforcing immigration laws, but the courts have upheld the process and the right of the government to keep names of those deported or detained secret (King 2004c; N. Lewis 2003; *Migration News* 2003b).

In "Listen to Our Voices," opinion pollster and founder of the Arab American Institute, James Zogby, raises his concerns about how government policies within the United States have created problems for Arab Americans but remains optimistic that these policies will be revisited and changed.

Consider the particular case of some 100,000 Afghan Americans, typically Muslim but, like the people of Afghanistan, not considered Arabs. After September 11, Afghan Americans found themselves specially targeted for prejudice and were understandably concerned when the United States bombed Afghanistan in search of terrorist groups. Some Afghan Americans talk of leaving for Afghanistan, generally out of a desire to reestablish family ties. Like other Muslim immigrants, Afghan Americans generally came to the United States seeking better education, improved housing, and a higher standard of living in a country they perceived as tolerant of religious diversity. Most came in the 1970s and now have children who are more American than Afghan. Increasingly, their family ties, not just the economic ones, are in the United States (Ritter and Squiteri 2002).

Issues of Prejudice and Discrimination

Al tikrar bialllem il hmar
(By repetition even the donkey learns)

Media scholar Jack Shaheen (2003, 171) uses this Arab proverb to underscore how the media has reinforced the negative image of Arabs and Muslims. Motion pictures such as *The Sheik* (1921), *The Mummy* (1932), *True Lies* (1994), and *The Mummy Returns* (2001) uniformly show Arabs and Muslims as savages and untrustworthy. Even Disney's 1995 animated film *Aladdin* referred to Arabs as "barbaric" and depicted, contrary to Islamic law, a guard threatening to cut off a young girl's hand for stealing food. In what ways do prejudice and discrimination manifest themselves with respect to Muslim and Arab Americans? In form and magnitude, they are much like what is shown toward other subordinate groups. Regrettably, the situation appears to have gone beyond Orientalism in which one sees people as "the other" and somewhat frightening. What makes current expressions of hostility strikingly different are that the events of the twenty-first century have been given a decidedly patriotic fervor; that is, for many who overtly express their anti-Muslim or anti-Arab feeling, they are also being pro-American.

Perhaps even more troubling to many Arab and Muslim Americans are the portrayals and images in the news and general information programming on television. To some, there is an overemphasis on the extreme representations, such as the wearing of opaque face veils by women, with little social context offered.

There are very few normalizing or positive images. Rarely are Arab and Muslim Americans shown doing "normal" behavior such as shopping, attending a sporting event, or even just eating without a subtext of terrorism lurking literally in the shadows. This is similar to the media portrayal of Native Americans. Like Arab and Muslim Americans, tribal people are rarely depicted just going about their daily routine as citizens. Furthermore, the interests of the United States are depicted either as leaning against the Arabs and Muslims, as in the Israeli-Palestinian violence, or presented as hopelessly dependent on them, in the case of our reliance on foreign oil production.

Not surprisingly, analysis of surveys done in the months after 9/11 found growing willingness to view Arabs and Muslims generally as a dangerous people and to require that Muslim and Arab Americans carry special identification cards. Nevertheless, there seemed little interest in repeating the internment camp experience of Japanese Americans following the attack on Pearl Harbor. One survey found that 65 percent were opposed to the federal government's holding Arabs who were U.S. citizens in camps until it could be determined whether they had links to terrorist organizations.

Evidence of hate crimes and harassment toward Arab and Muslim Americans rose sharply after 9/11, compared to studies done in the mid-1990s. It continued to remain high through 2004, according to more recent studies. Incidents have ranged from beatings to vandalism of mosques. Evidence of a backlash also includes Muslim Americans getting unwarranted eviction notices (Institute for Social Policy and Understanding 2004; J. Stewart 2002; Watanabe 2004).

Surveys show a complex view in the United States of Arab and Muslim Americans. Surveys since 2001 show one in four people believe a number of anti-Muslim stereotypes, such as the idea that Islam teaches violence and hatred. Curiously while harboring these views, people do recognize that Arab Americans are poorly treated. In 2006, 47 percent of White non-Hispanics felt that Arab Americans were ill-treated. Yet about 40 percent would require Muslim citizens of the United States to carry special identification and be subjected to greater surveillance (Council on American-Islamic Relations 2004; Jones 2006; Saad 2006a).

Arab Americans and Muslim Americans, like other subordinate groups, have not responded passively to their treatment. Organizations have been created in their communities to counter negative stereotypes and to offer schools material responding to the labeling that has occurred. Even before 2001, Arab Americans and Muslim Americans were beginning to become active in both major political parties in the United States. However, during the 2000 campaign, candidates already were distancing themselves from campaign contributions from Muslim and Arab organizations. As with other groups that have been disadvantaged and do not have clear access to the top levels of decision making in the public and private sectors, nonprofit organizations, such as the Council of American-Islamic Relations, the American Muslim Alliance, Muslim Public Affairs Council and the American Arab Anti-Discrimination Committee, have developed to represent their interests and to promote understanding as well as to bring attention to discrimination and expressions of prejudice in public life and the mass media.

Conclusion

We have seen the diversity within the Native American tribal community and among Latinos. Prejudice, discrimination, and responses of resistance have typified these groups and African Americans' long history in the United States. Now we can see in a special way that Arab Americans and Muslim Americans share in this experience. Not very numerous in absolute terms until the latter part of the twentieth century, both Arabs and Muslims have built upon a fragmented history that in the United States literally goes back 200 years. When Muslims were less numerous, it was difficult to maintain any sense of communal identity, but as their numbers increased, identifiable groups emerged (see Figure 11.5).

Diversity has marked both Arab Americans and Muslim Americans in the United States. For the descendants of earlier Arab settlers, their identity as Arab may be discounted by recent Arab immigrants through a process of the deficit model of ethnic identity. For the Muslim community, the divisions within the faith overseas are reproduced in the United States, with the added significant presence of African Americans who have embraced Islam.

The world and domestic events of recent years, and especially in the early years of the twenty-first century, have created some new challenges. In some respects, the continuing conflict in Israel and Palestine has served to create an Arab identity that was largely missing a few generations ago, when more strictly nationalistic agendas prevailed. Similarly, the agenda of fundamentalist and militant Muslims has created an us–them mentality found both in international organizations and on street corners of the United States. This lack of true understanding of one another is not totally new but is built upon the Orientalism that has its roots in the initial contacts between Europeans and the people of the Middle East and South Asia.

FIGURE 11.5   Intergroup Relations Continuum

To Chicago's Jahan Ghaemi, Seattle's Jawad al-Gheezi, and Cleveland's Rebecca Khoury—all mentioned at the beginning of this chapter—this is all ancient history. They, like other U.S. citizens, are seeking to define themselves and move ahead in their society. The challenges for them to do this seem measurably greater than they were just a few years ago, but their efforts to create bridges are also significant.

Key Terms

blended identity 306	hijab 312	jihad 305
deficit model of ethnic identity 303	hajj 305	Orientalism 300

Review Questions

1. What are the dimensions of diversity among Arab Americans and among Muslims?
2. What distinguishes African American Muslims from other practicing Muslims in the United States?
3. How has the immigration of Muslims and Arabs been influenced by the governmental policies of the United States?
4. What would you identify as the four most important differences between being a Christian in the United States and being a Muslim in this country?

Critical Thinking

1. Besides Arab Americans and Muslim Americans, identify other groups recently subjected to prejudice, perhaps in your own community.
2. Apply the deficit model of ethnic identity to another group besides Arab Americans.
3. What are some characteristics associated with Muslim and Arab Americans that have come to be viewed as negatives but when practiced by Christian Whites are seen as positives?
4. How are the Arab and Muslim communities composed of differences by language, social class, citizenship status, nationality, and religion?

Internet Connections—Research Navigator™

To access the full resources of Research Navigator™, please find the access code printed on the inside cover of *OneSearch with Research Navigator™: Sociology.* You may have received this booklet if your instructor recommended this guide be packaged with new textbooks. (If your book did not come with this printed guide, you can purchase one through your college bookstore.) Visit our Research Navigator™ site at www.ResearchNavigator.com. Once at this site, click on REGISTER under New Users and enter your access code to create a personal Login Name and Password. (When revisiting the site, use the same Login Name and Password.) Browse the features of the Research Navigator™ Web site and search the databases of academic journals, newspapers, magazines, and Web links.

For further information relevant to Chapter 11, you may wish to use such keywords as "Middle Eastern," "Islam," and "Patriot Act," and the search engine will supply relevant and recent scholarly and popular press publications. Use the *New York Times* Search-by-Subject Archive to find recent news articles related to sociology and the Link Library feature to locate relevant Web links organized by the key terms associated with this chapter.

12

Asian Americans: Growth and Diversity

CHAPTER OUTLINE

The "Model Minority" Image Explored

■LISTEN TO OUR VOICES
"Being Pakistani, Muslim, and Female in America"
by Fatima Arain

Political Activity

Diversity Among Asian Americans

Asian Indians

Filipino Americans

■RESEARCH FOCUS
Arranged Marriages in America

Southeast Asian Americans

Korean Americans

Hawaii and Its People

Conclusion

Key Terms/Review Questions/Critical Thinking/
Internet Connections—Research Navigator™

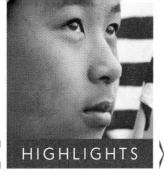

ASIAN AMERICANS AND PACIFIC ISLANDERS ARE A DIVERSE group that is one of the fastest-growing segments of the U.S. population. Asian Americans often are viewed as a model minority that has successfully overcome discrimination. This inaccurate image disguises lingering maltreatment and anti–Asian American violence. Furthermore, it denies Asian Americans the assistance afforded other racial minorities. Immigration is the primary source of growth among Asian Indians, Filipinos, Southeast Asians, and Koreans. All Asian groups, along with Blacks and Whites (or Haoles, as they are known there), coexist in Hawaii.

Madison Nguyen won election to the city council of San Jose, California, the nation's tenth largest city, in 2006. This was a significant event because she became the city council's first Vietnamese American member. Although San Jose has a large Asian American community, she attracted a lot of White, African American, and Latino voters as well. Was her Vietnamese ancestry an issue? That leads us to the second remarkable aspect of her election for attorney Madison Nguyen defeated another Vietnamese American, Linda Nguyen, who directs the popular New Year Tet parade in the city.

Pulitzer prize–winning writer Jhumpa Lahiri has lived all thirty-nine years of her life in the United States, except for her first two in London. She still sees her home being as much in Calcutta as in Rhode Island where she grew up. Still to this day, despite all her success her writing has had in English, she sees her life as a shifting equation between being a Bengali Indian and an American (Lahiri 2006; Vuong 2006).

Madison Nguyen and Jhumpa Lahiri, despite being public figures, could be speaking for all Asian Americans who are often aware of the country from which they or their parents came and their position in the United States. An elected official and successful writer remind us that the legacy of immigration to the United States is not merely quaint turn-of-the-century black-and-white photos taken at Ellis Island. It is not merely a thickly accented elderly person telling of the "old country." Immigration, race, and ethnicity are being lived out among people of all ages, and for no collective group is this truer than for Asian Americans who are living throughout the United States (Figure 12.1).

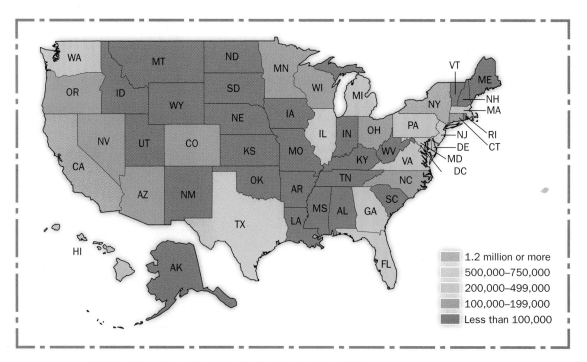

FIGURE 12.1 Where Most Asian Pacific Islanders Live, 2005

Source: Author based on American Community Survey 2005.

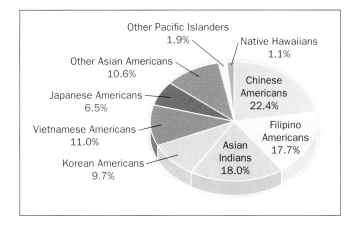

FIGURE 12.2   Asian Pacific Islanders, 2005

Source: Author based on American Community Survey 2005.

Asian Americans include groups such as Chinese Americans and Filipinos, whose nationality groups also include different linguistic groups and identifiable ethnic groups (Figure 12.2). Asian Americans also include ethnic groups such as the Hmong that do not correspond to any one nation. Finally, the U.S. population also includes Pacific Islanders, which include Hawaiians, Samoans, Tongans, and many smaller groups. Collectively, Asian Pacific Islanders in 2005 numbered 12.9 million—an 83 percent increase over 1990, compared with an overall population increase of only 16 percent.

Yet despite these large numbers—equivalent to the African American population after World War II—Asian Americans feel ignored. They see "race and ethnicity" in America framed as a Black–White issue or, more recently, as a "triracial" issue including Hispanics. But where are the Asian Americans in these pictures of the United States? For example, tens of thousands of Asian Americans, especially Vietnamese Americans, were displaced by Hurricane Katrina in 2005, but they received little media notice. Immigration issues understandably focus on Latin America, but what about challenges facing Asians seeking legal entry to the United States or the Asian Americans who are already here?

We need to remember in raising all these large numbers that, as with all racial and ethnic groups, most of the time life is played out on the individual level. In "Listen to Our Voices," a Pakistani American college student talks about what it is like to be immersed in American culture while also fully aware of the very different cultural tradition of her family.

To comprehend better the collective picture of Asian Americans, we will first consider the powerful image that many people have of Asian Americans of constituting some kind of perfect, model minority. We will then turn our attention to the role they play politically in the United States.

We will then consider four of the larger groups—Filipinos, Asian Indians, Southeast Asians, and Koreans—in greater depth. The chapter concludes by examining the coexistence of a uniquely mixed group of peoples—Hawaiians—among whom Asian Americans form the numerical majority. Chapter 13 concentrates on the Chinese and the Japanese, the two Asian groups with the longest historical tradition in the United States.

The "Model Minority" Image Explored

"Asian Americans are a success! They achieve! They succeed! There are no protests, no demands. They just do it!" This is the general image that people in the United States so often hold of Asian Americans as a group. They constitute a **model or ideal minority** because, although they have experienced prejudice and discrimination, they seem to have succeeded economically, socially, and educationally without resorting to

model or ideal minority
A group that, despite past prejudice and discrimination, succeeds economically, socially, and educationally without resorting to political or violent confrontations with Whites.

Voices Listen to Our Voices Listen to Ou

BEING PAKISTANI, MUSLIM, AND FEMALE IN AMERICA
BY FATIMA ARAIN

At first glance, I may look like a "White-washed" Pakistani American. I would not necessarily blame some for thinking this way. After all, I listen to indie and punk music; I have a White boyfriend; and most of my friends are White. However, it was not always this way.

My parents moved to the United States separately within 10 years of each other, in the 60's and 70's. Upon arrival, they knew that they were going to raise their children in American culture. So, naturally, when we were born they taught us Urdu, fed us Pakistani food, and dressed us in South Asian attire. We had Qur'an lessons and went to the mosque multiple times a week until we went off to college.

Originally, my parents settled in Brooklyn, but after they realized that they did not want to raise children in an urban environment, they finally settled in a western suburb of Milwaukee called Brookfield. Brookfield is almost 100% White. The minorities that do exist in the city are generally of East Asian or South Asian descent. There are hardly any African American or Latino residents. In my first years in Brookfield, I was made aware of my distinctiveness. I knew that I was different from most of the students. Still, I was raised to be proud of my heritage. I think that a huge reason that I was accepted in my community was because I also came from a wealthy family. Had I been in a similar city with similar racial demographics, without my wealthy background, I trust that I would not have had good experiences with my peers.

Gradually, Muslims became a more prominent part of Milwaukee. Our mosque grew with immigrants from South Asian and Arab countries. Since I was at the mosque all the time, I made many Muslim friends who understood the difficulties affiliated with growing up as a minority in a largely White area. However, being a part of Brookfield's community also led to me creating friendships with non-Muslim White youth as well.

In order to create a stronger sense of pride in our culture, my parents made it a point to travel to many Muslim countries. In my lifetime, I traveled to Pakistan several times, as well as Morocco, Turkey, Saudi Arabia and Afghanistan. However, my parents knew that it was important for us to learn

political or violent confrontations with Whites. Some observers point to the existence of a model minority as a reaffirmation that anyone can get ahead in the United States. Proponents of the model minority view declare that because Asian Americans have achieved success, they have ceased to be subordinate and are no longer disadvantaged. This is only a variation of blaming the victim; with Asian Americans, it is "praising the victim." An examination of aspects of their socioeconomic status will allow a more thorough exploration of this view (Fong 2002; Hurh and Kim 1989; Thrupkaew 2002).

Education and the Economy

Asian Americans as a group have impressive school enrollment rates in comparison to the total population. In 2004, 49.4 percent of Asian Americans 25 years old or older held bachelor's degrees, compared with 30.6 percent of the White population (Table 12.1).

s Listen to Our Voices Listen to Our Voices

about other cultures as well. Therefore, we traveled to Europe and all parts of the United States. Most of all, my parents wanted us to be proud to be a part of our country.

When I was a junior in high school, my friend told me that he would love for me to be a part of a program affiliated with the American Civil Liberties Union in Wisconsin. The program, which was targeted towards Milwaukee area high school students, created awareness about racism, sexism, classism, ableism, ageism, heterosexism, and religious discrimination. For the first time in my life, I was working with African American, Latino and Latina, and Jewish youth side by side on a regular basis. Similarly, it was the first time that I had ever had friends that were not either White, Muslim, or East Asian. I suddenly became aware of all the prejudices that were around me all the time.

The experience was so life-changing that, when senior year rolled around, I decided that I had to go to a college that was diverse. When I got to college, however, I was extremely disappointed. I was appalled to see the self-segregation amongst all the different ethnic and racial groups on campus. Right away, I befriended everybody I could. I went out of my way to be friends with South Asian students but, to my dismay, I was rejected based on the fact that I was willing to be friends with other people besides Muslims. I

realized that this must be a problem for many minority students. We will always face the issue of being either too American ("White-washed," "oreo," etc.) , or not American enough ("fresh off the boat").

Now, as I am getting older, I face the challenges of finding a suitable mate. My parents are obsessed with the idea of their daughter marrying a Pakistani Muslim. However, my boyfriend is a White Catholic. These are not problems that are exclusive to my life. I think that a lot of first-generation Americans face these issues as well.

Overall, I do not think that the problems that I have faced have held me back. I have had an extremely rich experience as far as multiculturalism is concerned. I have been exposed to a lot. However, being a minority does not necessarily mean that I am automatically more cultured than a White American. My parents went out of their way to make sure that we were not only proud of their culture, but of ours as well. I know very few Pakistani families who have tried to achieve that. Even though I was not exposed to class and economic diversity until later in my life, I still had a chance to have those experiences. ■

Source: F. Arain 2006.

These rates vary among Asian American groups, with Asian Indians, Chinese Americans, and Japanese Americans having higher levels of educational achievement than others.

This encouraging picture does have some qualifications, however, which call into question the optimistic model minority view. According to a study of California's state university system, although Asian Americans often are viewed as successful overachievers, they have unrecognized and overlooked needs and experience discomfort and harassment on campus. As a group, they also lack Asian faculty and staff members to whom they can turn for support. They confront many identity issues and have to do a "cultural balancing act" along with all the usual pressures faced by college students. The report noted that an "alarming number" of Asian American students appear to be experiencing intense stress and alienation, problems that have often been "exacerbated by racial harassment" (Ohnuma 1991; Zhou 2004).

Even the positive stereotype of Asian American students as "academic stars" or "whiz kids" can be burdensome to the people so labeled. Asian Americans who do only

TABLE 12.1
Selected Social and Economic Characteristics of Asian Americans

	Non-Hispanic White	Asian Americans
Percentage completing college, 25 years old and older	30.6%	49.4%
Percentage unemployed	5.1%	5.1%
Percentage of households with a single parent	18.2%	18.6%
Percentage of people living below poverty level	8.2%	11.8%
HOUSEHOLD INCOME		
Below $10,000	7.1%	10.7%
Over $50,000	54.4%	48.1%

Note: Income and poverty data for 2003; other data for 2004.

Source: Author based on Asian and Pacific Islander detailed tables (PPL-184) from 2004 *Current Population Survey*.

modestly well in school may face criticism from their parents or teachers for their failure to conform to the "whiz kid" image. Some Asian American youths disengage from school when faced with these expectations or receive little support for their interest in vocational pursuits or athletics (Kibria 2002).

That Asian Americans as a group work in the same occupations as Whites suggests that they have been successful, and many have. However, the pattern shows some differences. Asian immigrants, like other minorities and immigrants before them, are found disproportionately in the low-paying service occupations. At the same time, they are also concentrated at the top in professional and managerial positions. Yet as we will see, they rarely reach the very top. They hit the glass ceiling (as described in Chapter 3) or, as some others say, try to "climb a broken ladder," before they reach management. In 2002, only 2 percent of 11,500 people who serve on the boards of the nation's 1,000 largest corporations were Asian American (G. Strauss 2002).

The absence of Asian Americans as top executives also indicates that their success is not complete. Asian Americans have done well in small businesses and modest agricultural ventures. Although self-employed and managing their own businesses, Asian Americans have had very modest-sized operations. Because of the long hours, the income from such a business may be below prevailing wage standards, so even when they are business owners, they may still constitute cheap labor, although they also get the profits. Chinese restaurants, Korean American cleaning businesses and fruit and vegetable stores, and motels, gasoline stations, and newspaper vending businesses operated by Asian Indians fall into this category.

Asian Americans, therefore, are typical of what sociologists call **middlemen minorities**, groups that occupy middle positions rather than positions at the bottom of the social scale, where many racial and ethnic minorities typically are located, at least in the early years of residence here. Asian Americans involved in small businesses tend to maintain closer ties with other Asian Americans than do people who join larger corporations. These ethnic owners generally hire other ethnics, who are paid low wages in exchange for paternalistic benefits such as on-the-job training or even assistance in creating their own middleman businesses. However, the present high proportion of Asian Americans as middlemen often is the result of exclusion from other work, not of success. Furthermore, serving as shopkeepers, for example, often contributes to their outsider status because they are resented by both the economic movers of a community and the customers they serve (Bonacich 1988; Bonacich and Modell 1981; Kim and Kim 1998).

Another misleading sign of the apparent success of Asian Americans is their high incomes as a group. Like other elements of the image, however, this deserves closer inspection. Asian American family income approaches parity with that of Whites because of their greater achievement than Whites in formal schooling. If we look at specific

middlemen minorities
Groups such as Japanese Americans that typically occupy middle positions in the social and occupational stratification system.

Asian Americans are subject to stereotypes, one of which, "straight-A student," reflects the model minority image.

Source: © 2001 Oliver Chin. Reprinted by permission of Oliver Chin.

educational levels, Whites earn more than their Asian counterparts of the same age. Asian Americans' average earnings increased by at least $2,300 for each additional year of schooling, whereas Whites gained almost $3,000. As we see in Table 12.1, Asian Americans as a group have significantly more formal schooling but actually have lower household family income. We should note that, to some degree, some Asian Americans' education is from overseas and, therefore, may be devalued by U.S. employers. Yet in the end, educational attainment does pay off as much if you are of Asian descent as it does for White non-Hispanics (F. Wu 2002; Zeng and Xie 2004; Zhou and Kamo 1994).

There are striking contrasts among Asian Americans. Nevertheless, for every Asian American family with an annual income of $75,000 or more, another earns less than $10,000 a year. In New York City's Chinatown neighborhood, about one-quarter of all families live below the poverty level. In San Diego, dropout rates were close to 60 percent among Southeast Asians in 1997. Even successful Asian Americans continue to face obstacles because of their racial heritage. According to a study of three major public hospitals in Los Angeles, Asian Americans account for 34 percent of all physicians and nurses but fill only 11 percent of management positions at these hospitals (Dunn 1994; Reeves and Bennett 2003; Sengupta 1997).

At first, one might be puzzled to see criticism of a positive generalization such as "model minority." Why should the stereotype of adjusting without problems be a disservice to Asian Americans? The answer is that this incorrect view helps to exclude Asian Americans from social programs and conceals unemployment and other social ills. For example, Asian American participation has been questioned in **set-aside** programs that stipulate government contracts must be awarded to a minimum proportion of minority-owned business. More and more local governments are eliminating Asian Americans from the definition of minority in their set-aside programs, essentially buying into the model minority myth (Committee of 100 2001).

The Door Half Open

Despite the widespread belief that they constitute a model minority, Asian Americans are victims of both prejudice and violence. Reports released annually by the National Asian Pacific American Legal Consortium (2002) chronicle incidents of suspected and proven anti–Asian American incidents that occur. After the terrorist attacks of September 11, 2001, anti-Asian violence increased dramatically for several months in the United States. The first fatality was an Indian American who was shot and killed by a gunman in Mesa, Arizona, shouting, "I stand for America all the way."

set-asides
Programs stipulating that a minimum proportion of government contracts must be awarded to minority-owned businesses.

yellow peril
A term denoting a generalized prejudice toward Asian people and their customs.

This anti–Asian American feeling is built on a long cultural tradition. The term *yellow peril* dates back to the view of Asian immigration, particularly from China, as unwelcome. **Yellow peril** came to refer to the generalized prejudice toward Asian people and their customs. The immigrants were characterized as heathen, morally inferior, drug addicted, savage, or lustful. Although the term was first used around the turn of the twentieth century, this anti-Asian sentiment is very much alive today. Many contemporary Asian Americans find this intolerance very unsettling given their conscientious efforts to extend their education, seek employment, and conform to the norms of society (Hurh 1994).

What explains the increase in violence against Asian Americans? Prejudice against Asian Americans is fueled by how they are represented in the media. The Asian American Journalists Association (2000) annually conducts a "media watch" to identify how mainstream news media use ethnic slurs and stereotypes, demonstrate insensitivity, and otherwise exhibit bias in reporting. We can identify several ways in which this occurs—some subtle, some overt:

- *Inappropriate use of clichés.* News reports use the term *Asian invasion* even when referring to a small number of Asian Americans. For example, a 1994 *Sports Illustrated* article about Asians trying out for major league baseball teams was billed "Orient Express" and "Asian Invasion," yet the story noted only two Asians as examples.

- *Mistaken identity.* Not only are Asians identified by the wrong nationality, but also American citizens of Asian descent are presented as if they were foreigners.

- *Overgeneralization.* Inappropriate assumptions are made and too widely applied. For example, a newspaper article discussing the growth of Chinatown was headlined "There Goes the Neighborhood," implying that any increase in the number of Chinese Americans was undesirable.

- *Ethnic slurs.* Although the print media generally take great pains to avoid racially derogatory terms, radio talk shows offer frequent examples of racism.

- *Inflammatory reporting.* Unbalanced coverage of such events as World War II or Asian investment in the United States can needlessly contribute to ill feelings.

- *Japan bashing.* News accounts may unfairly blame Asian nations for economic problems in the United States. For example, as Japan-based automakers gained a foothold in the United States, much of the coverage failed to note that U.S. carmakers had not maintained their own competitive advantage.

- *Media invisibility.* News reports may ignore Asian Americans and rarely seek their views on issues related to Asia.

- *Model minority.* This positive portrayal can also have a negative effect.

Many Asian Americans seek out less traditional media outlets given the lack of Asian or Asian American images. Many Korean Americans followed with great interest the exploits of *Damo,* the multi-episode series of a female undercover detective in seventeenth-century Korea.

In its own way, each of these biases contributes to the unbalanced view we have developed of the large, diverse Asian American population.

The resentment against Asian Americans is not limited to overt incidents of violence. Like other subordinate groups, Asian Americans are subject to institutional discrimination. For example, some Asian American groups have large families and find themselves subject to zoning laws stipulating the number of people per room, which make it difficult to live together. Kinfolk are unable to take in family members legally. Whereas we may regard these family members as distant relatives, many Asian cultures view cousins, uncles, and aunts as relatives to whom they have a great deal of familial responsibility.

The marginal status of Asian Pacific Islanders leaves them vulnerable to both selective and collective oppression. In 1999, news stories implicated Wen Ho Lee, a nuclear physicist at Los Alamos National Laboratory in New Mexico, as a spy for China. Subsequent investigation, during which Lee was imprisoned under very harsh conditions, concluded that the naturalized citizen scientist had indeed downloaded secret files to an unsecured computer, but there was no evidence that the information ever went further.

In the aftermath of the Wen Ho Lee incident, a new form of racial profiling emerged. We introduced **racial profiling** in Chapter 2 as any police-initiated action that relies on race, ethnicity, or national origin rather than a person's behavior. Despite Lee's being found not guilty, Asian Americans were viewed as security risks. A survey found that 32 percent of the people in the United States felt that Chinese Americans are more loyal to China than to the United States. In fact, the same survey showed that 46 percent were concerned about Chinese Americans passing secrets to China. Subsequent studies found that Asian Americans were avoiding top-secret science labs for employment because they became subject to racial profiling at higher security levels (Committee of 100 2001; Department of Energy 2000; Lee with Zia 2006 F. Wu 2002).

For young Asian Americans, life in the United States often is a struggle for one's identity when their heritage is so devalued by those in positions of influence. Sometimes identity means finding a role in White America; other times, it involves finding a place among Asian Americans collectively and then locating oneself within one's own racial or ethnic community.

Political Activity

Against this backdrop of prejudice, discrimination, and searching for one's identity, it would not be surprising to see Asian Americans seeking to recognize themselves. Historically, Asian Americans have followed the pattern of other immigrant groups: They bring organizations from the homeland and later develop groups to respond to the

racial profiling
Any arbitrary police-initiated action based on race, ethnicity, or natural origin rather than a person's behavior.

Compared to the other groups discussed in this book, the national political agenda has paid almost no attention to issues particular to Asian Americans.
Source: Tak Toyoshima.

special needs identified in the United States. Recently, during the expressions of anti-immigrant sentiment that began in the late 1990s and that were given a boost by antialien feelings after 9/11, Asian Americans staged demonstrations in several cities, seeking to persuade people to become citizens and register to vote.

These efforts, similar to the recent steps taken by Hispanic groups discussed in previous chapters, have also met with mixed success. Asians and Pacific Islanders' political clout is still developing; many still are not citizens. At the time of the 2004 election, 32.5 percent were not citizens and were, therefore, ineligible to vote, compared with 41 percent of Hispanics and 2 percent of non-Hispanic Whites (Holder 2006).

For newly arrived Asians, grassroots organizations and political parties are a new concept. With the exception of Asian Indians, the immigrants come from nations where political participation was unheard of or looked upon with skepticism and sometimes fear. Using the sizable Chinese American community as an example, we can see why Asian Americans have been slow to achieve political mobilization. At least six factors have been identified that explain why Chinese Americans—and, to a large extent, Asian Americans in general—have not been more active in politics:

1. To become a candidate means to take risks, invite criticism, be assertive, and be willing to extol one's virtues. These traits are alien to Chinese culture.

2. Older people remember when discrimination was blatant, and they tell others to be quiet and not attract attention.

3. As noted earlier, many recent immigrants have no experience with democracy and arrive with a general distrust of government.

4. Like many new immigrant groups, Chinese Americans have concentrated on getting ahead economically and educating their children rather than thinking in terms of the larger community.

5. The careers that the brightest students pursue tend to be in business and science rather than law or public administration and, therefore, do not provide preparation for politics.

6. Chinatowns notwithstanding, Chinese and other Asian American groups are dispersed and cannot control the election of even local candidates.

Democrat Tammy Duckworth was named Illinois Director of Veterans' Affairs after an unsuccessfully attempt for Congress. Duckworth, a trained helicopter pilot who lost both her legs in the Iraq War where she rose to the rank of major, is of mixed European, Thai, and Chinese ancestry.

On the other hand, both Democrats and Republicans are increasingly regarding Asian Americans as a future political force in the United States (Gross 1989; Holmes 1996).

Many political observers expect Asian Americans to favor Democratic candidates, as most Latinos and especially African Americans do. Indeed, in the 2000 elections, the majority of Asian Americans favored Democratic candidates, compared with 43 percent of Whites. However, the Republicans, nationally and locally, continue to try to cut into this Democratic preference among these voters. In local politics, it is much easier to see Asian Americans getting involved in city council and school board elections, where they can more readily see the immediate impact of the democratic process on their lives (L. Romney 2004).

Diversity Among Asian Americans

The political activity of Asian Pacific Islanders occurs within a complex segment of the population: Asian Americans who reflect the diversity of their native lands. Asia is a vast region, holding more than half the world's population. The successive waves of immigrants to the United States from that continent have been composed of a large number of nationalities and cultures. In addition to the seven groups listed in Figure 12.2, the Census Bureau enumerates forty-seven groups, as shown in Table 12.2. Given this variety among Asian Pacific Islanders, we can apply to Asian Americans several generalizations made earlier about Native Americans. Both groups are a collection of diverse peoples with distinct linguistic, social, and geographic backgrounds.

TABLE 12.2
Asian Pacific Islander Groups in the United States

Asian	Pacific Islander
Asian Indian	Polynesian
Bangladeshi	Native Hawaiian
Bhutanese	Samoan
Burmese	Tongan
Cambodian	Tahitian
Chinese	Tokelauan
Filipino	Micronesian
Hmong	Guamanian or Chamorro
Indo Chinese	Mariana Islander
Indonesian	Saipanese
Iwo Jiman	Palauan
Japanese	Carolinian
Korean	Kosraean
Laotian	Pohnpeian
Malaysian	Chuukese
Maldivian	Yapese
Nepalese	Marshallese
Okinawan	I-Kiribati
Pakistani	Melanesian
Singaporean	Fijian
Sri Lankan	Papua New Guinean
Taiwanese	Solomon Islander
Thai	Ni-Varnualu
Vietnamese	

Note: Groups as enumerated separately in the 2000 census.

Source: Barnes and Bennett 2002; Grieco 2001.

Asian Americans, like Native Americans, are not evenly distributed across the United States. To lump these people together ignores the sharp differences between them. Any examination of Asian Americans quickly reveals their diversity, which will be apparent as we focus on individual Asian American groups, beginning with the largest group, Asian Indians.

Asian Indians

The second largest Asian American groups (after Chinese Americans) are the immigrants from India and their descendants numbering more than 2.3 million. Sometimes the immigrants from Pakistan, Bangladesh, and Sri Lanka are also included in this group.

Immigration

Like several other Asian immigrant groups, Asian Indians (or East Indians) are recent immigrants. Only 17,000 total came from 1820 to 1965, with the majority of those arriving before 1917. These pioneers were subjected to some of the same anti-Asian measures passed to restrict Chinese immigration. In the ten years after the Immigration and Naturalization Act, which eliminated national quotas, more than 110,000 arrived (Takaki 1989).

Immigration law, although dropping nationality preferences, gave priority to the skilled, so the Asian Indians arriving in the 1960s through the 1980s tended to be urban, educated, and English speaking. Three times the proportion of Asian Indians aged 25 and older had a college degree, compared with the general population. These families experienced a smooth transition from life in India to life in the United States. They usually settled here in urban areas or located near universities or medical centers. Initially, they flocked to the Northeast, but by 1990, California had edged out New York as the state with the largest concentration of Asian Indians. The growth of Silicon Valley information technology furthered the increase of Asian Indian professionals in northern California (Boxall 2001; Mogelonsky 1995).

More recent immigrants, sponsored by earlier immigrant relatives, are displaying less facility with English, and the training they have tends to be less easily adapted to the U.S. workplace. They are more likely to work in service industries, usually with members of their extended families. They are often in positions that many Americans

Reflecting the growth of the Indian American population, the landscape is changing. A Hindu priest makes his way toward the entrance to the largest Hindu temple in the United States, which is located outside Chicago.

reject because of the long hours, the seven-day workweek, and vulnerability to crime. Consequently, Asian Indians are as likely to be cab drivers or managers of motels or convenience stores as they are to be physicians or college teachers. Asian Indians see the service industries as transitional jobs to acclimatize them to the United States and to give them the money they need to become more economically self-reliant (Kalita 2003; Levitt 2004; Varadarajan 1999).

The Present Picture

It is difficult to generalize about Asian Indians because, like all other Asian Americans, they reflect a diverse population. With more than 1 billion people in 2000, India is soon to be the most populous nation in the world. Diversity governs every area. The Indian government recognizes eighteen official languages, each with its own cultural heritage. Some can be written in more than one type of script. Hindus are the majority in India and also among the immigrants to the United States, but significant religious minorities include Sikhs, Muslims, Jains, and Zoroastrians (Kurien 2004).

Religion among Asian Indians presents an interesting picture. Among initial immigrants, religious orthodoxy often is stronger than it is in India. Immigrants try to practice the Hindu and Muslim faiths true to their practices in India rather than joining the Caribbean versions of these major faiths already established in the United States by other immigrant groups. Although other Indian traditions are maintained, older immigrants see challenges not only from U.S. culture but also from pop culture from India, which is imported through motion pictures and magazines. It is a very dynamic situation as the Asian Indian population moves into the twenty-first century (Lessinger 1995; Rangaswamy 2005).

Maintaining traditions within the family household is a major challenge for Indian immigrants to the United States. These ties remain strong, and many Indians see themselves more connected to their relatives 10,000 miles away than Americans are to their kinfolk less than a hundred miles away. Parents are concerned about the erosion of traditional family authority among the desi. **Desi** (pronounced "DAY-see") is a colloquial name for people who trace their ancestry to South Asia, especially India.

Indian children, dressed like their peers, go to fast-food restaurants and eat hamburgers while out on their own, yet both Hindus and Muslims are vegetarian by practice. Sons do not feel the responsibility to the family that tradition dictates. Daughters, whose occupation and marriage could, in India, be closely controlled by the family, assert their right to choose work and, in an even more dramatic break from tradition, select a husband.

In "Research Focus," we consider one cultural practice faced by Indian and some other immigrant groups not a part of American mainstream culture: arranged marriages.

Filipino Americans

Little has been written about the Filipinos, although they are the third-largest Asian American group in the United States, with 2.2 million people now living here. Social science literature considers them Asians for geographic reasons, but physically and culturally, they also reflect centuries of Spanish colonial rule and the more recent colonial and occupation governments of the United States.

Immigration Patterns

Immigration from the Philippines is documented during the eighteenth and nineteenth centuries; it was relatively small but significant enough to create a "Manila Village" along the Louisiana coast around 1750. Increasing numbers of Filipino immigrants came as American nationals when, in 1899, the United States gained possession of the Philippine

 ASK Yourself

What are some of the advantages that can been seen in arranged marriages?

desi
Colloquial name for people who trace their ancestry to South Asia, especially India and Pakistan.

Focus Research Focus Research Fo

ARRANGED MARRIAGES IN AMERICA

The question becomes not does he or she love me but who do my parents want me to marry. An **arranged marriage** is when others choose the marital partners not based on any preexisting mutual attraction. Indeed, typically in arranged marriages the couple does not even know one another.

The idea of arranged marriages seems strange to most youth growing up in the United States whose culture romanticizes finding Mr. or Ms. Right. In an arranged marriage, the boy and girl start off on neutral ground with no expectations of each other. Then understanding develops between them as the relationship matures. The couple selected is assumed to be compatible because they are chosen from very similar social, economic, and cultural backgrounds. In an arranged marriage, the couple works to achieve the mutual happiness they expect to find. In contrast, in a romantic or sentimental marriage, couples start off from a high ground of dreams and illusions where there is little likelihood for things to get better and there are great chances of failure, as some of the dreams do not materialize after marriage.

Historically arranged marriages are not unusual and even today are common in many parts of Asia and Africa. In cultures where arranged marriage is common, young people tend to be socialized to expect and look forward to such unions. But what happens in cultures that send very different messages? For example, immigrants from India, Pakistan, and Bangladesh may desire that their children enter an arranged union, but their children are growing up in culture where most of their schoolmates are obsessed with dating as a prelude to marriage and endlessly discuss the latest episodes of *Bachelor* and *Bachelorette*.

Studies of young people in countries like Canada and the United States whose parents still cling to the tradition of arranging their children's marriage document the

---

Islands at the conclusion of the Spanish-American War. In 1934, the islands gained commonwealth status. The Philippines gained their independence in 1948 and with it lost their unrestricted immigration rights. Despite the close ties that remained, immigration was sharply restricted to only 50 to 100 people annually until the 1965 Immigration Act lifted these quotas. Before the restrictions were removed, pineapple growers in Hawaii lobbied successfully to import Filipino workers to the islands.

Besides serving as colonial subjects of the United States, Filipinos played another role in this country. The U.S. military accepted Filipinos in selected positions. In particular, the Navy put Filipino citizens to work in kitchens. Filipino veterans of World War II believed that their U.S. citizenship would be expedited. This proved untrue; the problem was only partially resolved by a 1994 federal court ruling. However, many of these veterans felt they were regarded not as former Navy employees but as unwanted immigrants (Espiritu 1996; Posadas 1999).

Filipino immigration can be divided into four distinct periods:

arranged marriage
Others choose one's marital partners not based on any pre-existing mutual attraction.

1. The first generation, immigrating in the 1920s, was mostly male and employed in agricultural labor.

2. A second group, also arriving in the early twentieth century, immigrated to Hawaii to serve as contract workers on Hawaii's sugar plantations.

challenges this represents. Many young people do still embrace the tradition of their parents. As one first-year female Princeton student of Indian ancestry puts it, "In a lot of ways it's easier. I don't have pressure to look for a boyfriend" (Herschthal 2004). Young people like her will look to their parents and other relatives to finalize a mate or even accept a match with a partner who has been selected in the country of their parents. Systematic, nationwide studies are lacking, but available research points to a trend away from arranged marriages toward romantic marriages even when the couples entered such unions over family objections.

Change has brought with it some variations as expectation for formally arranged marriages has been modified to *assisted marriages* in which parents identify a limited number of possible mates based on what is referred to as "bio-data"—screening for caste, family background, and geography. Children get final veto power but rarely head out on their own when seeking a mate. Young men and women may date on their own but, when it comes to marrying, they limit themselves to a very narrow field of eligibles brought to them by their parents. The combination of arranged and assisted marriages has meant that Indian immigrants have the highest rates of ethnic endogamy of any major immigrant group in the United States—about 90 percent in-group marriage in 2003.

For thousands of young people the pattern is not bringing a possible spouse home to meet the future in-laws but the other way around. Her father introduced Leona Singh of California, 25 years old, to an appropriate future mate living in Iowa. They met in the company of relatives and then went out alone. They married several months later when they felt they were "90 percent certain." Years later she looked back, "From the beginning, I felt there was a physical chemistry, but it took years to develop a mature bond, and I guess you could call that love" (Bellafante 2005 A15). ▪

Sources: Bellafante 2005; Herschthal 2004; Talbane and Hasanau 2000; Zaidi and Shuraydi 2002.

3. The post–World War II arrivals included many war veterans and wives of U.S. soldiers.

4. The newest immigrants, who include many professionals (physicians, nurses, and others), arrived under the 1965 Immigration Act (Min 1995; Posadas 1999).

As in other Asian groups, the people are diverse. Besides these stages of immigration, the Filipinos can also be defined by various states of immigration (different languages, regions of origin, and religions), distinctions that sharply separate people in their homeland as well. In the Philippines and among Filipino immigrants to the United States, eight distinct languages with an estimated 200 dialects are spoken. Yet assimilation is under way; a 1995 survey showed that 47 percent of younger Filipino Americans speak only English and do not speak Tagalog, the primary language of the Philippine people (Kang 1996; Pido 1986).

The Present Picture

The Filipino population increased dramatically when restrictions on immigration were eased in 1965. More than two-thirds of the new arrivals qualified for entry as professional and technical workers, but like Koreans, they have often worked at jobs ranked below those they left in the Philippines. Surprisingly, U.S.-born Filipinos often

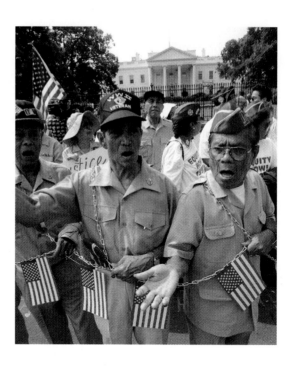

Filipino American World War II veterans protested in 1997 for full veterans' benefits for Filipinos who served in World War II.

have less formal schooling and lower job status than the newer arrivals. They come from poorer families that are unable to afford higher education, and they have been relegated to unskilled work, including migrant farm work. Their poor economic background means that they have little start-up capital for businesses. Therefore, unlike other Asian American groups, Filipinos have not developed small business bases such as retail or service outlets that capitalize on their ethnic culture.

Yet there is a significant segment of the immigration from the Philippines that constitutes a more professional educated class in the area of health professionals. Although a positive human resource for the United States, it has long been a brain drain on the medical establishment of the Philippines. This is apparent when we consider areas in the United States that reflect Filipino settlement in the last forty years. For example, in metropolitan Chicago, Filipino Americans have household incomes 30 percent higher than the general population and higher than that of Asian Indians. When the United States ceased giving preference to physicians from abroad, doctors in the Philippines began to enter the United States retrained as nurses, which dramatically illustrates the incredible income differences between the United States and the Philippines (Espiritu and Wolf 2001; Kim 2006; Lau 2006b; Zarembro 2004).

Despite their numbers, no significant single national Filipino social organization has formed, for several reasons. First, Filipinos' strong loyalty to family (*sa pamilya*) and church, particularly Roman Catholicism, works against time-consuming efforts to create organizations that include a broad spectrum of the Filipino community. Second, their diversity makes forming ties here problematic. Divisions along regional, religious, and linguistic lines present in the Philippines persist in the United States. Third, although Filipinos have organized many groups, they tend to be clublike or fraternal. They do not seek to represent the general Filipino population and, therefore, remain largely invisible to Anglos. Fourth, although Filipinos initially stayed close to events in their homeland, they show every sign of seeking involvement in broader non-Filipino organizations and avoiding group exclusiveness. The two terms of Filipino American Benjamin Cayetano as governor of Hawaii from 1994 to 2002 are an example of such involvement in mainstream political organizations (Bonus 2000; Espiritu 1996; Kang 1996; Lau 2006b; Posadas 1999).

Southeast Asian Americans

The people of Southeast Asia—Vietnamese, Cambodians, and Laotians—were part of the former French Indochinese Union. *Southeast Asian* is an umbrella term used for convenience; the peoples of these areas are ethnically and linguistically diverse. Ethnic Laotians constitute only half of the Laotian people, for example; a significant number of Mon-Khmer, Yao, and Hmong form minorities. Numbering more than 2.1 million in 2005, Vietnamese Americans are the largest group, with 1.4 million members, or 11 percent of the total Asian American population (see Figure 12.2).

The Refugees

The problem of U.S. involvement in Indochina did not end when all U.S. personnel were withdrawn from South Vietnam in 1975. The final tragedy was the reluctant welcome given to the refugees from Vietnam, Cambodia, and Laos by Americans and people of other nations. One week after the evacuation of Vietnam in April 1975, a Gallup poll reported that 54 percent of Americans were against giving sanctuary to the Asian refugees, with 36 percent in favor and 11 percent undecided. The primary objection to Vietnamese immigration was that it would further increase unemployment (Schaefer and Schaefer 1975).

Many Americans offered to house refugees in their homes, but others declared that the United States had too many Asians already and was in danger of losing its "national character." This attitude toward the Indochinese has been characteristic of the feeling that Harvard sociologist David Riesman called the **gook syndrome**. *Gook* is a derogatory term for an Asian, and the syndrome refers to the tendency to stereotype these people in the worst possible light. Riesman believed that the American news media created an unflattering image of the South Vietnamese and their government, leading the American people to believe they were not worth saving (Luce 1975).

The initial 135,000 Vietnamese refugees who fled in 1975 were joined by more than a million running from the later fighting and religious persecution that plagued Indochina. The United States accepted about half of the refugees, some of them the so-called boat people, primarily Vietnamese of ethnic Chinese background, who took to the ocean in overcrowded vessels, hoping that some ship would pick them up and offer sanctuary. Hundreds of thousands were placed in other nations or remain in overcrowded refugee camps administered by the United Nations.

The Present Picture

Like other immigrants, the refugees from Vietnam, Laos, and Cambodia face a difficult adjustment. Few expect to return to their homeland for visits, and fewer expect to return there permanently. Therefore, many look to the United States as their permanent home and the home of their children. However, the adult immigrants still accept jobs well below their occupational positions in Southeast Asia; geographic mobility has been accompanied by downward social mobility. For example, only a small fraction of refugees employed as managers in Vietnam have been employed in similar positions in the United States.

Language is also a factor in adjustment by the refugees; a person trained as a manager cannot hold that position in the United States until he or she is fairly fluent in English. The available data indicate that refugees from Vietnam have increased their earnings rapidly, often by working long hours. Partly because Southeast Asians comprise significantly different subgroups, assimilation and acceptance are not likely to occur at the same rate for all.

Although most refugee children spoke no English upon their arrival here, they have done extremely well in school. Studies indicate that immigrant parents place

gook syndrome
David Riesman's phrase describing Americans' tendency to stereotype Asians and to regard them as all alike and undesirable.

Vietnamese Americans are sometimes divided over their loyalty to their "home country." Some Vietnamese in the United States make a point of displaying the "heritage flag" on the left that was last used by South Vietnam. They regard those who display the flag on the right, the flag of Vietnam and formerly North Vietnam, as embracing the past injustices committed under communism.

great emphasis on education and are pleased by the prospect of their children going to college—something very rare in their homelands. The children do very well with this encouragement, which is not unlike that offered by Mexican immigrants to their children, as we discussed in Chapter 10. It remains to be seen whether this motivation will decline as the next young generation looks more to their American peers as role models.

The picture for young Southeast Asians in the United States is not completely pleasant. Crime is present in almost all ethnic groups, but some fear that in this case it has two very ugly aspects. Some of this crime may represent reprisals for the war: anti-Communists and communist sympathizers who continue their conflicts here. At the same time, gangs are emerging as young people seek the support of close-knit groups even if they engage in illegal and violent activities. Of course, this pattern is very similar to that followed by all groups in the United States. Indeed, defiance of authority can be regarded as a sign of assimilation. Another unpleasant but well-documented aspect of the present picture is the series of violent episodes directed at Southeast Asians by Whites and others expressing resentment over their employment or even their mere presence (Alvord 2000; Zhou and Bankston 1998).

In contrast to its inaction concerning earlier immigrant groups, the federal government involved itself conspicuously in locating homes for the refugees from Vietnam, Cambodia, and Laos. Pressured by many communities afraid of being overwhelmed by immigrants, government agencies attempted to disperse the refugees throughout the nation. Such efforts failed, mostly because the refugees, like European immigrants before them, sought out their compatriots. As a result, Southeast Asian communities and neighborhoods have become visible, especially in California and Texas. In such areas, where immigrants from Asia have reestablished some cultural practices from their homeland, a more pluralistic solution to their adjustment seems a possible alternative to complete assimilation. Also, Southeast Asians living outside metropolitan areas may make frequent trips to major urban areas, where they can stock up on food, books, and even videotapes in their native language (Aguillar-San Juan 1998; Mui 2001).

In 1995, the United States initiated normal diplomatic relations with Vietnam, which is leading to more movement between the nations. Gradually, Vietnamese Americans are returning to visit but generally not to take up permanent residence. **Viet Kieu**, Vietnamese living abroad, are making the return—some 270,000 in 1996 compared with only 80,000 four years earlier. Generational issues are also merging as time passes. In Vietnamese communities from California to Virginia, splits emerge over a powerful symbol—under what flag to unite a nationality. Merchants, home residents, and college Vietnamese student organizations take a stand by whether they decide to display the yellow with red bars flag of the now-defunct South Vietnam, sometimes called the "heritage flag," or the red with yellow star flag of the current (and communist) Vietnam (Avila 2004; Lamb 1997).

Meanwhile, for the more than 1.4 million Vietnamese Americans who remain, settlement patterns here vary. Little Saigons can be found in major cities in the United States long after the former South Vietnam capital of Saigon became Ho Chi Min City. Like many other immigrant groups in the second generation, some have moved into suburbs where residential patterns tend to be rather dispersed but one can still spot mini-malls with Vietnamese restaurants and grocery stores—some even sporting a sloping red-tiled roof. Other Vietnamese Americans remain in rural areas such as the Gulf Coast fisherman left homeless by Hurricane Katrina in 2005 (Aguilar-San Juan 2005; M. Cooper 2005).

Case Study: A Hmong Community

Wausau (population 38,000) is a community in rural Wisconsin, best known, perhaps, for the insurance company bearing its name. To sociologists, it is distinctive for its sizable Hmong (pronounced "Mong") population. Hmong come from rural areas of Laos and Vietnam where they had been recruited to work for the CIA during the Vietnam War. This association made life very difficult for them after the United States pulled out. Hence, many immigrated and the United States has a relatively open policy to their becoming permanent residents. Wausau finds itself with the greatest percentage of Hmong of any city in Wisconsin. Hmong and a few other Southeast Asians account for 12 percent of the city's population and 25 percent of its public school students (Chan 1994: T. Jones 2003; Torriero 2004a).

The Hmong, who now number 186,000, immigrated to the United States from Laos and Vietnam after the end of the U.S. involvement in Vietnam in April 1975. Like other refugees at the time, the first Hmong came to Wausau invited by religious groups. Others followed as they found the surrounding agricultural lands were places they could find work. Coming from a very rural peasant society, the immigrants faced dramatic adjustment upon arrival in the United States (Hein 2000; T. Jones 2003).

Viet Kieu
Vietnamese living abroad such as in the United States.

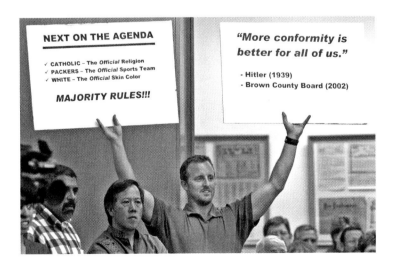

Despite objections by the Hmong and sympathetic White citizens, a Wisconsin county with a large presence of Hmong made English the official language—a move with little practical significance but one that spoke loudly in terms of symbolism.

Wausau school officials believed that progress in teaching the Hmong English was stymied because the newcomers continued to associate with each other and spoke only their native tongue. In the fall of 1993, the Wausau school board decided to distribute the Hmong and other poor students more evenly by restructuring its elementary schools in a scheme that required two-way busing.

Recalls of elected officials are rare in the United States, but in December 1993, opponents of the busing plan organized a special election that led to the removal of the five board members. This left the Wausau board with a majority who opposed the busing plan that had integrated Asian American youngsters into mostly White elementary schools. By 2006, neighborhood schools played an important role in Wausau so that among elementary schools, the proportion of Hmong children ranged from 2 percent Hmong, to 52 percent (Seibert 2002; Wausau School District 2006).

How events will unfold in Wausau are unclear. However, positive signs are identifiable in Wausau and other centers of Hmong life in the United States. Immigrants and their children are moving into nonagricultural occupations. Enrollment in citizenship classes is growing. The Wausau Area Hmong Mutual Association, funded by a federal grant and the local United Way, offers housing assistance. Although many struggle to make a go of it economically, large numbers are able to move off public assistance. Language barriers and lack of formal schooling still are barriers encountered by older Hmong residents, but the younger generation is emerging to face some of the same identity and assimilation questions experienced by other Asian American groups (Peckham 2002).

The challenges facing the Hmong extend well beyond Wausau, Wisconsin. In other cities with concentrations of Hmong immigrants, disputes break out over contemporary U.S. policies. Hmong were recruited by the U.S. military intelligence in the Vietnam War to gather information about communists. To this day, occasional violence occurs in the Hmong community over whether the United States might lift trade barriers with the communist-run government of Laos. Finally in 2004, the United States, recognizing the special role that the Hmong people played in the Vietnam conflict era, agreed to accept thousands of Hmong people that had been in overseas refugee camps for thirty years (Aglionby 2004; Torriero 2004b).

Korean Americans

The population of Korean Americans, with more than 1.2 million in 2005 (see Figure 12.2), is now the fifth largest Asian American group, yet Korean Americans often are overlooked in studies in favor of groups such as Chinese Americans and Japanese Americans, who have a longer historical tradition.

Historical Background

Today's Korean American community is the result of three waves of immigration. The initial wave of a little more than 7,000 immigrants came to the United States between 1903 and 1910, when laborers migrated to Hawaii. Under Japanese colonial rule (1910–1945), Korean migration was halted except for a few hundred "picture brides" allowed to join their prospective husbands.

The second wave took place during and after the Korean War, accounting for about 14,000 immigrants from 1951 through 1964. Most of these immigrants were war orphans and wives of American servicemen. Little research has been done on these first two periods of immigration.

The third wave was initiated by the passage of the 1965 Immigration Act, which made it much easier for Koreans to immigrate. In the four years before passage of the act, Koreans accounted for only 7 of every 1,000 immigrants. In the first four years after the act's passage, 38 of every 1,000 immigrants to the United States were Korean. This third wave, which continues today, reflects the admission priorities set up in the 1965 immigration law. These immigrants have been well educated and have arrived in the United States with professional skills (Min 1995).

However, many of the most recent immigrants must at least initially settle for positions of lower responsibility than those they held in Korea and must pass through a period of "exigency" or disenchantment, as described in Chapter 2. The problems documented reflect the pain of adjustment: stress, loneliness, alcoholism, family strife, and mental disorders. Korean American immigrants who accompanied their parents to the United States when young now occupy a middle, marginal position between the cultures of Korea and the United States. They have also been called the **ilchomose**, or "1.5 generation." Today, they are middle-aged, remain bilingual and bicultural, and tend to form the professional class in the Korean American community (Hurh 1998; Kim 2006).

The Present Picture

Today's young Korean Americans face many of the cultural conflicts common to any initial generation born in a new country. The parents may speak the native tongue, but the signs on the road to opportunity are in the English language, and the road itself runs through U.S. culture. It is very difficult to maintain a sense of Korean culture in the United States; the host society is not particularly helpful. Although the United States fought a war there and U.S. troops remain in South Korea, Korean culture is very foreign to contemporary Americans. In the few studies of attitudes toward Koreans, White Americans respond with vague, negative attitudes or simply lump Korean Americans with other Asian groups.

Studies by social scientists indicate that Korean Americans face many problems typical for immigrants, such as difficulties with language. In Los Angeles, home to the largest concentration, more than 100 churches have only Korean-language services, and local television stations feature several hours of Korean programs. The Korean immigrants' high level of education should help them cope with the challenge. Although Korean Americans stress conventional Western schooling as a means to success, Korean schools have also been established in major cities. Typically operated on Saturday afternoons, they offer classes in Korean history, customs, music, and language to help students maintain their cultural identity (Abelmann and Lie 1995; Hurh and Kim 1982, 1984; D. Lee 1992).

ilchomose
The 1.5 generation of Korean Americans-those who immigrated into the United States as children.

A large proportion of Asian Americans work as shop managers in neighborhoods serving minority clientele. Although typically the relationships are businesslike, for many low-income residents their only interaction with local merchants is with Asian Americans including this Korean American, shop owner pictured here.

Korean American women commonly participate in the labor force, as do many other Asian American women. About 60 percent of U.S.-born Korean American women and half the women born abroad work in the labor force. These figures may not seem striking compared with the data for White women, but the cultural differences make the figures more significant. Korean women come here from a family system with established, well-defined marital roles: The woman is expected to serve as homemaker and mother only. Although these roles are carried over to the United States, because of their husbands' struggles to establish themselves, women are pressed to help support their families financially as well.

Many Korean American men begin small service or retail businesses and gradually involve their wives in the business. Wages do not matter as the household mobilizes to make a profitable enterprise out of a marginal business. Under economic pressure, Korean American women must move away from traditional cultural roles. However, the move is only partial; studies show that despite the high rate of participation in the labor force by Korean immigrant wives, first-generation immigrant couples continue in sharply divided gender roles in other aspects of daily living.

Korean American businesses are seldom major operations; most are small. They do benefit from a special form of development capital (or cash) used to subsidize businesses, called a **kye** (pronounced "kay"). Korean Americans pool their money through the kye, an association that grants members money on a rotating basis to allow them to gain access to additional capital. Kyes depend on trust and are not protected by laws or insurance, as bank loans are. Kyes work as follows. Say, for example, that twelve people agree to contribute $500 a year. Then, once a year, one of these individuals receives $6,000. Few records are kept because the entire system is built on trust and friendship. Rotating credit associations are not unique to Korean Americans; West Indians and Ethiopians have used them in the United States, for example. Not all Korean business entrepreneurs use the kye, but it does represent a significant source of capital. A 1984 Chicago survey revealed that 34 percent of Korean merchants relied on a kye.

In the early 1990s, nationwide attention was given to the friction between Korean Americans and other subordinate groups, primarily African Americans but also Hispanics. In New York City, Los Angeles, and Chicago, Korean American merchants confronted African Americans who were allegedly robbing them. The African American neighborhood groups sometimes responded with hostility to what they perceived as the disrespect and arrogance of the Korean American entrepreneurs toward their Black customers. Such friction is not new; earlier generations of Jewish, Italian, and Arab merchants encountered similar hostility from what to outsiders seems an unlikely source, another oppressed subordinate group. The contemporary conflict was dramatized in Spike Lee's 1989 movie *Do the Right Thing*, in which African Americans and Korean Americans clashed. The situation arose because Korean Americans are the latest immigrant group prepared to cater to the needs of the inner city that has been abandoned by those who have moved up the economic ladder (Hurh 1998; Kang and Richardson 2002).

The tension that can arise between subordinate groups gained national attention during the 1992 riots in south central Los Angeles. In that city's poor areas, the only shops in which to buy groceries, liquor, or gasoline are owned by Korean immigrants. They have largely replaced the White business owners who left the ghetto area after the 1965 Watts riot. African Americans were well aware of the dominant role Korean Americans played in their local retail market. The 1991 fatal shooting of a 15-year-old Black girl by a Korean grocer in a dispute over a payment for orange juice had previously fueled some Blacks' resentment of the Koreans. The resentment grew when the grocer, convicted of manslaughter, had her prison sentence waived by a judge in favor of a five-year probation period.

kye
Rotating credit system used by Korean Americans to subsidize the start of businesses.

The 1992 riots focused in part on retailers in south central Los Angeles and, therefore, on Korean Americans. During the unrest, 2,000 Korean businesses valued at $400 million were destroyed. Desire to succeed had led Korean Americans to the inner city, where they did not face competition from Whites. But it also meant that they had to deal on a daily basis with the frustration of another minority group. As a direct outgrowth of the violence and tension, numerous cross-ethnic groups have been organized in Los Angeles and other cities, such as Chicago and New York City, to improve relations between Korean Americans and other subordinate groups (Yi 2006).

Among Korean Americans, the church is the most visible organization holding the group together. Half the immigrants were affiliated with Christian churches before immigrating. One study of Koreans in Chicago and Los Angeles found that 70 percent were affiliated with Korean ethnic churches, mostly Presbyterian, with small numbers of Catholics and Methodists. Korean ethnic churches are the fastest-growing segment of the Presbyterian and Methodist faiths. The church performs an important function, apart from its religious one, in giving Korean Americans a sense of attachment and a practical way to meet other Korean Americans. The churches are much more than simply sites for religious services; they assume multiple secular roles for the Korean community. As the second generation seeks a church with which to affiliate as adults, they may find the ethnic church and its Korean-language services less attractive, but for now, the fellowship in which Korean Americans participate is both spiritual and ethnic (Kwon et al. 2001).

Haoles
Hawaiian term for Caucasians.

Hawaii and Its People

The entire state of Hawaii (or Hawai'i) appears to be the complete embodiment of cultural diversity. Nevertheless, despite a dramatic blending of different races living together, prejudice, discrimination, and pressure to assimilate are very much present in Hawaii. As we will see, life on the island is much closer to that in the rest of the country than to the ideal of a pluralistic society. Hawaii's population is unquestionably diverse, as shown in Figure 12.3. To grasp contemporary social relationships, we must first understand the historical circumstances that brought races together on the islands: the various Asian peoples and the **Haoles** (pronounced "hah-oh-lehs"), the term often used to refer to Whites in Hawaii.

Historical Background

Geographically remote, Hawaii was initially populated by Polynesian people who had their first contact with Europeans in 1778, when English explorer Captain James Cook arrived. The Hawaiians (who killed Cook) tolerated the subsequent arrival of plantation operators and missionaries. Fortunately, the Hawaiian people were united under a monarchy and

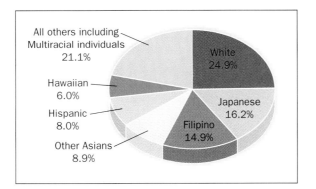

FIGURE 12.3   Hawaii: Racial Composition, 2005

Source: Author based on the American Community Survey 2005, Bureau of the Census.

received respect from the European immigrants, a respect that developed into a spirit of goodwill. Slavery was never introduced, even during the colonial period, as it was in so many areas of the Western Hemisphere. Nevertheless, the effect of the White arrival on the Hawaiians themselves was disastrous. Civil warfare and disease had reduced the number of full-blooded natives to fewer than 30,000 by 1900, and the number is probably well under 10,000 now. Meanwhile, large sugarcane plantations imported laborers from China, Portugal, Japan, and, in the early 1900s, the Philippines, Korea, and Puerto Rico.

In 1893, a revolution encouraged by foreign commercial interests overthrew the monarchy. During the revolution, the United States landed troops, and five years later, Hawaii was annexed as a territory to the United States. The 1900 Organic Act guaranteed racial equality, but foreign rule dealt a devastating psychological blow to the proud Hawaiian people. American rule had mixed effects on relations between the races. Citizenship laws granted civil rights to all those born on the islands, not just the wealthy Haoles. However, the anti-Asian laws still applied, excluding the Chinese and Japanese from political participation.

The twentieth century witnessed Hawaii's transition from a plantation frontier to the fiftieth state and an integral part of the national economy. During that transition, Hawaii became a strategic military outpost, although that role has had only a limited effect on race relations. Even the attack on Pearl Harbor had little influence on Japanese Americans in Hawaii.

The Present Picture

Hawaii has achieved some fame for its good race relations. Tourists, who are predominantly White, have come from the mainland and have seen and generally accepted the racial harmony. Admittedly, Waikiki Beach, where large numbers of tourists congregate, is atypical of the islands, but even their tourists cannot ignore the differences in intergroup relations. If they look closely they will see that the low-wage workers in the resorts and tourist industry tend to be disproportionately of Asian descent (Adler and Adler 2005).

One clear indication of the multicultural nature of the islands is the degree of exogamy: marrying outside one's own group. The out-group marriage rate varies annually but seems to be stabilizing; about 45 percent of all marriages performed in the state involving residents are exogamous. The rate varies by group, from a low of 41 percent among Haoles to 62 percent among Chinese Americans (Hawaii Department of Health 2001, Table 80).

A 2001 march of 1,500 people through downtown Honolulu protesting that insufficient progress has been made in the Hawaiian sovereignty movement. Note they are flying the Hawaiian state flag upside down.

A closer look shows that equality between the people is not absolute, let alone between the races as groups. The pineapple and sugarcane plantation legacy persists. As recently as 1972, an estimate placed 97 percent of Hawaiian workers in the employ of forty landholders. One estate alone owned nearly one-tenth of the state's territory. Native Hawaiians tend to be least well off, working land they do not own. Japanese Americans and Haoles dominate the economy. The **AJAs** (Americans of Japanese ancestry, as they are called in Hawaii) are especially important in education, where they account for nearly 58 percent of teachers, and in politics, where they dominate. The political activity of the AJAs certainly contrasts to that of mainland Japanese Americans. The majority of the state legislators are AJAs. Chinese Americans have been successful in business in Hawaii, but almost all top positions are filled by Haoles. Recent immigrants from Asia and, more significantly, even long-term residents of Filipino and Hawaiian descent showed little evidence of sharing in Hawaii's overall picture of affluence (Kaser 1977; W. Turner 1972; Wright and Gardner 1983).

Prejudice and discrimination are not alien to Hawaii. Attitudinal surveys show definite racial preferences and sensitivity to color differences. Housing surveys taken before the passage of civil rights legislation showed that many people were committed to nondiscrimination, but racial preferences were still present. Certain groups sometimes dominate residential neighborhoods, but there are no racial ghettos. The various racial groups are not distributed uniformly among the islands, but they are clustered rather than sharply segregated.

Discrimination by exclusive social clubs exists but is diminishing. Groups such as the Rotary and Lions' clubs opened their doors to Asians in Hawaii before they did on the mainland. Undoubtedly, Hawaii has gradually absorbed the mainland's racial consciousness, but a contrast between the islands and the rest of the nation remains. Evidence of racial harmony is much more abundant. Hawaii has never known forced school segregation, Jim Crow laws, slavery, or laws prohibiting racial intermarriage.

The multiracial character of the islands will not change quickly, but the identity of the native Hawaiians has already been overwhelmed. Though rich in cultural heritage, they tend to be very poor and often view the U.S. occupation as the beginning of their cultural and economic downfall. For centuries they traditionally placed the earthly remains of their loved ones in isolated caves. However, as these "archaeological sites" were found by Haoles, the funeral remains made their way to the Bishop Museum, which is the national historical museum located in Honolulu. Now Native Hawaiians are using the Native American Graces and Protection Act (NAGPRA) described in Chapter 6 to get the remains back and rebury them appropriately (LaDuke 2006).

"*E Heluuelu Kaqkou,*" Nako'hlani Warrington tells her third graders ("Let's read together"). She has no need to translate because is teaching at the public immersion school where all instruction is in the Hawaiian language. Not too long ago it was assumed that Hawaiian would only be spoken by linguistic scholars, but efforts to revive it in general conversation have resulted in its use well beyond "Aloha." In 1983, only 1,500 people were considered native speakers; now native speakers number 68,000. This goes well beyond symbolic ethnicity. Language perpetuity is being combined with a solid grade school education (Edles 2004; Staton 2004b).

The **sovereignty movement** is the effort by the indigenous people of Hawaii to secure a measure of self-government and restoration of their lands. Its roots and significance to the people are very similar to the sovereignty efforts by tribal people on the continental United States. The growing sovereignty movement has also sought restoration of the native Hawaiian land that has been lost to Anglos over the last century or compensation for it. Sometimes, the native Hawaiians successfully form alliances with environmental groups that want to halt further commercial development on the islands. In 1996, a native Hawaiian vote was held seeking a response to the question, "Shall the Hawaiian people elect delegates to propose a native Hawaiian government?" The results indicated that

AJAs
Americans of Japanese ancestry in Hawaii.

sovereignty movement
Effort by the indigenous people of Hawaii to secure a measure of self-government and restoration of their lands.

panethnicity
The development of solidarity between ethnic subgroups, as reflected in the terms Hispanic or Asian American.

73 percent voting were in favor of such a government structure. Since then, the state Office of Hawaiian Affairs has sought to create a registry of Hawaiians that is only about halfway to having all the estimated 200,000 people of significant Hawaiian descent on the islands to come forward (Cart 2001; Staton 2004a; Ward 1996).

Up to the present, Hawaii's congressional delegation has sought passage of the Native Hawaiian Government Reorganization Act, or the Akaka Bill as it is called after the state Senator's Daniel Akaka. It would give people of Hawaiian ancestry more say over resources, would provide affordable housing, take steps to preserve culture, and create a means by which they could better express their grievances. A recent vote in 2006 passed the House but fell short by four votes of overcoming a legislative roadblock to prevent it from even being discussed on the floor of the Senate (Akaka 2006; Niesse 2006).

In an absolute sense, Hawaii is not a racial paradise. Certain occupations and even social classes tend to be dominated by a single racial group. Hawaii is not immune to intolerance, and it is expected that the people will not totally resist prejudice as the island's isolation is reduced. However, newcomers to the islands do set aside some of their old stereotypes and prejudices. The future of race relations in Hawaii is uncertain, but relative to the mainland and much of the world, Hawaii's race relations are characterized more by harmony than by discord.

Conclusion

Despite the diversity among groups of Asian Americans or Asian Pacific Islanders, they have spent generations being treated as a monolithic group. Out of similar experiences have come panethnic identities in which people share a self-image, as do African Americans or Whites of European descent. As we noted in Chapter 1, **panethnicity** is the development of solidarity between ethnic subgroups. Are Asian Americans finding a panethnic identity? It is true that, in the United States, extremely different Asian nationalities have been lumped together in past discrimination and present stereotyping. Asian Americans now see the need to unify their diverse subgroups. After centuries of animosity between ethnic groups in Asia, any feelings of community among Asian Americans must develop anew here; they bring none with them.

Asian Americans are a rapidly growing group, with about 13 million now living in the United States. Despite striking differences between them, they are often viewed as if they arrived all at once and from one culture. Also, they are often characterized as a successful or model minority. However, individual cases of success and some impressive group data do not imply that the diverse group of peoples who make up the Asian American community are uniformly successful. Indeed, despite high levels of formal schooling, Asian Americans earn far less than Whites with comparable education and continue to be victims of discriminatory employment practices.

The diversity within the Asian American community belies the similarity suggested by the panethnic label *Asian American*. Chinese and Japanese Americans share a history of several generations in the United States. Filipinos are veterans of a half-century of direct U.S. colonization and a cooperative role with the military. In contrast, Vietnamese, Koreans, and Japanese are associated in a negative way with three wars. Korean Americans come from a nation that still has a major U.S. military presence and a persisting "cold war" mentality. Korean Americans and Chinese Americans have taken on middleman roles, whereas Filipinos, Asian Indians, and Japanese Americans tend to avoid the ethnic enclave pattern.

Who are the Asian Americans? This chapter has begun to answer that question by focusing on four of the larger groups: Asian Indians, Filipino Americans, Southeast Asian Americans, and Korean Americans. Hawaii is a useful model because its harmonious social relationships cross racial lines. Although it is not an interracial paradise, Hawaii does illustrate that, given proper historical and economic conditions, continuing conflict is not inevitable. Chinese and Japanese Americans, the subjects of Chapter 13, have experienced problems in American society despite striving to achieve economic and social equality with the dominant culture.

Key Terms

AJAs 347

arranged marriage 336

desi 335

gook syndrome 339

Haoles 345

ilchomose 343

kye 344

middlemen minorities 328

model or ideal minority 325

panethnicity 348

racial profiling 331

set-asides 329

sovereignty movement 347

Viet Kieu 341

yellow peril 330

Review Questions

1. How is the model minority image a disservice to both Asian Americans and other subordinate racial and ethnic groups?

2. In what respects has the mass media image of Asian Americans been both undifferentiated and negative?

3. How has the tendency of many Korean Americans to help each other been an asset but also been viewed with suspicion by those outside their community?

4. What critical events or legislative acts increased each Asian American group's immigration into the United States?

5. To what degree do race relations in Hawaii offer both promise and a chilling dose of reality to the future of race and ethnicity on the mainland?

Critical Thinking

1. How is the model minority image reinforced by images in the media?

2. Coming of age is difficult for anyone, given the ambiguities of adolescence in the United States. How is it doubly difficult for the children of immigrants? How do you think the immigrants themselves, such as those from Asia, view this process?

3. *American Indians*, *Hispanics*, and *Asian Americans* are all convenient terms to refer to diverse groups of people. Do you see these broad umbrella terms as being more appropriate for one group than for the others?

Internet Connections—Research Navigator™

Follow the instructions found on page 35 of this text to access the features of Research Navigator™. Once at the Web site, enter your Login Name and Password. Then, to use the ContentSelect database, enter keywords such as "arranged marriages," "desi," and "Hmong," and the search engine will supply relevant and recent scholarly and popular press publications. Use the *New York Times* Search-by-Subject Archive to find recent news articles related to sociology, and the Link Library feature to locate relevant Web links organized by the key terms associated with this chapter.

13 Chinese Americans and Japanese Americans

CHAPTER OUTLINE

Chinese Americans

■ **RESEARCH FOCUS**
Chinese Christians or Christian Chinese?

Japanese Americans

■ **LISTEN TO OUR VOICES**
"From Kawasaki to Chicago"
by Miku Ishii

Remnants of Prejudice and Discrimination

Conclusion

Key Terms/Review Questions/
Critical Thinking/Internet Connections—
Research Navigator™

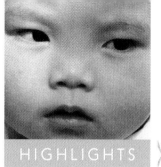

PRESENT-DAY CHINESE AMERICANS ARE DESCENDANTS OF both pre–Exclusion Act immigrants and those who immigrated after World War II. Although Chinese Americans are associated with Chinatown and its glitter of tourism, this facade hides the poverty of the newly arrived Chinese and the discontent of the U.S.-born Chinese Americans. Japanese Americans encountered discrimination and ill treatment in the early twentieth century. The involuntary wartime internment of 113,000 Japanese Americans was the result of sentencing without charge or trial. During wartime, merely to be of Japanese ancestry was reason enough to be suspected of treason. A little more than a generation later, Japanese Americans did very well, with high educational and occupational attainment. Today, Chinese Americans and Japanese Americans experience both prejudice and discrimination despite a measure of economic success.

he Los Angeles Japanese American festival was in full swing in mid-July 2004 when, during the opening ceremonies, a South Pasadena 24-year-old grabbed a heavy mallet and took a swing at a drum as she had practiced for months. Nicole Miyako Cherry, the daughter of a Japanese American mother and a White American father, had had little interest in her Japanese roots except for wearing a kimono for Halloween as a youngster. Yet in the last couple of years, she has begun to take interest in all things Japanese, including a visit to Japan. Looking to her future as a social work therapist, she says she would like her own children to learn Japanese, go to Japanese festivals, play in Japanese sports leagues, and have a Japanese first name (M. Navarro 2004).

Nicole's experience is certainly a case of the principle of third-generation interest—that ethnic awareness may increase among the grandchildren. But Nicole is of mixed ancestral background, so she is obviously making a choice to maintain her Japanese American identity as an important part of her future. But for many other Asian Americans, particularly recent immigrants, they are just trying to survive and to accumulate savings for their family here and kinfolk in the old country.

Many people in the United States find it difficult to distinguish between Japanese Americans and Chinese Americans physically, culturally, and historically. As we will see in this chapter, the two groups differ in some ways but also share similar patterns in their experiences in the United States.

Chinese Americans

China, the most populous country in the world, has been a source of immigrants for centuries. Many nations have a sizable Chinese population whose history there may be traced back more than five generations. The United States is such a nation. Even before the great migration from Europe began in the 1880s, more than 100,000 Chinese already lived in the United States. Today, Chinese Americans number more than 2.8 million (Table 13.1).

TABLE 13.1
Chinese American and Japanese American Population, 1860–2005

Year	Chinese Americans	Japanese Americans
1860	34,933	—
1880	105,465	148
1900	89,863	24,326
1930	74,954	138,834
1950	117,629	141,768
1960	237,292	464,332
1970	435,062	591,290
1980	806,027	700,747
1990	1,640,000	847,562
2000	2,314,533	796,700
2005	2,882,257	833,761

Note: Data beginning with 1960 include Alaska and Hawaii. Data are for responses of one race. In 2000, 2,734,841 reported Chinese American and another race, and 1,148,932 reported Japanese American and another race.

Source: Barnes and Bennett 2002; S. Lee 1998, 15; Ng 1991. Data for 2005 from American Community Survey of the Bureau of the Census.

From the beginning of Chinese immigration, Americans have held conflicting views about it. In one sense, Chinese immigration was welcome because it brought to these shores needed hardworking laborers. At the same time, it was unwelcome because the Chinese brought with them an alien culture that the European settlers were unwilling to tolerate. There was also a perception of economic competition by people in the western United States, and the Chinese newcomers proved to be very convenient and powerless scapegoats. As detailed in Chapter 4, the anti-Chinese mood led to the passage of the Exclusion Act in 1882, which was not repealed until 1943. Even then, the group that lobbied for repeal, the Citizens' Committee to Repeal Chinese Exclusion, encountered the old racist arguments against Chinese immigration (Ryo 2006).

Very gradually, the Chinese were permitted to enter the United States after 1943. Initially, the annual limit was 105, then several thousand wives of servicemen were admitted, and later, college students were allowed to remain after finishing their education. Not until after the 1965 Immigration Act did Chinese immigrants arrive again in large numbers, almost doubling the Chinese American community. Immigration continues to exert a major influence on the growth of the Chinese American population. It has approached 100,000 annually. The influx was so great in the 1990s that the number of new arrivals in that decade exceeded the total number of Chinese Americans present in 1980.

As the underside of immigration, illegal immigration is also functioning in the Chinese American community. The lure of perceived better jobs and a better life leads overseas Chinese to seek alternative routes to immigration if legal procedures are unavailable to them. The impact of illegal entry in some areas of the country can be significant. For example, every month in 2002, 340 illegal Chinese immigrants were apprehended at Chicago's O'Hare Airport and taken to a rural jail (Starks 2002).

A small but socially significant component of Chinese in the United States are those that have been adopted by American non-Chinese couples. Since 1991, China loosened its adoption laws to address the growing number of children, particularly girls, who were abandoned under the country's one-child policy. This policy strongly encourages couples to have one child and having more children can impede promotions and even cause a household to have to accept a less roomy dwelling. Numbers of adopted Chinese were small but recently about 7,000 are adopted annually. Although most are still young, they and their adopting parents face the complex issues of cultural and social identity. Organized efforts now exist to reconnect these children with their roots back in China, but for most of their lives they are adjusting to being Chinese American in a non Chinese American family (Olemetson 2005).

It is also important to appreciate that even *Chinese American* is a collective term. There is diversity within this group represented by nationality (China versus Taiwan, for example), language, and region of origin. It is not unusual for a church serving a Chinese American community to have five separate services, each in a different dialect. These divisions can be quite sharply expressed. For example, near the traditional Chinatown of New York City, a small neighborhood has emerged serving Chinese from the Fujian Province of China. In this area, job postings include annotation in Chinese that translates as "no north," meaning people from the provinces north of Fujian are not welcomed. Throughout the United States, Chinese Americans often divide along pro-China and pro-Taiwan allegiances (K. Guest 2003; Lau 2005b; Louie 2004; Sachs 2001).

Occupational Profile of Chinese Americans

The background of the contemporary Chinese American labor force lies in Chinatown. For generations, Chinese Americans were largely barred from working elsewhere. The Chinese Exclusion Act was only one example of discriminatory legislation. Many laws were passed that made it difficult or more expensive for Chinese Americans to enter certain occupations. Whites did not object to Chinese in domestic service

With the growth of the Chinese American population in the United States, businesses developed to cater to their needs. Bo Bo Poultry Market, located in upstate New York, produces Buddhist-style chicken—referring to birds sold with their heads and feet still attached and killed and prepared to precise specifications.

Source: John Sotomayor/ *The New York Times*

occupations or in the laundry trade because most White men were uninterested in such menial, low-paying work. When given the chance to enter better jobs, as they were in wartime, Chinese Americans jumped at the opportunities. Without such opportunities, however, many Chinese Americans sought the relative safety of Chinatown. The tourist industry and the restaurants dependent on it grew out of the need to employ the growing numbers of idle workers in Chinatown.

Chinatowns Today

Chinatowns represent a paradox. The casual observer or tourist sees them as thriving areas of business and amusement, bright in color and lights, exotic in sounds and sights. Behind this facade, however, they have large poor populations and face the problems associated with all slums. Most Chinatowns are in older, deteriorating sections of cities. There are exceptions, such as Monterey Park outside Los Angeles, where Chinese Americans dominate the economy. However, in the older enclaves, the problems of Chinatowns include the entire range of the social ills that affect low-income areas but with even greater difficulties because the glitter sometimes conceals the problems from outsiders and even social planners. A unique characteristic of Chinatowns, one that distinguishes them from other ethnic enclaves, is the variety of social organizations they encompass.

Organizational Life The Chinese in this country have a rich history of organizational membership, much of it carried over from China. Chief among such associations are the clans, or *tsu*; the benevolent associations, or *hui kuan*; and the secret societies, or *tongs*.

   The clans, or **tsu**, that operate in Chinatown have their origins in the Chinese practice in which families with common ancestors unite. At first, immigrant Chinese continued to affiliate themselves with those sharing a family name, even if a blood relationship was absent. Social scientists agree that the influence of clans is declining as young Chinese become increasingly acculturated. The clans in the past provided mutual assistance, a function increasingly taken on by government agencies. The strength of the clans, although diminished today, still points to the extended family's important role for Chinese Americans. Social scientists have found parent–child relationships stronger and more harmonious than those among non–Chinese Americans. Just as the clans have become less significant, however, so has the family structure changed. The differences between family life in Chinese and non-Chinese homes are narrowing with each new generation (Li 1976; Lyman 1986; Sung 1967).

 ASK Yourself

What are some of the elements that comprise life in contemporary Chinatowns?

tsu
Clans established along family lines and forming a basis for social organization by Chinese Americans.

The benevolent associations, or **hui kuan** (or *huiguan*), help their members adjust to a new life. Rather than being organized along kinship ties like the clans, hui kuan membership is based on the person's district of origin in China. Besides extending help with adjustment, the *hui kuan* lend money to and settle disputes between their members. They have thereby exercised wide control over their members. The various *hui kuan* are traditionally, in turn, part of an unofficial government in each city called the Chinese Six Companies, later changed to the Chinese Consolidated Benevolent Association (CCBA). The president of the CCBA is sometimes called the mayor of a Chinatown. The CCBA often protects newly arrived immigrants from the effects of racism. The organization works actively to promote political involvement among Chinese Americans and to support the democracy movement within the People's Republic of China. Some members of the Chinese community have resented, and still resent, the CCBA's authoritarian ways and its attempt to speak as the sole voice of Chinatown.

The Chinese have also organized in **tongs**, or secret societies. The secret societies' membership is determined not by family or locale but by interest. Some have been political, attempting to resolve the dispute over which China (the People's Republic of China or Taiwan) is the legitimate government, and others have protested the exploitation of Chinese workers. Other *tongs* provide illegal goods and services, such as drugs, gambling, and prostitution. Because they are secret, it is difficult to determine accurately the power of *tongs* today. Most observers concur that their influence has dwindled over the last sixty years and that their functions, even the illegal ones, have been taken over by elements less closely tied to Chinatown.

Some conclusions can be reached about these various social organizations. First, all have followed patterns created in traditional China. Even the secret societies had antecedents, organizationally and historically, in China. Second, all three types have performed similar functions, providing mutual assistance and representing their members' interests to a sometimes hostile dominant group. Third, because all these groups have had similar purposes and have operated in the same locale, conflict between them has been inevitable. Such conflicts were very violent in the nineteenth century, but in the twentieth century they tended to be political. Fourth, the old associations have declined in significance, notably since the mid-1970s, as new arrivals from Asian metropolises bring little respect for the old rural ways to which such organizations were important. Fifth, when communicating with the dominant society, all these groups have downplayed the problems that afflict Chinatowns. Only recently has the magnitude of social problems become known (Adams 2006; Lyman 1974, 1986; Soo 1999; Tong 2000; Wei 1993; Zhao 2002).

hui kuan
Chinese American benevolent associations organized on the basis of the district of the immigrant's origin in China.

tongs
Chinese American secret associations.

Chinatown, despite its tourist image, offers limited job opportunities for young people.

Social Problems It is a myth that Chinese Americans and Chinatowns have no problems. This false impression grows out of our tendency to stereotype groups as being all one way or the other, as well as the Chinese people's tendency to keep their problems within their community. The false image is also reinforced by the desire to maintain tourism. The tourist industry is a double-edged sword. It does provide needed jobs, even if some pay substandard wages. But it also forces Chinatown to keep its problems quiet and not seek outside assistance, lest tourists hear of social problems and stop coming. Slums do not attract tourists. This parallel between Chinese Americans and Native Americans finds both groups depending on the tourist industry even at the cost of hiding problems (Light et al. 1994).

In the late 1960s, White society became aware that all was not right in the Chinatowns. This awareness grew not because living conditions suddenly deteriorated in Chinese American settlements but because the various community organizations could no longer maintain the facade that hid Chinatowns' social ills. Despite Chinese Americans' remarkable achievements as a group, the inhabitants suffered by most socioeconomic measures. Poor health, high suicide rates, run-down housing, rising crime rates, poor working conditions, inadequate care for the elderly, and the weak union representation of laborers were a few of the documented problems.

These problems have grown more critical as Chinese immigration has increased. For example, the population density of San Francisco's Chinatown in the late 1980s was ten times that of the city as a whole. The problems faced by elderly Chinese are also exacerbated by the immigration wave because the proportion of older Chinese immigrants is more than twice that of older people among immigrants in general. The economic gap between Chinatown residents and outsiders is growing. As Chinese Americans become more affluent, they move out of Chinatowns. Census data showed the household income for Chinese Americans in New York City's Chinatown was 26 percent lower than those who lived outside the ethnic enclave (Logan et al. 2002; Wong 1995).

Life in Chinatown may seem lively to an outsider, but beyond the neon signs the picture can be quite different. Chinatown in New York City remained a prime site of sweatshops in the 1990s. Dozens of women labor over sewing machines, often above restaurants. These small businesses, often in the garment industry, consist of workers sewing twelve hours a day, six or seven days a week, and earning about $200 weekly—well below minimum wage. The workers, most of whom are women, can be victimized because they are either illegal immigrants who may owe labor to the smugglers who brought them into the United States, or legal residents unable to find better employment (Finder 1994; Kwong 1994).

The attacks on the World Trade Center in 2001 made the marginal economy of New York's Chinatown even shakier. Though not located by the World Trade Center, it was close enough to feel the drop in customary tourism and a significant decline in shipments to the garment industry. Initially, emergency relief groups ruled out assistance to Chinatown, but within a couple of months, agencies opened up offices in Chinatown. Within two months, 42,000 people had received relief as 60 percent of businesses cut staff. Like many other minority neighborhoods, New York City's Chinatown may be economically viable, but it always is susceptible to severe economic setbacks that most other areas could withstand much more easily (J. Lee 2001; Swanson 2004).

Increasingly, Chinese neither live nor work in Chinatowns; most have escaped them or have never experienced their social ills. Chinatown remains important for many of those who now live outside its borders, although less so than in the past. For many Chinese, movement out of Chinatown is a sign of success. Upon moving out, however, they soon encounter discriminatory real estate practices and White parents' fears about their children playing with Chinese American youths.

The movement of Chinese Americans out of Chinatowns parallels the movement of White ethnics out of similar enclaves. It signals the upward mobility of Chinese Amer-

The extended family is an important part of the Chinese American community.

icans, coupled with their growing acceptance by the rest of the population. This mobility and acceptance are especially evident in the presence of Chinese Americans in managerial and professional occupations.

However, with their problems and constant influx of new arrivals, we should not forget that, first and foremost, Chinatowns are communities of people. Originally, in the nineteenth century, they emerged because the Chinese arriving in the United States had no other area in which they were allowed to settle. Today, Chinatowns represent cultural decompression chambers for new arrivals and an important symbolic focus for long-term residents. Even among many younger Chinese Americans, these ethnic enclaves serve as a source of identity.

Family and Religious Life

Family life and religious worship are major forces shaping all immigrant groups' experience in the United States. Generally, with assimilation, cultural behavior becomes less distinctive. Family life and religious practices are no exceptions. For Chinese Americans, the latest immigration wave has helped preserve some of the old ways, but traditional cultural patterns have undergone change even in the People's Republic of China, so the situation is very fluid.

In the People's Republic of China, organized religion barely exists, with state policy sharply discouraging it and prohibiting foreign mission activity. In "Research Focus," we consider religion in the Chinese American community.

The contemporary Chinese American family often is indistinguishable from its White counterpart except that it is victimized by prejudice and discrimination. Older Chinese Americans and new arrivals often are dismayed by the more American behavior patterns of Chinese American youths. Change in family life is one of the most difficult cultural changes to accept. Children questioning parental authority, which Americans grudgingly accept, is a painful experience for the tradition-oriented Chinese.

Where acculturation has taken hold less strongly among Chinese Americans, the legacy of China remains. Parental authority, especially the father's, is more absolute, and the extended family is more important than is typical in White middle-class families. Divorce is rare, and attitudes about sexual behavior tend to be strict because the Chinese generally frown on public expressions of emotion. We noted earlier that Chinese immigrant women in Chinatown survive a harsh existence. A related problem beginning to surface is domestic violence. Although the available data do not indicate

Focus Research Focus Research

CHINESE CHRISTIANS OR CHRISTIAN CHINESE?

Religion plays an important role in most immigrant communities, but the Chinese are an unusual case because they come from a country where organized religion has been strongly discouraged for three generations. Many festivals are celebrated in the Chinese American community, such as Chingming or Tomb-Sweeping Day, but such observances have lost their religious significance and have become largely social occasions.

What about organized religion within the Chinese American community? A 1997 survey of Chinese Americans in southern California found that a large proportion have no ties to organized religion. When asked, "What religion—if any—do you currently consider yourself?" 44 percent said none, whereas 32 percent identified themselves as Christian and 20 percent as Buddhists. This is at least twice as high a proportion of no religious affiliation as the general population.

Most Christian Chinese are Protestant: about one in five Chinese Americans, compared with one in twenty who are Roman Catholic. What kind of Christianity is pursued by the Chinese Americans? On one level, it typically embraces what one would normally expect to be practices in a church, but on a second level, Chinese Americans often bring into the faith the moral virtues and filial piety (discussed in Chapter 11) that are taught by Buddhism.

Protestant churches attended by Chinese Americans often were initially sponsored by a major denomination such as the Methodists, Presbyterians, or United Church of Christ to serve an ethnic Chinese community. Services often are bilingual, making prolonged sermons a bit laborious to worshippers.

As in nonethnic churches, social events play a prominent role in the church calendar. However, there is little to distinguish these events in a Protestant Chinese church, except that the food served is typically Chinese, with some non-Chinese options for the young people. Distinctive touches do exist, such as celebration of the Chinese (or Lunar) New Year and the use of Chinese calligraphy or the playing of the lantern puzzle at get-togethers.

Although each Chinese American church has its own manner of approaching religious faith, one finds that the links to the larger Chinese American community, including non-Christian Chinese, tend to be stronger than the links to congregations of the same faith that are not of Chinese ancestry. This is not to say that religion is not important but that ethnicity ties the congregation together. Consequently, the Chinese American community of Christian worshippers probably is best seen as Christian Chinese, where Chinese is the operative identifier rather than Christian. ■

Source: J. Dart 1997; Guest 2003; Ng 1999, 2003.

---

that Asian American men are any more abusive than men in other groups, their wives, as a rule, are less willing to talk about their plight and to seek help. The nation's first shelter for Asian women was established in Los Angeles in 1981, but increasingly, the problem is being recognized in more cities (Banerjee 2000; Tong 2000).

Another problem for Chinese Americans is the rise in gang activity since the mid-1970s. Battles between opposing gangs have taken their toll, including the lives of some innocent bystanders. Some trace the gangs to the *tongs* and, thus, consider them an aspect, admittedly destructive, of the cultural traditions some groups are trying to maintain. However, a more realistic interpretation is that Chinese American youths from the lower classes are not part of the model minority. Upward mobility is not in their future. Alienated, angry, and with prospects of low-wage work in restaurants and laundries, they turn to gangs such as the Ghost Shadows and Flying Dragons and force Chinese American shopkeepers to give them extortion money. Asked why he became involved in crime, one gang member replied, "To keep from being a waiter all my life" (Takaki 1989, 451; see also Chin 1996).

Japanese Americans

The nineteenth century was a period of sweeping social change for Japan: It brought the end of feudalism and the beginning of rapid urbanization and industrialization. Only a few pioneering Japanese came to the United States before 1885 because Japan prohibited emigration. After 1885, the numbers remained small relative to the great immigration from Europe at the time.

With little consideration of the specific situation, the American government began to apply to Japan the same prohibitions it applied to China. The early feelings of yellow peril were directed at the Japanese as well. The Japanese who immigrated into the United States in the 1890s took jobs as laborers at low wages under poor working conditions. Their industriousness in such circumstances made them popular with employers but unpopular with unions and other employees.

Japanese Americans distinguish sharply between themselves according to the number of generations a person's family has been in the United States. Generally, each succeeding generation is more acculturated, and each is successively less likely to know Japanese. The **Issei** (pronounced "EE-say") are the first generation, the immigrants born in Japan. Their children, the **Nisei** ("NEE-say"), are American-born. The third generation, the **Sansei** ("SAHN-say"), must go back to their grandparents to reach their roots in Japan. The **Yonsei** ("YAWN-say") are the fourth generation. Because Japanese immigration is recent, these four terms describe almost the entire contemporary Japanese American population. Some Nisei are sent by their parents to Japan for schooling and to have marriages arranged, after which they return to the United States. Japanese Americans expect such people, called **Kibei** ("KEE-boy"), to be less acculturated than other Nisei. These terms sometimes are used loosely, and occasionally Nisei is used to describe all Japanese Americans. However, we will use them as they were intended to differentiate the four generational groups.

The Japanese arrived just as bigotry toward the Chinese had been legislated in the harsh Chinese Exclusion Act of 1882. For a time after the act, powerful business interests on the West Coast welcomed the Issei. They replaced the dwindling number of Chinese laborers in some industries, especially agriculture. In time, however, anti-Japanese feeling grew out of the anti-Chinese movement. The same Whites who disliked the Chinese made the same charges about the new yellow peril. Eventually, a stereotype developed of Japanese Americans as lazy, dishonest, and untrustworthy.

The attack on Japanese Americans concentrated on limiting their ability to earn a living. In 1913, California enacted the Alien Land Act, which 1920 amendments made still stricter. The act prohibited anyone who was ineligible for citizenship from owning land and limited leases to three years. The anti-Japanese laws permanently influenced the form that Japanese American business enterprise was to take. In California, the land laws drove the Issei into cities. In the cities, however, government and union restrictions prevented large numbers from obtaining the available jobs, leaving self-employment as the only option. Japanese, more than other groups, ran hotels, grocery stores, and other medium-sized businesses. Although this specialty limited their opportunities to advance, it did give urban Japanese Americans a marginal position in the expanding economy of the cities (Bonacich 1972; Light 1973; Lyman 1986).

Issei
First-generation immigrants from Japan to the United States.

Nisei
Children born of immigrants from Japan.

Sansei
The children of the Nisei-that is, the grandchildren of the original immigrants from Japan.

Yonsei
The fourth generation of Japanese Americans in the United States; the children of the Sansei.

Kibei
Japanese Americans of the Nisei generation sent back to Japan for schooling and to have marriages arranged.

 ASK Yourself

Why were Japanese Americans placed in prison-like camps during World War II?

The Wartime Evacuation

Japan's attack on Pearl Harbor on December 7, 1941, brought the United States into World War II and marked a painful tragedy for the Issei and Nisei. Almost immediately, public pressure mounted to "do something" about the Japanese Americans living on the West Coast. Many feared that if Japan attacked the mainland, Japanese Americans would fight on behalf of Japan, making a successful invasion a real possibility. Pearl Harbor was followed by successful Japanese invasions of one Pacific island after another. A Japanese submarine actually attacked a California oil tank complex early in 1943.

Rumors mixed with racism rather than facts explain the events that followed. Japanese Americans in Hawaii were alleged to have cooperated in the attack on Pearl Harbor by using signaling devices to assist the pilots from Japan. Front-page attention was given to pronouncements by the Secretary of the Navy that Japanese Americans had the greatest responsibility for Pearl Harbor. Newspapers covered in detail FBI arrests of Japanese Americans allegedly engaging in sabotage to assist the attackers. They were accused of poisoning drinking water, cutting patterns in sugarcane fields to form arrows directing enemy pilots to targets, and blocking traffic along highways to the harbor. None of these charges was substantiated, despite thorough investigations. It made no difference. In the 1940s, the treachery of the Japanese Americans was a foregone conclusion regardless of evidence to the contrary (Kashima 2003 Kimura 1988; Lind 1946; ten Brock et al. 1954;).

Executive Order 9066 On February 13, 1942, President Franklin Roosevelt signed Executive Order 9066. It defined strategic military areas in the United States and authorized the removal from those areas of any people considered threats to national security. The events that followed were tragically simple. All people on the West Coast of at least one-eighth Japanese ancestry were taken to assembly centers for transfer to evacuation camps. These camps are identified in Figure 13.1. This order covered 90 percent of the 126,000

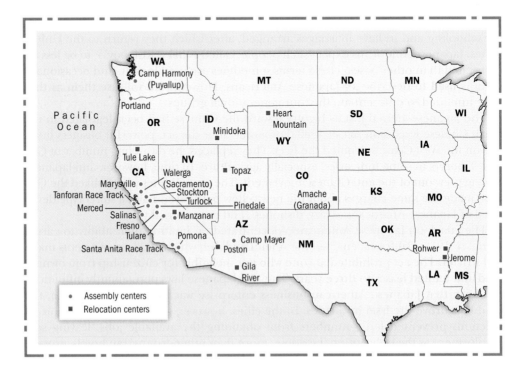

FIGURE 13.1 Japanese Americans were first ordered to report to "assembly centers," from which, after a few weeks or months, they were resettled in "relocation centers."

Source: Map "Evacuation Camps" from Michi Nishura Weglyn, *Years of Infamy: The Untold Story of America's Concentration Camps.* New York: Quill Paperbacks, John Hawkins & Associates, Inc., 1976.

Japanese Americans on the mainland. Of those evacuated, two-thirds were citizens, and three-fourths were under age 25. Ultimately, 120,000 Japanese Americans were in the camps. Of mainland Japanese Americans, 113,000 were evacuated, but to those were added 1,118 evacuated from Hawaii, 219 voluntary residents (Caucasian spouses, typically), and, most poignantly of all, the 5,981 who were born in the camps (Weglyn 1976).

The evacuation order did not arise from any court action. No trials took place. No indictments were issued. Merely having a Japanese great-grandparent was enough to mark a person for involuntary confinement. The evacuation was carried out with little difficulty. For Japanese Americans to have fled or militantly defied the order would only have confirmed the suspicions of their fellow Americans. There was little visible objection initially from the Japanese Americans. The Japanese American Citizens League (JACL), which had been founded by the Nisei as a self-help organization in 1924, even decided not to arrange a court test of the evacuation order. The JACL felt that cooperating with the military might lead to sympathetic consideration later when tensions subsided.

Even before reaching the camps, the **evacuees,** as Japanese Americans being forced to resettle came to be called officially, paid a price for their ancestry. They were instructed to carry only personal items. No provision was made for shipping their household goods. The federal government took a few steps to safeguard the belongings they left behind, but the evacuees assumed all risks and agreed to turn over their property for an indeterminate length of time. These Japanese Americans were destroyed economically. Merchants, farmers, and business owners had to sell all their property at any price they could get. Precise figures of the loss in dollars are difficult to obtain, but after the war, the Federal Reserve Bank estimated it to be $400 million. To place this amount in perspective, one estimate stated that, in 1995 dollars, the economic damages sustained, excluding personal income, would be more than $3.7 billion (Bureau of the Census 1996, 483; Commission on Wartime Relocation and Internment of Civilians 1982a, 1982b; Hosokawa 1969; Thomas and Nishimoto 1946).

The Camps Ten camps were established in seven states. Were they actually concentration camps? Obviously, they were not concentration camps constructed for the murderous purposes of those in Nazi Germany, but such a positive comparison is no compliment to the United States. To refer to them by their official designation as relocation centers ignores these facts: The Japanese Americans did not go there voluntarily, they had been charged with no crime, and they could not leave without official approval.

Japanese Americans were able to work at wage labor in the camps. The maximum wage was set at $19 a month, which meant that camp work could not possibly recoup the losses incurred by evacuation. The evacuees had to depend on the government for food and shelter, a situation they had not experienced in prewar civilian life. More devastating than the economic damage of camp life was the psychological damage. Guilty of no crime, the Japanese Americans moved through a monotonous daily routine with no chance of changing the situation. Forced community life, with such shared activities as eating in mess halls, weakened the strong family ties that Japanese Americans, especially the Issei, took so seriously (Kitsuse and Broom 1956).

Amid the economic and psychological devastation, the camps began to take on some resemblance to U.S. cities of a similar size. High schools were established, complete with cheerleaders and yearbooks. Ironically, Fourth of July parades were held, with camp-organized Boy Scout and Girl Scout troops marching past proud parents. But the barbed wire remained, and the Japanese Americans were asked to prove their loyalty.

A loyalty test was administered in 1943 on a form all had to fill out, the "Application for Leave Clearance." Many of the Japanese Americans were undecided how to respond to two questions:

No. 27. Are you willing to serve in the armed forces of the United States on combat duty, wherever ordered? No. 28. Will you swear to abide by the laws of the United States and to take no action which would in any way interfere with the war effort of the United States? (Daniels 1972, 113)

evacuees
Japanese Americans interned in camps for the duration of World War II.

The ambiguity of the questions left many confused about how to respond. For example, if Issei said yes to the second question, would they then lose their Japanese citizenship and be left stateless? The Issei would be ending allegiance to Japan but were unable, at the time, to gain U.S. citizenship. Similarly, would Nisei who responded yes be suggesting that they had been supporters of Japan? For whatever reasons, 6,700 Issei and Nisei, many because of their unacceptable responses to these questions, were transferred to the high-security camp at Tule Lake for the duration of the war (Bigelow 1992).

Overwhelmingly, Japanese Americans showed loyalty to the government that had created the camps. In general, security in the camps was not a problem. The U.S. Army, which had overseen the removal of the Japanese Americans, recognized the value of the Japanese Americans as translators in the war ahead. About 6,000 Nisei were recruited to work as interpreters and translators, and by 1943, a special combat unit of 23,000 Nisei volunteers had been created to fight in Europe. The predominantly Nisei unit was unmatched, and it concluded the war as the most decorated of all American units.

Japanese American behavior in the concentration camps can be seen only as reaffirming their loyalty. True, some refused to sign an oath, but that was hardly a treasonous act. More typical were the tens of thousands of evacuees who contributed to the U.S. war effort.

A few Japanese Americans resisted the evacuation and internment. Several cases arising out of the evacuation and detention reached the U.S. Supreme Court during the war. Amazingly, the Court upheld lower court decisions on Japanese Americans without even raising the issue of the whole plan's constitutionality. Essentially, the Court upheld the idea of the collective guilt of an entire race. Finally, after hearing *Mitsuye Endo v. United States*, the Supreme Court ruled, on December 18, 1944, that the detainment was unconstitutional and consequently the defendant (and presumably all evacuees) must be granted freedom. Two weeks later, Japanese Americans were allowed to return to their homes for the first time in three years, and the camps were finally closed in 1946 (Asahina 2006; ten Brock et al. 1954).

The immediate postwar climate was not pro–Japanese American. Whites terrorized returning evacuees in attacks similar to those against Blacks a generation earlier. Labor unions called for work stoppages when Japanese Americans reported for work. Fortunately, the most blatant expression of anti-Japanese feeling disappeared rather quickly. Japan stopped being a threat as the atomic bomb blasts destroyed Nagasaki and Hiroshima. For the many evacuees who lost relatives and friends in the bombings, however, it must have been a high price to pay for marginal acceptance (Maykovich 1972a, 1972b; Peterson 1971).

The Evacuation: What Does It Mean? The social significance of the wartime evacuation has often been treated as a historical exercise, but in the wake of the stigmatizing

Mournful Japanese Americans during World War II, as depicted in this present-day mural in Los Angeles.

of Arab and Muslim Americans after 9/11, singling out people of Japanese descent some sixty years ago takes on new meaning. Japanese American playwright Chay Yew reflected recently, "You think you can walk away from history and it takes you on the back" (Boehm 2004, E2). We will not know the consequences of the current focus on identifying potential disloyal Americans, but we do have some perspective on stigmatizing Japanese Americans during and after World War II.

The evacuation policy cost the U.S. taxpayers a quarter of a billion dollars in construction, transportation, and military expenses. Japanese Americans, as already noted, effectively lost at least several billion dollars. These are only the tangible costs to the nation. The relocation was not justifiable on any security grounds. No verified act of espionage or sabotage by a Japanese American was recorded. How could it happen?

Racism cannot be ignored as an explanation. Japanese Americans were placed in camps, but German Americans and Italian Americans were largely ignored. Many of those whose decisions brought about the evacuation were of German and Italian ancestry. The fact was that the Japanese were expendable. Placing them in camps posed no hardship for the rest of society, and, in fact, some profited by their misfortune. That Japanese Americans were evacuated because they were seen as expendable is evident from the decision not to evacuate Hawaii's Japanese. In Hawaii, the Japanese were an integral part of the society; removing them would have destroyed the islands economically (Hosokawa 1969; Kimura 1988; Miyamoto 1973).

Some argue that Japanese lack of resistance made internment possible. This seems a weak effort to transfer guilt—to blame the victim. In the 1960s, some Sansei and Yonsei were concerned about the alleged timidity of their parents and grandparents when faced with evacuation orders. However, many evacuees, if not most, probably did not really believe what was happening. "It just cannot be that bad," they may have thought. At worst, the evacuees can be accused of being naive. But even if they did see clearly how devastating the order would be, what alternatives were open? None (Haak 1970; Kitano 1976; Takezawa 1991).

The Commission on Wartime Relocation and Internment of Civilians in 1981 held hearings on whether additional reparations should be paid to evacuees or their heirs. The final commission recommendation in 1983 was that the government formally apologize and give $20,000 tax-free to each of the approximately 82,000 surviving internees. Congress began hearings in 1986 on the bill authorizing these steps, and President Ronald Reagan signed the Civil Liberties Act of 1988, which authorized the payments. The payments, however, were slow in coming because other

Six decades late! Ben Hara was a freshman at Lodi High School in May 1942 when he was taken and forced into an internment camp. In 2005, the California State Assembly authorized diplomas for the Japanese American internees.

federal expenditures had higher priority. Meanwhile, the aging internees were dying at a rate of 200 a month. In 1990, the first checks were finally issued, accompanied by President Bush's letter of apology. Many Japanese Americans were disappointed by and critical of the begrudging nature of the compensation and the length of time it had taken to receive it (Commission on Wartime Relocation and Internment of Civilians 1982a, 1982b; Department of Justice 2000).

Perhaps actor George Takei, of *Star Trek* fame, sums up best the wartime legacy of the evacuation of Japanese Americans. As a child, he had lived with his parents in the Tule Lake, California, camp. In 1996, on the fiftieth anniversary of the camp's closing and five years before 9/11 would turn the nation's attention elsewhere, he reflected on his arrival at the camp. "America betrayed American ideals at this camp. We must not have national amnesia; we must remember this" (S. Lin 1996, 10).

The Economic Picture

The socioeconomic status of Japanese Americans as a group is very different from that of Chinese Americans. Many of the latter are recent immigrants and refugees, who have fewer of the skills that lead to employment in higher-paying positions. In contrast, the Japanese American community is more settled and less affected by new arrivals from the home country, yet it continues to operate in a society in which tensions remain with Japan. We will first consider the Japanese American economic situation, which, on balance, has been very positive.

The camps left a legacy with economic implications; the Japanese American community of the 1950s was very different from that of the 1930s. Japanese Americans were more widely scattered. In 1940, 89 percent lived on the West Coast. By 1950, only 58 percent of the population had returned to the West Coast. Another difference was that a smaller proportion than before was Issei. The Nisei and even later generations accounted for 63 percent of the Japanese population. By moving beyond the West Coast, the Japanese Americans seemed less of a threat than if they had remained concentrated. Furthermore, by dispersing, Japanese American businesspeople had to develop ties to the larger economy rather than do business mostly with other Japanese Americans. Although ethnic businesses can be valuable initially, those who limit their dealings to those from the same country may limit their economic potential (Oliver and Shapiro 1995, 46).

After the war, some Japanese Americans continued to experience hardship. Some remained on the West Coast and farmed as sharecroppers in a role similar to that of the freed slaves after the Civil War. Sharecropping involved working the land of others, who provided shelter, seeds, and equipment and who also shared any profits at the time of harvest. The Japanese Americans used the practice to gradually get back into farming after being stripped of their land during World War II (Parrish 1995).

However, perhaps the most dramatic development has been the upward mobility that Japanese Americans collectively and individually have accomplished. By occupational and academic standards, two indicators of success, Japanese Americans are doing very well. The educational attainment of Japanese Americans as a group, as well as their family earnings, is higher than that of Whites, but caution should be used in interpreting such group data. Obviously, large numbers of Asian Americans, as well as Whites, have little formal schooling and are employed in poor jobs. Furthermore, Japanese Americans are concentrated in areas of the United States such as Hawaii, California, Washington, New York, and Illinois, where both wages and the cost of living are far above the national average. Also, the proportion of Japanese American families with multiple wage earners is higher than that of White families. Nevertheless, the overall picture for Japanese Americans is remarkable, especially for a racial minority that had been discriminated against so openly and so recently (Inoue 1989; Kitano 1980; Nishi 1995).

The Japanese American story does not end with another account of oppression and hardship. Today, Japanese Americans have achieved success by almost any standard. However, we must qualify the progress that *Newsweek* (1971) once billed as their "Success Story: Outwhiting the Whites." First, it is easy to forget that several generations of Japanese Americans achieved what they did by overcoming barriers that U.S. society had created, not because they had been welcomed. However, many, if not most, have become acculturated. Nevertheless, successful Japanese Americans still are not wholeheartedly accepted into the dominant group's inner circle of social clubs and fraternal organizations. Second, Japanese Americans today may represent a stronger indictment of society than economically oppressed African Americans, Native Americans, and Hispanics. There are few excuses apart from racism that Whites can use to explain why they continue to look on Japanese Americans as different—as "them."

Family and Religious Life

The contradictory pulls of tradition and rapid change that are characteristic of Chinese Americans are very strong among Japanese Americans today. Surviving Issei see their grandchildren as very nontraditional. Change in family life is one of the most difficult cultural changes for any immigrant to accept in the younger generations.

As cultural traditions fade, the contemporary Japanese American family seems to continue the success story. The divorce rate has been low, although it is probably rising. Similar conclusions apply to crime, delinquency, and reported mental illness. Data on all types of social disorganization show that Japanese Americans have a lower incidence of such behavior than all other minorities; it is also lower than that of Whites. Japanese Americans find it possible to be good Japanese and good Americans simultaneously. Japanese culture demands high in-group unity, politeness, respect for authority, and duty to community, all traits highly acceptable to middle-class Americans. Basically, psychological research has concluded that Japanese Americans share the high-achievement orientation held by many middle-class White Americans. However, one might expect that as Japanese Americans continue to acculturate, the breakdown in traditional Japanese behavior will be accompanied by a rise in social deviance (Nishi 1995).

As is true of the family and other social organizations, religious life in these groups has its antecedents in Asia, but there is no single Japanese faith. In Japan, religious beliefs tend to be much more accommodating than Christian beliefs are: One can be Shinto but also Buddhist at the same time. Consequently, when they came to the United States, immigrants found it easy to accept Christianity, even though doing so ultimately meant rejecting their old faiths. In the United States, a Christian cannot also be a Shintoist or a Buddhist. As a result, with each generation, Japanese Christians depart from traditional ways.

Although traditional temples are maintained in most places where there are large numbers of Japanese Americans, many exist only as museums, and few are places of worship with growing memberships. Religion is still a source of community attachment, but it is in the Protestant Chinese church, not in the temple. At the same time, some Eastern religions, such as Buddhism, are growing in the United States, but, overwhelmingly, the new adherents are Whites who are attracted to what they perceive as a more enriching value system. This has led to friction between more traditional Buddhist centers and those associated with the more Americanized Zen Buddhism (Ataiyero 2006; Kosmin and Lachman 1993).

ASK Yourself

What are Japanese American families like today?

FROM KAWASAKI TO CHICAGO

I was born a citizen of Japan in an area named Kawasaki, which is basically the suburbs of Tokyo. My parents raised me in a small apartment in Kawasaki until I was six years old. From then, my father's company decided to transfer him to the U.S. and my mother, my father and my brother all moved to Illinois. Japanese is my native language and as I came to America, I was forced to learn English. It took me 4 years in bilingual school to fully be able to speak English and get sent off to the "regular" school where there were no foreigners like me. Since we moved to the Northwest suburbs of Chicago, I grew up with mostly Caucasian kids and a mediocre percentage of Asians. There were hardly any African American people in the town of Schaumburg. In elementary school, I was mistreated so badly at my "regular" school that I hardly spoke and was incredibly shy.

Miku Ishii

The very first time I had experienced the excruciating pain of pure racism was when I was only in the second grade. A Caucasian girl with big bright blue eyes and short bouncy blonde hair had a habit of picking at me constantly. She said it was because of my slanted slim slits of an eye. It was because of my dark jet-black pigtails that hung thick as horses tail around my face. One afternoon during recess, I climbed up a dome that she also happened to be on. As she saw me coming near, she jumped back down on the ground and ran to the teacher. The next thing I knew, my teacher was punishing me, saying that I should not be pushing this grinning blonde haired blue-eyed girl. At the time, I was only a beginner in bilingual class so I was barely able to say anything but "Where is the bathroom?" and "I don't know." I tried to explain to the teacher. But all that came out were words in Japanese. Of course they looked at me wide

Remnants of Prejudice and Discrimination

The Fu Manchu image may be gone, but its replacement is not much better. In popular television series, Asian Americans, if they are present, usually are either karate experts or technical specialists involved in their work. Chinese Americans are ignored or misrepresented in history books. Even past mistakes are repeated. When the transcontinental railroad was completed in Utah in 1869, Chinese workers were barred from attending the ceremony. Their contribution is now well known, one of the stories of true heroism in the West. However, in 1969, when Secretary of Transportation John Volpe made a speech marking the hundredth anniversary of the event, he neglected to mention the Chinese contribution. He exclaimed, "Who else but Americans could drill tunnels in mountains 30 feet deep in snow? Who else but Americans could chisel through miles of solid granite? Who else but Americans could have laid 10 miles of track in 12 hours?" (Yee 1973, 100). The Chinese contribution was once again forgotten.

eyed, as I tried to speak broken English with Japanese. Finally, the teacher, who could not understand me to hear my self-defense, banned me from going out to recess for a week. I was furious and embarrassed and felt ashamed of my race.

Even the bus ride to school and back could not be near peaceful for me. The back of the bus was where all the cool white kids sat. When I would try to sit in the back because there were no other seats, those kids would call me Chinese or chink and make that obnoxious sound which clearly mocked the language. Some days they threw chewed gum at me. Not because I did anything to them. But because I was a chink and they wanted to see how crazy I would react. I would always just ignore it and stay quiet. I wanted to make it seem like it did not bother me, but inside, it was breaking my heart. Heck, I was not even Chinese but I was always called that in such disdainful manner. Going to school became something I feared. I remember I felt so miserable and ashamed to death for being born "Chinese." All I wanted was to be white.

I stand here today still remembering those days very vividly. In all essence, those experiences have molded me into person that I am today. I like to think that I am very open-minded and I love diversity. I love to learn about other cultures and I have a very ethnic variety of friends. I would say relative to others, my multicultural experience has been rich because of the fact that I am an immigrant, a minority. And as I have expressed before, for many years when I first came to the United States, I have experienced so much hate and prejudice for just being born my race. I am still a citizen of Japan to this day and I go back to Kawasaki about every 2 years. I feel that I have grown up in two different worlds. The experiences that I have undergone have made me accept people at face value. A lot of times for me, I forget about color because I never judge by race but I am also not oblivious or blind to the fact that racism does exist. I think as sad as it sounds, that it is an evil that will never go away. ■

Source: Ishii 2006.

Today, young Japanese Americans and Chinese Americans are very ambivalent about their cultural heritage. The pull to be American is intense, but so are the reminders that, in the eyes of many others, Asian Americans are "they," not "we." College student Miku Ishii comments in "Listen to Our Voices" about the prejudice she has experienced both because she is Japanese American and sometimes because others just think of her as being "Asian" or even "Chinese."

Chinese Americans and Japanese Americans believe that prejudice and discrimination have decreased in the United States, but subtle reminders remain. Third-generation Japanese Americans feel insulted when they are told, "You speak English so well." Adopting new tactics, Asian Americans are now trying to fight racist and exclusionary practices (Lem 1976).

Marriage statistics also illustrate the effects of assimilation. At one time, twenty-nine states prohibited or severely regulated marriages between Asians and non-Asians. Today, intermarriage, though not typical, is legal and certainly more common, and more than one-fourth of Chinese Americans under age 24 marry someone who is not

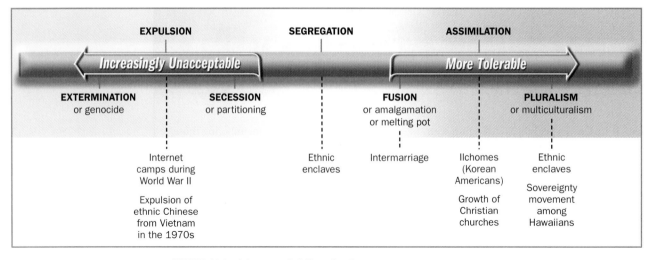

FIGURE 13.2 Intergroup Relations Continuum

Chinese. The degree of intermarriage is even higher among Japanese Americans: 1990 census data showed that two-thirds of all children born to a Japanese American had a parent of a different race.

The increased intermarriage indicates that Whites are increasingly accepting of Chinese Americans and Japanese Americans. It also suggests that Chinese and Japanese ties to their native cultures are weakening. As happened with the ways of life of European immigrants, the traditional norms are being cast aside for those of the host society. In one sense, these changes make Chinese Americans and Japanese Americans more acceptable and less alien to Whites. But this points to all the changes in Asian Americans rather than any recognition of diversity in the United States. As illustrated in Figure 13.2, intermarriage patterns reflect the fusion of different racial groups; but, compared with examples of assimilation and pluralism, they are a limited social process at present (S. Fong 1965, 1973; Kibria 2002; Onishi 1995).

The Japanese American community struggles to maintain its cultural identity while also paying homage to those who were interned during World War II. Paradoxically, as many see parallels between the collective guilt forced on people of Japanese ancestry during the 1940s and profiling of Arab and Muslim Americans, a few are seeking to justify the internment. Books and even a public middle school named after an internee in Washington state have been criticized; critics feel that when internment was taught it was too biased and that arguments for internment being the correct action should be included. For many Japanese Americans, the more things change, the more they stay the same (Malkin 2004; Tizon 2004).

It would be incorrect to interpret assimilation as an absence of protest. Because a sizable segment of the college youth of the 1960s and early 1970s held militant attitudes and because the Sansei are more heterogeneous than their Nisei and Issei relatives, it was to be expected that some Japanese Americans, especially the Sansei, would be politically active. For example, Japanese and other Asian Americans have emerged as activists for environmental concerns ranging from contaminated fish to toxic working conditions, and the targets of Japanese Americans' anger have included the apparent rise in hate crimes in the United States against Asian Americans in the 1990s. They also lobbied for passage of the Civil Rights

Restoration Act, extending reparations to the evacuees. They have expressed further activism through Hiroshima Day ceremonies, marking the anniversary of the detonation in World War II of the first atomic bomb over a major Japanese city. Also, each February, a group of Japanese American youths makes a pilgrimage to the site of the Tule Lake evacuation camp in a "lest we forget" observance. Such protests are modest, but they are a militant departure from the almost passive role played by the Nisei (Cart 2006).

Is pluralism developing? Japanese Americans show little evidence of wanting to maintain a distinctive way of life. The Japanese values that have endured are attitudes, beliefs, and goals shared by and rewarded by the White middle class in America. All Asian Americans, not only Japanese Americans, are caught in the middle. Any Asian American is culturally a part of a society that is dominated by a group that excludes him or her because of racial distinctions.

Conclusion

The presence of Asian and Pacific Islanders is unmistakable throughout much of the United States. As shown in Table 13.2, urban centers from coast to coast are homes of significant numbers of immigrants from Asia and their descendants.

Most White adults are confident that they can distinguish Asians from Europeans. Unfortunately, though, White Americans often cannot tell Asians apart from their physical appearance and are not disturbed about their confusion.

However, there are definite differences in the experience of the Chinese and the Japanese, as we have seen, in the United States. One obvious difference is in the degree of assimilation. The Chinese Americans have maintained their ethnic enclaves more than the Japan-

ese Americans have. Chinatowns live on, both as welcomed halfway points for new arrivals and as enclaves where many make very low wages. However, Little Tokyos are few because of the differences in the cultures of China and Japan. China was almost untouched by European influence, but even by the early 1900s, Japan had already been influenced by the West. Therefore, the Japanese arrived somewhat more assimilated than their Chinese counterparts. The continued migration of Chinese in recent years has also meant that Chinese Americans as a group have been less assimilated than Japanese Americans.

Both groups have achieved some success, but this success has not extended to all members. For Chinese Americans, a notable exception to success can be found in

TABLE 13.2		
Cities with the Largest Asian Pacific Islander Concentrations, 2000		
City	Number of Asian Pacific Islanders	Proportion of City's Population
New York City	792,477	9.9%
Los Angeles	375,167	10.2
San Jose	243,959	27.3
San Francisco	243,409	31.3
Honolulu	233,045	62.7
San Diego	172,821	14.1
Chicago	127,762	4.4
Houston	104,876	5.4
Fremont, California	75,984	37.4
Seattle	75,769	13.4

Source: Barnes and Bennett 2002; Grieco 2001.

Chinatowns, which, behind the tourist front, are much like other poverty-stricken areas in American cities. Neither Chinese Americans nor Japanese Americans have figured prominently in the executive offices of the nation's large corporations and financial institutions. Compared with other racial and ethnic groups, Asian Americans have shown little interest in political activity on their own behalf.

However, the success of Asian Americans, especially that of the Japanese Americans, belongs to them, not to U.S. society. First, Asian Americans have been considered successful only because they conform to the dominant society's expectations. Their acceptance as a group does not indicate growing pluralism in the United States.

Second, the ability of the Nisei, in particular, to recover from the camp experience cannot be taken as a precedent for other racial minorities. The Japanese Americans left the camps a skilled group, ambitious to overcome their adversity and placing a cultural emphasis on formal education. They entered a booming economy in which Whites and others could not afford to discriminate even if they wanted to. African Americans after slavery and Hispanic immigrants have entered the economy without skills at a time when the demand for manual labor has been limited. Many of them have

been forced to remain in a marginal economy, whether that of the ghetto, the barrio, or subsistence agriculture. For Japanese Americans, the post–World War II period marked the fortunate coincidence of their having assets and ambition when they could be used to full advantage.

Third, some Whites use the success of the Asian Americans to prop up their own prejudice. Bigoted people twist Asian American success to show that racism cannot possibly play a part in another group's subordination. If the Japanese or Chinese can do it, why cannot African Americans, the illogical reasoning goes. More directly, Japanese Americans' success may serve as a scapegoat for another's failure ("They advanced at my expense") or as a sign that they are clannish or too ambitious. Regardless of what a group does, a prejudiced eye will always view it as wrong.

As for other racial and ethnic minorities, assimilation seems to be the path most likely to lead to tolerance but not necessarily to acceptance. However, assimilation has a price that is well captured in the Chinese phrase *Zhancao zhugen:* "To eliminate the weeds, one must pull out their roots." To work for acceptance means to uproot all traces of one's cultural heritage and former identity (Wang 1991).

Key Terms

evacuees 361	Kibei 359	tongs 355
hui kuan 355	Nisei 359	tsu 354
Issei 359	Sansei 359	Yonsei 359

Review Questions

1. What has been the legacy of the "yellow peril"?
2. What made the placement of Japanese Americans in internment camps unique?
3. In what respects does diversity characterize Chinatowns?
4. How has Japanese American assimilation been blocked in the United States?
5. What are the most significant similarities between the Chinese American and Japanese American experience? What are the differences?

Critical Thinking

1. Considering the past as well as the present, are the moves made to restrict or exclude Chinese and Japanese Americans based on economic or racist motives?

2. What events can you imagine that could cause the United States to again identify an ethnic group for confinement in some type of internment camps?

3. What stereotypical images of Chinese Americans and Japanese Americans can you identify in the contemporary media?

Internet Connections—Research Navigator™

Follow the instructions found on page 35 of this text to access the features of Research Navigator™. Once at the Web site, enter your Login Name and Password. Then, to use the ContentSelect database, enter keywords such as "Chinatowns," "model minority," and "Tule Lake," and the search engine will supply relevant and recent scholarly and popular press publications. Use the *New York Times* Search-by-Subject Archive to find recent news articles related to sociology, and the Link Library feature to locate relevant Web links organized by the key terms associated with this chapter.

14 Jewish Americans: Quest to Maintain Identity

CHAPTER OUTLINE

The Jewish People: Race, Religion, or Ethnic Group?

Immigration of Jews to the United States

Anti-Semitism: Past and Present

■ **LISTEN TO OUR VOICES**
"Night"
by Elie Wiesel

Position of Jewish Americans

Religious Life

Jewish Identity

■ **RESEARCH FOCUS**
Intermarriage:
The Final Step to Assimilation?

Conclusion

Key Terms/Review Questions/
Critical Thinking/Internet Connections—
Research Navigator™

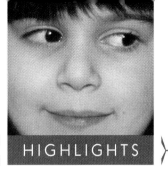

THE JEWISH PEOPLE ARE AN ETHNIC GROUP. THEIR IDENTITY rests not on the presence of physical traits or religious beliefs but on a sense of belonging that is tied to Jewish ancestry. The history of anti-Semitism is as ancient as the Jewish people themselves. Evidence suggests that this intolerance persists today in both thought and action. Jews in the United States may have experienced less discrimination than did earlier generations in Europe, but some opportunities are still denied them. Contemporary Jews figure prominently in the professions and as a group exhibit a strong commitment to education. Many Jews share a concern about either the lack of religious devotion of some members or the division within American Judaism over the degree of orthodoxy. Jews in the United States practice their faith as Orthodox, Conservative, or Reform. Paradoxically, the acceptance of Jews by Gentiles has made the previously strong identity of Jews weaker with each succeeding generation.

Two events reflect the complexity of Jewish life in the United States; one began with a lawsuit and the other with violence.

On December 21, 2001, the Second Court of Appeals upheld earlier court decisions that ruled in favor of Yale University and against the "Yale Five." The case began in 1997 when three Orthodox Jews felt that the Yale housing policy that requires unmarried freshmen and sophomores under age 21 to live on campus was discriminatory. The freshmen felt it would force Orthodox Jews to violate their faith's call for modesty in living by expecting them to live in co-ed residence halls. Even a compromise offered by Yale to place them in rooms with bathrooms on single-sex floors was rejected. The students contended that the dormitory atmosphere of sexual promiscuity is irreconcilable with their deeply held religious beliefs. Two sophomores, who had paid for university housing the year before while living off-campus, soon joined their lawsuit. Many supported the Yale Five, but even other Orthodox Jewish students at Yale expressed anger over the lawsuit, feeling that they could be respectful to their faith and still conform to the housing standards of the university (Itano 1997; Muller 2001).

Billings, Montana, does not have a large Jewish population, but it does have an established community of Jews. Billings had no history of visible anti-Jewish hostility. However, beginning in 1992, swastikas appeared outside a Jewish temple, tombstones in a Jewish cemetery were toppled, and bomb threats were made to a synagogue. Then, in the fall of 1993, rocks and bottles were thrown through the windows of homes of prominent members of the Jewish community in Billings. Police advised one of the victim households to remove the "Happy Hanukkah" pictures from their front windows. In light of this tension, local Christian ministers encouraged their members to place menorahs in their windows. Stores instantly sold out of them, and local newspapers printed color pictures of them for people to hang in their windows. As Christmas Day came in this overwhelmingly Christian community, home after home displayed symbols of Judaism, defying those who had attacked the Jews. The culprits were never identified, but they had succeeded in bringing a city together (Cohen 2005; Cohon 1995).

The United States has the largest Jewish population in the world. This nation's approximately 5.3 million Jews account for 41 percent of the world's Jewish population. Jewish Americans not only represent a significant group in the United States but also play a prominent role in the worldwide Jewish community. The nation with the second-largest Jewish population, Israel, is the only one in which Jews are in the majority, accounting for 75 percent of the population, compared with just under 2 percent in the United States. Figure 14.1 depicts the worldwide distribution of Jews (DellaPergola 2005).

The Jewish people form a contrast to the other subordinate groups we have studied. At least 1,500 years had passed since Jews were the dominant group in any nation until Israel was created in 1948. Even there, Jews are in competition for power. American Jews superficially resemble Asian Americans in that both are largely free from poverty, compared to Chicanos or Puerto Ricans. Unlike those groups, however, the Jewish cultural heritage is not nationalistic in origin. Perhaps the most striking difference is that the history of anti-Jewish prejudice and discrimination (usually called **anti-Semitism**) is nearly as old as relations between Jews and Gentiles (non-Jews).

anti-Semitism
Anti-Jewish prejudice or discrimination.

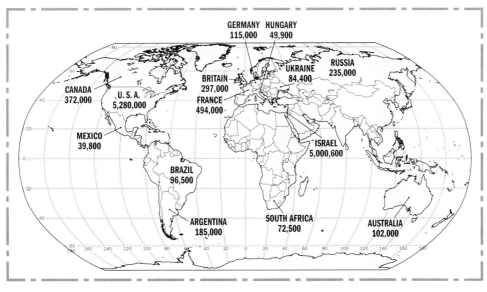

FIGURE 14.1 Worldwide Distribution of Jews, 2005

Note: Data include all nations with at least 40,000 Jews.

Source: Sergio Dellapergola, "World Jewish Population 2005," *American Jewish Yearbook*, ed. David Singer and Lawrence Grossman, American Jewish Committee, 2005b.

The most distinctive aspect of the Jewish population is its concentration in urban areas and in the Northeast. The most recent estimates place more than 45 percent of the Jewish population in the Northeast (Figure 14.2). Jews are concentrated especially in the metropolitan areas of New York City, Los Angeles, and Miami, where altogether they account for half of the nation's Jewish population.

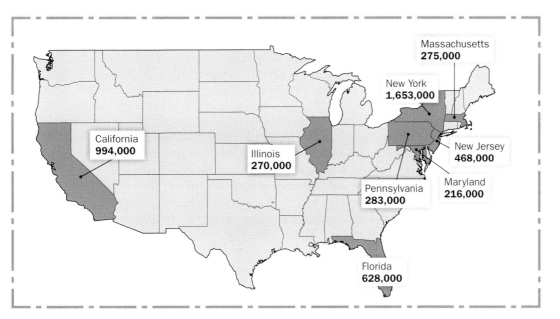

FIGURE 14.2 Jewish Population Distribution in the United States, 2001

Note: States highlighted have largest Jewish populations.

Source: Jim Schwartz and Jeffrey Scheckner, "Jewish Population in the United States, 2001." *American Jewish Yearbook*, ed. David Singer and Lawrence Grossman, American Jewish Committee, 2001.

The Jewish People: Race, Religion, or Ethnic Group?

Jews are a subordinate group. They fulfill the criteria set forth in Chapter 1:

- Jewish Americans experience unequal treatment from non-Jews in the form of prejudice, discrimination, and segregation.
- Jews share a cultural history that distinguishes them from the dominant group.
- Jews do not choose to be Jewish, in the same way that Whites do not choose to be White or Mexican Americans to be Mexican American.
- Jews have a strong sense of group solidarity.
- Jewish men and women tend to marry one another rather than marrying outside the group.

What are the distinguishing traits for Jewish Americans? Are they physical features, thus making Jews a racial group? Are these characteristics matters of faith, suggesting that Jews are best regarded as a religious minority? Or are they cultural and social, making Jews an ethnic group? To answer these questions, we must address the ancient and perennial question: What is a Jew?

The issue of what makes a Jew is not only a scholarly question; in Israel, it figures in policy matters. The Israel Law of Return defines who is a Jew and extends Israeli citizenship to all Jews. Currently, the law recognizes all converts to the faith, but pressure has grown recently to limit citizenship to those whose conversions were performed by Orthodox rabbis. Although the change would have little practical impact, symbolically this pressure shows the tension and lack of consensus even among Jews over who is a Jew.

The definition of race used here is fairly explicit. The Jewish people are not physically differentiated from non-Jews. True, many people believe they can tell a Jew from a non-Jew, but actual distinguishing physical traits are absent. Jews today come from all areas of the world and carry a variety of physical features. Most Jewish Americans are descended from northern and eastern Europeans and have the appearance of Nordic and Alpine people. Many others carry Mediterranean traits that make them indistinguishable from Spanish or Italian Catholics. Many Jews reside in North Africa, and although they are not significantly represented in the United States, many people would view them only as a racial minority, Black. The wide range of variation among Jews makes it inaccurate to speak of a Jewish race in a physical sense (Gittler 1981; Montagu 1972).

To define Jews by religion seems the obvious answer because there are Judaic religious beliefs, holidays, and rituals. But these beliefs and practices do not distinguish all Jews from non-Jews. To be a Jewish American does not mean that one is affiliated with one of the three religious groups: the Orthodox, the Reform, and the Conservative. A large segment of adult Jewish Americans, more than a third, do not participate in religious services or even belong, however tenuously, to a temple or synagogue. They have not converted to Christianity, nor have they ceased to think of themselves as Jews. Nevertheless, Jewish religious beliefs and the history of religious practices remain significant legacies for all Jews today, however secularized their everyday behavior. In a 1998 survey, half of all Jews felt that a "shared history or culture" much more so than religion defined what it means to be Jewish (*Los Angeles Times* Poll 1998).

The trend for some time, especially in the United States, has been toward a condition called **Judaization**, the lessening importance of Judaism as a religion and the substitution of cultural traditions as the ties that bind Jews. Depending on one's definition, Judaization has caused some Jews to become so assimilated in the United States that very traditional Jews no longer consider them acceptable spouses (Gans 1956).

Jewish identity is ethnic. Jews share cultural traits, not physical features or uniform religious beliefs. The level of this cultural identity differs for the individual Jew. Just as

Judaization
The lessening importance of Judaism as a religion and the substitution of cultural tradition as the tie that binds Jews.

some Apaches may be more acculturated than others, the degree of assimilation varies between Jewish people. Judaization may base identity on such things as eating traditional Jewish foods, telling Jewish jokes, and wearing the Star of David. For others, this cultural identity may be the sense of a common history of centuries of persecution. For still others, it may be an unimportant identification. They say, "I am a Jew," just as they say, "I am a resident of California."

The question of what constitutes Jewish identity is not easily resolved. The most appropriate explanation of Jewish identity may be the simplest. A Jew in contemporary America is a person who thinks of himself or herself as a Jew. That also means that being a Jew is a choice and, as we will return to later in the chapter, many Jews may not be making that choice (Abrahamson and Pasternak 1998; Himmelfarb 1982).

Immigration of Jews to the United States

As every schoolchild knows, 1492 was the year in which Christopher Columbus reached the Western Hemisphere, exploring on behalf of Spain. That year also marked the expulsion of all Jews from Spain. The resulting exodus was not the first migration of Jews, nor was it the last. This is but one illustration of several of the social processes in the intergroup relations continuum illustrated in Figure 14.3. Other examples will be presented throughout this chapter.

One of the most significant movements among Jews is the one that created history's largest concentration of Jews: the immigration to the United States. The first Jews arrived in 1654 and were of Sephardic origin, meaning that they were originally from Spain and Portugal. These immigrants sought refuge in America after they had been expelled from other European countries as well as from Brazil.

When the United States gained its independence from Great Britain, only 2,500 Jews lived here. By 1870 the Jewish population had climbed to about 200,000, supplemented mostly by Jews of German origin. They did not immediately merge into the older Jewish American settlements any more than the German Catholics fused immediately with native Catholics. Years passed before the two groups' common identity as Jews overcame nationality differences (Dinnerstein 1994; Jaher 1994; Sarna 2004).

The greatest migration of Jews to the United States occurred around the end of the nineteenth century and was simultaneous with the great European migration described in Chapter 4. Because they arrived at the same time does not mean that the

FIGURE 14.3 Intergroup Relations Continuum

movements of Gentiles and Jews were identical in all respects. One significant difference was that Jews were much more likely to stay in the United States; few returned to Europe. Although between 1908 and 1937, one-third of all European immigrants returned, only 5 percent of Jewish immigrants did. The legal status of Jews in Europe at the turn of the century had improved since medieval times, but their rights were still revoked from time to time (Sherman 1974).

Despite the legacy of anti-Semitism in Europe, past and present, most of the Jews who migrated to the United States up to the early twentieth century came voluntarily. These immigrants tended to be less pious and less observant of Judaic religious customs than those who remained in Europe. As late as 1917, there were only five small day schools, as Jewish parochial schools were called, in the entire nation. Nevertheless, although the earliest Jewish immigration was not a direct response to fear, the United States had special meaning for the Jewish arrivals. This nation had no history of anti-Semitism like that of Europe. Many Jews must have felt a new sense of freedom, and many clearly demonstrated their commitment to their new nation by becoming citizens at a rate unparalleled in other ethnic groups (Herberg 1983; Sklare 1971).

The immigration acts of the 1920s sharply reduced the influx of Jews, as they did for other European groups. Beginning in about 1933, the Jews arriving in the United States were not merely immigrants; they were also refugees. The tyranny of the Third Reich began to take its toll well before World War II. German and Austrian Jews fled Europe as the impending doom became more evident. Many of the refugees from Nazism in Poland, Hungary, and the Ukraine tended to be more religiously orthodox and adapted slowly to the ways of the earlier Jewish immigrants, if they adapted at all. As Hitler's decline and fall came to pass, the concentration camps, the speeches of Hitler, the atrocities, the war trials, and the capture of Nazi leaders undoubtedly made all American Jews—natives and refugees, the secular and the orthodox—acutely aware of their Jewishness and the price one may be required to pay for ethnicity alone.

Because the U.S. Citizenship and Immigration Services do not identify an immigrant's religion, precise data are lacking for the number of people of Jewish background migrating recently to the United States. Estimates of 500,000 have been given for the number of Jews who made the United States their home in the 1960s and 1970s. The majority came from Israel, but 75,000 came from the Soviet Union and another 20,000 from Iran, escaping persecution in those two nations. As the treatment of Jews in the Soviet Union improved in the late 1980s, U.S. immigration officials began to scrutinize

Jewish shoppers, many immigrants, crowd Orchard Street in New York City in 1923. Reprinted by permission of The American Jewish Committee.

requests for entry to see whether refugee status was still merited. Although some Soviet Jews had difficulty demonstrating that they had a "well-founded fear of persecution," the United States admitted more than 13,600 in 1988 (through the processing center in Rome alone). The situation grew more complicated with the collapse of the Soviet Union in 1991. Throughout the period, the immigrants' arrival brought about a growth in the Jewish community in the United States.

Anti-Semitism: Past and Present

The history of the Jewish people is a history of struggle to overcome centuries of hatred. Several religious observances, such as Passover, Hanukkah, and Purim, commemorate the past sacrifices or conflicts Jews have experienced. Anti-Jewish hostility, or anti-Semitism, has followed the struggle of the Jewish people since before the beginning of the Christian faith to the present.

Origins

Many anti-Semites justify their beliefs by pointing to the role of some Jews in the crucifixion of Jesus Christ, although he was also a Jew. For nearly 2,000 years various Christians have argued that all Jews share in the responsibility of the Jewish elders who condemned Jesus Christ to death. Much anti-Semitism over the ages bears little direct relationship to the crucifixion, however, and has more to do with the persisting stereotype that sees Jews as behaving treacherously to members of the larger society in which they live.

A 2004 survey found that 26 percent of Americans felt Jews were "responsible for Christ's death"—a significant increase over a similar survey nine years earlier. At the time of the survey, many Jews felt that Mel Gibson's *The Passion of the Christ* reinforces such a view. Indeed, the same survey shows that among those who had seen the film, 36 percent held Jews responsible for the crucifixion (Pew Research Center 2004).

What truth is there in such stereotypes? Even prominent celebrities and political leaders have publicly expressed stereotyped opinions about Jews. In 2006, Hollywood director and actor Mel Gibson while stopped for drunk driving, told the arresting office, who happened to be Jewish, "The Jews are responsible for all wars in the world" (Cohen 2006). In 1974, the chairman of the Joint Chiefs of Staff of the U.S. armed forces declared that Jews "own, you know, the banks in this country" (*Time* 1974, 16). Yet the facts show that Jewish Americans are dramatically underrepresented in management positions in the nation's leading banks. Even in New York City, where Jews account for half the college graduates, Jewish Americans represent only 4 percent of that city's senior banking officials. Similarly, a 1998 national survey found that 8 percent of Jews were business owners, compared with 9 percent of the total U.S. population (Getlin 1998; Slavin and Pradt 1979, 1982).

If the stereotype that Jews are obsessed with money is false, how did it originate? Social psychologist Gordon Allport (1979), among others, advanced the **fringe-of-values theory**. Throughout history, Jews have occupied positions economically different from those of Gentiles, often because laws forbade them to farm or practice trades. For centuries, the Christian church prohibited the taking of interest in the repayment of loans, calling it the sin of usury. Consequently, in the minds of Europeans, the sinful practice of money lending was equated with the Jew. In reality, most Jews were not moneylenders, and most of those who were did not charge interest. In fact, many usurers were Christians, but because they worked in secret, it was only the reputation of the Jews that was damaged. To make matters worse, the nobles of some European countries used Jews to collect taxes, which only increased the ill feeling. To the Gentile, such business practices by the Jews constituted behavior on the fringes of proper

fringe-of-values theory
Behavior that is on the border of conduct that a society regards as proper and is often carried out by subordinate groups, subjecting those groups to negative sanctions.

in-group virtues
Proper behavior by one's own group (in-group virtues) becomes unacceptable when practiced by outsiders (out-group vices).

out-group vices
Proper behavior by one's own group (in-group virtues) becomes unacceptable when practiced by outsiders (out-group vices).

conduct. Therefore, this theory about the perpetuation of anti-Semitism is called the fringe-of-values theory (American Jewish Committee 1965, 1966a, 1966b; *Time* 1974).

A similar explanation is given for other stereotypes, such as the assertion that Jews are clannish, staying among themselves and not associating with others. In the ancient world, Jews in the Near East area often were under attack by neighboring peoples. Throughout history, Jews have also at times been required to live in closed areas, or ghettos. This experience naturally led them to unify and rely on themselves rather than others. More recently, the stereotype of clannishness has gained support because Jews have been more likely to interact with Jews than with Gentiles. But this behavior is reciprocal because Gentiles have tended to stay among their own kind, too.

Being critical of others for traits for which you praise members of your own group is an example of **in-group virtues** becoming **out-group vices**. Sociologist Robert Merton (1968) described how proper behavior by one's own group becomes unacceptable when practiced by outsiders. For Christians to take their faith seriously is commendable; for Jews to withstand secularization is a sign of backwardness. For Gentiles to prefer Gentiles as friends is understandable; for Jews to choose other Jews as friends suggests clannishness. The assertion that Jews are clannish is an exaggeration and also ignores the fact that the dominant group shares the same tendency. It also fails to consider to what extent anti-Semitism has logically encouraged—and indeed, forced—Jews to seek out other Jews as friends and fellow workers (Allport 1979).

This only begins to explore the alleged Jewish traits, their origin, and the limited value of such stereotypes in accurately describing several million Jewish people. Stereotypes are only one aspect of anti-Semitism; another has been discrimination against Jews. In C.E.. 313, Christianity became the official religion of Rome. Within another two centuries, Jews were forbidden to marry Christians or to try to convert them. Because Christians shared with Jews both the Old Testament and the origin of Jesus, they felt ambivalent toward the Jewish people. Gentiles attempted to purge themselves of their doubts about the Jews by projecting exaggerated hostility onto the Jews. The expulsion of the Jews from Spain in 1492 is only one example. Spain was merely one of many countries, including England and France, from which the Jews were expelled. In the mid-fourteenth century, the bubonic plague wiped out a third of Europe's population. Because of their social conditions and some of their religious prohibitions, Jews were less likely to die from the plague. Anti-Semites pointed to this as evidence that the Jews were in league with the devil and had poisoned the wells of non-Jews. Consequently, from 1348 to 1349, 350 Jewish communities were exterminated, not by the plague but by Gentiles.

Germany's effort to move the population against Jews was clear well before the Holocaust. *The Poisonous Mushroom* published in 1938 was a *children's* book that shows children gleefully seeing Jewish teachers and children driven away from their school. Jews were presented as the poisonous mushrooms and Aryan Germans as the edible mushrooms.

Source: Reprinted by permission of The American Jewish Committee.

The Holocaust

The injustices to the Jewish people continued for centuries. However, it would be a mistake to say that all Gentiles were anti-Semitic. History, drama, and other literature record daily, presumably friendly interaction between Jews and Gentiles. At particular times and places, anti-Semitism was an official government policy. In other situations, it was the product of a few bigoted individuals and sporadically became very widespread. Regardless of the scope, anti-Semitism was a part of Jewish life, something that Jews were forced to contend with. By 1870, most legal restrictions aimed at Jews had been abolished in Western Europe. Since then, however, Jews have again been used as scapegoats by opportunists who blame them for a nation's problems.

The most tragic example of such an opportunist was Adolf Hitler, whose "final solution" to Germany's problems led to the Holocaust. The **Holocaust** is the state-sponsored systematic persecution and annihilation of European Jewry by Nazi Germany and its collaborators. The move to eliminate Jews from the European continent started slowly, with Germany gradually restricting the rights of Jews: preventing them from voting, living outside the Jewish ghetto, and owning businesses. Much of the anti-Semitic cruelty was evident before the beginning of the war. If there was any doubt, "Night of Broken Glass," or Kristallnacht, in Berlin on November 9, 1938, ended any doubt. Ninety Berlin Jews were murdered, hundreds of homes and synagogues were set on fire or ransacked, and thousands of Jewish store windows were broken.

Despite the obvious intolerance, Jews desiring to immigrate were turned back by government officials in the United States and elsewhere. Just a few months after Kristallnacht, 907 Jewish refugees aboard the liner *St. Louis* were denied entry to Cuba. Efforts to gain entry in the United States, including special appeals to Congress and President Roosevelt, were useless. Ultimately the ship returned, with many of the Jews later dying in the death camps. Between 1933 and 1945, two-thirds of Europe's total Jewish population were killed; in Poland, Germany, and Austria, 90 percent were murdered. Even today, there are still 17 percent fewer Jews than in 1940.

Many eyewitnesses to the events of the Holocaust remind us of the human tragedy involved. Among the most eloquent are the writings and speeches of Nobel Peace Prize winner, Romanian-born Elie Wiesel (pronounced EL-ee Vee-SELL). In "Listen to Our Voices," he recalls the moments before he, age 16 at the time, and other Jews were freed from the Buchenwald concentration camp.

Despite the enormity of the tragedy, a small but vocal proportion of the world community are **Holocaust revisionists** who claim that the Holocaust did not happen. Debates also continue between those who contend that this part of modern history must be remembered and others, in the United States and Europe, who feel that it is time to put the Holocaust behind us and go on. However, the poignant statements by Holocaust survivors such as Elie Wiesel and the release of such films as *Schindler's List* (1993) and *Life Is Beautiful* (1998) keep the tragedy of the Holocaust in our minds (Cooper and Brackman 2001; Stern 2001).

A new version of Holocaust revisionism emerged in the wake of 9/11. A small but vocal group of people in the United States contents that the attack on the World Trade Center was planned and actually carried out by Jews. The unfounded assertion even makes the false claim that Jewish employees at the World Trade Center did not show up for work because they were told in advance of the attacks (Foxman 2006).

Anti-Semitism is definitely not just a historical social phenomenon in Europe. After the attacks on the United States on September 11, 2001, fresh outbreaks occurred throughout the continent. Newspapers reported Jewish worshippers being subjected to rocks and insults as they walked to services. A growing Arab and Muslim population in Europe is also serving to offer an audience for Christian-generated anti-Semitism, especially after the U.S. occupation of Iraq beginning in 2003 and the continued uncertainty of Palestine's future (J. Fleishman 2004).

Holocaust
The state-sponsored systematic persecution and annihilation of European Jewry by Nazi Germany and its collaborators.

Holocaust revisionist
People who deny the Nazi effort to exterminate the Jews or who minimize the numbers killed.

Voices Listen to Our Voices Listen to

NIGHT

On April 10 [1945], there were still some twenty thousand prisoners in the camp, among them a few hundred children. It was decided to evacuate all of us at once. By evening. Afterward, they would blow up the camp.

And so we were herded into the huge *Appelplatz* [assembly square], in ranks of five, waiting for the gate to open. Suddenly, the sirens began to scream. Alert! We went back to the blocks. It was too late to evacuate us that evening. The evacuation was postponed to the next day.

Hunger was tormenting us; we had not eaten for nearly six days except for a few stalks of grass and some potato peels found on the grounds of the kitchens.

At ten o'clock in the morning, the SS took positions throughout the camp and began to herd the last of us toward the *Appelplatz*.

The resistance movement decided at that point to act. Armed men appeared from everywhere. Bursts of gunshots. Grenades exploding. We, the children stayed, remained flat on the floor of the block.

The battle did not last long. Around noon, everything was calm again. The SS had fled and the resistance had taken charge of the camp.

Elie Wiesel

At six o'clock that afternoon, the first American tank stood at the gates of Buchenwald.

Our first act as free men was to throw ourselves onto the provisions. That's all we thought about. No thought of revenge, or of our parents. Only of bread.

And then when we were no longer hungry, not one of us thought of revenge. The next day, a few of the young men ran into Weimar to bring back some potatoes and clothes—and to sleep with the girls. But still no trace of revenge.

Three days after the liberation of Buchenwald, I became very ill: some form of [food] poisoning. I was transferred to a hospital and spent two weeks between life and death.

One day when I was able to get up, I decided to look at myself in the mirror on the opposite wall. I had not seen myself since the ghetto.

From the depths of the mirror, a corpse was contemplating me.

The look in his eyes as he gazed at me has never left me. ◼

Source: Excerpt pp. 114–115 from *Night* by Elie Wiesel, translated from the French by Marion Wiesel. Copyright © 2006.

Originally published in 1958. Reprinted by permission of Hill & Wang, a division of Farrar, Straus & Giroux, LLC.

U.S. Anti-Semitism: Past

Compared with the brutalities of Europe from the time of the early Christian church to the rule of Hitler, the United States cannot be described as a nation with a history of severe anti-Semitism. Nevertheless, the United States has also had its outbreaks of anti-Semitism, though none have begun to approach the scope of that in Western Europe. An examination of the status of Jewish Americans today indicates the extent of remaining discrimination against Jews. However, contemporary anti-Semitism must be seen in relation to past injustices.

In 1654, the year Jews arrived in colonial America, Peter Stuyvesant, governor of New Amsterdam (the Dutch city later named New York), attempted to expel them from the city. Stuyvesant's efforts failed, but they were the beginning of an unending effort to separate Jews from the rest of the population. Because the pre-1880 immigration of Jews was small, anti-Semitism was little noticed except, of course, by Jews. Most nineteenth-century movements against minorities were targeted at Catholics and Blacks and ignored Jews. In fact, Jews occasionally joined in such movements. By the 1870s, however, signs of a pattern of social discrimination against Jews had appeared. Colleges limited the number of Jewish students or excluded Jews altogether. The first Jewish fraternity was founded in 1898 to compensate for the barring of Jews from campus social organizations. As Jews began to compete for white-collar jobs early in twentieth century, job discrimination became the rule rather than the exception (Higham 1966; Selzer 1972).

The 1920s and the 1930s were periods of the most virulent and overt anti-Semitism. In these decades, the myth of an internationally organized Jewry took shape. According to a forged document titled *Protocols of the Learned Elders of Zion,* Jews throughout the world planned to conquer all governments, and the major vehicle for this rise to power was communism, said by anti-Semites to be a Jewish movement. Absurd though this argument was, some respected Americans accepted the thesis of an international Jewish conspiracy and believed in the authenticity of the *Protocols.*

Henry Ford, founder of the automobile company that bears his name, was responsible for the publication of the *Protocols.* The *Dearborn Independent,* a weekly newspaper owned by Ford, published anti-Semitic material for seven years. Finally in 1927, faced with several million dollars' worth of civil suits for slandering well-known Jewish Americans, he published a halfhearted apology. In his later years, Ford expressed regret for his espousal of anti-Semitic causes, but the damage had been done; he had lent an air of respectability to the most exaggerated charges against Jewish people.

It is not clear why Henry Ford, even for a short period of his life, so willingly accepted anti-Semitism. But Ford was not alone. Groups such as the Ku Klux Klan and the German American Bund, as well as radio personalities, preached about the Jewish conspiracy as if it were fact. By the 1930s, these sentiments expressed a fondness for Hitler. Even famed aviator Charles Lindbergh made speeches to gatherings claiming that Jews were forcing the United States into a war so that Jewish people could profit by wartime production. When the barbarous treatment of the Jews by Nazi Germany was exposed, most Americans were horrified by such events, and people such as Lindbergh were as puzzled as anyone about how some Americans could have been so swept up by the pre–World War II wave of anti-Semitism (N. Baldwin 2001; Meyers 1943; Selzer 1972).

Historical anti-Semitism is never far below the surface. The discredited *Protocols* was sold online by Wal-Mart through 2004 and described as "genuine" until protests made the large retailer rethink its sale. In 2006, a Spanish-language version published in Mexico City enjoyed wide distribution (*Intelligence Report* 2004; Rothstein 2006).

The next section examines anti-Semitic feelings in contemporary America. Several crucial differences between anti-Semitism in Europe and in the United States must be considered. First, and most important, the U.S. government has never promoted anti-Semitism. Unlike its European counterparts, the U.S. government has never embarked on an anti-Semitic program of expulsion or extermination. Second, because anti-Semitism was never institutionalized in the United States as it sometimes has been in Europe, American Jews have not needed to develop a defensive ideology to ensure the survival of their people. A Jewish American can make a largely personal decision about how much to assimilate or how secular to become.

 ASK Yourself

How much prejudice is there toward Jews in the United States today?

Contemporary Anti-Semitism

Next to social research on anti-Black attitudes and behavior of Whites, anti-Semitism has been the major focus of studies of prejudice by sociologists and psychologists. Most of the conclusions described in Chapter 2 apply equally to the data collected on anti-Semitism. Little concern was expressed by Jews in the United States about anti-Semitism immediately after World War II. From the late 1960s through the 1990s, however, anti-Semitism has again appeared to be a threat in many parts of the world. A 2005 national survey found that 9 percent felt anti-Semitism was a "very serious problem" and 48 percent "somewhat of a problem" in the United States (J. Jones 2003b).

The Anti-Defamation League (ADL) of B'nai B'rith, founded in 1913, makes an annual survey of reported anti-Semitic incidents. Although the number has fluctuated, the 1994 tabulation reached the highest level in the twenty-two years during which the ADL has been recording such incidents. Figure 14.4 shows the rise of harassment, threats, and assaults, which, adding episodes of vandalism, brings the total to 1,757 incidents for 2005. Some incidents were inspired and carried out by neo-Nazis or skinheads, groups of young people who champion racist and anti-Semitic ideologies. In our mapping of racist fringe groups (see Figure 14.4), we see the widespread presence of such groups.

Particularly disturbing has been the number of reported anti-Semitic incidents on college campuses. Incidents continue to be reported. Anti-Jewish graffiti, anti-Semitic speakers, and swastikas affixed to predominantly Jewish fraternities were among the documented incidents. Another manifestation of it appears in editorial-style advertisements in college newspapers that argue that the Holocaust never occurred. A chilling development is the Internet as a growing vehicle for anti-Semitism, either delivering such messages or serving as a means of reaching Web sites that spread intolerance (Anti-Defamation League 1996, 2006).

Acts of anti-Semitic violence in the United States, along with the continuing conflict in the Middle East and the expression of anti-Semitic themes by some African Americans, have prompted renewed national attention to anti-Semitism.

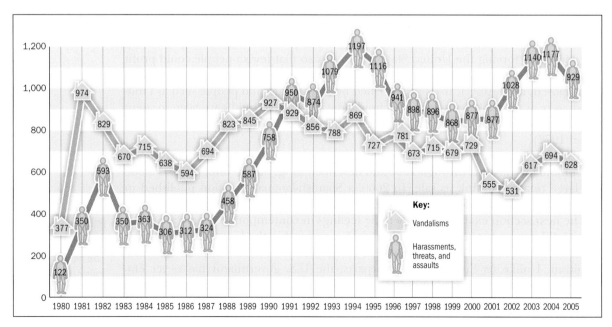

FIGURE 14.4 Anti-Semitic Incidents, 1980–2005

Source: Reprinted with permission of the Anti-Defamation League, *www.adl.org.*

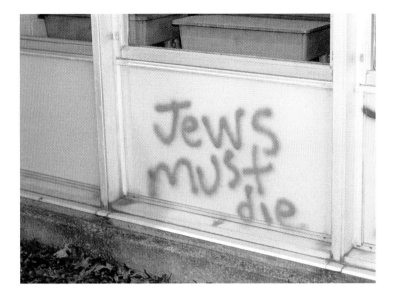

This anti-Semitic graffiti was painted on the outside walls of Pacadah, Kentucky's Temple Israel in 2004.

American Jews and Israel When the Middle East became a major hot spot in international affairs in the 1960's, a revival of 1930s anti-Semitism occurred. Many Jewish Americans expressed concern that because Jews are freer in the United States than they have been in perhaps any other country in their history, they would ignore the struggle of other Jews. Israel's precarious status has proven to be a strong source of identity for Jewish Americans. Major wars in the Middle East in 1967, 1973, and 1991 reminded the world of Israel's vulnerability. Palestinian uprisings in the Occupied Territories and international recognition of the Palestine Liberation Organization (PLO) in 1988 and 2002 eroded the strong pro-Israeli front among the Western powers. Some Jewish Americans have shown their commitment to the Israeli cause by immigrating to Israel.

Jewish American support is not uniform. Although not all American Jews agree with Israel's actions, many Jews express support for Israel's struggles by contributing money and trying to influence American opinion and policy to be more favorable to Israel. A survey taken in 2005 showed that 36 percent of Jewish Americans feel "very close" to Israel and another 41 percent feel "fairly close." But that still leaves more than a quarter (23 percent) who feel distant from Israel. A similar proportion disagree that caring about Israel is an important part of being a Jew (American Jewish Committee 2005a).

In the year after the oil embargo (1974), the United Nations General Assembly ignored American and Israeli objections and passed a resolution declaring that "Zionism is a form of racism and racial discrimination." **Zionism**, which initially referred to the old Jewish religious yearning to return to the biblical homeland, has been expressed in the twentieth century in the movement to create a Jewish state in Palestine. Ever since the **Diaspora**, the exile of Jews from Palestine several centuries before Christianity, many Jews have seen the destiny of their people only as the establishment of a Jewish state in the Holy Land.

The Zionism resolution, finally repealed by the United Nations in 1991, had no lasting influence and did not change any nation's foreign policy. However, it did increase Jewish fears of reawakened anti-Semitism thinly disguised as attacks on Zionist beliefs. Even the development of agreements between Israel and its Arab neighbors and the international recognition of Palestinian autonomy in Israel did not end the concern of Jewish Americans that continuing anti-Israeli feeling reflected anti-Semitism.

Zionism
Traditional Jewish religious yearning to return to the biblical homeland, now used to refer to support for the state of Israel.

Diaspora
The exile of Jews from Palestine.

American Jews and African Americans. The contemporary anti-Semitism of African Americans is of special concern to Jewish Americans. There is no reason why anti-Semites should be exclusively White, but Jews have been especially troubled by Blacks expressing ethnic prejudices, given their own history of oppression. Jewish Americans have been active in civil rights causes and have contributed generously to legal defense funds. Jewish neighborhoods and employers have also been quicker than their Gentile counterparts to accept African Americans. Therefore, there is a positive Black–Jewish alliance with a long history. For these reasons, some Jews find it especially difficult to understand why another group experiencing prejudice and discrimination should express anti-Semitic sentiments.

Beginning in the 1960s, some African American activists and the Black Panther party supported the Arabs in the Middle East conflict and called on Israel to surrender. Black–Jewish relations were again inflamed in 1984 by the Reverend Jesse Jackson during his campaign for the Democratic party's nomination for the presidency. His off-the-record reference to Jews as "Hymies" and the publicly broadcast anti-Semitic remarks by one of his supporters, Nation of Islam minister Louis Farrakhan, gave rise to new tensions between Blacks and Jews. During the 1988 campaign, Jackson distanced himself from anti-Semitic rhetoric, stating, "The sons and the daughters of the Holocaust and the sons and the daughters of slavery must find common ground again" (Schmidt 1988, 14).

In the 1990s, unrelated events again seemed to draw attention to the relationship between Jews and African Americans. On several college campuses, invited African American speakers made anti-Israeli statements, inflaming the Jewish students in attendance. In a 1991 New York City incident, a Hasidic Jew ran a red light, killing an African American child, and the ambulance that regularly serves the Hasidic community did not pick up the child. In the emotional climate that resulted, an Australian Jewish researcher was stabbed to death, and several days of rioting in the Brooklyn, New York, neighborhood of Crown Heights followed (Morris and Rubin 1993).

In response to these and other events, many Jewish and African American leaders perceived a crisis in intergroup relations, and calls for unity became very public. For example, in 1994, the Reverend Jesse Jackson sought to distance himself from the statements of Khalid Abdul Muhammad, an aide of Farrakhan, calling him "racist, anti-Semitic, divisive, untrue, and chilling" (Finder 1994, 21).

African American resentment, in many situations attracting notoriety, has rarely been anti-Jewish as such but rather has been opposed to White institutions. As author James Baldwin (1967, 114) said, Blacks "are anti-Semitic because they're anti-White." That racial prejudice is deep in the United States is shown by the fact that two groups suffering discrimination, groups that might unite in opposition to the dominant society, fight each other instead.

An old Yiddish saying, "Schwer zu sein a Yid," means "It is tough to be a Jew." Anti-Semitism past and present is related. The old hostilities seem never to die. The atrocities of Nazi Germany have not been forgotten, nor should they be. Racial and ethnic hostility, against whatever group, unifies the group against its attackers, and Jewish Americans are no exception. The Jewish people of the United States have come together, regardless of nationality, to form a minority group with a high degree of group identity.

Position of Jewish Americans

Jewish Americans have an important role in contemporary America. They are active participants in the fight for civil rights and work on behalf of Israel. These efforts are important but only begin to describe their role in the United States. For a better perspective on Jewish people in the United States, the following summarizes their present situation with respect to employment and income, education, organizational activity, and political activity.

Employment and Income

Discrimination conditions all facets of a subordinate group's life. Jews have experienced, and to a limited extent still experience, differential treatment in the American job market. The results of a 1998 national survey showed that 71 percent of Jews viewed anti-Semitism as a problem in the United States, although not necessarily in hiring practices. As shown in Table 14.1, through perseverance and emphasis on education, Jewish Americans as a group have overcome barriers to full employment and now enjoy high incomes (*Los Angeles Times* Poll 1998).

Using a variety of techniques, social science studies have documented declining discrimination against Jews in the business world. Sociologist Samuel Klausner interviewed business school graduates, comparing Jews with Protestants and Catholics who graduated from the same university in the same year. Klausner (1988) concludes, "(1) Jewish MBAs are winning positions in the same industries as their Catholic and Protestant classmates; (2) they are rising more rapidly in corporate hierarchies than their Catholic and Protestant colleagues; (3) they are achieving higher salaries than their Catholic and Protestant colleagues" (p. 33). Klausner adds that researchers tested

TABLE 14.1
Profile of Jews in the United States

	Jewish Americans	All U.S.
INCOME		
Less than $40,000	28%	52%
$40,000–$59,999	18	21
$60,000 or more	38	20
Don't know/refused	16	7
OCCUPATION		
Professional	40	15
Manager	24	20
White collar	19	19
Business owner	8	9
Unskilled blue collar	5	16
Skilled blue collar	3	19
IDEOLOGY		
Liberal	46	24
Moderate	28	31
Conservative	23	40
POLITICAL PARTY		
Democrat	45	32
Independent	29	31
Republican	12	23
EDUCATION		
High school or less	13	59
Some college	27	21
College graduate	24	10
Graduate school	35	9

Source: Los Angeles Times Poll 1998.

seven indicators of discrimination and in each case failed to find evidence of discrimination against Jewish executives. Interestingly, however, this same study detected substantial discrimination against African Americans and women.

The economic success of the Jewish people as a group obscures the poverty of many individual Jewish families. We reached a similar conclusion in Chapter 12 from income data on Asian Americans and their image as a model minority. Sociologists largely agree that Jews in 1930 were as likely to be poverty stricken and to be living in slums as any minority group today. Most have escaped poverty, but what Ann Wolfe (1972) calls "the invisible Jewish poor" remains invisible to the rest of society. Like Chinese Americans, the Jewish poor were not well served by the Economic Opportunity Act and other federal experiments to eradicate poverty in the 1960s and 1970s. Although the proportion of the poor among the Jews is not as substantial as among Blacks or Hispanics, it does remind us that not all Jewish families have affluent lifestyles (Gold 1965; Lavender 1977; Levine and Hochbaum 1974).

Education

Jews place great emphasis on education (see Table 14.1). This desire for formal schooling stems, it is argued, from the Judaic religion, which places the rabbi, or teacher, at the center of religious life.

In the United States today, all Jewish congregations emphasize religious instruction more than Protestants typically do. A 2000 estimate stated that there were 7,000 day schools with 200,000 pupils. Day schools are, in effect, private elementary schools with a substantial proportion of the curriculum given to Judaic studies and the learning of Hebrew. The less religiously committed may attend instruction on Sundays or on weekday afternoons after attending public schools. Seventy-six percent of Jews have received some form of formal Jewish education before they reach 30 years of age. The Jewish-sponsored component of higher education is not limited to strict religious instruction such as that found in rabbinical schools. Beginning in 1947, Jews founded graduate schools of medicine, education, social work, and mathematics, along with Brandeis University, which offers both undergraduate and graduate degrees. These institutions are nonsectarian (i.e., admission is not limited to Jews) and are conceived of as a Jewish-sponsored contribution to higher education (Abrahamson 1997; *Los Angeles Times* Poll 1998; *Religion Watch* 2000).

The religiously based tradition of lifelong study has left as a legacy a value system that stresses education. The poverty of Jewish immigrants kept them from devoting years to secular schooling, but they were determined that their children would do better. Despite their high levels of educational attainment, some members of the Jewish community express concern about Jewish education. They are disappointed with its highly secularized nature, not only because religious teaching has been limited but also because the Jewish sociocultural experience has been avoided altogether. It may even contribute to Judaization, the lessening of Judaism.

Organizational Activity

The American Jewish community has encompassed a variety of organizations since its beginnings. These groups serve many purposes: Some are religious, and others are charitable, political, or educational. No organization, secular or religious, represents all American Jews, but there are more than 300 nationwide organizations.

Among the most significant are the United Jewish Appeal (UJA), the American Jewish Committee, the American Jewish Congress, and B'nai B'rith. The UJA was founded in 1939 and serves as a fund-raising organization for humanitarian causes. Recently, Israel has received the largest share of the funds collected. The American Jewish Committee (founded in 1906) and American Jewish Congress (1918) work toward the similar purpose of improving Jewish–Gentile relations. B'nai B'rith (Sons of the Covenant) was founded in 1843 and claims 500,000 members in forty nations. It promotes cultural and social programs and, through its Anti-Defamation League, monitors and fights anti-Semitism and hate crimes directed at other groups.

Besides the national groups, many community-based organizations are active. Some local organizations, such as social and business clubs, were founded because the existing groups barred Jews from membership. The U.S. Supreme Court has consistently ruled that private social organizations such as country clubs and business clubs may discriminate against Jews or any other ethnic or racial group. Jewish community centers are also prominent local organizations. To Gentiles, the synagogue is the most visible symbol of the Jewish presence at the community level. However, the Jewish community center is an important focus of local activity. In many Jewish neighborhoods throughout the United States, it is the center of secular activity. Hospitals, nurseries, homes for the elderly, and child care agencies are only a few of the community-level activities sponsored by Jewish Americans (Rabinove 1970; Sklare 1971).

Political Activity

American Jews play a prominent role in politics as both voters and elected officials. Jews as a group are not typical in that they are more likely than the general population to label themselves liberal (refer back to Table 14.1). Although upper-middle-class voters tend to vote Republican, Jewish voters in that category have been steadfastly Democratic. About 54 percent identify themselves as Democrat compared to only 16 percent Republican (American Jewish Committee 2005a).

Jews have long been successful in being elected to office, but it was not until 1988 that an Orthodox Jew from Connecticut was elected to the U.S. Senate. Joseph Lieberman refrained from campaigning on the Sabbath each week; his religious views were not an issue. He went on to be named as the vice presidential running mate of Al Gore. Even during the campaign, he honored the Sabbath and did not actively campaign, even avoiding dialing a telephone to potential supporters. Many view the positive response to his campaign as a sign of openness to devout Jews as political candidates (Issacson and Foltin 2001; Pew Charitable Trust 2000).

As in all subordinate groups, the political activity of Jewish Americans has not been limited to conventional electoral politics. Radical Jewish politics has been dominated by college students. At the height of their involvement in the late 1960s, Jewish youths were active with Gentiles in the New Left movement and in working alone for causes unique to Jews, such as the support of Israel. Into the latter part of the twentieth century, some Jews backed the more extreme responses to the friction between Israel and its Arab neighbors. A few even settled in Israel and, though small in number, were often vocal backers of resistance to any accommodation to the Arab nations or the Palestinian Authority.

Religious Life

Jewish identity and participation in the Jewish religion are not the same. Many Americans consider themselves Jewish and are considered Jewish by others even though they have never participated in Jewish religious life. The available data indicate that 57 percent of American Jews are affiliated with a synagogue or temple, but only 10 percent view participation in religious worship as extremely important. Even in Israel, only 30 percent of Jews are religiously observant. Nevertheless, the presence of a religious tradition is an important tie among Jews, even secular Jews (American Jewish Committee 2005; S. Cohen 1991).

Typically Jews affiliated with Reform Congregations such as this one pictured in Seattle, Washington, at Yom Kippur Service have made up the largest segment of observant Jews. But the number of Conservative and Orthodox Jews is growing.

The Judaic faith embraces a number of factions or denominations that are similar in their roots but marked by sharp distinctions. No precise data reveal the relative numbers of the three major groups. Part of the problem is the difficulty of placing individuals in the proper group. For example, it is common for a Jew to be a member of an Orthodox congregation but consider himself or herself Conservative. The following levels of affiliation are based on a December 2005 national survey of Jewish Americans:

- Orthodox: 19 percent
- Conservative: 32 percent
- Reconstructionist: 2 percent
- Reform: 29 percent
- Just Jewish: 26 percent
- Not sure: 1 percent

There is a definite trend toward Jews being more Orthodox and Conservative. This trend results from the large Orthodox families, some conversion by less conservative Jews to orthodoxy, and immigration of traditional Jews to the United States. Young Jews ages 18 to 39 are nearly twice as likely to be Orthodox as the general Jewish population (American Jewish Committee 2001, 2005a; Ukeles et al. 2006).

We, will focus on two forms of Judaism at either end of the continuum: the Orthodox, faith, which attempts to uphold a very traditional practice of Judaism, and the Reform faith, which accommodates itself to the secular world.

The Orthodox Tradition

The unitary Jewish tradition developed in the United States into three sects, beginning in the mid-nineteenth century. The differences between Orthodox, Conservative, and Reform Judaism are based on their varying acceptance of traditional rituals. All three sects embrace a philosophy based on the Torah, the first five books of the Old Testament. The differences developed because some Jews wanted to be less distinguishable from other Americans. Another significant factor in explaining the development of different groups is the absence of a religious elite and bureaucratic hierarchy. This facilitated the breakdown in traditional practices.

Orthodox Jewish life is very demanding, especially in a basically Christian society such as the United States. Almost all conduct is defined by rituals that require an Orthodox Jew to reaffirm his or her religious conviction constantly. Most Americans are familiar with **kashrut**, the laws pertaining to permissible and forbidden foods. When strictly adhered to, kashrut governs not only what foods may be eaten (kosher) but also how the food is prepared, served, and eaten. Besides day-to-day practices, Orthodox Jews have weekly and annual observances. Women may not be rabbis among the Orthodox, although beginning in 2006, women were named to head a congregation, but only male members of the congregation could read publicly from the Torah (Luo 2006b).

Even Orthodox Jews differ in their level of adherence to traditional practices. Among the ultraorthodox are the Hasidic Jews, or Hasidim, who number some 2000,000 with half residing chiefly in several neighborhoods in Brooklyn. To the Hasidim, following the multitude of mitzvahs, or commandments of behavior, is as important today as it was in the time of Moses. Their spiritual commitment extends well beyond customary Jewish law even as interpreted by Orthodox Jews.

Hasidic Jews wear no garments that mix linen and wool. Men wear a yarmulke, or skullcap, constantly, even while sleeping. Attending a secular college is frowned on. Instead, the men undertake a lifetime of study of the Torah and the accompanying rabbinical literature of the Talmud. Women's education consists of instruction on how to run the home in keeping with Orthodox tradition. Hasidic Jews, who themselves are organized in separate communities, have courts with jurisdiction recognized by the faithful in many matters especially as they relate to family life.

Orthodox children attend special schools in order to meet minimal New York State educational requirements. The devotion to religious study is reflected in this comment by a Hasidic Jew: "Look at Freud, Marx, Einstein—all Jews who made their mark on the non-Jewish world. To me, however, they would have been much better off studying in a yeshiva [a Jewish school]. What a waste of three fine Talmudic minds" (H. Arden 1975, 294). Although devoted to their religion, the Hasidim participate in local elections and politics and are employed in outside occupations. All such activities are influenced by their orthodoxy and a self-reliance rarely duplicated elsewhere in the United States.

kashrut
Laws pertaining to permissible (kosher) and forbidden foods and their preparation.

A rabbi blesses a 13-year-old at her Bat Mitzvah in the temple. Jewish children often celebrate a coming-of-age ceremony. According to Jewish law, when Jewish children reach the age of maturity (12 years for girls, 13 years for boys), they become responsible for their actions. At this point a boy is said to become Bar Mitzvah; a girl is said to become Bat Mitzvah.

The Reform Tradition

Reform Jews, though deeply committed to the religious faith, have altered many of the rituals. Women and men sit together in Reform congregations, and both participate in the reading of the Torah at services. A few Reform congregations have even experimented with observing the Sabbath on Sunday. Circumcision for males is not mandatory. Civil divorce decrees are sufficient and recognized so that a divorce granted by a three-man rabbinical court is not required before remarriage. Reform Jews recognize the children of Jewish men and non-Jewish women as Jews with no need to convert. All these practices would be unacceptable to the Orthodox Jew.

Conservative Judaism is a compromise between the rigidity of the Orthodox and the extreme modification of the Reform. Because of the middle position, the national organization of Conservatives, the United Synagogue of America, strives to create its own identity and seeks to view its traditions as an appropriate, authentic approach to the faith.

Table 14.2 displays some results of a national survey on Jewish identification. The three sects here include both members and nonmembers of local congregations. Reform Jews are the least likely of the three religious groups to participate in religious events, to be involved in the Jewish community, or to participate in predominantly Jewish organizations. Yet in Reform temples, there has been an effort to observe religious occasions such as Rosh Hashanah (*Religion Watch* 1995b; Wertheimer 1996).

The one exception in Reform Jews' lower levels of participation is on issues concerning world Jewry, such as Israel or the treatment of Jews in such nations as the former Soviet Union and Iran. For the Orthodox Jew, these issues are less important than those strictly related to the observance of the faith. Although no nationwide organized movement advocates this, in recent years Reform Jews seem to have reclaimed traditions they once rejected.

Unlike people of other faiths in the United States, Jews historically have not embarked on recruitment or evangelistic programs to attract new members. Beginning in the late 1970s, Jews, especially Reform Jews, debated the possibility of outreach programs. Least objectionable to Jewish congregations were efforts begun in 1978 aimed at non-Jewish partners and children in mixed marriages. In 1981, the program was broadened to invite conversions by Americans who had no religious connection, but these very modest recruitment drives are still far from resembling those that have been carried out by Protestant denominations for decades (Luo 2006a).

Like Protestant denominations, Jewish denominations are associated with class, nationality, and other social differences. The Reform Jews are the wealthiest and have the best formal education of the group, the Orthodox are the poorest and least educated in years of formal secular schooling, and the Conservatives occupy a position between the

TABLE 14.2 Jewish Identification by Group				
Indices	Orthodox	Conservative	Reform	"Just Jewish"
Ethnic pride	86%	79%	73%	65%
Closeness to Jews	90	83	71	54
Observance of Jewish holidays	73	42	28	18
Observance of Christian holidays	6	6	17	28
Pro-Israel	78	71	56	50

Source: S. Cohen 1991, 58, 63, 74.

two. A fourth branch of American Judaism, Reconstructionism, an offshoot of the Conservative movement, has only recently developed an autonomous institutional structure with ritual practices similar to those of Reform Jews. Religious identification is associated with generation: Immigrants and older Jews are more likely to be Orthodox, and their grandchildren are more likely to be Reform (*Los Angeles Times* Poll 1998).

Yiddishkait
Jewishness.

halakha
Jewish laws covering obligations and duties.

Jewish Identity

Ethnic and racial identification can be positive or negative. Awareness of ethnic identity can contribute to a person's self-esteem and give that person a sense of group solidarity with similar people. When a person experiences an identity only as a basis for discrimination or insults, he or she may want to shed that identity in favor of one more acceptable to society. Unfavorable differential treatment can also encourage closer ties between members of the community being discriminated against, as it has for Jews.

Most would judge the diminishing of out-group hostility and the ability of Jews to leave the ghetto as a positive development (G. Friedman 1967). However, the improvement in Jewish–Gentile relations also creates a new problem in Jewish social identity. It has become possible for Jews to shed their "Jewishness," or **Yiddishkait**. Many retain their Yiddishkait even in suburbia, but it is more difficult there than in the ghetto. In the end, however, Jews cannot lose their identity entirely. Jews are still denied total assimilation in the United States no matter how much the individual ceases to think of himself or herself as Jewish. Social clubs may still refuse membership, and prospective non-Jewish in-laws may try to interfere with plans to marry.

Events in the world also remind the most assimilated Jew of the heritage left behind. A few such reminders in the past generation include Nazi Germany, the founding of Israel in 1948, the Six-Day War of 1967, Soviet interference with Jewish life and migration, the terrorist attack at the 1972 Munich Olympics, the Yom Kippur War of 1973, the 1973 oil embargo, the United Nations' 1974 anti-Zionism vote, and the Scud missile attacks during the 1991 Gulf War.

A unique identity issue presents itself to Jewish women, whose religious tradition has placed them in a subordinate position. For example, it was not until 1972 that the first female rabbi was ordained. Jewish feminism has its roots in the women's movement of the 1960s and 1970s, several of whose leaders were Jewish. There have been some changes in **halakha** (Jewish law covering obligations and duties), but it is still difficult for a woman to get a divorce recognized by the Orthodox Jewish tradition. Sima Rabinowicz of upstate New York has been hailed as the Jewish Rosa Parks for her recent

Young people gather at a Jewish school in Manhattan.

bus battle. Rabinowicz refused to give up her seat in the women's section of a Hasidic-owned, publicly subsidized bus to Orthodox men who wanted to pray in private, segregated from women as required by halakha. The courts defended her right to ride as she wished, just as an earlier court had ruled with Rosa Parks in the Birmingham bus boycott. Jewish women contend that they should not be forced to make a choice between their identity as a woman and as a Jew (Baum 1998; Frankel 1995).

We will now examine three factors that influence the ethnic identity of Jews in the United States: family, religion, and cultural heritage.

Role of the Family

ASK Yourself

What are the main challenges facing Jewish families today?

In general, the family works to socialize children, but for religious Jews it also fulfills a religious commandment. In the past, this compulsion was so strong that the *shadchan* (the marriage broker or matchmaker) fulfilled an important function in the Jewish community by ensuring marriage for all eligible people. The emergence of romantic love in modern society made the *shadchan* less acceptable to young Jews, but recent statistics show Jews more likely to marry than any other group.

Jews have traditionally remained in extended families, intensifying the transmission of Jewish identity. Numerous observers have argued that the Jewish family today no longer maintains its role in identity transmission and that the family is consequently contributing to assimilation. The American Jewish Committee released a report identifying ten problems that are endangering "the family as the main transmission agent of Jewish values, identity, and continuity" (Conver 1976, A2). The following issues are relevant to Jews today:

- More Jews marry later than members of other groups.
- Most organizations of single Jews no longer operate solely for the purpose of matchmaking. These groups are now supportive of singles and the single way of life.
- The divorce rate is rising; there is no presumption of the permanence of marriage and no stigma attached to its failure.
- The birthrate is falling, and childlessness has become socially acceptable.
- Financial success has taken precedence over child raising in importance and for many has become the major goal of the family.
- The intensity of family interaction has decreased, although it continues to be higher than in most other religious and ethnic groups.
- There is less socializing across generation lines, partly as a result of geographic mobility.
- The sense of responsibility of family members to other family members has declined.
- The role of Jewishness is no longer central to the lives of Jews.
- Intermarriage has lessened the involvement of the Jewish partner in Jewish life and the emphasis on Jewish aspects of family life.

Data and sample surveys have verified these trends. Nevertheless, to use a term introduced in Chapter 10 in connection with the Latino family, Jewish Americans still have a higher than typical degree of familism. Jews are more likely than other ethnic or religious groups to be members of a household that interacts regularly with kinfolk. Nonetheless, the trend is away from familism, a trend that could further erode Jewish identity.

Without question, of the ten problems cited by the American Jewish Committee, intermarriage has received the greatest attention from Jewish leaders. Therefore, it has been the subject of significant social research and not just idle speculation. This topic is the subject of our "Research Focus."

Focus Research Focus Research

INTERMARRIAGE: THE FINAL STEP TO ASSIMILATION?

Sex and the City's Charlotte York, the quintessential WASP character, descends again into a Jewish ritual bath marking her conversion to Judaism. Although this fictional portrayal was welcomed by Jewish viewers, is it representative of what happens when Jews take a spouse today?

Since Christianity's influence has grown in Europe and North America, a persistent fear among Jews has been that their children or grandchildren would grow up ignorant of the Torah. Equally bad, a descendant might become *apikoros*, an unbeliever who engages in intellectual speculation about the relevance of Judaism. These concerns are growing as Jewish Americans' resistance to intermarriage declines. In 2005, two-thirds of Jews felt anti-Semitism was the biggest threat to Jewish life, but one out of three saw it to be intermarriage.

Why does intermarriage emerge as a social issue rather than a personal dilemma? Intermarriage makes a decrease in the size of the Jewish community in the United States more likely. In marriages that occurred in the 1970s, more than 70 percent of Jews married Jews or people who converted to Judaism. In marriages since 1996, that proportion has dropped to 53 percent. This trend means that American Jews today are just as likely to marry a Gentile as a Jew. For many, religion is a nonissue—neither parent practices religious rituals. Two-thirds of the children of these Jewish–Gentile marriages are not raised as Jews.

Many Jewish Americans respond that intermarriage is inevitable and the Jewish community must build on whatever links the intermarried couple may still have with a Jewish ethnic culture. There are many programs throughout the United States to help Gentile spouses of Jews feel welcome so that the faith will not lose them both. Yet other Jews feel that such efforts may be sending a dangerous signal that intermarriage is inevitable. Therefore, it is not surprising to see that probably more than any other ethnic or religious group, organizations within the Jewish community commission research on the trends in intermarriage. ▨

Source: American Jewish Committee 2005a; Freedman 2003; Schwartz 2006; Snyder 2006; United Jewish Communities 2003.

Several trends come together to lead to a stabilization or decline in the number of active Jews in the United States. As shown in Figure 14.5, the continuation of a Jewish tradition varies dramatically by denomination. Conservative and Orthodox Jews have larger families, encourage formal Jewish instruction, and are much less likely to witness intermarriage than Reform or unaffiliated ("just Jewish") Jewish Americans. Analysts of these data are concerned that Jews, especially if they are not Orthodox, cannot take it for granted that they will have grandchildren with whom to share seders, Sabbath, and other Jewish moments.

Role of Religion

Devotion to Judaism appears to be the clear way to preserve ethnic identity. Yet Jews are divided about how to practice their faith. Many of the Orthodox see Reform Jews as little better than nonbelievers. Even among the Orthodox, some sects such as the Lubavitchers try to awaken less-observant Orthodox Jews to their spiritual obligation. Added to these developments is the continuing rise in Jewish out-marriages previously

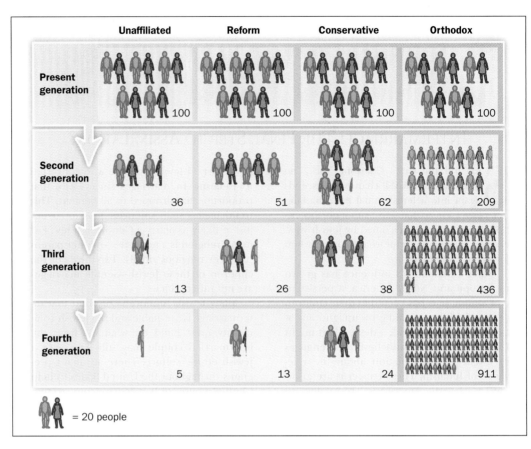

FIGURE 14.5 Generational Patterns by Denomination

Source: Gordon and Horowitz 1997. Based on the 1990 National Population Survey and the 1991 New York Jewish Population Study.
Note: Figure assumes each denomination begins with the same number of people.

noted. Many Jewish religious rituals are centered in the home rather than in the synagogue, from lighting Sabbath candles to observing dietary laws. Therefore, Jews are far more likely to feel that children cannot be brought up in the faith without that family support.

The religious question facing Jews is not so much one of ideology as of observing the commandments of traditional Jewish law. The religious variations among the nearly 6 million Jewish Americans are a product of attempts to accommodate traditional rituals and precepts to life in the dominant society. It is in adhering to such rituals that Jews are most likely to be at odds with the Christian theme advanced in public schools, even if it appears only in holiday parties. In Chapter 1, we introduced the term **marginality** to describe the status of living in two distinct cultures simultaneously. Jews who give some credence to the secular aspects of Christmas celebrations exemplify individuals' accommodating themselves to two cultures. For all but the most Orthodox, this acceptance means disobeying commandments or even accepting non-Jewish traditions by singing Christmas carols or exchanging greeting cards.

Is there a widespread pattern among Jewish Americans of reviving the old ways? Some Jews, especially those secure in their position, have taken up renewed orthodoxy. It is difficult to say whether the sporadic rise of traditionalism among Jews is a significant force or a fringe movement. Novelist Tom Ross at age 67 retook his birth name, Tom Rosenberg. Shortly after coming to the United States, his parents volun-

marginality
The status of being between two cultures at the same time, such as the status of Jewish immigrants in the United States.

Hillel Houses, such as this one at the University of Southern California, are both social and spiritual gathering places for Jewish students on college campuses.

tarily Anglicized their name. Now Tom wanted to take another step in reclaiming his roots. Still, at the beginning of the twenty-first century, Jewish leaders in North America and Europe are much more likely to express concern about the increase in the number of secularized Jews than to find reasons to applaud an increase in Yiddishkait (Rosenberg 2000).

Role of Cultural Heritage

For many Jews, religious observance is a very small aspect of their Jewishness. They express their identity instead in a variety of political, cultural, and social activities. For them, acts of worship, fasting, eating permitted foods, and the study of the Torah and the Talmud are irrelevant to being Jewish. Of course, religious Jews find such a position impossible to accept (Liebman 1973).

Many Gentiles mistakenly suppose that a measure of Jewishness is the ability to speak Yiddish. Few people have spoken as many languages as the Jews through their long history. Yiddish is only one, and it developed in Jewish communities in eastern Europe between the tenth and twelfth centuries. Fluency in Yiddish in the United States has been associated with the immigrant generation and the Orthodox. Sidney Goldstein and Calvin Goldscheider (1968) reported that evidence overwhelmingly supports the conclusion that linguistic assimilation among Jews is almost complete by the third generation. However, the 1960s and 1970s brought a slight increase in the use of Hebrew. This change probably resulted from increased pride in Israel and a greater interaction between that nation and the United States.

Overall, the differences between Jews and Gentiles have declined in the United States. To a large extent, this reduction is a product of generational changes typical of all ethnic groups. The first-generation Mexican American in Los Angeles contrasts sharply with the middle-class White living in suburban Boston. The convergence in culture and identity is much greater between the fourth-generation Mexican American and his or her White counterpart. A similar convergence is occurring among Jews. This change does not signal the eventual demise of the Jewish identity. Moreover, Jewish identity is not a single identity, as we can see from the heterogeneity in religious observance, dedication to Jewish and Israeli causes, and participation in Jewish organizations.

Being Jewish comes from the family, the faith, and the culture, but it does not require any one criterion. Jewishness transcends nation, religion, or culture. A sense of peoplehood is present that neither anti-Semitic bigotry nor even an ideal state of fellowship

peoplehood
Milton Gordon's term for a group with a shared feeling.

among all religions would destroy. American life may have drastically modified Jewish life in the direction of dominant society values, but it has not eliminated it. Milton Gordon (1964) refers to **peoplehood** as a group with a shared feeling. For Jews, this sense of identity originates from a variety of sources, past and present, both within and without (Goldscheider 2003).

Conclusion

Jewish Americans are the product of three waves of immigration originating from three different Jewish communities: the Sephardic, the western European, and the eastern European. They brought different languages and, to some extent, different levels of religious orthodoxy. Today, they have assimilated to form an ethnic group that transcends the initial differences in nationality.

Jews are not a homogeneous group. Among them are the Reform, the Conservative, and Orthodox denominations, listed in ascending order of adherence to traditional rituals. Nonreligious Jews make up another group, probably as large as any one segment, and still see themselves as Jewish.

Jewish identity is reaffirmed from within and outside the Jewish community; however, both sources of affirmation are weaker today. Identity is strengthened by the family, religion, and the vast network of national and community-based organizations. Anti-Semitism outside the Jewish community strengthens the in-group feeling and the perception that survival as a people is threatened.

Today, American Jews face a new challenge: They must maintain their identity in an overwhelmingly Christian society in which discrimination is fading and outbreaks of prejudice are sporadic. *Yiddishkait* may not so much have decreased as changed. Elements of the Jewish tradition have been shed in part because of modernization and social change. Some of this social change—a decline in anti-Semitic violence and restrictions—is certainly welcome. Although *kashrut* observance has declined, most Jews care deeply about Israel, and many engage in pro-Israel activities. Commitment has changed with the times, but it has not disappeared (S. Cohen 1988).

Some members of the Jewish community view the apparent assimilation with alarm and warn against the grave likelihood of the total disappearance of a sizable and identifiable Jewish community in the United States. Others see the changes not as erosion but as an accommodation to a pluralistic, multicultural environment. We are witness to a progressive change in the substance and style of Jewish life. According to this view, Jewish identity, the Orthodox and Conservative traditions notwithstanding, has shed some of its traditional characteristics and has acquired others. The strength of this view comes with the knowledge that doomsayers have been present in the American Jewish community for at least two generations. Only the passage of time will reveal the future of Jewish life in the United States (Finestein 1988; Glazer 1990).

Despite their successes, Jews experience discrimination and prejudice, as does any subordinate group. Michael Lerner (1993:33), editor of the liberal Jewish journal *Tikkun*, declares that "Jews can only be deemed 'white' if there is massive amnesia on the part of non-Jews about the monumental history of anti-Semitism." As we noted earlier, reported episodes of anti-Semitism are on the increase in Europe and North America and even on the college campuses in the United States.

Although discrimination against Jews has gone on for centuries, far more ancient than anti-Semitism and the experience of the Diaspora is the subordinate role of women. Women were perhaps the first to be relegated to an inferior role and may be the last to work collectively to struggle for equal rights. Studying women as a subordinate group will reaffirm the themes in our study of racial and ethnic groups.

Key Terms

anti-Semitism 374
Diaspora 385
fringe-of-values theory 379
halakha 393
Holocaust 381

Holocaust revisionists 381
in-group virtues 380
Judaization 376
kashrut 391
marginality 396

out-group vices 380
peoplehood 398
Yiddishkait 393
Zionism 385

Review Questions

1. Why are the Jewish people most accurately characterized as an ethnic group?
2. How have the patterns of anti-Semitism changed or remained the same?
3. Why do African American–Jewish American relationships receive special scrutiny?
4. Why is maintaining Jewish identity so difficult in the United States?
5. Why does the family play such a critical role in Jewish identity?

Critical Thinking

1. Most minority groups regard acceptance as a positive outcome. Why do some Jewish Americans seem threatened by being accepted in contemporary Gentile society?
2. Using the Jewish experience as a basis for comparison, how has fusion functioned or not functioned for any other subordinate group when compared with Jews in the United States?
3. In Chapter 5, we presented Marcus Hansen's principle of third-generation interest. How does that apply or not apply to the generational differences displayed by denomination in Figure 14.5?
4. How different and similar have the experiences of women in organized religion been, compared with those of women in the Jewish faith?

Internet Connections—Research Navigator™

Follow the instructions found on page 35 of this text to access the features of Research Navigator™. Once at the Web site, enter your Login Name and Password. Then, to use the ContentSelect database, enter keywords such as "anti-Semitism," "bar mitzvah," "genocide," and "Holocaust," and the search engine will supply relevant and recent scholarly and popular press publications. Use the *New York Times* Search-by-Subject Archive to find recent news articles related to sociology, and the Link Library feature to locate relevant Web links organized by the key terms associated with this chapter.

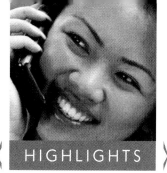
SUBORDINATE STATUS MEANS CONFINEMENT TO SUBORDINATE roles not justified by a person's abilities. Society is increasingly aware that women are a subordinate group. There are biological differences between males and females; however, one must separate differences of gender from those produced by sexism, distinctions that result from socialization. The feminist movement did not begin with the women's movement of the 1960s but has a long history and, like protest efforts by other subordinate groups, has not been warmly received by society. A comparison of the socioeconomic position of men and women leaves little doubt that they have unequal opportunities in employment and political power. Although men are taking on greater responsibilities with child care and housework, these are still disproportionately the responsibilities of women. Minority women occupy an especially difficult position in that they experience subordinate status by virtue of their race or ethnicity as well as their gender. Minority women are also more likely to be poor, which creates what sociologists have termed the matrix of domination.

VOTES FOR WOMEN ON THE SAME TERMS AS MEN

Women are an oppressed group even though they form the numerical majority. They are a social minority in the United States and throughout Western society. Men dominate in influence, prestige, and wealth. Women do occupy positions of power, but those who do are the exceptions, as evidenced by newspaper accounts that declare "She is the first woman" or "the only woman" to be in a particular position.

Many people, men and women, find it difficult to conceptualize women as a subordinate group. After all, not all women live in ghettos. They no longer have to attend inferior schools. They freely interact and live with their alleged oppressors, men. How, then, are they a subordinate group? Let us reexamine the five properties of a subordinate or minority group introduced in Chapter 1

1. Women do experience unequal treatment. Although they are not segregated by residence, they are victims of prejudice and discrimination.

2. Women have physical and cultural characteristics that distinguish them from the dominant group (men).

3. Membership in the subordinate group is involuntary.

4. Through the rise of contemporary feminism, women have become increasingly aware of their subordinate status and have developed a greater sense of group solidarity.

5. Women are not forced to marry, yet many women feel that their subordinate status is most irrevocably defined within marriage.

In this chapter, the similarities between women and racial and ethnic groups will become apparent.

The most common analogy about minorities used in the social sciences is the similarity between the status of African Americans and that of women. Blacks are considered a minority group, but, one asks, how can women of all groups be so similar in condition? We recognize some similarities in recent history; for example, an entire generation has observed and participated in both the civil rights movement and the women's movement. A background of suffrage campaigns, demonstrations, sit-ins, lengthy court battles, and self-help groups is common to the movements for equal rights for both women and African Americans. But similarities were recognized long before the recent protests against inequality. In *An American Dilemma* (1944), the famous study of race described in Chapter 1, Gunnar Myrdal observed that a parallel to the Blacks' role in society was found among women. Others, such as Helen Mayer Hacker (1951, 1974), later elaborated on the similarities.

What do these groups have in common besides recent protest movements? The negative stereotypes directed at the two groups are quite similar: Both groups have been considered emotional, irresponsible, weak, or inferior. Both are thought to fight subtly against the system: Women allegedly try to outwit men by feminine wiles, as historically Blacks allegedly outwitted Whites by pretending to be deferential or respectful. To these stereotypes must be added another similarity: Neither women nor African Americans are accepting a subordinate role in society any longer.

Nearly all Whites give lip service, even if they do not wholeheartedly believe it, to the contention that African Americans are innately equal to Whites. They are inherently the same. But men and women are not the same, and they vary most dramatically in their roles in reproduction. Biological differences have contributed to sexism.

Sexism is the ideology that one sex is superior to the other. Quite different is the view that there are few differences between the sexes. Such an idea is expressed in the concept of **androgyny.** An androgynous model of behavior permits people to see that humans can be both aggressive and expressive, depending on the requirements of the situation. People do not have to be locked into the behavior that accompanies the labels *masculine* and *feminine.* In the United States, people disagree widely as to what implications, if any, the biological differences between the sexes have for social roles. We will begin our discussion of women as a subordinate group with this topic.

Gender Roles

A college man, done with afternoon classes, heads off to get a pedicure and, while the nail polish is drying, sits on a nearby park bench finishing some needlepoint he started. Meanwhile, a college woman walks through the park chewing tobacco and spitting along the path. What is wrong with this picture? We are witnessing the open violation of how men and women are expected to act. So unlikely are these episodes that I have taken them from sociology teachers who specifically ask their students to go out, violate gender expectations, and record how they feel and how people react to their behavior (Nielsen et al. 2000, 287).

Gender roles are society's expectations of the proper behavior, attitudes, and activities of males and females. Toughness has traditionally been seen in the United States as masculine, desirable only in men, whereas tenderness has been viewed as feminine. A society may require that one sex or the other take the primary responsibility for the socialization of the children, economic support of the family, or religious leadership.

Without question, socialization has a powerful impact on the development of females and males in the United States. Indeed, the gender roles first encountered in early childhood often are a factor in defining a child's popularity. Sociologists Patricia Adler and her colleagues (1992, 1998) observed elementary school children and found that boys typically achieved high status on the basis of their athletic ability, coolness, toughness, social skills, and success in relationships with girls. By contrast, girls gained popularity based on their parents' economic background and their own physical appearance, social skills, and academic success.

It may be obvious that males and females are conditioned to assume certain roles, but the origin of gender roles as we know them is less clear. Many studies have been

sexism
The ideology that one sex is superior to the other.

androgyny
The state of being both masculine and feminine, aggressive and gentle.

gender roles
Expectations regarding the proper behavior, attitudes, and activities of males and females.

Women's roles have changed significantly since the early 1960s, when they were generally depicted in the media solely as wives and mothers, as shown in the popular television series of that time, *Leave It to Beaver.*

done on laboratory animals, such as injecting monkeys and rats with male and female hormones. Primates in their natural surroundings have been closely observed for the presence and nature of gender roles. Animal studies do not point to instinctual gender differences similar to what humans are familiar with as masculinity and femininity. Historically, women's work came to be defined as a consequence of the birth process. Men, free of child-care responsibilities, generally became the hunters and foragers for food. Even though women must bear children, men could have cared for the young. Exactly why women were assigned that role in societies is not known.

Women's role varies across different cultures. Furthermore, we know that acceptable behavior for men and women changes over time in a society. For example, the men in the royal courts of Europe in the late 1700s fulfilled present-day stereotypes of feminine appearance in their display of ornamental dress and personal vanity rather than resembling the men of a century later, although they still engaged in duels and other forms of aggression. The social roles of the sexes have no constants in time or space (Doyle and Paludi 1998).

Sociological Perspectives

Sociologist Estelle Disch (1997) points out that gender differences are maintained in our culture through the systematic socialization of babies and infants, children, adolescents, and adults. Even though different subcultures and even different families vary in child rearing, we teach our children to be boys and girls, even though men and women are more alike than they are different. But she noted that gender socialization is not something that stops with youth. "From the time we are born until we die, gender socialization is a constant part of our lives" (p. 74). Gender training persists, and the larger institutional structures reinforce it.

We are bombarded with expectations for behavior as men and women from many sources simultaneously. Many individual women hold positions involving high levels of responsibility and competence but may not be accorded the same respect as men. Similarly, individual men find the time to get involved with their children's lives only to meet with disbelief and occasional surprise from health-care and educational systems accustomed to dealing only with mothers. Even when individuals are motivated to stretch the social boundaries of gender, social structure and institutions often impede them. Gender differentiation in our culture is embedded in social institutions: the family, of course, but also education, religion, politics, the economy, medicine, and the mass media.

Through this lifelong socialization, people are labeled by virtue of their sex. Certain activities and behaviors are associated with men and others with women. Besides the labeling perspective, we can also use functionalist and conflict perspectives to grasp more firmly how gender roles develop.

Functionalists maintain that sex differentiation has contributed to overall social stability. Sociologists Talcott Parsons and Robert Bales (1955) argued that, to function most efficiently, the family needs adults who will specialize in particular roles. They believed that the arrangement of gender roles with which they were familiar had arisen because marital partners needed a division of labor.

The functionalist view is initially persuasive in explaining the way in which women and men are typically brought up in U.S. society. However, it would lead us to expect even girls and women with no interest in children to still become baby-sitters and mothers. Similarly, males with a caring feeling for children may be "programmed" into careers in the business world. Clearly, such a differentiation between the sexes can have harmful consequences for the person who does not fit into specific roles, while depriving society of the optimal use of many talented people who are confined by sex-

Suffragists struggled for many years to convince Congress and the states to pass the Nineteenth Amendment to the Constitution, extending to women the right to vote, beginning in 1920.

ual labeling. Consequently, the conflict perspective is increasingly convincing in its analysis of the development of gender roles.

Conflict theorists do not deny the presence of a differentiation by sex. In fact, they contend that the relationship between females and males has been one of unequal power, with men being dominant over women. Men may have become powerful in preindustrial times because their size, physical strength, and freedom from childbearing duties allowed them to dominate women physically. In contemporary societies, such considerations are not as important, yet cultural beliefs about the sexes are now long established.

Both functionalists and conflict theorists acknowledge that it is not possible to change gender roles drastically without dramatic revisions in a culture's social structure. Functionalists see potential social disorder, or at least unknown social consequences, if all aspects of traditional sex differentiation are disturbed. Yet for conflict theorists, no social structure is ultimately desirable if it has to be maintained through the oppression of its citizens.

The Feminist Movement

Women's struggle for equality, like the struggles of other subordinate groups, has been long and multifaceted. From the very beginning, women activists and sympathetic men who spoke of equal rights were ridiculed and scorned.

In a formal sense, the American feminist movement was born in upstate New York in a town called Seneca Falls in the summer of 1848. On July 19, the first women's rights convention began, attended by Elizabeth Cady Stanton, Lucretia Mott, and other pioneers in the struggle for women's rights. This first wave of feminists, as they are currently known, battled ridicule and scorn as they fought for legal and political equality for women, but they were not afraid to risk controversy on behalf of their cause. In 1872, for example, Susan B. Anthony was arrested for attempting to vote in that year's presidential election.

All social movements—and feminism is no exception—have been marked by factionalism and personality conflicts. The civil rights movement and pan-Indianism have been hurt repeatedly by conflicts over what tactics to use and which reforms to push for first, as well as personality conflicts. Despite similar divisiveness, the women's movement struggled on toward its major goal: to gain the right to vote.

The Suffrage Movement

The **suffragists** worked for years to get women the right to vote. From the beginning, this reform was judged to be crucial. If women voted, it was felt, other reforms would quickly follow. The struggle took so long that many of the initial advocates of women's suffrage died before victory was reached. In 1879, an amendment to the Constitution was introduced that would have given women the right to vote. Not until 1919 was it finally passed, and not until the next year was it ratified as the Nineteenth Amendment to the Constitution.

The opposition to giving women the vote came from all directions. Liquor interests and brewers correctly feared that women would assist in passing laws restricting or prohibiting the sale of their products. The South feared the influence that more Black voters (i.e., Black women) might have. Southerners had also not forgotten the pivotal role women had played in the abolitionist movement. Despite the opposition, the suffrage movement succeeded in gaining women the right to vote, a truly remarkable achievement because it had to rely on male legislators to do so.

The Nineteenth Amendment did not automatically lead to other feminist reforms. Women did not vote as a bloc and have not been elected to office in proportion to their numbers. The single-minded goal of suffrage was harmful to the cause of feminism in many respects. Many suffragists thought that any changes more drastic than granting the vote would destroy the home. They rarely questioned the subordinate role assigned to women. For the most part, agitation for equal rights ended when suffrage was gained. In the 1920s and 1930s, large numbers of college-educated women entered professions, but these individual achievements did little to enhance the rights of women as a group. The feminist movement as an organized effort that gained national attention faded, to regain prominence only in the 1960s (Freeman 1975; O'Neill 1969; Rossi 1964).

Nevertheless, the women's movement did not die out completely in the first half of the century. Many women carried on the struggle in new areas. Margaret Sanger fought for legalized birth control. She opened birth control clinics because the medical profession refused to distribute birth control information. Sanger and Katherine Houghton Hepburn (mother of actress Katharine Hepburn) lobbied Congress for reform throughout the 1920s and 1930s. The police closed Sanger's early clinics. Not until 1937 were nationwide restrictions on birth control devices lifted, and some state bans remained in force until 1965.

The Women's Liberation Movement

Ideologically, the women's movement of the 1960s had its roots in the continuing informal feminist movement that began with the first subordination of women in Western society. Psychologically, it grew in America's kitchens, as women felt unfulfilled and did not know why, and in the labor force, as women were made to feel guilty because they were not at home with families. Demographically, by the 1960s, women had attained greater control about when and whether to become pregnant if they used contraception and, hence, had greater control over the size of the population (Heer and Grossbard-Shectman 1981).

Sociologically, several events delayed progress in the mid-1960s. The civil rights movement and the antiwar movement were slow to embrace women's rights. The New Left seemed as sexist as the rest of society in practice, despite its talk of equality. Groups protesting the draft and demonstrating on college campuses generally rejected women as leaders and assigned them traditional duties like preparing refreshments and publishing organization newsletters. The core of early feminists often knew each other from participating in other protest or reform groups that had initially been

suffragists
Women and men who worked successfully to gain women the right to vote.

unwilling to accept women's rights as a legitimate goal. Beginning in about 1967, as Chapter 7 showed, the movement for Black equality was no longer as willing to accept help from sympathetic Whites. White men moved on to protest the draft, a cause not as crucial to women's lives. While somewhat involved in the antiwar movement, many White women began to struggle for their own rights, although at first they had to fight alone. Eventually, civil rights groups, the New Left, and most established women's groups endorsed the feminist movement with the zeal of new converts, but initially they resisted the concerns of feminists (Freeman 1973, 1983).

The movement has also brought about a reexamination of men's roles. Supporters of "male liberation" wanted to free men from the constraints of the masculine value system. The masculine mystique is as real as the feminine one. Boys are socialized to think that they should be invulnerable, fearless, decisive, and even emotionless in some situations. Men are expected to achieve physically and occupationally at some risk to their own values, not to mention those of others. Failure to take up these roles and attitudes can mean that a man will be considered less than a man. Male liberation is the logical counterpart of female liberation. If women are to redefine their gender role successfully, men must redefine theirs as workers, husbands, and fathers (Messner 1997; National Organization for Men Against Sexism 2006).

Amid the many changing concerns since the mid-1960s, the feminist movement too has undergone significant change. Betty Friedan, a founder of the National Organization for Women (NOW), argued in the early 1960s that women had to understand the **feminine mystique,** recognizing that society saw them only as their children's mother and their husband's wife. Later, in the 1980s, though not denying that women deserved to have the same options in life as men, she called for restructuring the "institution of home and wife." Friedan and others now recognize that many young women are frustrated when time does not permit them to do it all: career, marriage, and motherhood. Difficult issues remain, and feminists continue to discuss and debate concerns such as the limits businesses put on careers of women with children, domestic violence, and male bias in medical research (Ferree and Hess 1994; Friedan 1963, 1981, 1991; Somners 1994).

Where are women's rights in the early years of the twenty-first century? In "Listen to Our Voices," sociologist Arlie Russell Hochschild sees the women's movement as a stalled revolution in which women may have more opportunities in the workplace but now are forced to do everything.

A sign of progress? Changing images of gender roles has meant the gradual emergence of the depiction of women, such as Laura Croft, as aggressive and violent characters in video games.

The Economic Picture

He works. She works. They are both physicians—a high-status occupation with financial rewards. He makes $140,000. She makes $88,000. Those are the results of a detailed study of occupations by the U.S. Census Bureau in 2004. It looked at the earnings of 821 occupations ranging from chief executives to dishwashers, considering one's age, education, and work experience. The unmistakable conclusion was there is a substantial gap in median earnings between full-time male and female workers in the same occupation. He's an air traffic controller and makes $67,000. She earns $56,000. He's a housekeeper and makes $19,000. She earns $15,000. He's a teacher's assistant and makes $20,000. She earns $15,000.

Men do not always earn more. The Census Bureau found two occupations out of 821 in which women typically earn about 1 percent more—hazardous materials recovery workers and telecommunications line installers (Weinberg 2004).

Another aspect of women's subordinate status is that, more than any other group, they are confined to certain occupations. Some sex-typed jobs for women pay well

feminine mystique
Society's view of a woman as only her children's mother and her husband's wife.

Voices Listen to Our Voices Listen to

TIME FOR CHANGE

Nationwide, work absorbs more of a parent's time than it did 25 years ago. Women go back to work earlier after childbirth—in the 1960s, one in eight women returned to work less than a year after childbirth; in 1996, it was approximately one in two. Once back, more mothers now work full-time, year-round.

Arlie Russell Hochschild

Studies on hours vary, but one national study conducted by Families and Work Institute found that, of workers with children age 12 and under, only 4 percent of men and 13 percent of women worked less than 40 hours a week.

This is part of a larger pattern I refer to as "stalled revolution." In the last 25 years, women have changed, but everything else has not changed as fast or as much. Thus, tens of millions of women go out to work in offices and plants that demand long hours and inflexible schedules, live in a world without widespread quality child care, and come home to mates who don't share the domestic load. The family has become the shock absorber for the strains between faster-changing women and slower-changing men and workplaces. This was already true for some families in the 1950s and 1960s, but now it's true for most. And we've come to think of the family under these strained conditions as the "normal" family. Then we wonder why young people are scared to death to become working parents and why our divorce rate is one of the world's highest.

Thoughtful public discussion about this state of affairs has been oddly silenced by two opposing parties, both of which divert our attention from the project of transforming the workplace. First, there are what I call the "accusatory traditionals," who have an eagle eye out for the problems of working mothers. If working mothers are tired, have troubled kids or tense marriages, the traditionals admonish women to junk their careers and stay home. Men, they don't touch.

Responding to these scolding traditionals are the "sunshine moderns," who get cornered into saying, "Two-, three-, and four-year-olds in nine- and ten-hour child care? Fine." "Middle-school children home alone after school? Let's call it 'self-care.'" The sunshiners' motto is "Don't bring me any bad news." Or at least no news that isn't strictly about the external world. Anything internal—like the idea that we can become complicit in the very cultural pressures that end up hurting us—is too dangerous, because if you admit such a thing, you're playing into the hands of the scolding traditionals and you're back to square one. . . .

Other societies—Sweden, Norway, Canada—have led the way. And a number of organizations, inspired by the women's movement, are fighting the good fight here. The Women's Legal Defense Fund, for example, is trying to expand the 1993 Family and Medical Leave Act to cover more working people and more family needs, such as minor illnesses. It is also trying to make these leaves paid for low-wage workers. We can begin to think about a broader movement pressing for a shorter workweek and work-sharing as an alternative to layoffs. And we need men to join us in taking pressure off kids and putting it on the workplace. These are all ways we can unstall the feminist revolution in the next 25 years. ■

TABLE 15.1
Women as a Percentage of All Workers in Selected Occupations, 1950, 1980, and 2004

Occupation	1950	1980	2004
PROFESSIONAL WORKERS			
Accountants	14.9%	36.2%	60.5%
Engineers	1.2	4.0	13.8
Lawyers and judges	4.1	12.8	29.4
Physicians	6.5	12.9	29.4
Registered nurses	97.8	96.5	92.2
College professors	22.8	33.9	46.0
School teachers	74.5	70.8	73.3
OTHER OCCUPATIONS			
Carpenters	0.4	1.5	1.8
Protective services (firefighters, police, guards)	2.0	9.5	21.7
Sales clerks, retail	48.9	71.1	50.8
Cashiers	81.7	86.6	76.1
Bookkeepers	77.7	90.5	91.8
Food service workers	61.6	66.9	56.1
Private household workers	94.9	97.5	90.0

Sources: Bureau of the Census 1981, 2005a, 401–404.

above the minimum wage and carry moderate prestige, such as nursing and teaching. Nevertheless, they are far lower in pay and prestige than such stereotyped male positions as physician, college president, or university professor. When they do enter non-traditional positions, as we have seen, women as a group receive lower wages or salary.

The data in Table 15.1 present an overall view of the male dominance of high-paying occupations. Among the representative occupations chosen, men unquestionably dominate in those that pay well. Women dominate as receptionists, seamstresses, health-care workers, and domestic workers. Trends show the proportions of women increasing slightly in the professions, indicating that some women have advanced into better-paying positions, but these gains have not significantly changed the overall picture.

How pervasive is segregation by gender in the workforce? To what degree are women and men concentrated in different occupations? Bureau of Labor Statistics researchers have compiled a segregation index to estimate the percentage of women who would have to change their jobs to make the distribution of men and women in each occupation mirror the relative percentage of each sex in the adult working population. This study showed that 54 percent of women and men workers would need to switch jobs to create a labor force without sex segregation. There has been a steady decline in such segregation, but the decrease was not as great in the 1990s as in earlier decades (Wooton 1997).

Although occupational segregation by gender continues, women have increased their participation in the labor force. A greater proportion of women seek and obtain paid employment than ever before in U.S. history. In 1870, less than 15 percent of all workers were women, compared with 46 percent in 2004. The most dramatic rise in the female workforce has been among married women and mothers. Among new mothers, 56 percent return to the labor force within a year of giving birth. As recently as 1975, only 29 percent went back to work (Bureau of the Census 1975, 129, 133; 2005a, 389).

Women's earnings have increased significantly over the last quarter century. However, so have the earnings of men. As shown in Figure 15.1, the female–male wage gap has narrowed from women's weekly earnings being just over 62 cents on the dollar

? ASK Yourself

How can we measure the gap between men's and women's earnings?

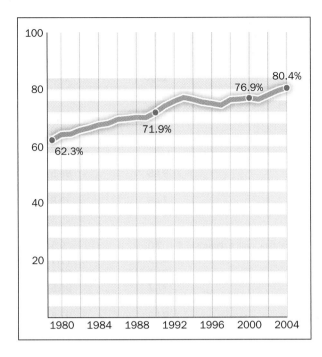

FIGURE 15.1 The Female-Male Earnings Gap: Closing but Still Massive

The gap has narrowed to women earning 80 cents on the men's dollar. However, this gap amounts to trillions of dollars a year because that means millions of working women every year, typically receive 80 cents rather than a full dollar.

Source: Department of Labor 2005.

earned by men as a group to 80 cents in 2004. One cannot assume that the trend will continue at the same rate because much of the increase in the last two decades represents women's gradual success moving into high-paying jobs, which has already leveled out significantly. A detailed analysis of all the components shows relatively little further narrowing in the near future, that is, through 2012 (Lips 2003).

Sources of Discrimination

If we return to the definition of discrimination cited earlier, are not men better able to perform some tasks than women, and vice versa? If ability means performance, there certainly are differences. The typical woman can sew better than the typical man, but the latter can toss a ball farther than the former. These are group differences. Certainly, many women outthrow many men, and many men outsew many women, but society expects women to excel at sewing and men to excel at throwing. The differences in those abilities result from cultural conditioning. Women usually are taught to sew, and men are less likely to learn such a skill. Men are encouraged to participate in sports requiring the ability to throw a ball much more than are women. True, as a group, males have greater potential for the muscular development needed to throw a ball, but U.S. society encourages men to realize their potential in this area more than it encourages women to pursue athletic skills.

Today's labor market involves much more than throwing a ball and using a needle and thread, but the analogy to these two skills is repeated time and again. Such examples are used to support sexist practices in all aspects of the workplace. Just as African Americans can suffer from both individual acts of racism and institutional discrimination, women are vulnerable to both sexism and institutional discrimination. Women are subject to direct sexism, such as sexist remarks, and also to differential treatment because of institutional policies.

Removing barriers to equal opportunity would eventually eliminate institutional discrimination. Theoretically, men and women would sew and throw a ball equally well. We say "theoretically" because cultural conditioning would take generations to change. In some formerly male jobs, such as gas station clerk and attendant, society

Source: Mike Luckovich and Creator's Syndicate, Inc.

seems quite willing to accept women. In other occupations, such as president, it will take longer; many years may pass before full acceptance can be expected in other fields, such as professional contact sports.

Many efforts have been made to eliminate institutional discrimination as it applies to women. The 1964 Civil Rights Act and its enforcement arm, the Equal Employment Opportunity Commission, address cases of sex discrimination. As we saw in Chapter 3, the inclusion of sex bias along with prejudice based on race, color, creed, and national origin was an unexpected last-minute change in the provisions of the landmark 1964 act. Federal legislation has not removed all discrimination against women in employment. The same explanations presented in Chapter 3 for the lag between the laws and reality in race discrimination apply to sex discrimination: lack of money, weak enforcement powers, occasionally weak commitment to using the laws available, and, most important, institutional and structural forces that perpetuate inequality.

What should be done to close the gap between the earnings of women and men? As shown in Figure 15.2, women earn more annually with more formal schooling, just like their male counterparts. However, as women continue their education, the wage gap does not narrow and even shows signs of growing.

In the 1980s, **pay equity,** or comparable worth, was a controversial solution presented to alleviate the second-class status of working women. It directly attempted to secure equal pay when occupational segregation by gender was particularly pervasive. Pay equity calls for equal pay for different types of work that are judged to be comparable by measuring such factors as employee knowledge, skills, effort, responsibility, and working conditions.

It is logical to assume that these percentages would be even higher if day care in the United States received more support. A number of European nations, including France, the Netherlands, Sweden, and the former Soviet Union, provide preschool care at minimal or no cost, although such benefits are underwritten through higher taxes. However, in the United States, these costs are borne entirely by the working parent. Recently, some employers have recognized the benefits of offering care and have

pay equity
The same wages for different types of work that are judged to be comparable by such measures as employee knowledge, skills, effort, responsibility, and working conditions; also called comparable worth.

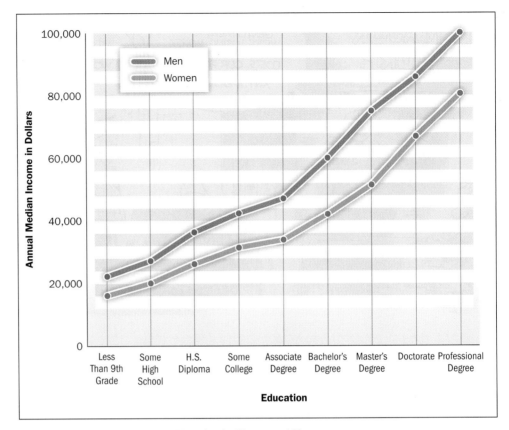

FIGURE 15.2   Financial Return on Education for Women and Men

Note: See Table 3.1.

Source: DeNavas-Walt et al. 2006.

begun to provide or subsidize this care, but they are the exception, not the rule (Schaefer 2007).

A primary goal of many feminists is to eliminate sex discrimination in the labor force and to equalize job opportunities for women. Without question, women earn less than men. As we noted earlier, in Table 3.1, and Figure 3.2 women earn less than men even when race and education are held constant; that is, college-educated women working full time make less than comparably educated men. Even when additional controls are introduced, such as previous work experience, a substantial earnings gap remains. A detailed analysis of the wage gap, considering schooling, employment history, time with the current employer, and medical leaves of absence, found that all these factors can explain less than 42 percent of the wage differences between men and women (Wellington 1994; also see Tomaskovic-Devey 1993).

This doctrine sounds straightforward, but it is not so simple to put into operation. How exactly does one determine the comparability of jobs to identify comparable worth? Should a zookeeper be paid more than a child-care worker? Does our society pay zookeepers more because we value caregiving for children less than for animals? Or do zookeepers earn more than child-care workers because the former tend to be male and the latter are generally female?

Despite some local initiatives, pay equity has not received much support in the United States except from the feminist movement. From a policy perspective, pay equity would have to broaden the 30-year-old Equal Pay Act and be initiated at the federal level. Proposed legislation such as the Paycheck Fairness Act and the Fair Pay Act has

TABLE 15.2
Major Barriers to Women's Executive Advancement

Initial placement and clustering in dead-end staff jobs or highly technical professional jobs
Lack of mentoring
Lack of management training
Lack of opportunities for career development
Lack of opportunities for training tailored to the individual
Lack of rotation to line positions or job assignments that produce revenue
Little or no access to critical developmental assignments, including service on highly visible task forces and committees
Different standards for performance evaluation
Biased rating and testing systems
Little or no access to informal communication networks
Counterproductive behavior and harassment by colleagues

Source: Glass Ceiling Commission, cited in Department of Labor 1995, 7–8.

failed to mobilize much support. With the government backing away from affirmative action, it is unlikely to launch an initiative on pay equity (Business and Professional Women 2002; Sorensen 1994).

What about women aspiring to crack the glass ceiling? The phrase **glass ceiling,** as noted in Chapter 3 and illustrated in Figure 3.3, refers to the invisible barrier blocking the promotion of a qualified worker because of gender or minority membership. Despite continuing debate over affirmative action, the consensus is that there is little room at the top for women and minorities. The glass ceiling operates so that all applicants may be welcomed by a firm, but when it comes to the powerful or more visible positions, there are limits—generally unstated—on the number of women and non-whites welcomed or even tolerated (Table 15.2).

Women are doing better in top-management positions than minorities, but they still lag well behind men, according to a study that showed that only 15 percent of the director seats of *Fortune* 1000's largest corporations were held by women. As for CEOs of the *Fortune* 500, there are so few—ten as of 2006—that the corporations can be named: Avon, Golden West Financial, eBay, Reynolds American, Rite Aid, Lucent, Sara Lee, Safeco, Radio Shack, and Xerox (CNN Money 2006; Strauss 2002).

Women are still viewed differently in the world of management. Although studies of top male executives show some improvement over their attitudes about executive woman in the last forty years, stereotypes still abound that block women's ascent up the corporate ladder. In making hiring decisions, executives may assume that women are not serious about their commitment to the job and will be "distracted" by family and home. They assume that women are on a **mommy track,** an unofficial career track that firms use for women who want to divide their attention between work and family. This assumption would be false if applied to all women. It also implies that corporate men are not interested in maintaining a balance between work and family. Even competitive, upwardly mobile women are not always taken seriously in the workplace (Carlson et al. 2006; Heilman 2001; Schwartz and Zimmerman 1992).

Sexual Harassment

Under evolving legal standards, **sexual harassment** is recognized as any unwanted and unwelcome sexual advances that interfere with a person's ability to perform a job and enjoy the benefits of a job. Increased national attention was given to harassment in the

 ASK Yourself

How much do men dominate the top corporate positions?

glass ceiling
The barrier that blocks the promotion of a qualified worker because of gender or minority membership.

mommy track
An unofficial corporate career track for women who want to divide their attention between work and family.

sexual harassment
Any unwanted and unwelcome sexual advances that interfere with a person's ability to perform a job and enjoy the benefits of a job.

1990s and into the present through allegations made against elected officials and high-ranking military officers.

The most obvious example of sexual harassment is the boss who tells an employee, "Put out or get out!" However, the unwelcome advances that constitute sexual harassment may take the form of subtle pressures regarding sexual activity, inappropriate touching, attempted kissing, or sexual assault. Indeed, in the computer age, there is growing concern that sexually harassing messages are being sent anonymously over computer networks through e-mail and picture phones.

In 1986, in a unanimous decision (*Meritor Savings Bank v. Vinson*), the Supreme Court declared that sexual harassment by a supervisor violates the federal law against sex discrimination in the workplace as outlined in the 1964 Civil Rights Act. If sufficiently severe, harassment is a violation even if the unwelcome sexual demands are not linked to concrete employment benefits such as a raise or promotion. Women's groups hailed the court's decisiveness in identifying harassment as a form of discrimination. A federal judge subsequently ruled that the public display of photographs of nude and partly nude women at a workplace constitutes sexual harassment. Despite these rulings, it is very difficult legally and emotionally for a person to bring forward a case of sexual harassment (Domino 1995).

Sexual harassment must be understood in the context of continuing prejudice and discrimination against women. Whether it occurs in the federal bureaucracy, the military, the corporate world, or universities, sexual harassment generally takes place where the hierarchy of authority finds White men at the top and in which women's work is valued less than men's. One survey of the private sector found that African American women were three times more likely than White women to experience sexual harassment. From a conflict perspective, it is not surprising that women, especially women of color, are most likely to become victims of sexual harassment. These groups typically are an organization's most vulnerable employees in terms of job security (J. Jones 1988).

Feminization of Poverty

Since World War II, an increasing proportion of the poor in the United States has been female, many of them divorced or never-married mothers. This alarming trend has come to be known as the **feminization of poverty.** In 2005, 12.6 percent of all families in the United States lived in poverty, but 28.7 percent of families headed by single mothers did so. Not only are female-headed families much more likely to be poor but also their income deficit relative to being non-poor is much greater than other types of poor families (DeNavas-Walt et al. 2006, 14, 18–19).

Poor women share many social characteristics with poor men: low educational attainment, lack of market-relevant job skills, and residence in economically deteriorating areas. However, conflict theorists believe that the higher rates of poverty among women can be traced to two distinct causes: Sex discrimination and sexual harassment on the job place women at a clear disadvantage when seeking vertical social mobility.

feminization of poverty
The trend since 1970 that has women accounting for a growing proportion of those below the poverty line.

displaced homemakers
Women whose primary occupation had been homemaking but who did not find full-time employment after being divorced, separated, or widowed.

The burden of supporting a family is especially difficult for single mothers, not only because of low salaries but also because of inadequate child support. The average child-support payment reported in 2005 (for money collected in 2001) for the 45 percent who received the *full* award was a mere $109 per week. This level of support is clearly insufficient for rearing a child in the early twenty-first century. In light of these data, federal and state officials have intensified efforts to track down delinquent spouses and ensure the payment of child support: Nearly 16 million cases were under investigation in 2004 (Bureau of the Census 2005a, 374).

According to a study based on census data by the advocacy group Women Work, families headed by single mothers and displaced homemakers are four times as likely to live in poverty as other households in the United States. **Displaced homemakers** are defined as women whose primary occupation had been homemaking but who did not find full-time employment after being divorced, separated, or widowed. Gilda Nardone, president of Women Work, noted that single mothers and displaced homemakers tend to work in service jobs, which offer low wages, few benefits, part-time work, and little job security. Moreover, single mothers and displaced homemakers are also more likely to have an unstable housing situation, including frequent changes of residence (Women Work 1998).

Many feminists feel that the continuing dominance of the political system by men contributes to government indifference to the problem of poor women. As more and more women fall below the official poverty line, policy makers will face growing pressure to combat the feminization of poverty.

Education

The experience of women in education has been similar to their experience in the labor force: a long history of contribution, but in traditionally defined terms. In 1833, Oberlin College became the first institution of higher learning to admit women, two centuries after the first men's college began in this country. In 1837, Wellesley became the first women's college. But it would be a mistake to believe that these early experiments brought about equality for women in education: At Oberlin, the women were forbidden to speak in public. Furthermore,

> *Washing the men's clothes, caring for their rooms, serving them at table, listening to their orations, but themselves remaining respectfully silent in public assemblages, the Oberlin "coeds" were being prepared for intelligent motherhood and a properly subservient wifehood. (Flexner 1959, 30)*

The early graduates of these schools, despite the emphasis in the curriculum on traditional roles, became the founders of the feminist movement.

Today, research confirms that boys and girls are treated differently in school: Teachers give boys more attention. In teaching students the values and customs of the larger society, schools in the United States have treated children as if men's education were more important than that of women. Professors of education Myra and David Sadker (2003) documented this persistence of classroom sexism: The researchers noted that boys receive more teacher attention than girls, mainly because they call out in class eight times more often. Teachers praise boys more than girls and offer boys more academic assistance. Interestingly, they found that this differential treatment was present with both male and female teachers.

Despite these challenges, in many communities across the nation, girls seem to outdo boys in high school, grabbing a disproportionate share of the leadership positions, from valedictorian to class president to yearbook editor—everything, in short, except captain of the boys' athletic teams. Their advantage numerically seems to be continuing after high school. In the 1980s, girls in the United States became more likely than boys to go to college. By 2003, women accounted for over 56 percent of college students nationwide. And in 2002, for the first time, more women than men in the United States earned doctoral degrees (Bureau of the Census 2005a, 178; Conlin 2003; Smallwood 2003).

At all levels of schooling, significant changes also occurred with congressional amendments to the Education Act of 1972 and the Department of Health, Education, and Welfare guidelines developed in 1974 and 1975. Collectively called Title IX provisions, the regulations are designed to eliminate sexist practices from almost all school systems. Schools must make these changes or risk the loss of all federal assistance:

1. Schools must eliminate all sex-segregated classes and extracurricular activities. This means an end to all-girl home economics and all-boy shop classes, although single-sex hygiene and physical education classes are permitted.

ASK Yourself

Student Voice: What does Title IX refer to?

The impact of Title IX over the last thirty years has been particularly apparent as more opportunities have emerged for women to participate in sports both in high school and in college.

2. Schools cannot discriminate by sex in admissions or financial aid and cannot inquire into whether an applicant is married, pregnant, or a parent. Single-sex schools are exempted.

3. Schools must end sexist hiring and promotion practices among faculty members.

4. Although women do not have to be permitted to play on all-men's athletic teams, schools must provide more opportunities for women's sports, intramural and extramural (*Federal Register,* June 4, 1975).

Title IX became one of the more controversial steps ever taken by the federal government to promote and ensure equality.

Efforts to bring gender equity to sports have been attacked as excessive. The consequences have not fully been intended: For example, colleges have often cut men's sports rather than build up women's sports. Also, most of the sports with generous college scholarships added for women over the last thirty years are in athletic fields that have not been traditionally attractive to minority women (Suggs 2002).

Family Life

Our society generally equates work with wages and holds unpaid work in low esteem. Women who do household chores and volunteer work are given little status in our society. Typically this unrecognized labor is done on top of wage labor in the formal economy. These demands traditionally placed on a mother and homemaker are so extensive that simultaneously pursuing a career is extremely difficult. For women, the family is, according to sociologists Lewis Coser and Rose Laub Coser (1974) a "greedy institution." More recently, other social scientists have also observed the overwhelming burden of the multiple social roles associated with being a mother and working outside the home.

Child Care and Housework

A man can act as a homemaker and caregiven for children, but in the United States, these roles are customarily performed by women. Studies indicate that men do not even think about their children as much as women do. Sociologist Susan Walzer (1996) was interested in whether there are gender differences in the amount of time that parents spend

Source: Kirk Anderson, www.kirktoons.com

thinking about the care of their children. Drawing on interviews, Walzer found that mothers are much more involved than fathers in the invisible mental labor associated with taking care of a baby. For example, while involved in work outside the home, mothers are more likely to think about their babies and to feel guilty later if they become so consumed with the demands of their jobs that they fail to think about their babies.

Is the gender gap closing in housework? In "Research Focus," we consider the latest scientific evidence in answer to this question.

Media attention in the early twenty-first century focused on the high-profile women who chose not to climb the last steps of the corporate ladder and devoted full-time effort to their family and nonwork interests. This "opting out" by privilege, educated women caused some observers to generalize about the commitment to work by *all* women. Yet careful analysis of women's labor force participation with children at home has shown no significant change up or down in recent years (Belkin 2003; Boushey 2005; Hewlett and Luce 2005).

Women are much more preoccupied than men in both thought and action with child care and housework, but it does not end there. Another challenge women disproportionately face is caring for aging parents. According to a Department of Labor (1998) study, 72 percent of caregivers are women, typically spending around 18 hours per week caring for a parent.

Given the stresses of performing most housework and caregiving, why do married women accept this arrangement? Psychologist Mary Clare Lennon and sociologist Sarah Rosenfield (1994) studied this issue using interviews of adults from a national sample. When questioned in that survey, almost 61 percent of the women and more than 67 percent of the men suggested that this uneven distribution of housework is fair to both spouses. According to the researchers, married women with the fewest alternatives and financial prospects outside marriage are most likely to accept unequal household arrangements as fair. Apparently, the more economically dependent a particular wife is, the more she will do (and justify) to preserve the marital relationship. In a striking finding, Lennon and Rosenfield reported that women who view unequal housework as unjust experience more symptoms of depression.

HOUSEWORK AND THE GENDER DIVIDE

It is a commonly held notion that in dual-income households men and women should equally share the housework, but this is not supported by the research. Study after study leads to the same conclusion: Men are gradually doing more housework, but women do far more even when they work full-time.

The latest study, released in 2004 by the Bureau of Labor Statistics, interviewed 21,000 married men and women ages 25 to 54 about their activities during a typical 24-hour period (Figure 15.3). This age group is used because it generally includes people who have completed going to school full-time but excludes retired people.

We can see that men generally spend about an hour more each day in paid labor, but mar-

ried women spend twice as much time as married men doing unpaid household work and caregiving, whether it be for their children or elderly parents and other relatives.

We have seen that almost as many women as men hold jobs. Yet the time-use study showed that two-thirds of all women said they prepared meals and did housework on an average day, compared with only 19 percent of men who said they did any housework and 34 percent who said they gave any assistance with meals or cleanup.

Over the last forty years, men have gradually been doing more housework, but women still account for the vast majority of all time a couple devotes to housework. ■

Source: Bureau of Labor Statistics 2004; Institute for Social Research 2002; Kaufman and Uhlenberg 2000.

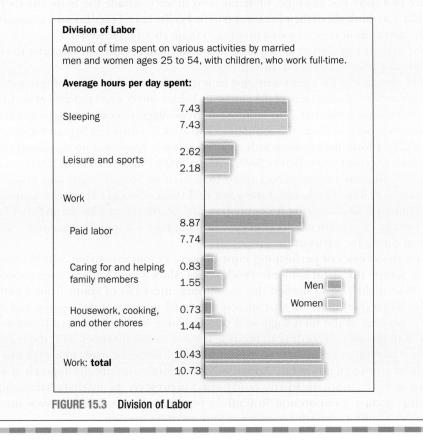

Division of Labor

Amount of time spent on various activities by married men and women ages 25 to 54, with children, who work full-time.

Average hours per day spent:

Activity	Men	Women
Sleeping	7.43	7.43
Leisure and sports	2.62	2.18
Work		
Paid labor	8.87	7.74
Caring for and helping family members	0.83	1.55
Housework, cooking, and other chores	0.73	1.44
Work: **total**	10.43	10.73

FIGURE 15.3   **Division of Labor**

Sociologist Arlie Hochschild has used the term **second shift** to describe the double burden—work outside the home followed by child care and housework—that many women face and that few men share equitably. As shown in Figure 15.4, this issue has become increasingly important as greater proportions of mothers work outside the home. On the basis of interviews with and observations of fifty-two couples over an eight-year period, Hochschild reports that the wives (and not their husbands) plan domestic schedules and play dates for children while driving home from the office and then begin their second shift (Hochschild 1990; Hochschild and Machung 1989).

Hochschild found that the married couples she studied were fraying at the edges psychologically and so were their careers and their marriages. The women she spoke with hardly resembled the beautiful young businesswomen pictured in magazine advertisements, dressed in power suits but with frilled blouses, holding briefcases in one hand and happy young children in the other. Instead, many of Hochschild's female subjects talked about being overtired and emotionally drained by the demands of their multiple roles. They were much more intensely torn by the conflicting demands of work outside the home and family life than were their husbands. Hochschild (1990) concludes that "if we as a culture come to see the urgent need of meeting the new problems posed by the second shift, and if society and government begin to shape new policies that allow working parents more flexibility, then we will be making some progress toward happier times at home and at work" (p. 73). Many feminists share this view.

There is an economic cost to this second shift. Households do benefit from the free labor of women, but women pay what has been called the **mommy tax:** the lower salaries women receive over their lifetime because they have children. Mothers earn less than men and other women over their lifetime because having children causes them to lose job experience, trade off higher wages for following the mommy track, and be discriminated against by employers. How high is this mommy tax? Estimates

second shift

The double burden—work outside the home followed by child care and housework—that is faced by many women and that few men share equitably.

mommy tax

Lower salaries women receive over their lifetime because they have children.

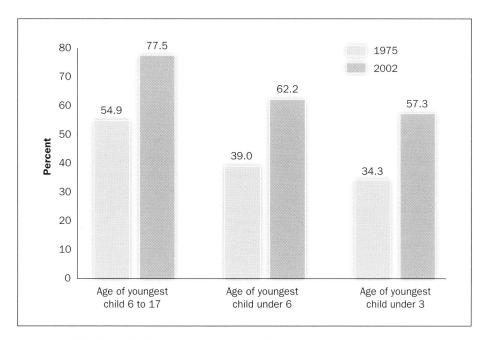

FIGURE 15.4 Labor Force Participation Rates Among Mothers

Source: Department of Labor 2001, 2005.

range from 5 to 13 percent of lifetime wages for the first child alone. Having two children lowers earnings 10 to 19 percent. There is no denying that motherhood and the labor market are intertwined (Budig and England 2001; Szegedy-Maszak 2001).

Abortion

A particularly controversial subject affecting family life in the United States has been the call for women to have greater control over their bodies, especially their reproductive lives, through contraceptive devices and the increased availability of abortions. Abortion law reform was one of the demands the National Organization for Women (NOW) made in 1967, and the controversy continues despite many court rulings and the passage of laws at every level of government.

On January 22, 1973, the feminist movement received unexpected assistance from the U.S. Supreme Court decision in *Roe v. Wade*. By a 7–2 margin, the justices held that the "right to privacy . . . founded in the Fourteenth Amendment's concept of personal liberty . . . is broad enough to encompass a woman's decision whether or not to terminate a pregnancy." However, the Court did set certain limits on a woman's right to abortion. During the last three months of pregnancy, the fetus was ruled capable of life outside the womb. Therefore, states were granted the right to prohibit all abortions in the third trimester except those needed to preserve the life, physical health, or mental health of the mother.

The Court's decision in *Roe v. Wade*, though generally applauded by pro-choice groups, which support the right to legal abortions, was bitterly condemned by those opposed to abortion. For people who call themselves "pro-life," abortion is a moral and often a religious issue. In their view, human life actually begins at the moment of conception rather than when the fetus could stay alive outside the womb. On the basis of this belief, the fetus is a human, not merely a potential life. Termination of this human's life, even before it has left the womb, is viewed as an act of murder. Consequently, antiabortion activists are alarmed by the more than 1 million legal abortions carried out each year in the United States (Luker 1984).

The early 1990s brought an escalation of violent antiabortion protests. Finally, a 1994 federal law made it a crime to use force or threats or to obstruct, injure, or interfere with anyone providing or receiving abortions and other reproductive health services. In a 6–3 decision, the Supreme Court's majority upheld the constitutionality of a 36-foot buffer zone that keeps antiabortion protesters away from a clinic's entrance and parking lot. Abortion remains a disputed issue both in society and in the courts. The law has apparently had some impact, but acts of violence, including deaths of clinic workers and physicians, continue.

In terms of social class, the first major restriction on the legal right to terminate a pregnancy affected poor people. In 1976, Congress passed the Hyde Amendment, which banned the use of Medicaid and other federal funds for abortions. The Supreme Court upheld this legislation in 1980. State laws also restrict the use of public funds for abortions. Another obstacle facing the poor is access to abortion providers: In the face of vocal pro-life public sentiment, fewer and fewer hospitals throughout the world are allowing their physicians to perform abortions, except in extreme cases. As of 2004, only about 3 percent of nonmetropolitan counties in the United States had even one provider able and willing to perform abortions (Guttmacher Institute 2004).

Political Activity

Women in the United States constitute 53 percent of the voting population and 49 percent of the labor force but only 8 percent of those holding high government positions. At the beginning of 2007, Congress included only 71 women (out of 435 members) in the House of Representatives and only 16 women (out of 100 members) in the Senate. As shown in Figure 15.5, the number of women serving in Congress has steadily

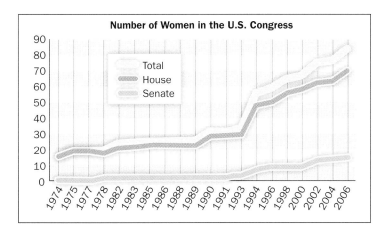

FIGURE 15.5   Women in the U.S. Congress

Electing women to Congress has enjoyed significant success over the last generation with 87 serving in 2007, but this compares to a total of 448 men in the House and Senate.

Source: Based on data from the Bureau of Census 2005a; Center for American Women and Politics, 2007; and 2006 newspaper coverage of runoff election.

increased. Only nine states—Arizona, Delaware, Hawaii, Kansas, Louisiana, Michigan, Montana, Connecticut, and Utah—had a woman governor as of 2007.

The low number of women officeholders until recently has not resulted from women's inactivity in politics. About the same proportion of eligible women and men vote in presidential elections. The League of Women Voters, founded in 1920, performs a valuable function in educating the electorate of both sexes, publishing newsletters describing candidates' positions, and holding debates among candidates. Perhaps women's most visible role in politics until recently has been as unpaid campaign workers for male candidates: doorbell ringers, telephone callers, newsletter printers, and petition carriers. Runs for elective office in the 1990s showed women overcoming one of their last barriers to electoral office: attracting campaign funds. Running for office is very expensive, and women candidates have begun to convince backers to invest in their political future. Their success as fund-raisers will also contribute to women's acceptance as serious candidates in the future (Carroll 2004).

Women have worked actively in both political parties, but women officeholders are more likely to be Democrats by a slight margin. A recent effective force is the National Women's Political Caucus (NWPC), which works to get more women elected. The NWPC was founded in 1971 by Betty Friedan, Gloria Steinem (founder of *Ms.* magazine), Bella Abzug, and Shirley Chisholm (the last two have been congresswomen from New York City). The NWPC oversees state caucuses that rally support for women's issues. It is difficult to represent all politically active women in the caucus because women's views encompass a whole range of ideologies, including women who are unmistakably antifeminists (NWPC 2006).

Matrix of Domination: Minority Women

We have seen the historical oppression of women that limits them by tradition and law to specific roles. Many women experience differential treatment not only because of their gender but also because of race and ethnicity. These citizens face a subordinate status twice defined. A disproportionate share of this low-status group also is poor. The African American feminist Patricia Hill Collins (2000) has termed this the **matrix of domination.** Whites dominate non-Whites; men dominate women, and the affluent dominate the poor.

Gender, race, and social class are not the only systems of oppression, but they do profoundly affect women and people of color in the United States. Other forms of categorization and stigmatization can also be included in this matrix, such as sexual orientation, religion, disability status, and age.

Feminists have addressed themselves to the needs of minority women, but the oppression of these women because of their sex is overshadowed by the subordinate status that

matrix of domination
Cumulative impact of oppression because of race, gender, and class as well as sexual orientation, religion, disability status, and age.

both White men and White women impose on them because of their race or ethnicity. The question for the Latina (Hispanic woman), African American woman, Asian American woman, Native American woman, and so on appears to be whether she should unify with her brothers against racism or challenge them for their sexism. The answer is that society cannot afford to let up on the effort to eradicate both sexism and racism (Beisel and Kay 2004; Epstein 1999).

The discussion of gender roles among African Americans has always provoked controversy. Advocates of Black nationalism contend that feminism only distracts women from full participation in the African American struggle. The existence of feminist groups among Blacks, in their view, simply divides the Black community and thereby serves the dominant White society. By contrast, Black feminists such as bell hooks (1994) argue that little is to be gained by accepting the gender-role divisions of the dominant society that place women in a separate, subservient position. African American journalist Patricia Raybon (1989) has noted that the media commonly portray Black women in a negative light: as illiterates, as welfare mothers, as prostitutes, and so forth. Black feminists emphasize that it is not solely Whites and White-dominated media that focus on these negative images; Black men (most recently, Black male rap artists) have also been criticized for the way they portray African American women.

Native Americans stand out as a historical exception to the North American patriarchal tradition. At the time of the arrival of the European settlers, gender roles varied greatly from tribe to tribe. Southern tribes, for reasons unclear to today's scholars, usually were matriarchal and traced descent through the mother. European missionaries sought to make the native peoples more like the Europeans, and this aim included transforming women's role. Some Native American women, like members of other groups, have resisted gender stereotypes (Pleck 1993).

The plight of Latinas usually is considered part of either the Hispanic or feminist movements, and the distinctive experience of Latinas is ignored. In the past, they have been excluded from decision making in the two social institutions that most affect their daily lives: the family and the church. The Hispanic family, especially in the lower class, feels the pervasive tradition of male domination. The Catholic Church relegates women to supportive roles while reserving for men the leadership positions (Browne 2001; De Andra 2004).

By considering the matrix of domination, we recognize how much of our discussion has focused on race and ethnicity coupled with data on poverty, low incomes, and meager wealth. Now we recognize that issues of gender domination must be included to fully understand what women of color experience.

Conclusion

omen and men are expected to perform, or at least to prefer to perform, specific tasks in society. The appropriateness to one gender of all but a very few of these tasks cannot be justified by the biological differences between females and males any more than differential treatment based on race can be justified. Psychologists Sandra Bem and Daryl Bem (1970) make the following analogy.

Suppose that a White male college student decided to room with a Black male friend. The typical White student would not blithely assume that his roommate was better suited to handle all domestic chores. Nor should his conscience allow him to do so even in the unlikely event that his roommate said, "No, that's okay. I like doing housework. I'd be happy to do it." We would suspect that the White student would still feel uncomfortable about taking advantage of the fact that his roommate has simply been socialized to be "happy with such an arrangement." But change this hypothetical Black roommate to a female marriage partner, and the student's conscience goes to sleep (p. 99).

The feminist movement has awakened women and men to assumptions based on sex and gender. New opportunities for the sexes require the same commitment from individuals and the government as they make to achieve equality between racial and ethnic groups.

Women are systematically disadvantaged in both employment and the family. Gender inequality is a serious problem, just as racial inequality continues to be a signifi-cant social challenge. Separate, socially defined roles for men and women are not limited to the United States. Chapter 16 concentrates on the inequality of racial and ethnic groups in societies other than the United States. Just as sexism is not unique to this nation, neither is racism nor religious intolerance.

Key Terms

androgyny 403

displaced homemakers 414

feminine mystique 407

feminization of poverty 414

gender roles 403

glass ceiling 413

matrix of domination 421

mommy tax 419

mommy track 413

pay equity 411

second shift 419

sexism 403

sexual harassment 413

suffragists 406

Review Questions

1. How is women's subordinate position different from that of oppressed racial and ethnic groups? How is it similar?

2. How has the focus of the feminist movement changed from the suffragist movement to the present?

3. How do the patterns of women in the workplace differ from those of men?

4. How has the changing role of women in the United States affected the family?

5. What are the special challenges facing women of subordinate racial and ethnic groups?

Critical Thinking

1. Women have many characteristics similar to those of minority groups, but what are some differences? For example, they are not segregated from men residentially.

2. Earlier in the 1990s, the phrase *angry white men* was used by some men who viewed themselves as victims. In what respect may men see themselves as victims of reverse discrimination? Do you think these views are justified?

3. How are men's and women's roles defined differently when it comes to such concepts as the mommy track, second shift, and the displaced homemaker?

Internet Connections—Research Navigator™

Follow the instructions found on page 35 of this text to access the features of Research Navigator™. Once at the Web site, enter your Login Name and Password. Then, to use the ContentSelect database, enter keywords such as "feminism," "sexual harassment," "equal rights amendment," and "Title IX," and the search engine will supply relevant and recent scholarly and popular press publications. Use the *New York Times* Search-by-Subject Archive to find recent news articles related to sociology and the Link Library feature to lo-cate relevant Web links organized by the key terms associated with this chapter.

16

Beyond the United States:
The Comparative Perspective

CHAPTER OUTLINE

Mexico

Canada

Brazil: Not a Racial Paradise

Israel and the Palestinians

Republic of South Africa

■ LISTEN TO OUR VOICES
"Africa, It Is Ours!"
by Nelson Mandela

■ RESEARCH FOCUS
Listening to the People

Conclusion

Key Terms/Review Questions/
Critical Thinking/Internet Connections—
Research Navigator™

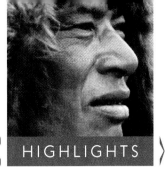

SUBORDINATING PEOPLE BECAUSE OF RACE, NATIONALITY, or religion is not a phenomenon unique to the United States; it occurs throughout the world. In Mexico, women and the descendants of the Mayans are given second-class status. Despite its being viewed as a homogeneous nation by some, Canada faces racial, linguistic, and tribal issues. Brazil is a large South American nation recognizing a long history of racial inequality. In Israel, Jews and Palestinians struggle over territory and the definition of each other's autonomy. In the Republic of South Africa, the legacy of apartheid dominates the present and the future.

Ironically, by bringing more and more diverse groups of people into contact, modernization has increased the opportunities for confrontation, both peaceful and violent, between culturally and physically different people. The decline in colonialism by European powers in the 1960s and the end of communist domination in Eastern Europe in the 1990s have also allowed interethnic rivalries to resume. Confrontations along racial or ethnic or religious lines, as Chapter 1 showed, can lead to extermination, expulsion, secession, segregation, fusion, assimilation, or pluralism. At the conclusion of this chapter, we will review how these processes have been illustrated in this chapter as we look beyond the United States.

C onfrontations between racial and ethnic groups have escalated in frequency and intensity in the twentieth century. In surveying these conflicts, we can see two themes emerge: the previously considered world systems theory and ethnonational conflict. **World systems theory** considers the global economic system as divided between nations that control wealth and those that provide natural resources and labor. Historically, the nations we will be considering reflect this competition between "haves" and "have-nots." Whether the laborers are poor Catholics in Ireland or Black Africans, their contribution to the prosperity of the dominant group created the social inequality that people are trying to address today (Wallerstein 1974; 2004).

Ethnonational conflict refers to conflicts among ethnic, racial, religious, and linguistic groups within nations. In some areas of the world, ethnonational conflicts are more significant than tension between nations as the source of refugees and even death. As you can see in Figure 16.1), countries in all parts of the world, including the most populous nations, have significant diversity within their borders. These conflicts remind us that the processes operating in the United States to deny racial and ethnic groups rights and opportunities are at work throughout the world (Connor 1994; Olzak 1998).

The sociological perspective on relations between dominant and subordinate groups treats race and ethnicity as social categories. As social concepts, they can be understood only in the context of the shared meanings attached to them by societies and their members. Although relationships between dominant and subordinate groups vary greatly, there are similarities across societies. Racial and ethnic hostilities arise out of economic needs and demands. These needs and demands may not always be realistic; that is, a group may seek out enemies where none exist or where victory will yield no rewards. Racial and ethnic conflicts are both the results and the precipitators of change in the economic and political sectors (Barclay et al. 1976; Coser 1956).

Relations between dominant and subordinate groups differ from society to society, as this chapter will show. Intergroup relations in Mexico, Canada, Brazil, Israel, and South Africa are striking in their similarities and contrasts. As shown in Figure 16.2, each society, in its own way, illustrates the processes of intergroup relations first introduced in Chapter 1. The examples range from the Holocaust, which precipitated the emergence of Israel, to the efforts to create a multiracial government in South Africa. A study of these five societies, coupled with knowledge of subordinate groups in the United States, will provide the background from which to draw some conclusions about patterns of race and ethnic relations in the world today.

world systems theory
A view of the global economic system as divided between nations that control wealth and those that provide natural resources and labor.

ethnonational conflicts
Conflicts between ethnic, racial, religious, and linguistic groups within nations replacing conflicts between nations.

Mexico

Usually in the discussions of racial and ethnic relations, Mexico is considered only as a source of immigrants to the United States. In questions of economic development, Mexico again typically enters the discussion only as it affects our own economy. However, Mexico, a nation of 108 million people (in the Western Hemisphere, only Brazil and the United States are larger) is an exceedingly complex nation (see Table 16.1). It is therefore appropriate that we understand Mexico and its issues of inequality better. This understanding will also shed light on the relationship of its people to the United States.

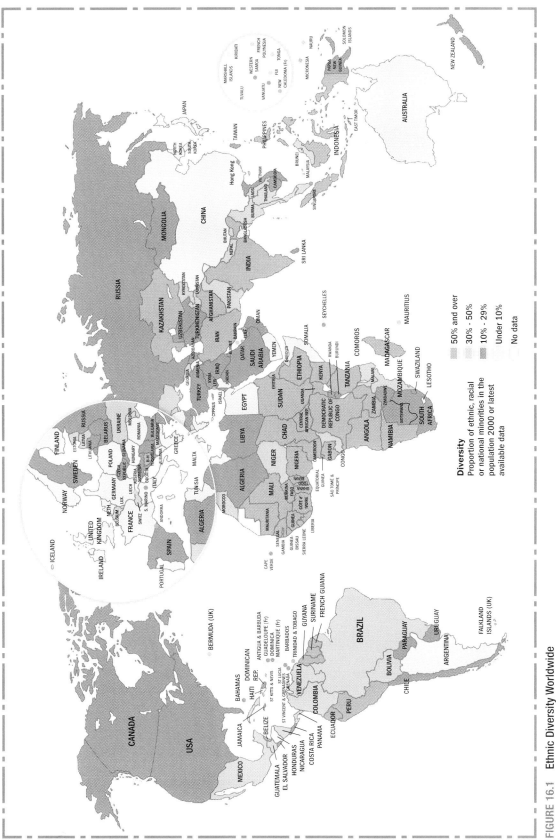

FIGURE 16.1   Ethnic Diversity Worldwide

Source: "Diversity," from *The Penguin State of the World Atlas* by Dan Smith, copyright © 2003 by Dan Smith. Illustration © 2003 by Myriad Editions Ltd. Used by permission of Penguin, a division of Penguin Group (USA) Inc.

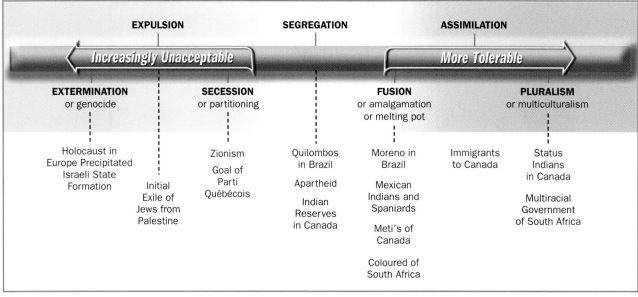

FIGURE 16.2 Intergroup Relations

Country	Population (in millions)	GNI/per capita (USA = $41,950)	Groups Represented	Current Nation's Formation
TABLE 16.1 Five-Nation Comparison, 2006				
Mexico	108.3	$10,030	Mexican Indians, 9%	1823: Republic of Mexico declared independent from Spain
Canada	32.6	$32,220	French speaking, 24% Aboriginal Peoples, 3–6% "Visible" minorities, 13%	1857: Colony of Canada formed independent of England
Brazil	186.8	$8,230	White, 53% Brown (moreno, mulatto), 39% Afro-Brazilians, 6% Asian and Indigenous Indians, 1%	Became independent of Portugal in 1889
Israel	7.2	$25,280	Jews, 80%	1948: Independence from British mandate under United Nations
Israel Occupied Territories	3.8	$4,247	Others (citizens), 1% Muslims, Christians, Palestinians (noncitizens), 19%	
South Africa	47.3	$12,120	Black Africans, 76% Whites, 13% Coloureds, 9% Asians, 3%	1948: Independence from Great Britain

Sources: Author estimates based on Canak and Swanson 1998; Dahlburg 1998; Haub 2006; Statistics Canada 2001, 2003a.

In the 1520s, Spain overthrew the Aztec Indian tribe that ruled Mexico. Mexico remained a Spanish colony until the 1820s. In 1836, Texas declared its independence from Mexico, and by 1846 Mexico was at war with the United States. As we described in Chapter 9, the Mexican-American War forced Mexico to surrender more than half of its territory. In the 1860s, France sought to turn Mexico into an empire under Austrian prince Maximilian but ultimately withdrew after bitter resistance led by a Mexican Indian, Benito Juárez, who later served as the nation's president.

The Mexican Indian People and the Color Gradient

In contemporary Mexico, a major need has been to reassess the relations between the indigenous peoples—the Mexican Indians, many descended from the Mayas, and the government of Mexico. In 1900, the majority of the Mexican population still spoke Indian languages and lived in closed, semi-isolated villages or tribal communities according to ancestral customs. Many of these people were not a part of the growing industrialization in Mexico and were not truly represented in the national legislature. Perhaps the major change for them in this century was that many intermarried with the descendants of the Europeans, forming a *mestizo* class of people of mixed ancestry. These *mestizos* have become increasingly identified with Mexico's growing middle class. Initially the subject of derision, the *mestizos* have developed their own distinct culture and, as the descendants of the European settlers are reduced in number and influence, have become the true bearers of the national Mexican sentiment.

Meanwhile, however, these social changes have left the Mexican Indian people even further behind the rest of the population economically. Indian cultures have been stereotyped as backward, resistant to progress and modern ways of living. Indeed, the existence of the many (at least fifty-six) Indian cultures has been seen in this century as an impediment to the development of a national culture in Mexico. In an effort to bring the indigenous people into the mainstream economy, in the late 1930s the Mexican government embarked on a government policy known as *indigenismo* or national integration. The Mexican Indians were given land rights to make them economically self-sufficient. This program was not unlike the U.S. policy in the 1880s with respect to the Native Americans (American Indians). However, *indigenismo* did not take place; the native people did not fade away culturally.

As noted in Chapter 9, a **color gradient** is the placement of people on a continuum from light to dark skin color rather than in distinct racial groupings by skin color. This is another example of the social construction of race in which social class is linked to the social reality (or at least the appearance) of racial purity. At the top of this gradient or hierarchy are the *criollos*, the 10 percent of the population who are typically White, well-educated members of the business and intellectual elites with familial roots in Spain. In the middle is the large impoverished *mestizo* majority, most of whom have brown skin and a mixed racial lineage as a result of intermarriage. At the bottom of the color gradient are the destitute Mexican Indians and a small number of Blacks, some the descendants of 200,000 African slaves brought to Mexico. The relatively small Black Mexican community received national attention in 2005 and 2006 following a series of racist events that received media attention. Ironically, although this color gradient is an important part of day-to-day life—enough so that some Mexicans use hair dyes, skin lighteners, and blue or green contact lenses to appear more European—nearly all Mexicans are considered part Mexican Indian because of centuries of intermarriage (Castañeda 1995; DePalma 1995; Thompson 2005).

On January 1, 1994, rebels from an armed insurgent group called the Zapatista National Liberation Army seized four towns in the state of Chiapas in southern Mexico. The rebels—who named their organization after Emiliano Zapata, a farmer and leader of the 1910 revolution against a corrupt dictatorship—were backed by 2,000

color gradient
The placement of people on a continuum from light to dark skin color rather than in distinct racial groupings by skin color.

The poverty of Mexican Indians is well documented and in some instances has led to violent protests for social change.

lightly armed Mayan Indians and peasants. Zapatista leaders declared that they had turned to armed insurrection to protest economic injustices and discrimination against the region's Indian population. The Mexican government mobilized the army to crush the revolt but was forced to retreat as news organizations broadcast pictures of the confrontation around the world. A cease-fire was declared after only twelve days of fighting, but 196 people had already died. Negotiations collapsed between the Mexican government and the Zapatista National Liberation Army, with sporadic violence ever since.

In response to the crisis, the Mexican legislature enacted the Law on Indian Rights and Culture, which went into effect in 2001. The act allows sixty-two recognized Indian groups to apply their own customs in resolving conflicts and electing leaders. Unfortunately, state legislatures must give final approval to these arrangements, a requirement that severely limits the rights of large Indian groups whose territories span several states. Tired of waiting for state approval, many indigenous communities in Chiapas have declared self-rule without obtaining official recognition (Bourdreaux 2002; J. Smith 2001).

Although many factors contributed to the Zapatista revolt, the subordinate status of Mexico's Indian citizens, who account for an estimated 14 percent of the nation's population, was surely important. More than 90 percent of the indigenous population live in houses without access to sewers, compared with 21 percent of the population as a whole. And whereas just 10 percent of Mexican adults are illiterate, the proportion for Mexican Indians is 44 percent (Bourdreaux 2002; *The Economist* 2004c; Thompson 2001).

The Status of Women

Often in the United States we consider our own problems to be so significant that we fail to recognize that many of these social issues exist elsewhere. Gender stratification is an example of an issue we share with almost all other countries, and Mexico is no exception. In 1975, Mexico City was the site of the first United Nations conference on the status of women. Much of the focus was on the situation of women in developing countries; in that regard, Mexico remains typical.

Women in Mexico did not receive the right to vote until 1953. They have made significant progress in that short period in being elected into office, but they have a long way to go. As of 2006, women accounted for 26 percent of Mexico's national assembly (Inter-Parliamentary Union 2006).

Even when Mexican women work outside the home, they are often denied recognition as active and productive household members, and men are typically viewed as heads of the household in every respect. As one consequence, women find it difficult to obtain credit and technical assistance in many parts of Mexico and to inherit land in rural areas.

In the larger economy in Mexico, women often are viewed as the "ideal workers." This appears to be particularly true of the foreign-owned factories or *maquiladoras* of the borderlands (discussed in Chapter 9) that rely heavily on women. For example, in a Tijuana electronics plant, women receive elementary training and work in the least-skilled and least-automated jobs because there is little expectation of advancement, organizing for better working conditions, or developing unions.

Men are preferred over women in the more skilled jobs, and women lose out entirely as factories, even in developing nations such as Mexico, require more complex skills. In 2003, only 42 percent of women were in the paid labor force, compared with about 73 percent in Canada and 70 percent in the United States (Bureau of the Census 2005a, 881).

In recent decades, Mexican women have begun to address an array of economic, political, and health issues. Often this organizing occurs at the grassroots level, outside traditional government forums. Because women continue to serve as household managers for their families, even when they work outside the home, they have been aware of the consequences of the inadequate public services in low-income urban neighborhoods. As far back as 1973, women in Monterrey, the nation's third-largest city, began protesting the continuing disruptions of the city's water supply. At first, individual women made complaints to city officials and the water authority, but subsequently, groups of female activists emerged. They sent delegations to confront politicians, organized protest rallies, and blocked traffic as a means of getting media attention. As a result of their efforts, there have been improvements in Monterrey's water service, although the issue of reliable and safe water remains a concern in Mexico and many developing countries (V. Bennett 1995).

Mexico is beginning to recognize that the issue of social inequality extends beyond poverty. A 2005 survey found that eight out of ten Mexicans felt it was as important to eliminate discrimination as poverty, yet 40 percent said that they did not want to live next to an Indian community and one-third considered it "normal" for women not to earn as much as men (Thompson 2005).

Canada

Multiculturalism is a fairly recent term in the United States; it is used to refer to diversity. In Canada, it has been adopted as a state policy for more than two decades. Still, many people in the United States, when they think of Canada, see it as a homogeneous nation with a smattering of Arctic-type people—merely a cross between the northern mainland United States and Alaska. This is not the social reality.

A railway bridge burns in Caledonia, Ontario, in April 2006 as First Nation people protest a housing development in town.

One of the continuing discussions among Canadians is the need for a cohesive national identity or a sense of common peoplehood. The immense size of the country, much of which is sparsely populated, and the diversity of its people have complicated this need.

In 1971, Canadian Prime Minister Pierre Trudeau presented to the House of Commons a policy of multiculturalism that sought to permit cultural groups to retain and foster their identity. Specifically, he declared that there should continue to be two official languages, French and English, but "no official culture" and no "ethnic group [taking] precedence over any other" (Labelle 1989, 2). Yet it is not always possible to legislate a pluralistic society, as the case of Canada demonstrates.

The First Nation

Canada, like the United States, has had an adversarial relationship with its native peoples. However, the Canadian experience has not been as violent. During all three stages of Canadian history—French colonialism, British colonialism, and Canadian nationhood—there has been, compared with the United States, little warfare between Canadian Whites and Canadian Native Americans. Yet the legacy today is similar. Prodded by settlers, colonial governments (and later Canadian governments) drove the Native Americans from their lands. Already by the 1830s, Indian reserves were being established that were similar to the reservations in the United States. Tribal members were encouraged to renounce their status and become Canadian citizens. Assimilation was the explicit policy until recently (Champagne 1994; Waldman 1985).

The 1.4 million native peoples of Canada are collectively referred to by the government as the First Nation or Aboriginal Peoples and represent about 3 to 6 percent of the population, depending on the definition used. This population is classified into the following groups:

Status Indians: The more than 600 tribes or bands officially recognized by the government, numbering about 690,000 in 2000, of whom the majority live on Indian reserves (or reservations).

Inuit: The 62,300 people living in the northern part of the country, who typically have been called the Eskimos.

Métis: Canadians of mixed ancestry, officially numbering 218,000; depending on definitions, they range in number from 100,000 to 850,000.

Non–Status Indians: Canadians of native ancestry who, because of voluntary decisions or government rulings, have been denied registration status. The group numbers about 425,000.

The Métis and Non–Status Indians have historically enjoyed no separate legal recognition, but efforts continue to secure them special rights under the law, such as designated health, education, and welfare programs. The general public does not understand these legal distinctions, so if a Métis or Non–Status Indian "looks like an Indian," she or he is subjected to the same treatment, discriminatory or otherwise (Indian and Northern Affairs Canada and Canadian Polar Commission 2000, 4).

The new Canadian Federal Constitution of 1982 included a Charter of Rights that "recognized and affirmed . . . the existing aboriginal and treaty rights" of the Canadian Native American, Inuit, and Métis peoples. This recognition received the most visibility through the efforts of the Mohawk, one of the tribes of Status Indians. At issue were land rights involving some property areas in Quebec that had spiritual significance for the Mohawk. Their protests and militant confrontations reawakened the Canadian people to the concerns of their diverse native peoples (Amnesty International 1993).

Some of the contemporary issues facing the First Nation of Canada are very similar to those faced by Native Americans in the United States. Contemporary Canadians are

Supporters of a Quebec separatist movement participate in a rally. In 1995, a referendum calling for separation from the rest of Canada was narrowly defeated; today support for such a drastic step appears to have declined.

shocked to learn of past mistreatment leading to belated remedies. Exposure of past sexual and physical abuse of tens of thousands in boarding schools led to compensation to former students. Tribal people document that environmental justice must be addressed because of the disproportionate pollution they experience. Seeking better opportunities, First Nation people move to urban areas in Canada where social services are slowly meeting the needs (Birchard 2006; Crenson 2005; Rosero 2006; Silver 2006).

A setback, occurred in 1992 when a national referendum, the Charlottetown Agreement, was defeated. This constitutional reform package embraced a number of issues, including greater recognition of the Aboriginal Peoples. Canadian Native American and Inuit leaders expressed anger over the defeat, and Ron George, leader of the Native Council of Canada, accused those who rejected the agreement of "perpetuating apartheid in this country." However, the federal government has declared its willingness to accept the right of the Inuit and the other aboriginal people of northern Canada to self-government ("Keesing's 1992 Canada" 39126; also see Champagne 1994).

The social and economic fate of contemporary Aboriginal Peoples reflects many challenges. Only 40 percent even graduate from high school compared to more than 70 percent for the country as a whole. The native peoples of Canada have unemployment rates twice as high and an average income one-third lower (Birchard 2006; Statistics Canada 2001).

In a positive step, in 1999 Canada created a new territory in response to a native land claim in which the resident Inuit (formerly called Eskimos) dominated. Nunavut ("NOO-nah-voot"), meaning "our land," as the territory was called, recognizes the territorial rights of the Inuit. Admirable as this event is, observers noted it was easier to grant such economic rights and autonomy to 27,000 people in the isolated expanse of northern Canada than to the Aboriginal Peoples of the more populated southern provinces of Canada (Krauss 2006b).

The Québécois

Assimilation and domination have been the plight of most minority groups. The French-speaking people of the province of Quebec—the Québécois, as they are known—represent a contrasting case. Since the mid-1960s, they have reasserted their identity and captured the attention of the entire nation.

Quebec accounts for about one-fourth of the nation's population and wealth. Reflecting its early settlement by the French, fully 80 percent of the province's population

 ASK Yourself

How can assimilation be applied to language use in Canada?

claims French as its first language, compared with only 24 percent in the nation as a whole (Statistics Canada 2002).

The Québécois have sought to put French Canadian culture on an equal footing with English Canadian culture in the country as a whole and to dominate in the province. At the very least, this effort has been seen as an irritant outside Quebec and has been viewed with great concern by the English-speaking minority in Quebec.

In the 1960s, the Québécois expressed the feeling that bilingual status was not enough. Even to have French recognized as one of two official languages in a nation dominated by the English-speaking population gave the Québécois second-class status in their view. With some leaders threatening to break completely with Canada and make Quebec an independent nation, Canada made French the official language of the province and the only acceptable language for commercial signs and public transactions. New residents are now required to send their children to French schools. The English-speaking residents felt as if they had been made aliens, even though many of them had roots extending back to the 1700s. These changes spurred residents to migrate from Quebec and some corporate headquarters to relocate to the neighboring English-speaking province of Ontario (Salée 1994).

The long debate over how much independence Quebec should be permitted reached a stalemate with the Meech Lake Accords. In 1987, at Meech Lake, a group of constitutional amendments was developed that would recognize Quebec as a distinct society, but the effort to pass the accords failed.

 ASK Yourself

What does the Parti Québécois stand for?

Throughout the past four decades of debate, the force both unifying and dividing the French-speaking people of Quebec has been the Parti Québécois. Since its establishment in 1968, the Parti Québécois has been a force in the politics of the provinces. It gained majority control of the province's assembly in 1994. The national version, Bloc Québécois, holding in 2004 about 18 percent of seats in Parliament, plays a role in the opposition coalition. The Bloc Québécois has advocated separatism: the creation of an independent nation of Quebec. Separatists contend that Quebec has the confidence, natural resources, and economic structure to stand on its own. However, not all Québécois who vote for the party favor this extreme position, although they are certainly sympathetic to preserving their language and culture.

In 1995, the people of Quebec were given a different referendum question that they would vote on alone: whether they wanted to separate from Canada and form a new nation. In a very close vote, 50.5 percent of the voters indicated a preference to remain united with Canada. The vote was particularly striking, given the confusion over how separation would be accomplished and its significance economically. Separatists vowed to keep working for secession and called for another referendum in the future, although surveys show the support for independence had dropped to 40 percent of the province by 2002. Independence for Quebec would not be easy because the Supreme Court of Canada ruled in 1998 that Quebec cannot secede without seeking the consent of the central government. Canadians opposed to separation spoke of reconciliation after the bitter election debate, but it was unclear what further concessions they were prepared to make to the separatists. Many French-speaking residents now seem to accept the steps that have been taken, but a minority still seeks full control of financial and political policies (C. Krauss 2003).

Canada is characterized by the presence of two linguistic communities: the Anglophone and the Francophone with the latter occurring largely in the one province of Quebec. Outside Quebec, Canadians are opposed to separatism, and within this province, they are divided. Language and cultural issues, therefore, both unify and divide a nation of 33 million people.

Immigration and Race

Immigration has also been a significant social force contributing to Canadian multiculturalism. Canada, proportionately to its population, receives consistently the most immigrants of any nation. Over 18 percent of its population is foreign born, with an increasing proportion being of Asian background rather than European. New arrivals particularly gravitate to urban areas. In recent years, 53 percent of immigrants have gone to Toronto, 15 percent to Vancouver, and 13 percent to Montreal.

Canada also speaks of its **visible minorities**—persons other than Aboriginal or First Nation people who are non-White in racial background. This would include much of the immigrant population as well as the Black population. In the 2001 census, the visible minority population accounted for 13.4 percent of the population compared to less than 5 percent twenty years earlier (Bauder 2003; Statistics Canada 2003a).

People in the United States tend to view Canada's race relations in favorable terms. In part, this view reflects Canada's role as the "promised land" to slaves escaping the U.S. South and crossing the free North to Canada, where they were unlikely to be recaptured. The view of Canada as a land of positive intergroup relations is also fostered by Canadians' comparing themselves with the United States. They have long been willing to compare their best social institutions to the worst examples of racism in the United States and to pride themselves on being more virtuous and high-minded (McClain 1979).

The social reality, past and present, is quite different. Africans came in 1689 as involuntary immigrants to be enslaved by French colonists. Slavery officially continued until 1833. It never flourished because the Canadian economy did not need a large labor force, so most slaves worked as domestic servants. Blacks from the United States did flee to Canada before slavery ended, but some fugitive slaves returned after Lincoln's issuance of the Emancipation Proclamation in 1863. The early Black arrivals in Canada were greeted in a variety of ways. Often they were warmly received as fugitives from slavery, but as their numbers grew in some areas, Canadians became concerned that they would overwhelm the White population (Winks 1971).

The contemporary Black Canadian population, about 3 percent of the nation's population, consists of indigenous Afro-Canadians with several generations of roots in Canada, West Indian immigrants and their descendants, and a number of post–World War II immigrants from the United States. Immigration has become significant, especially in cities where immigrants tend to settle (Statistics Canada 2003a).

Before 1966, Canada's immigration policy alternated between restrictive and more open, as necessary to assist the economy. As in the United States, there were some very exclusionary phases based on race. From 1884 to 1923, Canada levied a Chinese "head tax" that virtually brought Chinese immigration to a halt, although earlier it had been encouraged. Subsequent policies through 1947 were not much better. Current immigration policy favors those with specific skills that make an economic contribution to the country (Economist 2006a).

Public agitation to restrict immigration has been particularly intense in response to increased pressure from Latin Americans and Asians to gain entry. A national survey of Canadians in 2002 found that 54 percent felt immigration should be reduced, and only 26 percent favored an increase. Yet three-quarters or more agreed that immigrants make an economic and cultural contribution to their country (*Migration News* 2002a).

It is difficult to escape the parallels with the United States. For example, since the 1980s there has been a degree of resurgence in open racism. Its targets were Blacks, Asian immigrants, and Jewish Canadians. A government-commissioned national survey released in 2003 found that 20 percent of the visible minorities often feel discriminated against, compared to 5 percent of the rest of the population. The government and the courts have been far from silent on issues relevant to "the visible minorities"

visible minorities
In Canada, persons other than Aboriginal or First Nation people who are non-white in racial background.

and the Aboriginal Peoples. Canadian courts have liberally interpreted their Charter of Rights and Freedoms to prevent systematic discrimination, and equal rights legislation has been passed. Many Asian immigrants, including those from India, complain their skills and degrees are devalued. Yet institutional racism and continuing debates about immigration policy will remain a part of the Canadian scene for some time to come (Farnsworth 1996; Krauss 2006a; McKenna 1994; Statistics Canada 2003b).

In 1541, Frenchman Jacques Cartier established the first European settlement along the St. Lawrence River, but within a year he withdrew because of confrontations with the Iroquois. Almost 500 years later, the descendants of the Europeans and Aboriginal Peoples are still trying to resolve Canada's identity as it is shaped by issues of ethnicity, race, and language.

Brazil: Not a Racial Paradise

To someone knowledgeable about race and ethnic relations in the United States, Brazil seems familiar in a number of respects. Like the United States, Brazil was colonized by Europeans who overwhelmed the native people. Like the United States, Brazil imported Black Africans as slaves to meet the demand for laborers. Even today, Brazil is second only to the United States in the number of people of African descent, excluding nations on the African continent. Another similarity is treatment of indigenous people. Although the focus here is on Black and White people in Brazil, another continuing concern is the treatment of Brazil's native peoples, as this developing nation continues to industrialize.

Legacy of Slavery

The present nature of Brazilian race relations is influenced by the legacy of slavery, as is true of Black–White relations in the United States. It is not necessary to repeat here a discussion of the brutality of the slave trade and slavery itself or of the influence of slavery on the survival of African cultures and family life. Scholars agree that slavery was not the

Increasingly people of Brazil are coming to terms with the significant social inequality evident along color lines.

same in Brazil as it was in the United States, but they disagree on how different it was and how significant these differences are (Elkins 1959; Tannenbaum 1946).

Brazil depended much more than the United States on the slave trade. Estimates place the total number of slaves imported to Brazil at 4 million, eight times the number brought to the United States. At the height of slavery, however, both nations had approximately the same slave population: 4 to 4.5 million. Brazil's reliance on African-born slaves meant that typical Brazilian slaves had closer ties to Africa than did their U.S. counterparts. Revolts and escapes were more common among slaves in Brazil. The most dramatic example was the slave *quilombo* (or hideaway) of Palmores, whose 20,000 inhabitants repeatedly fought off Portuguese assaults until 1698. Interestingly these *quilombos* have reappeared in the news, as Black Brazilians still have sought to recognize their claims related to these settlements.

It is easier to recognize the continuity of African cultures among Brazil's Blacks than among Black Americans. The contributions of the African people to Brazil's history have been kept alive by the attention given them in the schools. Whereas U.S. schools have just recently begun to teach about the Black role in history, the Brazilian schoolchild has typically become acquainted with the historical role of the Africans and their descendants. As in the United States, however, the surviving African culture is overwhelmed by dominant European traditions (Andrews 1991; Degler 1971; Frazier 1942, 1943; Stouffer 2005; Telles 2004).

The most significant difference between slavery in the southern United States and in Brazil was the amount of *manumission*, the freeing of slaves. For every 1,000 slaves, 100 were freed annually in Brazil, compared to four per year in the U.S. South. It would be hasty to assume, however, as some have, that Brazilian masters were more benevolent. Quite the contrary. Brazil's slave economy was poorer than that of the U.S. South, and so slave owners in Brazil freed slaves into poverty whenever they became crippled, sick, or old. But this custom does not completely explain the presence of the many freed slaves in Brazil. Again unlike in the United States, the majority of Brazil's population was composed of Africans and their descendants throughout the nineteenth century. Africans were needed as craft workers, shopkeepers, and boatmen, not just as agricultural workers. Freed slaves filled these needs.

In Brazil, race was not seen as a measure of innate inferiority, as it was in the United States. Rather, even during the period of slavery, Brazilians saw free Blacks as contributing to society, which was not the view of White U.S. Southerners. In Brazil, you were inferior if you were a slave. In the United States, you were inferior if you were Black. Not that Brazilians were more enlightened than Americans. Quite the contrary, Brazil belonged to the European tradition of a hierarchical society that did not conceive of all people as equal. Unlike the English, who emphasized individual freedom, however, the Brazilian slave owner had no need to develop a racist defense of slavery. These distinctions help explain why Whites in the United States felt compelled to dominate and simultaneously fear both the slave and the Black man and woman. Brazilians did not have these fears of free Blacks and, thus, felt it unnecessary to restrict manumission (Davis 1966; Degler 1971; Harris 1964; Patterson 1982; Skidmore 1972; Sundiata 1987).

The "Racial Democracy" Illusion

For some time in the twentieth century, Brazil was seen by some as a "racial democracy" and even a "racial paradise." Indeed, historically the term *race* is rare in Brazil but rather the term *côr* or *color* is common. Historian Carl Degler (1971) identified the *mulatto escape hatch* as the key to the differences in Brazilian and American race relations. In Brazil, the mulatto or *moreno* (brown) is recognized as a group separate from either *brancos* (Whites) or *prêtos* (Blacks), whereas in the United States, mulattos are

What does it mean to describe Brazil as a "racial democracy"?

quilombo
Slave hideaways n Brazil.

mulatto escape hatch
Notion that Brazilians of mixed ancestry can move into high status positions.

classed with Blacks. Yet this escape hatch is an illusion because economically, mulattoes fare only marginally better than Black Brazilians or *Afro-Brazilians*, the term used here to refer to the dark end of the Brazilian color gradient and increasingly used by college-educated persons and activists in Brazil. In addition, mulattoes do not escape in the sense of mobility into the income and status enjoyed by White Brazilians. Labor market analyses demonstrate that Blacks with the highest levels of education and occupation experience the most discrimination in terms of jobs, mobility, and income (Fiola 1989; Freyre 1986; Motta 2000; Triner 1999; Winant 1989).

Today, the use of dozens of terms to describe oneself along the color gradient (see Chapter 12) is obvious in Brazil because, unlike in the United States, people of mixed ancestry are viewed as an identifiable social group. The 2000 census in Brazil classified 53 percent White, 39 percent brown or mulatto, 6 percent Afro-Brazilians, and 1 percent Asian and indigenous Brazilian Indians. Over the past fifty years, the mulatto group has grown, and the proportions of both Whites and Blacks declined (Brazil 1981).

The presence of mulattoes does not mean that color is irrelevant in society or that miscegenation occurs randomly. The incidence of mixed marriages is greatest among the poor and among those similar in color. About one-fourth of all marriages are between people of different color groupings. Marriages between partners from opposite ends of the color gradient are relatively uncommon—perhaps 1 percent. The absence of direct racial confrontation and the presence of mixed marriages lead some writers to conclude that Brazil is a "racial paradise." The lack of racial tension does not, however, mean that prejudice does not exist or that Blacks are fully accepted. For example, residential segregation is present in Brazil's urban areas, which extends beyond social class divisions. Furthermore, there is even greater regional segregation with about 75 percent of Whites living in the southern and southeastern regions where contact with Afro-Brazilians is limited (Telles 2004).

In Brazil, today as in the past, light skin color enhances status, but the impact is often exaggerated. When Degler advanced the idea of the "mulatto escape hatch," he implied that it was a means to success. The most recent income data controlling for gender, education, and age indicate that people of mixed ancestry earn 12 percent more than Blacks. Yet Whites earn another 26 percent more than the moreno. Clearly, the major distinction is between Whites and all "people of color" rather than between people of mixed ancestry and Afro-Brazilians (Dzidzienyo 1987; Silva 1985; Telles, 1992, 2004).

Brazilian Dilemma

Gradually in Brazil there has been the recognition that racial prejudice and discrimination do exist. A 2000 survey in Rio de Janeiro found that 93 percent believe racism exists in Brazil and 74 percent said there was a lot of bias. Yet 87 percent of the respondents said they themselves were not racist (Buckley 2000).

During the twentieth century, Brazil changed from a nation that prided itself on its freedom from racial intolerance to a country legally attacking discrimination against people of color. One of the first measures was in 1951 when the Afonso Arinos law was unanimously adopted, prohibiting racial discrimination in public places. Opinion is divided over the effectiveness of the law, which has been of no use in overturning subtle forms of discrimination. Even from the start, certain civilian careers, such as the diplomatic and military officer ranks, were virtually closed to Blacks. Curiously, the push for the law came from the United States, after a Black American dancer, Katherine Dunham, was denied a room at a São Paulo luxury hotel.

Today the income disparity is signficant in Brazil. As shown in Figure 16.3, people of color disproportionately clustered in the lowest income levels of society. Although not as disadvantaged as Blacks in South Africa, which we will take up later in this chapter,

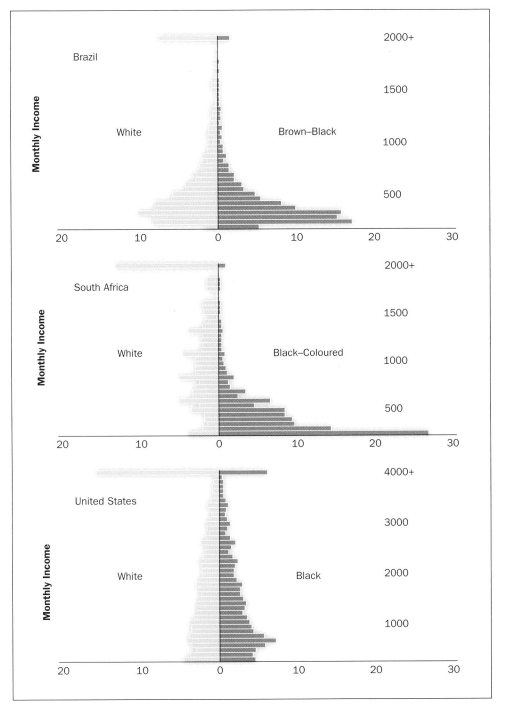

FIGURE 16.3 Income Distribution by Race

Note: Monthly income for 1996 for Brazil and United States, 1998 in South Africa.

Source: Government agencies as reported in Telles 2004, 108.

the degree of inequality between Whites and people of color is much greater in Brazil than in the United States.

As in other multiracial societies, women of color fare particularly poorly in Brazil. White men, of course, have the highest income, whereas Black men have earning levels comparable to those of White women, and Afro-Brazilian women are the furthest behind (Fiola 1989; Telles 2004).

Groups working on behalf of people of color in Brazil are gradually becoming more visible. Geledes/SOS Racism, a Black rights group, filed a protest with a television network for depicting a Black gardener cowering before a White man falsely accusing him of theft. Today such groups exist in a number of states, although actual convictions of discrimination are rare (Goering 1994).

The challenge to Afro-Brazilians becoming more organized is not that they fail to recognize the discrimination but that the society tends to think the distinctions are based on social class. After all, if problems are based on poverty, they are easier to overcome than if problems are based on color. However, this is also understandable because societal wealth is so unequal—the concentration of income and assets in the hands of a few is much greater than even in the United States. For Afro-Brazilians, even professional status can achieve only so much in one's social standing. An individual's blackness does not suddenly become invisible simply because he or she has acquired some social standing. The fame achieved by the Black Brazilian soccer player Pelé is a token exception and does not mean that Blacks have it easy or even have a readily available "escape hatch" through professional sports (Dzidzienyo 1979).

Is Brazilian society becoming more polarized, or are Brazilians as tolerant as they seem always to have been? There is no easy answer because Brazil has not been the subject of the intensive research and opinion polling found in the United States. Several scholars of Brazilian society believe that race has become more important. This does not mean that a belief in racial inferiority and the practice of de facto segregation will become common in Brazil. But also Brazil does not have, nor is it likely to have soon, a large Afro-Brazilian middle-class society separate from White middle-class society. By suggesting that Brazil is becoming more conscious of race, these scholars mean that coming generations will have a heightened awareness of race in Brazil and must try to address the racial divisions that are being increasingly documented (Economist 2006b).

Israel and the Palestinians

In 1991, when the Gulf War ended, hopes were high in many parts of the world that a comprehensive Middle East peace plan could be hammered out. Just a decade later, after the terrorist attacks of September 11, 2001, the expectations for a lasting peace were much dimmer. The key elements in any peace plan were to resolve the conflict between Israel and its Arab neighbors and to resolve the challenge of the Palestinian refugees. Although the issues are debated in the political arena, the origins of the conflict can be found in race, ethnicity, and religion.

Nearly 2,000 years ago, the Jews were exiled from Palestine in the **Diaspora**. The exiled Jews settled throughout Europe and elsewhere in the Middle East where they often encountered hostility and the anti-Semitism described in Chapter 14. With the conversion of the Roman Empire to Christianity, Palestine became the site of many Christian pilgrimages. Beginning in the seventh century, Palestine gradually fell under the Muslim influence of the Arabs. By the beginning of the twentieth century, tourism had become established. In addition, some Jews had migrated from Russia and established settlements that were tolerated by the Ottoman Empire, which then controlled Palestine.

Great Britain expanded its colonial control from Egypt into Palestine during World War I, driving out the Turks. Britain ruled the land but endorsed the eventual establishment of a Jewish national homeland in Palestine. The spirit of **Zionism**, the yearning to establish a Jewish state in the biblical homeland, was well under way. From the Arab perspective, Zionism meant the subjugation, if not the elimination, of the Palestinians.

Thousands of Jews came to settle from throughout the world; even so, in the 1920s, Palestine was only about 15 percent Jewish. Ethnic tension grew as the Arabs of Palestine were threatened by the Zionist fervor. Rioting grew to such a point that, in 1939,

Diaspora
The exile of Jews from Palestine.

Zionism
Traditional Jewish religious yearning to return to the biblical homeland, now used to refer to support for the state of Israel.

Britain yielded to Palestinian demands that Jewish immigration be stopped. This occurred at the same time as large numbers of Jews were fleeing Nazism in Europe. After World War II, Jews resumed their demand for a homeland, despite Arab objections. Britain turned to the newly formed United Nations to settle the dispute. In May 1948, the British mandate over Palestine ended, and the State of Israel was founded (Masci 2001).

The Palestinian people define themselves as the people who live in this former British mandate, along with their descendants on their fathers' side. They are viewed as an ethnic group within the larger group of Arabs. They generally speak Arabic, and most of them (97 percent) are Muslim (mostly Sunni). With a rapid rate of natural increase, the Palestinians have grown in number from 1.4 million at the end of World War II to about 7 million worldwide: 700,000 in Israel, 1.5 million in the West Bank, and 800,000 in the Gaza Strip (Third World Institute 2005, 434).

Arab-Israeli Conflicts

No sooner had Israel been recognized than the Arab nations, particularly Egypt, Jordan, Iraq, Syria, and Lebanon, announced their intention to restore control to the Palestinian Arabs, by force if necessary. As hostilities broke out, the Israeli military stepped in to preserve the borders, which no Arab nation agreed to recognize. Some 60 percent of the 1.3 million Arabs fled or were expelled from Israeli territory, becoming refugees in neighboring countries. An uneasy peace followed as Israel attempted to encourage new Jewish immigration. Israel also extended the same services that were available to the Jews, such as education and health care, to the non-Jewish Israelis. The new Jewish population continued to grow under the country's Law of Return, which gave every Jew in the world the right to settle permanently as a citizen. The question of Jerusalem remained unsettled, and the city was divided into two separate sections—Israeli Jewish and Jordanian Arab—a division both sides refused to regard as permanent.

In 1967, Egypt, followed by Syria, responded to Israel's military actions to take surrounding territory in what has come to be called the Six-Day War. In the course of defeating the Arab states' military, Israel occupied the Gaza Strip and the West Bank (Figure 16.4 on p. 442). The defeat was all the more bitter for the Arabs as Israeli-held territory expanded.

The October 1973 war (called the Yom Kippur War by Jews and the Ramadan War by Arabs), launched against Israel by Egypt and Syria, did not change any boundaries, but it did lead to huge oil price increases as Arab and other oil-rich nations retaliated for the European and U.S. backing of Israel. In 1979, Egypt, through the mediation of U.S. President Carter, recognized Israel's right to exist, for which Israel returned the Sinai, but there was no suggestion that the other occupied territories would be returned to neighboring Arab states. This recognition by Egypt, following several unsuccessful Arab military attacks, signaled to the Palestinians that they were alone in their struggle against Israel (Masci 2001).

Although our primary attention here is on the Palestinians and the Jews, another significant ethnic issue is present in Israel. The Law of Return has brought to Israel Jews of varying cultural backgrounds. European Jews have been the dominant force, but a significant migration of the more religiously observant Jews from North Africa and other parts of the Middle East has created what sociologist Ernest Krausz (1973) called "the two nations." Not only are the various Jewish groups culturally diverse, but there are also significant socioeconomic differences: The Europeans generally are more prosperous, better represented in the Knesset (Israel's parliament), and better educated. The secular Jews feel pressure from the more traditional and ultra-Orthodox Jews, who push for a nation more reflective of Jewish customs and law. Indeed, in a 1998 survey, more Israeli Jews see the lack of unity within the state as a major shortcoming than as a failure to end the Israeli-Arab conflict (*Los Angeles Times* Poll 1998; Miller 1998; Sela-Sheffy 2004).

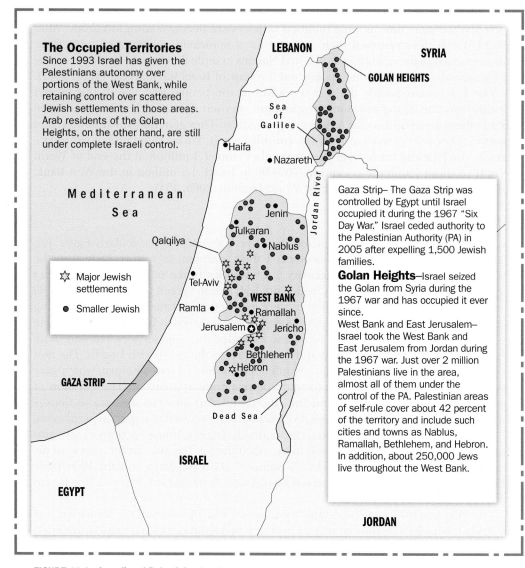

FIGURE 16.4   Israeli and Palestinian Lands

Source: Author based on Masci 2001; *The Economist* 2005b, 2005c, Tse 2005.

The Intifada

The occupied territories were regarded initially by Israel as a security zone between it and its belligerent neighbors. By the 1980s, however, it was clear that they were also serving as the location of new settlements for Jews migrating to Israel, especially from Russia. Palestinians, though enjoying some political and monetary support of Arab nations, saw little likelihood of a successful military effort to eliminate Israel. Therefore, in December 1987, they began the **Intifada**, the uprising against Israel by the Palestinians in the occupied territories through attacks against soldiers, the boycott of Israeli goods, general strikes, resistance, and noncooperation with Israeli authorities. The target of this first Intifada, lasting five years, was the Israelis.

The Intifada has been a grassroots, popular movement whose growth in support was as much a surprise to the Palestine Liberation Organization (PLO) and the Arab

Intifada
The Palestinian uprising against Israeli authorities in the occupied territories.

nations as it was to Israel and its supporters. The broad range of participants in the Intifada—students, workers, union members, professionals, and business leaders—showed the unambiguous Palestinian opposition to occupation.

Despite condemnation by both the United Nations and the United States, Israel continued to expel suspected activists from the occupied territories into neighboring Arab states. The Intifada began out of the frustration of the Palestinians within Israel, but the confrontations were later encouraged by the PLO, an umbrella organization for several Palestinian factions of varying militancy.

With television news footage of Israeli soldiers appearing to attack defenseless youths, the Intifada transformed world opinion, especially in the United States. Palestinians came to be viewed as people struggling for self-determination rather than as terrorists out to destroy Israel. Instead of Israel being viewed as the "David" and its Arab neighbors "Goliath," Israel came to take on the bully role and the Palestinians the sympathetic underdog role (Hubbard 1993).

Nearly half of the world's Palestinian people live under Israeli control. Of the Israeli Palestinians, about one-third are regarded as residents, and the rest live in the occupied territories. The Diaspora of Jews that the creation of Israel was to remedy has led to the displacement of the Palestinian Arabs. The Intifada and international reaction propelled Israel and the PLO to reach an agreement in 1993 known as the Oslo Accords.

The Search for Solutions Amid Violence

The Oslo Accords between Israeli Prime Minister Yitzhak Rabin and PLO Chairman Yasser Arafat and subsequent agreements ended the state of war and appeared to set in motion the creation of the first-ever self-governing Palestinian territory in the Gaza Strip and the West Bank. Hard-liners on both sides grew resistant to the move toward separate recognized Palestinian and Israel states. Prime Minister Rabin was assassinated at a peace rally by an Israeli who felt the government had given up too much. Succeeding governments in Israel took stronger stands against relinquishing control of the occupied territories. Meanwhile the anti-Israel Hamas party was elected to power following the death of Arafat in 2004.

Despite the assurances at Oslo, Israel did not end its occupation of the Palestinian territories by 1999, justifying its actions as necessary to stop anti-Israel violence originating in Palestinian settlements. Complicating the picture was the continued growth of 125 officially recognized Israeli settlements in the West Bank of 250,000 by 2006. Palestinians, assisted by Arabs in other countries, mounted a second Intifada beginning in September 2000, precipitated by the Israeli killing of several Palestinians at a Jerusalem mosque. This time militant Palestinians went outside the occupied territories and bombed civilian sites in Israel through a series of suicide bombings. This second Intifada, continuing through the present, has taken more Israeli lives. In the 1990s, about one Israeli died for every twenty-five Palestinians, but the recent violence has seen about one Israeli death for every three Palestinian deaths. Each violent episode brings a call for retaliation by the other side and desperate calls for a cease-fire from outside the region. Israel, despite worldwide denunciation, created a "security barrier" of 30-foot-high concrete walls, ditches, and barbed wire to try to protect its Jewish settlers, which served to limit the mobility of peaceful Palestinians trying to access crops, schools, hospitals, and jobs (*The Economist* 2006c; Segev 2006; Wilson 2006).

The immediate problem is to end the violence, but any lasting peace must face a series of difficult issues, including the following:

- The status of Jerusalem. It is Israel's capital but is also viewed by Muslims as the third most holy city in the world.
- The future of the Jewish settlements in the Palestinian Authority territories.
- The future of Palestinians and other Arabs with Israeli citizenship.
- The creation of a truly independent Palestinian national state with strong leadership. Israel-Palestinian Authority relations with the latter's government under control of the Hamas who are sworn to Israel's destruction.
- The future of Palestinian refugees elsewhere.

Beginning in 2005, Israel started constructing a 30-foot-high barrier for security purposes, but the wall also served to keep Palestinians from schools and jobs.

Added worries are the uneasy peace between Israel and its Arab neighbors and the sometimes interrelated events in Lebanon, Iraq, and Iran (Rouhana and Bar-Tal 1998).

The last sixty years have witnessed significant changes: Israel has gone from a land under siege to a nation whose borders are recognized by almost everyone. Israel has come to terms with the various factions of religious and secular Jews trying to coexist. The Palestinian people have gone from disfranchisement to having territory and welcoming back others from exile. The current solution is fragile and very temporary, as is any form of secession with a foundation for accommodation amid continuing violence.

Republic of South Africa

In every nation in the world, some racial, ethnic, or religious groups enjoy advantages denied to other groups. Nations differ in the extent of this denial and in whether it is supported by law or by custom. In no other industrial society has the denial been so entrenched in recent law as in the Republic of South Africa.

The Republic of South Africa is different from the rest of Africa because the original African peoples of the area are no longer present. Today, the country is multiracial, as shown in Table 16.2.

The largest group is the Black Africans who migrated from the north in the eighteenth century as well as more recent migrations from neighboring African countries over the last twenty years. The Coloured (or Cape Coloureds), the product of mixed race, and Asians (or Indians) make up the remaining non-Whites. The small White community consists of the English and the Afrikaners, the latter descended from Dutch and other European settlers. As in all other multicultural nations we have considered, colonialism and immigration have left their mark.

The Legacy of Colonialism

The permanent settlement of South Africa by Europeans began in 1652, when the Dutch East India Company established a colony in Cape Town as a port of call for shipping vessels bound for India. The area was sparsely populated, and the original inhabitants of the Cape of Good Hope, the Hottentots and Bushmen, were pushed inland like the indigenous peoples of the New World. To fill the need for laborers, the Dutch imported slaves from areas of Africa farther north. Slavery was confined mostly to areas near towns and involved more limited numbers than in the United States. The Boers, seminomads descended from the Dutch, did not remain on the coast but

---

TABLE 16.2
Racial Groups in the Republic of South Africa

	Whites	All Non-Whites	Black Africans	Coloureds	Asians
1904	22%	78%	67%	9%	2%
1936	21	79	69	8	2
1951	21	79	68	9	3
2005	9.4	90.6	79.4	8.8	2.5
2010 (proj.)	10	90	80	8	2

Note: "Non-White" totals subject to rounding error.

Sources: Author's estimates based on Statistics South Africa and Bureau of Market Research in MacFarlane 2006a, 8–9; van den Berghe 1978, 102.

A South African citizen displays the "passbook" that all non-Whites had to carry with them under apartheid. These internal passports required obedience to a complex series of laws and regulations.

trekked inland to establish vast sheep and cattle ranches. The trekkers, as they were known, regularly fought off the Black inhabitants of the interior regions. Sexual relations between Dutch men and slave and Hottentot women were quite common, giving rise to a mulatto group referred to today as Cape Coloureds.

The British entered the scene by acquiring part of South Africa in 1814, at the end of the Napoleonic Wars. The British introduced workers from India as indentured servants on sugar plantations. They had also freed the slaves by 1834, with little compensation to the Dutch slave owners, and had given Blacks almost all political and civil rights. The Boers were not happy with these developments and spent most of the nineteenth century in a violent struggle with the growing number of English colonists. In 1902, the British finally overwhelmed the Boers, leaving bitter memories on both sides. Once in control, however, they recognized that the superior numbers of the non-Whites were a potential threat to their power, as they had been to the power of the Afrikaners.

The growing non-White population consisted of the Coloureds, or mixed population, and the Black tribal groups, collectively called Bantus. The British gave both groups the vote but restricted the franchise to people who met certain property qualifications. **Pass laws** were introduced, placing curfews on the Bantus and limiting their geographic movement. These laws, enforced through "reference books" until 1986, were intended to prevent urban areas from becoming overcrowded with job-seeking Black Africans, a familiar occurrence in colonial Africa (van den Berghe 1965; W. Wilson 1973).

Apartheid

In 1948, South Africa was granted its independence from the United Kingdom, and the National Party, dominated by the Afrikaners, assumed control of the government. Under the leadership of this party, the rule of White supremacy, already well under way in the colonial period as custom, became more and more formalized into law. To deal with the multiracial population, the Whites devised a policy called apartheid to ensure their dominance. **Apartheid** (in Afrikaans, the language of the Afrikaners, it means "separation" or "apartness") came to mean a policy of separate development, euphemistically called multinational development by the government. At the time, these changes were regarded as cosmetic outside South Africa and by most Black South Africans.

The White ruling class was not homogeneous. The English and Afrikaners belonged to different political parties, lived apart, spoke different languages, and worshipped separately, but they shared the belief that some form of apartheid was necessary. Apartheid can perhaps be best understood as a twentieth-century effort to reestablish the master–slave relationship. Blacks could not vote. They could not move throughout the country freely. They were unable to hold jobs unless the government approved. To work at approved jobs, they were forced to live in temporary quarters at great distances from their real homes. Their access to education, health care, and social services was severely limited (W. Wilson 1973).

Events took a significant turn in 1990, when South African Prime Minister F. W. De Klerk legalized sixty banned Black organizations and freed Nelson Mandela, leader of the African National Congress (ANC), after twenty-seven years of imprisonment. Mandela's triumphant remarks after his release appear in "Listen to Our Voices."

The next year, De Klerk and Black leaders signed a National Peace Accord, pledging themselves to the establishment of a multiparty democracy and an end to violence. After a series of political defeats, De Klerk called for a referendum in 1992 to allow Whites to vote on ending apartheid. If he failed to receive popular support, he vowed to resign. A record high turnout gave a solid 68.6 percent vote favoring the

pass laws
Laws that controlled internal movement by non-Whites in South Africa.

apartheid
The policy of the South African government intended to maintain separation of Blacks, Coloureds, and Asians from the dominant Whites.

Voices Listen to Our Voices Listen to

Africa, it is Ours!

The following excerpts are from 71-year-old Black nationalist leader Nelson Mandela's speech, delivered in front of the Cape Town City Hall after his release from a 27-year imprisonment on February 12, 1990.

Nelson Mandela

Amandla! Amandla! i-Afrika, mayibuye! [Power! Power! Africa, it is ours!]

My friends, comrades and fellow South Africans, I greet you all in the name of peace, democracy and freedom for all. I stand here before you not as a prophet but as a humble servant of you, the people.

Your tireless and heroic sacrifices have made it possible for me to be here today. I therefore place the remaining years of my life in your hands.

On this day of my release, I extend my sincere and warmest gratitude to the millions of my compatriots and those in every corner of the globe who have campaigned tirelessly for my release.

Negotiations on the dismantling of apartheid will have to address the overwhelming demand of our people for a democratic nonracial and unitary South Africa. There must be an end to white monopoly on political power.

And [there must be] a fundamental restructuring of our political and economic systems to insure that the inequalities of apartheid are addressed and our society thoroughly democratized. . . .

Our struggle has reached a decisive moment. We call on our people to seize this moment so that the process toward democracy is rapid and uninterrupted. We have waited

too long for our freedom. We can no longer wait. Now is the time to intensify the struggle on all fronts.

To relax our efforts now would be a mistake which generations to come will not be able to forgive. The sight of freedom looming on the horizon should encourage us to redouble our efforts. It is only through disciplined mass action that our victory can be assured.

We call on our white compatriots to join us in the shaping of a new South Africa. The freedom movement is the political home for you, too. We call on the international community to continue the campaign to isolate the apartheid regime.

To lift sanctions now would be to run the risk of aborting the process toward the complete eradication of apartheid. Our march to freedom is irreversible. We must not allow fear to stand in our way.

Universal suffrage on a common voters' roll in a united democratic and nonracial South Africa is the only way to peace and racial harmony.

In conclusion, I wish to go to my own words during my trial in 1964. They are as true today as they were then. I wrote: I have fought against white domination, and I have fought against black domination. I have cherished the idea of a democratic and free society in which all persons live together in harmony and with equal opportunities.

It is an ideal which I hope to live for and to achieve. But if needs be, it is an ideal for which I am prepared to die. ■

continued dismantling of legal apartheid and the creation of a new constitution through negotiation. The process toward power-sharing ended symbolically when De Klerk and Mandela were jointly awarded the 1993 Nobel Peace Prize (Ottaway and Taylor 1992; Winant 2001).

The Era of Reconciliation and Moving On

In April 1994, South Africa held its first universal election. Apartheid had ended. Nelson Mandela's ANC received 62 percent of the vote, giving him a five-year term as president. The National Party's F. W. De Klerk is serving as one of two executive deputy presidents. Mandela enjoyed the advantage of wide personal support throughout the nation. He retired in 1999 when his second term ended and was succeeded by fellow ANC leader Thabo Mbeki, who is facing a daunting agenda because of the legacy of apartheid.

A significant step to help South Africa move past apartheid was the creation of the Truth and Reconciliation Commission (TRC). People were allowed to come forward and confess to horrors they had committed under apartheid from 1961 through 1993. If they were judged by the TRC to be truly remorseful, and most were, they were not subject to prosecution. If they failed to confess to all crimes they had committed, they were prosecuted. The stories gripped the country as people learned that actions taken in the name of the Afrikaner government were often worse than anyone had anticipated (Gobodo-Madikizela 2003).

The immediate relief that came with the end of apartheid has given way to greater concerns about the future of all South Africans. In "Research Focus" we consider the views expressed by contemporary South Africans.

With the emergence of the new multiracial government in South Africa, we see a country with enormous promise but many challenges that are similar to those of our own multiracial society. Some of the controversial issues facing the ANC-led government are very familiar to citizens in the United States:

> *Desperate poverty.* Despite the growth of a small but conspicuous middle class among Black South Africans, poverty rates stand at 60.6 percent, compared to 4.0 percent of White South Africans.
>
> *Affirmative action.* Race-based employment goals and other preference programs have been proposed, yet critics insist that such efforts constitute reverse apartheid.
>
> *Medical care.* The nation is trying to confront the duality of private care for the affluent (usually Whites) and government-subsidized care (usually for people of color). AIDS has reached devastating levels, with 10 percent of the population having HIV/AIDS as of the beginning of 2005 but less than 3 percent are receiving antiretroviral medication as of 2006.
>
> *Crime.* Although the government-initiated violence under apartheid has ended, the generations of conflict and years of intertribal attacks have created a climate for crime, illegal gun ownership, and disrespect for law enforcement.
>
> *School integration.* Multiracial schools are replacing the apartheid system, but for some, the change is occurring too fast or not fast enough. Although 17 percent of Whites hold a college degree, only 1.9 percent of Black South Africans are so advantaged.

These issues must be addressed with minimal increases in government spending as the government seeks to reverse deficit spending without an increase in taxes that would frighten away needed foreign investment. As difficult as all these challenges are, perhaps the most difficult is land reform (Cronje 2006; Dimant 2006; Lebone 2006; MacFarlane 2006b).

The government has pledged to address the issue of land ownership. Between 1960 and 1990, the government forced Black South Africans from their land and often allowed Whites to settle on it. Beginning in 1994, the government took steps to transfer 30 percent of agricultural land to Black South Africans. Where feasible, the government plans to restore the original inhabitants to their land; where this is not feasible, the gov-

ASK Yourself

What are the major social issues facing the people of South Africa?

Focus Research Focus Research

LISTENING TO THE PEOPLE

In the United States, we take for granted the regular release of opinion or survey data about what people think about the sensitive issues in their country. However, public opinion surveying does not typically occur in totalitarian countries such as South Africa under apartheid. Today, surveying is now a regular part of South African life and, not too surprisingly, the subject sometimes turns to race relations.

We can examine national surveys of opinions conducted in 2001, 2003, and 2005 to find out what adults from all racial groups thought about racism in everyday life. Reviewing these studies, the data reveal a racial divide on many issues.

Nearly two-thirds of Black Africans (65 percent) indicated in 2003 that they felt the country was headed in the right direction, whereas only about one-third (36 percent) of Whites felt the same way. Blacks overwhelmingly see unemployment as the major problem facing the nation, whereas Whites place crime and security as the top problem, with government corruption as number two. Blacks, meanwhile, do not see the government as a problem but give priority to both housing and water supply—two issues not ranked highly by their fellow White citizens.

On a more personal level, acceptance of intermarriage is limited, especially among White South Africans. When asked if one would approve of a close relative marrying someone of another color, only 14 percent of Whites endorsed such an idea compared to 53 percent of Blacks and Asians and 67 percent of Coloureds.

All South Africans—whether Black, Coloured, Indian, or White—agree that democracy is preferable to any other kind of government and that South Africa will remain democratic. Blacks are much more likely to see the gap between the rich and poor as a threat to democracy. Blacks are more likely to see education and health care as improving over the ten years of postapartheid South Africa, whereas Whites see it as actually getting worse. Just 19 percent of White respondents said they would consider a return to apartheid.

In summary, the survey revealed deep concerns among all South Africans about a number of social and economic issues, but the specific factor of race is not viewed as the dominant problem. Yet the consciousness of racism has not vanished. The majority still see racism as a serious concern. Yet when asked, they generally see their own group as the victim of racism with little recognition of the problems of prejudice and discrimination facing the other groups.

There seemed little doubt from this survey that, as during the apartheid era, South Africa still has a racial problem to solve. ▨

Sources: The Economist 2005a; Kaiser Family Foundation 2004, Schlemmer 2001a, 2001b.

ernment is to make "just and equitable compensation." By 2006, less than 7 percent of the farmland had been transferred. The magnitude of this land reform issue cannot be minimized. Originally the goal was to achieve the land transfer by 2004, but this has now been deferred to 2015. Certain critics say at the current rate it will take until 2060 to reach the 2004 objective. With its other economic problems and now the decision to invest hundreds of millions of dollars in hosting the 2010 Football (soccer) World Cup, more new land is likely to be occupied by Black South Africans through squatter arrangements than through government-approved transfer (Lebone 2006).

Conclusion

By looking beyond our borders, we gather new insights into the social processes that frame and define intergroup relationships. The colonial experience has played a role in all cases under consideration in this chapter but particularly in South Africa. In Mexico and South Africa, which have long histories of multiethnic societies, intergroup sexual relations have been widespread but with different results. *Mestizos* in Mexico occupy a middle racial group and experience less tension, whereas in South Africa, the Cape Coloureds had freedoms under apartheid almost as limited as those of the Black Africans. South Africa enforced *de jure* segregation, whereas Israeli communities seem to have de facto segregation. Israel's and South Africa's intergroup conflicts have involved the world community. Indigenous people figure in the social landscape of Canada, Brazil, and Mexico. Policies giving preference to previously devalued racial groups are in place in both Brazil and South Africa. Complete assimilation is absent in all five societies considered in this chapter and is unlikely to occur in the near future; the legal and informal barriers to assimilation and pluralism vary for subordinate people choosing either option. Looking at the status of women in Mexico reminds us of the worldwide nature of gender stratifi-

cation and also offers insight into the patterns present in developing nations.

If we add the United States to these societies, the similarities become even more striking. The problems of racial and ethnic adjustment in the United States have dominated our attention, but they parallel past and present experiences in other societies with racial, ethnic, or religious heterogeneity. The U.S. government has been involved in providing educational, financial, and legal support for programs intended to help particular racial or ethnic groups, and it continues to avoid interfering with religious freedom. Bilingual, bicultural programs in schools, autonomy for Native Americans on reservations, and increased participation in decision making by residents of ghettoes and barrios are all viewed as acceptable goals, although they are not pursued to the extent that many subordinate-group people would like.

The analysis of this chapter has reminded us of the global nature of dominant–subordinate relations along dimensions of race, ethnicity, religion, and gender. In the next chapter, we will take an overview of racial and ethnic relations but also explore social inequality along the dimensions of age, disability status, and sexual orientation.

Key Terms

apartheid 446
color gradient 429
Diaspora 440
ethnonational conflict 426

Intifada 442
mulatto escape hatch 437
pass laws 446
quilombo 437

visible minorities 435
world systems theory 426
Zionism 440

Review Questions

1. Identify who the native peoples are and what their role has been in each of the societies discussed in this chapter.
2. On what levels can one speak of an identity issue facing Canada as a nation?
3. What role has secession played in Canada and Israel?
4. How have civil uprisings affected intergroup tensions in Mexico and Israel?
5. To what extent are the problems facing South Africa today a part of apartheid's legacy?

Critical Thinking

1. Social construction of race emphasizes how we create arbitrary definitions of skin color that then have social consequences. Drawing on the societies discussed, select one nation and identify how social definitions work in other ways to define group boundaries.

2. Apply the functionalist and conflict approaches of sociology first introduced in Chapter 1 to each of the societies under study in this chapter.

3. The conflicts summarized are examples of ethnonational conflicts, but how have the actions or inactions of the United States contributed to these problems?

Internet Connections—Research Navigator™

Follow the instructions found on page 35 of this text to access the features of Research Navigator™. Once at the Web site, enter your Login Name and Password. Then, to use the ContentSelect database, enter keywords such as "apartheid," "Palestine," "Mandela," and "Inuit," and the search engine will supply relevant and recent scholarly and popular press publications. Use the *New York Times* Search-by-Subject Archive to find recent news articles related to sociology and the Link Library feature to locate relevant Web links organized by the key terms associated with this chapter.

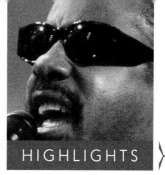

THE EXPERIENCE OF SOCIAL DISADVANTAGE IS NOT LIMITED to groups defined by race, ethnicity, gender, or religion. Despite an improving medical and financial situation, the elderly are still as a group at a disadvantage, given the ageism in our society. People with disabilities also have sought to achieve both respect and opportunities. Although the Americans with Disabilities Act (ADA) is a significant step forward, serious advocacy efforts continue. Long-term homophobia has made it a challenge for gays and lesbians to go about their lives. Progress has been mixed; some civil rights legislation has been passed at the local level, but the federal government took positions against avowed homosexuals in the military and sought to prevent legal recognition of gay and lesbian marriage. For each of these groups, as well as the racial and ethnic minorities discussed earlier, it is easy to applaud the progress already made. However, given the level of inequality that still persists, a full agenda for further progress remains.

What metaphor do we use to describe a nation whose racial, ethnic, and religious minorities are on the way to becoming numerical majorities in many cities and, now in the twenty-first century, in several states? For several generations, the image of the melting pot has been used as a convenient description of our culturally diverse nation. The analogy of an alchemist's cauldron was clever, even if a bit ethnocentric. It originated in the Middle Ages, when the alchemist used a melting pot to attempt to change less costly metals into gold and silver.

The Melting Pot was the title of a 1908 play by Israel Zangwill. In this play, a young Russian immigrant to the United States composes a symphony that portrays a nation that serves as a crucible (or pot) where all ethnic and racial groups melt together into a new, superior stock.

The vision of the United States as a melting pot became popular in the first part of the twentieth century, particularly because it suggested that the United States had an almost divinely inspired mission to destroy artificial divisions and create a single humankind. However, the image did not mesh with reality, as the dominant group indicated its unwillingness to welcome Native Americans, African Americans, Hispanics or Latinos, Jews, and Asians, among many others, into the melting pot.

The image of the melting pot is not invoked as much today. Instead, people speak of a salad bowl to describe a country that is ethnically diverse. As we can distinguish the lettuce from the tomatoes from the peppers in a tossed salad, we can see ethnic restaurants and the persistence of foreign languages in conversations on street corners. The dressing over the ingredients is akin to the shared value system and culture, covering but not hiding the different ingredients of the salad.

Yet even the notion of a salad is wilting. Like the melting pot that came before, the image of a salad is static, certainly not indicative of the dynamic changes we see in the United States. It also fails to conjure up the myriad cultural pieces that make up the fabric or mosaic of our diverse nation.

The kaleidoscope offers another familiar and more useful analogy. Patented in 1817 by Scottish scientist Sir David Brewster, the kaleidoscope was a toy and then became a table ornament in the parlors of the rich. Users of this optical device turn a set of mirrors and observe the seemingly endless colors and patterns that are reflected off pieces of glass, tinsel, or beads. The growing popularity of the phrase "people of color" fits well with the idea of the United States as a kaleidoscope. The changing images correspond to the often bewildering array of groups found in our country (Schaefer 1992).

The images created by a kaleidoscope are hard to describe because they change dramatically with little effort. Similarly, in the kaleidoscope of the United States, we find it a challenge to describe the dynamic multiracial nature of this republic. Yet even as we begin to understand the past, present, and future of all the many racial and ethnic groups, we recognize that there are still other people who are stigmatized in society by virtue of group membership. In this chapter, we will continue our effort to understand the people excluded in varying degrees from society by considering the cases of the aged, people with disabilities, and the gay and lesbian community.

The Aged: A Social Minority

Older people in the United States are subject to a paradox. They are a significant segment of the population who, as we shall see, often are viewed with negative stereotypes and are subject to discrimination. Yet they also have successfully organized into a potent collective force that wields significant political clout on certain social issues. Unlike other social groups subjected to differential treatment, this social category will include most of us someday. So in this one case, the notion of the elderly as "them" will eventually give way to "us."

The elderly share the characteristics of subordinate or minority groups that we introduced in Chapter 1. Specifically,

1. The elderly experience unequal treatment in employment and may face prejudice and discrimination.
2. The elderly share physical characteristics that distinguish them from younger people. In addition, their cultural preferences and leisure-time activities often differ from those of the rest of society.
3. Membership in this disadvantaged group is involuntary.
4. Older people have a strong sense of group solidarity, as reflected in senior citizens' centers, retirement communities, and advocacy organizations.
5. Older people generally are married to others of comparable age.

There is one crucial difference between older people and other subordinate groups, such as racial and ethnic minorities or women: All of us who live long will eventually assume the ascribed status of being an older person (Barron 1953; Wagley and Harris 1958).

Who Are the Elderly?

As shown in Figure 17.1, an increasing proportion of the population will be composed of older people. This trend is expected to continue well through the twenty-first century as mortality declines and the postwar baby boomers age. While the elderly population continues to increase, the "oldest old" segment of the population (i.e., people 85 years old and over) is growing at an even faster rate.

Compared with the rest of the population, the elderly are more likely to be female, White, and living in certain states. Men generally have higher death rates than women

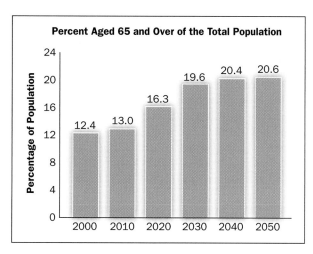

FIGURE 17.1 Actual and Projected Growth of the Elderly Population of the United States

Sources: Bureau of the Census data in Steinmetz 2006, 13.

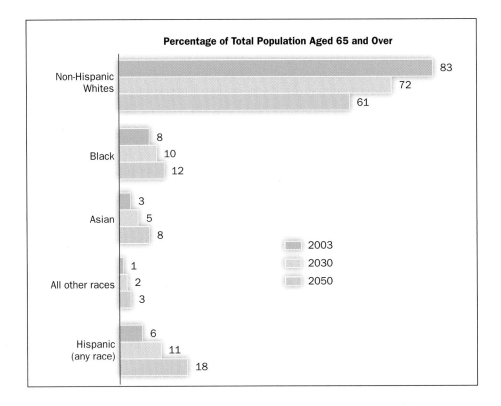

FIGURE 17.2 Population Aged 65 and Over by Race and Ethnicity

Source: Bureau of the Census in Steinmetz 2006, 6.

at every age. As a result, elderly women outnumber men by a ratio of 3 to 2. The difference grows with advancing age, so that among the oldest-old group, women outnumber men 5 to 2. About 83 percent of the elderly are White and non-Hispanic. Although the aged population is growing more racially and ethnically diverse, the higher death rates of members of racial and ethnic minorities, coupled with immigration to the United States of younger Latinos and Asians, are likely to keep the older population more White than the nation as a whole. Yet the overall pattern of a more diversified population will also be present among our oldest Americans. As seen in projections in Figure 17.2, the population aged 65 and over will become increasingly non-White and Latino.

Ageism

Respected gerontologist Bernice Neugarten (1996) observed that negative stereotypes of old age are strongly entrenched in a society that prides itself on being oriented toward youth and the future. In 1968, physician Robert Butler, the founding director of the National Institute on Aging, coined the term **ageism** to refer to prejudice and discrimination against the elderly. Ageism reflects a deep uneasiness among young and middle-aged people about growing old. For many, old age symbolizes disease and death; seeing the elderly serves as a reminder that they too may someday become old and infirm. By contrast, society glorifies youth, seeing it as interchangeable with beauty and the future. Ageism is so common that Robert Butler (1990, 178) notes that it "knows no one century, nor culture, and is not likely to go away any time soon."

If there is any doubt how pervasive ageism is, we need only consider an experiment conducted by sociologist William Levin, as described in "Research Focus."

How do these images described in Levin's experiment develop? Partly, we tend to see the elderly only in situations that reinforce the image. For example, physicians see more sick old people, so "all old people are sick." Social workers see only the indigent;

ageism
Prejudice and discrimination against the elderly.

Focus Research Focus Research

THE FACE OF AGEISM

For more than eighty years, sociologists have documented in their research how we stereotype groups of people. Using the checklist approach, studies identify how respondents tend to associate certain adjectives such as *wise* or *lazy* with certain racial and ethnic groups. Much more recently, research has documented the same stereotyping pattern when it comes to age.

"Does this person appear to you to be competent or incompetent? Generous or selfish?" Sociologist William Levin asked such questions of college students in California, Massachusetts, and Tennessee after showing them photographs of men who appeared to be about 25, 52, and 73 years old. Levin's findings confirmed that a widespread age bias is evident across the United States.

The students questioned in Levin's experiment were not told that the three photographs were of the same man at different stages of his life. Special care was taken to select old photographs that had a contemporary look. Levin asked the college students to evaluate the "three men" for a job using nineteen measures. The 25-year-old man was found to be active, powerful, healthy, fast, attractive, energetic, involved, and in possession of a good memory. Students thought that the 52-year-old man had a high IQ and was reliable. By contrast, the 73-year-old man was evaluated as inactive, weak, sickly, slow, ugly, unreliable, lazy, socially isolated, and possessing a low IQ and a poor memory. Clearly, the negative stereotypes of older people evident in this study could contribute to discrimination in the paid labor force and other areas of our society. ■

Source: Levin 1988.

therefore, "all aged are poor." We see the aged sitting on park benches but do not notice them rushing to and from jobs or volunteer work, so "all old people are inactive with no interests to keep them involved with society." The needy aged have come to represent all the elderly in the public mind (Birren and Gribbin 1973; Neugarten 1996).

For many, old age symbolizes the stigma of disease. With ageism all too common in the Untied States, it is hardly surprising that older people are barely visible on television. In 2002, the Senate Special Committee on Aging convened a panel on the media's portrayal of older people and sharply criticized media and marketing executives for bombarding audiences with negative images of the aged. The social consequences of such images are significant. Research shows that older people who have positive perceptions of aging live an average of 7.5 years longer than those who have negative perceptions (M. Gardner 2003; Levy et al. 2002; E. Ramirez 2002).

The federal Age Discrimination in Employment Act (ADEA), which went into effect in 1968, was passed to protect workers 40 years of age or older from being fired because of their age and replaced with younger workers who presumably would receive lower salaries. The Supreme Court strengthened federal protection against age discrimination in 1996, ruling unanimously that such lawsuits can be successful even if an older worker is replaced by someone older than 40. Consequently, if a firm unfairly fires a 65-year-old employee to make way for a 45-year-old, this still can constitute age discrimination.

Research shows that prior to the enactment of the ADEA, there was evidence of hiring discrimination against older workers as well as discrimination in promotions and

Being older does not mean that employment is not available, although sometimes jobs that are open are unrelated to one's career. Here a retiree has a "second career" as a greeter at a discount department store in Fishkill, New York.

training. Even with the ADEA, age continues to work against many older people as evidenced by how long it takes them to find employment, the wage loss they experience when they do become reemployed, and the size of court awards to victims of age discrimination (He et al. 2005).

Although firing workers simply because they are old violates federal law, courts have upheld the right to lay off older workers for economic reasons. Critics contend that later the same firms hire young, cheaper workers to replace experienced older workers. When economic growth began to slow in 2001 and companies cut back on their workforces, complaints of age bias grew sharply as older workers began to suspect they were bearing a disproportionate share of the layoffs. According to the Equal Employment Opportunity Commission, between 1999 and 2004, complaints of age discrimination rose more than 41 percent. However, evidence of a countertrend has emerged. Some firms have been giving larger raises to older workers to encourage their retirement at the higher salary—a tactic that prompts younger workers to complain of age discrimination (Novelli 2004; Uchitelle 2003).

The American Association of Retired Persons (AARP) conducted an experiment that confirmed that older people often face discrimination when applying for jobs. Comparable résumés for two applicants—one 57 years old and the other 32 years old—were sent to 775 large firms and employment agencies around the United States. In situations for which positions were available, the younger applicant received a favorable response 43 percent of the time. In contrast, the older applicant received favorable responses less than half as often (only 17 percent of the time). One *Fortune* 500 corporation asked the younger applicant for more information but informed the older applicant that no appropriate positions were open (Bendick et al. 1993).

Yet in contradiction to these negative stereotypes present in an ageist society, researchers have found that an older worker can be an asset for employers. According to a 1991 study, older workers can be retrained in new technologies, have lower rates of absenteeism than younger employees, and often are more effective salespeople. The study focused on two corporations based in the United States (the hotel chain Days Inns of America and the holding company Travelers Corporation of Hartford) and a British retail chain, all of which have long-term experience in hiring workers age 50 and over. Clearly, the findings pointed to older workers as good investments. Yet despite such studies, complaints of age bias grew during the economic slowdown beginning in 2001, when companies cut back on their workforces (Equal Employment Opportunity Commission 2001; Telsch 1991, A16).

A degree of conflict is emerging along generational lines that resemble other types of intergroup tension. Although the conflict involves neither violence nor the degree of subjugation found with other dominant–subordinate relations in the United States, a feeling still prevails that jobs and benefits for the elderly are at the expense of younger generations. Younger people are increasingly unhappy about paying Social Security taxes and underwriting the Medicare program, especially because they speculate that they themselves will never receive benefits from these fiscally insecure programs.

The Economic Picture

The elderly, like the other groups we have considered, do not form a single economic profile. The perception of "elderly" and "poor" as practically synonymous has changed in recent years to a view that the noninstitutionalized elderly are economically better off than the population as a whole. Both views are too simplistic; income varies widely among the aged.

There is significant variation in wealth and poverty among the nation's older people. Some individuals and couples find themselves poor in part because of fixed pensions and skyrocketing healths care costs. As shown in Figure 17.3, poverty has declined among the elderly of all racial groups.

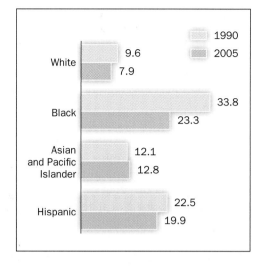

FIGURE 17.3 **Poverty Rate Among the Elderly, 2005**

Note: Data for Whites are for non-Hispanic Whites.

Source: DeNavas-Walt et al. 2006, 53-57.

As a group, older people in the United States are neither homogeneous nor poor. The typical elderly person enjoys a standard of living that is much higher than at any point in the nation's past. Class differences among the elderly tend to narrow somewhat: Retirees who had middle-class incomes while younger tend to remain better off after retirement than those who had lower incomes, but the financial gap is declining (He et al. 2005).

The decline in poverty rates is welcome. However, advocates of the position that the elderly are receiving too much at the expense of the younger generations point to the rising affluence of the aged as evidence of an unfair economic burden placed on the young and future generations of workers.

As we can see in the previously mentioned data, the aged who are most likely to experience poverty are the same people more likely to be poor earlier in their lives: female-headed households and racial and ethnic minorities. Although overall the aged are doing well economically, poverty remains a particularly difficult problem for the thousands of elderly who are impoverished annually by paying for long-term medical care (Quadagno 2005).

Advocacy Efforts by the Elderly

As we have seen with racial, ethnic, and gender groups, efforts to bring about desired change often require the formation of political organizations and advocacy groups. This is true with the elderly and, as we will see later, is also true for people with disabilities, gay men, and lesbian women. One such group working on behalf of the elderly is the Gray Panthers. As of 1995, this organization had 40,000 members in thirty-two states and five foreign countries working to combat prejudice and discrimination against older people. In early 1995, Maggie Kuhn, the best known of the Gray Panthers' founders, died at age 89. Kuhn had spent the last twenty-five years of her life as a leader in the battle against ageism and other forms of injustice. Her desire to create an advocacy group of the elderly began when she was forced to retire at age 65 from her position on a church staff. Only two weeks before her death, she joined striking transit workers on a picket line (Folkart 1995; R. Thomas 1995).

The growing collective consciousness among older people also contributed to the establishment of the Older Women's League (OWL) in 1980. OWL focuses on access to health insurance, Social Security benefits, and pension reform. OWL leaders and the group's 15,000 members hope that the organization will serve as a critical link between the feminist movement described in Chapter 15 and activists for "gray power" (Kening 2004).

The largest organization representing the nation's elderly is the American Association of Retired Persons (AARP), which was founded in 1958 by a retired school principal who was having difficulty obtaining insurance because of age prejudice. Many of AARP's services involve discounts and insurance for its 35 million members (44 percent of Americans aged 50 or older); recognizing that many elderly are still gainfully employed, it has dropped its full name, American Association of Retired Persons.

The potential power of AARP is enormous; it represents one out of every four registered voters in the United States. AARP has endorsed voter registration campaigns, nursing home reforms, and pension reforms. Acknowledging its difficulties in recruiting members of racial and ethnic minority groups, AARP began a Minority Affairs Initiative. The spokeswoman for this initiative, Margaret Dixon, became AARP's first African American president in 1996 (AARP 2003).

ASK Yourself

What special challenges are faced by members of racial and ethnic groups who are over the age 65?

People grow old in many different ways. Not all the elderly face the same challenges or enjoy the same resources. Whereas AARP lobbies to protect the elderly in general, other groups work in more specific ways. For example, the National Committee to Preserve Social Security and Medicare, founded in 1982, unsuccessfully lobbied Congress to keep Medicare benefits for the ailing poor elderly. Other large special-interest groups represent retired federal employees, retired teachers, and retired union workers (Quadagno 2005).

The elderly in the United States are better off today financially and physically than ever before. Many of them have strong financial assets and medical care packages that will take care of almost any need. But, as we have seen, a significant segment is impoverished, faced with the prospect of declining health and mounting medical bills. Older people of color may have to add being aged to a lifetime of discrimination. As in all other stages of the life course, the aged constitute a diverse group in the United States and around the world.

Although organizations such as the Gray Panthers, OWL, and AARP are undoubtedly valuable, the diversity of the nation's older population necessitates many different responses to the problems of the elderly. For example, older African Americans and Hispanics tend to rely more on family members, friends, and informal social networks than on organizational support systems. Because of their lower incomes and greater incapacity resulting from poor health, older Blacks and Hispanics are more likely to need substantial assistance from family members than are older Whites. In recent years, older people of color have emerged as a distinct political force, independent of the larger elderly population, in some urban centers and in the Southwest. Advocacy groups for the aged are still in their early stages, and low-income elderly often are the least represented (Achenbaumm 1993; Neugarten 1996; Schaefer 2007).

People with Disabilities: Moving On

George Lane was scheduled to appear in court in September 1997, arising from a reckless driving misdemeanor charge following an accident that left him unable to walk. Arriving at the Polk County, Tennessee, courthouse, he found that the courtroom was on the second floor in a building without an elevator. The court refused to make any allowance, so he dragged himself up the steps only to learn the case had been postponed. Refusing to repeat the experience at the next hearing date, Lane was forced to have his attorney shuttle information back and forth from the courtroom. The court felt it was not obligated to make any accommodation to his disability, and finally, seven years later, the Supreme Court ruled 5–4 that Lane's rights had been denied (Greenhouse 2004).

Throughout history, people have been socially disadvantaged, not because of the limits of their own skills and abilities but because assumptions are made about them

George Lane got his day in court—finally. A Tennessee courthouse held Mr. Lane's trial without him because he was unable to reach the courtroom, which was located in a building without an elevator. The court refused to accommodate him, and the Tennessee Supreme Court upheld the trial. Finally, after seven years, the U.S. Supreme Court held that the county court must hold the trial in a room that the paraplegic could reach.

based on some group characteristics. People with disabilities are such a group. The very term *disabilities* suggests lack of ability in some area, but as we shall see, society often assumes that a person with a disability is far less capable than she or he is. Furthermore, society limits the life chances of people with disabilities in ways that are unnecessary and unrelated to any physical infirmity.

Disability in Contemporary Society

Societies have always had members with disabilities. Historically, they have dealt differently with people who had physical or mental limitations, but rarely have they been treated as equals. According to the Bureau of the Census, an estimated 51.2 million people had a disability in 2002, or more than one in six in the population. **Disability** is considered a reduced ability to perform tasks one would normally do at a given stage in life. This includes everyone from people who have difficulty carrying 10 pounds to people who use a wheelchair, crutches, or a walker. As shown in Figure 17.4, many people with disabilities are otherwise in good health (Steinmetz 2006).

disability
Reduced ability to perform tasks one would normally do at a given stage in life.

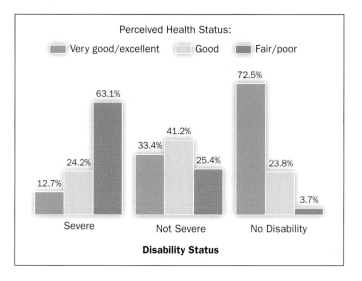

FIGURE 17.4   Perceived Health Status by Disability Status (age 25 to 64 years, percentage with specified health status)

Source: Based on 2002 Survey of Income and Program Participation as released by the Bureau of the Census in Steinmetz 2006, 7.

The proportion of people with disabilities continues to increase. Because of advances in medicine, many people who once would have died from an accident or illness now survive. Also, as more people live longer, they are more likely to experience diseases that have disabling consequences.

Disabilities are found in all segments of the population, but racial and ethnic minorities are disproportionately more likely to experience them and also to have less access to assistance. Fewer African Americans and Hispanic people with disabilities are graduating from college compared with White people with disabilities. They also have incomes consistently lower than their White counterparts (Steinmetz 2006).

Although disability knows no social class, about two-thirds of working-age people with a disability in the United States are unemployed. African Americans and Hispanics with disabilities are even more likely to be jobless. Most of them believe that they would be able to work if they were offered the opportunity or if some reasonable accommodation could be made to address the disability. These accommodations can be modest. Between 1978 and 1992, Sears Roebuck found that, on average, it cost only $126 to accommodate a worker's disability with some measures involving little or no cost, such as flexible work schedules, back-support belts, and rest periods (Kirkpatrick 1994; B. Noble 1995; Shapiro 1993).

Labeling the Disabled

Labeling theorists, drawing on the work of sociologist Erving Goffman (1963), suggest that society attaches a stigma to many forms of disability and that this stigma leads to prejudicial treatment. Indeed, people with disabilities often observe that people without disabilities see them only as blind, deaf, wheelchair users, and so forth, rather than

A significant stigma is attached to having a major visible disability. Not wishing to present an image of a "disabled" president, Franklin Roosevelt enlisted the cooperation of the press corps to avoid being shown in a wheelchair or using crutches. This picture shows the president leaving a New York City townhouse in 1933, with a rare view of the president's leg braces.
Source: © New York Daily News, L. P. Reprinted with permission.

THE MAGIC WAND

Quick-change artist
extraordinaire,
I whip out my folded
cane
and change from black
man to blind man
With a flick of my wrist.
It is a profound
metamorphosis-
From God-gifted wizard of
roundball
dominating backboards across America
To God-gifted idiot savant
Pounding out chart-busters on a cock-
eyed whim;
From sociopathtic gangbanger with
death for eyes

Lynn Manning

to all-seeing soul with saintly
spirit;
From rape driven misogynist
to poor motherless child;
From welfare-rich pimp
to disability-rich gimp;
And from 'white man's burden'
to every man's burden.
It is always a profound meta-
morphosis.
Whether from cursed by man
to cursed by God;
or from a scripture-condemned to God-or-
dained,
my final form is never of my choosing;
I only wield the wand;
You are the magician. ■

as complex human beings with individual strengths and weaknesses whose blindness or deafness is merely one aspect of their lives.

In "Listen to Our Voices," poet Lynn Manning discusses both the subtle and the more overt ways society assigns labels to people with disabilities and the special input it has on an African American male.

In this regard, a review of studies of women with disabilities disclosed that most academic research on people with disabilities does not even differentiate by gender, thereby perpetuating the view that when a disability is present, no other personal characteristic can matter. When gender differences are recognized, such recognition may deny a person's dignity. One study found that women with disabilities were more likely to be discouraged from having children and much more likely to be advised to have hysterectomies than women without disabilities but with similar medical conditions (Fine and Asch 1981, 1988a, 1988b; Gove 1980; Karkabi 1993).

As with other subordinate statuses, the mass media have contributed to the stereotyping of people with disabilities. Too often, they are treated with a mixture of pity and fear. Nationwide charity telethons promote a negative image of people with disabilities as being childlike and nonproductive, suggesting that, until they are "cured," they cannot contribute to society like other people. At the very least, the poster child image proclaims that it is not okay to have a disability. By contrast, in literature and film, evil characters with disabilities—from Captain Hook to Dr. Strangelove to Freddy Krueger—reinforce the view that disability is a punishment for evil. Efforts to encourage sober driving or safety in the workplace use images of people with disabilities to frighten people into the appropriate behavior.

Even the more favorable treatments of characters with disabilities tend to focus on courageous and inspirational characters who achieve striking personal successes against great odds, such as Tiny Tim in *A Christmas Carol* or the idiot savant in the film *Rain Man,* rather than on the impact of prejudice and discrimination on ordinary people with disabilities. The press coverage received by people with disabilities who excel also minimizes the day-to-day reality of most people with a disability (Bennetts 1993; Gartner and Joe 1987; Norden 1994).

Negative attitudes are not the only challenge facing people with disabilities. Among men and women with any kind of disability, 60 percent are employed compared to 81 percent without a disability. Even for those employed, research shows that people with disabilities are often marginalized, devalued, and even harassed (Robert and Harlan 2006; Steinmetz 2006, 25).

Through institutional discrimination, society is sometimes organized in a way that limits people with disabilities. Architectural barriers and transportation difficulties often add to the problems of people with disabilities when they seek and obtain employment. Simply getting around city streets can be quite difficult for people with mobility challenges. Many streets are not properly equipped with curb cuts for wheelchair users. A genuinely barrier-free building needs more than a ramp; it should also include automatic doors, raised letters and Braille on signs, and toilets that are accessible to people with disabilities. Even if a person with disabilities finds a job, and even if the job is in a barrier-free building, he or she still faces the problem of getting to work in a society where many rail stations and most buses remain inaccessible to wheelchair users and others with disabilities.

For so many people with disabilities, it is not just a glass ceiling they face; they are even refused entrance through the door. They face challenges to being taken seriously as job applicants, and research shows that the problems intensify further for members with disabilities of racial and ethnic minorities. The Glass Ceiling Commission took a special look at employment opportunities for people with disabilities who are also members of racial and ethnic minorities. The analysis revealed that White people with disabilities are twice as likely to be employed full-time as African American or Hispanic people with disabilities. The primary reason for this is that minorities with disabilities experience dual sources of discrimination: subordinate-group status as a member of a minority race and having a disability. The negative stereotype of having disabilities is added on top of the stereotypes associated with racial and ethnic minorities (Braddock and Bachelder 1994).

Advocacy for Disability Rights

Until recently, people with disabilities as a group have scarcely been thought of in any terms except perhaps pity. Often history has forgotten how deep the mistreatment has been. There has been a steadily growing effort to ensure not only the survival of people with disabilities but also the same rights as enjoyed by others. In the early 1960s, Ed Roberts and some other young adults with disabilities wanted to attend the University of California at Berkeley. Reluctant at first, the university was eventually persuaded to admit them and agreed to reserve space in the university infirmary as living quarters for students with disabilities. These students and others established their own student center and became known as the Rolling Quads. They eventually turned their attention to the surrounding community and established the Berkeley Center for Independent Living, which became a model for hundreds of independent living centers (Brannon 1995).

By the early 1970s, following the example of the Rolling Quads, a strong social movement for disability rights had emerged across the United States, which drew on the experiences of the Black civil rights movement and the feminist movement. This movement now includes a variety of organizations; some work on behalf of people with a single disability (such as the National Federation of the Blind), and others represent people with any of many disabilities (such as New York City's Disabled in Action). The large number of Vietnam veterans with disabilities who joined the effort gave a boost to advocacy efforts and a growing legitimacy in larger society.

Like other advocacy and resistance efforts, women and men involved in the disability rights movement are working to challenge negative views of people with disabilities; to gain a greater voice for people with disabilities in all agency and public policy decisions that affect them; and to reshape laws, institutions, and environments so that people with disabilities can be fully integrated into mainstream society. Disability rights activists argue that there is an important distinction between organizations for people with disabilities and organizations of people with disabilities. The former include service providers, charitable associations, and parents' groups. Some activists maintain that because people with disabilities do not control these organizations, they do not give priority to the goals of independence and self-help emphasized by the disability rights movement (Scotch 1989, 2001).

Many of these organizations worked for the 1990 passage of the Americans with Disabilities Act (ADA). This law in many respects is the most sweeping antidiscrimination legislation since the 1964 Civil Rights Act. The ADA went into effect in 1992, covering people with a disability, defined as a condition that "substantially limits" a "major life activity" such as walking or seeing. It prohibits bias in employment, transportation, public accommodations, and telecommunication against people with disabilities. Businesses with more than twenty-five employees cannot refuse to hire a qualified applicant with a disability; these companies are expected to make a "reasonable accommodation" to permit such a worker to do the job. Commercial establishments such as office buildings, hotels, theaters, supermarkets, and dry cleaners are barred from denying service to people with disabilities (Kilborn 1992).

The ADA represents a significant framing of the issues of people with disabilities. Basically, we can see it taking a civil rights view of disabilities that seeks to humanize the way society sees and treats people with disabilities. The ADA does not take the perspective adopted in other nations, such as Great Britain, of seeing disability as totally an entitlement issue; that is, because you have a disability, you automatically receive certain benefits. Rather, its perspective is that peopled with disabilities are being denied certain rights. As disability rights activist Mark Johnson said, "Black people fought for the right to ride in the front of the bus. We're fighting for the right to get on the bus" (Shapiro 1993, 128; also see Albrecht 1995, 1997; Farrell 2006; Gooding 1994).

Colleges are also being asked to reconsider what constitutes a student athlete and what competitive programs should be supported with coaches and even scholarships. Although athletes with some disabilities have long participated in intercollegiate athletics, the concept of developing programs for people with disabilities is not very common. Currently, only six universities support wheelchair basketball and two support track and field events for people with disabilities. Some activists are asking that colleges change their conception of what constitutes an athletic program, much like Title IX forced higher education to see women as college athletes (W. Suggs 2004).

A more specific concern relevant to people with disabilities has arose at Gallaudet University, the school founded in 1864 to serve deaf students. This institution located in the District of Columbia has been the scene of unrest during the last twenty years concerning the selection of its president. For many students and sympathetic supporters, the president of this institution must not only be deaf but embrace the primacy of American Sign Language (ASL). First in 1988 and then again 2006, students mounted "Deaf President Now" campaigns after presidents were proposed who were not "deaf enough" because they relied too much on reading lips or spoke without using ASL. The disability rights movement has caused people both with and without disabilities to rethink what constitutes fairness and equity (Farrell 2006).

Rethinking the rights of people with disabilities began with the ADA but has now come with the call for visitability. **Visitability** refers to making private homes built to be accessible for visitors with disabilities. In the mid-1990s, cities such as Atlanta and Austin, Texas, as well as Great Britain passed ordinances encouraging new homes to have at least one no-step entrance, wider doorways, grab bars in bathrooms, and other accommodations. This new idea suggests that all environments should be accessible—not just public places, such as courtrooms or token handicapped-accessible accommodations in hotels, but all living spaces. Many oppose such a move as unnecessary government interference; others see it as, at last, a recognition that people with disabilities should be able to move freely throughout the country (Buchholz 2003; *Ragged Edge* 1998).

Activists remain encouraged since the passage of the ADA. Although the act has been in effect for only a decade, studies reveal that people with disabilities feel empowered and perceive increased access to employment opportunities. However, one must remember that civil rights activists felt a measure of optimism after passage of the major civil rights legislation more than forty years ago (Pfeiffer 1996; Scotch 1988).

Gays and Lesbians: Coming Out for Equality

When and how did you first realize you were a heterosexual?

What do you think caused your heterosexuality?

Is it possible that your heterosexuality is just a phase you may grow out of?

Why are heterosexuals so promiscuous?

visitability
Building private homes to be accessible for visitors with disabilities.

These are not questions heterosexuals are likely to hear being asked because these queries assume something is wrong with being attracted to members of the opposite sex. On the other hand, we are all accustomed to hearing homosexuals questioned about their orientation.

Homosexuality has been forbidden in most periods of Western history, but it has not always been a social issue. For example, at certain times in many societies, it was possible to acknowledge same-sex love and act on it without necessarily encountering open hostility. Yet in general, societies have barely tolerated people who have sexual intimacy in any manner other than heterosexual.

The focus in this chapter is on differential treatment because one is a homosexual, that is, gay or lesbian, but human sexuality is very diverse. Yet typically in the United States, sexual orientation is constructed as either homosexual or heterosexual and ignores people who are *bisexuals,* that is, individuals sexually attracted to both sexes. Sometimes included in discussions about gays, lesbians, and bisexuals are *transgendered persons,* which refers to people whose gender identity does not match their physical identity at birth so, for example, transgender individuals may see themselves as both male and female. *Transexuals* are people who see themselves as the sex opposite of their birth identity and may take surgical measures to bring their physical being closer to their gender identity. Sometimes confused with these issues of gender identity and sexual orientation are *transvestites,* which today usually refers to cross-dressers who wear clothing of the opposite sex. These are typically men choosing to wear women's clothing, who may be either gay or heterosexual in their orientation.

Being Gay and Lesbian in the United States

There are anecdotal accounts of public recognition of homosexuality throughout U.S. history, but it was not until the 1920s and 1930s that it became visible. By that time, clubs for gays and lesbians were growing in number, typically in urban areas. Plays, books, and organizations were created to meet the social needs of gays and lesbians. As homosexuality has become more visible, efforts to suppress it have been institutionalized. At about the same time, the U.S. Army hired psychiatrists to screen recruits for evidence of homosexuality and dismissed volunteers who were gay (P. Schwartz 1992).

The studies published by Alfred Kinsey and his research group (1948, 1953) shocked the general public when they documented that almost half of all men had had same-sex fantasies and that about one-third had experienced a homosexual encounter after childhood. Although women reported less homosexual activity, the very fact that lesbian behavior was even raised in a national discussion was unprecedented. The Kinsey reports also launched a public debate about the number of homosexuals in the United States.

Given that gay men and lesbians are severely stigmatized, accurate data are hard to obtain. Researchers for the National Health and Life Survey and the Voter News Service in their election exit polls estimate that 2 to 5 percent of U.S. adults identify themselves as gay or lesbian. An analysis of the 2005 American Community Survey of the Bureau of the Census estimates at least 777,000 gay households and a gay and lesbian population between 8.8 and 10 million (Dang and Frazer 2004; Gates 2006; Laumann et al. 1994; Smith and Gates 2001).

Discussion and growing recognition of a sizable gay population did not lead to a consistent effort to promote understanding over the last sixty years. The general focus was to explore ways to prevent and control homosexuality as a disease, which is what psychiatrists thought it was. Well into the 1960s, discrimination against gays and lesbians was common and legal. Bars frequented by people seeking same-sex partners were raided and people jailed, with their names often published in local newspapers. Although not surprising, it was disappointing to hear that the county board in Rhea County, Tennessee, passed unanimously a measure in 2004 that allowed the county to prosecute someone for being gay or lesbian as a "crime against nature." A few days

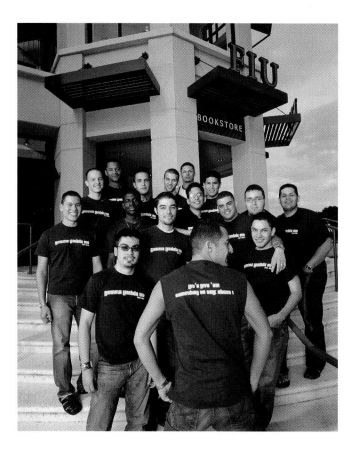

All students wish to take advantage of what college life offers. Here students at Florida International University took the step of forming a fraternity, Gamma Lambda Mu, aimed at gay men.

later, after recognizing the losing court battle they would face, the county commissioners rescinded the antigay motion, but clearly they did not take back their view of gays and lesbians (Barry 2004).

Prejudice and Discrimination

Homophobia, the fear of and prejudice toward homosexuality, is present in every facet of life: the family, organized religion, the workplace, official policies, and the mass media. Like the myths and stereotypes of race and gender, those about homosexuality keep gay men and lesbian women oppressed as a group and may also keep sympathetic members of the dominant group, the heterosexual community, from joining in support.

Homophobia is considered a much more respectable form of bigotry than the voicing of ill feelings against any other oppressed groups. People still openly avoid homosexuals, and group members are stereotyped on television and in motion pictures. Although homophobia has decreased, many people still feel at ease in expressing their homophobic feelings that a homosexual lifestyle is unacceptable.

As we will see later, gays and lesbians have made extensive efforts to make their feelings known, to ask for respect and a variety of rights, and to have their sexual orientation accepted. Their efforts seem to have had some impact on public opinion. In 2006, 56 percent of the public felt that homosexual relations should be legal—close to what it was in 1977, when it was about 40 percent. Yet there is a recognition that homosexual men and women should have equal rights in terms of job opportunities. This support has increased to 89 percent in 2006, compared with 56 percent in 1977 (Newport 2003; Saad 2006b).

The stigmatization of gays and lesbians was seen as a major factor in the slow initial response to the presence of AIDS (acquired immunodeficiency syndrome), which,

homophobia
The fear of and prejudice toward homosexuality.

when it first appeared in the United States, overwhelmingly claimed gay men as its victims. The inattention and the reluctance to develop a national policy forced gay communities in major cities to establish self-help groups to care for the sick, educate the healthy, and lobby for more responsive public policies. The most outspoken AIDS activist group has been the AIDS Coalition to Unleash Power (ACT-UP), which has conducted controversial protests and sit-ins in the halls of government and at scientific conferences. Although initially such efforts may have siphoned away participants from the broader gay rights effort, ultimately, new constituencies of gay men and lesbians were created, along with alliances with sympathetic supporters from the heterosexual community (Adam 1995; Shilts 1982).

In some instances, antigay prejudice has led to violence. Most notable were the 1978 killings of San Francisco Supervisor Harvey Milk (at one time the nation's most prominent openly gay public official) and Mayor George Moscone (a heterosexual supporter of gay rights) by a former police officer and supervisor. The National Coalition of Anti-Violence Programs (2004) released a report documenting more than 2,000 bias-motivated incidents against lesbians and gay men in the United States in 2003. Nationwide, 27 percent of the victims hurt in these attacks suffered injury or death. In a sobering finding in this study, about 60 percent of the attacks were not reported to police.

In 1998, the nation was shocked by the unprovoked, brutal murder of Matthew Shepard, a University of Wyoming student, by two men. Subsequent investigation showed that Shepard's being gay was the reason for his attackers' murdering him rather than leaving him alone after robbing the young man. This tragic event galvanized a move to include sexual orientation as a basis of hate crimes in many states. Gays and lesbians themselves began to actively resist their mistreatment, sometimes working with local law enforcement agencies and prosecutors to end antigay violence (J. Cloud 2003; Jenness 1995).

Advocacy for Gay and Lesbian Rights

The first homosexual organization in the United States was founded in Chicago in 1924. Such groups grew steadily over the next fifty years, but they were primarily local and were more likely to be self-help and social rather than confrontational. The social movements of the 1950s and 1960s on behalf of African Americans and women caused lesbians and gay men also to reflect more directly on the oppression their sexual orientation caused.

The contemporary gay and lesbian movement marks its beginning in New York City on June 28, 1969. Police raided the Stonewall Inn, an after-hours gay bar, and forced patrons into the street. Instead of meekly dispersing and accepting the disruption, the patrons locked police inside the bar and rioted until police reinforcements arrived. For the next three nights, lesbians and gay men marched through the streets of New York, protesting police raids and other forms of discrimination. Within months, gay liberation groups appeared in cities and campuses throughout the United States. (Armstrong and Crage 2006).

Despite the efforts of the lesbian and gay rights movement, in 1986 the Supreme Court in *Bowers v. Hardwick* ruled by a 5–4 vote that the Constitution does not protect homosexual relations between consenting adults, even in the privacy of their own homes. This position held until the Court reversed itself in 2003 by a 6–3 vote in *Lawrence v. Texas*. The divisiveness of the issue nationally was reflected among the justices. Justice Anthony Kennedy declared that gays are "entitled to respect for their private lives" while Justice Antonio Scalia complained that the decision indicated that the Court had "largely signed on to the so-called homosexual agenda" (Duberman 1993; Humphreys 1972; Moser 2005).

? ASK Yourself

How has the Supreme Court ruled on gay rights?

domestic partnership
Two unrelated adults who have chosen to share one another's lives in a relationship of mutual caring, who reside together, and who agree to be jointly responsible for their dependents, basic living expenses, and other common necessities.

In 2000, the Supreme Court hurt the gay rights movement when it ruled 5–4 that the Boy Scouts organization had a constitutional right to exclude gay members because opposition to homosexuality was part of the organization's message. The Court clearly stated in its ruling that it was not endorsing this view but supporting the right of the organization to hold this position and to limit participation based on it. Despite this and earlier Supreme Court decisions, gays and lesbians worked to establish the principle that sexual orientation should not be the basis for discrimination.

Issues involving gays and lesbians have always been present, but because of advocacy efforts, the concerns are being advanced by political leaders and the courts. In 1993, President Bill Clinton, under pressure from the gay community, reviewed the prohibition of homosexuals from the military. However, he encountered even greater pressure from opponents and eventually compromised in 1994 with the "don't ask, don't tell" policy. The policy allows lesbians and gay men to continue to serve in the military as long as they keep their homosexuality secret, but commanders can still investigate and dismiss military personnel if they find any evidence that they have committed homosexual acts. Indeed, according to a 2003 report, the military is discharging three or four service members every day (Hull 2003).

For many gay and lesbian couples, the inability to have their relationships recognized legally is the most personal restriction they have to face. Several dozen cities have begun to recognize **domestic partnerships,** defined as two unrelated adults who have chosen to share one another's lives in a relationship of mutual caring, who reside together and agree to be jointly responsible for their dependents, basic living expenses, and other common necessities. Domestic partnership benefits can apply to inheritance, parenting, pensions, taxation, housing, immigration, workplace fringe benefits, and health care. Although the advocacy efforts for legally recognizing domestic partnerships have come from the lesbian and gay community, the majority of the relationships that would benefit would be cohabiting heterosexual couples.

The most vocal debate is over whether gay and lesbian couples should be able to legally get married. Congress enacted the Defense of Marriage Act in 1996, which would deny federal recognition of same-sex marriages. Despite criticism from the gay community and those supportive of legal recognition of same-sex marriage, the

Despite the stability of many same-sex couples, the same people who are concerned over family instability often are opposed to legal recognition of gay and lesbian couples.
Source: Signe Wilkinson/Cartoonists & Writer's Syndicate/cartoonweb.com

SIGNE WILKINSON, Philadelphia Daily News

measure was immensely popular with the public. Despite this action, Vermont in 1999 and Massachusetts in 2005 have given same-sex couples the legal benefits of marriage through civil union in 1999. In response, thirteen states in various 2004 elections passed amendments to their own constitutions to prevent same-sex marriages from receiving any recognition. Another eight ratified such action in 2006: A 2006 survey showed that 39 percent felt that same-sex marriages should be legal. Yet efforts in Congress to propose a constitutional amendment that would limit marriage to heterosexual couples has failed even to come to a vote (Human Rights Campaign 2006; Saad 2006b).

We have used assimilation throughout this book to describe the process by which individuals forsake their own heritage to become a part of a different culture. Assimilation has emerged as a hot issue in the gay community. Some argue that promoting gay marriage is merely trying to assimilate or to become like the oppressor, adopting their social conventions. Efforts to downplay overt expression of homosexuality are yet another example of assimilation. Critics of assimilation argue that equal treatment is the real issue and should not be the result of conforming to the ways of the heterosexual dominant society. The debate is unlikely to be resolved soon because full acceptance of gays and lesbians is far removed from today's social and political agenda. But this discussion repeats a pattern found with every subordinate group of how to maintain one's unique identity and become part of a multicultural society (Hartocollis 2006; Hequembourg and Arditi 1999).

The Glass Half Empty

A common expression makes reference to a glass half full or half empty of water. If one is thirsty, it is half empty and in need of being replenished. If one is attempting to clear dirty dishes, it is half full. For many people, especially Whites, the progress of subordinate groups or minorities makes it difficult to understand calls for more programs and new reforms and impossible to understand when minority neighborhoods erupt in violence.

In absolute terms, the glass of water has been filling up, but people in the early twenty-first century do not compare themselves with people in the 1960s. For example, Latinos and African Americans regard the appropriate reference group to be Whites today; compared with them, the glass is half empty at best.

In Figure 17.5, we have shown the present picture and recent changes by comparing African Americans and Hispanics with Whites as well as contemporary data for Native Americans (American Indians). We see that the nation's largest minority groups—African Americans and Hispanics—have higher household income, complete more schooling, and enjoy longer life expectancy today than in 1975. White Americans have made similar strides in all three areas. The gap remains and, if one analyzes it closely, has actually increased in some instances. Both Blacks and Latinos in 2005 had just edged out the income level that Whites had exceeded back in 1975. Three decades behind! Also, Black Americans today have barely matched the life expectancy that Whites had a generation earlier. Similarly, many minority Americans remain entrenched in poverty: nearly one out of four Hispanics and African Americans.

Little has changed since 1975. We have chosen 1975 because that was a year for which we have comparable data for Latinos, Whites, and African Americans. However, the patterns would be no different if we considered 1950, 1960, or 1970.

These data provide only the broadest overview. Detailed analyses do not yield a brighter picture. For example, about 1 in 9 Whites were without health insurance in

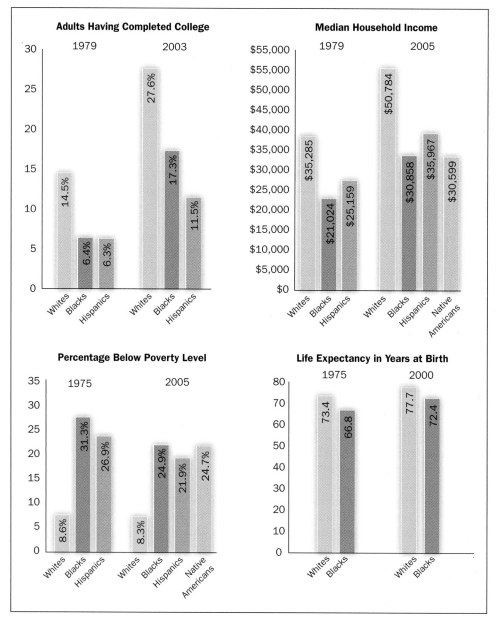

FIGURE 17.5   Changes in Schooling, Income, and Life Expectancy

Note: Native American data are for 2000. Education data include people age 25 and over. Hispanic education 1975 data estimated by author from data for 1970 and 1980. White data are for non-Hispanic (except in education).

Source: Bureau of the Census 1988, 167, 2005a, 44; DeNavas-Walt et al. 2006, 6,15; Ogunwole 2006.

2005 compared to 1 of 5 African Americans and 1 of 3 Latinos. Similarly, 3.9 percent of all doctorates were awarded to African Americans in 1981. By 2002, the proportion had increased only to 5.4 percent. The United States continues to rely on overseas students to fill the places on the educational ladder. The number of doctorates awarded to nonresident aliens (that is, immigrants who gained entry for schooling with no other ties to U.S. citizens) was three times that of Blacks, Asian Americans, Latinos, and American Indians *combined* (Bureau of the Census 2005a; DeNavas-Walt et al. 2006; Hoffer et al. 2001).

Conclusion

As the United States promotes racial, ethnic, and religious diversity, it strives also to impose universal criteria on employers, educators, and realtors so that subordinate racial and ethnic groups can participate fully in the larger society. In some instances, to bring about equality of results—not just equality of opportunity—programs have been developed to give competitive advantages to women and minority men. Only more recently have similar strides been made on behalf of people with disabilities. These latest answers to social inequality have provoked much controversy over how to achieve the admirable goal of a multiracial, multiethnic society, undifferentiated in opportunity and rewards.

The huge outpouring of information for the census documents the racial and ethnic diversity of the entire nation. And as we see in Figure 17.6, although the proportion of specific minorities present may be different in different regions and different communities, the tapestry

of racial and ethnic groups is always close at hand wherever one is in the United States.

Relations between racial, ethnic, or religious groups take two broad forms, as situations characterized by either consensus or conflict. Consensus prevails where assimilation or fusion of groups has been completed. Consensus also prevails in a pluralistic society in the sense that members have agreed to respect differences between groups. By eliminating the contending group, extermination and expulsion also lead to a consensus society. In the study of intergroup relations, it is often easy to ignore conflict where there is a high degree of consensus because it is assumed that an orderly society has no problems. In some instances, however, this assumption is misleading. Through long periods of history, misery inflicted on a racial, ethnic, or religious group was judged to be appropriate, if not actually divinely inspired.

In recent history, harmonious relations between all racial, ethnic, and religious groups have been widely

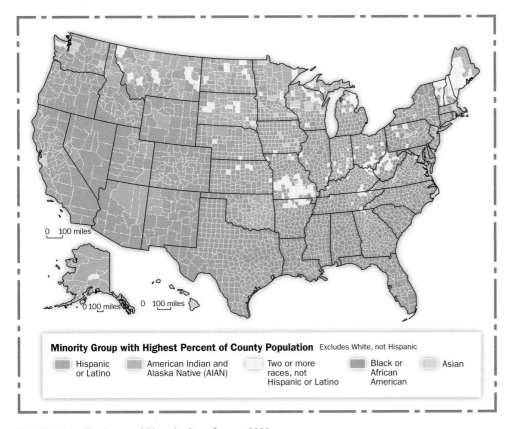

FIGURE 17.6   **The Image of Diversity from Census 2000**

Source: Brewer and Suchan 2001, 20.

accepted as a worthy goal. The struggle against oppression and inequality is not new. It dates back at least to the revolutions in England, France, and the American colonies in the seventeenth and eighteenth centuries. The twentieth century was unique in the extension of equality to the less-privileged classes, many of whose members are racial and ethnic minorities. Conflict along racial and ethnic lines is especially bitter now because it evokes memories of slavery, colonial oppression, and overt discrimination. Today's African Americans are much more aware of slavery than contemporary poor people are of seventeenth-century debtors' prison.

Racial and ethnic equality implies the right of the individual to choose his or her own way of life. As Hunt and Walker (1979) observed, however, individual rights may conflict with the group consensus. Gay and lesbian marriages and accommodating the needs of people with disabilities in the workplace are the latest examples. This conflict makes the situation exceedingly complex; even if a society allows a group to select its own destiny, individual members of the group may be unable to freely pursue their own course of action. If Native Americans as a group choose to emphasize their cultural distinctiveness, individuals who want to integrate into White society may be looked on by their peers as traitors to their tribe.

Unquestionably, the struggle for justice among racial and ethnic groups has not completely met its goals. Many people are still committed to repression, although they may see it only as the benign neglect of those less privileged. Such repression leads to the dehumanization of both the subordinated individual and the oppressor. Growth in equal rights movements and self-determination for Third World countries largely populated by non-White people has moved the world onto a course that seems irreversible. The old ethnic battle lines now renewed in Iran, Sudan, and Chechnya in Russia have only added to the tensions. Philip (1970) acknowledged that people are more willing to reject stability if preserving it means inequality.

Self-determination, whether for groups or individuals, often is impossible in societies as they are currently structured. Bringing about social equality, therefore, will entail significant changes in existing institutions. Because such changes are not likely to come about with everyone's willing cooperation, the social costs will be high. However, if there is a trend in racial and ethnic relations in the world today, it is the growing belief that the social costs, however high, must be paid to achieve self-determination.

It is naive to foresee a world of societies in which one person equals one vote and all are accepted without regard to race, ethnicity, religion, gender, age, disability status, or sexual orientation. It is equally unlikely to expect to see a society, let alone a world, that is without a privileged class or prestigious jobholders. Contact between different peoples, as we have seen numerous times, precedes conflict. Contact also may initiate mutual understanding and appreciation.

In a commencement address at American University in 1963, President John F. Kennedy declared, "If we cannot end now our differences, at least we can help make the world safe for diversity" (Cleveland 1995, 23). Yet today, with conflicts along ethnic, racial, and religious lines jeopardizing peace and fostering terrorism, such a goal seems very distant. What may well emerge from contemporary and future unrest is the recognition by human beings that people are fundamentally alike and share the same abilities, weaknesses, and dreams.

Key Terms

ageism 456	domestic partnership 470	visitability 466
disability 461	homophobia 468	

Review Questions

1. What contributes to the changing image of diversity in the United States?
2. In what ways are the aged, people with disabilities, and gays and lesbians stereotyped?
3. What are common and differing aspects of the effort to mobilize the elderly, people with disabilities, and gay men and lesbians to achieve equality?
4. What has been the role of the federal government in the effort to achieve equality by the aged, people with disabilities, and the gay and lesbian community?
5. What does it mean to overcome "exclusion"?

Critical Thinking

1. Sociologists use the term *master status* to describe a status that dominates others and thereby determines a person's general position in society. To what degree can that term be applied to the three groups considered in this chapter?

2. The media—in advertisements, humor, dramas, and situation comedies—portray life in society. What are some examples, both positive and negative, of how the elderly, people with disabilities, and gays and lesbians are presented in the media that you have seen? In what ways are these groups stereotyped?

3. How might advances in technology, including innovations for the home and computer chat rooms, have a unique effect on each of the groups trying to overcome exclusion discussed in this chapter?

4. How do policy makers trying to bring about change use the model of "half full" and "half empty" either to argue for change on behalf of minorities or to use the same concepts to maintain that the status quo is adequate for addressing issues of social inequality?

Internet Connections—Research Navigator™

Follow the instructions found on page 35 of this text to access the features of Research Navigator™. Once at the Web site, enter your Login Name and Password. Then, to use the ContentSelect database, enter keywords such as "domestic partnership," "ADA," "Stonewall," and "retirement," and the search engine will supply relevant and recent scholarly and popular press publications. Use the *New York Times* Search-by-Subject Archive to find recent news articles related to sociology and the Link Library feature to locate relevant Web links organized by the key terms associated with this chapter.

Internet Resource Directory

The following is a sample of the thousands of Web sites that offer information on topics discussed in this book. Most of these sites have links to other resources.

General

All of Us are Related, Each of Us is Unique (Syracuse University)
http://allrelated.syr.edu/

Hate Crimes Laws
http://www.adl.org/99hatecrime/intro.asp

U.S. Citizenship and Immigration Services
http://www.uscis.gov/graphics/

Race Traitor (constructing whiteness)
http://www.racetraitor.org

Southern Poverty Law Center (tolerance education)
http://splccenter.org and www.tolerance.org

U.S. Census Bureau
http://www.census.gov
and specifically www.census.gov/pubinfo/www/hotlinks.html

U.S. Commission on Civil Rights
http://www.usccr.gov

African Americans

African Americna History and Culture (The Smithsonian)
http://www.si.edu/resource/faq/nmah/afroam.htm

Black Collegian Online
http://www.black-collegian.com/

Kwanzaa Information Center
http://www.melanet.com/kwanzaa/

MelaNET (The UnCut Black Experience)
http://www.melanet.com/

Asian Americans

Asian American Network
http://www.aan.net/

Asian American Studies, Yale University Guide to
http://www.library.yale.edu/rsc/asian-american/

Hmong Home Page
http://www.stolaf.edu/people/cdr/hmong/

Little India (magazine website)
http://www.littleindia.com/

Little Saigon Net
http://www.littlesaigon.com/

Hispanics and Latinos

Afro Cubans as well as Cuba and the Caribbean
   http://www.afrocubaweb.com/
Julian Samora Research Institute (Michigan State University)
   http://www.jsri.msu.edu/
Latin American National Information Center
   http://lanic.utexas.edu
Mexican American Studies and Research Center (University of Arizona)
   http://masrc.arizona.edu/
Pew Hispanic Center
   http://pewhispanic.org/
Puerto Ricans and the American Dream
   http://prdream.com/

Jews and Judaism

American Jewish Committee
   http://www.ajc.org
Anti-Defamation League
   http://www.adl.org
Jewish culture
   http://myjewishlearning.com
Judaism and Jewish Resources
   http://shamash.org

Muslim and Arab Americans

Arab American Institute
   http://www.aaiusa.org/
American-Arab Anti-Discrimination Committee
   http://www.adc.org
Muslim Students' Association
   http://msa-natl.org

Native Americans

Bureau of Indian Affairs
   http://www.doi.gov/bureau-indian-affairs.html
Nation of Hawai'i
   http://hawaii-nation.org/
Native Web
   http://www.nativeweb.org
Smithsonian National Museum of the American Indian
   http://www.nmai.si.edu

Women and Men

National Organization for Women
   http://www.now.org
National Women's History Project
   http://www.nwhp.org/
Womensnet (South Africa)
   http://www.womensnet.org.za

Outside the United States

Abya Yala Net (South and Meso American Indian Rights Center)
http://abyayala.nativeweb.org
African National Congress (South Africa)
http://www.anc.org.za/
Information (general) on countries (CIA World Factbook)
http://www.odci.gov/cia/publications/factbook
Peace People (Northern Ireland)
http://www.peacepeople.com

Ethnic Groups and Other Subordinate Groups

Administration on Aging
http://www.aoa.dhhs.gov
American Institute of Polish Culture
http://www.ampolinstitute.org
American Irish Historical Society
http://www.aihs.org
Catholics for a Free Choice
http://www.cath4choice.org
Disability Social History Project
http://www.disabilityhistory.org
German Americans (German Embassy site)
http://www.germany-info.org/
Human Rights Web
http://www.hrweb.org
Interracial Voice (people of mixed racial background)
http://www.webcom.com/~intvoice
Polish American Association
http://www.polish.org
SeniorLink
http://www.seniorlink.com/
Society and Culture: Disabilities (Yahoo)
http://www.yahoo.com/Society_and_Culture/Disabilities/
Sons of Norway
http://www.sofn.com

The Author

Richard T. Schaefer (for e-mail correspondence)
schaeferrt@aol.com
www.schaefersociology.net

Glossary

Parenthetical numbers refer to the pages on which the term is introduced.

abolitionists Whites and free Blacks who favored the end of slavery. (205)

absolute deprivation The minimum level of subsistence below which families or individuals should not be expected to exist. (69)

acting White Taking school seriously and accepting the authority of teachers and administrators. (231)

affirmative action Positive efforts to recruit subordinate group members, including women, for jobs, promotions, and educational opportunities. (85)

Afrocentric perspective An emphasis on the customs of African cultures and how they have pervaded the history, culture, and behavior of Blacks in the United States and around the world. (33)

ageism Prejudice and discrimination against the elderly. (456)

AJAs Americans of Japanese ancestry in Hawaii. (347)

amalgamation The process by which a dominant group and a subordinate group combine through intermarriage to form a new group. (25)

androgyny The state of being both masculine and feminine, aggressive and gentle. (403)

anti-Semitism Anti-Jewish prejudice or discrimination. (374)

apartheid The policy of the South African government intended to maintain separation of Blacks, Coloureds, and Asians from the dominant Whites. (446)

apartheid schools All-Black schools. (230)

arranged marriage Others choose one's marital partner not based on any preexisting mutual attraction. (336)

assimilation The process by which a subordinate individual or group takes on the characteristics of the dominant group. (25)

asylees Foreigners who have already entered the United States and now seek protection because of persecution or a well-founded fear of persecution. (119)

authoritarian personality A psychological construct of a personality type likely to be prejudiced and to use others as scapegoats. (45)

bilingual education A program designed to allow students to learn academic concepts in their native language while they learn a second language. (143)

bilingualism The use of two or more languages in places of work or education and the treatment of each language as legitimate. (28)

biological race The mistaken notion of a genetically isolated human group. (12)

blaming the victim Portraying the problems of racial and ethnic minorities as their fault rather than recognizing society's responsibilities. (18)

blended identity Self-image and worldview that is a combination of religious faith, cultural background based on nationality, and current residency. (306)

Bogardus scale Technique to measure social distance toward different racial and ethnic groups. (51)

borderlands The area of a common culture along the border between Mexico and the United States. (262)

bracero Contracted Mexican laborers brought to the United States during World War II. (276)

brain drain Immigration to the United States of skilled workers, professionals, and technicians who are desperately needed by their home countries. (107)

chain immigration Immigrants sponsor several other immigrants who upon their arrival may sponsor still more. (97)

Chicanismo An ideology emphasizing pride and positive identity among Mexican Americans. (281)

civil disobedience A tactic promoted by Martin Luther King, Jr., based on the belief that people have the right to disobey unjust laws under certain circumstances. (216)

civil religion The religious dimension in American life that merges the state with sacred beliefs. (152)

class As defined by Max Weber, people who share similar levels of wealth. (15)

colonialism A foreign power's maintenance of political, social, economic, and cultural dominance over people for an extended period. (21)

color gradient The placement of people on a continuum from light to dark skin color rather than in distinct racial groupings by skin color. (268)

comparable worth *See* pay equity. (411)

conflict perspective A sociological approach that assumes that the social structure is best understood in terms of conflict or tension between competing groups. (17)

contact hypothesis An interactionist perspective stating that intergroup contact between people of equal status in noncompetitive circumstances will reduce prejudice. (59)

creationists People who support a literal interpretation of the biblical book of Genesis on the origins of the universe and argue that evolution should not be presented as established scientific thought. (158)

crossover effect An effect that appears as previously high-scoring Native American children score as below average in intelligence when tests are given in English rather than their native languages. (188)

culture of poverty A way of life that involves no future planning, no enduring commitment to marriage, and no work ethic; this culture follows the poor even when they move out of the slums or the barrio. (278)

curanderismo Hispanic folk medicine. (294)

de facto segregation Segregation that is the result of residential patterns. (230)

deficit model of ethnic identity One's ethnicity is viewed by others as a factor of subtracting away the characteristics corresponding to some ideal ethnic type. (303)

de jure segregation Children assigned to schools specifically to maintain racially separated schools. (214)

denomination A large, organized religion not officially linked with the state or government. (147)

desi Colloquial name for people who trace their ancestry to South Asia, especially India and Pakistan. (335)

Diaspora The exile of Jews from Palestine. (385)

differential justice Whites being dealt with more leniently than Blacks, whether at the time of arrest, indictment, conviction, sentencing, or parole. (245)

disability Reduced ability to perform tasks one would normally do at a given stage in life. (461)

discrimination The denial of opportunities and equal rights to individuals and groups because of prejudice or for other arbitrary reasons. (41)

displaced homemakers Women whose primary occupation had been homemaking but who did not find full-time employment after being divorced, separated, or widowed. (414)

domestic partnership Two unrelated adults who have chosen to share one another's lives in a relationship of mutual caring, who reside together, and who agree to be jointly responsible for their dependents, basic living expenses, and other common necessities. (470)

dry foot, wet foot Policy toward Cuban immigrants allowing entry to those who manage to reach the United States (dry foot) to remain whereas those picked up at sea (wet foot) are sent back to Cuba. (266)

dual labor market Division of the economy into two areas of employment, the secondary one of which is populated primarily by minorities working at menial jobs. (75)

dysfunction An element of society that may disrupt a social system or decrease its stability. (17)

Ebonics Distinctive dialect with a complex language structure found among many Black Americans. (204)

emigration Leaving a country to settle in another. (20)

English immersion Teaching in English by teachers who know the students' native language but use it only when students do not understand the lessons. (144)

environmental justice Efforts to ensure that hazardous substances are controlled so that all communities receive protection regardless of race or socioeconomic circumstances. (85)

ethclass The merged ethnicity and class in a person's status. (152)

ethnic cleansing Policy of ethnic Serbs to eliminate Muslims from parts of Bosnia. (22)

ethnic group A group set apart from others because of its national origin or distinctive cultural patterns. (9)

ethnicity paradox The maintenance of one's ethnic ties in a way that can assist with assimilation in larger society. (129)

ethnocentrism The tendency to assume that one's culture and way of life are superior to all others. (39)

ethnonational conflicts Conflicts between ethnic, racial, religious, and linguistic groups within nations replacing conflicts between nations. (426)

ethnophaulism Ethnic or racial slurs, including derisive nicknames. (41)

evacuees Japanese Americans interned in camps for the duration of World War II. (361)

exploitation theory A Marxist theory that views racial subordination in the United States as a manifestation of the class system inherent in capitalism. (45)

familism Pride and closeness in the family that result in placing family obligation and loyalty before individual needs. (292)

feminine mystique Society's view of a woman as only her children's mother and her husband's wife. (407)

feminization of poverty The trend since 1970 that has women accounting for a growing proportion of those below the poverty line. (414)

fish-ins Tribes' protests over government interference with their traditional rights to fish as they like. (178)

fringe-of-values theory Behavior that is on the border of conduct that a society regards as proper and is often carried out by subordinate groups, subjecting those groups to negative sanctions. (379)

functionalist perspective A sociological approach emphasizing how parts of a society are structured to maintain its stability. (16)

fusion A minority and a majority group combining to form a new group. (25)

gender roles Expectations regarding the proper behavior, attitudes, and activities of males and females. (403)

genocide The deliberate, systematic killing of an entire people or nation. (22)

gerrymandering Redrawing districts bizarrely to create politically advantageous outcomes. (248)

glass ceiling The barrier that blocks the promotion of a qualified worker because of gender or minority membership. (90)

glass escalator The male advantage experienced in occupations dominated by women. (92)

glass wall A barrier to moving laterally in a business to positions that are more likely to lead to upward mobility. (91)

globalization Worldwide integration of government policies, cultures, social movements, and financial markets through trade, movements of people, and the exchange of ideas. (20)

gook syndrome David Riesman's phrase describing Americans' tendency to stereotype Asians and to regard them as all alike and undesirable. (339)

hajj Pilgrimage to Mecca to be completed at least once in a Muslim's lifetime. (305)

halakha Jewish laws covering obligations and duties. (393)

Haoles Hawaiian term for Caucasians. (345)

hate crimes Criminal offense committed because of the offender's bias against a race, religion, ethnic/national origin group, or sexual orientation group. (39)

hijab Refers to a variety of garments that allow women to follow the guidelines of modest dress. (312)

Holocaust The state-sponsored systematic persecution and annihilation of European Jewry by Nazi Germany and its collaborators. (381)

Holocaust revisionists People who deny the Nazi effort to exterminate the Jews or who minimize the numbers killed. (381)

hometown clubs Nonprofit organizations that maintain close ties to immigrants' hometowns in Mexico and other Latin American countries. (263)

homophobia The fear of and prejudice toward homosexuality. (468)

hui kuan Chinese American benevolent associations organized on the basis of the district of the immigrant's origin in China. (355)

ilchomose The 1.5 generation of Korean Americans—those who immigrated into the United States as children. (343)

immigration Coming into a new country as a permanent resident. (20)

income Salaries, wages, and other money received. (83)

informal economy Transfers of money, goods, or services that are not reported to the government. Common in inner-city neighborhoods and poverty-stricken rural areas. (75)

in-group virtues Proper behavior by one's own group (in-group virtues) becomes unacceptable when practiced by outsiders (out-group vices). (380)

institutional discrimination A denial of opportunities and equal rights to individuals or groups resulting from the normal operations of a society. (72)

intelligence quotient (IQ) The ratio of a person's mental age (as computed by an IQ test) to his or her chronological age, multiplied by 100. (13)

intelligent design View that life is so complex that must have been created by a higher intelligence. (159)

internal colonialism The treatment of subordinate peoples as colonial subjects by those in power. (22)

Intifada The Palestinian uprising against Israeli authorities in the occupied territories. (442)

irregular or underground economy *See* informal economy. (75)

Issei First-generation immigrants from Japan to the United States. (359)

jihad Struggle against the enemies of Allah, usually taken to mean one's own internal struggle. (305)

Jim Crow Southern laws passed in the late nineteenth century that kept Blacks in their subordinate position. (206)

Judaization The lessening importance of Judaism as a religion and the substitution of cultural traditions as the tie that binds Jews. (376)

kashrut Laws pertaining to permissible (kosher) and forbidden foods and their preparation. (391)

Kibei Japanese Americans of the *Nisei* generation sent back to Japan for schooling and to have marriages arranged. (359)

kickouts or pushouts Native American school dropouts who leave behind an unproductive academic environment. (187)

kye Rotating credit system used by Korean Americans to subsidize the start of businesses. (344)

labeling theory A sociological approach introduced by Howard Becker that attempts to explain why certain people are viewed as deviants and others engaging in the same behavior are not. (18)

La Raza 'The People"—a term referring to the rich heritage of Mexican Americans and, therefore, used to denote a sense of pride among Mexican Americans today. (277)

life chances People's opportunities to provide themselves with material goods, positive living conditions, and favorable life experiences. (151)

maquiladoras Foreign-owned companies on the Mexican side of the border with the United States. (263)

marginality The status of being between two cultures at the same time, such as the status of Jewish immigrants in the United States. (31)

Marielitos People who arrived from Cuba in the third wave of Cuban immigration, most specifically those forcibly deported by way of Mariel Harbor. The term is generally reserved for refugees seen as especially undesirable. (264)

matrix of domination Cumulative impact of oppression because of race, gender, and class as well as sexual orientation, religion, disability status, and age. (421)

melting pot Diverse racial or ethnic groups or both, forming a new creation, a new cultural entity. (25)

middlemen minorities Groups such as Japanese Americans that typically occupy middle positions in the social and occupational stratification system. (328)

migradollars (or remittances) The money that immigrant workers send back to families in their native societies. (114)

migration A general term that describes any transfer of population. (20)

millenarian movements Movements, such as the Ghost Dance, that prophesy a cataclysm in the immediate future, to be followed by collective salvation. (171)

minority group A subordinate group whose members have significantly less control or power over their own lives than do the members of a dominant or majority group. (7)

model or ideal minority A group that, despite past prejudice and discrimination, succeeds economically, socially, and educationally without resorting to political or violent confrontations with Whites. (325)

mojados "Wetbacks"; derisive slang for Mexicans who enter illegally, supposedly by swimming the Rio Grande. (277)

mommy tax Lower salaries women receive over their lifetime because they have children. (419)

mommy track An unofficial corporate career track for women who want to divide their attention between work and family. (413)

mulatto escape hatch Notion that Brazilians of mixed ancestry can move into high-status positions. (437)

nativism Beliefs and policies favoring native-born citizens over immigrants. (100)

naturalization Conferring of citizenship on a person after birth. (105)

neocolonialism Continuing dependence of former colonies on foreign countries. (285)

Neoricans Puerto Ricans who return to the island to settle after living on the mainland of the United States (also Nuyoricans). (284)

Nisei Children born of immigrants from Japan. (359)

normative approach The view that prejudice is influenced by societal norms and situations that encourage or discourage the tolerance of minorities. (46)

Orientalism The simplistic view of the people and history of the Orient with no recognition of change over time or the diversity within its many cultures. (300)

out-group vices Proper behavior by one's own group (ingroup virtues) becomes unacceptable when practiced by outsiders (out-group vices). (380)

panethnicity The development of solidarity between ethnic subgroups, as reflected in the terms *Hispanic* or *Asian American*. (30)

pan-Indianism Intertribal social movements in which several tribes, joined by political goals but not by kinship, unite in a common identity. (178)

pass laws Laws that controlled internal movement by non-Whites in South Africa. (446)

pay equity The same wages for different types of work that are judged to be comparable by such measures as employee knowledge, skills, effort, responsibility, and working conditions; also called comparable worth. (411)

Pentecostalism A religion similar in many respects to evangelical faiths that believes in the infusion of the Holy Spirit into services and in religious experiences such as faith healing. (295)

peoplehood Milton Gordon's term for a group with a shared feeling. (398)

pluralism Mutual respect between the various groups in a society for one another's cultures, allowing minorities to express their own culture without experiencing prejudice or hostility. (26)

powwows Native American gatherings of dancing, singing, music playing, and visiting, accompanied by competitions. (181)

prejudice A negative attitude toward an entire category of people, such as a racial or ethnic minority. (41)

principle of third-generation interest Marcus Hansen's contention that ethnic interest and awareness increase in the third generation, among the grandchildren of immigrants. (127)

quilombo Slave hideaways n Brazil. (437)

Quinceañera (or Quinceañero) Celebration of Latinas turning 15 years of age. (258)

racial formation A sociohistorical process by which racial categories are created, inhibited, transformed, and destroyed. (15)

racial group A group that is socially set apart because of obvious physical differences. (8)

racial profiling Any arbitrary police-initiated action based on race, ethnicity, or natural origin rather than a person's behavior. (50)

racism A doctrine that one race is superior. (14)

redlining The pattern of discrimination against people trying to buy homes in minority and racially changing neighborhoods. (82)

refugees People living outside their country of citizenship for fear of political or religious persecution. (118)

relative deprivation The conscious experience of a negative discrepancy between legitimate expectations and present actualities. (69)

remittances (or migradollars) The monies that immigrants return to their country of origin. (114)

repatriation The 1930s' program of deporting Mexicans. (276)

respectable bigotry Michael Lerner's term for the social acceptance of prejudice against White ethnics, when intolerance against non-White minorities is regarded as unacceptable. (130)

restrictive covenants Private contracts or agreements that discourage or prevent minority-group members from purchasing housing in a neighborhood. (211)

reverse discrimination Actions that cause better-qualified White men to be passed over for women and minority men. (88)

riff-raff theory Also called the rotten-apple theory; the belief that the riots of the 1960s were caused by discontented youths rather than by social and economic problems facing all African Americans. (219)

rising expectations The increasing sense of frustration that legitimate needs are being blocked. (219)

Sansei The children of the *Nisei*—that is, the grandchildren of the original immigrants from Japan. (359)

scapegoating theory A person or group blamed irrationally for another person's or group's problems or difficulties. (43)

secessionist minority Groups, such as the Amish, that reject both assimilation and coexistence. (158)

second shift The double burden—work outside the home followed by child care and housework—that is faced by many women and that few men share equitably. (419)

segregation The physical separation of two groups, often imposed on a subordinate group by the dominant group. (23)

self-fulfilling prophecy The tendency to respond to and act on the basis of stereotypes, a predisposition that can lead one to validate false definitions. (19)

set-asides Programs stipulating that a minimum proportion of government contracts must be awarded to minority-owned businesses. (329)

sexism The ideology that one sex is superior to the other. (403)

sexual harassment Any unwanted and unwelcome sexual advances that interfere with a person's ability to perform a job and enjoy the benefits of a job. (413)

sinophobes People with a fear of anything associated with China. (101)

slave codes Laws that defined the low position held by slaves in the United States. (202)

slavery reparations Act of making amends for the injustices of slavery. (206)

social distance Tendency to approach or withdraw from a racial group. (51)

sociology The systematic study of social behavior and human groups. (15)

sovereignty Tribal self-rule. (181)

sovereignty movement Effort by the indigenous people of Hawaii to secure a measure of self-government and restoration of their lands. (347)

states' rights The principle, reinvoked in the late 1940s, that holds that each state is sovereign and has the right to order its own affairs without interference by the federal government. (81)

stereotypes Unreliable, exaggerated generalizations about all members of a group that do not take individual differences into account. (18)

stratification A structured ranking of entire groups of people that perpetuates unequal rewards and power in a society. (15)

suffragists Women and men who worked successfully to gain women the right to vote. (406)

sundown towns Communities where non-Whites were systematically excluded from living. (212)

symbolic ethnicity Herbert Gans's term that describes emphasis on ethnic food and ethnically associated political issues rather than deeper ties to one's heritage. (128)

tongs Chinese American secret associations. (355)

total discrimination The combination of current discrimination with past discrimination created by poor schools and menial jobs. (70)

tracking The practice of placing students in specific curriculum groups on the basis of test scores and other criteria. (230)

transnationals Immigrants who sustain multiple social relationships linking their societies of origin and settlement. (118)

tsu Clans established along family lines and forming a basis for social organization by Chinese Americans. (354)

underemployment Work at a job for which the worker is overqualified, involuntary part-time instead of full-time employment, or intermittent employment. (236)

underground economy *See* informal economy. (75)

victim discounting Tendency to view crime as less socially significant if the victim is viewed as less worthy. (246)

victimization surveys Annual attempts to measure crime rates by interviewing ordinary citizens who may or may not have been crime victims. (245)

visible minorities In Canada, persons other than Aboriginal or First Nation people who are non-White in racial background. (435)

Viet Kieu Vietnamese living abroad such as in the United States. (341)

visitability Building private homes to be accessible for visitors with disabilities. (466)

wealth An inclusive term encompassing all of a person's material assets, including land and other types of property. (83)

White primary Legal provisions forbidding Black voting in election primaries, which in one-party areas of the South effectively denied Blacks their right to select elected officials. (206)

world systems theory A view of the global economic system as divided between nations that control wealth and those that provide natural resources and labor. (21)

xenophobia The fear or hatred of strangers or foreigners. (100)

yellow peril A term denoting a generalized prejudice toward Asian people and their customs. (330)

Yiddishkait Jewishness. (393)

Yonsei The fourth generation of Japanese Americans in the United States; the children of the Sansei. (359)

Zionism Traditional Jewish religious yearning to return to the biblical homeland, now used to refer to support for the state of Israel. (385)

zoning laws Legal provisions stipulating land use and the architectural design of housing, often used to keep racial minorities and low-income people out of suburban areas. (244)

References

AARP. 2003. *AARP Home.* Accessed May 12, 2003, at http://www.aarp.org.

___. 2004. *Civil Rights and Labor Relations.* Princeton, NJ: Gallup Organization.

ABC News. 1992. *Primetime Live:* "True Colors." Transcript of November 26 episode.

Abdo, Geneive. 2004. "A Muslim Rap Finds Voice." *Chicago Tribune,* June 30, 1, 19.

___. 2004b. "New Generation Lifting Muslims." *Chicago Tribune,* September 3, 1, 8.

Abelmann, Nancy and John Lie. 1995. *Blue Dreams: Korean Americans and the Los Angeles Riots.* Cambridge, MA: Harvard University Press.

Abraham, Nabeel and Andrew Shyrock. 2000. *Arab Detroit: From Margin to Mainstream.* Detroit, MI: Wayne State University Press.

Abrahamson, Alan. 1997. "School Growth: A New Chapter for U.S. Jews." *Los Angeles Times,* October 22, B2.

Abrahamson, Alan and Judy Pasternak. 1998. "For U.S. Jews, Era of Plenty Takes Many Far from Roots." *Los Angeles Times,* April 20, A1, A10–11.

Abrahamson, Mark. 1996. *Urban Enclaves: Identity and Place in America.* New York: St. Martin's Press.

Achenbaumm, W. A. 1993. "Old Age." In *Encyclopedia of American Social History,* edited by Mary Kupeic Coyton, Elliot J. Gorn, and Peter W. Williams, 2051–2062. New York: Scribner's.

ACLU. 1996. *Racial Justice.* New York: American Civil Liberties Union.

Adam, Barry D. 1995. *The Rise of a Gay and Lesbian Movement,* rev. ed. New York: Twayne.

Adams, Jane Meredith. 2006. "Mystery Shrouds Slaying of Chinatown Businessman." March 31, p. 5.

Adler, Patricia A. and Peter Adler. 1998. *Peer Power: Preadolescent Culture and Identity.* New Brunswick, NJ: Rutgers University Press.

___. Steven J. Kess, and Peter Adler. 1992. "Socialization to Gender Role: Popularity among Elementary School Boys and Girls." *Sociology of Education,* July, 65: 169–187.

___. and Peter Adler. 2004. *Paradise Laborers: Hotel Work in the Global Economy.* Ithaca, NY: Cornell University Press.

Adorno, T. W., Else Frenkel-Brunswik, Daniel J. Levinson, and R. Nevitt Sanford. 1950. *The Authoritarian Personality.* New York: Wiley.

Aglionby, John. 2004. "US Pays Debt at Last to Vietnam War Allies." *The Guardian,* August 24, 11.

Aguirre Jr., Adalberto. 2004. "Profiling Mexican American Identity." *American Behavioral Scientist,* March, 47: 928–942.

Aguillar-San Juan, Karin. 1998. "Creating Ethnic Places in 'Little Saigon': History, Memory and Citizenship." Paper presented at American Sociological Association Annual Meeting, San Francisco.

___. 2005. "Staying Vietnamese: Community and Place in Orange County and Boston." *City and Community* March, 4: 37–65.

Akaka, Daniel. 2006. Akaka Bill: S. 147. Accessed June 5, 2006 at http://akaka.senate.gov.

Akwesasne Notes. 1972. "Columbus a Trader in Indian Slaves," Early Autumn, 4:22.

Alárcon, Odette. 1995. An Interview. Research Report (Center for Research on Women, Wellesley College), Fall, 15: 3–4.

Alba, Richard and Dalia Abdel-Hady. 2005. "Galileo's Children: Italian Americans' Difficult Entry into the Intellectual Elite." *Sociological Quarterly* 46: 3–18.

Albrecht, Gary L. 1995. "Review of Disabling Laws, Enabling Acts: Disability Rights in Britain and America." *Contemporary Sociology,* 24(5): 627–629.

___. 1997. "Disability Is Area Rich with Sociological Opportunity." *Footnotes,* December, 25: 6.

Allport, Gordon W. 1979. *The Nature of Prejudice, 25th Anniversary Edition.* Reading, MA: Addison-Wesley.

Alvord, Lori Arviso and Elizabeth Cohen Van Pelt. 1999. *The Scalpel and the Silver Bear.* New York: Bantam.

Alvord, Valerie. 2000. "Refugees' Success Breeds Pressure, Discrimination." *USA Today,* May 1, 74.

American Community Survey. 2006. *American Community Survey 2005.* Released August 2006 at http://www.census.gov.

American Indian Higher Education Consortium. 1999. *Tribal Colleges: An Introduction.* Alexandra, VA: A.I.H.E.C.

American Jewish Committee. 1965. *Mutual Savings Banks of New York City.* New York: American Jewish Committee.

___. 1966a. *Mutual Savings Banks: A Follow-Up Report.* New York: American Jewish Committee.

___. 1966b. *Patterns of Exclusion from the Executive Suite: Corporate Banking.* New York: American Jewish Committee.

___. 2001. *American Jewish YearBook 2001.* New York: AJC.

___. 2005a. *2005 Annual Survey of American-Jewish Opinion.* New York: AJC.

___. 2006. *American Jewish Yearbook 2005.* New York: AJC.

Amnesty International. 1993. *Amnesty International Report 1993.* New York: Amnesty International.

___. 2004. *Threat and Humiliation: Racial Profiling, Domestic Security, and Human Rights in the United States.* New York: Amnesty International.

Andrew, George Reid. 1991. *Blacks and Whites in São Paulo, Brazil, 1888–1988.* Madison: University of Wisconsin Press.

Angier, Natalie. 1993. "U.S. Opens the Door Just a Crack to Alternative Forms of Medicine." *New York Times,* January 10, 1, 13.

Ansari, Zafar Ishaq. 2004. "Islam among African Americans: An Overview." Pp. 222–267 in *Muslims' Place in the American Public Square,* edited by Zahid H. Bukhari et al. Walnut Creek, CA: Atamira Press.

Anti-Defamation League (ADL). 1996. *The Web of Hate: Extremists Exploit the Internet.* New York: Anti-Defamation League.

___. 2006. *Audit of Anti-Semitic Incidents 2005.* New York: ADL.

Aponte, Robert. 1991. "Urban Hispanic Poverty: Disaggregations and Explanations." *Social Problems,* November, 38: 516–528.

Applebome, Peter. 1996. "70 Years after Scopes Trial, Creation Debate Lives." *New York Times,* March 10, 1, 22.

___. 1997. "Dispute over Ebonics Reflects a Volatile Mix That Roils Urban Education." *New York Times,* March 1, p. 8.

Arain, Fatima. 2006. *Being Pakistani, Muslim, and Female in America.* Unpublished paper. April 3. Chicago: DePaul University.

Aran, Kenneth, Herman Arthur, Ramon Colon, and Harvey Goldenberg. 1973. *Puerto Rican History and Culture: A Study Guide and Curriculum Outline.* New York: United Federation of Teachers.

Archuleta, Glenda. 1998. Interview with Archuleta (Council for Energy Resource Tribes) by Richard T. Schaefer, September 18.

Arden, Harvey. 1975. "The Pious Ones." *National Geographic,* August, 168: 276–298.

Arias, Elizabeth and Betty Smith. 2003. "Deaths: Preliminary Data for 2001." *National Vital Statistics Reports* 51 (March 14).

Armstrong, Elizabeth A. and Suzanna M. Crage. 2006. Movements and Memory: The Making of the Stonewall Myth. *American Sociological Review* 71 (October): 724–751.

Asahina, Robert. 2006. *Just Americans: How Japanese Americans Won a War at Home and Abroad: The Story of the 100th Battalion/442d Regimental Combat Team in World War II*. New York: Gotham.

Asante, Molefi Kete and Mark T. Mattson. 1991. *The Historical and Cultural Atlas of African Americans*. New York: Macmillan.

Asian American Journalists Association. 2000. *All-American: How to Cover Asian America*. San Francisco, CA: AAJA.

Associated Press. 2003. "U.S. Withholds Approval for Nuclear Waste Storage on Indian Reservation." *New York Times*, March 11.

___. 2006a. "Church Blaze—Alabama's 10th—'Definitely Arson,' Official Says." *Chicago Tribune* February 14, 3.

___. 2006b. "Braceros Will Get 3,500." *Los Angeles Times*, October 28, A9.

Association of American Medical Colleges. 2005. *Facts—Applicants, Matriculants and Graduates*. Accessed August 5, 2004, at http://www.aamc.org.

Ataiyero, Kayce T. 2006. "Faith Outgrows Space for Japanese Church." *Chicago Tribune*, February 6, sect. 2, 3.

Avila, Oscar. 2003. "Muslim Holiday Testing Schools." *Chicago Tribune*, November 24, 1, 16.

___. 2004. "The Conflicting Colors of Vietnam." *Chicago Tribune*, February 22, sect. 4, 1, 6.

___. 2006. "Legal Immigrants Feel Overlooked." *New York Times*, October 13, A1, A29.

Ayala, César J. and Viviana Carro-Figueroa. 2006. "Expropriation and Displacement of Civilians in Vieques, 1940–1950." Pp. 172–205 in *Puerto Rico Under Colonial Rule*, edited by Ramón Bosque-Pérez and José Javier Colón Morera, Albany: State University of New York Press.

Badgett, M. V. Lee and Heidi I. Hartmann. 1995. "The Effectiveness of Equal Employment Opportunity Policies." In *Economic Perspectives in Affirmative Action*, edited by Margaret C. Simms, 55–83. Washington, DC: Joint Center for Political and Economic Studies.

Bagby, Ishan. 2004. *A Portrait of Detroit Mosques: Muslim Views on Policy, Politics and Religion*. Clinton Township, MI: Institute for Social Policy and Understanding.

Baldwin, James. 1967. "Negroes Are Anti-Semitic Because They're Anti-White." *New York Times*, May 21, 114.

Baldwin, Neil. 2001. *Henry Ford and the Jews: The Mass Production of Hate*. Public Affairs.

Baltzell, E. Digby. 1964. *The Protestant Establishment: Aristocracy and Caste in America*. New York: Vintage Books.

Bamshad, Michael J. and Steve E. Olson. 2003. "Does Race Exist?" *Scientific American*, December, 78–85.

Banerjee, Neela. 2000. "Fighting Back against Domestic Violence: Asian American Women Organize to Break the Silence." *AsianWeek*, November 30, 22:13–15.

___. 2006. "Clergywomen Find Hard Path to Bigger Pulpit." *New York Times*, August 26, A1, A11.

Barbaro, Fred. 1974. "Ethnic Resentment." *Society*, March–April 11: 67–75.

Barclay, William, Krishna Kumar, and Ruth P. Simms. 1976. *Racial Conflict, Discrimination, and Power: Historical and Contemporary Studies*. New York: AMS Press.

Barnes, Edward. 1996. "Can't Get There from Here." *Time*, February 19, 147: 33.

Barnes, Jessica S. and Claudette L. Bennett. 2002. *The Asian Population: 2000*. Census Brief C2KBR/01-16. Washington, DC: U.S. Government Printing Office.

Barnes, Patricia M., Patricia F. Adams, and Eric Powell-Grener. 2005. "Health Characteristics of the American Indian and Alaska Native Adult Population: United States, 1999–2003." *Advance Data*, April 27.

Barrera, Mario, Carlos Munos, and Charles Ornelas. 1972. "The Barrio as an Internal Colony." Pp. 465–549 in *People and Politics in Urban Society*, edited by Harlan Mahlan. Beverly Hills, CA: Sage Publications.

Barrett, David B. and Todd M. Johnson. 2001. "Worldwide Adherents of All Religions by Six Continental Areas, Mid-2000." P. 302 in *Britannica Book of the Year 2001*. Chicago: Encyclopedia Britannica.

Barringer, Felicity. 2004. "Bitter Division for Sierra Club on Immigration." *New York Times*, March 14, A1, A16.

Barron, Milton L. 1953. "Minority Group Characteristics of the Aged in American Society." *Journal of Gerontology*, October, 8: 477–482.

Barry, Ellen. 2004. "County Rescinds Vote." *Los Angeles Times*, March 19, A16.

Bartlett, Donald L. and James B. Steele. 2002. "Casinos: Wheel of Misfortune." *Time*, December 10, 160: 44–53, 56–58.

___. 2004 "Who Left the Door Open." *Time*, September 20, 164: 51–66.

Bash, Harry M. 1979. *Sociology, Race and Ethnicity*. New York: Gordon & Breach.

___. 2001. "If I'm So White, Why Ain't I Right?: Some Methodological Misgivings on Taking Identity Ascriptions at Face Value." Paper presented at the Annual Meeting of the Midwest Sociological Society, St. Louis.

Basu, Moni. 2004. "In Troubled Times, U.S. Muslims Get Political." *Atlanta Journal-Constitution*, July 24, 1.

Bauder, Harald. 2003. "'Brain Abuse', or the Devaluation of Immigrant Labour in Canada." *Antipode*, September, 35: 699–717.

Bauer, Raymond A. and Alice H. Bauer. 1942. "Day to Day Resistance to Slavery." *Journal of Negro History*, October, 27: 388–419.

Baum, Geraldine. 1998. "New Power of Women Recasts Judaism." *Los Angeles Times*, April 21, A1, A14, A15.

Baylor Institute for Studies of Religion. 2006. *American Piety in the 21st Century: New Insights to the Depth and Complexity of Religion in the US*. Waco, TX: Baylor ISR.

Ba-Yunus, Ilyas and Kassim Kone. 2004. "Muslim Americans: A Demographic Report." Pp. 299–322 in *Muslims' Place in the American Public Square*, edited by Zahid H. Bukhari et al. Walnut Creek, CA: Atamira Press.

Bean, Frank D., Jennifer Lee, Jeanne Batalova, and Mark Leach. 2004. *Immigration and Fading Color Lines in America*. New York: Russell Sage Foundation.

Beisel, Nicola and Tamara Kay. 2004. Abortion: Race and Gender in Nineteenth Century America. *American Sociological Review* 69 (August): 498–518.

Belkin, Lisa. 2003. "The Opt-Out Revolution." *New York Times Magazine*, October 26, 43–47, 58.

Bell, Derrick. 1994. "The Freedom of Employment Act." *The Nation*, May 23, 258: 708, 710–714.

Bell, Wendell. 1991. "Colonialism and Internal Colonialism." In Richard Lachmann, ed., *The Encyclopedic Dictionary of Sociology*, 4th ed., pp. 52–53 Guilford, CT: Dushkin Publishing Group.

Bellafante, Ginia. 2005. "Young South Asians in America Embrace 'Assisted' Marriages." *New York Times*, August 23, A1, A15.

Bellah, Robert. 1967. "Civil Religion in America." *Daedalus*, Winter, 96: 1–21.

Belliard, Juan Carlos and Johnny Ramirez-Johnson. 2005. "Medical Pluralism in the Life of a Mexican Immigrant Woman." *Hispanic Journal of Behavioral Sciences*, August, 27: 267–285.

Belluck, Pam. 1997. A New Window to Run Welfare is a Tight Squeeze for Many Tribes. *New York Times*, September 9, pp. A1. A15.

Belt, Don. 2002. "The World of Islam." *National Geographic*, January, 76–85.

Bem, Sandra L. and Daryl J. Bem. 1970. "Case Study of a Nonconscious Ideology: Training the Woman to Know Her Place." Pp. 89–99 in *Beliefs, Attitudes, and Human Affairs*, edited by Daryl J. Bem. Belmont, CA: Brooks/Cole Publishing Co.

Bendavid, Naftali. 2006. "Primary Colors" *Chicago Tribune*, October 24, pp. 17–21, 32.

Bendick, Marc, Jr., Charles W. Jackson, and J. Horacio Romero. 1993. *Employment Discrimination against Older Workers: An Experimental Study of Hiring Practices*. Washington, DC: Fair Employment Council of Greater Washington.

Bendyna, Mary E. and Paul M. Pearl. 2000. *Political Preferences of American Catholics at the Time of Election 2000*. Washington, DC: Center for Applied Research in the Apostolate, Georgetown University.

Bennett, Lerone, Jr. 1966. *Before the Mayflower*, rev. ed. Baltimore: Penguin.

Bennett, Phillip. 1993. "Ethnic Labels Fail to Keep Up with Reality." *The Cincinnati Enquirer,* November 18, A10.

Bennett, Vivienne. 1995. "Gender, Class, and Water: Women and the Politics of Water Service in Monterrey, Mexico." *Latin American Perspective,* September, 22: 76–99.

Bennetts, Leslie. 1993. "Jerry vs. the Kids." *Vanity Fair,* September, 56: 83–84, 86, 90, 92, 94, 96, 98.

Bertrand, Mariane and Sendhil Mullainathan. 2003. *Are Emily and Greg More Employable Than Lakisha and Jamal? A Field Experiment on Labor Market Discrimination.* Cambridge, MA: National Bureau of Economic Research.

Best, Joel. 2001. "Social Progress and Social Problems: Toward a Sociology of Gloom." *Sociological Quarterly* 42 (1): 1–12.

Bigelow, Rebecca. 1992. "Certain Inalienable Rights." *Friends Journal,* November, 38: 6–8.

Billson, Janet Mancini 1988. "No Owner of Soil: The Concept of Marginality Revisited on Its Sixtieth Birthday." *International Review of Modern Sociology,* Autumn, 18: 183–204.

Birchard, Karen. 2006. "Native Suspicion." *Chronicle of Higher Education,* January 13, 52: A46–A49.

Birren, James E. and Kathy Gribbin. 1973. "The Elderly." In *Outsiders USA,* edited by Don Spiegel and Patricia Keith-Spiegel. San Francisco: Rinehart Press.

Blackfeet Preservation Development Fund 2006. *The Facts v. the Brochure.* Blackfeet Restoration.

Blackstock, Nelson. 1976. *COINTELPRO: The FBI's Secret War on Political Freedom.* New York: Vintage Press.

Blanchard, Fletcher A., Lilly, Teri, and Vaughn, Leigh Ann. 1991. "Reducing the Expression of Racial Prejudice." *Psychological Science,* March, 2: 101–105.

Blauner, Robert. 1969. "Internal Colonialism and Ghetto Revolt." *Social Problems,* Spring, 16: 393–408.

___. 1972. *Racial Oppression in America.* New York: Harper & Row.

Bloch, Hannah. 1996. Cutting Off the Brains. *Time* 147, February 5, 46

Blood, Michael R. 2006. "Schwarzenegger's Hot-Blooded Ethnic Remarks Draw Mixed Reaction." *San Jose Mercury News,* September 9.

Bobo, Lawrence, James R. Kluegel, and Ryan A. Smith. 1997. "Laissez-Faire Racism: The Crystallization of a Kinder, Gentler, Antiblack Ideology." Pp. 15–42 in *Racial Attitudes in the 1990s: Continuity and Change,* edited by Steven A. Tuch and Jack K. Martin. Westport, CT: Praeger.

___. and Mia Tuan. 2006. *Prejudices in Politics: Group Position, Public Opinion, and the Wisconsin Treaty Rights Dispute.* Cambridge, MA: Harvard University Press.

Bocian, Debbie Gruenstein, Keith S. Ernst, and Wei Li. 2006. *Unfair Lending: The Effect of Race and Ethnicity on the Price of Subprime Mortgages.* Oakland, CA: Center for Responsible Lending.

___. Keith S. Ernst and Wei Li. 2006. *Unfair Lending: The Effect of Race and Ethnicity on the Price of Subprime Mortgages.* Durham, NC: Responsible Lending.

Bogardus, Emory. 1968. "Comparing Racial Distance in Ethiopia, South Africa, and the United States." *Sociology and Social Research,* January, 52 149–156.

Bohland, James R. 1982. "Indian Residential Segregation in the Urban Southwest: 1970 and 1980." *Social Science Quarterly,* December, 63: 749–761.

Bonacich, Edna. 1972. "A Theory of Ethnic Antagonism: The Split Labor Market." *American Sociological Review, October,* 37: 547–559.

___. 1976. "Advanced Capitalism and Black/White Race Relations in the United States: A Split Labor Market Interpretation." *American Sociological Review,* February, 41: 34–51.

___. 1988. "The Social Costs of Immigrant Entrepreneurship." *Amerasia,* Spring, 14: 119–128.

___. and Appelbaum, Richard. 2000. *Behind the Label: Inequality in the Los Angeles Apparel Industry.* Berkeley: University of California Press.

___. and John Modell. 1981. *The Economic Basis of Ethnic Solidarity.* Berkeley: University of California Press.

Bonilla-Silva, Eduardo. 1996. "Rethinking Racism: Toward a Structural Interpretation." *American Sociological Review,* June, 62: 465–480.

___. 2002. "The Linguistics of Color Blind Racism: How to Talk Nasty about Blacks without Sounding Racist." *Critical Sociology,* No. 1–2, 28: 41–64.

___. 2006. *Racism Without Racists,* 2nd ed. Lanham: Rowman and Littlefield.

Bonus, Rick. 2000. *Locating Filipino Americans: Ethnicity and the Cultural Politics of Space.* Philadelphia, PA: Temple University Press.

Boorstein, Michelle. 2006. Efforts Aims to Push Muslims to the Polls. September 29, A7.

Bordt, Rebecca L. 2005. "Using a Research Article to Facilitate a Deep Structure Understanding of Discrimination." *Teaching Sociology,* October, 33: 403–410.

Bork, Robert H. 1995. "What to Do About the First Amendment." *Commentary,* February, 99: 23–29.

Bositis, David A. 1996. "The Farrakhan Factor." *Washington Post National Weekly Edition,* December 16, 14: 24.

___. 2003. "Black Elected Officials Reach Historic Highs." *Focus,* November/December, 31: 3–4.

Bosque-Pérez, Ramon and José Javier Colón Morera. 2006. *Puerto Rico Under Colonial Rule: Political Persecution and the Quest for Human Rights.* Albany: State University of New York Press.

Boudreaux, Ruhid. 2002. "Indian Rights Law Is Upheld in Mexico." *Los Angeles Times,* September 7, A3.

Boushey, Heather. 2005. *Are Women Opting Out? Debunking the Myth.* Washington, DC: Center for Economic and Policy Research.

Bowles, Scott. 2000. "Bans on Racial Profiling Gain Steam." *USA Today,* June 2, 3A.

Bowman, Tom. 1998. "Evangelicals Allege Bias in U.S. Navy, Marine Chaplain Corps." *Baltimore Sun,* August 23, A12.

Bowser, Benjamin and Raymond G. Hunt, eds. 1996. *Impacts of Racism on White Americans.* Beverly Hills, CA: Sage Publications.

Boxall, Bettina. 2001. "Asian Indians Remake Silicon Valley." *Los Angeles Times,* July 6, A1, A26.

Brachear, Manya A. 2003. "Muslim-Run Food Pantry Feeds Body and Soul." *Chicago Tribune* December 14, sect. 4, 1, 5.

Braddock, D., and Bachelder, L. 1994. *The Glass Ceiling and Persons with Disabilities.* Washington, DC: The Glass Ceiling Commission.

Brannon, Ruth. 1995. "The Use of the Concept of Disability Culture: A Historian's View." *Disability Studies Quarterly,* Fall, 15: 3–15.

Braxton, Greg. 1999. "A Mad Dash for Diversity." *Los Angeles Times,* August 9, F1, F10.

Brazil. 1981. *IX Recenseamento Geral do Brasil—1980,* 1, P + 1. Rio de Janeiro: Secretaria de Planejamento da Presidencia da República, Fundacão Instituto Brasilerio de Geografia e Estatistica.

Brewer, Cynthia A. and Trudy A. Suchan. 2001. *Mapping Census 2000: The Geography of U.S. Diversity.* Washington, DC: U.S. Government Printing Office.

Briggs, David. 1996. "Greeley Poll Says Catholics Want Democratic Church." *Chicago Tribune,* May 31, sect. 2, 9.

Brimmer, Andrew. 1995. "The Economic Cost of Discrimination against Black Americans." Pp. 9–29 in *Economic Perspectives in Affirmative Action,* edited by Margaret C. Simms. Washington, DC: Joint Center for Political and Economic Studies.

Brittingham, Angela and G. Patricia de la Cruz. 2004. "Ancestry 2000." *Census 2000* Brief c2kbr-35. Washington, DC: U.S. Government Printing Office.

Broder, John M. 2006. "Immigrants and the Economics of Hard Work." *New York Times,* April 2, Section wk, p. 3.

Brodie, Mollyann, Annie Steffenson, Jamie Valdez, Rebecca Levin, and Roberto Suro. 2002. *2002 National Survey of Latinos.* Menlo Park, CA: Henry J. Kaiser Foundation and Pew Hispanic Center.

Brooke, James. 1995. "Attacks on U.S. Muslims Surge Even as Their Faith Holds." *New York Times,* August 28, A1, B7.

___. 1998. "Indians Striving to Save Their Languages." *New York Times*, April 9, A1, A20.

Brooks-Gunn, Jeanne, Pamela K. Klebanov, and Greg J. Duncan. 1996. "Ethnic Differences in Children's Intelligence Test Scores: Role of Economic Deprivation, Home Environment, and Maternal Characteristics." *Child Development*, April, 67: 396–408.

Brown, Dee. 1971. *Bury My Heart at Wounded Knee*. New York: Holt, Rinehart & Winston.

Brown, Patricia Leigh. 2003. "For the Muslim Prom Queen, There Are No Kings Allowed." *New York Times*, June 9, A1, A24.

Browne, Irene, ed. 2001. *Latinas and African American Women at Work: Race, Gender, and Economic Inequality*. New York: Russell Sage Foundation.

Brownstein, Andrew. 2001. "A Battle over a Name in the Land of the Sioux." *Chronicle of Higher Education*, February 23, 47: A46–A49.

Bruchfeld, Stéphane and Paul A. Levine. 2003. *Tell ye your children*. Stockholm: Living History Forum.

Bryan, Susan Montoya. 2006. "Navajo Power Plant Lease Approved, Opponents Vow To Fight." News from *Indian Country*, May 29, p. 6.

Bryson, Ken and Lynne M. Casper. 1999. "Co-Resident Grandparents and Grandchildren." *Current Population Reports* Ser. 823, No. 198. Washington, DC: U.S. Government Printing Office.

Buchholz, Barbara Ballinger. 2003. "Expanded Access." *Chicago Tribune*, January 26, sect. 16, 1R, 5R.

Buckley, Stephen. 2000. "Brazil's Racial Awakening." *Washington Post*, June 12, A 12.

Budig, Michelle J. 2002. "Male Advantage and the Gender Composition of Jobs: Who Rides the Glass Escalator?" *Social Problems*, 49(2): 258–277.

___. and Paula England. 2001. "The Wage Penalty for Motherhood." *American Sociological Review*, April, 66: 204–225.

Bukowcyk, John J. 1996. *Polish Americans and Their History: Community, Culture and Politics*. Pittsburgh: University of Pittsburgh Press.

Bunche Center. 2003. *Prime Time in Black and White: Not Much Is New for 2002*. Bunche Research Report 1 (1).

Bureau of the Census. 1975. *Historical Statistics of the United States, Colonial Times to 1970*. Washington, DC: U.S. Government Printing Office.

___. 1981. *Statistical Abstract of the United States, 1981*. Washington, DC: U.S. Government Printing Office.

___. 1988. *Statistical Abstract of the United States, 1988*. Washington, DC: U.S. Government Printing Office.

___. 1996. *Statistical Abstract of the United States, 1996*. Washington, DC: U.S. Government Printing Office.

___. 2001c. *Census 2000 PHC-T.6., Population by Race and Hispanic or Latino Origin in the United States*. Accessed February 5, 2001, at http://www.census.gov.

___. 2001d. *March 2001 Current Population Survey*. From Table HINC-01. Accessed February 1, 2002, at http://www.census.gov/hhes/www/income.html.

___. 2001e. *(NP-D1-A) Projections of the Resident Population by Age, Sex, Race, and Hispanic Origin: 1999 to 2100*. Washington, DC: U.S. Government Printing Office.

___. 2002a. *Table 1. United States—Race and Hispanic Origin: 1790–1990*. Internet Release Date: September 13, 2002.

___. 2002b. March 2002. "Current Population Survey." From Table HINC03. Accessed October 18, 2002, at http://www.census.gov.

___. 2003a. *Statistical Abstract of the United States, 2003*. Washington, DC: U.S. Government Printing Office.

___. 2003b. *Detailed List of Languages Spoken at Home for the Population 5 Years Ago Over by State: 2000*. Released February 5, 2003. Accessed August 1, 2003, at http://www.census/gov/population/www/cen2000/phc-t20.html.

___. 2003c. *Florida Leads in Growth of School-Age Population: Census Bureau Estimates Also Show Increasing State Diversity*. September 18, 2003, News Release, Table 3.

___. 2003d. *Characteristics of American Indians and Alaska Natives by Tribe and Language: 2000*. Washington, DC: U.S. Government Printing Office.

___. 2004a. *Statistical Abstract of the United States, 2004*. Washington, DC: U.S. Government Printing Office.

___. 2004b. *U.S. Interim Projections by Age, Sex, Race, and Hispanic Origin*. Released March 18, 2004, at http://www.census.gov/ipc/www/usinterimproj.

___. 2004c. *American Fact Finder: Census 2000 Survey File 3 (SF3)-Sample Data*, Tables P19 and P20. Accessed August 11, 2004, at http://factfinder.census.gov.

___. 2005a. *Statistical Abstract of the United States, 2004–2005*. Washington, DC: U.S. Government Printing Office.

___. 2005b. *Texas Becomes Nation's Newest "Majority-Minority" States*, Census Bureau Announces. CBO5-118. Washington, DC: U.S. Government Printing Office.

___. 2005c. *College Degree Nearly Doubles Annual Earnings, Census Bureau Reports*. CB05-38. Accessed October 1, 2006, at http://www.census.gov.

___. 2005d. Foreign-Born Population of the United States Current Population Survey–March 2004. Detailed Tables (PPL-176). Accessed at http://www.census.gov.

___. 2006a. *Statistical Abstract of the United States, 2005–2006*. Washington, DC: U.S. Government Printing Office.

___. 2006c. *2005 March Current Population Reports*. Detailed Tables. Accessed October 2 at http://www.census.gov.

Bureau of Citizenship and Immigration Services. 2003a. *Fiscal Year 2002 Yearbook of Immigrant Statistics*. http://www.bcis.gov.

___. 2006. Civics Flash Cards. Accessed February 3, 2006, at http://uscis.gov/graphics/citizenship/flashcards/questionaire.htm.

Bureau of Indian Affairs. 1970. *Answers to Your Questions about Indians*. Washington, DC: U.S. Government Printing Office.

___. 1986. *American Indians Today: Answers to Your Questions*. Washington, DC: U.S. Government Printing Office.

___. 1988. *Report of BIA Education: Excellence in Indian Education through the Effective School Process*. Washington, DC: U.S. Government Printing Office.

Bureau of Justice Statistics. 2004. *First Release from State Prisons 2001*. Washington, DC: Bureau of Justice Statistics.

Bureau of Labor Statistics. 2004a. *Women in the Labor Force: A Databook*. Washington, DC: U.S. Government Printing Office.

___. 2004. *Time-Use Survey*. Accessed September 14, 2004, at http://www.bls.gov/tus.

Burgess, Mike. 1992. "American Indian Religious Freedom Act Hearings". *News from Indian Country*, Late December, 8–9.

Bush, George W. 2001. *Islam Is Peace*. Accessed October 16, 2004, at http://www.whitehouse.gov/news/releases.

___. 2005. "President, Lieutenant General Honore Discuss Hurricane Relief in Louisiana." September 12. Accessed January 31, 2006, at http://www.whitehouse.gov.

Business and Professional Women. 2002. *Equal Pay Day 2002 Legislative Bankguard*, April 14, 2002, at http://www.bpwusa.org/Content/FairPay/Docy/NCPE.

Bustillo, Miguel. 2006. "Remarks Leave Nagin in a Not-So-Sweet Spot." *Los Angeles Times*, January 22.

Butler, John Sibley. 1996. "The Return of Open Debate." *Society*, March/April, 39: 11–18.

Butler, Robert N. 1990. "A Disease Called Ageism." *Journal of the American Geriatrics Society*, February, 38: 178–180.

Cainkar, Louise. 2006. Immigrants from the Arab World. Pp. 182–196 in *The New Chicago* edited by John P. Koval et al. Philadelphia, PA: Temple University Press.

Cairns, Ed and John Darby. 1998. "The Conflict in Northern Ireland." *American Psychologist* 56(7): 754–760.

Camarillo, Albert. 1993. "Latin Americans: Mexican Americans and Central Americans." Pp. 855–872 in *Encyclopedia of American Social History*, edited by Mary Koplec Coyton, Elliot J. Gorn, and Peter W. Williams. New York: Charles Scribner.

Camarota, Steven A. 2002. *Immigrants from the Middle East*. Washington DC: Center for Immigration Studies.

Canak, William and Laura Swanson. 1998. *Modern Mexico*. New York: McGraw-Hill.

Cañas, Jesus; Roberto Coronado and Robert W. Gilmer. 2006. "U.S. Mexico Deepen Economic Ties." *Southwest Economy* 1 (January/February). Accessible at http://www.dallasfed.org.

Capps, Randy, Ku Leighton, and Michael Fix. 2002. *How Are Immigrants Faring After Welfare Reform? Preliminary Evidence from Los Angeles and New York City*. Washington, DC: Urban Institute.

Carberry, Maegan. 2006. "Multicultural Chic", Chicago, *Red Eye*. February 16: 4–5.

Card, David, John DiNardo, and Eugena Estes. 1998. "The More Things Change: Immigrants and the Children of Immigrants in the 1940s, the 1970s, and the 1990s." Paper presented at the Joint Center for Poverty Research, Northwestern University of Chicago, April 9.

Carlson, Dawn S., K. Michele Kacmar, and Dwayne Whitten. 2006. "What Men Think They Knew About Executive Women." *Harvard Business Review*, September, 84: 28.

Carmichael, Stokely with Ekwueme Michael Thelwell. 2003. *The Life and Struggles of Stokely Carmichael (Kwame Ture)*. New York: Scribner.

Carnegie Foundation for the Advancement of Teaching. 1990. Native Americans and Higher Education: New Mood of Optimism. *Change*. January-February: 27–30.

Carrell, Michael R., Norbert F. Elbert, and Robert D. Hatfield. 2000. *Human Resource Management: Strategies for Managing a Diverse and Global Workforce*. 6th ed. Orlando, FL: Dryden Press.

Carrier, Jim. 2000. *Ten Ways to Fight Hate*. 2nd ed. Montgomery, AL: Tolerance.org.

Carroll, Joseph. 2006. "Public National Anthem Should Be Sung in English." The Gallup Poll, May 3.

Cart, Julie. 2001. "Natives Brace for a Paradise Loss." *Los Angeles Times*, May 23, A15.

___. 2006. "Painful Past, Iffy Future." *Los Angeles Times*, July 23, B1, B6.

Carter, Bill. 2001. "'Los Simpsons': Don't Have a Vaca, Man." *New York Times*, February 18, sec. WK, 3.

Carvajal, Doreen. 1996. "Diversity Pays Off in a Babel of Yellow Pages." *New York Times*, December 3, 1, 23.

Castañeda, Jorge G. 1995. "Ferocious Differences." *Atlantic Monthly*, July, 276: 68–69, 71–76.

___. 1996. "A Tale of Two Islands." *Los Angeles Times*, February 12, B5.

Catalano, Shannan M. 2006. Criminal Victimization, 2005. Bureau of Justice Statistics Bulletin, September: 1–12.

Catalyst. 2001. "Women Satisfied with Current Job in Financial Industry but Barriers Still Exist." Press Release July 25, 2001. Accessed January 31, 2002, at http://www.catalystwomen.org.

CBS New York. 2003. "Shame On You: Rockstar Video Games." Accessed November 15, 2003, at cbsnewyork.com.

Cerar, K. Melissa. 1995. *Teenage Refugees from Nicaragua Speak Out*. New York: Rosen Publishing.

CERT. 2006. "About CERT." Accessed September 25, at http://www.certredearth.com.

Chambers. 2005 Chambers Book of Facts. Edinburgh: Chambers Harrap Publishers.

Champagne, Duane. 1994. *Native America. Portrait of the Peoples*. Detroit: Visible Ink.

Chan, Sucheng. 1991. Asian Americans: An Interpretive History. 1994. Hmong Means Free Pb.

Chang, Patricia M. Y. 1997. "Female Clergy in the Contemporary Protestant Church: A Current Assessment." *Journal for the Scientific Study of Religion*, December, 36: 565–573.

Chase-Dunn, Christopher and Thomas D. Hall. 1998. "World-Systems in North America: Networks, Rise and Fall and Pulsations of Trade in Stateless Systems." *American Indian Culture and Research Journal*, 22(1): 23–72.

Chen, David W. and Somini Sengupta. 2001. "Not Yet Citizens but Eager to Fight for the U.S." *New York Times*, October 22, A1, B2.

Chicago Tribune. 2006. "Newark Is No. 1 in U.S. Ordinations," May 26: 12.

Children Now. 1998. *A Different World: Children's Perceptions of Race, Class, and the Media*. Oakland, CA: Children Now.

___. 2004. *2003–04 Fall Colors Prime Time Diversity Report*. Oakland, CA: Children Now.

Chin, Ko-lin. 1996. *Chinatown Gangs: Extortion, Enterprise, and Ethnicity*. New York: Oxford University Press.

Chirot, Daniel and Jennifer Edwards. 2003. "Making Sense of the Senseless: Understanding Genocide." *Contexts*, Spring, 12–19.

Christopulos, Diana. 1974. "Puerto Rico in the Twentieth Century: A Historical Survey." Pp. 123–163 in *Puerto Rico and Puerto Ricans: Studies in History and Society*, edited by Adalberto Lopez and James Petras. New York: Wiley.

Chu, Jeff and Nadia Mustafa 2006 "Between Two Worlds." *Time*, January 16:167:64–68.

Clark, Kenneth B. and Mamie P. Clark. 1947. "Racial Identification and Preferences in Negro Children." Pp. 169–178 in *Readings in Social Psychology*, edited by Theodore M. Newcomb and Eugene L. Hartley. New York: Holt, Rinehart & Winston.

Clary, Mike. 1997. "A City That Still Is Consumed by Castro," *Los Angeles Times*, January 1, A1, A26.

Cleaver, Kathleen. 1982. "How TV Wrecked the Black Panthers." *Channels*, November–December, 98–99.

Clemetson, Lynette. 2003. "Arab-Americans Gain a Higher Political Profile." *New York Times*, October 19.

___. 2004. "Some Younger U.S. Arabs Reassert Ethnicity." *New York Times*, January 11, 12.

Clemmitt, Marcia. 2005. "Intelligent Design." *CQ Researcher*, July 29, 95: 637–660.

Cloud, John. 2003. "The New Face of Gay Power." *Time*, October 13, 162: 52–56.

CNN Money. 2006. "Women CEOs for Fortune 500 Companies." Accessed October 11, at http://money.cnn.com.

Coates, Rodney D. 2004. "Critical Racial and Ethnic Studies—Profiling and Reparations." *American Behavioral Scientist*, March, 47: 873–878.

Cockburn, Andrew. 2003. "True Colors: Divided Loyalty in Puerto Rico." March, 203: 34–55.

Cognard-Black, Andrew J. 2004. "Will They Stay, or Will They Go? Sex—Atypical Among Token Men Who Teach." *Sociological Quarterly*, 45(1): 113–139.

Cohen, Sandy. 2006. "Gibson: 'I am not an anti-Semite.'" *Chicago Tribune*, August 2, 2.

Cohen, Steven M. 1988. *American Assimilation or Jewish Revival?* Bloomington: Indiana University Press.

___. 1991. *Content or Continuity? Alternative Bases for Commitment*. New York: American Jewish Committee.

Cohon, Samuel M. 1995. "Not in Our Town. The Courage to Resist Hatred." *The Chronicle*, 6–9, 36, 38, 44, 48–50.

Cole, David. 1999. *No Equal Justice: Race and Class in the American Criminal Justice System*. New York: The New Press.

Coleman, Arica L. 2006. "'Tell the Court I Love My (Indian) Wife' Interrogating Race and Self-Identity in *Loving v. Virginia*." *Souls*, 8 (1): 67–80.

Collins, Patricia Hill. 2000. *Black Feminist Thought: Knowledge, Consciousness, and the Politics of Empowerment*. 2nd ed. New York: Routledge.

Colón Morera, José Javier and José E. Rivera Santana. 2006. "New Dimensions in Civil Society Mobilization: The Struggle for Peace in Vieques." Pp. 207–236 in *Puerto Rico Under Colonial Rule*, edited by Ramón Bosque-Pérez and José Javier Colón Morera. Albany: State University of New York Press.

Comas-Díaz, Lillian, M. Brinton Lykes, and Renato D. Alarcón. 1998. "Ethnic Conflict and the Psychology of Liberation in Guatemala, Peru, and Puerto Rico." *American Psychologist*, July, 53: 778–792.

Comer, James P. and Alvin F. Poussaint. 1992. *Raising Black Children*. New York: Plume.

Commission on Civil Rights. 1976. *Fulfilling the Letter and Spirit of the Law: Desegregation of the Nation's Public Schools*. Washington, DC: U.S. Government Printing Office.

___. 1981. *Affirmative Action in the 1980s: Dismantling the Process of Discrimination*. Washington, DC: U.S. Government Printing Office.

___. 2003. *A Quiet Crisis: Federal Funding and Unmet Needs in Indian Country*. Washington, DC: U.S. Government Printing Office.

Commission on Wartime Relocation and Internment of Civilians. 1982a. *Recommendations*. Washington, DC: U.S. Government Printing Office.

___. 1982b. *Report*. Washington, DC: U.S. Government Printing Office.

Committee of 100. 2001. *American Attitudes towards Chinese Americans and Asian Immigrants*. New York: Committee of 100.

Conlin, Michelle. 2003. "The New Gender Gap." *Business Week*, May 26.

Connor, Walter. 1994. *Ethnonationalism: The Quest for Understanding*. Princeton, NJ: Princeton University Press.

Conver, Bill. 1976. "Group Chairman Lists Problems Endangering Jewish Family." *Peoria Journal Star*, December 4, A2.

"Converts to Judaism." 1982. *New York Times*, August 29, 23.

Conyers, James L., Jr. 1996. "A Case Study of Social Stratification: An Afrocentric Edification." *Western Journal of Black Studies*, Spring, 20: 9–15.

Coogan, Michael D. 2003. *The Illustrated Guide to World Religions*. Oxford University Press.

Cooper, Abraham and Harold Brackman. 2001. "Holocaust Deniers Spread Their Lies in the Middle East." *USA Today*, March 8, 15A.

Cooper, Mary H. 2004 "Voting Rights." *CQ Researcher*, October 29, 14: 901–924.

Cooper, Michael. 2005. "Vietnamese Shrimpers in the Gulf Become Refugees Again." *New York Times*, August 10, A12.

Cooper, Richard S., Charles N. Rotimi, and Ryk Ward. 1999. "The Puzzle of Hypertension in African Americans." *Scientific American*, February, 56–63.

Cooperman, Alan. 2005. "One Way to Pray?" *Washington Post National Weekly Edition*, September 5, 22: 10–11.

Cornacchia, Eugene J. and Dale C. Nelson. 1992. "Historical Differences in the Political Experiences of American Blacks and White Ethnics: Revisiting an Unresolved Controversy." *Ethnic and Racial Studies*, January, 15: 102–124.

Cornell, Stephen. 1984. "Crisis and Response in Indian–White Relations: 1960–1984." *Social Problems*, October, 32: 44–59.

___. 1996. "The Variable Ties That Bind: Content and Circumstance in Ethnic Processes." *Ethnic and Racial Studies*, April, 19: 265–289.

Cornell, Stephen and Joseph P. Kalt. 1990. "Pathways from Poverty: Economic Development and Institution-Building on American Indian Reservations." *American Indian Culture and Research Journal*, 14(1): 89–125.

___. 2003. *Alaska Native Self-Government and Service Delivery: What Works?* Tucson: Native Nations Institute for Leadership, Management, and Policy.

Correll, Joshua et al. 2002. "The Police Officer's Dilemma: Using Ethnicity to Disambiguate Potentially Threatening Individuals." *Journal of Personality and Social Psychology*, 83(6): 1314–1329.

Cose, Ellis. 1993. *The Rage of a Privileged Class*. New York: Harper-Collins.

Coser, Lewis A. 1956. *The Functions of Social Conflict*. New York: Free Press.

Coser, Lewis A. and Rose Laub Coser. 1974. *Greedy Institutions*. New York: Free Press.

Council on American-Islamic Relations. 2004. *Poll: 1-in-4 Americans Holds Anti-Muslim Views*. Accessed October 7, 2004, at http://www.cair-net.org.

Cox, James. 2002. "Activists Challenge Corporations That They Say Are Tied to Slavery." *USA Today*, February 21, 1A, 8A, 9A.

Cox, Oliver C. 1942. "The Modern Caste School of Social Relations." *Social Forces*, December, 21: 218–226.

Crenson, Matt. 2005. "Polluted Town Alarmed by Shortage of Sons." *Associated Press*, Accessed on December 18 at aol.com.

Cronje, Frans. 2006. "Education." Pp. 257–334 in *South Africa Survey 2004/2005*. Johannesburg: Institute of Race Relations.

Dahlburg, John-Thor. 1998. "Deal Okd to End 30 Years of 'Trouble' in Northern Ireland." *Los Angeles Times*, April 11, A1, A8–A9.

___. 2001. "A New World for Haitians." *Los Angeles Times*, September 4, A1, A9.

___. 2004a. "The Spanish-Speaking Heritage of the State Now Reflects All of Latin America, Not Just Cuba." *Los Angeles Times*, June 28, A1, A12.

___. 2004b. "The Cuban Americans Rush to Visit Kin While They Can." *Los Angeles Times*, June 30, A27.

Daitz, Ben. 2003. "Navajo Miners Battle a Deadly Legacy of Yellow Dust." *New York Times*, May 13, D5, D8.

Dang, Alain and Somjem Frnzer. 2004. *Black Same-Sex Households in the United States*. Washington, DC: National Gay and Lesbian Task Force Policy Institutes.

Daniels, Roger. 1972. *Concentration Camps, USA*. New York: Holt, Rinehart & Winston.

___. 1990. *Coming to America*. New York: HarperCollins.

Dannin, Robert. 2002. *Black Pilgrimage to Islam*. Cambridge, England: Oxford University Press.

Dansie, Roberto. 2004. "Curanderisno." *Indian Country Today*, December 8, C5.

Dart, Bob. 1998. "Preserving America: Lancaster County, PA." *Atlanta Journal and Constitution*, June 28.

Dart, John. 1997. "Poll Studies Chinese Americans, Religion." *Los Angeles Times*, July 5, B5.

David, Gary C. 2003. "Rethinking Who's an Arab American: Arab-American Studies in the New Millennium." *Al-Jadid*, Fall, 9.

___. 2004a. "Being Arab and Becoming Americanized: Forms of Mediated Assimilation in Metropolitan Detroit." Pp. 125–142 in *Muslim Minorities in the West*, edited by Yvonne Yazbeck Haddad and Jane I. Smith. Lanham, MD: Rowman and Littlefield.

___. 2004b. "Scholarship on Arab Americans Distorted Past 9/11." *Al-Jadid*, Winter/Spring, 26–27.

___. and Kenneth Kahtan Ayouby. 2004. "Perpetual Suspects and Permanent Others: Arab Americans and the War and Terrorism." Pp. 30–71 in *Guerras e Imigracioes*, edited by Marco Aurélio Machado de Oliveira. Universida de Federal de Mato Grosso Do Sul.

___. 2005. "Studying the Exotic Other in the Classroom: The Portrayal of Arab Americans in Educational Source Materials." *Multicultural Perspectives*, (July).

___. 2006. "The Creation of 'Arab American': Political Activism and Ethnic (Dis)Unity." *Critical Sociology* 32: forthcoming.

Davis, David Brion. 1966. *The Problem of Slavery in Western Culture*. Ithaca, NY: Cornell University Press.

Davis, James A, Tom W. Smith, and Peter V. Marsden. 2005. *General Social Surveys, 1972-2004: Cumulative Codebook*. Chicago: NORC.

Dawson, Michael C. and Rovana Popoff. 2004. "Reparations: Justice and Greed in Black and White." *DuBois Review* 1(1): 47–91.

De Anda, Roberto M. 2004. *Chicanas and Chicanos in Contemporary Society*. 2nd ed. Lanham, MD: Rowman and Littlefield & Bacon.

Death Penalty Information Center. 2006. *Facts About the Death Penalty, September 27, 2006*. Accessed October 1, 2006, at http://www.deathpenaltyinfo.org.

Degler, Carl N. 1971. *Neither Black nor White: Slavery and Race Relations in Brazil and the United States*. New York: Macmillan.

de la Garza, Rodolfo O., Louis DeSipio, F. Chris Garcia, John Garcia, and Angelo Falcon. 1992. *Latino Voices: Mexican, Puerto Rican, and Cuban Perspectives on American Politics*. Boulder, CO: Westview Press.

Dell'Angela, Tracy. 2005. "Dakota Indians Say Kids Trapped in 'School-to-Prison' Pipeline." *Chicago Tribune*, November 29, 1, 12.

DellaPergola, Sergio. 2005. "World Jewish Population, 2005." Pp. 87–122 in *American Jewish Yearbook 2005*, edited by David Singer and Lawrence Grossman. New York: American Jewish Committee.

Del Olmo, Frank. 2003. "Slow Motion Carnage at the Border." *Los Angeles Times*, May 18, M5.

Deloria, Vine, Jr. 1969. *Custer Died for Your Sins: An Indian Manifesto*. New York: Avon.

___. 1971. *Of Utmost Good Faith*. New York: Bantam.

___. 1992. "Secularism, Civil Religion, and the Religious Freedom of *American Indians.*" *American Indian Culture and Research Journal,* 16(2): 9–20.

___. 1995. *Red Earth, White Lies.* New York: Scribner's.

___. 2004. "Promises Made, Promises Broken." Pp. 143–159 in *Native Universe: Voices of Indian America,* edited by Gerald McMaster and Clifford E. Trofzer. Washington, DC: National Geographic.

___. and Clifford M. Lytle. 1983. *American Indians, American Justice,* Austin: University of Texas Press.

DeNavas-Walt, Carmen, Bernadette D. Proctor, and Cheryl Hill Lee. 2006. *Income, Poverty, and Health Insurance Coverage in the United States: 2005.* Current Population Reports, pp. 60–231. Washington, DC: U.S. Government Printing Office.

DePalma, Anthony. 1995. "Racism? Mexico's in Denial." *New York Times,* June 11, E4.

Department of Energy. 2000. *Final Report: Task Force against Racial Profiling.* Washington, DC: U.S. Government Printing Office.

Department of Interior. 2005. *Historical Accounting for Individual Indian Monies: A Progress Report.* Washington, DC: U.S. Government Printing Office.

Department of Justice. 2000. *The Civil Liberties Act of 1988: Redress for Japanese Americans.* Accessed June 29, 2000, at http://www.usdoj.gov/crt/ora/main.html.

___. 2001a. *Report to the Congress of the United States: A Review of Restrictions on Persons of Italian Ancestry During World War II.* Accessed February 1, 2002, at http://www.house.gov/judiciary/Italians.pdf.

___. 2004. *Uniform Crime Reports, 2004.* Washington, DC: U.S. Government Printing Office.

___. 2005. *Uniform Crime Reports, 2005.* Washington, DC: U.S. Government Printing Office.

Department of Labor. 1965. *The Negro Family: The Case for National Action.* Washington, DC: U.S. Government Printing Office.

___. 1995. *Good for Business: Making Full Use of the Nation's Capital.* Washington, DC: U.S. Government Printing Office.

___. 1998. *Work and Elder Care: Facts for Caregivers and Their Employers.* Accessed November 20, 1998, at http://www.dol.gov/dol/wb/public/wb_pubs/elderc.htm.

___. 2001. *Working in the 21st Century.* Washington, DC: U.S. Government Printing Office.

___. 2005. *Women in the Labor Force: A Databook.* Washington, DC: U.S. Government Printing Office.

Deutscher, Irwin, Fred P. Pestello, and H. Frances Pestello. 1993. *Sentiments and Acts.* New York: Aldine de Gruyter.

Diamond, Jared. 2003. "Globalization, Then." *Los Angeles Times,* September 14, M1, M3.

DiMaggio, Paul. 2005. "Cultural Capital." Pp. 167–170 in *Encyclopedia of Social Theory,* edited by George Ritzer. Thousand Oaks, CA: Sage Publications.

Dimant, Tamara. 2006. "The Economy." Pp. 51–256 in *South Africa Survey 2004/2005.* Johannesburg: South African Institute of Race Relations.

Dinnerstein, Leonard. 1994. *Anti-Semitism in America.* New York: Oxford University Press.

Dionne, E. J., Jr. 1988. "Jackson Share of Votes by Whites Triples in '88." *New York Times,* June 13, B7.

Disch, Estelle. 1997. *Reconstructing Gender: A Multicultural Anthology.* Mountain View, CA: Mayfield.

Dixon, Robyn. 2003. "Crime in South Africa More Vexing and Vicious." *Los Angeles Times,* May 4,. A1, A5.

Dolan, Maura. 2000. "State Justices Deal New Set Back to Affirmative Action." *Los Angeles Times,* December 1.

Domino, John C. 1995. *Sexual Harassment and the Courts.* New York: HarperCollins.

Dorris, Michael. 1988. "For the Indians, No Thanksgiving." *New York Times,* November 24, A23.

Doyle, James A. and Michele A. Paludi. 1998. *Sex and Gender: The Human Experience,* 4th ed. New York: McGraw-Hill.

Drinkard, Jim. 2006. "Tubes' Special Status a Product of Law and History." *USA Today,* January 31, 6A.

2006. "Tribes' Political Giving Targeted." *USA Today,* January 31, A1.

Du Bois, W. E. B. 1903. *The Souls of Black Folks: Essays and Sketches.* Reprinted in 1961. New York: Facade Publications.

___. 1935. "Does the Negro Need Separate Schools?" *Journal of Negro Education,* July, 1: 328–335.

___. 1939. *Black Folk: Then and Now.* New York: Holt, Rinehart & Winston.

___. 1952. *Battle for Peace: The Story of My 83rd Birthday.* New York: Masses and Mainstream.

___. 1961. *The Souls of Black Folk.* New York: Fawcett.

___. 1968. *Dusk of Dawn.* New York: Schocken.

___. 1969a. [1900] *An ABC of Color.* New York: International Publications.

___. 1969b. *The Suppression of the African Slave-Trade to the United States of America, 1638–1870.* New York: Schocken.

___. 1970. *The Negro American Family.* Cambridge, MA: MIT Press.

___. 1996. *The Philadelphia Negro: A Social Study.* Philadelphia: University of Pennsylvania Press (originally published in 1899).

Duberman, Martin. 1993. *Stonewall.* New York: Dutton.

Dudley, Carl S. and David A. Roozen. 2001. *Faith Communities Today.* Hartford, CT: Hartford Seminary.

Dunn, Ashley. 1994. "Southeast Asians Highly Dependent on Welfare in U.S." *New York Times,* May 19, A1, A20.

Durant, Thomas J., Jr. and Joyce S. Louden. 1986. "The Black Middle Class in America: Historical and Contemporary Perspectives." *Phylon,* December, 47: 253–263.

Duszak, Thomas. 1997. "Lattimer Massacre Centennial Commemoration." *Polish American Journal,* August.

Dyson, Michael Eric. 1995. *Making Malcolm: The Myth and Meaning of Malcolm X.* New York: Oxford University Press.

___. 2005. *Is Bill Cosby Right?* Perseus Books.

Dzidzienyo, Anani. 1987. Brazil. In Jay A. Sigler, ed., *International Handbook on Race and Race Relations.* New York: Greenwood Press.

Early, Gerald. 1994. "Defining Afrocentrism". *Journal of Blacks in Higher Education,* Winter, 1: 46.

Echaveste, Maria. 2005. "Target Employees." *American Prospect,* November, A10–A11.

Eckholm, Erik. 2006. "Plight Deepens for Black Men, Studies Warn." *New York Times,* March 20, A1, A18.

Eckstrom, Kevin. 2001. "New, Diverse Take Spot on Catholic Altars." *Chicago Tribune,* August 31, 8.

The Economist. 2004a. "An Amish Exception." *The Economist,* February 7, 33.

___. 2004b. "Who's Winning the Fight?" *The Economist,* July 3, 38.

___. 2004c. "Indigenous People in South America: A Political Awakening." *The Economist,* February 21, 35–37.

___. 2004d. "The Curse of Nepotism." *The Economist,* January 10, p. 27.

___. 2005a. "South African Race Relations: If Only the Adults Would Behave Like the Children." *The Economist,* April 23, 25–27.

___. 2005b. "The Status of Gaza: Now Who Takes the Blame?" *The Economist,* August 27, 39.

___. 2005c. "Israel and Palestine: Even More Separate." *The Economist,* October 22, 47–48.

___. 2006a. "Canada: Ulterior Motives." *The Economist,* June 24, 44.

___. 2006b. "Brazil: No Black and White Matter." *The Economist,* July 15, 38.

___. 2006c. "Chasing the Rainbow: A Survey of South Africa" April 8: 1–12.

Edles, Laura Desfor. 2004. "Rethinking 'Race', 'Ethnicity' and 'Culture': Is Hawaii the 'Model Minority' State?" *Ethnic and Racial Studies,* January, 27: 37–45.

Edmonds, Patricia. 1995. "Gambling's Backers Find It Isn't a Sure Bet." *USA Today,* December 29, A1, A2.

Egan, Timothy. 1998. "New Prosperity Brings New Conflict to Indian Country." *New York Times,* March 8, 1, 22.

Eitle, Tamela McNulty. 2002. "Special Education on Racial Segregation: Understanding Variation in the Representation of Black Students in Educable Mentally Handicapped Programs." *Sociological Quarterly,* 43(4): 575–605.

El Nasser, Haya. 1997. "Varied Heritage Claimed and Extolled by Millions." *USA Today*, May 8, 1A, 2A.

Elkins, Stanley. 1959. *Slavery: A Problem in American Institutional and Intellectual Life*. Chicago: University of Chicago Press.

Elliott, Andrea. 2006. "More Muslims Are Coming to U.S. After a Decline in Wake of 9/11" *New York Times*, September 10, 1, 24.

Ely, Robin J., Debra E. Meyerson, and Martin N. Davidson. 2006. Rethinking Political Correctness. *Harvard Business Review*, September, 84: 79–87.

Engen, Rodney L., Sara Stern, and George S. Bridges. 2002. "Racial Disparities in the Punishment of Youth: A Theoretical and Empirical Assessment of the Literature." *Social Problems*, 49(2): 194–220.

Epstein, Cynthia Fuchs. 1999. "The Major Myth of the Women's Movement." *Dissent*, Fall, 83–111.

Equal Employment Opportunity Commission. 2001. Age Discrimination in Employment Act (ADEA) Changes FY 1992–FY 2000. Accessed December 10, 2001, at http://www.eeoc.gov/stats/adea.html.

Erdmans, Mary Patrice. 1998. *Opposite Poles: Immigrants and Ethnics in Polish Chicago, 1976–1990*. University Park: Pennsylvania State University.

___. 2006. "New Chicago Polonia: Urban and Suburban." Pp. 115–127 in *The New Chicago*, edited by John Koval et al. Philadelphia: Temple University Press.

Eschbach, Karl and Kalman Applebaum. 2000. "Who Goes to Powwows? Evidence from the Survey of American Indians and Alaskan Natives." *American Indian Culture and Research Journal*, 24(2): 65–83.

Espiritu, Yen Le. 1992. *Asian American Panethnicity: Bridging Institutions and Identities*. Philadelphia: Temple University Press.

___. 1996. "Colonial Oppression, Labour Importation, and Group Formation: Filipinos in the United States." *Ethnic and Racial Studies*, January, 19: 29–48.

___. and Diane L. Wolf. 2001. "The Paradox of Assimilation: Children of Filipino Immigrants in San Diego." Pp. 157–186 in *Ethnicities: Children of Immigrants in America*, edited by Ruben G. Rumbaut and Alejandro Portes. Berkeley: University of California Press.

Fallows, Marjorie R. 1979. *Irish Americans: Identity and Assimilation*. England Cliffs, NJ: Prentice-Hall.

Farnsworth, Clyde H. 1996. "Canada's Justice System Faces Charges of Racism." *New York Times*, January 28, 3.

Farrell, Elizabeth F. 2006. A Protest Topples a President. *Chronicle of Higher Education*, 53, November 10: A39–A41.

Feagin, Joe R., Hernán Vera, and Pinar Batur. 2000. *White Racism*. 2nd ed. New York: Routledge.

___. and Eileen O'Brien. 2003. *White Men on Race, Power, Privilege, and the Shaping of Cultural Consciousness*. Boston: Beacon Press.

Fernandez, Manny and Kareem Fahim. 2006. "5 on Plane Are Detained at Newark, but Later Freed." *New York Times*, May 7, 29.

Ferree, Myra Marx and Beth B. Hess. 1994. *Controversy and Coalition: The New Feminist Movement across Three Decades of Change*, rev. ed. New York: Twayne.

Files, John. 2004. "U.S. Is Ordered to Tell Indians Before Selling Trust Property." *New York Times* October 4, A17.

Finder, Alan. 1994. "Muslim Gave Racist Speech, Jackson Says." *New York Times*, January 23, 21.

Fine, Gary Alan. 2004. "Forgotten Classic: The Robbers Cave Experiment." *Sociological Forum*, December, 19: 663–666.

Fine, Michelle and Adrienne Asch. 1981. "Disabled Women: Sexism without the Pedestal." *Journal of Sociology and Social Welfare*, July, 8: 233–248.

___. 1988a. "Disability beyond Stigma: Social Interaction, Discrimination, and Activism." *Journal of Social Issues*, 44(1): 3–21.

___. 1988b. *Women with Disabilities: Essays in Psychology, Culture, and Politics*. Philadelphia: Temple University Press.

Finestein, Israel. 1988. "The Future of American Jewry." *The Jewish Journal of Sociology*, December, 30:121–125.

Fing, Jing, Shantha Madhavan, and Michael H. Alderman. 1996. "The Association between Birthplace and Mortality from Cardiovascular Causes among Black and White Residents of New York City." *New England Journal of Medicine*, November 21, 335: 1545–1551.

Fiola, Jan. 1989. Race Relations in Brazil: A Reassessment of the "Racial Democracy" Thesis. Paper presented at the annual meeting of the Midwest Sociological Society, St. Louis.

Fix, Michael, Wendy Zimmerman, and Jeffery S. Passel. 2001. *The Integration of Immigrant Families in the United States*. Washington, DC: The Urban Institute.

Fixico, Donald L. 1988. "The Federal Policy of Termination and Relocation, 1945–1960." Pp. 260–277 in *The American Indian Experience*, edited by Phillip Weeks. Arlington Heights, IL: Forum Press.

Fleischman, Jeffrey. 2004. "New Anti-Semitism Stirs Old Anxieties." *Los Angeles Times*, March 27, A1, A6.

Flexner, Eleanor. 1959. *Century of Struggle: The Women's Rights Movement in the United States*. Cambridge, MA: Harvard University Press.

Foerstrer, Amy. 2004. "Race, Identity, and Belonging: 'Blackness' and the Struggle for Solidarity in a Multiethnic Labor Union." *Social Problems*, 51(3): 386–409.

Folkhart, Bart A. 1995. "Maggie Kuhn, 89; Iconoclastic Founder of Gray Panthers." *Los Angeles Times*, April 23, A34.

Foner, Eric. 2006. *Forever Free: The Story of Emancipation and Reconstruction*. New York: Knopf.

Fong, Stanley L. M. 1965. "Assimilation of Chinese in America: Changes in Orientation and Perception." *American Journal of Sociology*, November, 71: 265–273.

___. 1973. "Assimilation and Changing Social Roles of Chinese Americans." *Journal of Social Issues*, 29(2): 115–127.

___. 2002. *The Contemporary Asian American Experience: Beyond the Model Minority*. 2nd ed. Upper Saddle River, NJ: Prentice Hall.

Fox, Elaine. 1992. "Crossing the Bridge: Adaptive Strategies among Navajo Health Care Workers." *Free Inquiry in Creative Sociology*, May, 20: 25–34.

Fox, Stephen. 1990. *The Unknown Internment*. Boston: Twayne.

Foxman, Abraham H. 2006. "9/11 Conspiracy Theories Take Root in Arab/Muslim World." *Jewish News Weekly*, September 8.

Foy, Paul. 2006. "Interior Rejects Goshute Nuclear Waste Stockpile." *Indian Country Today* September 18, 20: 1.

Frankel, Bruce. 1995. "N.Y.'s 'Jewish Rosa Parks' Wins Bus Battle." *USA Today*, March 17, 4A.

Frankenberg, Erica, Chungmei Lee, and Gary Orfield. 2003. *A Multiracial Society with Segregated Schools: Are We Losing the Dream?* Cambridge, MA: Civil Rights Project, Harvard University.

Franklin, John Hope and Alfred A. Moss, Jr. 2000. *From Slavery to Freedom: A History of African Americans*. 8th ed. New York: McGraw-Hill.

Frazier, E. Franklin. 1942. The Negro Family in Bahia, Brazil. *American Sociological Review*, August, 7: 465–478.

___. 1957. *Black Bourgeois: The Rise of a New Middle Class*. New York: Free Press.

___. 1964. *The Negro Church in America*. New York: Schocken.

Freedman, Samuel G. 2003. "*Sex and the City* Celebrates Judaism." *USA Today*, July 17, 13A.

___. 2004. "Latino Parents Decry Bilingual Programs." *New York Times*, July 14, A21.

Freeman, Jo. 1973. "The Origins of the Women's Liberation Movement." *American Journal of Sociology*, January, 78: 792–811.

___. 1975. *The Politics of Women's Liberation*. New York: David McKay.

___. 1983. "On the Origins of Social Movements. Pp. 1–30 in *Social Movements of the Sixties and Seventies*, edited by Jo Freeman. New York: Longman.

Freyre, Gilberto. 1986. *The Masters and the Slaves: A Study in the Development of Brazilian Civilization*. Berkeley: University of California Press.

Friedan, Betty. 1963. *The Feminine Mystique*. New York: Dell.

___. 1981. *The Second Stage*. New York: Summit Books.

___. 1991. "Back to the Feminine Mystique?" *The Humanist,* January–February, 51: 26–27.

Friends Committee on National Legislation. 1993. "American Indian Religious Freedom." *News from Indian Country,* Mid-February, 8.

Fryer, Ronald G. 2006. "Acting White." *Education Next,* Winter: 53–59.

Fuchs, Estelle and Robert J. Havighurst. 1972. *To Live on This Earth: American Indian Education.* Garden City, NY: Doubleday.

Fuller, Chevon. 1998. "Service Redlining." *Civil Rights Journal,* Fall, 3: 33–36.

Gaines, Patrice. 2005. "Political Report: Black Women, White Men Face Similar Confinement Rates." *Focus,* January/February, 33: 7.

Galarza, Ernesto. 1964. *Merchants of Labor: The Mexican Bracero Story.* Santa Barbara, CA: McNally & Loften.

Gallagher, Mari. 2005. *Chain Reaction: Income, Race, and Access to Chicago's Major Player Grocers.* Chicago: Metro Chicago Information Center.

Gallup. 2004a. *Poll Topics and Trends: Religion.* Accessed August 2, 2004, at http://www.gallup.com.

___. 2004b. *Focus on Gay and Lesbian Marriages.* Accessed April 14, 2004, at http://www.gallup.com.

___. 2006a. *Gallup Poll: Immigration June 8–25.* Accessed September 15, 2006, at http://www.pollingreport.com.

___. 2006b. Religion. Accessed November 26, 2006 at http://www.gallup.com.

Gallup, George H. 1972. *The Gallup Poll, Public Opinion, 1935–1971.* New York: Random House.

Gans, Herbert J. 1956. "American Jewry: Present and Future." *Commentary,* May, 21: 424–425.

___. 1979. "Symbolic Ethnicity: The Future of Ethnic Groups and Cultures in America." *Ethnic and Racial Studies,* January, 2: 1–20.

___. 1995. *The War against the Poor: The Underclass and Antipoverty Policy.* New York: Basic Books.

Gardner, Marilyn. 2003. "This View of Seniors Just Doesn't 'Ad' Up." *Christian Science Monitor,* January 15, 15.

Garfinkel, Herbert. 1959. *When Negroes March.* New York: Atheneum.

Garner, Roberta. 1996. *Contemporary Movements and Ideologies.* New York: McGraw-Hill.

Gartner, Alan and Tom Joe, eds. 1987. *Images of the Disabled, Disabled Images.* New York: Praeger.

Gary, Lawrence E., Lula A. Beatty, Greta L. Berry, and Mary D. Price. 1983. *Stable Black Families: Final Report.* Washington, DC: Institute for Urban Affairs and Research, Howard University.

Gates, Gary J. 2006. *Same-Sex Couples and the Gay, Lesbian, Bisexual Population: New Estimates from the American Community Survey.* Los Angeles: Williams Institute.

Gerstenfeld, Phyllis B. and Diana R. Grant. 2003. "Hate Online: A Content Analysis of Extremist Internet Sites." *Analysis of Social Issues and Public Policy,* 3(No. 1): 29–44.

Gerth, H. H. and C. Wright Mills. 1958. *From Max Weber: Essays in Sociology.* New York: Galaxy Books.

Getlin, Josh. 1998. "Leaving an Impact on American Culture." *Los Angeles Times,* April 22, A1, A26, A27.

Gibbs, Nancy. 2001. "A Whole New World." *Time,* June 11, 36–45.

Girardelli, Davide. 2004. "Commodified Identities: The Myth of Italian Food in the United States." *Journal of Communication Inquiry,* October, 28: 307–324.

Gittler, Joseph B., ed. 1981. *Jewish Life in the United States: Perspectives from the Social Sciences.* New York: New York University Press.

Gladwell, Malcolm. 1996. "Discrimination: It's Just a Bus Stop Away." *Washington Post National Weekly Edition,* February 19, 13: 33.

Glanz, James. 2000. "Amid Race Profiling Claims, Asian Americans Avoid Labs." *New York Times,* July 25, A1, A12.

Glazer, Nathan. 1971. "The Issue of Cultural Pluralism in America Today." Pp. 2–8 in *Pluralism beyond Frontier: Report of the San Francisco Consultation on Ethnicity.* San Francisco: American Jewish Committee.

___. 1990. "American Jewry or American Judaism?" *Society,* November–December, 28 14–20.

___. and Daniel Patrick Moynihan. 1970. *Beyond the Melting Pot: The Negroes, Puerto Ricans, Jews, Italians, and Irish of New York City.* 2nd ed. Cambridge: MIT Press.

Gleason, Philip. 1980. "American Identity and Americanization." pp. 31–58 in *Harvard Encyclopedia of American Ethnic Groups,* edited by Stephen Therstromm. Cambridge: Belknap Press of Harvard University Press.

Glionna, John M. 2004. "Finding a Voice in Politics." *Los Angeles Times,* May 22, A1, A22.

Gobodo-Madikizela, Pumla. 2003. *A Human Being Died That Night.* New York: Houghton Mifflin.

Goering, John M. 1971. "The Emergence of Ethnic Interests: A Case of Serendipity." *Social Forces,* March, 48: 379–384.

Goering, Laurie. 1994. "Beneath Utopian Façade, Brazilians Uncover Racism" *Chicago Tribune,* December 20: 1, 11.

Gold, Michael. 1965. *Jews without Money.* New York: Avon.

Gold, Steven J. 2001. *Arab Americans in Detroit.* Accessed October 15, 2004, at http://www.commurb.org/features/sgold/detroit.html.

Goldscheider, Calvin. 2003. "Are American Jews Vanishing Again?" *Contexts,* Winter, 18–24.

Goldstein, Sidney and Calvin Goldscheider. 1968. *Jewish Americans: Three Generations in a Jewish Community.* Englewood Cliffs, NJ: Prentice Hall.

Gompers, Samuel and Herman Gustadt. 1908. *Meat vs. Rice: American Manhood against Asiatic Coolieism: Which Shall Survive?* San Francisco: Asiatic Exclusion League.

Gooding, Caroline. 1994. *Disabling Laws, Enabling Acts: Disability Rights in Britain and America.* Boulder, CO: Westview.

Goodnough, Abby. 2004. "Honor for Dr. King Splits Florida City, and Faces Reversal." *New York Times,* May 10, A1, A20.

Goodstein, Laurie. 2001. "As Attacks' Impact Recedes a Return to Religion as Usual." *New York Times,* November 26, A1, B6.

___. 2004. "Muslim Women Seeking a Place in the Mosque." New York Times, July 22, A1, A16.

___. 2005. "Issuing Rebuke, Judge Rejects Teaching of Intelligent Design." *New York Times,* December 21, A1, A21.

Gordon, Anthony and Richard M. Horowitz. 1997. "Will Your Grandchildren Be Jewish?" Unpub. research based on a 1990 National Jewish Population Survey and the 1991 New York Jewish Population Study.

Gordon, Milton M. 1964. *Assimilation in American Life: The Role of Race, Religion, and National Origins.* New York: Oxford University Press.

Gordon, Wendell. 1975. "A Case for a Less Restrictive Border Policy." *Social Science Quarterly,* December, 56: 485–491.

Gouldner, Alvin. 1970. *The Coming Crisis in Western Sociology.* New York: Basic Books.

Gove, Walter R. 1980. *The Labeling of Deviance.* 2nd ed. Beverly Hills, CA: Sage Publications.

Graham, Lawrence Otis. 1995. *Member of the Club: Reflections on Life in a Racially Polarized World.* New York: HarperCollins.

Greeley, Andrew M. 1974a. *Ethnicity in the United States: A Preliminary Reconnaissance.* New York: Wiley.

___. 1974b. "Political Participation among Ethnic Groups in the United States: A Preliminary Reconnaissance." *American Journal of Sociology,* July, 80: 170–204.

___. 1977. *The American Catholic.* New York: Basic Books.

___. 1981. The *Irish Americans: The Rise to Money and Power.*

Greenhouse, Linda. 1996. "Case on Government Interface in Religion Tied to Separation of Powers." *New York Times,* October 16, C23.

___. 2003a. "Justices Back Affirmative Action by 5–4. But Wider Vote Bans a Racial Point System." *New York Times,* June 24, A1, A25.

___. 2003b. "Justices, 6-3, Legalize Gay Sexual Conduct in Sweeping Reversal of Courts '86 Ruling." *New York Times,* June 27, A1, A16–A17.

___. 2004. "Justices Find States Can Be Liable for Not Making Townhouses Accessible to Disabled." *New York Times,* May 18.

Greenhouse, Steven. 2001. "Fear and Poverty Sicken Many Migrant Workers in the U.S." *New York Times,* May 13, 14.

Greenwald, Anthony G., Mark A. Oakes, and Hunter Hoffman. 2003. "Targets of Discrimination: Effects of Race on Responses to Weapon Holders." *Journal of Experimental Social Psychology*, July, 39: 399–405.

Grieco, Elizabeth M. 2001. *The Native Hawaiian and Other Pacific Islander Population 2000*. Brief C2KBR/01-14. Washington, DC: U.S. Government Printing Office.

___. and Rachel C. Cassidy. 2001. "Overview of Race and Hispanic Origin." *Current Population Reports* Ser. CENBR/01-1. Washington, DC: U.S. Government Printing Office.

Grimshaw, Allen D. 1969. *Racial Violence in the United States*. Chicago: Aldine.

Grodsky, Eric and Devah Pager. 2001. "The Structure of Disadvantage: Individual and Occupational Determinants of the Black-White Wage Gap." *American Sociological Review*, August, 66: 542–567.

Guerin-Gonzales, Camille. 1994. *Mexican Workers and American Dreams*. New Brunswick, NJ: Rutgers University Press.

Guest, Kenneth J. 2003. *God in Chinatown: Religion and Survival in New York's Evolving Immigrant Community*. New York, New York: University Press.

Guglielmo, Jennifer and Saleno Salvatore, eds. 2003. *Are Italians White?* New York: Routledge.

Guttmacher Institute, The Alan. 2004. *An Overview of Abortion in the United States*. Accessed September 27, 2004 at http://www.agi-usa.org.

Guzmán, Betsy. 2001. *The Hispanic Population*. Census 2000 Brief Series C2kBR/01-3. Washington, DC: U.S. Government Printing Office.

Haak, Gerald O. 1970. "Co-opting the Oppressors: The Case of the Japanese-Americans." *Society*, October, 7: 23–31.

Hacker, Andrew. 1995. *Two Nations: Black and White, Separate, Hostile, and Unequal*, expanded and updated ed. New York: Ballantine.

Hacker, Helen Mayer. 1951. "Women as a Minority Group." *Social Forces*, October, 30: 60–69.

___. 1974. "Women as a Minority Group: Twenty Years Later." Pp. 124–134 in *Who Discriminates against Women*, edited by Florence Denmark. Beverly Hills, CA: Sage Publications.

Haeri, Shaykh Fadhilalla. 2004. *The Thoughtful Guide to Islam*. Alresford, UK: O Books.

Hagenbaugh, Barbara. 2006. "Sending Money Back Has Vital Role." *USA Today*, April 11, 2B.

Hallinan, Maureen T. 2003. *Ability Grouping and Student Learning*. Pp. 95–140 in Brookings Papers on Education Policy, edited by Diane Ravitch. Washington, DC: Brookings Institution Press.

Handlin, Oscar. 1951. *The Uprooted: The Epic Story of the Great Migrations that Made the American People*. New York: Grossett and Dunlap.

Hansen, Marcus Lee. 1952. "The Third Generation in America." *Commentary*, November, 14: 493–500.

Harlan, Louis R. 1972. *Booker T. Washington: The Making of a Black Leader*. New York: Oxford University Press.

Harlow, Caroline Wolf. 2005. *Hate Crime Reported by Victims and Police*. Bureau of Justice Statistics Special Report, November.

Hartocullis, Anemona. 2006. "For Some Gays, a Right They Can Forsake." *New York Times*, July 30, sect. ST, 2.

Harris, Marvin. 1964. *Patterns of Race in the Americas*. New York: Norton.

Hassaballa, Hesham A. 2004. "The Koran Commands Muslims to Use Vote." *Chicago Tribune*, September 12, sec. 2, 1, 6.

Haub, Carl. 2006. *2006 World Population Data Sheet*. Washington, DC: U.S. Population Reference Bureau.

Hawaii Department of Health. 2001. Annual Statistics 2000, A46–A55. Accessed March 20, 2002, at http://www.hawaii.gov.

Hawkins, Hugh. 1962. *Booker T. Washington and His Critics: The Problem of Negro Leadership*. Boston: Heath.

Hays, Kristen L. 1994. "Topeka Comes Full Circle." *Modern Maturity*, April–May, 34.

He, Wan, Manisha Sengupta, Victoria A. Velkoff, and Kimberly A. DeBarros. 2005. "65+ in the United States: 2005." *Current Population Reports*. Ser. P23. No. 209. Washington, DC: U.S. Government Printing Office.

Hechinger, Fred M. 1987. "Bilingual Programs." *New York Times*, April 7, C10.

Heer, David M. and Amgra Grossbard-Shectman. 1981. "The Impact of the Female Marriage Squeeze and the Contraceptive Revolution on Sex Roles and the Women's Liberation Movement in the United States, 1960 to 1975." *Journal of Marriage and the Family*, February, 43: 49–76.

Heilman, Madeline E. 2001. "Description and Prescription: How Gender Stereotypes Present Women's Ascent Up the Organizational Ladder." *Journal of Social Issues*, 57 (4): 657–674.

Hein, Jeremy. 2000. "Interpersonal Discrimination against Hmong Americans: Parallels and Variation in Microlevel Racial Inequality." *Sociological Quarterly*, 41(3): 413–429.

Hemlock, Doreen A. 1996. "Puerto Rico Loses Its Edge." *New York Times*, September 21, 17, 30.

Henig, Samantha. 2006. "Colleges Reach Out to American Indians." *Chronicle of Higher Education*, September 15 (53): A39–A41.

Hennessy-Fiske, Molly. 2006. "The Town That Didn't Look Away." *Los Angeles Times*, July 23, A1, A26.

Henry, William A., III. 1994. "Pride and Prejudice." *Time*, February 28, 143: 21–27.

Hentoff, Nicholas. 1984. "Dennis Banks and the Road Block to Indian Ground." *Village Voice*, October, 29: 19–23.

Hequembourg, Amy and Jorge Arditi. 1999. "Fractured Resistances: The Debate over Assimilationism among Gays and Lesbians in the United States." *Sociological Quarterly*, 40(4): 663–680.

Herberg, Will. 1983. *Protestant—Catholic—Jew: An Essay in American Religious Sociology*, rev. ed. Chicago: University of Chicago Press.

Hero, Rodney. 1995. *Latinos and U.S. Politics*. New York: HarperCollins.

Herrnstein, Richard J. and Charles Murray. 1994. *The Bell Curve: Intelligence and Class Structure in American Life*. New York: Free Press.

Herschthal, Eric. 2004. "Indian Students Discuss Pros, Cons of Arranged Marriages." *Daily Princetonian*, October 20.

Herskovits, Melville J. 1930. *The Anthropometry of the American Negro*. New York: Columbia University Press.

___. 1941. *The Myth of the Negro Past*. New York: Harper.

Hewlett, Sylvia Ann and Carolyn Buck Liace. 2005. "Off-Ramps and On-Ramps: Keeping Talented Women on the Road to Success." *Harvard Business Review*, March: 43–54.

Hickman, Matthew J. 2003. *Tribal Law Enforcement, 2000*. Bureau of Justice Statistics Fact Sheet (January).

Higham, John. 1966. "American Anti-Semitism Historically Reconsidered." Pp. 237–258 in *Jews in the Mind of America*, edited by Charles Herbert Stember. New York: Basic Books.

Hilberg, Soleste, and Tharp, Ronald G. 2002. *Theoretical Perspectives, Research Findings, and Classroom Implications of the Learning Styles of American Indian and Alaska Native Students*. Washington, DC: Eric Digest.

Hill, Herbert. 1967. "The Racial Practices of Organized Labor: The Age of Gompers and After." Pp. 365–402 in *Employment, Race, and Poverty*, edited by Arthur M. Ross and Herbert Hill. New York: Harcourt, Brace & World.

Hill, Robert B. 1999. *The Strengths of African American Families: Twenty-Five Years Later*. Lanham, MD: University Press of America.

Himmelfarb, Harold S. 1982. "Research on American Jewish Identity and Identification: Progress, Pitfalls, and Prospects." Pp. 56–95 in *Understanding American Jewry*, edited by Marshall Sklare. New Brunswick, NJ: Transaction Books.

Hirsley, Michael. 1991. "Religious Display Needs Firm Count." *Chicago Tribune*, December 20, Section 2, 10.

Hochschild, Arlie Russell. 1990. "The Second Shift: Employed Women Are Putting in Another Day of Work at Home". *Utne Reader*, March–April, 38: 66–73.

___. 1997. "Time for Change." *Ms.*, September/October, 8: 39–40.

___. and Anne Machung. 1989. *The Second Shift*. New York: Viking.

Hochschild, Jennifer L. 1995. *Facing Up to the American Dream: Race, Class, and the Soul of the Nation*. Princeton, NJ: Rutgers University Press.

Hoffer, Thomas B. et al. 2001. *Doctorate Recipients from United States Universities: Summary Report 2000*. Chicago: National Opinion Research Center.

Holder, Kelly. 2006. "Voting and Registration in the Election of November 2004." *Current Population Reports*. Series P20. No. 556. Washington, DC: U.S. Government Printing Office.

Hooks, Bell. 1994. "Black Students Who Reject Feminism." *The Chronicle of Higher Education*, July 13, 60: A44.

Hosokawa, Bill. 1969. *Nisei: The Quiet Americans*. New York: Morrow.

Hubbard, Amy S. 1993. "U.S. Jewish Community Responses to the Changing Strategy of the Palestinian Nationalist Movement: A Pilot Study." Paper presented at the Annual Meeting of the Eastern Sociological Society, Boston.

Hudgins, John L. 1992. "The Strengths of Black Families Revisited." *The Urban League Review*, Winter, 15: 9–20.

Hull, Anne. 2003. Translating "Don't Ask, Don't Tell." *Washington Post National Weekly Edition*, December 21: 30–31.

Human Rights Campaign. 2006. Marriage, Relationship Recognition. Accessed December 11, 2006 at http://www.hrc.org.

Human Rights Watch. 1998. *Losing the Vote: The Impact of Felony Disenfranchisement Laws in the United States*. Washington, DC: Human Rights Watch.

___. 2002. "Florida Ex-Offenders Barred from Vote Decisive in Election." Accessed February 1, 2002, at http://www.hrw.org/campaign/elections/results.htm.

Humphreys, Laud. 1972. *Out of the Closets*. Englewood Cliffs, NJ: Prentice Hall.

Hunt, Larry L. 1999. "Hispanic Protestantism in the United States: Trends by Decade and Generation." *Social Forces*, 77(4): 1601–1624.

Hurh, Won Moo. 1994. "Majority Americans' Perception of Koreans in the United States: Implications of Ethnic Images and Stereotypes." Pp. 3–21 in *Korean Americans: Conflict and Harmony*, edited by H. Kwon. Chicago: Center for Korean Studies.

___. 1998. *The Korean Americans*. Westport, CT: Greenwood Press.

Hurh, Won Moo and Kwang Chung Kim. 1982. "Race Relations Paradigms and Korean American Research: A Sociology of Knowledge Perspective." Pp. 219–255 in *Koreans in Los Angeles*, edited by E. Yu, E. Phillips, and E. Yang. Los Angeles: Center for Korean American and Korean Studies, California State University.

___. and ___. 1984. *Korean Immigrants in America: A Structural Analysis of Ethnic Confinement and Adhesive Adaptation*. Cranbury, NJ: Fairleigh Dickinson University Press.

___. and ___. 1989. "The 'Success' Image of Asian Americans: Its Validity, and Its Practical and Theoretical Implications." *Ethnic and Racial Studies*, October, 12: 512–538.

Ignatiev, Noel. 1994. "Treason to Whiteness Is Loyalty to Humanity." Interview with Noel Ignatiev. *Utne Reader*, November/December, 83–86.

___. 1995. *How the Irish Became White*. New York: Routledge.

Immigration and Refugee Services of America. 2004 "Refugees Admitted to the United States." December, 31: 25.

Indian and Northern Affairs Canada and Canadian Polar Commission. 2000. *2000–2001 Estimates*. Ottawa: Canadian Government Publishing.

Indian Country. 1999. "Parents Ask for Both Traditional and Modern Medical Treatments." May 24, B2.

IndianTrust. 2006. "Corbell v. Kempthrone: Case Chronology." Accessed September 24, 2006, at http://www.IndianTrust.com.

Indianz.com. 2004. Tribal authority over the Indians still unsettled question. Accessed August 9, 2004, at http://www.Indianz.com.

Inoue, Miyako. 1989. "Japanese Americans in St. Louis: From Internees to Professionals." *City and Society*, December, 3: 142–152.

Institute for Social Policy and Understanding. 2004. *The USA Patriot Act: Impact on the Arab and Muslim American Community*. Clinton Township, MI: ISPU.

Institute for Social Research. 2002. "U.S. Husbands Are Doing More Housework While Wives Are Doing Less." March 12 Press Release. Ann Arbor, MI: ISR.

Intelligence Project. 2006. "Hatewatch for the Record." Accessed August 30, 2006, at Southern Poverty Law Center at http://www.splcenter.org.

Intelligence Report. 2004. *Wal-Mart Drops Protocols, But Controversy Lives On*, Winter: 3.

Inter-Parliamentary Union. 2006. Women in National Parliaments. Accessed October 4, 2006, at http://www.ipu.org.

Issacson, Jason and Richard Foltin. 2001. *Election 2000: Post Election*. New York: American Jewish Committee.

Ishii, Miku. 2006. *Multicultural Autobiography*. Unpublished Paper. Chicago: DePaul University.

Itano, Nicole. 1997. "Lawsuit Draws Little Support from Student Body." *Yale Daily News*, October 31.

Jaher, Frederic Caple. 1994. *A Scapegoat in the New Wilderness*. Cambridge, MA: Harvard University Press.

James, Keith, et al. 1995. "School Achievement and Dropout among Anglo and Indian Females and Males: A Comparative Examination." *American Indian Culture and Research Journal*, 19(3): 181–206.

Jaroszynska-Kirchman, Anna D. 1996 "Displaced Persons, Émigrés, Refugees, and Other Polish Immigrants: World War II Through the Solidarity Era." Pp. 152–179 in *Polish Americans and Their History: Community, Culture and Politics*, edited by John J. Bukowcyk. Pittsburgh: University of Pittsburgh Press.

Jenness, Valerie. 1995. "Hate Crimes in the United States: The Transformation of Injured Persons into Victims and the Extension of Victim Status to Multiple Constituencies." Pp. 213–237 in *Images of Issues: Typifying Contemporary Social Problems*, edited by Joel Best. 2nd ed. New York: Aldine de Gruyter.

Jimenez, Alfredo. 2005. *Leaving Cuba*. Unpublished paper. Depaul University, Chicago.

Johnson, Greg 2005. "Narrative Remains: Articulating Indian Identities in the Repatriation Context." *Society for Comparative Study of Society and History*, 47 (July): 480–506.

Johnson, Kevin. 1992. "German Ancestry Is Strong Beneath Milwaukee Surface." *USA Today*, August 4, 9A.

___. 2004. *Immigration and Civil Rights*. Philadelphia: Temple University Press.

Johnson, Peter. 2001. "Minorities Lose Time on Network News." *USA Today*, February 28, 4 D.

Johnson, Troy R. 1996. "Roots of Contemporary Native American Activism." *American Indian Culture and Research Journal*, 20(2): 127–154.

Jolidon, Laurence. 1991. "Battle Builds over Indians' Fishing Rights." *USA Today*, March 21, 1A–2A.

Jones, Charisse 2003 "Newcomers Give Old City a Look at Itself." *USA Today*, February 7, 13A.

Jones, Dale E., Sherri Doty, James E. Horsch, Richard Houseal, Mac Lynn, John P. Marcum, Kenneth M. Sanchagrin, and Richard H. Taylor. 2002. *Religious Congregations and Membership in the United States 2000: An Enumeration by Region, State, and County Based on Data Reported by 149 Religious Bodies*. Nashville, TN: Glenmary Research Center.

Jones, James T., IV. 1988. "Harassment Is Too Often Part of the Job." *USA Today*, August 8, 5D.

Jones, Jeffrey M. 2003a. "Nearly Half of Americans Say Immigration Levels Should be Decreased." *Poll Analysis*, July 10, 2003. Accessed August 6, 2003, at http://www.gallup.com.

___. 2003b. "Majority of American Say Anti-Semitism a Problem in U.S." Released June 11, 2003, at http://www.gallup.com.

___. 2006. Whites, Blacks, Hispanics Disagree About Way Minority Groups Treated. The Gallup Poll July 11, 2006. Accessed October 6, 2006 at http://www.galluppoll.com.

Jones, Nicholas and Amy Symens Smith. 2001. *The Two or More Races Population: 2000*. Series C2KBR/01-6. Washington, DC: U.S. Government Printing Office.

Jones, Tim. 2003. "In Wausau, Hmong at Another Crossroads." *Chicago Tribune*, June 16, 8.

Jonsson, Patrik. 2005. "Noncitizen Soldiers: The Quandaries of Foreign-Born Troops." *Christian Science Monitor*, July 5, 1.

Joseph, Peniel E. 2006. "Black Power's Powerful Legacy." *Chronicle of Higher Education*, June 21, 52: B6–B7.

Kagan, Jerome. 1971. "The Magical Aura of the IQ." *Saturday Review of Literature*, December 4, 4: 92–93.

Kaiser Family Foundation. 2004. *South Africa at Ten Years of Democracy*. Washington, DC: Washington Post/ Kaiser Family Foundation/ Harvard University at http://www.kff.org/kaiserpolls/southafrica.cfm.

Kalita, S. Mitra. 2003. *Suburban Sahibs: Three Immigrant Families and Their Passage from India to America*. New Brunswick, NJ: Rutgers University Press.

Kalt, Joseph P. and Joseph W. Singer. 2004. *Myths and Realities of Tribal Sovereignty: The Law and Economics of Indian Self-Rule*. Cambridge, MA: Harvard University Native American Program.

Kanamine, Linda. 1992. "Amid Crushing Poverty, Glimmers of Hope." *USA Today*, November 30, 7A.

Kanellos, Nicholas. 1994. *The Hispanic Almanac: From Columbus to Corporate America*. Detroit: Visible Ink Press.

Kaneya, Rui. 2004. "Native Tongue." *The Chicago Reporter*, November, 7: 6–7.

Kang, K. Connie. 1996. "Filipinos Happy with Life in U.S., but Lack United Voice." *Los Angeles Times*, January 26, A1, A20.

___. and Lisa Richardson. 2002. "We Can't All Get Along Yet." *Los Angeles Times*, April 27, A1, A18–A19.

Kao, Grace and Kara Joyner. 2004. "Do Race and Ethnicity Matter Among Friends?" *Sociological Quarterly*, 45 (No. 3): 557–573.

Kapur, Deuesh and John McHale. 2003. "Migration's New Payoff." *Foreign Policy*, November/December, 48–57.

Karkabi, Barbara. 1993. "Researcher in Houston Surveys Disabled Women about Sexuality." *Austin American–Statesman*, May 26, E8.

Kaser, Tom. 1977. "Hawaii's Schools: An Ethnic Survey." *Integrated Education*, May–June, 15: 31–36.

Kashima, Tetsuden. 2003. *Judgement Without Trial: Japanese Americans Imprisonment During World War II*. Seattle, WA: University of Washington Press.

Katel, Peter. 2005. "Illegal immigration." *CQ Researcher*, May 6, 15: 393–420.

___. 2006. "American Indians." *CQ Researcher*, April 28, 16.

Kaufman, Gayle and Peter Uhlenberg. 2000. "The Influence of the Work Effort of Married Men and Women." *Social Forces*, 78(3): 931–949.

"Keesing's 1992 Canada: Rejection of Charlottetown Constitutional Reform Package." *Keesing's Record of World Events*, October, 39126.

Kelly, David. 2003. "Spanish Spoken Here—and Hmong, Narago, Arabic." *Chicago Tribune*, March 5, 16.

Kelly, Kimbriell 2005 "Retail Runaround." *Chicago Reporter*, November/December, 14: 8–12.

Kening, Dan. 2004. "OWL Keeps an Eye Out for Issues Affecting Women." *Chicago Tribune*, March 12, sec. 9, 1,12.

Kibria, Nazli. 2002. *Becoming Asian American: Second-Generation Chinese and Korean American Identities*. Baltimore: Johns Hopkins Press.

Kieh, George Klay, Jr. 1995. "Malcolm X and Pan-Africanism." *Western Journal of Black Studies*, 19(4): 293–299.

Kilborn, Peter T. 1992. "Big Change Likely as Law Bans Bias toward Disabled." *New York Times*, July 19, 1, 24.

Killian, Caitlin. 2003. "The Other Side of the Veil: North Africa Women in France Respond to the Headscarf Affair." *Gender and Society*, August, 17: 567–590.

Killian, Lewis M. 1975. *The Impossible Revolution, Phase 2: Black Power and the American Dream*. New York: Random House.

Kilson, Martin. 1995. "Affirmative Action." *Dissent*, Fall, 42: 469–470.

Kim, Kiljoong. 2006. "The Korean Presence in Chicago." In *The New Chicago*, edited by John Koval et al. Philadelphia: Temple University Press.

Kim, Kwang Chung and Shin Kim. 1998. "Korean Middleman Merchants: A Conceptual Revision of Middleman Minority Theory." Paper presented at Midwest Sociological Society Annual Meeting, April 2.

Kim, T.C. 2005. "Electronic Storm." *Intelligence Report*, Summer: 50–57.

Kimura, Yukiko. 1988. *Issei: Japanese Immigrants in Hawaii*. Honolulu: University of Hawaii Press.

King, Martin Luther, Jr. 1958. *Stride Towards Freedom: The Montgomery Story*. New York: Harper.

___. 1963. *Why We Can't Wait*. New York: Mentor.

___. 1967. *Where Do We Go from Here: Chaos or Community?* New York: Harper & Row.

___. 1971. "I Have a Dream." Pp. 346–351 in *Black Protest Thought in the Twentieth Century*, edited by August Meier, Elliott Rudwick, and Francis L. Broderick. Indianapolis: Bobbs-Merrill.

King, Peter. 2004a. "Still Living in the Shadow of a September Day." *Los Angeles Times*, August 3, A1, A12, A13.

___. 2004b. "Their Spiritual Thirst Found a Desert Spring." *Los Angeles Times*, August 4, A1, A16, A17.

___. 2004c. "Private Moments in the Public Eye." *Los Angeles Times*, August 5, A1, A16, A17.

Kinsey, Alfred G., Wardell B. Pomeroy, and Clyde E. Martin. 1948. *Sexual Behavior in the Human Male*. Philadelphia: Saunders.

___. Wardell B. Pomeroy, and Paul H. Gebhard. 1953. *Sexual Behavior in the Human Female*. Philadelphia: Saunders.

Kinzer, Stephen. 2000. "Museums and Tribes: A Tricky Truce." *New York Times*, December 24, sec. 2, 1, 39.

Kirkpatrick, P. 1994. "Triple Jeopardy: Disability, Race and Poverty in America." *Poverty and Race*, 3: 1–8.

Kitagawa, Evelyn. 1972. "Socioeconomic Differences in the United States and Some Implications for Population Policy." Pp. 87–110 in *Demographic and Social Aspects of Population Growth*, edited by Charles F. Westoff and Robert Parke, Jr. Washington, DC: U.S. Government Printing Office.

Kitano, Harry H. L. 1976. *Japanese Americans: The Evolution of a Subculture*, 2nd ed. Englewood Cliffs, NJ: Prentice Hall.

___. 1980. Japanese. In *Harvard Encyclopedia of American Ethnic Groups*, edited by Stephen Thernstrom. Cambridge, MA: Belknap Press of Harvard University Press.

Kitsuse, John I. and Leonard Broom. 1956. *The Managed Casualty: The Japanese American Family in World War II*. Berkeley: University of California Press.

Klausner, Samuel Z. 1988. "Anti-Semitism in the Executive Suite: Yesterday, Today, and Tomorrow." *Moment*, September, 13: 32–39, 55.

Knudson, Thomas J. 1987. "Zoning the Reservations for Enterprise." *New York Times*, January 25, E4.

Koch, Wendy. 2006a. 'Mixed Status' Tears Apart Families. *USA Today*, March 26, 3A.

___. 2006b. "Push for 'Official' English Heats Up." *USA Today*, October 9, 1A.

Kochhar, Rakesh. 2004. *The Wealth of Hispanic Households: 1966 to 2002*. Washington, DC: Pew Hispanic Center.

Korecki, Natasha. 2003. "Rebuilding Mexico from the Suburbs." *Daily Herald* (Arlington Heights, IL), November 20.

Kosmin, Barry A. 1991. *The National Survey of Religious Identification*. New York: City University of New York.

___. and Seymour P. Lachman. 1993. *One Nation Under God: Religion in Contemporary American Society*. New York: Harmony Books.

___. Egon Mayer, and Ariela Keysar. 2001. *American Religious Identification Survey 2001*. New York: New York Graduate Center of the City University of New York.

Kozlowicz, John. 2001. *Regaining the Language*. Accessed February 10, 2002, at http://www.hocakworak.com.

Krauss, Clifford. 2003. "Immigrant Families Québec Seeking to End Its Old Cultural Divide." *New York Times*, April 13, A6.

___. 2006a. "Some Skilled Foreigners Find Jobs Scarce in Canada." *New York Times*, June 5, 6.

___. 2006b. "7 Years Into Self-Rule, Inuit Are Struggling." *New York Times*, June 18, 4.

Krausz, Ernest. 1973. Israel's New Citizens. In *1973 Britannica Book of the Year*, pp. 385–387. Chicago: Encyclopedia Britannica.

Kraybill, Donald B. 2001. *The Riddle of Amish Culture*, rev. ed. Baltimore: Johns Hopkins University Press.

___. ed. 2003. *The Amish and the State*. 2nd ed. Baltimore: John Hopkins University Press.

___. and Steven M. Nolt. 1995. *Amish Enterprises: From Plows to Profits.* Baltimore: Johns Hopkins Press.

Krueger, Alan B. 2002. "Economic Scene." *New York Times,* December 11, C2.

Krueger, Brooke. 2004. "When a Dissertation Makes a Difference." Accessed January 15, 2005 at www.racematters.org/devahpager.html.

Kugel, Seth. 2004. "Destination, Neza York." *New York Times,* February 15, 4.

Kwon, Ho-Youn, Kwag Chung Kem, and R. Stephen Warner, eds. 2001. *Korean Americans and Their Religions: Pilgrims and Missionaries from a Different Shore.* Philadelphia: Pennsylvania State University Press.

Kwong, Peter. 1994. "The Wages of Fear." *Village Voice,* April 26, 39: 25–29.

Labelle, Huguette. 1989. "Multiculturalism and Government." Pp. 1–7 in *Multiculturalism and Intergroup Relations,* edited by James S. Frideres. New York: Greenwood Press.

Lacy, Dan. 1972. *The White Use of Blacks in America.* New York: McGraw-Hill.

Lahiri, Jhumpa. 2006. "My Two Lives." *Newsweek,* March 6, 43.

Lal, Barbara Ballis. 1995. "Symbolic Interaction Theories." *American Behavioral Scientist,* January, 38: 421–441.

Lamb, David. 1997. "Viet Kieu: A Bridge between 2 Worlds." *Los Angeles Times,* November 4, A1, A8.

Landale, Nancy S. and Nimfa B. Ogena. 1995. "Migration and Union Dissolution among Puerto Rican Women." *International Migration Review,* Fall, 29: 671–692.

___. and R. S. Oropesa. 2002. "White, Clack, or Puerto Rican? Racial Self-Identification among Mainland and Island Puerto Ricans." *Social Forces,* 81(1): 231–254.

___. ___. and Bridget K. Gorman. 2000. "Migration and Infant Death: Assimilation or Selective Migration among Puerto Ricans?" *American Sociological Review,* December, 65: 888–909.

LaDuke, Winona. 2006. "Hui Na Iwa—The Bones Live: Hawaiians and NAGPRA." *News from Indian Country,* April 3, 17.

LaPiere, Richard T. 1934. "Attitudes vs. Actions". *Social Forces,* October, 13: 230–237.

___. 1969. "Comment of Irwin Deutscher's Looking Backward." *American Sociologist,* February, 4: 41–42.

Lara, Marielena, Cristina Gramboa, M. Iya Kahramanian, Leo S. Morales, and David E. Hayes Bautista. 2005. "Acculturation and Latino Health in the United States: A Review of the Literature and its Sociopolitical Context." In *Annual Review of Public Health 2005,* pp. 367–397. Palo Alto, CA: Annual Reviews Inc.

Lareau, Annette. 2002. "Juvenile Inequality: Social Class and Childrearing in Black Families and White Families." *American Sociological Review,* October, 67: 747–776.

Latino Coalition. 2006. *2005 National Latino Survey Topline.* Washington, DC: The Latino Coalition.

Lau, Yvonne. 2006a. "Chicago's Chinese Americans: From Chinatown and Beyond." In *The New Chicago* edited by John Koval et al. Philadelphia: Temple University Press.

___. 2006b. "Filipino Americans in Chicago: Success at What Cost?" In *The New Chicago,* edited by John Koval et al. Philadelphia: Temple University Press.

Lauerman, Connie. 1993. "Tribal Wave." *Chicago Tribune,* April 5, sec. 2, 1–2.

Laumann, Edward O., John H. Gagnon, Robert T. Michael, and Stuart Michaels. 1994. *The Social Organization of Sexuality: Sexual Practices in the United States.* Chicago: University of Chicago Press.

Lavender, Abraham D., ed. 1977. *A Coat of Many Colors: Jewish Subcommunities in the United States.* Westport, CT: Greenwood Press.

Laxson, Joan D. 1991. "'We' See 'Them': Tourism and Native Americans." *Annals of Tourism Research,* 18(3): 365–391.

Leavitt, Paul. 2002. "Bush Calls Agent Kicked Off Flight 'Honorable Fellow.'" *USA Today,* January 8.

Lebone, Kerwin. 2006 "Living Conditions and Communications." and "Crime and Security." Pp. 383–517 in *South African Survey 2004/2005.* Johannesburg: South African Institute of Race Relations.

Lee, Don. 1992. "A Sense of Identity." *Kansas City Star,* April 4, E1, E7.

Lee, J. J. and Marion R. Casey. 2006. *Making the Irish American.* New York: New York University Press.

Lee, Jennifer. 2001. "Manhattan's Chinatown Reeling from the Effects of September 11." *New York Times,* November 21, B1, B9.

Lee, Sharon M. 1998. "Asian Americans: Diverse and Growing." *Population Bulletin,* June, 53.

___. and Barry Edmonston. 2005. "New Marriages, New Families: U.S. Racial and Hispanic Intermarriages." *Population Bulletin* 60. (No. 2): 1–36.

Lee, Wen Ho with Helen Zia. 2006. *My Country Versus Me: The First-Hand Account by the Los Almos Scientist Who Was Falsely Accused of Being a Spy.* New York: Hyperion.

Leehotz, Robert. 1995. "Is Concept of Race a Relic?" *Los Angeles Times,* April 15, A1, A14.

LeinWand, Donna. 2004. "Muslims See New Opposition to Building Mosques Since 9/11." *USA Today,* March 9, A1, A2.

Lem, Kim. 1976. "Asian American Employment." *Civil Rights Digest,* Fall, 9: 12–21.

Lennon, Mary Clare and Sara Rosenfeld. 1994. Relative Fairness and the Dimensional Housework: The Importance of Options. *American Journal of Sociology,* 100: 506–531.

Leonard, Karen Isaksen. 2003. *Muslims in the United States: The State of Research.* New York: Russell Sage Foundation.

Lerner, Michael. 1969. "Respectable Bigotry." *American Scholar,* August, 38: 606–617.

Lessinger, Johanna. 1995. *From the Ganges to the Hudson: Indian Immigrants in New York City.* Boston: Allyn & Bacon.

Let Puerto Rico Decide. 2005. Status Choices. Accessed October 7, 2006 at http://www.letpuertoricodecide.com. Citizens' Educated Foundation 2005.

Levin, William C. 1988. "Age Stereotyping: College Student Evaluations." *Research on Aging,* March, 10: 134–148.

Levine, Naomi and Martin Hochbaum, eds. 1974. *Poor Jews: An American Awakening.* New Brunswick, NJ: Transaction Books.

Levitt, Peggy. 2004. "Salsa and Ketchup: Transnational Migrants Struggle Two Worlds." *Contexts,* Spring, 20–26.

Levy, Becca R., Martin D. Slade, Suzanne R. Kunkel, and Stanislav V. Kasl. 2002. "Longevity Increased by Positive Self-Perceptions of Aging." *Journal of Personality and Social Psychology,* 83(2): 261–270.

Levy, Jacques E. 1975. *César Chávez: Autobiography of La Causa.* New York: Norton.

Lewin, Tamar. 2006. "Campaign to End Race Preferences Splits Michigan" *New York Times,* October 31, A1, A19.

Lewinson, Paul. 1965. *Race, Class, and Party: A History of Negro Suffrage and White Politics in the South.* New York: Universal Library.

Lewis, Amanda E. 2004. "'What Group?' Studying Whites and Whiteness in the Era of 'Color-Blindness'." *Sociological Theory,* (December), 22: 623–646.

Lewis, Neil A. 2003. "Secrecy Is Barked on 9/11 Detainees." *New York Times,* June 18, A1, A16.

Lewis, Oscar. 1959. *Five Families: Mexican Case Studies in the Culture of Poverty.* New York: Basic Books.

___. 1965. *La Vida: A Puerto Rican Family in the Culture of Poverty—San Juan and New York.* New York: Random House.

___. 1966. "The Culture of Poverty." *Scientific American,* October, 19–25.

Lewis Mumford Center. 2001. *Ethnic Diversity Grows, Neighborhood Integration Is at a Standstill.* Albany, NY: Lewis Mumford Center.

Li, Wen Lang. 1976. "Chinese Americans: Exclusion from the Melting Pot." Pp. 297–324 in Anthony Dworkin and Rosalind Dworkin, eds., *Minority Report.* New York: Praeger.

Lichtblau, Eric. 2003. "Bush Issues Racial Profiling Ban But Exempts Security Information." *New York Times,* June 18, A1, A16.

___. 2005. "Profiling Report Leads to a Clash and a Demotion." *New York Times,* August 24, A1, A9.

Libman, Jeff (ed.). 2004. *An Immigrant Class: Oral Histories from Chicago's Newest Immigrants.* Chicago: Flying Kite.

Liebman, Charles S. 1973. *The Ambivalent American Jew.* Philadelphia: Jewish Publication Society of America.

Light, Ivan H. 1973. *Ethnic Enterprise in America: Business and Welfare among Chinese, Japanese, and Blacks.* Berkeley: University of California Press.

___. Georges Sabagh, Mendi Bozorgmehr, and Claudia Der-Martirosian. 1994. "Beyond the Ethnic Enclave Economy." *Social Problems,* February, 41: 65–80.

Lin, Sam Chu. 1996. "Painful Memories." *AsianWeek,* July 12, 17: 10.

Lincoln, C. Eric. 1994. *The Black Muslims in America,* 3rd ed. Grand Rapids, MI: William B. Eerdmans.

Lind, Andrew W. 1946. *Hawaii's Japanese: An Experiment in Democracy.* Princeton, NJ: Princeton University Press.

___. 1969. *Hawaii: The Last of the Magic Isles.* London: Oxford University Press.

Lindner, Eileen, ed. 2006. *Yearbook of American and Canadian Churches 2006.* Nashville: Abingden Press.

Linn, Mike 2006. "Ferry Carries Symbolic Weight." *USA Today* August 21, p. 3A.

Linthicum, Leslie. 1993. "Navajo School Working to Revive Language." *News from Indian Country,* Late June, 5.

Lips, Hilary M. 2003. "The Gender Pay Gap: Concrete Indicator of Women's Progress Toward Equality." *Analyses of Social Issues and Public Policy,* 3 (1): 87–109.

Lodder, LeeAnn, Scott McFarland, Diana White. 2003. *Racial Preference and Suburban Employment Opportunities.* Chicago: Chicago Urban League.

Loewen, James W. 2005. *Sundown Towns: A Hidden Dimension of American Racism.* New York: The New Press.

___. 2008. "Sundown Towns." In *Encyclopedia of Race, Ethnicity and Society,* edited by Richard Schaefer. Thousand Oaks, CA: Sage.

Logan, John R. 2001a. *The New Latinos: Who They Are, Where They Are.* Albany: Lewis Mumford Center for Comparative Urban and Regional Research, State University of New York at Albany.

___. 2001b. *The New Ethnic Enclaves in America Suburbs.* Albany, NY: Lewis Mumford Center for Comparative Urban and Regional Research, State University of New York at Albany.

___. Alba Richard D., and Werquan Zhang. 2002. "Immigrant Enclaves and Ethnic Communities in New York and Los Angeles." *American Sociological Review,* April, 67: 299–322.

___. and Glenn Deane. 2003. *Black Diversity in Metropolitan Area.* Albany, NY: Lewis Mumford Center for Comparative Urban and Regional Research, State University of New York at Albany.

Logan, Rayford W. 1954. *The Negro in American Life and Thought: The Nadir, 1877–1901.* New York: Dial Press.

Lomax, Louis E. 1971. *The Negro Revolt,* rev. ed. New York: Harper & Row.

Lopata, Helena Znaniecka. 1994. 2nd ed. *Polish Americans.* New Brunswick, NJ: Transaction Books.

Lopez, Ana Alicia Peña López. 2004. "Central American Labor Migration, 1980–2000." *Diálgo,* Spring: 3–14.

Lopez, David and Yen Espiritu. 1990. "Panethnicity in the United States: A Theoretical Framework." *Ethnic and Racial Studies,* April, 13: 198–224.

Lopez, Julie Amparano. 1992. "Women Face Glass Walls as Well as Ceilings." *Wall Street Journal,* March 3.

Los Angeles Times Poll. 1997. Hong Kong Transition Project Survey. Los Angeles: Los Angeles Times.

___. 1998. American and Israeli Jews. Los Angeles: Los Angeles Times and Yedioth Ahronoth.

Lotke, Eric. 2004. "Racial Disparity in the Justice System: More Than the Sum of Its Parts." *Focus,* May/June, 32: 3–4.

Louie, Andrea. 2004. *Chineseness across Borders: Renegotiation Chinese Identities in China and the United States.* Durham, NC: Duke University Press.

Loury, Glenn C. 1996. "Joy and Doubt on the Mall." *Utne Reader,* January–February, 73: 70–73.

Lowenstein, Roger. 2006. "What Is She Really Doing to American Jobs and Wages?" *New York Times Magazine,* July 9, 36–43ff.

Luce, Clare Boothe. 1975. "Refugees and Guilt." *New York Times,* May 11, E19.

Luconi, Stefano. 2001. *From Paesani to White Ethnics: The Italian Experience in Philadelphia.* Albany: State University Press of New York.

Ludwig, Jack, 2004 *Has the Civil Rights Movement Overcome?* Accessed July 15, 2004, at http://www.gallup.com.

Luker, Kristin. 1984. *Abortion and the Politics of Motherhood.* Berkeley: University of California Press.

Luo, Michael. 2006a. "Reform Jews Hope to Unmix Mixed Marriages" *New York Times,* February 12, 1, 30.

___. 2006b. "An Orthodox Jewish Woman and Soon, a Spiritual Leader." *New York Times,* August 21, B1, B4.

Lyman, Stanford M. 1974. *Chinese Americans.* New York: Random House.

___. 1986. *Chinatown and Little Tokyo.* Milwood, NY: Associated Faculty Press.

Lynch, David J. 2000. "Papal Visit Elicits Painful Ambivalence." *USA Today,* March 24, 12A.

MacFarguhar, Neil. 2006. "A Muslim's Election is Celebrated Here and in Mideast" *New York Times,* November 10: A25.

MacFarlane, Marco. 2006a. "Demographics." And "Health and Welfare." Pp. 1–50; 335–381 in *South African Survey 2004/2005.* Johannesburg: South African Institute of Race Relations.

___. 2006. HIV/AIDS: Best in the World? Let's Hope Not. *Fast Facts,* 7, July: 1.

Mack, Raymond W. 1996. "Whose Affirmative Action?" *Society,* March/April, 33: 41–43.

MacRae, Neil C., Stangor, Charles, and Hewstone, Miles. 1996. *Stereotypes and Stereotyping.* New York: Guilford Press.

Major, Aline K., Airlen Egley, Jr., James C. Howell, Barbara Mendenhall, and Troy Armstrong. 2004. *Youth Gangs in Indian Country.* Washington, DC: Office of Juvenile Justice and Delinquency Prevention.

Malcolm X. 1964. *The Autobiography of Malcolm X.* New York: Grove Press.

Malkin, Michelle. 2004. *In Defense of the Interment: The Case for Racial Profiling in World War II and the War on Terror.* Regency Books.

Malone, Tara. 2005. "Student Rebuked for Sitting During the Mexican Anthem." *Daily Herald,* October 6.

Mandela, Nelson. 1990. "Africa, It Is Ours." *New York Times,* February 12, A10.

Mandelbaum, Robb. 2000. "Sour Grapes." *New York Times,* December 10, 62.

Manning, Robert D. 1995. "Multiculturalism in the United States: Clashing Concepts, Changing Demographics, and Competing Cultures." *International Journal of Group Tensions,* Summer, 117–168.

Marshall, Patrick. 2001. "Religion in Schools." *CQ Research,* July 12, 11: 1–24.

Marshall, Susan E. and Jen'nam Ghazal Read. 2003. Identity Politics Among Arab-American Women. *Social Science Quarterly,* 84, December: 875–891.

Martin, Joel W. 2001. *The Land Looks After Us: A History of Native American Religion.* New York: Oxford University Press.

Martin, Lydia. 1996. "A Question of Tolerance" *Miami Herald,* July 14: 11, 71.

Martinez, Michael. 2006a. "Indians Decry Banishment by Their Tribes." *Chicago Tribune,* January 14, . 9.

___. 2006b. "Yuma: 'The Devil's Highway' for Immigrants." *Chicago Tribune,* May 18, . 9.

Marvasti, Amir. 2005. Being Middle Eastern American: Identity Negotiation in the Context of the War on Terror. *Symbolic Interaction* 28(4): 525–547.

Marvasti, Amir and Karyn McKinney. 2004. *Middle Eastern Lives in America.* New York: Rowman and Littlefield.

Marx, Anthony. 1998. *Making Race and Nation: A Companion of the United States, South Africa, and Brazil.* Cambridge: Cambridge University Press.

Marx, Karl and Frederick Engels. 1955. *Selected Works in Two Volumes.* Moscow: Foreign Languages Publishing House.

Masci, David. 2001. "Middle East Conflict." *CQ Researcher,* April 6, 11: 273–296.

Masayesva, Vernon. 1994. The Problem of American Indian Religious Freedom: A Hopi Perspective. *American Indian Religions: An Interdisciplinary Journal* 1 (Winter), pp. 93–96.

Mason, Heather. 2003. *Does Bilingual Education Translate to Success?* Accessed July 8, 2003, at http://www.gallup.com.

Massey, Douglas S., Jorge Durand, and Nolan Malone. 2002. *Beyond Smoke and Mirrors: Mexican Immigration in an Age of Economic Integration.* New York: Russell Sage Foundation.

Massey, Douglas. 2004. "Segregation and Stratification: A Biosocial Perspective." *DuBois Review,* 1(1): 7–25.

___. 2005. "Racial Discrimination in Housing: A Moving Target." *Social Problems,* 52 (No. 2): 148-151.

___. 2006. "The Wall That Keeps Illegal Workers In." *New York Times,* April 4, . A 13.

___. and Nancy A. Denton. 1993. *American Apartheid: Segregation and the Making of the Underclass.* Cambridge, MA: Harvard University Press.

Matthiessen, Peter. 1991. *In the Spirit of Crazy Horse.* New York: Peking.

Matza, David. 1964. *Delinquency and Drift.* New York: Wiley.

Mauer, Marc. 2004. "Disenfranchising Felons Hurts Entire Communities." *Focus,* May/June, 32: 5–6.

Mauro, Tony. 1995. "Ruling Helps Communities Set Guidelines." *USA Today,* December 21, A1, A2.

Maykovich, Minako Kurokawa. 1972a. *Japanese American Identity Dilemma.* Tokyo: Waseda University Press.

___. 1972b. "Reciprocity in Racial Stereotypes: White, Black and Yellow." *American Journal of Sociology,* March, 77: 876–877.

McClain, Paula Denice. 1979. *Alienation and Resistance: The Political Behavior of Afro-Canadians.* Palo Alto, CA: R & E Research Associates.

McCloud, Aminah Beverly. 1995. *African American Islam.* New York: Routledge.

___. 2004. "Conceptual Discourse: Living as a Muslim in a Pluralistic Society." Pp. 73–83 in *Muslims Place in the American Public Square,* edited by Zahid H. Bukhari et al. Walnut Creek, CA: Altamira Press.

McCoy, Ron. 2004. "Truth-in-Marketing. Law Indian Arts and Crafts Act Regulations Published." *American Indian Art Magazine,* Spring, 29: 84–85.

McGhee, Bernard. 2006. "Young Resigns from Wal-Mart Committee Amid Criticism of Remarks". *Chicago Tribune,* August 19, . 3.

McIntosh, Peggy. 1988. *White Privilege: Unpacking the Invisible Knapsack.* Wellesley, MA: Wellesley College Center for Research on Women.

McKenna, Ian. 1994. "Legal Protection against Racial Discrimination Law in Canada." *New Community,* April, 20: 415–436.

McKinley, Jr. James C. 2005. "Mexican Pride and Death in U.S. Service." *New York Times,* March 22, . A6.

McKinney, K.D. 2003 "I Feel "Whiteness" When I Hear People Blaming Whites: Whiteness as Cultural Victimization." *Race and Society,* 6: 39–55.

McNamara, Mary. 2006. "Friends Tell of Complicated Man." *Chicago Tribune,* August 4, . 8.

McNickle, D'Arcy. 1973. *Native American Tribalism: Indian Survivals and Renewals.* New York: Oxford University Press.

Meagher, Timothy J. 2005. *The Columbia Guide to Irish American History.* New York: Columbia University Press.

Meier, August and Elliott Rudwick. 1966. *From Plantation to Ghetto: An Interpretive History of American Negroes.* New York: Hill & Wang.

Meier, Matt S. and Feliciano Rivera. 1972. *The Chicanos: A History of Mexican Americans.* New York: Hill & Wang.

Meléndez, Edwin. 1994. "Puerto Rico Migration and Occupational Selectivity, 1982–1981." *International Migration Review,* Spring, 28: 49–67.

Merton, Robert A. 1968. Social Theory and Social Structure. *New York Free Press.*

Merton, Robert K. 1949. "Discrimination and the American Creed." Pp. 99–126 in *Discrimination and National Welfare,* edited by Robert M. MacIver. New York: Harper & Row.

___. 1976. *Sociological Ambivalence and Other Essays.* New York: Free Press.

Messner, Michael A. 1997. *Politics of Masculinities: Men in Movements.* Thousand Oaks, CA: Sage.

Meyers, Gustavus. 1943. *History of Bigotry in the United States.* Rev. by Henry M. Christman, 1960. New York: Capricorn Books.

Migration News. 1998. Mexico, Dual Nationality, 5, April. Accessed at http://migration.ucdavis.edu.

___. 2000. Hometown Clubs, 7, July. Accessed at http://migrationnews .ucdavis.edu.

___. 2002a. Canada: Polls Data, April. Accessed at http://migrationnews .ucdavis.edu.

___. 2002b. Income, Education, Politics, October. Accessed at http://migrationnews.ucdavis.edu.

___. 2002c. Mexico: Bush IDs Remittances, December. Accessed at http://migrationnews.ucdavis.edu.

___. 2003 DHS: 9/11 Aftermath, Visas, July. Accessed at http://migrationnews.ucdavis.edu.

___. 2004 NAFTA at 10. January 11. Accessed at http://migrationnews.ucdavis.edu.

Mihesuah, Devon A., ed. 2000. *Reparation Reader: Who Owns American Indian Remains?* Lincoln: University of Nebraska Press.

Miller, David L. and Richard T. Schaefer. 1998. "Promise Keepers and Race: The Stand in the Gap Rally, Washington, DC, 1997." Paper presented at the annual meeting of the Midwest Sociological Society, April, Kansas City, MO.

Miller, Marjorie. 1998. "Cultural Battles Fall along a Religious Divide." *Los Angeles Times,* April 12, 59.

Miller, Norman. 2002. "Personalization and the Promise of Contact Theory." *Journal of Social Issues,* Summer, 58: 387–410.

Min, Pyong Gap. 1995. *Asian Americans: Contemporary Trends and Issues.* Thousand Oaks, CA: Sage.

Minton, Todd D. 2002. "Jails in Indian Country, 2001." *Bureau of Justice Statistics Bulletin,* May.

Mitchel, Gary. 1996. "Native Languages Go Silent." *News from the Indian Country,* Late April, 10: 1A, 7A.

Miyamoto, S. Frank. 1973. "The Forced Evacuation of the Japanese Minority during World War II." *Journal of Social Issues,* 29(2): 11–31.

Mocha, Frank (ed.) 1998. *American "Polonia" and Poland.* New York: Columbia University Press.

Mogelonsky, Marcia. 1995. "Asian–Indian Americans." *American Demographics,* August, 17: 32–39.

Montagu, Ashley. 1972. *Statement on Race.* New York: Oxford University Press.

Moore, David W. 2002. "Americans' View of Influences of Religion Settling Back to pre-September 11th Levels." *Gallup Poll Tuesday Briefly,* December 31, 2002. Accessed at http://www.gallup.com.

Moore, Joan W. 1970. "Colonialism: The Case of the Mexican Americans." *Social Problems,* Spring, 17: 463–472.

___. and Harry Pachon. 1985. *Hispanics in the United States.* Englewood Cliffs, NJ: Prentice Hall.

___. and Raquel Pinderhughes, eds. 1993. *In the Barrios: Latinos and the Underclass Debate.* New York: Sage.

Moore, Stephen. 1998. *A Fiscal Report of the Newest Americans.* Washington, DC: National Immigration Forum and Cato Institute.

Morris, Milton D. and Gary E. Rubin. 1993. "The Turbulent Friendship: Black–Jewish Relations in the 1990s." *Annals,* November, 42–60.

Morse, Samuel F. B. 1835. *Foreign Conspiracy against the Liberties of United States.* New York: Leavitt, Lord.

Moser, Bob. 2005. "The Religious Crusade Against Gays Has Been Building for 30 Years." *Intelligence Report,* Spring: 8–28.

Moskos, Charles C. and John Sibley Butler, eds. 1996. *All That We Can Be: Black Leadership and Racial Integration the Army Way.* New York: Basic Books.

Mostofi, Nilou. 2003. Who We Are: The Perplexity of Iranian-American Identity. *Sociological Quarterly,* 44, Fall: 681–703.

Motta, Roberto. 2000. "Paradigms in the Study of Race Relations in Brazil." December, 15: 665–682.

Moulder, Frances V. 1996. "Teaching about Race and Ethnicity: A Message of Despair or a Message of Hope?" Paper presented at the Annual Meeting of the American Sociological Association, New York City.

Mui, Yian Q. 2001. "Videos Revive Viet Memories." *Chicago Tribune,* July 19, 8B.

Mullen, Fitzhugh. 2005 "The Metrics of the Physician Brain Drain." *New England Journal of Medicine,* 353, October 27: 1810–1818.

Muller, Eli. 2001. "Orthodox Jews Relieved by 'Yale 5' Loss." *Yale Daily News,* January 12.

Murphy, Dean, and Neela Banerjee. 2005. "Catholics in U.S. Keep Faith but Live with Contradictions," *New York Times,* April 11, A1, A16.

Muschkin, Clara G. 1993. "Consequences of Return Migrant Status for Employment in Puerto Rico." *International Migration Review,* 27 Spring: 79–102.

Muslims in the American Public Square. 2001. *American Muslim Poll.* Washington, DC: Project MAPS.

Myrdal, Gunnar. 1944. *An American Dilemma: The Negro Problem and Modern Democracy.* New York: Harper.

Nabokov, Peter. 1970. *Tijerina and the Courthouse Raid,* 2nd ed. Berkeley, CA: Ramparts Press.

Naff, Alika. 1980. "Arabs". *In Harvard Encyclopedia and Asian Ethnic Groups,* edited by Richard Thernstrom. Cambridge, MA: Harvard University Press.

Nagel, Joane. 1988. "The Roots of Red Power: Demographic and Organizational Bases of American Indian Activism 1950–1990." Paper presented at the Annual Meeting of the American Sociological Association, Atlanta.

___. 1996. *American Indian Ethnic Renewal: Red Power and the Resurgence of Identity and Culture.* New York: Oxford University Press.

Nash, Manning. 1962. "Race and the Ideology of Race." *Current Anthropology,* June, 3: 285–288.

National Advisory Commission on Civil Disorders. 1968. *Report.* New York: Bantam.

National Conference of Christians and Jews (NCCJ). 1994. *Taking America's Pulse.* New York: NCCJ.

National Indian Gaming Association. 2006. Indian Gaming Facts. Accessed September 27, 2006, at http://www.indiangaming.org.

National Italian American Foundation. 2001. National Survey: American Teen-Agers and Stereotyping. Accessed October 1, 2003, at http://www.niaf.org.

2006 "Stop Ethnic Bashing." *New York Times,* January.

National Organization for Men Against Sexism. 2006. NOMAS Home. Accessed May 11, at www.nomas.org.

National Women's Political Center. 2006. About NWPC. Accessed April 14, 2006, at http://www.nwpc.org/abort_home.html.

Navarro, Mireya. 1995. "Puerto Rico Reeling under Scourge of Drugs and Rising Gang Violence." *New York Times,* July 23, 11.

___. 1998. "With a Vote for 'None of the Above,' Puerto Ricans Endorse Island's Status Quo." *New York Times,* December 14, A12.

___. 2000. "Puerto Rican Presence Wanes in New York." *New York Times,* February 28, A1, A20.

___. 2004. "Young Japanese-Americans Honor Ethnic Roots." *New York Times,* August 2, A1, A15.

NCAA (National Collegiate Athletic Association). 2003a: Executive Committee Reviews American Indian Mascot Input. Press Release, April 25.

___. 2003b. NCAA Executive Committee Passes Recommendations Regarding American Indian Mascots, Confederate Flag and NCAA Budget, Press Release, August 11.

___. 2005. NCAA Executive Committee Issues Guidelines for Use of Native American Mascots at Championship Events. August 5, 2005. Accessed February 1, 2006, at http://www.ncaa.org

Network Omni. 2006. Anywhere, Anytime, Any Language. Accessed January 11, 2006 at http://www.networkomni.com.

Neugarten, Bernice L. 1996. *The Meanings of Age.* Selected Papers of Bernice L. Neugarten. Ed. with a forward by Dail A. Neugarten.

Newport, Frank. 2003. Six out of 10 Americans Say Homosexual Relations Should Be Recognized as Legal. Accessed May 15, 2003, at http://www.gallup.com.

New York Times. 1917a. "Illiteracy Is Not All Alike". February 8, . 12.

___. 1917b. "The Immigration Bill Veto." January 31, . 210.

___. 1991. "For 2, An Answer to Years of Doubt on Use of Peyote in Religious Rite" July 9, A14.

___. 2005a. "U.S. Panel Backs Nuclear Dump on Indian Reservation in Utah." September 10, A10.

___. 2005b. "Warnings Raised About Exodus of Philippine Doctors and Nurses." November 27, .13.

Newman, William M. 1973. *American Pluralism: A Study of Minority Groups and Social Theory.* New York: Harper & Row.

Ng, Kwai Hang. 1999. Chinese Christian, Christian Chinese? Ethnicity and Religion: An Ethnographic Study of a Chinese Protestant Church. Paper presented at Conference on Sociological Ethnography, Evanston.

___. 2003. "Seeking the Christian Tutelage: Agency and Culture in Chinese Immigrants' Conversion to Christianity." *Sociology of Religion,* 63(2): 195–214.

Nie, Norman H., Barbara Currie, and Andrew M. Greeley. 1974. "Political Attitudes among American Ethnics: A Study of Perceptual Distortion." *Ethnicity,* December, 1: 17–343.

Niebuhr, Gustav. 1998. "Southern Baptists Declare Wife Should 'Submit' to Her Husband." *New York Times,* June 10, A1, A20.

Nielsen, Joyce McCarl, Glenda Walden, and Charlotte A. Kunkel. 2000. "Gendered Heteronormality: Empirical Illusions in Everyday Life." *Sociological Quarterly,* 41(2): 283–296.

Niesse, Mark. 2006. "Bill to Recognize Native Hawaiians with Self-Government Fails Senate." *News from Indian Country,* June 26, 2.

Nishi, Setsuko Matsunga. 1995. "Japanese Americans." Pp. 95–133 in *Asian Americans: Contemporary Trends and Issues,* edited by Pyong Gap Min. Thousand Oaks, CA: Sage Publications.

Noble, Barbara Presley. 1995. "A Level Playing Field, for Just $121." *New York Times,* March 5, F21.

Noel, Donald L. 1972. *The Origins of American Slavery and Racism.* Columbus, OH: Charles Merrill Publishing Co.

Norden, Martin E. 1994. *The Cinema of Isolation: A History of Physical Disability in the Movies.* New Brunswick, NJ: Rutgers University Press.

Novak, Michael. 1996. *Unmeltable Ethnics: Politics and Culture in American Life,* 2nd. ed. New Brunswick, NJ: Transaction Books.

Novelli, William D. 2004. "Common Sense: The Case for Age Discrimination Law." Pp. 4, 7 in *Global Report on Aging.* Washington, DC: AARP.

___. 1999. "Roar of Soccer at Coliseum." *Los Angeles Times,* April 29, A1.

Oakes, James. 1993. "Slavery." Pp. 1407–1419 in *Encyclopedia of American Social History,* edited by Mary Kupiec Clayton, Elliot J. Gorn, and Peter W. Williams. New York: Scribner's.

Oberschall, Anthony. 1968. "The Los Angeles Riot of August 1965." *Social Problems,* Winter, 15: 322–341.

O'Connor, Anne-Marie. 1998. "Church's New Wave of Change." *Los Angeles Times,* March 25, A1, A16.

Office of Immigration Statistics. 2006. *2004 Yearbook of Immigration Statistics.* Washington, DC: US Government Printing Office.

Office of the Inspector General. 2004. *A Review of the Federal Bureau of Prisons' Selection of Muslim Religion Services Providers.* Washington DC: U.S. Department of Justice.

Ogbu, John V. with Astrid Davis. 2003. *Black American Students in an Affluent Suburb: A Study of Academic Disengagement.* Mahwah, NJ: Lawrence Erlbaum Associates.

Ogunwole, Stella V. 2002. "The American Indian and Alaskan Native Population." *Census 2000* Brief C2KBR/01:15. Washington, DC: U.S. Government Printing Office.

___. 2006. *We the People: American Indians and Alaska Natives in the United States.* CENSR-28. Washington, DC: U.S. Government Printing Office.

Ohnuma, Keiko. 1991. "Study Finds Asians Unhappy at CSU." *AsianWeek,* August 8, 12: 5.

Olemetson, Lynette. 2005. "Adopted in China, Seeking Identity in America." *New York Times,* March 23, p. A1.

Oliver, Melvin L. and Thomas M. Shapiro. 1996. *Black Wealth/White Wealth: New Perspective on Racial Inequality.* New York: Routledge.

___. and ___. 2006. *Black Wealth/White Wealth. 10th Anniversary Edition.* New York: Routledge.

Olzak, Susan. 1998. "Ethnic Protest in Core and Periphery States." *Ethnic and Racial Studies,* March, 21: 187–217.

Omi, Michael and Howard Winant. 1994. *Racial Formation in the United States*, 2nd ed. New York: Routledge.

O'Neill, William. 1969. *Everyone Was Brave: The Rise and Fall of Feminism in America*. Chicago: Quadrangle.

Onishi, Norimitsu. 1995. "Japanese in America Looking beyond Past to Shape Future." *New York Times*, December 25, 1.

Orfield, Gary. 2002. *Schools More Separate: Consequences of a Decade of Resegregation*. Cambridge, MA: The Civil Rights Project, Harvard University.

___. and Holly J. Liebowitz, eds. 1999. *Religion, Race, and Justice in a Changing America*. New York: The Twentieth Century Fund.

___. Susan E. Eaton, and the Harvard Project on School Segregation. 1996. *Dismantling Desegregation: The Quiet Reversal of Brown v. Board of Education*. New York: The New Press.

Orlov, Ann and Reed Ueda. 1980. "Central and South Americans." Pp. 210–217 in *Harvard Encyclopedia of American Ethnic Groups*, edited by Stephan Thernstrom. Cambridge, MA: Belknap Press of Harvard University Press.

Ottaway, David S. and Paul Taylor. 1992. "A Minority Decides to Stand Aside for Majority Rule." *Washington Post National Weekly Edition*, April 5, 9: 17.

Padget, Martin. 2004. *Indian Country: Travels in the American Southwest, 1840–1935*. Albuquerque, NM: University of New Mexico Press.

Pager, Devah. 2003. "The Mark of a Criminal." *American Journal of Sociology*, 108: 937–975.

___. and Lincoln Quillian 2005 "Walking the Talk? What Employers Say Versus What They Do." *American Sociological Review*, 70 (No. 3): 355–380.

Paik, Nancy. 2001. One Nation: Islam in America. Accessed March 15, 2001, at http://www.channelonenews.com/special/islam/media.html.

Park, Robert E. 1928. "Human Migration and the Marginal Man." *American Journal of Sociology*, May, 33: 881–893.

___. 1950. *Race and Culture: Essays in the Sociology of Contemporary Man*. New York: Free Press.

___. and Ernest W. Burgess. 1921. *Introduction to the Science of Sociology*. Chicago: University of Chicago Press.

Parker, Laura. 2001. "USA Just Wouldn't Work without Immigrant Labor." *USA Today*, July 23, A1, A2.

Parrish, Michael. 1995. "Betting on Hard Labour and a Plot of Land." *Los Angeles Times*, July 7, A1, A20.

Passel, Jeffrey S. 2006. *The Size and Characteristics of the Unauthorized Migrant Population in the US: Estimates Based on the March 2005 Current Population Survey*. Washington, DC: Pew Hispanic Center.

Patterson, Orlando. 1982. *Slavery and Social Death*. Cambridge: Harvard University Press.

Pawel, Miriam 2006. "Farmworkers Reap Little as Union Strays From Its Roots." *Los Angeles Times*, January 8, A1, A28–A30.

Payne, Charles M. 1995. *I've Got the Light of Freedom*. Berkeley: University of California Press.

Pearson, Rick and John McCormick. 2004. "Election 2004: Faith, Values Fueled Win." *Chicago Tribune* November 4, 32.

Pease, John and Lee Martin. 1997. "Want Ads and Jobs for the Poor: A Glaring Mismatch." *Sociological Forum*, 12(4): 545–564.

Peckham, Pat. 2002. "Hmong's Resettlement Changes Agency's Focus." *Wausau Daily Herald*, February 10, 1A, 2A.

Pedder, Sophie 1991 "Social Isolation and the Labour Market: Black Americans in Chicago." Paper presented at the Chicago Urban Poverty and Family Life Conference, Chicago.

Peek, Lori. 2002. *Religious and Ethnic Issues after September 11, 2001: Examining Muslim University Student Expenses*. Boulder: University of Colorado, Natural Hazards Research and Applications Information Center.

Peréz, Linsandro. 2001. "Growing Up in Cuban Miami: Immigrants, the Enclave, and New Generations." Pp. 91–125 in *Ethnicities*, edited by Ruben G. Rumbaut and Alejandro Portes. Berkeley: University of California Press.

Perusse, Roland I. 1990. *The United States and Puerto Rico: The Struggle for Equality*. Malabor, FL: Robert E. Krieger Publishing Company.

Pessar, Patricia R. 1995. *A Visa for a Dream: Dominicans in the United States*. Boston: Allyn & Bacon.

Peterson, William. 1971. *Japanese Americans: Oppression and Success*. New York: Random House.

Pew Charitable Trust. 2000. "Jews and the American Public Square Data." Accessed May 23, 2001, at http://www.pewtrusts.org.

Pew Hispanic Center. 2006a. *Hispanics at Mid-Decade*. Washington, DC: Pew Hispanic Center.

___. 2006b. *Hispanics: A People in Motion*. Washington, DC: Pew Hispanic Center.

___. 2006c. *Hispanics and the 2006 Election*. Washington, DC: Pew Hispanic Center.

Pew Research Center. 2004. *Beliefs That Jews Were Responsible for Christ's Death Increase*. Washington, DC: Pew Research Center.

___. 2005. *Huge Racial Divide Over Katrina and Its Consequences*. Washington, DC: Pew Research Center.

Pewewardy, Cornel. 1998. "Our Children Can't Wait: Recapturing the Essence of Indigenous Schools in the United States." *Cultural Survival Quarterly*, Spring, 29–34.

Pfeiffer, David. 1996. "A Critical Review of ADA Implementation Studies Which Use Empirical Data." *Disability Studies Quarterly*, Winter, 16: 30–47.

Pido, Antonio J. A. 1986. *The Filipinos in America*. New York: Center for Migration Studies.

Pincus, Fred L. 2003. *Reverse Discrimination: Dismantling the Myth*. Boulder: Lynne Rienner.

Pinderhughes, Raquel. 1996. "The Impact of Race on Environmental Quality: An Empirical and Theoretical Discussion." *Sociological Perspectives*, Summer, 39: 231–248.

Pinkney, Alphonso. 1975. *Black Americans*, 2nd ed. Englewood Cliffs, NJ: Prentice Hall.

___. 1984. *The Myth of Black Progress*. New York: Cambridge University Press.

Pleck, Elizabeth H. 1993. "Gender Roles and Relations." Pp. 1945–1960 in *Encyclopedia of American Social History*, edited by Mary Kupiec Clayton, Elliot J. Gorn, and Peter W. Williams. New York: Scribner's.

Polzin, Theresita. 1973. *The Polish Americans: Whence and Whither*. Pulaski, WI: Franciscan Publishers.

Porter, Eduardo. 2005. "Illegal Immigrants Are Bolstering Social Security with Billions." *New York Times*, April 5, A1, C6.

___. 2006. "Flow of Immigrants' Money to Latin America Surges." *New York Times*, October 19, A23.

Posadas, Barbara M. 1999. *The Filipino Americans*. Westport, CT: Greenwood Press.

President's Task Force on Puerto Rico's Status. 2005. *Report by the President's Task Force on Puerto Rico's Status*. Washington, DC: U.S. Government Printing Office.

Public Broadcasting System. 1998. Weekend Edition: National Public Radio with Eric Westervelt and Scott Simon, May 30.

Purdy, Matthew. 2001. "Ignoring and Then Embracing the Truth about Racial Profiling." *New York Times*, March 11, .

Quadagno, Jill. 2005. *Aging and the Life Course: An Introduction to Social Gerontology*, 3rd ed. New York: McGraw-Hill.

Quillian, Lincoln. 2006. "New Approaches to Understanding Racial Prejudice and Discrimination." Pp. 299–328 in *Annual Reviews of Sociology 2006*, edited by Karen S. Cook and Douglas S. Massey. Palo Alto, CA: Annual Review of Sociology.

Quintanilla, Ray. 2006. "Islanders Ask: Where's the Cleanup?" *Chicago Tribune*, March 27, 3.

Rabinove, Samuel. 1970. "Private Club Discrimination and the Law." *Civil Rights Digest*, Spring, 3: 28–33.

Rachlin, Carol. 1970. "Tight Shoe Night: Oklahoma Indians Today." Pp. 160–183 in *The American Indian Today*, edited by Stuart Levine and Nancy Oestreich Lurie. Baltimore: Penguin.

Ragged Edge. 1998. "Austin, Texas Becomes Second City in the Nation to Require Basic Access in Single-Family Homes." November/December, 5.

Rainey, James. 2000. "Farm Workers Union Ends 16-Year Boycott of Grapes." *Los Angeles Times*, November 22, A3, A36, A37.

Ramirez, Eddy. 2002. "Ageism in the Media Is Seen as Harmful to Health of the Elderly." *Los Angeles Times*, September 5, A20.

Ramirez, Margaret. 2000. "Study Finds Segregation of Latinos in Catholic Church." *Los Angeles Times*, March 1, A1, A24.

Ramirez, Roberto R. and Patricia de la Cruz. 2003. "The Hispanic Population in the United States: March 2003." *Current Population Reports*. Ser. P20, No. 545. Washington, DC: U.S. Government Printing Office.

Rangaswamy, Padma. 2005. "Asian Indians in Chicago." In *The New Chicago*, edited by John Koval et al. Philadelphia: Temple University Press.

Rawick, George P. 1972. *From Sundown to Sunup: The Making of the Black Community*. Westport, CT: Greenwood Press.

Read, Jen'nan Ghazal. 2003. "The Source of Gender Role Attitudes Among Christian and Muslim Arab-American Women." *Sociology of Religion*, Summer, 64: 207–222.

———. 2004. Family, Religion, and Work Among Arab American Women. *Journal of Marriage and Family*, November, 66: 1042–1050.

Remini, Robert V. 2001. *Andrew Jackson and His Indian Wars*. New York: Viking.

Renzulli, Linda and Lorraine Evans. 2005. School Choice, Charter Schools, and White Flight. *Social Problems* 52 (No.2): 398–418.

Reese, Debbie. 1996. "Teaching Young Children about Native Americans." *ERIC Digest*, May, ED0-PS-96-3.

Reeves, Terrance and Claudette Bennett. 2003. "The Asian and Pacific Islander Population in the United States: March 2002." *Current Population Reports*. Ser. P20. No. 540. Washington, DC: U.S. Government Printing Office.

Religion Watch. 1995a. "Women Religious Leadership Facing Mainline Decline, Conservative Growth." November, 11: 1–3.

———. 1995b. "Reform Synagogues Increasingly Adopting Orthodox Practices." March, 10: 7.

———. 2000. "Future of Jewish Day Schools Threatened by Finances, Ideology." January, 4.

Religious Diversity News. 2004. "The Oklahoma Headscarf Case." Accessed October 16, 2004, at http://www.pluralism.org.

Remini, Robert V. 2001. *Andrew Jackson and His Indian Wars*. New York: Viking.

Reyhner, Jon. 2001a. "Cultural Survival vs. Forced Assimilation." *Cultural Survival Quarterly*, Summer, 25: 22–25.

———. 2001b. "Family, Community, and School Impacts on American Indian and Alaskan Native Students Success." Paper presented at the annual meeting of the National Indian Education Association, October 29.

Richmond, Anthony H. 2002. "Globalization: Implications for Immigrants and Refugees." *Ethnic and Racial Studies*, September, 25: 707–727.

Ritter, John and Tom Squitieri, 2002. "Afghan-Americans Hear Call to Return" *USA Today*, January 21, 6A.

Rivera-Batiz, Francisco and Carlos E. Santiago. 1996. *Island Paradox: Puerto Rico in the 1990s*. New York: Russell Sage Foundation.

———. 1992. "People of Color: The 'Kaleidoscope' May Be a Better Way to Describe America Than 'The Melting Pot.'" Peoria Journal Star January 19, A7.

Rivlin, Gary. 2005 "Hate Messages on Google Site Draw Concern." *New York Times*, February 7, C1, C7.

Robert, Pamela M. and Sharon L. Harlan. 2006. Mechanisms of Disability Discrimination in Large Bureaucratic Organizations: Ascriptive Inequalities in the Workplace. *The Sociological Quarterly*, 47: 599–630.

Rodríguez, Clara E. 1989. *Puerto Ricans: Born in the USA*. Boston: Unwin Hyman.

———. 2000. *Changing Race: Latinos, the Census, and the History of Ethnicity in the United States*. New York: New York University Press.

———. ed. 1997. *Latin Looks: Image of Latinas and Latinos in the U.S. Media*. Boulder, CO: Westview Press.

Rodríquez, Robert. 1994. "Immigrant Bashing: Latinos Besieged by Public Policy Bias." *Black Issues in Higher Education*, February 24, 10: 31–34.

Roediger, David R. 1994. *Towards the Abolition of Whiteness: Essays on Race, Politics, and Working Class History (Haymarket)*. New York: Verso Books.

———. 2006. "Whiteness and Its Complications." *Chronicle of Higher Education*, July 14, 52: B6–B8.

Rohter, Larry. 1993. "Trade Pact Threatens Puerto Rico's Economic Rise." *New York Times*, January 3, 1, 14.

Romney, Lee. 2004 "Chinese Americans Emerge as a Political Power in S.F." *Los Angeles Times*, February 1, B1, B12.

Rosales, F. Arturo. 1996. *Chicano! The History of the Mexican American Civil Rights Movement*. Houston, TX: Arte Público Press.

Rose, Arnold. 1951. *The Roots of Prejudice*. Paris: UNESCO.

Rosenbaum, James E. and Patricia Meaden. 1992. "Harassment and Acceptance of Low-Income Black Youth in White Suburban Schools." Paper presented at the Annual Meeting of the American Sociological Association, Pittsburgh.

Rosenberg, Tom. 2000. "Changing My Name after 60 Years." *Newsweek*, July 17, 136: 10.

Rosero, Karla. 2005. Canada Agrees to Boarding School Reparations. *Cultural Survival Quarterly* (Fall): 7.

Rosin, Hanna. 2002. "To Be Arab and American." *Washington Post National Weekly Edition*, November 18, 20: 9.

Rossi, Alice S. 1964. "Equality between the Sexes: An Immodest Proposal." *Daedalus*, Spring, 93: 607–652.

Rothstein, Edward. 2006. "The Anti-Semitic Hoax That Refuses to Die." *New York Times*, April 21, B27, B37.

Rouhana, Nadim N. and Daniel Bar-Tal. 1998. "Psychological Dynamics of Intractable Ethnonational Conflicts: The Israeli–Palestinian Case." *American Psychologist*, July, 761–770.

Rudwick, Elliott. 1957. "The Niagara Movement." *Journal of Negro History*, July, 42: 177–200.

Rusk, David. 2001. *The "Segregation Tax": The Cost of Racial Segregation to Black Homeowners*. Washington, DC: Brookings Institution.

Ryan, William. 1976. *Blaming the Victim*, rev. ed. New York: Random House.

Ryo, Emily. 2006. "Through the Back Door: Applying Theories of Legal Compliance to Illegal Immigration During the Chinese Exclusion Era." *Law and Social Enquiry*, 109–146.

Saad, Lydia. 1998. "America Divided Over Status of Puerto Rico." *Gallup Poll Monthly*, March, 390: 278.

———. 2006a. "Anti-Muslim Sentiments Fairly Commonplace." *The Gallup Poll*, August 10.

———. 2006b. "Americans at Odds Over Gay Rights". *The Gallup Poll*, October 15.

Sachs, Susan. 2001. "For Newcomers, a Homey New Chinatown." *New York Times*, July 22, A1, A44.

Sadker, Myra Pollack and David Miller Sadker. 2003. *Teachers, Schools, and Sociology*. 6th ed. New York: McGraw-Hill.

Saeed, Agha. 2002. The American Muslim Paradox. In *Muslim Minorities in the West*, edited by Yvonne Yazbeck Haddad and Jane I. Smith, pp. 39–58. Walnut Creek, CA: Altamira Press.

Sahagun, Louis. 2004. "Tribes Fear Backlash to Prosperity." *Los Angeles Times*, May 3, B1, B6.

Said, Edward. 1978. *Orientalism*. New York: Viking.

St. Espada, Martín. 2000. "!Viva Vieques" *The Progressive*, July, 64: 27–29.

Salée, Daniel. 1994. "Identity Politics and Multiculturalism in Quebec." *Cultural Survival Quarterly*, Summer–Fall, 89–94.

Salopek, Paul. 1996. "Assimilation Puts Tribal Cultures at Loss for Words." *Chicago Tribune*, February 25, 1, 13.

Salzberger, Ronald P. and Mary G. Turck. 2004. *Reparations for Slavery: A Reader*. London: Rowman and Little Field.

Samhan, Helen. 2001. "Arab Americans." *In Grolier's Multimedia Encyclopedia*. Accessed March 15, 2001, at http://www.grolier.com.

Sanchez, Rene. 1998. "The Winter of Their Discontent." *Washington Post National Weekly Edition*, December, 16: 20.

Sanders, Irwin T. and Ewa T. Morawska. 1975. *Polish-American Community Life: A Survey of Research*. Boston: Community Sociology Training Program.

Sarna, Jonathan D. 2004. "American Jewish History: A Chance to Reflect" *Chronicle of Higher Education*, October 1, B9–B10.

Schaefer, Richard T. 1971. "The Ku Klux Klan: Continuity and Change." *Phylon*, Summer, 32: 143–157.

___. 1976. *The Extent and Content of Racial Prejudice in Great Britain.* San Francisco: R & E Research Associates.

___. 1980. "The Management of Secrecy: The Ku Klux Klan's Successful Secret." Pp. 161–177 in *Secrecy: A Cross-Cultural Perspective* edited by Stanton K. Tefft. New York: Human Sciences Press.

___. 1986. "Racial Prejudice in a Capitalist State: What Has Happened to the American Creed?" *Phylon*, September, 47: 192–198.

___. 1992. People of Color: The "'Kaleidoscope' May Be a Better Way to Describe America Than 'The Melting Pot.'" *Peoria Journal Star*, January 19, A7.

___. 1996. "Education and Prejudice: Unraveling the Relationship." *Sociological Quarterly*, January, 37: 1–16.

___. 2007. *Sociology.* 10th ed. New York: McGraw-Hill.

___. and Sandra L. Schaefer. 1975. "Reluctant Welcome: U.S. Responses to the South Vietnamese Refugees." *New Community*, Autumn, 4: 366–370.

Schlemmer, Laurence. 2001a. "Between a Rainbow and a Hard Place." *Fast Facts*, December, 2–12.

___. 2001b. "Race Relations and Racism in Everyday Life." *Fast Facts*, September, 2–12.

Schodolski, Vincent J. 2002. "Demographic Shift Pits Blacks against Latinos." *Chicago Tribune*, April 25, 1, 12.

Schulz, Amy J. 1998. "Navajo Women and the Politics of Identity." *Social Problems*, August, 45: 336–352.

Schwartz, Felice and Jean Zimmerman. 1992. *Breaking with Tradition: Women and Work, The New Facts of Life.* New York: Warner Books.

Schwartz, Jim and Jeffery Scheckner. 2001. "Jewish Population in the United States." Pp. 253–277 in *American Jewish Yearbook 2001*, edited by David Singer and Lawrence Grossman. New York: American Jewish Committee.

Schwartz, John. 1994. "Preserving Endangered Speeches." *Washington Post National Weekly Edition*, March 21, 11: 38.

Schwartz, Margaret. 2006. "A Question in the Shape of Your Body." Pp. 9–14 in *Half/Life: Jewish Tales from Interfaith Homes*, edited by Laurel Synder. Brooklyn NY: Soft Skull Press.

Schwartz, Pepper. 1992. "Sex as a Social Problem." Pp. 794–819 in *Social Problems*, edited by Craig Calhoun and George Ritzer. New York: McGraw-Hill.

Scotch, Richard K. 1988. "Disability as the Basis for a Social Movement: Advocacy and the Politics of Definition." *Journal of Social Issues*, 44(1): 159–172.

___. 1989. "Politics and Policy in the History of the Disability Rights Movement." *The Milbank Quarterly*, Supplement 2, 6: 380–400.

___. 2001. *From Good Will to Civil Rights: Transforming Federal Disability Policy*, 2nd ed. Philadelphia: University of California Press.

Scott, Janny. 2003. "Debating White Private Clubs Are Acceptable and Private." *New York Times*, December 8, Sec. 7, 5.

Sears, David O. and J. B.McConahay. 1969. "Participation in the Los Angeles Riot." *Social Problems*, Summer, 17: 3–20.

___. 1970. "Racial Socialization, Comparison Levels, and the Watts Riot." *Journal of Social Issues*, Winter, 26: 121–140.

___. 1973. *The Politics of Violence: The New Urban Blacks and the Watts Riots.* Boston: Houghton-Mifflin.

Seibert, Deborah. 2002. Interview with Author. *Wausau Daily Herald* Staff Member, March 27.

Sela-Sheffy, Rakefet. 2004. "'What Makes One an Israeli' Negotiating Identities in Everyday Representations of 'Israeliness.'" *Nations and Nationalism*, 10 (40): 479–497.

Selzer, Michael. 1972. *"Kike": Anti-Semitism in America.* New York: Meridian.

Sengupta, Somini. 1997. "Asians' Advances Academically Are Found to Obscure a Need." *New York Times*, November 9, 17.

The Sentencing Project. 2006. Racial Disparity. Accessed September 4, 2006 at http://www.sentencingproject.org.

Servin, Manuel P. 1974. "The Beginnings of California's Anti-Mexican Prejudice." Pp. 2–26 in *An Awakened Minority: The Mex-ican Americans*, 2nd ed, edited by Manuel P. Servin. Beverly Hills, CA: Glencoe Press.

Sever, Tom. 2006. "A Bitter Prize: Israel and the Occupied Territories." *Foreign Affairs*, May/June, 145–150.

Shaheen, Jack. 2003. "Reel Bad Arabs: How Hollywood Vilifies a People." *Annals*, July, 558: 171–193.

Shapiro, Joseph P. 1993. *No Pity: People with Disabilities Forging a New Civil Rights Movement.* New York: Times Books.

Shapiro, Thomas M. 2004. *The Hidden Cost of Being African American: How Wealth Perpetuates Inequality.* New York: Oxford University Press.

Sherif, Musafer and Carolyn Sherif. 1969. *Social Psychology.* New York: Harper & Row.

Sherkat, Darren E. and Christopher G. Ellison. 1999. "Recent Developments and Current Controversies in the Sociology of Religion." Pp. 363–394 in *Annual Review of Sociology 1999*, edited by Karen S. Cook and John Hagan. Palo Alto, CA: Annual Reviews.

Sherman, C. Bezalel. 1974. "Immigration and Emigration: The Jewish Case." Pp. 51–55 in *The Jew in American Society*, edited by Marshall Sklare. New York: Behrman House.

Shilts, Randy. 1982. *The Mayor of Castro Street: The Life and Times of Harvey Milk.* New York: St. Martin's.

Shin, Hyon S. and Rosalind Bruno. 2003. "Language Use and English-Speaking Ability: 2000." *C2KBR-29.* Washington, DC: U.S. Government Printing Office.

Sigelman, Lee and Steven A. Tuch. 1997. "Metastereotypes: Blacks' Perception of Whites' Stereotypes of Blacks." *Public Opinion Quarterly*, Spring, 61: 87–101.

Silberman, Charles E. 1971. *Crisis in the Classroom: The Remaking of American Education.* New York: Random House.

Silva, Helga. 1985. *The Children of Mariel.* Miami: Cuban American National Foundation.

Silver, Jim, ed. 2006. *In Their Own Voices: Building Urban Aboriginal Communities.* Halifax NS: Fernwood Publishing.

Simon, Stephanie. 2004. "Muslim Call to Prayer Stirs a Midwest Town," *Los Angeles Times*, May 8, A17.

Simpson, Jacqueline C. 1995. "Pluralism: The Evolution of a Nebulous Concept." *American Behavioral Scientist*, January, 38: 459–477.

Skidmore, Thomas E. 1972. "Toward a Comparative Analysis of Race Relations Since Abolition in Brazil and the United States" *Journal of Latin American Studies*, May, 4: 1–28.

Sklare, Marshall. 1971. *America's Jews.* New York: Random House.

Slavin, Robert E. and Alan Cheung. 2003. *Effective Reading Programs for English Language Learners.* Baltimore: Center for Research on the Education of Students Placed at Risk, Johns Hopkins University.

Slavin, Steven and Mary Pradt. 1979. "Anti-Semitism in Banking." *The Bankers Magazine*, July–August, 162: 19–21.

___. 1982. *The Einstein Syndrome: Corporate Anti-Semitism in America Today.* Washington, DC: University Press of America.

Smallwood, Scott. 2003. "American Women Surpass Men in Earning Doctorates." *Chronicle of Higher Education*, December 12, A10.

Smith, Dan. 2003. *The Penguin State of the World Atlas.* 7th ed. London: Penguin Books.

Smith, David M. and Gary J. Gates. 2001. *Gay and Lesbian Families in the United States: Same-Sex Unmarried Partner Households.* Washington, DC: Human Rights Campaign.

Smith, James F. 2001. "Mexico's Forgotten Find Cause for New Hope." *Los Angeles Times*, February 23, A1, A12, A13.

Smith, Paul Chaat and Robert Allen Warrior. 1996. *Like a Hurricane: The Indian Movement from Alcatraz to Wounded Knee.* New York: The New Press.

Smith, Tom W. 2000. *Taking America's Pulse II: A Survey of Intergroup Relations.* New York: National Conference for Community and Justice.

___. 2001. *Religious Diversity in America: The Emergence of Muslims, Buddhists, Hindus, and Others.* New York: American Jewish Committee.

___. 2006. *Taking America's Pulse III. Intergroup Relations in Contemporary America.* Chicago: National Opinion Research Center, University of Chicago.

Snipp, C. Matthew. 1989. *American Indians: The First of This Land.* New York: Sage.

Snyder, Laurel, ed. 2006. *Half/Life: Jewish Tales from Interfaith Homes.* Brooklyn, NY: Soft Skull Press.

Snyder, Susan 2006. "Defying Church, Organization Ordains 8 Women as Priests." *Philadelphia Inquirer*, August 1.

Society for Human Resource Management. 2002. "Diversity Aspects Covered in Corporate America." *New York Times Magazine*, August 15, 100.

Soltero, Sonia White. 2004. *Dual Language: Teaching and Learning in Two Languages.* Boston: Allyn and Bacon.

Somners, Christina Hoff. 1994. *Who Stole Feminism?* New York: McGraw-Hill.

Song, Tae-Hyon. 1991. "Social Contact and Ethnic Distance between Koreans and the U.S. Whites in the United States." Paper, Western Illinois University, Macomb.

Soo, Julie D. 1999. "Strained Relations: Why Chinatown's Venerable Associations Are Ending Up in Court." *AsianWeek*, January 14, 15–18.

Sorensen, Elaine. 1994. *Comparable Worth. Is It a Worthy Policy?* Princeton, NJ: Princeton University Press.

Southern, David W. 1987. *Gunnar Myrdal and Black–White Relations.* Baton Rouge: Louisiana State University.

Southern Poverty Law Center. 2006a. "Active Hate Groups in the United States in 2005." Intelligence Report, Spring.

___. 2006b "Intelligence Project: Top Hate Watch Headlines." Accessed February 12, 2006, at http://www.splcenter.org.

Squitieri, Tom. 1999. "FALN Brought Bloody Battle into American Streets." *USA Today*, September 21, 15A.

Stampp, Kenneth M. 1956. *The Peculiar Institution: Slavery in the Ante-Bellum South.* New York: Random House.

Starks, Carolyn. 2002. "Sitting Here in Limbo." *Chicago Tribune*, March 26.

Statistics Canada. 2001. *Aboriginal Peoples in Canada.* Ottawa: Canadian Centre for Justice.

___. 2002. Population. Accessed May 13, 2002, at http://www.statcan.ca/english.

___. 2003a. *2001 Census: Analysis Serves Canada's Ethnocultural Portrait: The Changing Mosaic.* Ottawa: Statistics Canada.

___. 2003b. *Ethnic Diversity Survey: Portrait of a Multicultural Society.* Ottawa: Statistics Canada.

Statistics South Africa. 2004. Key Finds at Mid-2004. Accessed October 9, 2004, at http://www.statsaa.gov.za.

Staton, Ron. 2004a. "Still Fighting for National Hawaiian Recognition." *Asian Week*, January 22, 8.

___. 2004b. "Beyond Aloha: A Hawaiian Renaissance." *Chicago Tribune*, March 29, sect. 5, 1, 4.

Stauffer, John. 2005. "Across the Great Divide." *Time*, July 4, 59–65.

Steinberg, Stephen. 2005 "Immigration, African Americans, and Race Discourse." *New Politics*, Winter, 10.

Steiner, Stan. 1968. *The New Indians.* New York: Harper and Row.

Steinhauer, Jennifer. 2006. "An Unwelcome Light on Club Where Legends Teed Off." *New York Times*, September 23, A8.

Steinmetz, Erica. 2006. Americans with Disabilities: 2002. *Current Population Reports*, Ser. P70, No. 107. Washington, DC: U.S. Government Printing Office.

Stern, Kenneth S. 2001. "Lying about the Holocaust." *Intelligence Report*, Fall, 50–55.

Stewart, Jocelyn Y. 2002. "Groups Fight Increased Bias Against Arabs." *Los Angeles Times*, July 8, B3.

Stoddard, Ellyn R. 1973. *Mexican Americans.* New York: Random House.

___. 1976a. "A Conceptual Analysis of the 'Alien Invasion': Institutionalized Support of Illegal Mexican Aliens in the U.S." *International Migration Review*, Summer, 10: 157–189.

___. 1976b. "Illegal Mexican Labor in the Borderlands: Institutionalized Support of an Unlawful Practice." *Pacific Sociological Review*, April, 19: 175–210.

Stonequist, Everett V. 1937. *The Marginal Man: A Study in Personality and Culture Conflict.* New York: Scribner's.

Stout, David. 2000. "At Indian Bureau, A Milestone and an Apology." *New York Times*, September 9, A47.

Strauss, Gary. 2002. "Good Old Boys' Network Still Rules Corporate Boards." *USA Today*, November 1, B1, B2.

Suggs, Welch. 2002. "Title IX at 30." *Chronicle of Higher Education*, June 21, 48: A38–A42.

___. 2004. "'Varsity' with an Asterisk." *Chronicle of Higher Education*, February 13, A35–A37.

Sullivan, Cheryl. 1986. "Seeking Self-Sufficiency." *Christian Science Monitor*, June 25, 16–17.

Sullivan, Keith. 2005 "Desperate Moves." *Washington Post National Weekly Edition.* March 14: 9–10

Sundiata, Ibrahim K. 1987. "Late Twentieth Century Patterns of Race Relations in Brazil and the United States" *Phylon*, March, 48: 62–76.

Sung, Betty Lee. 1967. *Mountains of Gold: The Story of the Chinese in America.* New York: Macmillan.

Suro, Roberto. 1998. *Strangers among Us: Latino Lives in a Changing America.* New York: Vintage Books.

___. and Gabriel Escobar. 2006. *2006 National Survey of Latinos: The Immigration Debate.* Washington, DC: Pew Hispanic Center.

Swagerty, William R. 1983. "Native Peoples and Early European Contacts." Pp. 15–16 in *Encyclopedia of American Social History*, edited by Mary Kupiec Clayton, Elliot J. Gorn, and Peter W. Williams. New York: Scribner's.

Swanson, Stevenson. 2004. "Chinatown: Hopes for a Mini-boom." *Chicago Tribune*, August 1, 1, 5.

Swarns, Christina. 2004. "The Uneven Scales of Capital Justice." *American Prospect*, July, A14–A15.

Swartz, Jon. 2003. "Internet Firms Woo Hispanics." *USA Today*, January 27, 3B.

Szegedy-Maszak, Marianne. 2001. "Guess Who's Footing the 'Mommy Tax?'" *U.S. News and World Report*, March 19, 130: 48.

Tafoya, Sonya M., Hans Johnson, and Laura E. Hill. 2004. *Who Chooses to Choose Two?* New York: Russell Sage Foundation and Population Reference Bureau.

Takaki, Ronald. 1989. *Strangers from a Different Shore: A History of Asian Americans.* Boston: Little, Brown.

Takezawa, Yasuko I. 1991. "Children of Inmates: The Effects of the Redress Movement among Third Generation Japanese Americans." *Qualitative Sociology*, Spring, 14: 39–56.

Talbani, Aziz and Parveen Hasanav. 2000. "Adolescent Females Between Tradition and Modernity: Gender Role Socialization in South Asian Immigrant Culture." *Journal of Adolescence*, 23: 615–627.

Tannenbaum, Frank. 1946. *Slave and Citizen.* New York: Random House.

Taylor, Jonathan B. and Joseph P. Kalt. 2005. *American Indians on Reservations: A Databook of Socioeconomic Change Between the 1990 and 2000 Censuses.* Cambridge, MA: The Harvard Project on American Indian Development.

Taylor, Stuart, Jr. 1987. "High Court Backs Basing Promotion on a Racial Quota." *New York Times*, February 26, 1, 14.

___. 1988. "Justices Back New York Law Ending Sex Bias by Big Clubs." *New York Times*, June 21, A1, A18.

Taylor, T. Shaun. 2004. "Blacks Find Progress Slow in Joining Trade Unions." *Chicago Tribune*, August 1, 1, 12–13.

Telles, Edward E. 1992. "Residential Segregation by Skin Color in Brazil" *American Sociological Review*, April, 57: 186–197.

___. 2004. *Race in Another America: The Significance of Skin Color in Brazil.* Princeton, NJ: Princeton University Press.

Telsch, Kathleen. 1991. "New Study of Older Workers Finds They Can Become Good Investments." *New York Times*, May 21, A16.

ten Brock, Jacobus, Edward N. Barnhart, and Floyd W. Matson. 1954. *Prejudice, War and the Constitution.* Berkeley: University of California Press.

Terba, Harallamb. 2004. "My Name is Harallamb Terba." Pp. 184–195 in Jeff Libman (ed.) *An Immigrant Class: Oral Histories from Chicago's Newest Immigrants.* Chicago: Flying Kite.

Therrien, Melissa and Roberto R. Ramirez. 2001. "The Hispanic Population in the United States, March 2000." *Current Population Reports* Ser. P20, No. 535. Washington, DC: U.S. Government Printing Office.

Third World Institute, 2005. *Third World Guide 05/06.* Toronto: Garamond Press.

Thomas, Curlew O. and Barbara Boston Thomas. 1984. "Blacks' Socioeconomic Status and the Civil Rights Movement's Decline, 1970–1979: An Examination of Some Hypotheses." *Phylon,* March, 45: 40–51.

Thomas, Dorothy S. and Richard S. Nishimoto. 1946. *The Spoilage: Japanese-American Evacuation and Resettlement.* Berkeley: University of California Press.

Thomas, Robert M., Jr. 1995. "Maggie Kuhn, 89, the Founder of the Gray Panthers, Is Dead." *New York Times,* April 23, 47.

Thomas, William Isaac. 1923. *The Unadjusted Girl.* Boston: Little, Brown.

___. and Florian Znaniecki. 1918–1920. *The Polish Peasant in Europe and America.* (5 volumes), edited by Eli Zaretsky. 1996. Urbana: University of Illinois Press.

Thompson, Ginger. 2001. "Fallout of U.S. Recession Drifts South into Mexico." *New York Times,* December 26, C1, C2.

___. 2003. "Money Sent Home by Mexicans Is Booming." *New York Times,* October 28, A12.

___. 2005. "Uneasily, a Latin Land Looks at Its Own Complexion." *New York Times,* May 19, A5.

Thornburgh, Nathan. 2005 "Serving Up a Conflict." *Time,* August 1, 33.

Thornton, Russell. 1981. "Demographic Antecedents of the 1890 Ghost Dance." *American Sociological Review,* February, 46: 88–96.

___. 1991. "North American Indians and the Demography of Contact." Paper presented at the Annual Meeting of the American Sociological Association, Cincinnati.

Thrupkaew, Noy. 2002. "The Myth of the Model Minority." *The American Prospect,* April 8, 13: 38–47.

Time. 1974. "Are You a Jew?" September 2, 104: 56, 59.

Tizon, Thomas Alex. 2004. "Internment Lesson Plan Is Under Attack." *Los Angeles Times,* September 12, A21.

Tomaskovic-Devey, Donald. 1993. "The Gender and Race Composition of Jobs and the Male/Female, White/Black Pay Gaps." *Social Forces,* September, 72: 45–76.

Tomlinson, T. M. 1969. "The Development of a Riot Ideology among Urban Negroes." Pp. 226–235 in *Racial Violence in the United States,* edited by Allen D. Grimshaw. Chicago: Aldine.

Tong, Benson. 2000. *The Chinese Americans.* Westport, CT: Greenwood Press.

Torriero, E. A. 2004a. "Political Strife Hits Hmong in St. Paul." *Chicago Tribune,* June 14, 12.

___. 2004b. "Taste of Success, Sorrow." *Chicago Tribune,* December 4, 1, 17.

Tough, Paul. 2004. "The 'Acting White' Myth." *New York Times,* December 12.

Tran, Quynh-Giang. 2001. "Black Men's Pay in Top Jobs Lags." *Chicago Tribune,* August 15, 1, 13.

Triner, Gail D. 1999 "Race, With or Without Color? Reconciling Brazilian Histography." *Educación y Política en América Latina* June, 10.

Triplett, William. 2004. "Migrant Farmworkers." *CQ Researcher* October 8, 14.

Tse, Archie. 2005. "Gaza Pullout: Cooperation or Resistance." *New York Times,* August 7, 14.

Tucker, M. Belinda and Claudia Mitchell-Kernan, eds. 1995. *The Decline in Marriage among African Americans.* New York: Russell Sage.

Tumulty, Karen. 2006. "Should They Stay or Should They GO?" *Time,* April 10: 28–41.

Ture, Kwame and Charles Hamilton. 1992. *Black Power: The Politics of Liberation.* New York: Vintage Books.

Turner, Margery Austin, Fred Freiburg, Erin Godfrey, Clark Herbig, Diane K. Levy, and Robin S. Smith. 2002. All *Other Things Being Equal: A Paired Testing Study of Mortgage Lending Institutions.* Washington, DC: Urban Institute.

Turner, Ralph H. 1994. "Race Riots Past and Present: A Cultural-Collective Approach." *Symbolic Interaction,* 17(3): 309–324.

Turner, Richard Brent. 2003. *Islam in the African-American Experience.* 2nd ed. Bloomington, IN: Indiana University Press.

Turner, Wallace. 1972. "New Hawaii Economy Stirs Minority Upset." *New York Times,* August 13, 1, 46.

Tyler, S. Lyman. 1973. *A History of Indian Policy.* Washington, DC: U.S. Government Printing Office.

Tyson, Karolyn, William Darity, Jr., and Domini R. Castellino 2005. "It's Not 'a Black Thing': Understanding the Burden of Acting White and Other Dilemmas of High Achievement." *American Sociological Review,* August, 70: 582–605.

Uchitelle, L. 2003. "Older Workers Are Thriving Despite Recent Hard Times." *New York Times,* September 8, 2003. A1, A15.

Ukeles, Jacob B., Ron Miller, and Pearl Beck. 2006. *Young Jewish Adults in the United States Today: Harbingers of the American Jewish Community of Tomorrow?* New York: AJC.

Umberger, Mary. 2006. "Mortgage Law under Fire." *Chicago Tribune* August 18, 1, 8.

United Jewish Communities. 2003. *The National Jewish Population Survey 2000–01.* New York: United Jewish Community.

United Nations. 1997. *The Rights of Indigenous Peoples.* Geneva: United Nations.

UPI. 1997. "Carrier to Change Offensive Manual." *Chicago Defender,* August 21, 10.

U.S. Committee for Refugees. 2003. *World Refugee Survey 2003.* Washington, DC: U.S. Committee for Refugees.

U.S. English. 2006. "Official English: States with Official English Laws." Accessed January 28, 2006, at http://www.us-english.org.

Usdansky, Margaret L. 1992. "Old Ethnic Influences Still Play in Cities." *USA Today,* August 4, 9A.

Valentine, Charles A. 1968. *Culture and Poverty: Critique and Counter-Proposals.* Chicago: University of Chicago Press.

Van Ausdale, Debra and Joe R. Feagin. 2002. *The First R: How Children Learn Race and Racism.* New York: Rowman & Littlefield.

Van Den Berghe, Pierre L. 1965. *South Africa: A Study in Conflict.* Middletown, CT: Wesleyan University.

___ 1978. *Race and Racism: A Comparative Perspective,* 2nd ed. New York: Wiley.

Varadarajan, Tunko. 1999. "A Patel Motel Cartel?" *New York Times Magazine,* July 4, 36–39.

Vega, William A. et al. 1986. "Cohesion and Adaptability in Mexican-American and Anglo Families." *Journal of Marriage and Family,* November, 48: 857–867.

Vigil, Maurilio. 1990. "The Ethnic Organization as an Instrument of Political and Social Change: MALDEF, a Case Study." *The Journal of Ethnic Studies,* Spring, 18: 15–31.

Vuong, Vu-Duc. 2006. "In the Year of the Hen, Viet-Am Women Rock, What Went Right in San Jose Election." *AsianWeek,* June 16.

Wagley, Charles and Marvin Harris. 1958. *Minorities in the New World: Six Case Studies.* New York: Columbia University Press.

Wagner, Angie. 2004. "Invisible Indian Tribes." *Fort Lauderdale Sun-Sentential,* May 23.

Waitzkin, Howard. 1986. *The Second Sickness: Contradictions of Capitalistic Health Care.* Rev. ed. New York: Free Press.

Waldman, Carl. 1985. *Atlas of North American Indians.* New York: Facts on File.

Waller, David. 1996. "Friendly Fire: When Environmentalists Dehumanize American Indians." *American Indian Culture and Research Journal,* 20(2): 107–126.

Wallerstein, Immanuel. 1974. *The Modern World System.* New York: Academic Press.

___. 2004. *World-Systems Analysis: An Introduction.* Durham, NC: Duke University Press.

Walzer, Susan. 1996. "Thinking about the Baby: Gender and Divisions of Infant Care." *Social Problems,* May, 43: 219–234.

Wang, L. Ling-Chi. 1991. "Roots and Changing Identity of the Chinese in the United States." *Daedalus,* Spring, 120: 181–206.

Ward, Deborah L. 1996. "Native Hawaiian Vote: The 'Aes Have It." *Ka Wai Ola O Oha,* October 1996.

Warner, W. Lloyd and Leo Srole. 1945. *The Social Systems of American Ethnic Groups.* New Haven, CT: Yale University Press.

Warren, Jeve. 2000. "Poll: Custody Fight Sharply Divides Dade." *Miami Herald*, April 9, 1A, 24A.

Washburn, Wilcomb E. 1984. "A Fifty-Year Perspective on the Indian Reorganization Act." *American Anthropologist*, June, 86: 279–289.

Washington, Booker T. 1900. *Up from Slavery: An Autobiography*. New York: A. L. Burt.

Watanabe, Teresa. 2004. "Anti-Muslim Incidents Rise, Study Finds." *Los Angeles Times*, May 31, B1, B8.

___. and Susana Enriquez 2005. "Church Redefined." *Los Angeles Times*, April 24, 54.

Waters, Mary. 1990. *Ethnic Options. Choosing Identities in America*. Berkeley: University of California Press.

Watson, Jamal E. 2004. "Going Extra Mile to Worship." *Chicago Tribune*, August 8, sect. 4, 1, 4.

Wausau School District. 2006. *Enrollment Reports 2005–2006*. Wausau WI: Wausau School District.

Wax, Murray L. 1971. *Indian Americans: Unity and Diversity*. Englewood Cliffs, NJ: Prentice Hall.

___. and Robert W. Buchanan. 1975. *Solving "the Indian Problem": The White Man's Burdensome Business*. New York: New York Times Book Company.

Wax, Rosalie. 1967. "The Warrior Drop-Outs" *Trans-Action*, May, 4: 40–46.

Weber, Max [1913–1922]. 1947. *The Theory of Social and Economic Organization*. Translated by A. Henderson and T. Parsons. New York: Free Press.

Weglyn, Michi. 1976. *Years of Infamy: The Untold Story of America's Concentration Camps*. New York: Quill Paperbacks.

Wei, William. 1993. *The Asian American Movement*. Philadelphia: Temple University Press.

Weinberg, Daniel H. 2004. Evidence from Census 2000 about Earnings by Detailed Occupation for Men and Women. CENSR-15. Washington, DC: U.S. Government Printing Office.

Weiner, Tim. 2004. "Of Gringos and Old Grudges: This Land Is Their Land." New York Times, January 9, A4.

Wellington, Alison J. 1994. "Accounting for the Male/Female Wage Gap among Whites: 1976 and 1985." *American Sociological Review*, December, 59: 839–848.

Wells, Robert N., Jr. 1989. "Native Americans' Needs Overlooked by Colleges." Paper, Canton, New York: St. Lawrence University.

___. 1991. "Indian Education from the Tribal Perspective: A Survey of American Indian Tribal Leaders." Paper, Canton, New York: St. Lawrence University.

Werner, Erica. 2006. "Casinos Bank Another Record Year of Revenues." *Indian Country Today*, July 26, 26: B4.

Wernick, Robert. 1996. "The Rise, and Fall, of a Fervid Third Party." *Smithsonian*, November, 27: 150–152, 154–158.

Wertheimer, Jack. 1996. *Conservative Synagogues and Their Members*. New York: Jewish Theological Seminary of America.

Wertsman, Vladima. 2001. "Arab Americans: A Comparative and Critical Analysis of Leading Reference Sources." *Multicultural Review*, June, 42–47.

Wessel, David. 2001. "Hidden Costs of Brain Drain." *Wall Street Journal*, March 1, 1.

White, Jack E. 1997. "I'm Just Who I Am." *Time*, May 5, 149: 32–34, 36.

White House Initiative. 2006. *White House Initiative on Historically Black Colleges and Universities*. Accessed October 1, at http://www.ed.gov/about/inits/list/whhbcu/edlite-index.html

Whitman, David. 1987. "For Latinos, a Growing Divide." *U.S. News and World Report*, August 10, 103: 47–49.

Whyte, John H. 1986. "How Is the Boundary Maintained between the Two Communities in Northern Ireland?" *Ethnic and Racial Studies*, April, 9: 219–234.

Wickham, DeWayne. 1993. "Subtle Racism Thrives." *USA Today*, October 25, 2A.

Wieberg, Steve 2005. "Mascots Create Divisiveness on Some Campuses." *USA Today*, May 16, p. 3C.

Wiesel, Elie. 2006. *Night*. Translated from the French by Marion Wiesel. New York: Hill and Wang.

Wilgoren, Jodi. 2001. "On Campus and on Knees, Facing Mecca." *New York Times*, February 15, A1, A26.

Willeto, Angela A. A. 1999. "Navajo Culture and Female Influences on Academic Success: Traditional Is Not a Significant Predictor of Achievement among Young Navajos." *Journal of American Indian Education*, Winter, 38: 1–24.

Williams, Carol J. 2006a. "Puerto Rico Could Soon Get Real Vote on Status." *Los Angeles Times*, February 17, A15.

2006b. "In Miami, Graying Anti-Castro Movement Is Losing Steam." *Los Angeles Times*, August 11, A13.

Williams, Chris. 2004. "In Minnesota, Tribes Complain of Profiling." *Chicago Tribune*, October 2, 15.

Williams, L. Susan, Sandra D.Alvarez, and Kevin S. Andrado Hauck. 2002. "My Name Is Not Maria: Young Latinas Seeking Home in the Heartland." *Social Problems*, 49(4): 563–584.

Williams, Patricia J. 1997. *Of Race and Risk. The Nation Digital Edition*, December 12, 1997. Accessed at http://www.thenation.com

Willie, Charles V. 1978. "The Inclining Significance of Race." *Society*, July–August, 15: 10, 12–13.

___. 1979. *The Caste and Class Controversy*. Bayside, NY: General Hall.

Wilson, James Q. and Edward C. Banfield. 1964. "Public Regardingness as a Value Premise in Voting Behavior." *American Political Science Review*, December, 58: 876–887.

Wilson, Scott. 2006. "The Village of Nowhere." *Washington Post National Weekly Edition*, June 5, 23: 9–11.

Wilson, William Julius 1973. *Power, Racism and Privilege: Race Relations in Theoretical and Sociohistorical Perspectives*. New York: Macmillan.

___. 1980. *The Declining Significance of Race: Blacks and Changing American Institutions*, 2nd ed. Chicago: University of Chicago Press.

___. 1988. "The Ghetto Underclass and the Social Transformation of the Inner City." *The Black Scholar*, May–June, 19: 10–17.

___. 1996. *When Work Disappears: The World of the New Urban Poor*. New York: Knopf.

___. 2003. "There Goes the Neighborhood. *New York Times*, June 16, A19.

Winant, Howard. 1989. The Other Side of the Process: Racial Formation in Contemporary Brazil. Paper presented at the annual meeting of the American Sociological Association, San Francisco.

___. 1991 Indian Education from the Tribal Perspective: A Survey of American Indian Tribal Leaders. Paper, Canton, New York: St. Lawrence University.

___. 1994. *Racial Conditions: Politics, Theory, Comparisons*. Minneapolis: University of Minnesota Press.

___ 2001. *The World Is a Ghetto: Race and Democracy Since World War II*. New York: Basic Books.

Winkler, Karen. 1990. "Researcher's Examination of California's Poor Latino Population Prompts Debate over the Traditional Definitions of the Underclass." *Chronicle of Higher Education*, October 10, 37: A5, A8.

Winks, Robin W. 1971. *The Blacks in Canada: A History*. Montreal, Quebec: McGill-Queen's University Press.

Withrow, Brian L. 2006. Racial Profiling: From Rhetoric to Reason. Upper Saddle River, NJ: Prentice Hall.

Wolfe, Kathi. 2001. "Debunk Those Stereotypes." *Washington Post National Weekly Edition*, July 9, 18: 23.

"Women Religious Leadership Facing Mainline Decline, Conservative Growth." 1995a. *Religion Watch*, November, 11: 1–3.

Women Work. 1998. *Women Work: Poverty Persists*. Washington, DC: Women Work.

Wong, Morrison G. 1995. "Chinese Americans." Pp. 58–94 in *Asian Americans: Contemporary Trends and Issues*, edited by Pyong Gap Min. Thousand Oaks, CA: Sage Publications.

Woodson, Carter G. 1968. *The African Background Outlined*. Washington, DC: Association Press, 1936. Reprinted New York: Negro Universities Press.

Woodward, C. Vann. 1974. *The Strange Career of Jim Crow*, 3rd ed. New York: Oxford University Press.

Wooton, Barbara H. 1997. "Gender Differences in Occupational Employment." *Monthly Labor Review*, April, 120: 15–24.

Wright, Paul and Robert W. Gardner. 1983. *Ethnicity, Birthplace, and Achievement: The Changing Hawaii Mosaic.* Honolulu: East–West Population Institute.

Wrong, Dennis H. 1972. "How Important Is Social Class?" *Dissent,* Winter, 19: 278–285.

Wu, Frank M. 2002. *Yellow: Race in America beyond Black and White.* New York: Basic Books.

Wyman, Mark. 1993. *Round-Trip to America. The Immigrants Return to Europe, 1830–1930.* Ithaca, NY: Cornell University Press.

Yancey, George. 2003. *Who Is White? Latinos, Asians, and the New Black-Nonblack Divide.* Boulder, CO: Lynne Rienner.

Ybarra, Michael J. 1996. "Limitations of Statuses: In the Light of Today." *New York Times,* June 9, E4.

Yee, Albert H. 1973. "Myopic Perceptions and Textbooks: Chinese Americans' Search for Identity." *Journal of Social Issues,* 29(2): 99–113.

Yi, Daniel. 2006. "Koreatown Immigrants Blending In." *Los Angeles Times,* June 3, A1.

Yinger, John. 1995. *Closed Doors, Opportunities Lost: The Continuing Costs of Housing Discrimination.* New York: Russell Sage Foundation.

Young, Jeffrey R. 2003. "Researchers Change Racial Bias on the SAT." *Chronicle of Higher Education,* October 10, A34–A35.

Younge, Gary. 2004. Election Trail. (Manchester, England). *Guardian Weekly,* November 4, 8.

Zaidi, Arishia U. 2002 "Perceptions of arranged marriages by young Pakistani Muslim women living in a western society." *Journal of Comparative Family Studies,* Autumn, 33: 495–515.

Zambrana, Ruth E., ed. 1995. *Understanding Latino Families: Scholarship, Policy, and Practice.* Thousand Oaks, CA: Sage.

Zarembro, Alan. 2004. "Physician, Remake Thyself: Lured by Higher Pay and Heavy Recruiting, Philippine Doctors Are Getting Additional Degrees and Starting Over in the U.S. as Nurses." *Los Angeles Times,* January 10, A1, A10.

Zeng, Zhen and Yu Xie. 2004. "Asian-Americans' Earnings Disadvantage Reexamined: The Role of Place of Education." *American Journal of Sociology,* 109 (March): 1075–1108.

___. 2004b. "Race and Religion: The Protestant-Catholic Divide." *Gallup Poll Tuesday Briefing,* August 12.

Zernike, Kate. 2005 "Cultural Differences Complicate a Georgia Drug Sting Operation." *New York Times,* August 4: A1, A16.

Zhao, Yilu. 2002. "Chinatown Gentrifies, and Evicts." *New York Times,* August 23, A13.

Zhou, Min. 2004. "Are Asian Americans Becoming 'White?'" *Contexts,* Winter, 29–37.

___. and Carl L. Bankston, III. 1998. *Growing Up American: How Vietnamese Children Adapt to Life in the United States.* New York: Russell Sage Foundation.

___. and Yoshinori Kamo. 1994. "An Analysis of Earnings Patterns for Chinese, Japanese, and Non-Hispanic White Males in the United States." *Sociological Quarterly,* 35(4): 581–602.

Zia, Helen. 2000. *Asian American Dreams: The Emergence of an American People.* New York: Farrar, Straus & Giroux.

Zogby, James J. 1998. Arab Americans Challenge Official Violations. Accessed October 17, 2000, at http://www.arabaai.org/newsandviews/washingtonwatch/032898.html.

___. 2001. *Arab American Attitudes and the September 11 Attacks.* Washington DC: Arab American Institute Foundation.

___. 2003. Arab Pendulum Swings on Civil Liberties. Accessed July 20, 2004, at http://www.aaiusa.org/wwatch/112403.htm.

Photo Credits

288: Frank Espada/Professor Martin Espada; **291:** Redux Pictures.

Chapter 11 Page 298 (from top): © John Van Hasselt/Corbis Sygma; © Cheryl Diaz Meyer/Dallas Morning News/Corbis; © Ed Kashi/Corbis; © Bettmann/Corbis; **299 (from top):** © Hulton-Deutsch Collection/Corbis; © Sherwin Crasto/Reuters/ Corbis; © Ricki Rosen/Corbis Saba; **304:** Atwater Kent Museum of Philadelphia; **307:** Pictorial Parade/Getty Images, Inc.; **309:** © CORBIS All Rights Reserved; **311:** Azizah Magazine; **312:** Bill Aron/PhotoEdit Inc.; **314:** Ed Kashi/CORBIS - NY; **315:** The Image Works; **317:** Arab American Institute; **318:** Lawrence K. Ho/Tribune Media Services TMS Reprints.

Chapter 12 Page 322 (from top): Richard Ellis/Corbis/Sygma; Kelly Mooney/CORBIS - NY; Kelly Mooney/CORBIS - NY; Anne. W. Krause/CORBIS - NY; Craig Aurness/CORBIS - NY; **323 (from top):** Annie Griffiths Belt/CORBIS - NY; © Chris Carroll/Corbis; **330:** David Young/PhotoEdit Inc.; **332:** © CORBIS All Rights Reserved; **334:** John Lee/The Chicago Tribune; **338:** AP Wide World Photos; **340 (left):** Lawrence Migdale/Pix **(right):** Index Stock Imagery, Inc.; **341:** Mike Roemer Photography, Inc.; **343:** PhotoEdit Inc.; **346:** Corbis/Bettmann.

Chapter 13 Page 350 (from top): Reed Kaestner/CORBIS - NY; David Paterson/CORBIS - NY; Phil Schermeister/CORBIS - NY; Nik Wheeler/CORBIS - NY; © Lucidio Studio Inc./Corbis; **351 (from top):** Piere Vauthey/CORBIS - NY; Catherine Karnow/CORBIS - NY; **354:** John Sotomayor/The New York Times; **355:** David Turnley/Corbis/Bettmann; **357:** Rob Lewine/Corbis/Bettmann; **362:** © Tony Freeman/PhotoEdit; **363:** Amanda Marsalis Photography; **366:** Provided by M. Ishii.

Chapter 14 Page 372 (from top): Annie Griffiths Belt/CORBIS - NY; Nathan Benn/CORBIS - NY; Najlah Feanny/CORBIS - NY; Bettmann/ALBERT EINSTEIN and related rights TM/© of The Hebrew University of Jerusalem, used under license. Represented exclusively by Corbis Corporation.; © Scott Speakes/Corbis; **373 (from top):** Richard T. Nowitz/CORBIS - NY; David Wells/CORBIS - NY; **378:** Corbis/Bettmann; **380:** The Wiener Library; **382:** Ulf Andersen/SIPA Press; **385:** AP Wide World Photos; **390:** © CORBIS All Rights Reserved; **391:** H. Gans/The Image Works; **393:** A. Ramey/Stock Boston; **397:** Bill Aron/PhotoEdit Inc.

Chapter 15 Page 400 (from top): © Nathan Benn/Corbis; © Earl & Nazima Kowall/Corbis; © LWA-Dann Tardif/Corbis; © Patrik Giardino/Corbis; **401 (from top):** © Bettmann/Corbis; © Jack Hollingsworth/Corbis; © Jose Luis Pelaez, Inc./Corbis; **403:** Photofest; **405:** Photo Researchers, Inc.; **407:** Edios Interactive **408:** © Sigrid Estrada; **416:** AP Wide World Photos.

Chapter 16 Page 424 (from top): Charles Lenars/Corbis/Bettmann; © Christie's Images/CORBIS; © Lindsay Hebberd/CORBIS; © Brooks Kraft/CORBIS; © John Garrett/CORBIS; **425 (from top):** © Richard A. Cooke/CORBIS; © Jonathan Blair/CORBIS; **430:** Wesley Bocxe/Photo Researchers, Inc.; **431:** Frank Gunn/AP Wide World Photos; **433:** Andrew Wallace/Getty Images, Inc.-Liaison; **436:** The Image Works; **443:** Cagle Cartoons Inc.; **444:** Landov LLC; **446:** Corbis/Bettmann; **447:** Louis Gubb/The Image Works.

Chapter 17 Page 452 (from top): Charles H. Hewitt/© Hulton-Deutsch Collection/CORBIS; © Ed Eckstein/CORBIS; Bob Krist/© CORBIS; © Norbert Schaeer/CORBIS; **453 (from top):** © Richard Hamilton Smith/CORBIS;/© Neal Preston/CORBIS; © Cat Gwynn/CORBIS; **458:** Jack Kurtz/The Image Works; **461:** AP Wide World Photos; **462:** Martin McEbilly/© New York Daily News, L. P. Reprinted with permission; **463:** Vivian Zink; **465:** Copley News Service/Mike Thompson; **468:** Brian Smith/Corbis/Outline.

Index

Abdel-Hady, Dalia, 138
Abdo, Geneive, 307–10
Abeenaki Indians, 44*f*
Abelmann, Nancy, 343
Abolitionists, defined, 205, 479
Aboriginal peoples. *See* First Nation (Canada)
Abortion, 420
Abraham, Nabeel, 311
Abrahamson, Alan, 377, 388
Abrahamson, Mark, 264
Abramoff, Jack, 185
Absolute deprivation
    defined, 69, 479
    relative deprivation *vs.*, 69–70
Abzug, Bella, 421
Accomodation, politics of, 208–9
Achenbaumm, W.A., 460
Acknowledgement process, 182
Acting White, defined, 231–32, 231*f*, 479
Adain, Fatima, 326–27
Adam, Barry D., 469
Adams, Jane Meredith, 355
Adler, Patricia, 346, 403
Adler, Peter, 346
Adorno, T.W., 45
Aetna Insurance, 207
Affirmative action
    defined, 85, 479
    in education, 57–58
    ending discrimination with, 80–82, 86–89, 88*t*
    legal debate over, 87–88
    trends in prejudice and, 52–53
Afghan Americans, 318–19
Afonso Arinos law, 438
Africa
    African-American view of, 204
    slave trade in, 200–1, 201*f*
    tribal groups during slave trade, 201*f*
African Americans
    accomodation politics and, 208–9
    Africa and, 200–1, 201*f*, 204
    Black Power movement and, 219–22
    in Brazil, 436–37
    businesses of, 238
    Civil Rights movement and, 214–18, 215*f*, 216*f*
    control over their lives, 7
    criminal justice system and, 245
    economic conditions for, 234–38
    education of, 209–10, 228–33
    elderly among, 460
    employment data on, 236–38, 238*f*
    family life of, 203, 238–42
    gains and losses of, 211
    gender issues and, 422
    health care for, 245–47
    higher education, 232–33, 233*f*
    history of, 200
    housing discrimination for, 243–45
    income and wealth among, 83–84, 234–36, 234*f*, 235*f*
    institutional discrimination against, 72–75
    internet resource directory, 476
    Irish immigrant fear of, 135
    Jewish Americans and, 385–86
    Korean Americans tensions with, 344–45
    leadership challenges for, 208–11

lynching of, 209, 209*f*
middle class of, 241–42
migration patterns of, 210–11, 210*f*
as Muslims, 23, 223, 307*f*, 309–10, 315
police officers, 238*f*
in politics, 248–49, 248*f*
population data, 202*t*
prejudice among, 55–56
protest movements of, 211–13
racial profiling and, 50
rebuilding after Hurricane Katrina, 4
recent changes in schooling, income
    and life expectancy, 471–72, 472*f*
redlining experienced by, 82
religious beliefs of, 148, 203–4, 222–23, 222*f*
school segregation of, 214–16, 230–31
secession proposed by, 23
slavery of, 200–8, 201*f*, 206*f*
underrepresentation in mass media of, 58–59, 58*f*
views of prejudice by, 53–55
violence and, 209*f*, 210–11, 218–19, 221*f*
voting, 200
white ancestry of, 12
White attitudes toward, 52–53
white ethnic hostility toward, 130, 231
women's issues and, 421–22
women's status compared with, 402–3
African National Congress, 446, 448
Afro-Brazilians, 438–40
Afro-Canadians, 435
Afrocentric perspective, 128
    of African Americans, 204
    defined, 33, 479
    in education curriculums, 230
Age Discrimination in Employment Act (ADEA), 457
Aged as social minority, 455–60, 455*f*
Ageism, 456–58, 479
Aglionby, John, 346
Aguillar-San Juan, Karin, 340, 341
Aguirre, A., 277
Ahmed, Pareha, 96
AIDS Coalition to Unleash Power (ACT-UP), 469
AIDS epidemic
    gays and lesbians and, 468–69
    in South Africa, 448
Airport screening and institutional discrimination, 73–74
Akaka, Daniel, 348
al-Gheezi, Jawad, 300
al-Saud, Faisal, 307*f*
Aladdin, 319
Alárcon, Odette, 292
Alaska Native Settlement Act of 1971, 179
Alaskan Federation of Natives (AFN), 179
Alba, Richard, 138
Albrecht, Gary L., 466
Alcatraz Island, tribal occupation of, 179
Aleut tribes, 179
Ali, Noble Drew, 308
Alien Act of 1798, 100
Alien Land Act of 1913, 359

Allotment Act, 165, 172–73
Allport, Gordon, 45, 58, 379
Alonso-Zaldivar, Ricardo, 74
Alvord, Lois Arviso, 191–92
Alvord, Valerie, 340
Amalgamation
    defined, 25, 479
    fusion and, 25
American Airlines, 254
American Apartheid, 23
American Arab Anti-Discrimination Committee, 319
American Association of Retired Persons (AARP), 458, 460
American Colonization Society, 23
American Dilemna, The, 18, 402
American Federation of Labor (AFL), 102
American Indian Movement (AIM), 178–80
American Indian Religious Freedom Act, 192, 193
American Indians. *See* Native Americans
American Jewish Committee, 388–89, 394
American Jewish Congress, 388–89
American Muslim Alliance, 319
American Protective Association, 133
American Society of Muslims (ASM), 308–9
Americans of Japanese ancestry (AJAs), 347, 479
Americans with Disabilities Act (ADA), 465–66
Amish, 158
    lifestyle of, 159–60, 160*f*
    in society, 160–62
Ancient Order of Hibernians, 132
Andretti, Mario, 138
Andrews, George Reid, 437
Androgyny, 403, 479
Angier, Natalie, 192
Anglo culture
    Cuban Americans and, 267
    Hispanic references to, 255–57
    language and, 143
    Mexican Americans and, 275, 281, 291f
Animal sacrifice as religious ritual, 158
Annexation of subordinate groups, 20
Ansari, Zafar Ishaq, 308
Anthony, Susan B., 405
Anti-Catholic crusade, 101
Anti-Chinese movement, 101–3, 102*f*
Anti-Defamation League (ADL) of B'nai B'rith, 40, 384, 389
Anti-Muslim attitudes, 316–19
Anti-Semitism
    of Black Muslims, 309
    contemporary trends in, 384–86, 384*f*, 385*f*
    defined, 374, 479
    history of, 382–83
    Holocaust and, 22, 381–82
    Jewish American migration and, 378
    in Montana, 374
    origins of, 379–86
    social construction of race and, 14
    in United States, 382–86
Apache tribe, 195

Apartheid. *See also* Racism
defined, 479
schools, 230, 479
in South Africa, 446–47
Apikoros, 395
Aponte, Robert, 279
Applebaum, Kalman, 181
Applebome, Peter, 159, 204
Arab Americans, 301–4, 302*f*
conditions for, 300–1
contemporary life in U.S., 311–15, 311*f*
education for, 314, 314*f*
family life and gender issues, 312–13
immigration to U.S., 310–11
internet resource directory, 477
language of, 301–2
Muslims as, 300–1, 301*f*
politics of, 314–15
population data on, 302–3, 303*f*
prejudice and discrimination against, 46, 319–20
as racial identity, 31
racial profiling and, 49
U.S. attitudes toward, 316–19
Arab countries, 302*f*
Arab-Israeli conflict, 310, 441, 442*f*
Arafat, Yasser, 443
Aran, Kenneth, 283
Archulta, Glenda, 194
Arden, H., 391
Arditi, Jorge, 471
Arias, Elizabeth, 246
Armed Forces of National Liberation, 287
Armstrong, Elizabeth A., 470
Arranged marriage, 336–37, 479
Arrest rates for African Americans, 245–46
Asahina, Robert, 362
Asante, Molefi Kete, 32–33, 201*f*
Asch, Adrienne, 464
Asian American Journalists Association, 330
Asian Americans
Asian Indians as, 334–35
Chinese Americans, 352–59
diversity among, 333, 333*t*
economic conditions, 326–29, 328*t*
education, 326–29, 328*t*
ethnic categories, 325*f*
ethnic diversity of, 333–34
Filipino Americans, 335–38
in Hawaii, 345–48
illegal immigration policies and, 106–10
institutional discrimination against, 74
internet resource directory, 476
Japanese Americans, 352, 359–65
Korean Americans, 342–45
as "model minority," 325–31
panethnicity and, 30, 348
political activity, 331–33, 331*f*
population data on, 324*f*, 325*f*
prejudice among, 55–56
racial profiling of, 330–31
rebuilding after Hurricane Katrina, 4
segregation of, 24
Southeast Asian Americans, 339–42
women's issues, 422
workplace discrimination against, 78
Asian Indians, 334–35
current issues for, 335
immigration patterns, 334–35
violence against, 327
Assimilation
of African Americans, 214–15, 250
Americanization of Roman Catholic church, 154–55

by Arab and Muslim Americans, 303–4
of Asian Americans, 367–69
Black Power *vs.*, 219–22
of Chinese Americans, 357–59
defined, 25–26, 479
of Filipino Americans, 337
by gays and lesbians, 471
Hispanic Catholicism and, 294–95
Hmong community case study in, 341–42
immigrant health care and, 293
of Italian Americans, 135–38, 136*f*
of Jewish Americans, 376–77, 393–95
of Mexican Americans, 277–78, 280–82, 293
of Native Americans, 172–74, 189
of Southeast Asian Americans, 339–40
of subordinate groups, 3, 25–26
symbolic ethnicity and, 128–29
Asylees, defined, 119, 479
Atague, 294
Ataiyero, Kayce, 365
Atlanza Federal de Mercedes (Federal Alliance of Land Grants), 281
Attitudes, trends in prejudice and, 52–53
Austria, German annexation of, 20
Authoritarian Personality, The, 45
Authoritarian personality theory of prejudice, 45, 479
Autobiography of Malcolm X, 308
Avila, Oscar, 314, 341
Ayala, César J., 287
Ayouby, Kenneth Kahtan, 300, 311, 316
Azizah (magazine), 311*f*
Aztec civilization, 167, 274, 429

Ba-Yunus, Ilyas, 306, 308
Bachelder, L., 464
Badgett, M.V. Lee, 87
Bagby, Ishan, 311
Bahr, Howard, 177
Bakke, Allan, 87
Baldwin, James, 386
Baldwin, N., 383
Bales, Robert, 404
Baltzell, E. Digby, 137
Bamshad, Michael J., 13
Banerjee, Neela, 153, 157, 358
Banfield, Edward, 131
Banks, Dennis, 178–80
Bankston, Carl L., 340
Baptist Church, 154–55
Bar Mitzvah, 391*f*
Bar-Tal, Daniel, 445
Barbaro, Fred, 131
Barclay, William, 426
Barnes, Edward, 268
Barnes, Jessica S., 352, 369
Barnes, Patricia M., 100
Baron, Milton L., 455
Barrera, Mario, 281
Barrett, David B., 146
Barringer, Felicity, 108
Barry, Ellen, 468
Bartlett, Donald L., 185
Bartlett, Jed, 58
Bash, Harry M., 14
Basrietos, Gonzala, 261*f*
Basu, Moni, 300
Bat Mitzvah, 391*f*
Battle of Little Big Horn, 170, 176
Battle of Wounded Knee, 171
Battle of Wounded Knee II, 179
Bauder, Harald, 435
Bauer, Raymond A., 205
Baum, Geraldine, 394
Bean, Frank D., 108–9
Becker, Howard, 18
Beisel, Nicola, 422

Belkin, Lisa, 417
Bell, Derrick, 92
Bell, Wendel, 21
Bell Curve, The, 13–14
Bell hooks, 422
Bellafante, Ginia, 337
Bellah, Robert, 152–53
Bellecourt, Clyde, 178
Belliard, Juan Carlos, 294
Belluck, Pam, 183
Belt, Don, 305, 307
Bem, Sandra and Daryl, 422
Bendavid, Naftali, 248
Bendick, Marc Jr., 458
Bendyna, Mary E., 130
Benedetto, Richard, 262
Benevolent associations, of Chinese Americans, 354–55
Bennett, Claudette, 333, 352, 369
Bennett, L., 205–6, 216
Bennett, P., 31
Bennett, V., 431
Bennetts, Leslie, 464
Benny, Jack, 141
Berkeley Center for Independent Living, 464
Bertrand, Marianne, 62
Best, Joel, 32
Bilingual Education, 143–45
Act, 144
Bilingualism
defined, 28, 143, 479
in education, 143–45, 479
education for Puerto Ricans and Mexicans and, 290–91
of Hispanic Americans, 143–45, 261
official language movement and, 145–46
pluralism and, 28
politics and, 261–62
of Puerto Ricans, 285
Billson, Janet Mancini, 32
Biological race, defined, 12–13, 479
Biracial couples, challenges of, 15, 29–32, 30*f*–31*f*
Birchard, Karen, 433
Birren, James E., 457
Birth control issues, 406
Bisexuals, 467
Bishop Museum, 347
Black English, 204
Black Entertainment Television (BET), 59
Black Hills Sioux Nation Act, 176
Black Muslims, 307–10, 307*f*
secession proposed by, 23
Black Panther Party, 221, 386
Black Power, 130, 199, 219–22
Blackfeet tribe, 175
Blackstock, Nelson, 218
Blaming the victim perspective, 18
culture of poverty theory and, 278–79
defined, 479
Blauner, Robert, 22
Blended identity, 306–7, 307*f*, 479
Bloc Québécois, 436
Bloch, Hannah, 107
Blood, Michael R., 254
Blue-collar workers
ethnicity among, 128
white ethnics as, 130
Blyden, Edward Wilmot, 308
B'nai B'rith (Sons of the Covenant), 388–89
"Boat people"
from Cuba, 264–66
from Haiti, 119
from Vietnam, 20, 23, 339
Bob Jones University, 130
Bobo, Lawrence D., 179

Bocian, Debbie, 72
Boehm, M., 363
Boers, 446
Bogardus, Emory, 51
Bogardus scale, 51, 479
Bohland, James R., 177
Bon Jovi, 140f, 141
Bonacich, Edna, 76, 328, 359
Bonilla-Silva, Eduardo, 14, 52, 126
Bonus, Rick, 338
Boorstein, Michelle, 315
Border militarization, 111–12
Border Patrol, 110–11
Borderlands, 262–64, 263f, 479
Bordt, Rebecca L., 76
Boricua, 282
Borinquén, 282
Bork, Robert H., 159
Bositis, David A., 248f, 309
Bosnia, ethnic cleansing in, 22
Bosque-Pérez, Ramon, 287
Bourke-White, Margaret, 214f
Boushey, Heather, 417
Bowers v. Hardwick, 469
Bowles, Scott, 50
Bowman, Tom, 155
Bowser, Benjamin, 17
Boxall, Bettina, 334
Boy Scouts, 470
Bracero program, 276, 479
Brachear, Manya A., 300
Brackman, Harold, 381
Braddock, D., 464
Brain drain
    defined, 107, 479
    immigration patterns and, 107–8,
        107t, 269
Brannon, Ruth, 464
Braxton, Greg, 59
Brazil
    prejudice and discrimination in,
        438–40
    racial democracy and, 437–38
    slavery and, 436–37
Brazilians, as racial identity, 31
Brewer, Cynthia, 210f, 473f
Brewster, David (Sir), 454
Briggs, David, 156
Brimmer, Andrew, 80
Brittingham, Angela, 6t, 303f
Broder, John M., 109
Brodie, Mollyann, 143, 256, 259
Brody, Adrien, 141
Brooke, James, 166, 316
Brooks-Gunn, Jeanne, 13
Broom, Leonard, 361
Brotherhood of Sleeping Car Porters, 211
Brown, Dee, 171
Brown, Linda, 214
Brown, Patricia Leigh, 307
Brown vs. Board of Education, 53, 81,
    214–16, 224, 230
Browne, Irene, 422
Brownstein, Andrew, 61
Bruno, Rosalind, 138, 141, 146
Bryan, Susan M., 194
Brynner, Yul, 47f
Bryson, Ken, 241
Buchanan, Robert W., 174, 176
Buchenwald, 382
Buchholz, Barbara Ballinger, 466
Buckley, Stephen, 438
Buddhists
    Chinese Americans as, 358
    Japanese Americans as, 365
    in United States, 147
Budig, Michelle J., 92, 420
Bukowcyk, John J., 141
Bullard, Robert, 85
Bureau of Citizenship and Immigration

Services, 112, 318
Bureau of Indian Affairs, 169–70, 173,
    175, 178, 185, 190
Burgess, Ernest, 51
Burgess, Mike, 192
Bush, George W., 4, 46, 76, 130, 152,
    248–49, 261, 315–17, 364
    race/ethnicity guidelines of, 50
Bushmen, 445
Businesses
    of African Americans, 238
    of Arab and Muslim Americans,
        311–12
    of Asian Americans, 326–29
    of Chinese Americans, 354–56, 354f
    of Korean Americans, 343–46
Bustillo, Miguel, 4
Butler, John Sibley, 213, 215
Butler, Robert, 456

Cage, Nicholas, 138
Cainkar, Louise, 312
California, immigrant legislation in,
    115–16
California Civil Rights Initiative, 89
Calvary Chapel, 150
Camarillo, Albert, 269
Cambodia, refugees from, 339
Canada
    ethnic and racial diversity in, 431–36
    First Nation in, 432–33
    immigration and race in, 435–36
    Québécois, 433–34, 433f
Canak, William, 428t
Cañas, Jesus, 263
Canyonlands National Park, 194
Capone, Al, 137
Capps, Randy, 115f
Card, David, 114
Carey, Mariah, 29, 135
Carlson, Dawn S., 413
Carmichael, Stokely, 72, 220
Carrier, Jim, 63–64
Carro-Figueroa, Viviana, 287
Carroll, Joseph, 145
Carroll, S., 421
Cart, Julie, 348, 369
Carter, Bill, 59
Carter, Jimmy, 264, 441
Cartier, Jacques, 436
Carvajal, Doreen, 125
Casey, Marion R., 78t
Casinos, Native American operation of,
    184–85, 184f
Casper, Lynne M., 241
Cassidy, Rachel C., 6f, 31f
Castañeda, Jorge G., 290, 429
Castro, Fidel, 264, 267
Catalano, Shannan M., 245
Catalyst, 91
Cayetano, Benjamin, 338
Census data
    on Arab Americans, 302–3, 303f
    of Asian Americans, 333, 333t
    black population, 202t, 435
    black-white segregation figures, 24f
    on economic conditions of women,
        407, 409t
    on ethnic diversity, 124
    on gays and lesbians, 467
    on Hispanic Americans, 254–55
    illegal immigrant statistics, 106
    on Native Americans, 166–67
    Native   Americans   reservations,
        180–82, 182t
    on race and ethnicity, 27f
    race questions on, 30–31, 31f
    white-latino segregation figures, 24f
    on women clergy, 156
Central Americans, 268–70, 268f

Cerar, K. Melissa, 269
Chain immigration, 479
    defined, 97–98
Champagne, Duane, 432–33
Chan, Sucheng, 196
Chang, Patricia M.Y., 157
Charlottetown Agreement, 433
Charter of Rights (Canada), 432, 436
Charter schools, 230
Chase-Dunn, Christopher, 168
Chavez, Julio Cesar, 279–80, 279f
Chen, David W., 4
Cherokee tribe, 170, 187
Cherry, Nicole Miyako, 352
Cheung, Alan, 144
Cheyenne tribe, 170
Chicanismo, 281, 479
Chicano movement, 281–82, 295
Chicksaw tribe, 170, 187
Child care issues, 416–20
Child labor among Amish, 161–62
Children's living arrangements, 239f
Chin, Ko-lin, 359
Chinatowns, 354–57
Chinese, expulsion by Vietnam, 23
Chinese Americans, 352–59
    current conditions for, 354–57
    family and religious life of, 357–59,
        357f
    immigration restrictions of, 95
    occupational profile of, 353–54
    organizational life of, 354–55, 354f
    political activity by, 332, 355, 368
    population data on, 352–53, 352t
    prejudice and discrimination against,
        43, 366–69
    restrictionist sentiment and, 101–3,
        102f
    social problems of, 356–57
Chinese Canadians, 435
Chinese   Consolidated   Benevolent
    Association (CCBA), 355
Chinese Exclusion Act, 101–3, 353–54,
    359
Chinese immigrants
    anti-Chinese movement, 101–3
    LaPiere's study concerning, 42–43
Chinese Six Companies, 355
Chippewa tribe, 179, 188
Chirot, Daniel, 22
Chisholm, Shirley, 421
Choctaw tribe, 170
Christian Science church, 156
Christianity
    of African Americans, 203–4, 222–23,
        222f
    of Chinese Americans, 358
    compared to Islam, 304
    denominations by U.S. county, 147,
        147f
    of Japanese Americans, 365
    of Native Americans, 192–93
    segregation of, 147–48
Christmas Carol, A, 464
Christopulos, Diana, 283
Chu, Jeff, 96
Chulalongkorn, king, 47f
Church membership
    for African Americans, 222–23, 222f
    statistics on, 148, 148t, 150
Church of God in Christ, 156
Church of Jesus Christ of Latter-Day
    Saints, 156
Churchill, Winston, 14
*Cisneros v. Corpus Christi Independent School
    District*, 143
Citizens' Committee to Repeal Chinese
    Exclusion, 353
Citizenship
    denial of, to Chinese immigrants, 102

Citizenship *(cont.)*
  for Hispanic Americans, 261
  immigration restrictions and, 104–6, 105*f*
  for Mexican Americans, 275
  for Puerto Ricans, 274, 283
City of Richmond v. Croson, 88*t*
Civil disobedience
  African Americans and, 215–18
  defined, 216, 479
Civil Liberties Act of 1988, 363
Civil religion
  defined, 152, 479
  Protestant denomination of, 156
Civil Rights Act of 1964, 81–82, 218, 411, 414
  disabled persons and, 465
Civil Rights Movement, 214–18, 215*f*, 216*f*
Civil Rights movement, 224
Civil Rights Project (Harvard University), 230
Civil Rights Restoration Act, 368–69
Clark, Kenneth, 53
Clark, Mamie, 53
Clary, Mike, 267
Class
  African American middle class, 241–42
  defined, 15, 242, 479
  ethnicity awareness and, 128
  Mexican Americans, 279–80
  in Mexico, 429–30
  religion and ethnicity and, 149*f*, 151–52
  stratification of, 15–16
  white ethnics and issue of, 129–30
Classroom sexism, 415–16
Cleaver, Eldridge, 221
Cleaver, Kathleen, 221
Clemetson, Lynette, 300, 315
Clemmitt, Marcia, 159
Cleveland, Grover, 208
Clinton, Bill, 247*f*, 470
Cloud, John, 469
Coates, Rodney D., 50
Cochran, Floyd, 64
Cockburn, Andrew, 282
Cognard-Black, Andrew J., 92
Cohen, Sandy, 374, 379
Cohen, Steven M., 389, 392, 398
Cohon, Samuel M., 374
Cole, David, 246
Coleman, Arica L., 25
Coleman, James S., 188
Colleges and universities
  affirmative action, 87
  anti-Semitism at, 374
  disabled persons at, 464, 466
  gay students in, 468*f*
  Jewish Americans at, 388
  Native Americans at, 189–90
Collier, John, 176
Collins, Patricia Hill, 421
Colombia, immigrants from, 269
Colón Morera, José Javier, 287
Colonialism
  defined, 21, 479
  South Africa and, 445–46
  of subordinate group, 21–22, 21*f*
  world systems theory, 21
Color gradient, 268, 289, 479
  in Brazil, 438
  in Mexico, 429
Coloured, 445–46
Columbian Coalition, 130
Columbus, Christopher, 167–68, 284
Comas-Díaz, Lillian, 295
Comer, James, 241
Commission on Civil Rights, 191, 278

Commission on Wartime Relocation and Internment of Civilians, 363
Communist Party of the United States, 221
Comparable worth. *See also* Pay equity
  defined, 479
Conflict perspective, defined, 17
Conflict theory
  ageism and, 458
  Amish society and, 160–62
  anti-Chinese movement and, 102
  bilingual education and, 143
  brain drain and, 108
  criminal justice for African Americans and, 245
  culture of poverty theory and, 279
  defined, 17–18, 479
  gender issues, 405
  Mexican Americans immigration and, 276
  sexual harassment and, 414
Congregationalists, beliefs of, 154
Congress of Racial Equality (CORE), 211
Conlin, Michelle, 415
Connecticut Mashantucket Pequot Indians, 184
Connor, Walter, 426
Conscription, 133–34
Conservative Judaism, 390–93
Contact hypothesis, defined, 59, 479
Conver, Bill, 394
Conyers, James L. Jr., 209–10
Conyers, John, 207
Coogan, Michael D., 302*f*
Cook, James (Capt.), 345
Cooper, Abraham, 381
Cooper, Mary, 75, 341
Cooper, Richard S., 247
Cooperman, Alan, 155
Coppola, Francis Ford, 138
Corbell, Eloise, 175
Corbell class action lawsuit, 175–76
Cornacchia, Eugene J., 137
Cornell, Stephen, 174, 178–79, 186
Corporate response to prejudice, 60–62, 61*f*
Correll, Joshua, 38
Cortéz, Hernando, 281
Cosby, Bill, 231–32, 239
Cose, Ellis, 90
Coser, Lewis, 416
Coser, Rose Laub, 416
Council of American-Islamic Relations, 319
Council of Energy Resource Tribes (CERT), 194
Court of Claims (U.S.), 175
Coury, Joseph, 300
Coury, Rebecca, 300
Cox, James, 208
Cox, Oliver C., 45
Crage, Suzanna M., 470
Crazy Horse, 170
Creationism, 158–59
Creationists, defined, 158, 479
Creek tribe, 170, 187
Crenson, Matt, 433
Crèvecoeur, Hector St. John de, 25
Crime
  among Southeast Asian Americans, 340
  for Native Americans, 192
  trends in prejudice and, 52–53, 137
Criminal justice for African Americans, 245
Criollos class, 429
Croft, Laura, 407*f*
Cronje, Frans, 448
Crosby Show, The, 59
Crossover effect

  defined, 188, 479–80
  Native American education, 188
Cuban-American National Foundation, 267
Cuban Americans, 264–67
  current status of, 266–67, 266*f*
  immigration, 264–66
  refugees, 118
Cultural bias, intelligence testing and, 13
Cultural freedom and pluralism, 27
Cultural identity
  of Asian Indians, 334–35
  of Hispanic Americans, 258–59
  of Japanese Americans, 367–69
  of Jewish Americans, 393–94
Culture of poverty theory, 278–79, 480
Curanderismo, 293–94, 480
Curanderos, 294
Currie, Barbara, 130
Custer, George, 170
Czechoslovakia, German annexation of, 20

Dahlburg, John-Thor, 120, 266–67, 428*t*
Daitz, Ben, 194
Dang, Alain, 467
Daniels, Roger, 361
Dannin, Robert, 309
Dansie, Roberto, 294
Dart, Bob, 162
Dart, John, 358
David, Gary, 300, 303, 311, 316
Davis, Astrid, 231
Davis, David Brion, 437
Davis, James A., 52, 154–55
Davis, Stacey, 30
Dawson, Michael C., 207
Day care, gender issues in labor force and, 408, 411, 418
Days Inns of America, 458
De Diego, Jose, 288*f*
De facto segregation, 215, 230, 480
De jure segregation, 214, 480
  bilingual education and, 143–44
De Klerk, F.W., 446–48
de la Cruz, Patricia, 4*t*, 6, 255, 266, 278, 291, 303*f*
de la Garza, Rodolfo O., 31
Dearborn Independent, 383
Death penalty, African Americans, 246
Declining Significance of Race, The, 242
Defense of Marriage Act, 470
Deficit model of ethnic identity, 303, 480
Degler, Carl, 437–38
Del Olmo, Frank, 113
Dell'Angela, Tracy, 187
DellaPergola, Sergio, 374, 375*f*
Deloria, Vine Jr., 167, 173–74, 176, 192
DeNavas-Watt, Carmen, 78*f*, 220*f*, 234*f*, 235, 241, 257*f*, 293, 412*f*, 414, 459*f*, 472*f*
Denomination
  defined, 147, 480
  education and, 154, 155*f*
  income and, 155*f*
Denton, Nancy, 23, 243
DePalma, Anthony, 429
Department of Homeland Security, immigration policies of, 112
Department of Justice, 317–18
Deportations of Mexican Americans, 276–78
Desegregation, 213–16
  Puerto Rican and Mexican Americans students and, 291–92
Desi, 335, 480
Deutscher, Irwin, 43
Devil's Tower, 193*f*, 195
Día de los Muertos (Day of the Dead), 295

Diamond, Jared, 118
Diaspora, 385, 440, 443, 480
Differential justice, 245, 480
DiMaggio, Joe, 138
Dimant, Tamara, 448
Diné College, 190
Dinnerstein, Leonard, 377
Disability, defined, 461, 480
Disabled in Action, 465
Disabled persons. *See* People with disabilities
Disch, Estelle, 404
Discrimination
    affirmative action, 85–88, 88*t*
    ageism and, 457–58
    apartheid and, 446
    against Arab and Muslim Americans, 319–20
    of Asian Americans, 329–31, 366–69
    in Brazil, 438–40
    characteristics of, 68–69
    of Chinese Americans, 353–54
    current trends in, 77–80
    defined, 37, 69, 480
    elimination of, 80–83
    environmental justice and, 84–85
    against gays and lesbians, 467–69
    glass ceiling and, 89–92
    on Hawaii, 345, 347
    institutional, 72–75
    against Japanese Americans, 366–69
    of Jewish Americans, 380, 387–88
    job seeking and, 76
    low-wage labor and, 75–77, 76*f*
    measurement of, 78–80, 78*f*, 79*t*
    of people with disabilities, 460–6
    prejudice and, 41–43, 42*f*
    relative *vs.* absolute deprivation, 69–70
    reverse discrimination, 88–89
    total discrimination, 70–72
    wealth inequality and, 83–84
    of women, 410–15
Displaced homemakers, 414–15, 480
Ditka, Mike, 141
Diversity training
    as corporate response to prejudice, 60–62, 61*f*
    in education, 58
Dixon, Margaret, 460
Do the Right Thing, 344
Dolan, Maura, 89
Domestic partnerships, 470, 480
Dominant groups
    assimilation fostered to, 25–26
    defined, 7
    expulsion of subordinate groups by, 22–23
    fusion process and, 25
    resistance to change from, 32–33
    stereotypes held by, 47
    subordination group relations with, 426
    tribal resistance to, 174
    whiteness of, 125
Dominican Republic, immigrants from, 118, 270
Domino, John C., 414
"Don't ask don't tell" policy, 470
Dora the Explorer, 270
Dorris, Michael, 196
"Double consciousness" concept, 31–32
Douglass, Frederick, 205, 208, 223
Doyle, James A., 404
Drabelle, Dennis, 175
"Draft Riots of 1863," 134
Dred Scott decision, 81
Drinkard, Jim, 185
"Driving While Black" (DWB) stereotype, 50

Dropout rates of Native Americans, 187
Drug trafficking in Puerto Rico, 289–90
"Dry foot, wet foot" policy, 266, 480
Du Bois, W.E.B.
    on Africa, 204
    on Black capitalism, 241–42
    on class issues, 241–42
    on color line, 9–10
    "double consciousness" concept of, 31–32
    on education, 233
    leadership by, 208–9
    Niagara movement and, 209–11
    on prejudice, 53
    on slavery, 203–4
    theories of, 33
Dual housing market, 244
Dual labor market
    defined, 75, 480
    for Hispanic Americans, 270
Dual national laws, 281–82
Duberman, Martin, 469
Duckworth, Tammy, 332*f*
Dudley, Carl S., 151
Duncan, Greg J., 13
Dunham, Katherine, 438
Dunn, Ashley, 329
Duston, Hannah, 44*f*
Duszak, Thomas, 139
Dutch East India Company, 445
Dysfunction, defined, 17, 480
Dyson, Michael, 232, 309

Early, Gerald, 33
Ebonics, 230
    defined, 204, 480
Echaveste, Maria, 111
Eckholm, Erik, 236–37
Eckstrom, Kevin, 153
Economic conditions. *See also* Income
    for African Americans, 234–38, 241–42
    of Asian Americans, 326–29, 328*t*
    for Chinese Americans, 356–57
    for Cuban and South Americans, 266–67, 266*f*
    for elderly, 458–59
    feminization of poverty, 480
    of Filipino Americans, 337–38
    government employment of Native Americans, 183–84
    on Hawaii, 346–47
    for Hispanic Americans, 257–61, 257*f*, 260*f*
    for Japanese Americans, 364–65
    of Jewish Americans, 387–88
    for Korean Americans, 343–45
    for Mexican Americans, 278–80, 278*f*, 280*f*
    Native American casino gambling operations, 184–85
    for Native Americans, 183–86
    for Puerto Ricans, 278*t*, 289–90
    slavery's impact on, 205
    for women, 407–15
Economic Opportunity Act, 388
Ecuadorian Americans, prejudice against, 4–5
Ecuavolley, 4–5
Edles, Laura Desfor, 347
Edmonds, Patricia, 168
Edmonston, Barry, 114–15
Education. *See also* Higher education
    affirmative action and, 87–89
    of African Americans, 209–10, 228–33
    of Arab and Muslim Americans, 314, 314*f*
    of Asian Americans, 326–29, 328*t*
    of Asian Indians, 335
    bilingual, 143–45

desegregation of, 214–15
discrimination despite constants in, 79–80, 79*t*
    of Filipino Americans, 338
    financial return on for women and men, 412*f*
    for Hmong communities, 341–42
    Italian-American attitudes toward, 137
    of Japanese Americans, 364
    of Jewish Americans, 388
    life expectancy, comparison of white, African Americans and Hispanic Americans, 471–72, 472*f*
    of Native Americans, 166*f*, 187–90, 188*f*
    for Puerto Ricans and Mexicans, 290–92
    quantity and quality of, for African Americans, 229–30
    reduction of prejudice and, 57–59
    religious denomination and levels of, 154, 155*f*
    for Southeast Asian Americans, 326–29
    of women, 412*f*, 415–16
Education Act of 1972, 415
Edwards, Jennifer, 22
Edwards v. Aguillard, 158–59
Egan, Timothy, 183
Egypt, 303, 441
Eid-al-Fitr, 314
Eitle, Tamela McNulty, 231
El Salvador, immigrants from, 268–69, 268*f*
Elderly
    advocacy by, 459–60
    economic conditions for, 458–59
    Korean Americans community and care for, 344
    as minority group, 455–60, 455*f*
Elkins, Stanley, 203, 437
Elliott, Andrea, 310
Ellison, Christopher G., 151
Ellison, Keith, 315
Emancipation Proclamation, 205, 435
Emerald Society, 134
Emigration
    defined, 20, 480
    of Hispanic Americans, 262–63
Employment Assistance Program, 165, 175, 177–78
Employment data
    on African Americans, 236–38, 238*f*
    of women, 409, 409*t*
Engel v. Vitale, 157
Engels, Frederick, 69
Engen, Rodney L., 245
England, Paula, 420
English as a second language (ESL), 144
English immersion, 144, 480
English immigrants, Whiteness defined by, 125–26
Enriquez, Susana, 295
Environmental justice
    defined, 84–85, 194, 480
    health care for African Americans, 247
    for Native Americans, 193–95
Environmental Protection Agency (EPA), 85
Episcopal church
    characteristics of, 154–55
    West Indian immigration and, 148
Epstein, Cynthia Fuchs, 422
Equal Employment Opportunity Commission (EEOC), 81, 411, 458
Equal Pay Act, 412
Equal-status contract, 59–60
Erdmans, Mary Patrice, 141
Eriksson, Leif, 167

Eschbach, Karl,   181
Escobar, Gabriel,   262
Espiritu, Yen Le,   30, 31, 336, 338
Estado Libre Asociado,   283
Esteves, Ramon,   58
Ethclass
    African American middle class and,
        241–42
    defined,   152, 257, 480
    of Hispanic Americans,   257
Ethnic cleansing
    defined,   22, 480
    of subordinate groups,   22
Ethnic diversity,   124–25
    among Asian-Americans,   315–16,
        316f, 366–69
    worldwide distribution of,   427f
Ethnic groups. *See also* Intergroup rela-
        tions
    characteristics of,   9–10
    defined,   9, 480
    Jewish Americans,   376–79
    secession by,   23
Ethnic identity
    of Asian Americans,   333–34
    of Chinese Americans,   353
    deficit model of,   303
    of Jewish Americans,   376–77, 393–95
    marginality and,   31–32
Ethnicity
    in 15 largest U.S. cities,   27f
    conflicts over,   9–10
    hate crimes and,   39
    of Hispanic Americans,   30–31
    income differences and,   78–80, 78f, 79t
    internet resource directory,   478
    of Italian Americans,   135–38
    paradox,   129, 480
    prejudice of,   130–31
    rediscovery of,   127
    religion and social class and,   149f,
        151–52
    religious practices and,   148, 149f
    sociology and study of,   15–19
    symbolic ethnicity,   128
    third-generation principle,   127–28
    in U.S. states,   8f
Ethnocentrism
    defined,   39, 480
    prejudice and,   39
Ethnonational conflict,   426, 427f, 480
Ethnophaulism,   41, 480
Evacuees,   361, 480
Evans, Lorraine,   230
Evolution, creationism *vs.*,   158–59
Exclusion Act (1882),   95
Executive Order 9066,   360–61
Exogamy,   346
Expansionism, Eurocentric and Native
    American views of,   169f
Exploitation theory of prejudice,   45–46, 480
Expulsion of subordinate groups,   22–23
Extermination of subordinate groups,   22

Fair Employment Practices Commission
    (FEPC),   81, 211
Fair Pay Act,   412
Fallows, Marjorie R.,   134
Familism, defined,   292, 480
Family and Medical Leave Act,   408
Family life
    of African Americans,   203, 238–42
    of Arab Americans,   312–13
    of Asian Indians,   335
    of Chinese Americans,   354–55,
        357–59, 357f
    of Filipino Americans,   338
    of Hispanic Americans,   258
    of Japanese Americans,   365, 366
    for Jewish Americans,   394–95

for Korean Americans,   344–45
of Muslim Americans,   312–13
of Puerto Ricans and Mexican
    Americans,   292
women and,   416–20, 417f
Fannie Lou Hamer, Rosa Parks and
    Coretta Scott King Voting Rights
    Reauthorization and Amendments
    Act,   249
Farm laborers
    Mexican Americans as,   279–80, 279f
    Puerto Ricans as,   290
Farnsworth, Clyde H.,   436
Farrakhan, Louis,   239, 309, 386
Farrell, Elizabeth F.,   466
Feagin, Joe R.,   17, 25
Federal Fair Housing Law,   243
Federal government
    affirmative action measures of,   86–89,
        88t
    anti-discrimination efforts of,   81–82
    anti-slavery discouraged by,   205–6
    education of Native Americans by,
        187–90
    employment of Native Americans,
        185–86
    impact on Native Americans of,   172–78
    Native American sovereignty and,
        181–82
    Native Americans legal claims and,
        175–76
    slavery reparations legislation and,
        206–7
Feminine mystique,   407, 480
Feminist movement,   405–7, 405f, 407f,
        422–23
    African Americans and,   422
    minority women in,   421–22
Feminization of poverty,   414–15, 480
Ferraro, Geraldine,   137
Ferree, Myra Marx,   407
Fifteenth Amendment (U.S. Constitution),
        205
Files, John,   175
Filipino Americans
    current issues facing,   337–38, 338f
    as farm laborers,   338
    on Hawaii,   345
    immigration patterns of,   335–37
Finder, Alan,   356, 386
Fine, Gary Alan,   60
Fine, Michelle,   464
Finestein, Israel,   398
Fing, Jing,   245
Fiola, Jan,   438–39
First Nation (Canada),   432–33
Fish-ins, defined,   178–79, 480
Fix, Michael,   114–15
Fixico, Donald L.,   176
Flames,   64
Fleischman, Jeffrey,   381
Flexner, Eleanor,   415
Flores, Betty,   262
Flying Dragons (gang),   359
Foltin, Richard,   389
Foner, Eric,   205, 208
Fong, Stanley L.,   326, 368
Ford, Henry,   383
*Foreign Conspiracy Against the Liberties of the
    United States, A*,   133
Foreign population
    in United States,   98, 98f, 118–19
    in world,   100, 100t
Fort Laramie Treaty,   170, 171f, 176
Forty-Niners,   168
Fourteenth Amendment (U.S. Constitution),
        214
Fox, Elaine,   192
Fox, Stephen,   137
Foxman, Abraham H.,   381

Foxwoods Resort,   184
Foy, Paul,   194
Frankel, Bruce,   394
Frankenberg, Erica,   230
Franklin, John Hope,   203, 205, 218
Frazer, Somjem,   467
Frazier,   59
Frazier, E. Franklin,   204, 241, 437
Freedman, Samuel G.,   125, 145, 395
Freedom Bus,   215f
Freedom flotilla,   264–65
Freedom riders,   211
Freeman, Jo,   406–7
Freyre, Gilberto,   438
Friedan, Betty,   407, 421
Friedman, G.,   393
Friends,   48
Fringe-of-values theory,   379–80, 480
Fryer, Ronald G.,   231
Fuchs, Estelle,   188
Fuller, Chevon,   83
Fugitive slave acts,   205
Full Employment Action Council,   186
Functionalist perspective
    defined,   16, 480
    gender issues,   404–5
    millenarian movement and,   171
    theory of,   16–17
Fusion
    of Asian Americans,   367–68
    defined,   25, 480
    social construction of race and,   289
    of subordinate groups,   25

Gabriel,   304
Gaines, Patrice,   245
Galarza, Ernesto,   277
Gallagher, Mari,   77
Gallup, George H.,   98, 151, 218
Gambling, Native American operation of,
        184–85, 184f
Gandhi, Mahatma,   211
Gangs
    in Chinese American community,
        358–59
    of Italian Americans,   137
Gans, Herbert J.,   128, 279, 376
Gardner, Alexander,   171f
Gardner, Marilyn,   457
Gardner, Robert W.,   347
Garfinkel, Herbert,   211
Garner, Roberta,   219
Gartner, Alan,   464
Gary, Lawrence,   241
Gates, Gary J.,   467
Gays and lesbians,   466–71
    advocacy by,   469–71
    prejudice and discrimination against,
        468–69
Gaza Strip,   441, 442f
Gee's Bend Ferry,   200
Geledes/SOS Racism,   440
Gender groups, characteristics of,   11–12
Gender issues
    abortion,   420
    for African Americans,   422
    for Arab and Muslim Americans,
        312–13
    for Asian Indians,   335
    childcare and housework,   416–20,
        418f
    for Chinese Americans,   357
    discrimination,   78–79
    division of labor and,   416–20, 417f,
        418f
    elderly women,   455–56
    feminization of poverty,   414–15
    for Hispanic Americans,   259
    income differences and,   78–80, 78f, 79t
    for Jewish Americans,   391

for Korean Americans, 343–44
people with disabilities and, 463
politics and, 420–21
research on, 11
sexual harassment, 413–14
sociological perspectives on, 404–5
stratification of, 15–16
Title IX provisions, 415–16, 416*f*
Gender roles, 403–4, 480
Genocide
defined, 22, 480
of subordinate groups, 22
Gentlemen's Agreement, 103
George, Ron, 433
George III, king, 100
George Lopez Show, 58
German American Bund, 383
German Americans in U.S. population, 124–25
Germany, Holocaust in, 22
Gerrymandering, 248, 249*f*, 480
Gerstenfeld, Phyllis B., 41
Gerth, H.H., 15
Getlin, Josh, 379
Ghaemi, Jahan, 300
Gheezi, Jawad al-, 300, 321
Ghost Dance, 171, 178, 192
Ghost Shadows (gang), 359
Gibbs, Nancy, 262
Gibson, Mel, 44, 379
Girardelli, Davide, 137
Gittler, Joseph B., 376
Giullani, Rudolph, 138
Gladwell, Malcolm, 68
Glass ceiling, 89–92, 91*f*
for African Americans, 237–38
for Asian Americans, 328
defined, 90, 480
for disabled people, 464
for women, 413, 413*t*
Glass Ceiling Commission, 90, 464
Glass escalator, 480
defined, 92
Glass wall
characteristics of, 91–92
defined, 91–92, 480
Glazer, Nathan, 129, 131, 152, 398
Gleason, Philip, 25
Glionna, John M., 185
Globalization
defined, 20, 117, 480–81
immigration and, 117–18
informal economy and, 75, 77
Puerto Rico economics and, 289–90
Glock, Charles, 154
Glover, Danny, 49*f*
Gobodo-Madikizela, Pumla, 448
Goering, John, 127–28
Goering, Laurie, 440
Goffman, Erving, 462
Gold, Michael, 388
Gold, Steven J., 311
Goldscheider, Calvin, 397–98
Goldstein, Sidney, 397
Gomez, David, 295
Gompers, Samuel, 102
Gonzales, Rodolpho "Corky," 280
Gonzalez, Elián, 266–67
Gooding, Caroline, 466
Goodstein, Laurie, 151, 159, 313
Gook syndrome, 339, 481
Gordon, Anthony, 396
Gordon, Milton, 129, 152, 241–42, 398
Gordon, Wendell, 277
Gore, Al, 248, 389
Gorman, Bridget, 293
Gouldner, Alvin, 241
Gove, Walter R., 464
Graham, Lawrence Otis, 68–69, 68*f*, 83
Grand Canyon National Park, 194

"Grand Theft Auto: Vice City" video game, 38
Grant, Diana R., 41
Grape boycott, 279
Gray-Little, Bernadette, 55
Gray Panthers, 459
Great Britain
in Republic of South Africa, 446
secession of Palestine from, 23
Greek Orthodox Archdiocese of North and South America, 156
Greeley, Andrew, 130, 152
Greenhouse, Linda, 88, 158, 460
Greenhouse, Steven, 280
Greenwald, Anthony G., 38
Gribbin, Kathy, 457
Grieco, Elizabeth M., 6*f*, 31*f*, 333, 369
Grimshaw, Allen D., 211
Grodsky, Eric, 238
Gross, Jane, 333
Gross domestic product (GDP) discrimination and loss of, 80
Grossbard-Shechtman, 406
Guadalupe-Hidalgo Treaty Claims Act, 281
Guatemala, immigrants from, 269
Guer, Kevin, 174
Guerin-Gonzales, Camille, 276
Guest, Kenneth J., 353, 358
Guglielmo, Jennifer, 137
Gulf War of 1991, 393, 440
Gustadt, Herman, 102
Guttmacher Institute, 420
Guzmán, Betsy, 269

Haak, Gerald O., 363
Hacker, Andrew, 239
Hacker, Helen Mayer, 402
Haeri, Shaykh Fadhilalla, 312
Hafdahl, Adam R., 55
Hagenbaugh, Barbara, 115
Haitian refugees, 119–20
Haitians, as racial identity, 31
Hajj (pilgrimage), 305, 481
Halakha, 393, 481
Hall, Thomas D., 168
Hallinan, Maureen T., 231
Hamilton, Charles, 72, 220
Handlin, Oscar, 127
Hansen, Marcus, 127
Haoles, 345–46, 481
Harlan, Louis R., 209
Harlan, Sharon L., 464
Harlow, Caroline Wolf, 39, 40
Harris, Barbara, 156*f*
Harris, Marvin, 7, 437, 455
Hartmann, Heidi, 87
Hartocollis, Anemona, 471
Hasidim, 391
Hassaballa, Hesham, 315
Hate Crime Statistics Act, 39
Hate crimes
active hate groups map, 40*f*
against Arab and Muslim Americans, 319
against Asian Americans, 368
defined, 39, 481
distribution of, 39*f*
fighting against, 63
prejudice and, 39–41
Haub, Carl, 428
Havighurst, Robert J., 188
Hawaii
ethnic groups of, 345–48, 345*f*
Japanese Americans in, 347
sovereignty movement on, 346–48, 346*f*
Hawkins, Hugh, 209
Hays, Kristen L., 224
He, Wan, 459
Head Start program, 229
Healing traditions, Native Americans, 191–92

Health care
for African Americans, 245–47
for Native Americans, 190–92
for Puerto Ricans and Mexican Americans, 292–94
Hechinger, Fred M., 144
Heer, David M., 406
Heilman, Madeline E., 413
Hein, Jeremy, 341
Hemlock, Doreen A., 290
Henig, Samantha, 188
Hennessy-Fiske, Molly, 96
Henry, William A., 309
Hentoff, Nicholas, 180
Hepburn, Katherine Houghton, 406
Hequembourg, Amy, 471
Herberg, Will, 152, 378
Hero, Rodney, 281
Herrnstein, Richard J., 13–14
Herschthal, Eric, 337
Herskovits, Melville, 204
Hess, Beth B., 407
Hewlett, Sylvia Ann, 417
Hewstone, Miles, 47
Hickman, Matthew, 192
Higham, John, 383
Higher education. *See also* Education
for African Americans, 232–33, 233*f*
desegregation of, 215
for Native Americans, 189–90
for Puerto Ricans and Mexican Americans, 290–92
Hijab, 312, 481
Hilberg, Soleste, 187
Hill, Herbert, 102
Hill, Laura E., 31
Hill, Robert, 240–41
Hillel Houses, 397
Himmelfarb, Harold S., 377
Hindus, Asian Indians as, 334*f*, 335
Hirsley, Michael, 159
Hispanic Americans
attitudes toward racial profiling, 50
bilingualism issue for, 28, 143
borderlands area and, 262–64, 263*f*
census questions for, 30–31
Central and South Americans, 268–70, 268*f*
citizenship issues for, 275
Cuban Americans, 264–67
cultural influence of, 258–59
economic conditions of, 257–61, 257*f*, 260*f*
effect on African Americans elections, 249
elderly among, 460
as farm laborers, 278–80
illegal immigration policies and, 109–14
as immigrants, 255–57
internet resource directory, 477
Korean Americans tensions with, 344
language divide for, 141–46
Latino identity of, 255–57, 256*f*
official language movement and, 145–46
panethnic labeling of, 30–31
in politics, 248–49, 261–62
population data, 254–55, 254*f*, 255*f*, 296*t*
prejudice among, 4, 55–56
recent changes in schooling, income and life expectancy, 471–72, 472*f*
religion among, 294–95, 294*f*
Roman Catholic church and, 153–54
segregation patterns of, 23–24, 24*f*
underrepresentation in mass media of, 58–59, 59*f*
views of prejudice, 55–57
women's issues, 422

Historically black colleges and universities (HBCUs), 232–33
Hitler, Adolf, genocide of Jews and, 14, 43–44, 378, 381, 383
Hmong community, 341–42, 341*f*
Ho-chunk tribe, 166, 189
Hochbaum, Martin, 388
Hochschild, Arlie Russell, 407–8, 419
Hochschild, Jennifer, 18
Hoffer, Thomas B., 108, 472
Hoffman, Philip Seymour, 135
Holder, Kelly, 261, 332
Holmes, Steven A., 332
Holocaust, 22, 380*f*, 381–82, 481
Holocaust revisionists, 381
Hometown clubs, 263–64, 481
Homophobia, 468, 481
Homosexuality. *See* Gays and lesbians
Hondurans, 268–69
Hoover, Herbert, 137
Hope Chapel, 150
Hopi tribe, 192
Horowitz, Richard, 396
Hosokawa, Bill, 361, 363
Hottentots, 445
Housework issues, 416–20
Housing discrimination
    for African Americans, 243–45
    race and, 70–72
Howard, Ayana, 233*f*
Hubbard, Amy, 443
Hudgins, John, 240
Hui kuan, 354–55, 481
Hull, Anne, 470
Human Genome Project, biological race characteristics of, 12–13
Humphreys, Laud, 469
Hungarian refugees, 118–19
Hunt, Larry L., 295
Hunt, Raymond G., 17
Hurh, Won Moo, 326, 330, 343, 344
Hurricane Katrina, 4
Hyde Amendment, 420

Ideal minority, 325, 481
Ignatiev, Noel, 125–26, 133
Ilchomose, 343, 481
Illegal immigration, 109–14, 109*f*–11*f*
    from Central and South America, 268–69
    in Chinese American community, 353
    of Mexican Americans, 276–78
Illegal Immigration Reform and Immigrant Responsibility Act of 1996, 112
Illiniwek, Chief, 182*f*
Imams, 306
Immigrants
    African Americans as, 200–1, 201*f*
    in Canada, 435–36
    health care of, 292–94
    Hispanic Americans as, 275–78
    institutional discrimination against, 74
    legal issues facing, 96
    Mexican Americans as, 276–78
    military enlistment by, 4
    Polish Americans as, 138–40
    refugees as, 118–20
    by region of last residence, 105*f*
    socioeconomic status of, 115
    transnationals, 118
Immigration
    from Africa, 5
    by Asian Indians, 334–35
    benefits and concerns, 107, 107*t*
    brain drain and, 107–8, 107*t*
    in Canada, 435–36
    from Central and South Americans, 268–69
    of Chinese Americans, 352–53

of Cuban Americans, 264–66
current issues in, 107–14
defined, 20, 481
early patterns in U.S. of, 100–3
economic impact of, 114–18, 115*f*
of Filipino Americans, 335–37
global phenomenon of, 97–98, 97*f*
illegal immigration, 109–14, 109*f*–11*f*
    from Ireland, Italy, and Poland, 132*f*
by Irish, 131–33
of Jewish Americans, 377–79
major U.S. policies of, 109*t*
management trends in, 113*t*
by Muslims, 305–6
of Muslims and Arabs, 310–11
patterns of, 98, 98*f*
population growth of, 108–9
restrictionist sentiment, 95–96, 101–6
social concerns of, 107–9
social forces behind, 98
by Southeast Asian Americans, 326
trends in prejudice and, 52
women and, 116–17
Immigration Act of 1965, 342–43, 353
Immigration and Naturalization Act of 1965, 95, 104–7, 105*f*–6*f*, 310
Immigration and Naturalization Service (INS), 112
Immigration Reform and Control Act of 1986 (IRCA), 109–10
In-group virtues, 380, 481
Incident at Oglala, 180
Income
    of African Americans, 219, 220*f*, 227, 234–36, 234*f*, 235*f*
    of Asian Americans, 328–29
    of Brazilians, 439*f*
    of Chinese Americans, 354–56
    comparison of white, African Americans and Hispanic Americans, 471–72, 472*f*
    defined, 83, 234, 481
    of Filipino Americans, 338
    of Hispanic Americans, 60*f*, 257, 257*f*, 260
    of Jewish Americans, 387–88, 387*t*
    median income, by race, ethnicity, and gender, 78–80, 78*f*, 79*t*
    of Native Americans, 184–85
    racial/ethnic differences in, 83–84
    religious denomination and levels of, 154, 155*f*
    of women, 407, 409–10, 410*f*, 410*t*
Index of dissimilarity, segregation and, 23
India, secession of Pakistan from, 23
Indian Arts and Crafts Act, 184
Indian Arts and Crafts Board, 184
Indian Claims Commission, 172, 175, 178
Indian culture, 167
Indian Gaming Regulatory Act, 184
Indian Health Service, 190
"Indian Nations at Risk," 188
Indian Removal Act, 170
Indian Reorganization Act, 173–74
Indigenismo policy, 429
Indigenous peoples, annexation of, 20
Informal economy
    defined, 75, 481
    low-wage labor in, 75–77
Inoue, Miyako, 365
Institutional discrimination, 481
    affirmative action measures and, 86–87
    characteristics of, 72–75
    defined, 72
    people with disabilities and, 464
Insurance industry and slavery reparations, 207
Intelligence quotient (IQ)

defined, 13, 481
    racial issues and, 13–14
Intelligent design, 481
    defined, 159
Intergroup relations
    in Canada, 435
    continuum of, 22*f*, 250*f*, 284*f*, 320*f*, 368*f*, 377*f*, 428*f*
    hostility, 55–56, 56*f*
    between whites and blacks, 200
Intermarriage. *See also* Marriage patterns
    biological race characteristics of, 13–14
    increased rates of, 25
    of Jewish Americans, 395
Internal colonialism
    defined, 21, 172
    federal policy toward Native Americans as, 172, 172*t*
    as oppression, 21
Internal colonialism, defined, 481
Interpreters, need for, 28
Intifada, 442–43, 481
Inuit tribes, 179
    in Canada, 432–33
Iraq, 381, 441, 445
Irish immigrants in U.S., 101
    case study of in U.S., 131–35
    English attitudes toward, 125
    immigration patterns of, 132*f*
    Roman Catholic church and, 131–33
    statistics on, 100
    symbolic ethnicity of, 128–29
    third-generation principle, 127–28
    as white ethnic group, 131–35
Iroquois tribe, 178
Irregular economy, 75, 481
Ishii, Miuku, 366–67
Islam. *See* Muslim Americans and Muslims
Israel
    Arab-Israeli conflict and, 441, 442*f*
    creation of, 23
    Intifada and, 442–43
    Jewish Americans and, 374, 385–86
    occupied territories map, 442*f*
    Palestinians and, 440–45
Israel Law of Return, 376
Issacson, Jason, 389
Issei, 359, 364, 366–67, 481
Italian Americans
    case study of, 135–38
    immigration patterns of, 132*f*, 135–36
    stereotypes of, 47, 130
    third-generation principle, 127–28
Itano, Nicole, 363, 365, 374

Jackson, Jesse, 386
Jaher, Frederic Caple, 377
Jamaicans, as racial identity, 31
James, Keith, 187, 189
James, LeBron, 19
Japan bashing, 330
Japanese American Citizens League (JACL), 361
Japanese Americans, 359–69
    current conditions for, 366–69
    economic conditions for, 364–65
    evacuation camps for, 362–64, 362*f*, 363*f*
    family life of, 365
    immigration restrictions and, 103
    population data on, 352–53, 352*t*
    prejudice and discrimination against, 366–69
    religion of, 365
    wartime evacuation of, 360–64
    workplace discrimination against, 69
Jaroszynska-Kirchman, Anna D., 141
Jean, Wyclef, 120
Jenness, Valerie, 469

Jesus Christ, 304, 379
Jewish Americans
  African Americans and, 386
  anti-Semitism and, 374
  cultural heritage of, 397–98
  current issues facing, 374–75, 386–89
  education of, 388
  employment and income, 387–88, 387*t*
  ethnic identity, 376–77, 393–98
  family life for, 394–95
  generational denomination patterns, 396*f*
  identity of, 393–98
  immigration to U.S., 377–79
  Israel and, 374, 385–86
  organizational activity of, 388–89
  politics of, 389
  religious life of, 389–93, 392*t*, 395–97
Jewish Canadians, 435
Jihad (struggle), 305, 481
Jim Crow, 205–6, 210–11, 481
Jimenez, Alfredo, 265
Job seeking and discrimination, 76
Joe, Tom, 464
John Paul II, pope, 140
Johnson, Gary, 193
Johnson, Hans, 31
Johnson, Kevin, 117, 125, 192
Johnson, Lyndon B., 104, 218
Johnson, Mark, 466
Johnson, Peter, 59
Johnson, Todd M., 146
Johnson, Troy R., 180
Johnson O'Malley Act, 187
Jolidon, Laurence, 179
Jones, Charisse, 5
Jones, Dale E., 147*f*
Jones, James T., 414
Jones, Jeffrey M., 98, 320
Jones, Nicholas, 31*f*
Jones, Tim, 341, 384
Jones Act of 1917, 283
Jones v. Mayer, 243
Jonsson, Patrik, 270
Jordan, 441
Joseph, Peniel E., 221
Joyner, Kara, 51
Juárez, Benito, 429
Judaism. *See also* Anti-Semitism
  Arab-Israeli conflict and, 441, 442*f*
  Diaspora of, 385, 440, 443, 480
  internet resource directory, 477
  Orthodox Judaism, 156, 390–91
  Reform Judaism, 392–93
  state of Israel and, 23, 440–41
  in United States, 148
  women in, 156
  world Jewish population, 374–75, 375*f*
Judaization, 376, 481
Judiciary, anti-discriminatory measures of, 81
Juneteenth celebration, 207*f*

Kaczmarek, Jane, 141
Kagan, Jerome, 13
Kalita, S. Mitra, 335
Kalota tribe, 166
Kalt, Joseph P., 179, 182, 185–86
Kamo, Yoshinori, 329
Kanamine, Linda, 186
Kanellos, Nicholas, 292
Kaneya, Rui, 141
Kang, K. Connie, 337–38, 344
Kao, Grace, 51
Kapur, Deuesh, 118
Karkabi, Barbara, 464
Kaser, Tom, 347
Kashima, Tetsuden, 360

Kashrut, 391, 398, 481
Katel, Peter, 116, 184–85
Kaufman, Gayle, 418
Kay, Tamara, 422
Keen, Judy, 262
Kelly, Kimbriell, 77
Kening, Dan, 459
Kennedy, Anthony (Justice), 469
Kennedy, John F., 85, 135, 214–15, 218, 243, 474
Kerry, John, 261
Keysar, Ariela, 145
Khoury, Rebecca, 321
Kibei, 359
Kibria, Nazli, 328, 368
Kickout, defined, 187, 481
Kieh, George Klay Jr., 309
Kilborn, Peter T., 465
Killian, Caitlin, 313
Killian, Lewis M., 216
Kilson, Martin, 89
Kim, Kiljoong, 338, 343
Kim, Kwang Chung, 326, 328, 343
Kim, Shin, 328
Kim, T.C., 38
Kimura, Yukiko, 360, 363
King, Martin Luther, Jr., 200, 215–220, 308
King, Martin Luther Jr., 199, 200, 215–18
King, Peter, 306, 318
King and I, 47*f*
Kinloch, Graham, 45
Kinsey, Alfred, 467
Kinship relations of African Americans, 239–40
Kinzer, Stephen, 200
Kirkpatrick, P., 462
Kit Carson National Forest, 281
Kitagawa, Evelyn, 247
Kitano, Harry H. L., 363, 365
Kitsuse, John I., 361
Kitzmiller v. Dove Area School District, 159
Klausner, Samuel Z., 387
Klebanov, Pamela K., 13
Knesset, 441
Know-Nothing party, 133
Knudson, Thomas J., 186
Koch, Wendy, 106, 145
Kochhar, Rakesh, 260
Kone, Kassim, 306, 308
Korean Americans, 330*f*, 342–45
  current issues facing, 343–45
  historical background, 342–43
Korecki, Natasha, 264
Kosciuszko, Thaddeus, 138
Kosmin, Barry A., 145, 222, 294, 365
Kozlowicz, John, 166
Krauss, Clifford, 433–34, 436
Krausz, Ernest, 441
Kraybill, Donald B., 162
Krueger, 76
Krueger, Alan B., 62
Ku Klux Klan, 133, 211
  anti-Semitism of, 383
  hate crimes and, 40, 63
Kubrick, Stanley, 141
Kugel, Seth, 284
Kuhn, Maggie, 459
Kwon, Ho-Youn, 345
Kwong, Peter, 356
Kye system, 344, 481

La opinión, 254
La Raza, defined, 277, 481
La Raza Unida (LRU), 280–81
Labeling theory
  defined, 18, 481
  disabled people and, 462–64
  sociological research, 18–19
  trends in stereotypes and, 49

Labelle, Huguette, 432
Labor force
  Amish child labor, 161–62
  Chinese Americans, 101–2, 353–54, 356–57
  gender segregation in, 409–13
  Hispanic Americans in, 257, 260
  illegal immigrants in, 111–12
  immigration restrictions and, 103–4
  impact of immigration on, 114–16, 116*f*
  Japanese Americans in, 364–65
  Korean Americans participation in, 343–44
  low-wage labor, 75–77, 76*f*
  Mexican Americans in, 275–80, 278*t*, 279*f*
  slavery as, 206–7
  women's participation in, 407–10, 409*t*, 419*f*
Lachman, Seymour P., 222*f*, 294, 294*f*, 365
Lacy, Dan, 206
LaDuke, Winoma, 347
LaGuardia, Fiorello, 137
Lahiri, Jhumpa, 324
Lal, Barbara Ballis, 129
Lamb, David, 341
Land disputes
  of Mexican Americans, 262–64
  of Native Americans, 194
Landale, Nancy, 292–93
Lane, George, 460, 461*f*
Language issues
  for African Americans, 204
  for Arab Americans, 301–2
  Central and South Americans, 268
  as dividing factor, 141–46
  for Hispanic Americans, 143
  Hmong community case study, 341–42, 341*f*
  for Jewish Americans, 397–98
  for Korean Americans, 343
  for Native Americans, 166
  for Puerto Ricans, 283–85
  Québécois movement, 434
  for Southeast Asian Americans, 335
  speaking languages other than English, 146*f*
  spoken at home other than English and Spanish, 141*f*
Laos, refugees from, 339–40
LaPiere, Richard, 42
  prejudice studies of, 42–43
Lara, Marielena, 293, 294
Lareau, Annette, 242
Latinos. *See also* Hispanic Americans
  terminology of, 253, 255–56
Lau, Yvonne, 338, 353
Lauerman, Connie, 178
Laumann, Edward O., 467
Lavender, Abraham D., 388
Law of Return, 376, 441
Law on Indian Rights and Culture (Mexico), 430
Lawrence, Jacob, 38*f*
Lawrence v. Texas, 469
Laxson, Joan D., 183
Lazarus, Emma, 103
League of Women Voters, 421
Leave It to Beaver, 403*f*
Leavitt, Paul, 46
Lebanon, 303, 310–11, 441–42
Lebone, Kerwin, 448–49
Lee, Don, 343
Lee, Jennifer, 356
Lee, J.J., 78*f*
Lee, Sharon M., 25, 352
Lee, Spike, 308, 344
Lee, Wen Ho, 331

Lee v. Weisman, 158
Leehotz, 12
Legal Assistance Foundation of Metropolitan Chicago, 77
Leinwand, Donna, 306
Lem, Kim, 367
Lennon, Mary Clare, 417
Leno, Jay, 138
Leonard, Karen Isaksen, 306, 308, 314
Lerner, Michael, 130, 398
Lessinger, Johanna, 335
"Letter from Birmingham Jail," 217
Levi Strauss, 63
Levin, William, 456–57
Levine, Naomi, 388
Levitt, Peggy, 335
Levy, Becca R., 457
Levy, Jacques E., 279
Lewin, Tamar, 89
Lewinson, Paul, 205
Lewis, Amanda E., 126
Lewis, Neil A., 318
Lewis, Oscar, 276, 278–79
Lewis Mumford Center, 24
Li, Wen Lang, 354
Liace, Carolyn Buck, 417
Liberace, 141
Liberia, 23
Libman, Jeff, 142
Lichtblau, Eric, 50
Lie, John, 343
Lieberman, Joseph, 389
Liebman, Charles S., 397
Liebowitz, Holly J., 148
Life chances, defined, 151, 292, 481
Life expectancy, comparison of white, African Americans and Hispanic Americans, 471–72, 472*f*
Life is Beautiful, 381
Light, Ivan H., 356, 359
Lin, Sam Chu, 364
Lincoln, Abraham, 205
Lincoln, C. Eric, 308–9
Lind, Andrew, 360
Linda Brown et al. v. Board of Education of Topeka, Kansas, 214
Lindbergh, Charles, 383
Lindner, Eileen, 148
Lindsley, Sheryl L., 61
Linn, Mike, 200
Linthicum, Leslie, 190
Lips, Hilary M., 410
Literacy test, immigration restrictions and, 103–4
Little Havana, 267
Lodder, LeeAnn, 78
Loewen, James W., 69, 212–13
Logan, John R., 24, 244, 250, 255, 267, 270, 284, 356
Lomax, Louis E., 220
Lopata, Helen Z., 129, 141
Lopez, Ana, 269
Lopez, David, 30
Lopez, George, 255
Lopez, Jennifer, 19
Lopez, Julie, 92
Lotke, Eric, 245
Louie, Andrea, 353
Louisiana Purchase of 1803, 20
Loury, Glenn C., 309
Low-wage labor, discrimination through, 75–77, 76*f*
Lowenstein, Roger, 114
Loyal League, 205
Loyalty test for Japanese Americans, 361–62
Lubavitchers, 395
Luce, Clare Boothe, 339
Luconi, Stefano, 136
Ludwig, Jack, 223

Luker, Kristin, 420
Luo, Michael, 391–92
Lutheran church, characteristics of, 148, 154
Lutheran Church-Missouri Synod, 156
Lyman, Stanford M., 354–55, 359
Lynch, Jessica, 173*f*
Lynching, of African Americans, 209, 209*f*
Lynn (poet), 463
Lytle, Clifford M., 173

MacFarlane, Marco, 445, 448
Mack, Raymond W., 89
MacRae, Neil C., 47
Madonna, 138
Major, Aline K., 192
Majority groups
    cultural dominance of, 18–19
    defined, 7
Malcolm X, 307*f*, 308–9
Male liberation, 407
Malinche, 281
Malkin, Michelle, 368
Malone, Tara, 5
Mandela, Nelson, 446–48
Mandelbaum, Robb, 280
Manila Village, 335
Manin, Alexandr, 4–5
Maning, Anita, 84
Manning, Robert D., 27
Manumission, 437
Maquiladoras, 263, 263*f*, 431, 481
March on Washington for Jobs and Freedom, 218
Marginality, 396
    defined, 31, 481
    ethnic identity and, 31–32
"Mariel" boatlift, 114, 264
Marielitos, 264, 481
Marmout, Yarrow, 304*f*
Maronite Church, 300
Marriage patterns. *See also* Intermarriage
    of African Americans, 201–3
    arranged, 336–37
    of Asian Americans, 367–68
    for gays and lesbians, 470–71
    resistance to fusion in, 25
    second shift issue and, 419
Marsden, Peter V., 52, 154–55
Marshall, Patrick, 158
Marshall, Susan E., 313
Martin, Joel W., 193, 195
Martin, Lee, 77
Martin, Lydia, 267
Martinez, Michael, 182, 263
Marvasti, Amir, 301, 315
Marx, Karl, 45, 69, 125
Masayesva, Vernon, 192
Masci, David, 441–42
Masculine mystique, 407
Mason, Heather, 145
Mass media
    Asian American images in, 325, 366
    disabled people in, 463
    elderly in, 457–58
    for Hispanic Americans, 262
    Italian-Americans in, 137
    Muslim Americans and, 311*f*, 312, 319
    portrayal of black women in, 422
    prejudice toward white ethnics in, 130–131
    reduction of prejudice and role of, 57–59
    religious issues in, 152, 158
    Southeast Asian Americans in, 330
    women in, 403*f*, 417
Massey, Douglas, 23–24, 28, 109–111, 243
Mathiessen, Peter, 180
Matrix of domination, 421, 481

Mattson, Mark T., 201*f*
Matza, David, 130
Mauro, Tony, 159
Max, Murray, 174, 176
Mayan civilization, 274, 430
Mayer, Egon, 145
Maykovich, Minako K., 362
Mbeki, Thabo, 448
McClain, Paula Denice, 435
McCloud, Aminah Beverly, 308, 310
McConahay, J.B., 219
McCormick, John, 262
McCourt, Frank, 135
McCoy, Ron, 184
McGhee, Bernard, 44
McHale, John, 118
McIntosh, Peggy, 126–27, 126*f*
McKenna, Ian, 436
McKinley, James C., Jr., 270
McKinney, Karyn, 301, 315
McKinney, K.D., 126
McNamara, Mary, 44
McNickle, D'Arcy, 174
Meagher, Timothy J., 131, 134
Means, Russell, 179–80
Media income by race, ethnicity, and gender, 78–79, 78*f*, 79*t*
Medicare, 460
Medicine man of Native Americans, 170, 181, 462
Meech Lake Accords, 434
Meidung (shunning), 160
Meier, August, 209, 211
Meier, Matt S., 274, 276
Meléndez, Edwin, 290
Melting pot
    defined, 25, 481
    fusion and, 25
Melting Pot, 454
Meredith, James, 214, 219–20
Meritor Savings Bank v. Vinson, 414
Merton, Robert, 37, 41, 380
    prejudice typology of, 41–42, 42*f*
Messner, Michael A., 407
Mestizo culture, 429
Methamphetamine raid, 5
Methodist church, characteristics of, 154–55
Mexican American Legal Defense and Education Fund (MALDEF), 277, 281
Mexican-American War of 1848, 20, 275, 429
Mexican Americans
    bilingualism of, 143
    borderlands region and, 262–64
    citizenship issues for, 275
    current issues for, 290–95
    economic conditions for, 280*f*, 278–80, 278*f*
    education for, 290–92
    family life, 292
    as farm laborers, 279–80, 279*f*
    health care, 292–94
    illegal crossing into United States, 110–11
    as immigrants, 275–78
    Native American roots of, 274
    in politics, 280–82
    population data, 254–55, 254*f*, 255*f*
    religion among, 294–95, 294*f*
Mexican Independence Day, 4
Mexican Revolution of 1909–1922, 276
Mexico
    Chiapas conflict in, 429–40
    Indians and color gradient in, 429–30
    race and ethnic relations in, 426, 429–30
    women's status in, 430–31
Meyers, Gustavus, 383

Miami and Cuban Americans, 266–67
Middle class, African Americans, 241–42
Middle East, defined, 301
Middlemen minorities, 328, 481
Migradollars, 263, 481
  defined, 114
  globalization and, 115–16, 118
Migrant workers, 279–80
Migration
  defined, 20, 481
  of Jewish Americans, 377–79
  by Puerto Ricans, 283–84, 290
  of subordinate groups, 20
Mihesuah, Devon A., 193
Mikulski, Barbara, 141
Military service
  African Americans participation in, 211–212
  desegregation of, 211, 213
  of Filipinos, 336, 338, 338*f*
  gays in, 470
Milk, Harvey, 469
Millenarian movement, 171, 481
Miller, David I., 441
Miller, Marjorie, 151
Miller, Norman, 60
Millikin v. Bradley, 230
Million Man March, 239, 309
Mills, C. Wright, 15
Milwaukee Brewers, 16
Min, Pyong Gap, 337, 343
Minority Affairs Initiative, 460
Minority groups. *See also* Subordinate group
  aged as, 455–60
  characteristics of, 7–8
  defined, 3, 7, 481
  elderly in, 455
  environmental racism and, 84–85
  equal-status contact among, 59–60
  intergroup hostility in, 55–56
  low self-esteem of, 53–55
  population data by county, 473*f*
  underrepresentation in mass media of, 57–59
  violence among, 55
  women, 402–3, 421–22
Minton, Todd D., 192
Mission San Xavier del Bac, 274*f*
Mitchel, Gary, 166
Mitchell-Kernan, Claudia, 239
Mitsuye Endo v. United States, 362
Mixed race, concepts of, 125, 129
Miyamoto, S. Frank, 363
Mocha, Frank, 141
Model minority, 325, 329, 481
Modell, John, 328
Mogelonsky, Marcia, 334
Mojados, 482
  defined, 277
Mommy tax, 419–20, 482
Mommy track, 413, 482
Montagu, Ashley, 14, 376
Monterey Park, 354
Montgomery Improvement Association, 215
Moore, David W., 150
Moore, Joan W., 279, 281
Moore, Stephen, 114
Moorish Science Temple, 308
Morawska, Eda T., 131
Morbidity and mortality rates of African Americans, 245–46
Morris, Milton D., 386
Morse, Samuel F.B., 133
Morton v. Mancari, 185
Moscone, George, 469
Moser, Bob, 469
Moskos, Charles C., 213
Mosques, 306, 311

Moss, Alfred A., 203, 205, 218
Moss, Paul, 186*f*
Mostofi, Nilou, 307
Motion pictures, Hispanic influence in, 255
Mott, Lucretia, 405
Motta, Roberto, 436
Moulder, Frances V., 32
Moynihan, Daniel Patrick, 129, 131, 152, 241
Mt. Graham, 195
MTV, 255
MTV Ritmo, 255
Muhammad, Elijah, 308, 309
Muhammad, Khalid Abdul, 386
Muhammad, W. Fard, 308
Muhammad, Warith Deen, 308–09
Muhammad (prophet), 304, 315
Mui, Yian Q., 340
Mulatoo escape hatch, 437–38, 482
Mullainathan, Sendhil, 62
Muller, Eli, 374
Multiculturalism
  in Canada, 431–32
  in education, 57–59
  on Hawaii, 346–48
  measurements of, 30
  in South Africa, 445–46, 445*t*
Multiracial couples, challenges of, 15, 30–32, 31*f*
Mummy, The, 319
Mummy Returns, The, 319
Munich Olympics attack, 316, 393
Murphy, Dean, 153
Murray, Charles, 13–14
Musal, Stan, 141
Muschkin, Clara G., 284
Museum of Intervention, 275
Muslim American Society, 315
Muslim Americans, 300, 304–10. *See also* Nation of Islam
  African Americans as, 222, 307–8
  Asian Indians as, 335
  black Muslims, 307–10, 307*f*
  blended identity of, 306–7, 307*f*
  contemporary life in U.S., 311–15, 311*f*
  education for, 314, 314*f*
  family life and gender issues, 312–13
  immigration to U.S., 310–11
  internet resource directory, 477
  politics of, 314–15
  population data on, 146, 305–6
  prejudice and discrimination against, 319–20
  U.S. attitudes toward, 60, 316–19
Muslim countries, 302*f*
Muslim Public Affairs Council, 319
Muslims
  Arab Americans as, 300–1, 301*f*
  ethnic cleansing by, 22
  in Palestine, 23
  Palestinians as, 440
  racial profiling and, 50
  stereotypes of, 46–47, 50
Mustafa, Nadia, 96
Mutattoes, 438
Myers, 115
Myrdal, Gunnar, 18, 120, 402

Nabokov, Peter, 281
Nader, Ralph, 314
Naff, Alika, 310
Nagel, Joane, 175, 180
Names, interview success linked to, 62, 62*t*
Nardone, Gilda, 415
Nash, Manning, 17
Nashimoto, Richard S., 361
Nation of Islam, 23, 223, 239, 304–5,

308–9
National Advisory Commission on Civil Disorders, 220
National Asian Pacific American Legal Consortium, 329
National Association for the Advancement of Colored People (NAACP), 58
  formation of, 210
  Legal Defense and Education Fund, 214
National Coalition of Anti-Violence Programs, 469
National Collegiate Athletic Association, 61, 182
National Committee to Preserve Social Security and Medicare, 460
National Congress of American Indians (NCAI), 178
National Farm Workers Association, 279
National Federation of the Blind, 465
National Gay and Lesbian Task Force, 40
National Health and Life Survey, 467
National Institute Against Prejudice and Violence, 40
National Organization for Women (NOW), 407, 420
National Origins System, 104
  Italian American immigration and, 137
  Muslim immigration and, 310
National Party (South Africa), 446–47
National Peace Accord (South Africa), 446
National Survey of Black Americans, 241
National Women's Political Caucus (NWPC), 421
Native American Church (NAC), 193
Native American Education Service College, 178
Native American Graces and Protection Act, 347
Native American Graves Protection and Repatriation Act of 1990, 192–93
Native Americans. *See also* specific tribes
  Allotment Act, 172–73
  athletic mascots named after, 182, 182*f*
  and bilingualism, 28
  casino gambling, 184–85, 184*f*
  Chinese Americans compared with, 356
  collective action by, 178–81
  current conditions for, 182–95
  early European contacts, 167–68
  economic development of, 183–86
  education of, 187–90, 188*f*
  Employment Assistance Program, 175, 177–78
  enrollment and dropout rates, 187
  environmental issues, 85, 193–95
  ethnic identity among, 128, 170*f*
  expulsion of, 22
  federal policies concerning, 172–78, 172*t*
  First Nation of Canada, 431*f*, 432–33, 433*f*
  genocide of, 22
  government employment of, 185–86
  health care issues, 190–92
  higher education, 189–90
  internet resource directory, 477
  intertribal network, 177
  land disputes, 194
  lands and communities of, 174*f*
  languages of, 166
  legal claims of, 175–76
  Mexican American ancestry and, 274
  in Mexico, 429–30, 430*f*
  pan-Indianism, 180–81
  panethnic labeling of, 30

Native Americans. *(cont.)*
  population patterns of, 167–68
  poverty of, 185–86
  powwows, 181*f*
  protest efforts by, 178–80
  rebuilding after Hurricane Katrina, 4
  relics stockpiling, 192–93, 193*f*
  religious practices of, 158, 192–93
  Reorganization Act, 173–74
  reservation life, 174–78
  schooling quality or, 187–89
  segregation of, 24, 177–78
  sovereignty, 181–82
  Termination Act, 175, 176
  tourism opportunities, 183–84
  treaties and warfare with, 168–70
  tribal councils, 177*f*
  tribal identification of, 29, 173*f*, 180*f*
  unemployment of, 185–86
  in urban areas, 182*t*
  view of expansionism by, 169*f*
  women's issues, 422
Native Claims Settlement Act, 179
Native Council of Canada, 433
Native Hawaiian Government Reorganization
    Act, 348
Nativism, 133
  defined, 100–1, 482
Naturalization, defined, 105, 482
Navajo Community College, 190
Navajo tribes, 187, 189, 191, 194
Navarro, Mireya, 21, 284, 289–290, 352
NCAA. *See* National Collegiate Athletic
    Association
*Negro Family: The Case for National Action,
    The,* 241
Neocolonialism, 285, 482
Neoricans (Nuyoricans), 283, 482
NetworkOmni, 28
Neugarten, Bernice, 456, 460
New Age savage, 194
New Left movement, 389, 406–07
New York City, Puerto Ricans in, 283–84,
    283*f*
*New York State Clubs Association v. City of
    New York,* 83
Newman, William M., 25–27
Newport, Frank, 468
Newton, Huey, 221
Ng, Kwai Hang, 352, 358
Nguyen, Linda, 324
Nguyen, Madison, 324
Niagara Movement, 209–11
Nicaragua, immigrants from, 269
Nie, Norman H., 130
Niebuhr, Gustav, 155
Nielsen, Joyce McCarl, 403
Niesse, Mark, 348
Nineteenth Amendment, 405*f*, 406
Nisei, 359, 362, 364, 366–69, 371, 482
Nishi, Setsuko Matsunaga, 365
Nixon, Richard, 316
"No Spanish" laws, 143
Nobel Peace Prize, 381, 447
Noble, Barbara Presley, 462
Noel, Donald L., 202
Nolt, Steven M., 162
Non-Christian religion, 146–47, 358
  of African Americans, 223
Norden, Martin E., 464
Normative theory of prejudice, 46, 482
North American Free Trade Agreement
    (NAFTA), 262, 290
Notimex, 254
Novak, Michael, 131
Novelli, William D., 458
Nuestro Himmo, 145
Nunavut territory, 433

Oakes, James, 205
Oberlin College, 415

Oberschall, Anthony, 219
O'Brien, Conan, 135
O'Connor, Anne-Marie, 254, 295
Official language movement, 145, 145*f*
Ogbu, John V., 231
Ogena, Nimfa B., 292
Oglala Sioux tribe, 179
Ogunwole, Stella V., 174, 179–80, 182,
    188, 472
Ohnuma, Keiko, 327
Ojibwee tribe, 166
O'Keefe, Betty, 124
Oklahoma City bombing, 152, 316
Old Order Amish, 160
Older Women's League (OWL), 459
Oldham, Jennifer, 74
Oliver, Melvin L., 84, 235, 364
Olson, Steve E., 13
Olzak, Susan, 426
Omi, Michael, 15, 31
"One-drop rule," social construction of
    race and, 15
Oneida tribe, 187
O'Neill, William, 406
Onishi, Norimitsu, 368
Operation Boulder, 316
Operation Pipeline and racial profiling,
    50
Operation Wetback, 277
Opinión, La, 254
Orapesa, R.S., 293
Ordnung (understanding), 160
Orfield, Gary, 148, 230, 291
Organic Act, 346
Organization of Afro-American Unity,
    309
Organizational membership
  of Chinese Americans, 354–55
  of Jewish Americans, 388–89
Organized crime, Italian Americans and,
    137
Orientalism, 299, 306, 310, 319, 482
  defined, 300
Orlov, Ann, 268
Orthodox Church in America, 148
Orthodox Jews, 374, 390–91
Oslo Accords, 443
Ottaway, David S., 447
Out-group vices, 380, 482

Pachon, Harry, 281
Pacific Islanders, 224*f*, 325, 325*f*
Padget, Martin, 183
Padrone system, 136
Pager, Devah, 76, 238
Paik, Nancy, 306
Paiute tribe, 171
Pakistan, secession from India of, 23
Pakistani Americans, 326–27
Palestine, 303
  secession from Great Britain of, 23
Palestine Liberation Organization (PLO),
    385, 442–43
Palestinians, Israel and, 385, 440–45
Palmores, 437
Paludi, Michele A., 404
Pan-Indianism
  defined, 178, 482
  origins of, 178–79
  overview of, 180–81
Panamanians, 268–69
Panethnicity, 482
  Asian Americans and, 348
  census questions and issues of, 30–31
  defined, 30, 255
  of Hispanic Americans, 255–57
  pan-Indianism as example of, 178
Park, Robert E., 32, 51, 127
Parker, Laura, 120
Parks, Rosa, 215
Parrish, Michael, 364

Parsons, Talcott, 404
Parti Québécois, 436
Pass laws, 446, 482
Passel, Jeffrey S., 109, 112
Passion of the Christ, The, 379
Pasternak, Judy, 377
Paterno, Joe, 138
Patterson, Orlando, 437
Pawel, Miriam, 280
Pay equity, 411–12, 482
Paycheck Fairness Act, 412
Payne, Charles M., 217
Peace and Freedom Party, 221
Pearl, Paul M., 130
Pearl Harbor, 360
Pearson, Rick, 262
Pease, John, 77
Peckham, Pat, 343
Pedder, Sophie, 77
Peek, Lori, 318
Peele, Charles Wilson, 304*f*
Pelé, 440
Peltier, Leonard, 180
Pentecostal religions, 150, 295
Pentecostalism, 295, 482
People with disabilities, 460–66
  advocacy by, 464–66
  contemporary issues for, 461–62
  health status of, 461–62, 461*f*
  labeling of, 462–64
Peoplehood, 129, 398, 482
Pequot tribe, 184
Peréz, Linsandro, 266
Perusse, Roland I., 296
Pessar, Patricia R., 270
Pestello, Fred P., 43
Pestello, H. Frances, 43
Pestewa, Lori, 173*f*
Peterson, William, 362
Petit Jean Poultry Plant, 96
Pew Hispanic Center, 254–55, 262
Pewewardy, Cornel, 187
Peyote, 158, 193
Pfeiffer, David, 466
Philip, 474
Pido, Antonio J.A., 337
Pincus, Fred L., 89
Pinderhughes, Raquel, 247, 279
Pine Ridge Reservation, 172, 178–80,
    186–87
Pinkney, Alphonso, 209, 221, 242, 309
Plains Indians, 171, 180, 195
Plastic reindeer rules, 159
Pleck, Elizabeth H., 422
Plessy v. Ferguson, 206
Pluralism
  defined, 26, 34, 482
  perspective on subordinate groups, 3,
    26–28
  religious pluralism, 146–51, 146*f*
Poisonous Mushroom, The, 380*f*
Poland, suppression by Russia, 20
Polish-American Congress, 129–30
Polish Americans
  case study of, 138–41
  immigration patterns of, 132*f*
  prejudice towards, 129–30
Polish Peasant in Europe and America, The,
    139
Polish National Alliance, 139
Polish Roman Catholic Union, 139
Politics
  of accomodation, 208–9
  African Americans in, 248–49, 248*f*
  of Arab and Muslim Americans,
    314–15
  of Asian Americans, 331–33, 331*f*
  of Chinese Americans, 353
  Cuban Americans and, 265–66
  elderly and, 459–60
  of Filipino Americans, 338

of gays and lesbians, 469–71, 470*f*
Hispanic Americans in, 261–62
Italian American participation in, 137
Jewish Americans and, 389
Mexican Americans in, 280–82
people with disabilities and, 464–66, 465*f*
women and, 420–21, 421*f*
Poll taxes, 206
Pollution, environmental justice and, 84–85
Polonia, 139–40
Polzin, Theresita, 141
Popoff, Rovana, 207
Population growth, immigration patterns and, 5, 108–9
Porter, Eduardo, 114
Posadas, Barbara M., 336–38
Potato famine (Ireland), 132
Poussaint, Alvin, 241
Poverty
of African Americans, 235, 235*f*
among elderly, 458–59, 459*f*
culture of, 278–79
feminization of, 414–15
of Hispanic Americans, 260, 260*f*
of Jewish Americans, 338
of Mexican Americans, 278–79, 278*t*
in Mexico, 430, 430*f*
of Native Americans, 183–84
in South Africa, 448–49
"Poverty pockets," white hostility toward, 131
Powwows, 181*f*
defined, 181, 482
Pradt, Mary, 379
"Praising the victim," 326
Prejudice
against Amish, 160–61
against Arab and Muslim Americans, 319–20
against Asian Americans, 325, 329–30, 366
authoritarian personality theory, 45
in Brazil, 438–40
characteristics of, 37
defined, 37, 482
discrimination, 41–43, 42*f*
diversity training and corporate response, 60–62, 61*f*
education and mass media and reduction of, 57–59
equal-status contract and, 59–60
experiments in, 38
exploitation theory, 45–46
extent of, 51–53
against gays and lesbians, 468–69
hate crimes and, 39–41
on Hawaii, 347
intergroup hostility and, 55–56, 56*f*
against Japanese Americans, 48, 366–69
LaPiere's study of, 42–43
Merton's typology of, 41–42
normative approach, 46
prevalence of, 38
reduction of, 57–62
scapegoating theory, 43–44
social construction of race and, 289
social distance scale and, 51–52, 51*f*
stereotypes, 46–50
theories of, 43–46, 46*t*
trends in, 52–53
views of oppressed groups on, 53–55
of white ethnics, 129–31
Presbyterian church
characteristics of, 223
Korean Americans in, 345
Presidential election and institutional discrimination, 74–75
Primetime Live, 228

Principle of third-generation interest, 125–26, 482
Prisoners' voting rights, 248
Project Lemonade, 63
Project RACE, 30
Promise Keepers, 151
Proposition 187 (California), 116
Proposition 209 (California), 89
Protestant Church
African Americans in, 222
diversity of, 154–55
women in, 156–57
Protocols of the Learned Elders of Zion, 383
Public Health Service
Native American health care and, 190–92
policies toward Native Americans, 190–92
Puerto Ricans, 282–95
bilingualism of, 143–45, 285
citizenship issues for, 274, 283
commonwealth status issue and, 288–89
current issues for, 290–95
economic conditions of, 278*t,* 289–90
education for, 290–92
family life, 292
health care, 292–94
identity of, 255–57
neocolonialism and, 285
population data on, 255, 290
religion among, 294–95, 294*f*
social construction of race, 289
statehood and self-rule issues for, 282–83, 282*f*
stereotyping of, 47
Vieques dispute, 287–88, 287*f*
Puerto Rico
geography and history, 282–89, 282*f*
island economy, 289–90
world systems theory and, 21
Pulaski, Casimir, 138
Purdy, Matthew, 50
Pushout, defined, 187, 481
Puzo, Mario, 138

Quadagno, Jill, 459–60
Québécois, 433–34, 433*f*
Quillian, Lincoln, 52, 76
Quilombo, 437, 482
Quinceañera, 258–59, 482
Quinceañero, 258–59
Quintanilla, 287
Quota system, immigration restriction with, 104
Qur'an, 301, 304–5, 312

Rabin, Yitzhak, 443
Rabinove, Samuel, 389
Rabinowicz, Sima, 393–94
Race
anti-Chinese movement and, 102
biological basis of, 12–14
in Brazil, 437
in Canada, 435–36
census questions on, 27, 27*f*
class and, 241–43, 242*f*
cultural importance of, 4–5
groups in Republic of South Africa, 445*t*
hate crimes and, 39–41, 39*f*
income differences and, 78–80, 78*f,* 79*t*
income distribution by, 439*f*
intelligence controversy concerning, 13–14
Jewish Americans and, 376–77
lifestyle differences and, 228
mixed race characteristics, 125
privilege and, 125–27, 125*f*
religious practices and, 148, 149*f*
risk and, 70–71

social construction of, 14–15, 289
social importance of, 3
sociology and study of, 15–19
in U.S. cities, 27*f*
in U.S. states, 8*f*
Race relations
current status of, 53–55, 54*f*
equal rights and, 5
Rachlin, Carol, 186
Racial attitudes
role of education in, 56–57
social conduct and, 42–43
Racial democracy, 437–38
Racial formation, 29
defined, 15, 482
Racial group
characteristics of, 8–9
defined, 8, 482
Racial profiling
of Asian Americans, 330–31
defined, 49, 482
of Muslims and Arab Americans, 316
stereotypes and, 49–50
Racism, 52*f. See also* Apartheid
in Canada, 435–36
defined, 14–15, 482
environmental racism, 84–85
institutional racism, 72
Japanese Americans and, 363–64
permanence of, 92
sexism and, 422
in South Africa, 449
toward Asian Indians, 327–28
in workplace, 60–62
Railroads
Chinese immigrant labor on, 101–02, 102*f*
slave labor on, 207
Rain Man, 464
Rainey, James, 280
Raising Black Children, 241
Ramadan War, 441
Ramirez, Eddy, 457
Ramirez, Margaret, 295
Ramirez, Roberto, 6, 255, 266, 278, 291
Ramirez-Johnson, Johnny, 294
Randolph, A. Philip, 211–13, 218
Randolph, Elmo, 50
Rangaswamy, Padma, 335
Rawick, George P., 204
Ray, Rachel, 138
Raybon, Patricia, 422
Read, Jen'nan Ghazal, 313
Reagan, Ronald, 152, 363
Recién llegados, 267
Reconstruction period
African American politicians in, 248–49, 248*t*
black-white relations during, 205–6
Reconstructionism, 393
Red Cloud (Chief), 170
Red Power movement, 179
Redford, Robert, 180
Redlining
defined, 82, 244, 482
residential segregation and, 244
social impact of, 82
Reese, Debbie, 189
Reeves, Terrance, 329
Reform Jews, 392–93
Reform Judaism, 390–91
Refugees
defined, 118, 482
immigration by, 118–20
Southeast Asian Americans as, 339
Regents of the University of California v. Bakke, 87
Relative deprivation
absolute deprivation *vs.,* 69–70
of African Americans, 219
defined, 69, 482

Religion
  of African Americans, 203–4, 222–23, 222*f*
  of Asian Indians, 335
  of Chinese Americans, 357–59, 357*f*
  ethnicity and racial makeup, 149*f*
  ethnicity and social class and, 149*f*, 151–52
  of Filipino Americans, 337
  of Hispanic Americans, 153, 294–95, 294*f*
  income and education and denomination patterns, 154–56, 155*f*
  for Japanese Americans, 365
  of Jewish Americans, 389–93, 392*t*, 395–97
  of Korean Americans, 345
  measuring importance of, 150–51, 151*f*
  of Muslim Americans, 304–10
  of Native Americans, 192–93
  pluralism, 146–51
  Polish Americans and, 139
  in United States, 146–59
  women and, 156–57, 156*f*
Religious cults, 11
Religious displays, controversy over, 159
Religious Freedom Restoration Act, 158
Religious groups
  Amish, 159–62
  characteristics of, 10–11
  hate crimes against, 39
Religious pluralism, 146–51, 147*f*, *148t*, 149*f*
  of Native Americans, 193
  Supreme Court and, 157–59
Remini, Robert V., 170
Remittances
  defined, 114, 482
  globalization and, 115–16, 118
  for Hispanic Americans, 263
Renzulli, Linda, 230
Reorganization Act of 1934, 165
Repatriation
  defined, 276, 482
  of Mexican Americans, 276–77
Republic of South Africa, 445–49
  segregation in, 23
Republican Party, 262
Reservations for Native Americans, 174–78
Residential segregation, 24, 230, 243–44
Reskin, Barbara, 87
Respectable bigotry
  against Baptists, 155–56
  defined, 130, 482
  toward Italian Americans, 137
Restrictionist sentiment, immigration policy and, 103–6, 105*f*
Restrictive covenants, 211–12, 482
Reverse discrimination
  affirmative action and, 88–89
  defined, 88, 482
Reyhner, Jon, 166, 189
Richardson, Lisa, 344
Richmond, Anthony H., 20
Riesman, David, 339
Riff-raff theory, 219, 482
Rising expectations
  of African Americans, 219
  defined, 482
Ritter, John, 319
Rivera, Feliciano, 274, 276
Rivera, George, 274, 276
Rivera-Batiz, Francisco, 290
Rivlin, Gary, 41
Robert, Pamela M., 464
Roberts, Ed, 464
Rockstar Video, 38
Rodríquez, Clara E., 255, 289, 291

Rodríquez, Robert, 256
Roe v. Wade, 420
Roediger, David R., 125–26, 133
Rohter, Larry, 290
Rolling Quads center, 464
Roman Catholicism
  diversity of, 153–54, 153*f*
  Filipino Americans and, 338
  Hispanic Americans and, 136, 294–95, 294*f*
  of Irish Americans, 131
  of Italian Americans, 136
  Mexican Americans and, 274*f*
  Polish Americans and, 139
  restrictionist sentiment, 101
  white ethnics and, 130
  women and, 156, 422
Romney, Lee, 333
Roosevelt, Franklin D., 81, 137, 209, 211, 360, 381, 462*f*
Roozen, David A., 151
Rosales, F. Arturo, 281, 295
Rose, Arnold, 17
Rosenberg, Tom (Tom Ross), 396–97
Rosenfield, Sarah, 417
Rosero, Karla, 433
Rosh Hashanah, 392
Rosin, Hanna, 300
Rossi, Alice S., 406
Rothstein, Edward, 383
Rouhana, Nadim, 445
Rousseau, Jean-Jacques, 152
Rubin, Gary E., 386
Rudwick, Elliott, 209–11
Rumspringe (running around), 161
Rush, Bobby, 222
Rusk, David, 82
Rwanda, ethnic cleansing in, 22
Ryan, William, 18, 279
Ryo, Emily, 353

Saad, Lydia, 21, 60, 289, 320, 459, 471
Sabeel Food Pantry, 300
Sabin, Albert, 141
Sachs, Susan, 353
Sadker, Myra and David, 231, 415
Sahagun, Louis, 185
Said, Edward, 300
Sajak, Pat, 141
Salée, Daniel, 434
Salopek, Paul, 166
Salvatore, Saleno, 137
Salzberger, Ronald P., 208
Sambora, Richie, 140*f*, 141
San Francisco Indian Center, 179
Sanchez, Rene, 280
Sanders, Irwin T., 131
Sanger, Margaret, 406
Sansei, 359, 363, 368, 482
Santana, José E. Rivera, 287
Santiago, Carlos E., 290
Sarna, Jonathan D., 377
Sawyer, Diane, 228
Scalia, Antonio (Justice), 137, 469
Scapegoating theory of prejudice, 43–44, 482
Schaefer, Richard, 58–59, 151, 211, 291, 339, 412, 441, 454, 460
Schaefer, Sandra L., 339
Scheckner, Jeffrey, 82
Schindler's List, 381
Schmidt, William E., 386
Schodolski, Vincent J., 249
School prayer, 157–58, 157*f*
School segregation, 214–16, 230–31
School-to-discipline pipeline, 187
Schulz, Amy J., 180
Schwartz, Felice, 413
Schwartz, Jim, 82

Schwartz, John, 167, 375
Schwartz, Margaret, 395
Schwartz, Pepper, 467
Schwarzenegger, Arnold, 254
Scopes, John, 158
Scotch, Richard K., 465–66
Scott, Janny, 83
Scrabble, 28
Seale, Bobby, 221–22
Sears, David O., 219
Sears Roebuck, 462
Secession by subordinate groups, 23
Secessionist minorities
  Amish, 158, 159–62
  defined, 158, 482
Second shift, 419, 482
Secret societies, of Chinese Americans, 354–55
Segregation, 52*f*
  census figures on, 23, 24*f*
  Civil Rights movement and gains in, 214–16
  de jure, 214, 450
  defined, 23, 482
  institutionalization of, 205–6
  of Native Americans, 177–78
  in religious practices, 147–48
  residential segregation, 243–44
  of schools, 214–16, 230–31
  social consequences of, 24–25
  of subordinate groups, 23–25
Segregation index, 409
Seibert, Deborah, 342
Seinfeld, 48, 59
Sela-Sheffy, Rakefet, 441
Self-determination, 474
  of Muslim Americans, 308–9
  of Native Americans, 180
Self-fulfilling prophecy, 483
  defined, 19, 19*f*
  impact on minority groups, 19, 19*f*
  of low-wage labor, 77
  in racial profiling, 49
Self-hatred, prejudice and oppression and, 53–55
Self-segregation by Amish, 159
Selzer, Michael, 383
Seminole tribe, 170, 187
Senate Special Committee on Aging, 457
Seneca Falls, 405
Sengupta, Somini, 4, 329
Separate but equal doctrine, 81, 206, 214
September 11, 2001 attacks, 4, 50, 299, 316–18, 318*f*, 381
  Anti-Semitism and, 381
  attitudes toward Muslims and Arabs and, 316–18
  effect on religion, 150–51
  immigration and, 95
Sequoyah, 187
Serbs, ethnic cleansing of, 22
Set-asides, 483
  for Asian Americans, 329
Sex differentiation, 404–5
Sex discrimination
  affirmative action and, 82–83
  federal legislation against, 90
  in religion, 157
  women in labor force and, 411–12, 414
Sexism, 403, 483
  classroom, 415–16
  racism and, 422
  in workplace, 60–61, 410–11
Sexual harassment, 413–14, 483
Sexual orientation, hate crimes involving, 39, 39*f*
Shabazz, Malik El-, 309
Shadchan, 394
Shaheen, Jack, 319

Shapiro, Joseph P., 462, 466
Shapiro, Thomas M., 84, 235, 364
Shater, Walied, 46
Shaw, Herman, 247
Sheen, Martin, 58
Sheik, The, 319
Shelly v. Kramer, 212
Shepard, Matthew, 469
Sherif, Carolyn, 60
Sherif, Musafer, 60
Sherkat, Darren E., 151
Shiite Muslims, 305
Shilts, Randy, 469
Shin, Hyon S., 138, 141, 146
Shinto, 365
Shyrock, Andrew, 311
Sierra Club, 108
Sigelman, Lee, 49
Silberman, Charles E., 188
Silva, Helga, 438
Silver, Jim, 433
Simon, Stephanie, 305
Simpson, Jacqueline C., 27
Singer, Joseph W., 182
Singh, Leona, 337
Single-parent families, 239–40
Sinophobes, defined, 101, 483
Sioux tribe, 170–71, 176, 179, 187
Sit-ins, 211, 287
Sitting Bull, 170
Six-Day War of 1967, 393, 441
Skidmore, Thomas E., 437
Skin color as determination of race, 8–9
Sklare, Marshall, 378, 389
Skull Valley Goshote tribe, 85–86, 86*f,* 194
Slave codes, defined, 202–4, 483
Slavery
    of African Americans, 200–8, 201*f,* 206f
    aftermath of, 205–6
    attack on, 204–5
    auctions, 203*f*
    Brazil and, 436–37
    Canada and, 435
    Muslims and, 308
    on Puerto Rico, 285
    reparations, 206–8, 206*f,* 483
    slave codes, 202–3
Slavin, Robert E., 144
Slavin, Steven, 379
Smallwood, Scott, 415
Smith, Amy Symens, 31*f*
Smith, Betty, 246
Smith, Dan, 427
Smith, David M., 467
Smith, James F., 430
Smith, James P., 114–15
Smith, Paul Chaat, 180
Smith, Tom W., 52, 56, 154–55, 306
Smith v. Allwright, 211
Smithsonian Museum of the American Indian, 184
Smits, Jimmy, 58
Snipp, C. Matthew, 168
Snyder, Laurel, 395
Snyder, Susan, 156
Social clubs, discrimination by, 82–83
Social conduct, racial attitudes and, 42–43
Social construction of race, 14–15
    for Puerto Ricans, 289
Social distance, defined, 51, 483
Social distance scale, measuring extent of prejudice and, 51–52, 51*f*
Social identity of Italian immigrants, 136, 136*f*
Social minority, women as, 11
Social Service Employees Union, 59–60
Sociology

conflict perspective, 17–18
defined, 15, 483
functionalist perspective, 16–17
labeling approach, 18–19
theoretical perspectives, 16–19
women's issues in, 404–5
Soltero, Sonia White, 145
Somalis and immigration to the United States, 5
Somners, Christina Hoff, 407
Song, Tae-Hyon, 51
Soo, Julie D., 355
Sorensen, Elaine, 413
South Africa. *See also* Republic of South Africa
    apartheid in, 446–47
    colonialism and, 445–46
    era of reconciliation in, 448–49
    racial groups in, 445*t*
South Americans, in U.S., 268–70, 268*f*
South Los Angeles, 221*f*
Southeast Asian Americans, 339–42
    current issues, 339–41
    Hmong community case study, 341–42, 341*f*
    refugees among, 118, 339
Southern, David W., 18
Southern Baptist Convention, 155–56
Southern Baptists, characteristics of, 155–57
Southern Christian Leadership Conference (SCLC), 218
Southern Poverty Law Center (SPLC), 40, 63
Sovereignty, 347, 483
    defined, 181, 483
Spanish-American War, 282, 336
Special Force Operation, 277
Squitieri, Tom, 319
Srole, Leo, 26, 127
St. Espada, Martín, 287–88, 288*f*
St. Louis, 381
St. Patrick's Day, 135
St. Patrick's Day Parade, 128, 128*f*
Stable Black Families Project, 241
Stampp, Kenneth M., 203–4
Stangor, Charles, 47
Stanton, Elizabeth Cady, 405
Stark, Rodney, 154
Starks, Carolyn, 353
States' rights, defined, 81, 483
Staton, Ron, 347–48
Statue of Liberty, 103, 104
Steele, James B., 185
Steinberg, Stephen, 114
Steinem, Gloria, 421
Steiner, Stan, 179
Steinhauer, Jennifer, 83
Steinmetz, Erica, 455–56, 461–62, 464
Stereotypes
    of Asian Americans, 326–29, 329*f,* 359
    characteristics of, 47
    of Chinese Americans, 356
    defined, 18, 47, 483
    of disabled people, 462–64
    of elderly, 456–58
    of immigrants, 114–16
    of Jewish Americans, 379–80
    labeling theory and, 18–19
    of prejudice, 46–50
    racial profiling and, 49–50
    trends in, 47–49
    of white ethnics, 130–31
    of women, 402–3
Stern, Kenneth S., 381
Stewart, Jocelyn Y., 319
Stewart, Martha, 141
Stoddard, Ellyn R., 277
Stonequist, Everett V., 32
Stonewall Inn, 469

Stout, David, 174
Stratification
    by class and gender, 15–16
    defined, 15, 483
Strauss, Gary, 91, 328, 413
Student Nonviolent Coordinating Committee (SNCC), 220
Students for a Democratic Society (SDS), 221
Stuyvesant, Peter, 383
Subordinate group
    affirmative action and, 86–89, 88*t*
    Amish as, 160–62
    annexation of, 20
    assimilation of, 25–26
    characteristics of, 7–8
    colonialism of, 21–22
    consequences of status for, 22–28
    contact hypothesis and, 59
    defined, 3
    dominant group relations with, 426
    expulsion of, 22–23
    extermination of, 22
    fusion of, 25
    income differences among, 78–79
    Jewish Americans as, 376–77
    migration of, 20
    Native Americans as, 172
    opinions of, 53–55
    pluralism perspective on, 26–28
    resistance and change in, 32–33
    secession of, 29
    segregation, 23–25
    status, creation of, 19–22
    types of, 8–12
    women as, 402–3
Suchan, Trudy A., 210*f,* 473*f*
Suffrage movement, 405*f,* 406
Suffragists, 406, 483
Suggs, Welch, 416, 466
Sullivan, Cheryl, 186
Sullivan, Keith, 113
Summer, William Graham, 7
Sundiata, Ibrahim K., 437
Sundown towns, 69, 212, 213*f,* 483
Sung, Betty Lee, 354
Sunnah, 304
Sunni Muslims, 305, 311
Supreme Court (U.S.). *See also* specific rulings
    abortion rulings, 420
    affirmative action rulings, 87–88, 88*t*
    age discrimination rulings, 457
    anti-discrimination rulings, 81–82
    bilingual education rulings, 143
    desegregation, 214–15
    disability rulings by, 460–61
    gays and lesbians rulings by, 469–70
    housing discrimination rulings, 243
    immigration rulings by, 120
    Japanese Americans rulings by, 362
    Native American legal rulings, 179, 181–82, 185, 187
    racial profiling ruling, 50
    religious decisions by, 157–59
    segregation rulings by, 206, 211–12
    sexual harassment decisions, 414
    slavery rulings by, 206
Suro, Roberto, 262, 270
Susto, 294
Swagerty, William R., 167–68
Swanson, Laura, 428*t*
Swanson, Stevenson, 356
Swarns, Christina, 246
Swartz, Jon, 254
Sweatshops in Chinatown, 356
Swedish Americans, statistics on, 125
Symbolic ethnicity
    defined, 128, 483
    of Irish Americans, 128–29, 128*f*

Syria, 303, 441–42
Szegedy-Maszak, Marianne, 420

Tafoya, Sonya M., 31
Taft, William Howard, 209
Taino Indians, 282
Takaki, Ronald, 101, 334, 359
Takei, George, 364
Takezawa, Yasuko I., 363
Talented tenth theory, 209
Tannenbaum, Frank, 437
Taylor, Jonathan B., 185
Taylor, Paul, 447
Taylor, Stuart Jr., 82–83
Television
    for African Americans, 58–59
    Hispanic Americans and, 58, 255, 270*f*
    stereotypes on, 48
Telles, Edward E., 437–39
Telsch, Kathleen, 438
ten Brock, Jacobus, 360, 362
Terba, Harallamb, 141–42
Termination Act, 165, 175–76
Terrorism
    attitudes toward Muslims and Arabs and, 316–20
    September 11, 2001 attacks, 4, 50, 299, 316–18, 318*f*, 381
Tharp, Ronald, 187
Therrien, Melissa, 6, 266, 278, 291
Third-generation principle, 352
    defined, 127, 482
Thomas, Barbara Boston, 219
Thomas, Curlew O., 219
Thomas, Dorothy S., 361
Thomas, Robert M. Jr., 459
Thomas, William Isaac, 18, 138–39
Thompson, Ginger, 263, 429–31
Thornburgh, Nathan, 5
Thornton, Russell, 168, 171
Thrupkaew, Noy, 326
Thunderheart, 180
Tijerina, Reies López, 281
Tikkun, 398
Tiny Tim, 464
Title IX provisions, 415–16, 416*f*
Tizon, Thomas Alex, 368
Tomaskovic-Devey, Donald, 412
Tomlinson, T.M., 219
Tong, Benson, 355
Tongs, 354–55, 358, 483
Torah, 390
Torriero, E.A., 341–42, 346
Total discrimination
    defined, 70, 483
    theory of, 70–72, 72*f*
Tough, Paul, 232
Tourism
    Chinese Americans and, 356
    on Hawaii, 346
    Native American employment in, 183–84
    Puerto Rico economics and, 290
Tracking
    defined, 230–31
    of minority students, 483
    of Puerto Ricans and Mexican American students, 291
Trail of Tears, 170
Tran, Quynh-Giang, 238
Transexuals, 467
Transgendered persons, 467
Transnationals, defined, 118, 483
Transport Security Administration, 73
Transvestites, 467
Travelers Corporation of Hartford, 458
Treaties with Native Americans, 168–70
Treaty of Guadalupe Hidalgo, 20, 143, 275

Treaty of Medicine Creek, 178–79
Treaty of Paris, 282
Tribal councils, 177*f*
    sovereignty of, 180
Triner, Gail D., 438
Triplett, William, 280
Trudeau, Pierre, 432
True Lies, 319
Truman, Harry S., 213, 287
Truth, Sojourner, 205
Truth and Reconciliation Commission (TRC), 448
Tryzmanie bortnków, 139
Tse, Archie, 442*f*
Tsu (clans), 354, 483
Tuan, Mia, 179
Tubman, Harriet, 205, 223
Tuch, Steven A., 49
Tucker, M. Belinda, 239
Tule Lake security camp, 362, 364, 369
Tumulty, Karen, 114
Turck, Mary G., 208
Ture, Kwame, 72, 220
Turner, Margery Austin, 82
Turner, Ralph H., 219
Turner, Richard Brent, 308
Turner, Wallace, 347
Tuskegee Institute, 208, 291
Tuskegee Syphilis study, 247
Tyler, S. Lyman, 175, 176
Tyson, Karolyn, 232

Uchitelle, L., 458
Ueda, Reed, 268
Uhlenberg, Peter, 418
Ukeles, Jacob B., 390
Ukraine, suppression by Russia, 20
Umberger, Mary, 74
Underclass
    among Hispanic Americans, 260–61
    culture of poverty theory and, 279
    lack of job accessibility for, 77–78
Underemployment, 236, 483
Underground economy, 75, 483
Underground Railroad, 205
Unemployment
    of African Americans, 236
    of Central and South American immigrants, 269
    of disabled people, 462, 465–66
    of Native Americans, 185–86
    of Puerto Ricans, 284
UNESCO Statement on Race, 14
Uniform Crime Report, 245
Union League, 205
Union organizations by Chinese laborers, 102
United Farm Workers (UFW), 279, 295
United Jewish Appeal (UJA), 388
United States
    African population in, 202*t*
    anti-Semitism in, 382–86
    attitudes toward Muslims and Arabs in, 316–19
    Chinese population in, 352–53, 353*t*
    diversity of population in, 26–28, 27*f*
    diversity of religious groups in, 10–11
    early immigration patterns in, 100–3
    elderly population in, 455–456, 455*f*
    ethnic diversity in, 124–25
    foreign-born population in, 99–100, 99*f*–100*f*
    Hispanic population in, 245*f*, 254–55, 255*f*
    illegal immigration in, 109–14, 109*t*, 113*t*
    immigrant population in, 98, 98*f*, 104, 105*f*, 108–9
    Jewish population in, 374–75, 375*f*, 377–79

    major immigration policies of, 109*t*
    Mexican American immigration to, 275–78
    population by race and ethnicity, 5, 6*f*
    population growth in, 108–9
    Puerto Rican population in, 284
    Puerto Rico and, 283–84
    racial and ethnic groups in, 4–5, 6*t*
    refugee assistance programs in, 118–19
    religion in, 147–59
    religious pluralism in, 146–47, 146*f*, 147*t*, 148*t*, 149*f*
United States v. Lara, 181
United Synagogue of America, 392
University of Alabama, 214
University of Michigan, 87, 89
University of Mississippi, 214
University of North Dakota, 61
Univision, 59
Uprooted, 127
Urban Institute, 115
Urban Poverty and Family Life Study (UPFLS), 237
Urbanization of Native Americans, 177–78, 182*t*
U.S. Citizenship and Immigration Services, 378
USA Patriot Act, 316
Usdansky, Margaret L., 125

Valentine, Charles A., 279
Van Den Berghe, Pierre L., 445*t*, 446
Varadarajan, Tunko, 335
Vega, William A., 292
Vendidos, 281
Verhovek, Sam, 84
Victim discounting, 246, 483
Victimization surveys, 245, 483
Vieques dispute, 287–88, 287*f*
Viet Kieu, 341, 483
Vietnam, expulsion of Chinese by, 23
Vietnamese Americans as refugees, 339–40, 340*f*
Vineyard, 150
Vinton, Bobby, 141
Violence
    African Americans and, 209*f*, 210–11, 218–19, 221*f*
    among Cuban Americans, 267
    Arab-Israeli conflicts, 441–45
    against Asian Americans, 329–30
    against gays and lesbians, 469
    in Puerto Rico, 289
Virgil, Maurilio, 281
Visible minorities, 435, 483
Visitability, 466, 483
Volpe, John, 366
Voluntary associations, ending discrimination with, 82–83
Voter News Service, 467
Voting rights
    of African Americans, 205–6, 211, 218–19, 249
    federal legislation for, 81–82
    of Hispanic Americans, 261–62
    for Mexican women, 430
    for Native Americans, 173
    of women, 405*f*, 406
Voting Rights Act, 145, 218–19
Vuong, Vu-Duc, 324

Wages
    of African Americans, 238
    of Hispanic Americans, 263
    of women, 407–11
Wagley, Charles, 7, 455
Wagner, Angie, 182
Waitzkin, Howard, 246
Waldman, Carl, 432

Walesa, Lech, 140
Walk for Justice, 180
Wallace, George, 214
Waller, David, 194
Wallerstein, Immanuel, 21, 426
Walzer, Susan, 416–17
Wang, L. Ling-Chi, 370
Ward, Deborah L., 348
Warner, W. Lloyd, 26, 127
Warren, Earl (Chief Justice), 214
Warren, Jeve, 266
Warrington, Nako'hlani, 347
Warrior, Robert Alan, 180
Washburn, Wilcomb E., 174
Washington, Brooker T., 33, 208–10, 223
Watanabe, Teresa, 295, 319
Waters, Mary, 124, 128
Watson, Jamal E., 223
Watts riot, 344–45
Wausau, Wisconsin, Hmong case study in,
    341–42, 341*f*
Wausau Area Hmong Mutual Association,
    342
Wax, Murray, 183, 186
Wax, Murray L., 174, 176, 183
Wax, Rosalie, 187
Wealth
    of African Americans, 234–36, 234*f*,
        235*f*
    defined, 83, 234, 483
    inequality and discrimination, 83–84
Weber, Max, 15, 91, 151, 242
Weglyn, Michi, 360*f*, 361
Wei, William, 355
Weinberg, Daniel H., 407
Weiner, Tim, 275
Wellesley, 415
Wellington, Alison J., 412
Wells, Robert N. Jr., 189, 190
Wen Ho Lee, 331
Werner, Erica, 184
Wertheimer, Jack, 392
Wertsman, Vladima, 303
Wessel, David, 108
West, Kanye, 4
West Bank, 441, 442*f*
West Wing, 58
"Wetbacks," 277
Wheeler-Howard Act, 173
White, Jack E., 29
White ethnics
    Black Power alliance with, 221
    Irish Americans and, 133–34
    Native American treaties and warfare
        with, 168–71
    prejudice of, 130–31
    prejudice toward, 129–30
    price paid by, 129–31
    recent changes in schooling, income
        and life expectancy, 471–72, 472*f*
White primary, 206, 211, 223, 483
White supremacy, 208–11
Whiteness
    ethnicity and, 125–26
    research on, 127–29
Whites
    attitudes toward racial profiling, 50
    dominance of mass media by, 57–59
    prejudice among, 53–54

privileges of, 126*f*, 127
support for integration among, 52–53
views of prejudice by, 52–53
Whitman, David, 270
Whren v. United States, 50
Wickham, De Wayne, 90
Wiesel, Elie, 381, 382
Wiggins, Cynthia, 68
Wilgoren, Jodi, 306
Willeto, Angela A., 189
Williams, Carol J., 266, 286*t*
Williams, K., 31*f*
Williams, L. Susan, 259
Williams, Patricia J., 70–71, 244
Williams v. Mississippi, 206
Willie, Charles V., 242
Wilson, James, 131
Wilson, Richard, 179
Wilson, Scott, 444
Wilson, William Julius, 219, 236–37, 242,
    260, 446
Wilson, Woodrow, 103–4
Winant, George, 15, 31
Winant, Howard, 15–16, 31, 102, 438, 447
Winkler, Karen, 279
Winks, Robin W., 435
Winnebago tribe, 166
Winseman, Albert L., 148, 294
Withrow, Brian L., 50
Wojtyla, Karol Józef, 140
Wolf, Diane L., 338
Wolfe, Ann, 388
Wolfe, Diane L., 30, 31, 336, 338
Women. *See also* Gender issues; Sex dis-
        crimination
    abortion and, 420
    affirmative action and, 86–88
    as Arab and Muslim Americans,
        312–13
    child care and housework issues,
        416–20
    disabilities and, 463
    discrimination against, 82, 410–15
    economic conditions for, 407–15,
        409*t*
    education of, 415–16
    elderly women's issues, 459
    family life and, 416–20, 417*f*
    federal legislation against, 80–81
    feminist movement and, 405–7, 405*f*,
        407*f*
    feminization of poverty and, 414–15
    glass ceiling for, 91–92, 91*f*, 413, 413*t*
    glass wall and, 91–92
    as heads of African American families,
        239–40
    hijab for, 312–13
    immigration and, 116–17
    income differences of, 78–79, 78*t*, 79*t*
    internet resource directory, 477
    in Korean American community, 343*f*,
        344
    in Mexico, 430–31
    minority women, 402–3, 421–22
    in politics, 420–21, 421*f*
    religion and, 156–57, 156*f*
    sexual harassment and, 413–14
    slavery for, 203
    sociological perspectives on, 404–5

as subordinate group, 402–3
Women's Legal Defense Fund, 408
Women's liberation movement, 406–7
Wong, Morrison G., 356
Woodard, C. Vann, 206, 221
Woods, Tiger, 29, 83
Woodson, Carter, 204
Wooton, Barbara H., 409
Workplace
    diversity training in, 60–62
    racial/ethnic composition of, 61–62,
        61*f*
World systems theory, 426
    defined, 21, 168, 483
    Native Americans and, 168
    Puerto Ricans and, 290
World War II, African American participa-
    tion in, 211–13
Wounded Knee II, 179
Wright, Paul, 347
Wrong, Dennis H., 128
Wu, Frank M., 329, 331
Wyman, Mark, 100

Xenophobia, defined, 100, 483
Xie, Yu, 329

"Yale Five" lawsuit, 374
Yancey, George, 126
Yankee City series, 127
Ybarra, Michael J., 168
Ye, Albert H., 366
Yellow peril, 101, 330, 483
Yew, Chay, 363
Yi, Daniel, 345
Yiddish language, 386, 397
Yiddishkait, 393, 397–98, 483
Yinger, John, 82
Yoder v. Wisconsin, 160, 161
Yom Kippur War of 1973, 393, 441
Yonsei, 359, 363, 483
York, Charlotte, 395
Young, Andrew, 44
Young, Jeffrey R., 12–13
Young Lords, 221
Young Patriots, 221
Younge, Gary, 34

Za Chlebem, 138
Zaidi, Arishia U., 337*f*
Zambrana, Ruth E., 292
Zangwill, Israel, 454
Zapata, Emiliano, 429
Zapatista National Liberation Army,
    429–30
Zarembro, Alan, 338
Zeng, Zhen, 329
Zernike, Kate, 5
Zhao, Yilu, 355
Zhou, Min, 327, 329, 340
Zia, Helen, 47–48, 331
Zimmerman, Jean, 413
Zion National Park, 194
Zionism, 385, 440, 483
Znaniecki, Florian, 138–39
Zogby, James J., 316–18
Zoning laws, residential segregation and,
    243*f*, 244, 483